NE능률 영어교과서

대한민국 고등학생 **10**명 중 **4.7**명이 보는 교과서

영어 고등 교과서 점유율 1위
[7차, 2007 개정, 2009 개정, 2015 개정]

리딩튜터

그동안 판매된
리딩튜터 1,900만 부
차곡차곡 쌓으면 19만 미터

에베레스트 21배 높이

190,000m

에베레스트 8,848m

능률보카

그동안 판매된
능률VOCA 1,100만 부

대한민국 박스오피스
천만명을 넘은 영화 단 28개

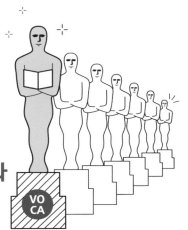

그래머존

그동안 판매된 450만 부의 그래머존을 바닥에 쭉 ~ 깔면

1000km 서울 - 부산 왕복가능

서울

부산

KB013919

교재 검토에 도움을 주신 선생님들

The 상승  어법·어휘 + 유형편

지은이	김경태
선임연구원	김지현
외주연구원	콘텐츠 인앤아웃
영문 교열	Angela Lan
디자인	조가영, 기지영
영업	한기영, 이경구, 박인규, 정철교, 김남준, 이우현
마케팅	박혜선, 남경진, 이지원, 김여진

**NE능률이
미래를
창조합니다.**

건강한 배움의 고객가치를 제공하겠다는 꿈을 실현하기 위해
40년이 넘는 시간 동안 열심히 달려왔습니다.

앞으로도 끊임없는 연구와 노력을 통해
당연한 것을 멈추지 않고

고객, 기업, 직원 모두가 함께 성장하는 NE능률이 되겠습니다.

The 상승

독해 기본기에서
수능 실전 대비까지
The 상승

어법·어휘
+ 유형편

STRUCTURE & FEATURES

STEP 1 어휘

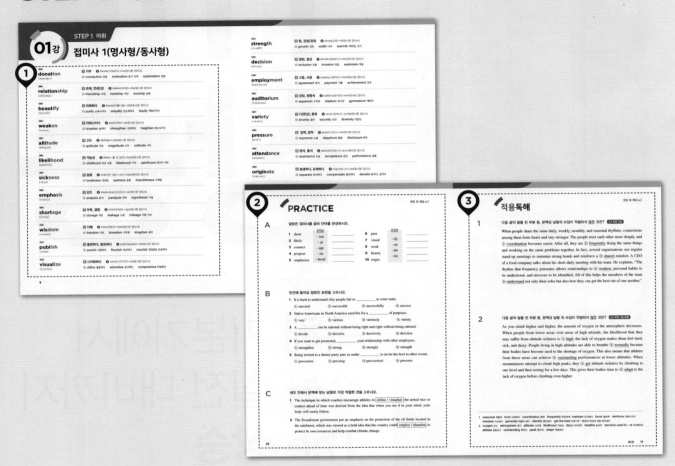

수능 핵심 어휘 학습

어원 및 테마별로 한 강에 25개씩, 총 750개 어휘를 수록하였습니다. 또한 파생어, 유의어, 반의어 등을 함께 제시하여 풍부한 어휘 학습이 될 수 있게 구성하였습니다.

PRACTICE

파생어, 빈칸에 알맞은 형태 고르기, 네모 안에서 문맥에 맞는 단어 고르기 등 다양한 유형으로 어휘 확인학습을 할 수 있습니다.

적용독해

수능 및 전국연합학력평가에서 선별한 기출 지문 속에서 학습한 어휘를 적용해 봄으로써 수능 실전 감각을 기를 수 있습니다.

STEP 2 어법

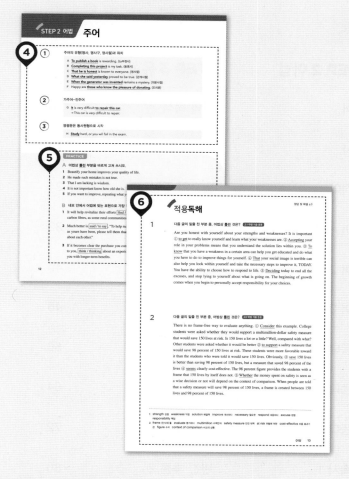

STEP 3 유형

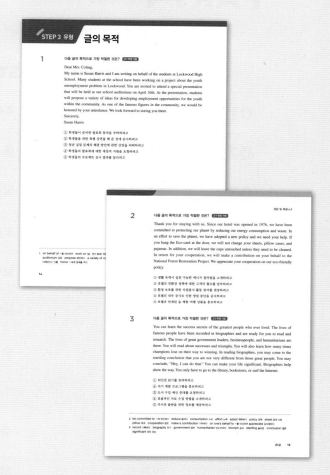

④ 수능 필수 어법

수능 필수 어법을 선별하여 간결하고 명확하게 설명하였습니다.

⑤ PRACTICE

학습한 어법을 다양한 유형으로 간단히 확인할 수 있습니다.

⑥ ✏ 적용독해

수능 및 전국연합학력평가에서 선별한 기출 지문 속에서 수능 어법을 적용해 봄으로써 수능 실전 감각을 기를 수 있습니다.

수능 독해 유형 학습

수능 독해 유형을 총 15개로 분류하여 각 유형별로 두 번씩 반복 학습할 수 있도록 구성하였습니다. 또한 수능 및 전국연합학력평가에서 선별한 기출 지문으로 유형 학습을 함으로써 수능 실전 감각을 기를 수 있습니다.

CONTENTS

PART 1

PART 2

PART 1

1강 - 15강

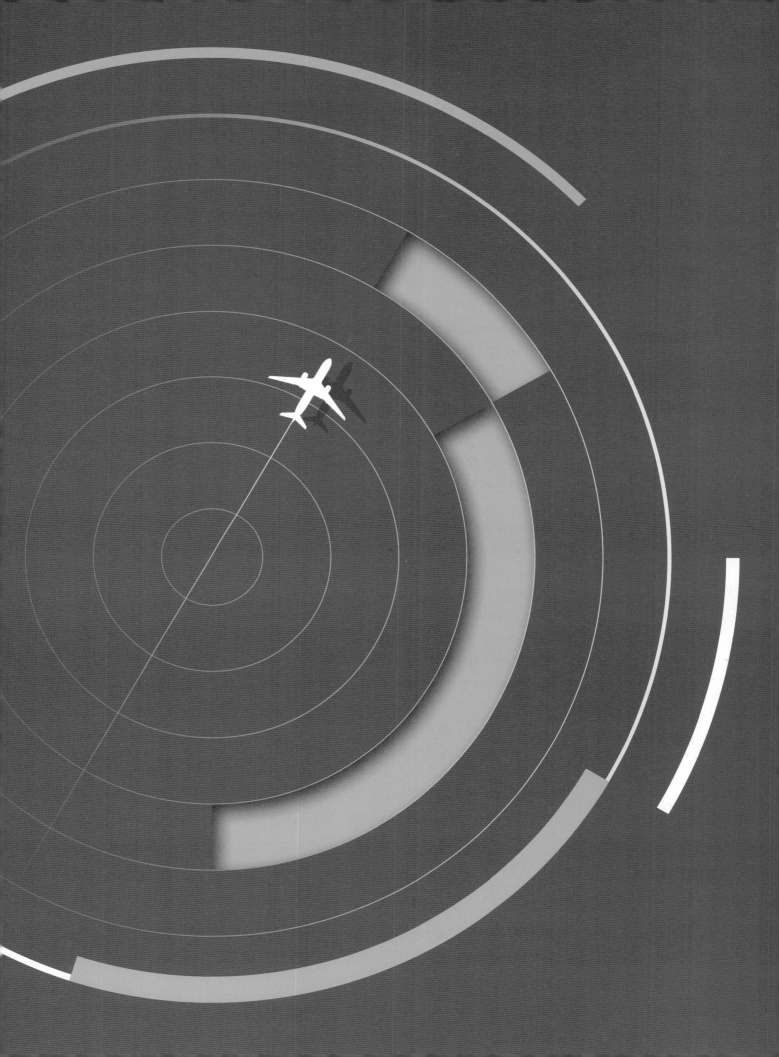

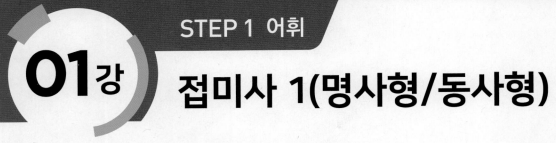

01강 접미사 1(명사형/동사형)

001

donat**ion**
[dounéiʃən]

명 기부 ❯ donate(기부하다)+ion(명사형 접미사)

⊕ connection 연결　motivation 동기 부여　explanation 설명

002

relations**hip**
[riléiʃənʃip]

명 관계, 연관(성) ❯ relation(관계)+ship(명사형 접미사)

⊕ friendship 우정　hardship 역경　worship 숭배

003

beauti**fy**
[bjúːtəfài]

동 미화하다 ❯ beauty(아름다움)+(i)fy(동사형 접미사)

⊕ purify 순화시키다　simplify 단순화하다　liquify 액화시키다

004

weake**n**
[wíːkən]

동 약화시키다 ❯ weak(약한)+en(동사형 접미사)

⊕ broaden 넓히다　strengthen 강화하다　heighten 향상시키다

005

altit**ude**
[ǽltitjùːd]

명 고도 ❯ alti(high)+tude(명사형 접미사)

⊕ aptitude 적성　magnitude 규모　solitude 고독

006

likelih**ood**
[láiklihùd]

명 가능성 ❯ likely(~할 것 같은)+hood(명사형 접미사)

⊕ childhood 유년 시절　falsehood 거짓　sainthood 성인의 지위

007

sickn**ess**
[síknis]

명 질병 ❯ sick(아픈, 멀미 나는)+ness(명사형 접미사)

⊕ loneliness 외로움　sadness 슬픔　impoliteness 무례함

008

emphas**is**
[émfəsis]

명 강조 ❯ emphasize(강조하다)+sis(명사형 접미사)

⊕ analysis 분석　paralysis 마비　hypothesis 가설

009

shorta**ge**
[ʃɔ́ːrtidʒ]

명 부족, 결핍 ❯ short(부족한)+age(명사형 접미사)

⊕ storage 저장　leakage 누출　mileage 주행 거리

010

wisd**om**
[wízdəm]

명 지혜 ❯ wise(현명한)+dom(명사형 접미사)

⊕ freedom 자유　boredom 지루함　kingdom 왕국

011

publis**h**
[pʌ́bliʃ]

동 출판하다, 발표하다 ❯ public(people)+ish(동사형 접미사)

⊕ punish 처벌하다　flourish 번성하다　nourish 영양분을 공급하다

012

visuali**ze**
[víʒuəlàiz]

동 시각화하다 ❯ visual(시각적인)+ize(동사형 접미사)

⊕ utilize 활용하다　advertise 광고하다　compromise 타협하다

013
strength
[streŋkθ]

명 힘, 강점/장점 ❯ strong(강한)+th(명사형 접미사)
⊕ growth 성장   width 너비   warmth 따뜻함, 온기

014
decision
[disíʒən]

명 결정, 결심 ❯ decide(결정하다)+sion(명사형 접미사)
⊕ inclusion 포함   invasion 침입   explosion 폭발

015
employment
[implɔ́imənt]

명 고용, 사용 ❯ employ(고용하다)+ment(명사형 접미사)
⊕ agreement 동의   payment 지불   achievement 성과

016
auditorium
[ɔ̀ːditɔ́ːriəm]

명 강당, 청중석 ❯ auditory(청각의)+ium(명사형 접미사)
⊕ aquarium 수족관   stadium 경기장   gymnasium 체육관

017
variety
[vəráiəti]

명 다양(성), 종류 ❯ vary(다양하다)+(e/i)ty(명사형 접미사)
⊕ anxiety 불안   security 보안   diversity 다양성

018
pressure
[préʃər]

명 압력, 압박 ❯ press(누르다)+ure(명사형 접미사)
⊕ exposure 노출   departure 출발   disclosure 폭로

019
attendance
[əténdəns]

명 참석, 출석 ❯ attend(참석하다)+ance(명사형 접미사)
⊕ assistance 도움   acceptance 용인   performance 실행

020
originate
[ərídʒənèit]

동 발생하다, 유래하다 ❯ orig(rise)+in+ate(동사형 접미사)
⊕ separate 분리하다   compensate 보상하다   elevate 올리다, 높이다

021
proposal
[prəpóuzəl]

명 제안, 계획, 청혼 ❯ propose(제안하다)+al(명사형 접미사)
⊕ refusal 거절   survival 생존   arrival 도착

022
resident
[rézidənt]

명 거주자, 주민 ❯ reside(거주하다)+(e/a)nt(명사형 접미사)
⊕ president 대통령   applicant 지원자   accountant 회계사

023
humanitarian
[hjuːmænité(ː)əriən]

명 인도주의자 ❯ humanity(인간성)+ian(명사형 접미사)
⊕ veterinarian 수의사   vegetarian 채식주의자   pedestrian 보행자

024
mountaineer
[màuntəníər]

명 산악인, 등반가 ❯ mountain(산)+ee/eer(명사형 접미사)
⊕ retiree 퇴직자   engineer 공학자   pioneer 선구자, 개척자

025
tendency
[téndənsi]

명 경향, 추세 ❯ tend(경향이 있다)+(en)cy(명사형 접미사)
⊕ urgency 긴급함   efficiency 효율성   deficiency 부족, 결핍

PRACTICE

A   알맞은 접미사를 골라 단어를 완성하시오.

		보기	
1	short	- ion	_____
2	likely	- al	_____
3	connect	- age	_____
4	propose	- sis	_____
5	emphasize	- hood	_____

		보기	
6	pure	- ify	_____
7	visual	- en	_____
8	weak	- ate	_____
9	beauty	- ize	_____
10	origin		_____

B   빈칸에 들어갈 알맞은 표현을 고르시오.

1 The movie director said he had no intention to _____ violence.

① beautify   ② beautiful   ③ beautifully   ④ beauty

2 Native Americans in North America used fire for a _____ of purposes.

① vary   ② various   ③ variously   ④ variety

3 A _____ can be rational without being right and right without being rational.

① decide   ② decisive   ③ decisively   ④ decision

4 If you want to get promoted, _____ your relationship with other employees.

① strengthen   ② strong   ③ strongly   ④ strength

5 Being invited to a dinner party puts us under _____ to invite the host to other events.

① pressurize   ② pressing   ③ pressurized   ④ pressure

C   네모 안에서 문맥에 맞는 낱말로 가장 적절한 것을 고르시오.

1 The technique in which coaches encourage athletes to utilize / visualize the actual race or contest ahead of time was derived from the idea that when you see it in your mind, your body will surely follow.

2 The Ecuadorean government put an emphasis on the protection of the oil fields located in the rainforest, which was viewed as a bold idea that the country could employ / abandon to protect its own resources and help combat climate change.

적용독해

1 다음 글의 밑줄 친 부분 중, 문맥상 낱말의 쓰임이 적절하지 <u>않은</u> 것은? `고1 학평 기출`

When people share the same daily, weekly, monthly, and seasonal rhythms, connections among them form faster and stay stronger. The people trust each other more deeply, and ① <u>coordination</u> becomes easier. After all, they are ② <u>frequently</u> doing the same things and working on the same problems together. In fact, several organizations use regular stand-up meetings to maintain strong bonds and reinforce a ③ <u>shared</u> mindset. A CEO of a food company talks about his short daily meeting with his team. He explains, "The rhythm that frequency generates allows relationships to ④ <u>weaken</u>, personal habits to be understood, and stressors to be identified. All of this helps the members of the team ⑤ <u>understand</u> not only their roles but also how they can get the best out of one another."

2 다음 글의 밑줄 친 부분 중, 문맥상 낱말의 쓰임이 적절하지 <u>않은</u> 것은? `고2 학평 기출 응용`

As you climb higher and higher, the amount of oxygen in the atmosphere decreases. When people from lower areas visit areas of high altitude, the likelihood that they may suffer from altitude sickness is ① <u>high</u>; the lack of oxygen makes them feel tired, sick, and dizzy. People living in high altitudes are able to breathe ② <u>normally</u> because their bodies have become used to the shortage of oxygen. This also means that athletes from those areas can achieve ③ <u>outstanding</u> performances at lower altitudes. When mountaineers attempt to climb high peaks, they ④ <u>get</u> altitude sickness by climbing to one level and then resting for a few days. This gives their bodies time to ⑤ <u>adapt</u> to the lack of oxygen before climbing even higher.

---

1 seasonal 계절의 trust 신뢰하다 coordination 협력 frequently 빈번하게 maintain 유지하다 bond 결속력 reinforce 강화시키다
mindset 사고방식 generate 만들어 내다 identify 확인하다 get the best out of ~에게서 최상의 것을 얻어내다
2 oxygen 산소 atmosphere 대기 altitude 고지대 likelihood 가능성 dizzy 어지러운 breathe 숨쉬다 become used to ~에 익숙해지다
athlete 운동선수 outstanding 뛰어난 peak 봉우리 adapt 적응하다

주어

① 주어의 유형(명사, 명사구, 명사절)과 위치

A **To publish a book** is rewarding. (to부정사)
B **Completing this project** is my task. (동명사)
C **That he is honest** is known to everyone. (명사절)
D **What she said yesterday** proved to be true. (관계사절)
E **When the generator was invented** remains a mystery. (의문사절)
F Happy are **those who know the pleasure of donating**. (도치문)

② 가주어-진주어

G **It** is very difficult **to repair this car**.
= This car is very difficult to repair.

③ 명령문은 동사원형으로 시작

H **Study** hard, or you will fail in the exam.

PRACTICE

A 어법상 **틀린** 부분을 바르게 고쳐 쓰시오.

1 Beautify your home improves your quality of life.
2 He made such mistakes is not true.
3 That I am lacking is wisdom.
4 It is not important know how old she is.
5 If you want to improve, repeating what you're learning.

B 네모 안에서 어법에 맞는 표현으로 가장 적절한 것을 고르시오.

1 It will help revitalize their efforts find / to find an economical way to use coal to produce carbon fibers, as some rural communities are suffering from the decline in coal production.

2 Much better is said / to say , "To help make sure that other people provide answers as useful as yours have been, please tell them that you and another person answered some questions about each other."

3 If it becomes clear the purchase you consider making will provide only short-term benefits to you, think / thinking about an experience you could purchase instead that would provide you with longer-term benefits.

적용독해

1 다음 글의 밑줄 친 부분 중, 어법상 <u>틀린</u> 것은? 고1 학평 기출 응용

Are you honest with yourself about your strengths and weaknesses? It is important ① <u>to get</u> to really know yourself and learn what your weaknesses are. ② <u>Accepting</u> your role in your problems means that you understand the solution lies within you. ③ <u>To know</u> that you have a weakness in a certain area can help you get educated and do what you have to do to improve things for yourself. ④ <u>That</u> your social image is terrible can also help you look within yourself and take the necessary steps to improve it, TODAY. You have the ability to choose how to respond to life. ⑤ <u>Deciding</u> today to end all the excuses, and stop lying to yourself about what is going on. The beginning of growth comes when you begin to personally accept responsibility for your choices.

2 다음 글의 밑줄 친 부분 중, 어법상 <u>틀린</u> 것은? 고2 학평 기출 응용

There is no frame-free way to evaluate anything. ① <u>Consider</u> this example. College students were asked whether they would support a multimillion-dollar safety measure that would save 150 lives at risk. Is 150 lives a lot or a little? Well, compared with what? Other students were asked whether it would be better ② <u>to support</u> a safety measure that would save 98 percent of 150 lives at risk. These students were more favorable toward it than the students who were told it would save 150 lives. Obviously, ③ <u>save</u> 150 lives is better than saving 98 percent of 150 lives, but a measure that saved 98 percent of the lives ④ <u>seems</u> clearly cost-effective. The 98 percent figure provides the students with a frame that 150 lives by itself does not. ⑤ <u>Whether</u> the money spent on safety is seen as a wise decision or not will depend on the context of comparison. When people are told that a safety measure will save 98 percent of 150 lives, a frame is created between 150 lives and 98 percent of 150 lives.

---

1 strength 강점　weakness 약점　solution 해결책　improve 개선하다　necessary 필요한　respond 대응하다　excuse 변명
responsibility 책임

2 frame (인식의) 틀　evaluate 평가하다　multimillion 수백만의　safety measure 안전 대책　at risk 위험에 처한　cost-effective 비용 효과가 큰
figure 수치　context of comparison 비교의 상황

글의 목적

1 다음 글의 목적으로 가장 적절한 것은? `고1 학평 기출 응용`

Dear Mrs. Coling,

My name is Susan Harris and I am writing on behalf of the students at Lockwood High School. Many students at the school have been working on a project about the youth unemployment problem in Lockwood. You are invited to attend a special presentation that will be held at our school auditorium on April 16th. At the presentation, students will propose a variety of ideas for developing employment opportunities for the youth within the community. As one of the famous figures in the community, we would be honored by your attendance. We look forward to seeing you there.

Sincerely,

Susan Harris

① 학생들이 준비한 발표회 참석을 부탁하려고

② 학생들을 위한 특별 강연을 해 준 것에 감사하려고

③ 청년 실업 문제의 해결 방안에 관한 강연을 의뢰하려고

④ 학생들의 발표회에 대한 재정적 지원을 요청하려고

⑤ 학생들의 프로젝트 심사 결과를 알리려고

---

1 on behalf of ~을 대신하여 work on (일·연구 등에) 작업하다 youth 청년 unemployment 실업 attend 참석하다 presentation 발표회 auditorium 강당 propose 제안하다 a variety of 다양한 develop 만들다, 개발하다 opportunity 기회 community 지역 사회 figure (저명)인사, 인물 honor ~에게 영예를 주다

2 다음 글의 목적으로 가장 적절한 것은? `고1 학평 기출`

Thank you for staying with us. Since our hotel was opened in 1976, we have been committed to protecting our planet by reducing our energy consumption and waste. In an effort to save the planet, we have adopted a new policy and we need your help. If you hang the Eco-card at the door, we will not change your sheets, pillow cases, and pajamas. In addition, we will leave the cups untouched unless they need to be cleaned. In return for your cooperation, we will make a contribution on your behalf to the National Forest Restoration Project. We appreciate your cooperation on our eco-friendly policy.

① 생활 속에서 실천 가능한 에너지 절약법을 소개하려고
② 호텔의 친환경 정책에 대한 고객의 협조를 당부하려고
③ 환경 보호를 위한 자원봉사 활동 참여를 권장하려고
④ 호텔의 내부 공사로 인한 영업 중단을 공지하려고
⑤ 호텔과 연계된 숲 체험 여행 상품을 홍보하려고

3 다음 글의 목적으로 가장 적절한 것은? `고3 학평 기출`

You can learn the success secrets of the greatest people who ever lived. The lives of famous people have been recorded in biographies and are ready for you to read and research. The lives of great government leaders, businesspeople, and humanitarians are there. You will read about successes and triumphs. You will also learn how many times champions lose on their way to winning. In reading biographies, you may come to the startling conclusion that you are not very different from those great people. You may conclude, "Hey, I can do that." You can make your life significant. Biographies help show the way. You only have to go to the library, bookstores, or surf the Internet.

① 위인전 읽기를 장려하려고
④ 자기 계발 프로그램을 홍보하려고
③ 도서 구입 예산 증대를 요청하려고
④ 효율적인 자료 수집 방법을 소개하려고
⑤ 자서전 출판을 위한 정보를 제공하려고

---

2 be committed to ~에 헌신하다 reduce 줄이다 consumption 소비 effort 노력 adopt 채택하다 policy 정책 sheet 침대 시트 pillow 베개 cooperation 협조 make a contribution 기부하다 on one's behalf to ~를 대신하여 appreciate 감사하다
3 record 기록하다 biography 전기 government 정부 humanitarian 인도주의자 triumph 승리 startling 놀라운 conclusion 결론 significant 의미 있는

02강 접미사 2(부사형/형용사형)

026
silently
[sáiləntli]
📖 튄 조용히, 말없이 ▸ silent(조용한)+ly(부사형 접미사)
➕ ironically 역설적이게도　probably 아마　roughly 대략

027
forward
[fɔ́:rwərd]
튄 앞(쪽)으로 ▸ for(forward, 앞에)+ward(부사형 접미사)
➕ toward ~쪽으로　backward 뒤(쪽으)로　upward 위(쪽으)로

028
otherwise
[ʌ́ðərwàiz]
튄 그렇지 않다면, 다르게 ▸ other(다른)+wise(부사형 접미사)
➕ clockwise 시계 방향으로　crabwise 게처럼 옆으로

029
beneficial
[bènəfíʃəl]
혱 이로운 ▸ benefit(이점)+ial(형용사형 접미사)
➕ financial 재정적인　industrial 산업의　sacrificial 희생적인

030
surrounding
[səráundiŋ]
혱 둘러싼, 주위의 ▸ surround(둘러싸다)+ing(형용사형 접미사)
➕ leading 선도적인　wanting 부족한　outstanding 뛰어난

031
western
[wéstərn]
혱 서양의, 서쪽의 ▸ west(서쪽)+ern(형용사형 접미사)
➕ eastern 동쪽의　southern 남쪽의　northern 북쪽의

032
incredible
[inkrédəbl]
혱 대단한, 믿을 수 없는 ▸ in(not)+cred(trust)+(a/i)ble(형용사형 접미사)
➕ edible 식용의　considerable 상당한　compatible 호환되는

033
humanoid
[hjú:mənɔ̀id]
혱 인간 모양의, 로봇의 ▸ human(인간)+oid(형용사형 접미사)
➕ deltoid 삼각형의　typhoid 장티푸스의　tabloid 타블로이드판(신문)의

034
aimless
[éimlis]
혱 목적 없는 ▸ aim(목적)+less(형용사형 접미사)
➕ worthless 쓸모없는　reckless 무분별한　restless 불안한

035
athletic
[æθlétik]
혱 운동의, 체육의 ▸ athlete(운동선수)+ic(형용사형 접미사)
➕ economic 경제의　tragic 비극적인　chronic 만성적인

036
extensive
[iksténsiv]
혱 광범위한 ▸ extend(넓히다)+sive(형용사형 접미사)
➕ intensive 집중적인　massive 대규모의　passive 수동적인

037
obvious
[ábviəs]
혱 분명한 ▸ ob(against)+vi(see)+ous(형용사형 접미사)
➕ ambiguous 애매한　tremendous 엄청난　nervous 신경의

038

excellent
[éksələnt]

형 뛰어난, 훌륭한　❯ excel(뛰어나다)+(e/a)nt(형용사형 접미사)

⊕ confident 자신 있는　　pleasant 즐거운　　transparent 투명한

039

particular
[pərtíkjələr]

형 특별한　❯ part(i)+cul(small)+ar(형용사형 접미사)

⊕ familiar 친숙한　　peculiar 특이한　　singular 단수의

040

individual
[ìndəvídʒuəl]

형 개개인의　❯ in(not)+divide(나누다)+ual(형용사형 접미사)

⊕ gradual 점진적인　　mutual 상호 간의　　punctual 시간을 엄수하는

041

physical
[fízikəl]

형 신체적인, 물리적인　❯ physic(body)+cal(형용사형 접미사)

⊕ typical 전형적인　　tropical 열대의　　philosophical 철학적인

042

friendly
[fréndli]

형 친화적인, 우호적인　❯ friend(친구)+ly(형용사형 접미사)

⊕ costly 값비싼　　deadly 치명적인　　leisurely 여유 있는

043

induced
[indjú:sd]

형 유발된, 야기된　❯ induce(유발하다)+ed(형용사형 접미사)

⊕ learned 학식 있는　　accustomed 익숙한　　qualified 자격이 있는

044

doubtful
[dáutfəl]

형 의심스러운　❯ doubt(의심)+ful(형용사형 접미사)

⊕ harmful 해로운　　fruitful 보람 있는　　grateful 감사하는

045

lengthy
[léŋkθi]

형 긴, 오랜　❯ length(길이)+y(형용사형 접미사)

⊕ wealthy 부유한　　thirsty 갈증 난　　trustworthy 신뢰할 수 있는

046

desperate
[déspərit]

형 절망적인　❯ de(away)+sper(hope)+ate(형용사형 접미사)

⊕ passionate 열정적인　　fortunate 행운의　　moderate 적당한

047

elementary
[èləméntəri]

형 기본의, 초등의　❯ element(원소, 기본)+ary(형용사형 접미사)

⊕ sanitary 위생적인　　military 군대의　　extraordinary 뛰어난

048

preparatory
[pripǽrətɔ̀:ri]

형 준비의, 대비의　❯ prepare(준비하다)+ory(형용사형 접미사)

⊕ satisfactory 만족하는　　introductory 도입의　　auditory 청각의

049

selfish
[sélfiʃ]

형 이기적인　❯ self(자아)+ish(형용사형 접미사)

⊕ childish 유치한　　sluggish 느린　　roundish 둥그스름한

050

hostile
[hástəl]

형 적대적인　❯ host(enemy)+ile(형용사형 접미사)

⊕ fertile 비옥한　　fragile 깨지기 쉬운　　sterile 살균한

PRACTICE

A   알맞은 접미사를 골라 단어를 완성하시오.

		보기				보기	
1	self	-ary	_____	6	host	-ful	_____
2	silent	-ish	_____	7	for	-ile	_____
3	length	-y	_____	8	doubt	-oid	_____
4	element	-ly	_____	9	human	-wise	_____
5	surround	-ing	_____	10	other	-ward	_____

B   빈칸에 들어갈 알맞은 표현을 고르시오.

1 Your research proposal should have a _____ discussion of your goals.

① lengthen   ② longing   ③ lengthy   ④ length

2 The _____ committee is busy preparing the funeral ceremony.

① prepare   ② preparable   ③ preparatory   ④ preparatorily

3 Your success depends mainly on how _____ you have studied.

① extend   ② extensive   ③ extensively   ④ extension

4 Considering the year of publication, the books are in _____ condition.

① excel   ② excellent   ③ excellently   ④ excellence

5 It is not _____ that each time we repeat an act, we learn something new.

① doubt   ② doubtful   ③ doubtfully   ④ undoubtedly

C   네모 안에서 문맥에 맞는 낱말로 가장 적절한 것을 고르시오.

1 Writers such as Shakespeare, through their works, imply that all of the characters are constantly wearing masks: Evil types such as Iago in the play *Othello* are able to conceal their fertile / hostile intentions behind a friendly smile.

2 When discovering that Isaac Singer had stolen the patent of a sewing machine he invented, Elias Howe took Singer to court, where he could get royalties from Singer after a(n) lengthy / aimless court fight — two decades.

적용독해

1 다음 글의 밑줄 친 부분 중, 문맥상 낱말의 쓰임이 적절하지 <u>않은</u> 것은? 고1 학평 기출

To rise, a fish must reduce its overall density, and most fish do this with a swim bladder. A fish fills its bladder with oxygen collected from the ① surrounding water. As it is filled, the bladder expands. Then, the fish has a greater volume, but its weight is not greatly ② increased. This means that its density has been decreasing, so the fish experiences a greater rising force. Finally, when the bladder is fully expanded, the fish is at its ③ minimum volume and is pushed to the surface. Most fish ④ rise using this method, but not all do. Some species don't need a swim bladder because they spend all their lives moving along the ocean floor. Other fish float and sink by propelling themselves ⑤ forward.

* swim bladder: (물고기의) 부레

2 다음 글의 밑줄 친 부분 중, 문맥상 낱말의 쓰임이 적절하지 <u>않은</u> 것은? 고2 학평 기출

It can be helpful to read your own essay aloud to hear how it sounds, and it can sometimes be even more beneficial to hear someone else read it. Either reading will help you to hear things that you might otherwise not notice when editing ① silently. If you feel uncomfortable having someone read to you, however, or if you simply don't have someone you can ask to do it, you can have your computer ② read your essay to you. Granted, it's not quite the same thing, and the computer is not going to tell you when something doesn't "sound right." The computer also won't stumble over things that are ③ awkward — it will just plow right on through. But hearing the computer read your writing is a very ④ similar experience from reading it yourself. If you have never tried it, you might find that you notice areas for revision, editing, and proofreading that you didn't ⑤ notice before.

* stumble: 말을 더듬다

---

1 density 밀도　surrounding 주위의　expand 팽창하다　volume 부피, 양　surface 수면, 표면　species 종　propel 헤엄쳐 나아가다　forward 앞(쪽)으로
2 aloud 큰소리로　beneficial 이로운, 유익한　otherwise 그렇지 않으면　notice 알아차리다　edit 편집하다　uncomfortable 불편한　granted 물론　awkward 어색한, 서투른　plow on 계속해 나가다　revision 수정　proofreading 교정

① 동사의 종류

A The sun **rises** in the east. (1형식 완전자동사)

B My wife **is** an English teacher. (2형식 불완전자동사)

C David and I **play** tennis every day. (3형식 완전타동사)

D She **gave** me a nice birthday gift. (4형식 수여동사) ▶p.60

E My friend **made** his parents happy. (5형식 불완전타동사) ▶p.44

② 동사의 위치

F The man in the store **looks** very old. (문장의 본동사)

G Some cars which **have** bad brakes are dangerous. (관계대명사절의 동사)

H What **made** me happy was her kind attitude. (관계대명사절의 동사)

I The park where we **take** a walk is near my house. (관계부사절의 동사)

J That she **made** a mistake makes me feel sad. (명사절의 동사)

K He asked me whether I would **accept** the invitation. (명사절의 동사) ▶p.84

L I don't know where this car **was** made. (의문사절의 동사) ▶p.84

M They got home safely before it **was** too dark. (부사절의 동사)

N Never **have** I **dreamed** that I would become a pilot. (도치문의 동사) ▶p.230

O So happy **was** I that I called my parents right away. (도치문의 동사)

PRACTICE

A 밑줄 친 부분을 어법에 맞게 고쳐 쓰시오.

1 The dictionary I bought yesterday <u>be</u> for elementary students.

2 The number of students <u>suffer</u> from bullying is increasing.

3 Humanoid robots <u>design</u> to imitate human behavior are widely used.

4 She avoids sending messages that <u>including</u> unnecessary information.

5 No sooner <u>having</u> I come home than I realized my phone was gone.

B 네모 안에서 어법에 맞는 표현으로 가장 적절한 것을 고르시오.

1 The introduction of alien plants resulted in the disruption and impoverishment of natural plant communities in South Africa, where Australian shrubs introduced to its western region ⸤degraded / degrading⸥ species-rich fynbos plant communities.

2 The introduction of extensive vehicle and roadway safety laws ⸤started / starting⸥ in the mid-1960s led to the number of highway deaths decreasing from roughly 51,000 in 1966 to 42,000 in 2000, even as the number of miles driven per year increased nearly 300%.

적용독해

1 다음 글의 밑줄 친 부분 중, 어법상 틀린 것은? 고3 학평 기출 응용

In the mid-1970s some scientists observed employees of two manufacturing plants in the United States. Sadly, both plants were scheduled to shut down. The employees ① working at their respective plants for twenty years on average were about to lose their jobs without any preparation. Scientists who followed these workers ② found that the employees experienced more days of illness before the plants were shut than during the weeks of unemployment that followed. The anxiety induced by anticipating the loss of their jobs ③ damaged their health and well-being. Ironically, once unemployed, the workers became healthier. It's because the uncertainty of how life would be without a job ④ being removed. Anxiety was reduced, and attention turned to finding a new job, rather than ⑤ worrying aimlessly about what might be.

2 다음 글의 밑줄 친 부분 중, 어법상 틀린 것은? 고2 학평 기출

Although sports nutrition is a fairly new academic discipline, there have always been recommendations made to athletes about foods that could enhance athletic performance. It is reported that one ancient Greek athlete ate dried figs to enhance training. There are reports that marathon runners in the 1908 Olympics ① drank cognac to improve performance. The teenage running phenomenon, Mary Decker, ② surprised the sports world in the 1970s reported that she ate a plate of spaghetti noodles the night before a race. Such practices may be suggested to athletes because of their real or perceived benefits by individuals who ③ excelled in their sports. Obviously, some of these practices, such as drinking alcohol during a marathon, ④ are no longer recommended, but others, such as a high-carbohydrate meal the night before a competition, ⑤ have stood the test of time.

* phenomenon: 천재

---

1 observe 관찰하다 employee 근로자 manufacture 제조하다 plant 공장 schedule 예정하다 respective 각각의 average 평균 preparation 대비, 준비 unemployment 실직 anxiety 불안감 induce 야기하다 anticipate 예상하다 ironically 역설적으로

2 nutrition 영양학, 영양 discipline (학문의) 분야 recommendation 충고, 추천 enhance 향상시키다 athletic 운동의 fig 무화과 training (경기의) 컨디션 perceive 인식하다 individual 개인 excel 탁월한 능력을 보이다 obviously 분명히, 명백하게 carbohydrate 탄수화물 competition 경기, 경쟁 stand the test 검증을 견뎌내다

심경

1   다음 글에 드러난 'I'의 심경으로 가장 적절한 것은? 고1 학평 기출

The match finished over an hour ago and there is no need for me to feel especially under pressure. I am tired, physically and emotionally, and I sit down to enjoy a cold drink, trying to make myself comfortable. But for some reason, I can't switch off. In my mind I go over every decision I made. I wonder, in particular, what other referees will think of how I did. I am concerned about having made mistakes, and the objections of the spectators are still ringing in my ears. I keep telling myself: "Forget the game," "My colleagues and I agreed on everything," "On the whole, I did a good job." And yet there are still concerns despite all my efforts to brush them aside.

① bored and irritated
② shocked and scared
③ touched and grateful
④ worried and doubtful
⑤ relieved and satisfied

2   다음 글에 드러난 Garnet의 심경 변화로 가장 적절한 것은? 고1 학평 기출

Garnet blew out the candles and lay down. It was too hot even for a sheet. She lay there, sweating, listening to the empty thunder that brought no rain, and whispered, "I wish the drought would end." Late in the night, Garnet had a feeling that something she had been waiting for was about to happen. She lay quite still, listening. The thunder rumbled again, sounding much louder. And then slowly, one by one, as if someone were dropping pennies on the roof, came the raindrops. Garnet held her breath hopefully. The sound paused. "Don't stop! Please!" she whispered. Then the rain burst strong and loud upon the world. Garnet leaped out of bed and ran to the window. She shouted with joy, "It's raining hard!" She felt as though the thunderstorm was a present.

* rumble: (천둥·지진 따위가) 우르르 울리다

① wishful → excited
② embarrassed → proud
③ ashamed → satisfied
④ indifferent → frightened
⑤ grateful → disappointed

---

1 pressure 중압감, 압박   physically 신체적으로   in particular 특히   referee 심판   concerned 걱정하는   objection 이의   despite ~에도 불구하고

2 blow 불다   sweat 땀을 흘리다   empty 공허한   whisper 속삭이다   drought 가뭄   pause 잠시 멈추다   leap out 뛰쳐나오다

3

다음 글에 드러난 Rowe의 심경 변화로 가장 적절한 것은? 고2 학평 기출

Rowe jumps for joy when he finds a cave because he loves being in places where so few have ventured. At the entrance he keeps taking photos with his cell phone to show off his new adventure later. Coming to a stop on a rock a few meters from the entrance, he sees the icy cave's glittering view. He says, "Incredibly beautiful!" stretching his hand out to touch the icy wall. Suddenly, his footing gives way and he slides down into the darkness. He looks up and sees a crack of light about 20 meters above him. 'Phone for help,' he thinks. But he realizes there's no service this far underground. He tries to move upward but he can't. He calls out, "Is anyone there?" There's no answer.

① delighted → grateful

② disappointed → ashamed

③ indifferent → regretful

④ bored → frightened

⑤ excited → desperate

---

3 cave 동굴 venture 탐험하다 entrance 입구 glittering 빛나는 incredibly 믿을 수 없을 정도로 stretch 뻗다, 늘이다 crack 틈 above ~보다 위에 realize 깨닫다

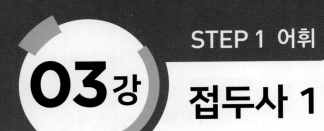

03강 접두사 1

051
accumulate
[əkjúːmjəlèit]
동 축적하다 ▶ ac(to)+cumul(pile)+ate
⊕ accustomed 익숙한   accurate 정확한   achieve 성취하다

052
adequate
[ǽdəkwit]
형 충분한, 적합한 ▶ ad(to)+equ(equal)+ate
⊕ adapt 적응하다   adhere 고수하다   adjust 조정하다

053
afford
[əfɔ́ːrd]
동 ~ (살/할) 여유가 있다 ▶ af(to)+ford(go)
⊕ affect 영향을 미치다   affirm 단언하다   affluent 풍부한

054
apply
[əplái]
동 지원하다, 적용하다, 바르다 ▶ ap(to)+ply(fold)
⊕ applaud 박수치다   appease 달래다   approximately 대략

055
associate
[əsóuʃièit]
동 연관시키다 ▶ as(to)+soci(companion)+ate
⊕ assign 할당하다   asset 자산   assault 폭행

056
attention
[əténʃən]
명 주목, 관심 ▶ at(to)+tend(stretch)+tion
⊕ attitude 태도   attempt 시도   attain 달성하다

057
intellectual
[ìntəléktʃuəl]
형 지성의 명 지식인 ▶ inter/intro(inward)+lect(select)+ual
⊕ intelligence (비밀) 정보   introvert 내성적인 사람

058
interstellar
[ìntərstélər]
형 (행)성간의 ▶ inter(between)+stell(star)+ar
⊕ interfere 간섭하다   interpret 통역하다   interrupt 방해하다

059
telescope
[téləskòup]
명 망원경 ▶ tele(far from)+scope(look)
⊕ telepathy 정신 감응   telegram 전보   teleconference 원격 회의

060
observe
[əbzɔ́ːrv]
동 관찰하다, 준수하다 ▶ ob(to, against)+serve(see)
⊕ object 반대하다   obstacle 장애물   obvious 분명한

061
occasion
[əkéiʒən]
명 경우, 행사 ▶ oc(to, against)+cas(fall)+ion
⊕ occur 일어나다   occupy 점유하다   Occidental 서양의

062
opportunity
[àpərtjúːnəti]
명 기회 ▶ op(to, against)+portus(harbor)+ity
⊕ oppose 반대하다   opposite 반대쪽의   oppress 억압하다

063

impress
[imprés]

동 깊은 인상을 주다 ▶ im(in)+press(push)

⊕ import 수입하다　imprison 수감하다　immigrate 이민 가다

064

inherent
[inhí(:)ərənt]

형 내재된, 타고난 ▶ in(in)+her(달라붙다)+ent

⊕ insert 삽입하다　infect 감염시키다　inspect 조사하다

065

undergo
[ʌ̀ndərgóu]

동 겪다, 받다 ▶ under(beneath)+go

⊕ underage 미성년의　underlying 근본적인　undertake 떠맡다

066

reexamine
[rì:igzǽmin]

동 재조사하다 ▶ re(again)+examine

⊕ refreshed 상쾌한　restore 회복하다　reconcile 화해하다

067

reservation
[rèzərvéiʃən]

명 예약 ▶ re(back)+serve(keep)+tion 동 reserve 예약하다

⊕ reflection 반사, 반영　retirement 퇴직　resignation 사임

068

upcoming
[ʌ́pkʌ̀miŋ]

형 다가오는, 곧 있을 ▶ up(up)+coming

⊕ upbringing 교육, 양육　upright 직립한　uprising 봉기, 반란

069

anticipate
[æntísəpèit]

동 예상하다, 기대하다 ▶ ance/ante(before)+cip(take)+ate

⊕ ancient 고대의　ancestor 조상　antecedent 선례, 선행사

070

abnormal
[æbnɔ́ːrməl]

형 비정상적인 ▶ ab(away)+normal(정상적인)

⊕ abandon 버리다　absorb 흡수하다　abuse 남용, 학대

071

postpone
[poustpóun]

동 연기하다 ▶ post(after)+pone(put)

⊕ postwar 전후의　postscript 추신　posterior 뒤의, 후면의

072

parasite
[pǽrəsàit]

명 기생충, 기생 생물 ▶ para(beside)+site(food)

⊕ paragraph 문단, 단락　parachute 낙하산　paradox 역설

073

device
[diváis]

명 장치, 기기 ▶ de(apart)+vice(see) 동 devise 고안하다

⊕ deceive 속이다　derive 도출되다　depart 출발하다

074

descend
[disénd]

동 내려오다, 기원하다 ▶ de(down)+scend(climb)

⊕ decline 감소하다　destroy 파괴하다　despise 경멸하다

075

deny
[dinái]

동 부정하다 ▶ de(completely)+ny(not) 명 denial 부정

⊕ devote 전념하다　delicate 섬세한　desolate 황량한

PRACTICE

A

알맞은 접두사를 골라 단어를 완성하시오.

보기		
de	1 -cumulate	_____
ab	2 -normal	_____
ac	3 -vice	_____
inter	4 -serve	_____
ob	5 -stellar	_____

보기		
af	6 -ny	_____
de	7 -ford	_____
re	8 -tire	_____
under	9 -scope	_____
tele	10 -go	_____

B

밑줄 친 부분의 의미가 <u>다른</u> 하나를 고르시오.

1 ① <u>im</u>press   ② <u>im</u>port   ③ <u>im</u>migrate   ④ <u>im</u>possible

2 ① <u>in</u>herent   ② <u>in</u>spect   ③ <u>in</u>convenient   ④ <u>in</u>fect

3 ① <u>ab</u>normal   ② <u>ac</u>cumulate   ③ <u>af</u>ford   ④ <u>at</u>tention

C

알맞은 단어를 〈보기〉에서 골라 빈칸을 채우시오.

〈보기〉	undergo	anticipate	abnormal	adequate	impress

1 His teacher was _____(e)d by his abilities.

2 The country is _____ing a financial crisis.

3 The journey took longer than we _____(e)d.

4 This computer is not _____ for progamers.

5 It's not _____ to feel nervous before an interview.

D

네모 안에서 문맥에 맞는 낱말로 가장 적절한 것을 고르시오.

1 Advertising experts have learned that the commercials that we remember will hook us into a story because the most memorable and effective advertisements of all time involve a(n) monotonous / impressive storyline.

2 While scheduled breaks keep you on track by being strategic methods of self-reinforcement, unscheduled breaks derail you from your goal, as they offer you opportunities to postpone / advance your schedule by making you feel as if you've got "free time."

적용독해

1 다음 글의 밑줄 친 부분 중, 문맥상 낱말의 쓰임이 적절하지 <u>않은</u> 것은? `고1 학평 기출 응용`

Everyone knows a young person who is impressively "street smart" but does poorly in school. We think it is a waste that one who is so intelligent about so many things in life seems unable to ① <u>apply</u> that intelligence to academic work. What we don't realize is that schools and colleges might be at ② <u>fault</u> for missing the opportunity to draw such street smarts and guide them toward good academic work. Nor do we consider one of the major reasons why schools and colleges ③ <u>notice</u> the intellectual potential of street smarts: the fact that we ④ <u>associate</u> those street smarts with anti-intellectual concerns. We associate the educated life, the life of the mind, too ⑤ <u>narrowly</u> with subjects and texts that we consider inherently weighty and academic.

2 다음 글의 밑줄 친 부분 중, 문맥상 낱말의 쓰임이 적절하지 <u>않은</u> 것은? `고1 학평 기출`

People have higher expectations as their lives get better. However, the higher the expectations, the more difficult it is to be satisfied. We can increase the satisfaction we feel in our lives by ① <u>controlling</u> our expectations. Adequate expectations leave room for many experiences to be pleasant surprises. The challenge is to find a way to have ② <u>proper</u> expectations. One way to do this is by keeping wonderful experiences ③ <u>rare</u>. No matter what you can afford, save great wine for special occasions. Make an elegantly styled silk blouse a special treat. This may seem like an act of ④ <u>accepting</u> your desires, but I don't think it is. On the contrary, it's a way to make sure that you can continue to experience ⑤ <u>pleasure</u>. What's the point of great wines and great blouses if they don't make you feel great?

---

1 **street smart** 처세술 **apply** 적용하다 **intellectual** 지적인 **potential** 잠재력 **associate** 연관시키다 **narrowly** 좁게 **inherently** 본질적으로 **weighty** 중요한

2 **expectation** 기대감 **satisfied** 만족한 **adequate** 적절한 **rare** 드문 **afford** 여유가 되다 **occasion** 행사 **elegantly** 품위 있게, 우아하게 **treat** 한 턱, 즐거움 **accept** 받아들이다 **desire** 욕구 **on the contrary** 그와 반대로

목적어

① 목적어의 유형(명사, 명사구, 명사절)과 위치

A He finished **writing** a book. (동명사) ▶p.134

B She refused **to take** the money. (to부정사)

C Galileo discovered **that the earth goes around the sun**. (명사절)

D We exactly know **what we have to do**. (의문사가 이끄는 명사절)

E He was excited about **going** to Africa. (전치사 + (동)명사) ▶p.100

F There are some tips on **how you can prevent gray hair**. (전치사 + 명사절)

② 가목적어—진목적어: to부정사나 명사절이 5형식 문장의 목적어일 때

G He found **it** easy **to take** a walk every morning.

H He found to take a walk every morning easy. (×)

③ 재귀대명사: 주어와 목적어가 같으면 목적어는 재귀대명사

I Narcissus loved **himself** too much.

J Lisa is proud of her for winning the award. (Lisa ≠ her)

PRACTICE

A 밑줄 친 부분을 어법에 맞게 고쳐 쓰시오.

1 She planned <u>do</u> exercise regularly.

2 I attempted <u>cross</u> the lake.

3 Jane finished <u>eat</u> breakfast.

4 After he was wounded, he struggled <u>do</u> the work.

5 They talked about <u>become</u> a teacher.

6 The plan allowed us to help the kid without <u>embarrass</u> him.

7 The committee won't accept <u>that</u> he suggests.

8 He thought it hard <u>write</u> an email in English.

9 Dolphins don't limit <u>them</u> to imitating each other.

10 Using its poison, the fish protects <u>it</u> against predators.

B 네모 안에서 어법에 맞는 표현으로 가장 적절한 것을 고르시오.

1 Studies show that / what many parasites actually force their hosts to attack other potential hosts or to be killed and eaten so that the parasites are passed on.

2 Most visitors to the Dudley zoo find it convenient make / to make a reservation on the zoo's website as the ticket booth can be crowded.

적용독해

1 다음 글의 밑줄 친 부분 중, 어법상 틀린 것은? **고1 학평 기출**

Though he probably was not the first to do it, Dutch eyeglass maker Hans Lippershey gets credit for putting two lenses on either end of a tube in 1608 and ① creating a "spyglass." Even then, it was not Lippershey but his children who discovered ② that the double lenses made a nearby weathervane look bigger. These early instruments were not much more than toys because their lenses were not very strong. The first person to turn a spyglass toward the sky ③ to be an Italian mathematician and professor named Galileo Galilei. Galileo, who heard about the Dutch spyglass and began making his own, realized right away ④ how useful the device could be to armies and sailors. As he made better and better spyglasses, which were later named telescopes, Galileo decided ⑤ to point one at interstellar space.

* weathervane: 풍향계

2 다음 글의 밑줄 친 부분 중, 어법상 틀린 것은? **고1 학평 기출**

There are many methods for ① finding answers to the mysteries of the universe, and science is only one of these. However, science is unique. Instead of making guesses, scientists follow a system designed to prove ② if their ideas are true or false. They constantly reexamine and test their theories and conclusions. Old ideas are replaced when scientists find new information that they cannot explain. Once somebody makes a discovery, others review ③ it carefully before using the information in their own research. This way of building new knowledge on older discoveries ensures ④ what scientists correct their mistakes. Armed with scientific knowledge, people build tools and machines that ⑤ transform the way we live, making our lives much easier and better.

---

1 Dutch 네덜란드의 spyglass 소형 망원경 discover 발견하다 instrument 도구, 기구 mathematician 수학자 professor 교수 useful 유용한 sailor 선원 telescope 망원경 interstellar 행성 간의

2 unique 독특한 instead of ~ 대신에 guess 추측하다 prove 증명하다 reexamine 재검토하다 theory 이론 conclusion 결론 replace 대체하다 knowledge 지식 ensure 보장하다 armed (지식 등으로) 무장한 transform 변화시키다

필자의 주장

1 다음 글에서 필자가 주장하는 바로 가장 적절한 것은? [고2 학평 기출]

Engaged in procrastination, how do you move from being stuck to doing the day's most difficult tasks? I say, "Eat the frogs!" The idea comes from a Mark Twain quote: "Eat a live frog first thing in the morning, and nothing worse will happen to you the rest of the day." Every morning, commit to dealing with the item on your to-do list that you're dreading the most, and do it before anything else. Mornings are especially ideal for when you need to be productive on creative tasks, such as writing, because you have fewer distractions and your mind is free of the stresses that accumulate over the course of a workday. While diving into undesirable tasks first thing, imagine how good it will feel to have gotten over that hurdle and still have a whole day ahead of you.

* procrastination: 미루는 버릇

① 하기 싫은 일에 시간을 낭비하지 말아야 한다.
② 어렵고 싫은 일을 하루 중 가장 먼저 해야 한다.
③ 업무가 주는 과도한 스트레스에서 벗어나야 한다.
④ 힘든 일을 해결하려면 여러 명이 협동해야 한다.
⑤ 해야 할 일의 목록을 저녁에 작성해야 한다.

---

1 engage 관여하다 stick (계획 등을) 벽에 부딪치게 하다 quote 인용 어구 commit to ~에 전념하다 deal with 처리하다, 다루다 dread 두려워하다 distraction 정신을 산만하게 하는 것 accumulate 쌓이다, 축적하다 undesirable 달갑지 않은, 불쾌한 get over ~을 극복하다 hurdle 장애물

2 다음 글에서 필자가 주장하는 바로 가장 적절한 것은? 고1 학평 기출

Most people don't assess their roles frequently enough and so stay in positions for years longer than they should, settling for suboptimal situations. There isn't a magic number for the amount of time you should stay in one role before evaluating whether it's right or not. But it makes sense to think about how often you do. Some people readjust their lives daily or weekly, constantly optimizing. Others wait years before noticing that they've ended up far from where they had hoped to be. The more frequently you assess your situation, looking for ways to fix problems, the more likely you are to find yourself in a position where things are going well.

① 실패에 대비하여 차선책을 마련해라.
② 구체적인 계획을 세워 시행착오를 줄여라.
③ 문제 해결을 위해 일의 우선순위를 정해라.
④ 업무능력 향상을 위해 충분한 휴식을 취해라.
⑤ 자신의 상황을 자주 평가하고 삶을 재조정해라.

3 다음 글에서 필자가 주장하는 바로 가장 적절한 것은? 고2 학평 기출

Mike Michalowicz, the author of *The Pumpkin Plan*, argues that comedians are the ultimate public speakers. For example, comedians have to hold an audience's attention for an hour or more, they don't get a break during their presentation, and they can't interact with the audience for a Q&A. They are also expected to make the audience laugh constantly. And they don't even get to use presentation software programs, because they want the audience looking at them, not trying to read a screen. These facts don't mean you need to be a comedian on stage to perform well. You aren't even required to tell jokes. To enhance your own presentations, however, start to observe the techniques comedians use, and employ them in your own speech.

① 말을 할 때는 요점을 정확히 전달하라.
② 코미디언들의 테크닉을 발표에 활용하라.
③ 청중과 관련이 있는 소재를 활용해 강연하라.
④ 청중의 눈높이에 맞춰 유머 감각을 발휘하라.
⑤ 뛰어난 코미디언이 되려면 유머 감각을 키워라.

---

2 assess 평가하다 frequently 자주, 빈번히 position 위치 suboptimal 차선의 evaluate 평가하다 readjust 재조정하다 optimize 최적화하다

3 author 작가, 저자 argue 주장하다 attention 주의, 관심 interact with ~와 상호 작용을 하다 expect 기대하다, 예상하다 require 필요로 하다, 필요하다 enhance 향상시키다 observe 관찰하다 technique 기술

04강 접두사 2

076

agreement
[əgríːmənt]

명 동의, 협정, 합의 ❯ ag(to)+gre(즐겁게 만들다)+ment

⊕ aggression 공격   aggrieve 괴롭히다   aggravate 악화시키다

077

amazing
[əméiziŋ]

형 놀라운, 훌륭한 ❯ am(to)+maze(confuse)+ing

⊕ amount 양   amused 기분 좋은   amass 모으다

078

arrival
[əráivəl]

명 도착, 당도 ❯ ar(to)+river(강)+al

⊕ arrange 배열하다   arrest 체포하다   array 다수

079

available
[əvéiləbl]

형 이용 가능한, 시간이 있는 ❯ av(to)+vail(value)+able

⊕ avenge 복수하다   avenue 방법   avow 공약하다

080

disconnected
[dìskənéktid]

형 단절된 ❯ dis(away)+connect(연결하다)+ed

⊕ disprove 반증하다   disposal 처리   discrimination 차별

081

hemisphere
[hémisfiər]

명 반구 ❯ hemi/semi(half)+sphere(globe)

⊕ semiconductor 반도체   demisemi 4분의 1의

082

transmit
[trænsmít]

동 전(송)하다, 전염시키다 ❯ trans(across)+mit(send)

⊕ transform 바꾸다   transport 운송하다   transplant 이식하다

083

atomic
[ətámik]

형 원자의, 원자력의 ❯ a(not)+tom(cut)+ic

⊕ amoral 도덕관념이 없는   anonymous 익명의   atheism 무신론

084

perceive
[pərsíːv]

동 인지하다, 인식하다 ❯ per(completely)+ceive(take)

⊕ persuade 설득하다   perplexed 당혹스런   persecution 박해

085

diverse
[daivə́ːrs]

형 다양한 ❯ di(away)+verse(turn)

⊕ dimension 차원   dilute 희석시키다   digress 일탈하다

086

select
[silékt]

동 선택하다, 선별하다 ❯ se(apart)+lect(choose)

⊕ secure 안전한   secret 비밀   separate 분리하다

087

contrast
[kántræst]

명 대조, 대비 ❯ contra(against)+st(stand)

⊕ contradict 반박하다   controversy 논쟁   control 통제, 제어

088

unrivaled
[ʌnráivəld]

형 경쟁 상대가 없는 ▶ un(not)＋rival(경쟁자)＋ed

⊕ unnoticed 눈에 띄지 않는   unconditioned 무조건적인

089

output
[áutpùt]

명 생산(량), 산출(물) ▶ out(out)＋put(두다)

⊕ outcome 결과   outbreak 발발   outstanding 현저한

090

subtle
[sʌ́tl]

형 미묘한, 섬세한 ▶ sub(under)＋tle(짜 놓은)

⊕ suburb 교외   submarine 잠수함   submerge 물속에 잠기다

091

suggest
[səgdʒést]

동 제안하다, 시사하다 ▶ sug(under)＋gest(carry)

⊕ sudden 갑작스런   suffix 접미사   suspicion 의심, 의혹

092

supplement
[sʌ́pləmènt]

명 보조 식품 동 보완하다 ▶ sup(under)＋ple(fill)＋ment

⊕ support 뒷받침하다   supply 공급(량)   suppress 억압하다

093

impossible
[impásəbl]

형 불가능한 ▶ im(not)＋possible(가능한)

⊕ immature 미숙한   immortal 불멸의   immune 면역의

094

inevitable
[inévitəbl]

형 필연적인, 불가피한 ▶ in(not)＋evitable(명확한)

⊕ inanimate 무생물의   incompetent 무능한   infinite 무한한

095

present
[prizént]

형 현재의, 참석한 ▶ pre(before)＋sent(being)

⊕ predict 예측하다   prefix 접두사   precede 선행하다

096

process
[práses, próuses]

명 과정 동 처리하다 ▶ pro(before)＋cess(go)

⊕ profound 심오한   prolong 연장하다   pronoun 대명사

097

by-product
[bai-prádəkt]

명 부산물 ▶ by(secondary)＋product(제품)

⊕ by-election 보궐선거   bypass 우회로   bystander 방관자

098

diameter
[daiǽmitər]

명 직경, 지름 ▶ dia(across)＋meter(measure)

⊕ diagonal 대각선의   diagnosis 진단   dialog 대화

099

supernatural
[sjùːpərnǽtʃərəl]

형 초자연적인 ▶ super(over)＋natural(자연적인)

⊕ superb 훌륭한   supreme 최고의   superlative 최상급의

100

downside
[dáunsàid]

명 단점, 하락세 ▶ down(down)＋side(측면)

⊕ downsize 축소하다   run-down 낡은   downslide 하락

PRACTICE

A 알맞은 접두사를 골라 단어를 완성하시오.

	보기		
1		-lect	_____
2	di	-verse	_____
3	dia	-meter	_____
4	se	-sphere	_____
5	trans	-mit	_____
	hemi		

	보기		
6		-ceive	_____
7	out	-put	_____
8	per	-sent	_____
9	down	-side	_____
10	pre	-natural	_____
	super		

B 밑줄 친 부분의 의미가 <u>다른</u> 하나를 고르시오.

1 ① <u>a</u>tomic   ② <u>per</u>ceive   ③ <u>un</u>rivaled   ④ <u>in</u>evitable

2 ① <u>down</u>size   ② <u>sub</u>tle   ③ <u>dis</u>connected   ④ <u>under</u>go

3 ① <u>pre</u>sent   ② <u>an</u>cestor   ③ <u>post</u>pone   ④ <u>pro</u>cess

C 알맞은 단어를 〈보기〉에서 골라 빈칸을 채우시오.

〈보기〉	subtle	inevitable	agree	downsides	diverse

1 Getting married early has merits and _____.

2 They discussed topics as _____ as sports and engineering.

3 Conflict is sometimes _____, but it can often be avoided with effort.

4 Most scientists _____ that global warming is a serious problem.

5 The facial expressions are so _____ that we can't figure them out exactly.

D 네모 안에서 문맥에 맞는 낱말로 가장 적절한 것을 고르시오.

1 The output that falls from a tree — an acorn — is an important input for a squirrel that eats it. The side effect / by-product of that delicious meal — the squirrel's poop — is an important input for the microbes that consume it.

2 The reason why the human brain(around 1.5 kg, 1,500 cc, and 15 cm in diameter), is so big compared to that of other similarly sized mammals is that big brains are disconnected / specialized for dealing with problems that typically arise when individuals need to interact with others in large groups.

적용독해

1

다음 글의 밑줄 친 부분 중, 문맥상 낱말의 쓰임이 적절하지 <u>않은</u> 것은? **고1 학평 기출 응용**

Creativity is a skill we usually consider uniquely human. For all of human history, we have been the most ① creative beings on Earth. Birds can make their nests, ants can make their hills, but no other species on Earth comes ② close to the level of creativity we humans display. However, just in the last decade we have ③ acquired the ability to do amazing things with computers, like developing robots. With the artificial intelligence ④ setback of the 2010s, computers can now recognize faces, translate languages, take calls for you, write poems, and beat players at the world's most complicated board game, to name a few things. All of a sudden, we must face the possibility that our ability to be creative is not ⑤ unrivaled.

2

다음 글의 밑줄 친 부분 중, 문맥상 낱말의 쓰임이 적절하지 <u>않은</u> 것은? **고2 학평 기출**

I was sitting outside a restaurant in Spain one summer evening, waiting for dinner. The aroma of the kitchens excited my taste buds. My future meal was coming to me in the form of molecules drifting through the atmosphere, too small for my eyes to see but ① detected by my nose. The ancient Greeks first came upon the idea of atoms this way; the smell of baking bread suggested to them that small particles of bread ② existed beyond vision. The cycle of weather ③ disproved this idea: a puddle of water on the ground gradually dries out, disappears, and then falls later as rain. They reasoned that there must be particles of water that turn into steam, form clouds, and fall to earth, so that the water is ④ conserved even though the little particles are too small to see. My paella in Spain had inspired me, four thousand years too ⑤ late, to take the credit for atomic theory.

* taste bud: 미뢰(혀의 감각 기관) ** paella: 파에야(스페인 요리의 하나)

---

1 nest 둥지 display 보여 주다 decade 10년 acquire 습득하다 setback 몰락 recognize 인식하다 translate 번역하다 complicated 복잡한 unrivaled 경쟁자가 없는

2 aroma 향기 excite 자극하다, 흥분시키다 drift 떠다니다, 떠돌다 detect 감지하다, 알아채다 come upon an idea 생각이 떠오르다 suggest 생각나게 하다, 암시하다 particle 알갱이, 입자 vision 시야 puddle 물웅덩이 gradually 점차 reason 추론하다 steam 수증기 conserve 보존하다 inspire 영감을 주다 take the credit for ~에 대한 공로를 인정받다 atomic 원자의 theory 이론

보어 1(2형식)

① 명사형(명사, 명사구, 명사절) 보어

> **A** She became **a class president**. (명사)
> **B** One of my bucket list is **to get a Ph. D**. (to 부정사)
> **C** His aim was **visiting** over 100 countries. (동명사)
> **D** The common myth is **that habits are hard to break**. (명사절)

② 형용사형 보어

① be 동사	am / are / is, was / were, been
② 감각동사	look, feel, seem, appear, sound, taste, 등
③ 상태동사	keep, remain, stay, 등
④ 변화동사	become, get, grow, turn, go, fall, 등

> **E** King Edward was **different** from fairy tale kings.
> **F** Considering his age, he looks **old**.
> **G** This mattress seems **comfortable**.
> **H** I stayed **awake** all night in the laboratory.
> **I** You have the right to remain **silent**.
> **J** Because it was growing **dark**, I became **scared**.

PRACTICE

A 어법상 **틀린** 부분을 바르게 고쳐 쓰시오.

1 Breakfast is the most importantly of the three meals of the day.

2 Remember that regular exercise makes your body keep healthily.

3 A significant change in mapping in the past decade is that it has become personally.

4 In all corners of the world thousands of species quietly go extinction.

5 Never let yourself get thirstily because your brain is being shrunk.

B 네모 안에서 어법에 맞는 표현으로 가장 적절한 것을 고르시오.

1 It is │possible / possibly│ for a person to interpret consequences for their actions in different ways. This inevitably has an effect on their future motivation and behavior.

2 Because fur pelts do not adhere closely to the body, the more air gets between the body and the clothing, the less │effective / effectively│ they are at trapping an insulating layer of air close to the skin.

적용독해

1 다음 글의 밑줄 친 부분 중, 어법상 틀린 것은? `고1 학평 기출 응용`

Clothing doesn't have to be expensive to provide comfort during exercise. Select clothing ① <u>appropriate</u> for the temperature and environmental conditions in which you will be doing exercise. In warm environments, clothes that have a wicking capacity are ② <u>helpful</u> in letting off heat from the body. In contrast, it is ③ <u>best</u> to face cold environments with layers so you can adjust your body temperature to avoid sweating and remain ④ <u>comfortably</u>. Clothing that is appropriate for exercise in chilly weather can make us feel ⑤ <u>warm</u> and improve the exercise experience.

* wick: (모세관 작용으로) 수분을 흡수하거나 배출하다

2 다음 글의 밑줄 친 부분 중, 어법상 틀린 것은? `고1 학평 기출 응용`

Each species of animals can detect a different range of odours. No species can detect all the molecules that are ① <u>present</u> in the environment in which it lives — there are some things that we cannot smell but which some other animals can, and vice versa. There are also differences between individuals, relating to the ability to smell an odour, or how ② <u>pleasantly</u> it seems. For example, some people like the taste of coriander — known as cilantro in the USA — while others find it soapy and ③ <u>unpleasant</u>. This effect has an underlying genetic component due to differences in the genes controlling our sense of smell. Ultimately, the selection of scents detected by a given species, and ④ <u>how</u> that odour is perceived, will depend upon the animal's ecology. Through this, locating the sources of smell that are ⑤ <u>relevant</u> to each species and responding accordingly is possible.

* coriander: 고수

---

1 comfort 편안함 appropriate 적절한 temperature 기온 environmental condition 환경 조건 capacity 기능 in contrast 반면에 layer 겹 adjust 조절하다 avoid 피하다 improve 향상시키다

2 detect 감지하다 odour 냄새 molecule 분자 relate 관련시키다 underlying 내재된, 근본적인 genetic 유전의 component (구성) 요소 gene 유전자 perceive 인식하다 depend upon ~에 달려있다 accordingly 따라서, 그러므로

1 밑줄 친 information blinded가 다음 글에서 의미하는 바로 가장 적절한 것은? 고1 학평 기출

Technology has doubtful advantages. We must balance too much information versus using only the right information and keeping the decision-making process simple. The Internet transmits so much free information on any issue that we think we have to consider all of it in order to make a decision. So we keep searching for answers on the Internet. This makes us information blinded, like deer in headlights, when trying to make personal, business, or other decisions. To be successful in anything today, we have to keep in mind that in the land of the blind, a one-eyed person can accomplish the seemingly impossible. The one-eyed person understands the power of keeping any analysis simple and will be the decision maker when he uses his one eye of intuition.

① unwilling to accept others' ideas
② unable to access free information
③ unable to make decisions due to too much information
④ indifferent to the lack of available information
⑤ willing to take risks in decision-making

2 밑줄 친 by reading a body language dictionary가 의미하는 바로 가장 적절한 것은? 고1 학평 기출

Authentic, effective body language is more than the sum of individual signals. When people work from this rote-memory, dictionary approach, they stop seeing the bigger picture, all the diverse aspects of social perception. Instead, they see a person with crossed arms and think, "Reserved, angry." They agree that they see a smile and think, "Happy." They use a firm handshake to show other people "who is boss." Trying to use body language by reading a body language dictionary is like trying to speak French by reading a French dictionary. Things tend to fall apart in an inauthentic mess. Your actions seem robotic; your body language signals are disconnected from one another. You end up confusing the very people you're trying to attract because your body language just rings false.

---

1 **doubtful** 의문의 여지가 있는 **advantage** 이점, 이익 **balance ~ versus …** …에 맞추어 ~을 조절하다[등가로 만들다] **decision-making process** 의사 결정 과정 **consider** 고려하다 **blinded** 눈 먼 **accomplish** 이루다 **seemingly** 겉보기에 **analysis** 분석 **decision maker** 의사 결정자 **intuition** 직관

① by learning body language within social context

② by comparing body language and French

③ with a body language expert's help

④ without understanding the social aspects

⑤ in a way people learn their native language

3

밑줄 친 The body works the same way가 다음 글에서 의미하는 바로 가장 적절한 것은?

`고2 학평 기출 응용`

The body tends to accumulate problems, often beginning with one small, seemingly minor imbalance. This problem causes another subtle imbalance, which triggers another, then several more. In the end, you get a symptom. It's like lining up a series of dominoes. All you need to do is knock down the first one and many others will fall too. What caused the last one to fall? Obviously it wasn't the one before it, or the one before that, but the first one. The body works the same way. The initial problem is often unnoticed. It's not until some of the later "dominoes" fall that more obvious clues and symptoms appear. In the end, you get a headache, fatigue or depression — or even disease. The last domino is not a destination. When you try to treat just the end-result symptom, the cause of the problem isn't addressed. The first domino is the cause, or primary problem.

① There is no definite order in treating an illness.

② Minor health problems are solved by themselves.

③ You get more and more inactive as you get older.

④ It'll never be too late to cure the end-result symptom.

⑤ The final symptom stems from the first minor problem.

---

2 authentic 실제적인 rote-memory 기계적 암기 approach 접근법 diverse 다양한 fall apart 분리되다 inauthentic 실효성 없는, 진짜가 아닌 mess 엉망, 난장판 robotic (동작 · 표정 등이) 로봇같은 attract 마음을 끌다 ring false 잘못 전달되다, 거짓으로 들리다

3 cause 유발하다; 원인 subtle 미묘한 imbalance 불균형 trigger 유발하다 symptom 증상 line up ~을 한 줄로 세우다 knock down ~을 쓰러뜨리다 obviously 분명히 initial 처음의 unnoticed 눈에 띄지 않는 fatigue 피로 depression 우울증 end-result 최종 결과의 address 해결하다, 처리하다 primary 가장 중요한, 첫 번째의

05강 접두사 3

101
illogical
[ilɑ́dʒikəl]

형 비논리적인 ▶ il(not)+logical(논리적인)
⊕ illegal 불법의   illiberal 편협한   illiterate 문맹의

102
irrational
[irǽʃənəl]

형 비합리적인 ▶ ir(not)+rational(합리적인)
⊕ irregular 불규칙적인   irrelevant 무관한   irresponsible 무책임한

103
embrace
[imbréis]

동 포용하다, 받아들이다 ▶ em(into)+brace(arm)
⊕ emphasize 강조하다   embarrass 당황하게 만들다

104
ensure
[inʃúər]

동 보증하다 ▶ en(make)+sure(확실한)
⊕ enlarge 확대하다   enact 제정하다   enrich 풍요롭게 하다

105
overwhelming
[òuvərhwélmiŋ]

형 압도적인, 매우 힘든 ▶ over(above)+whelm(짓누르다)+ing
⊕ overcome 극복하다   overlook 간과하다   overflow 범람하다

106
alone
[əlóun]

부 혼자서, 홀로 ▶ al(all)+one(한 사람)
⊕ already 이미, 벌써   altogether 전적으로   almighty 전능한

107
supplement
[sʌ́pləmènt]

동 보충하다, 보완하다 ▶ sup(over)+ple(full)+ment
⊕ support 지지하다   supply 공급하다   suppress 억압하다

108
survival
[sərváivəl]

명 생존 ▶ sur(over)+viv(life)+al
⊕ surpass 능가하다   surrender 항복하다   surrealism 초현실주의

109
cooperate
[kouɑ́pərèit]

동 협력하다, 협조하다 ▶ co(with)+oper(work)+ate
⊕ coed 남녀 공학   coworker 직장 동료   coincidence 우연의 일치

110
collective
[kəléktiv]

형 집단적인, 공동의 ▶ col(with)+lect(gather)+ive
⊕ collapse 붕괴   colleague 동료   collide 충돌하다

111
compromise
[kɑ́mprəmàiz]

동 타협하다, 손상시키다 ▶ com(with)+promise(약속)
⊕ commit 저지르다   commission 위원회   complement 보어

112
consequently
[kɑ́nsəkwèntli]

부 결과적으로, 그 결과로 ▶ con(with)+sequ(follow)+ent+ly
⊕ conceal 숨기다   condemn 비난하다   conflict 대립, 모순

113

antisocial
[æ̀ntaisóuʃəl]

형 반사회적인 ▶ anti(against)+social(사회적인)

➕ antibiotic 항생제　antipathy 반감　Antarctic 남극

114

symbolic
[simbálik]

형 상징적인 ▶ sym(with, same)+bol(throw)+ic

➕ symphony 교향곡　sympathy 공감　asymmetrical 비대칭적인

115

syndrome
[síndroum]

명 증후군 ▶ syn(with, same)+drome(run)

➕ synthetic 합성의　synonym 동의어　synergy 공동 작용

116

sustain
[səstéin]

동 지속하다, 유지하다 ▶ sus(under)+tain(hold)

➕ suspense 긴장감　suspect 의심하다　susceptible 민감한

117

malfunction
[mælfʌ́ŋkʃən]

명 오작동, 고장 ▶ mal(bad)+function(기능)

➕ maladjusted 부적응의　malnutrition 영양실조　malady 질병

118

misunderstand
[mìsʌndərstǽnd]

동 잘못 이해하다, 오해하다 ▶ mis(bad)+understand

➕ mistrust 불신하다　misguid 오도하다　mischievous 짓궂은

119

evolution
[èvəlú:ʃən]

명 진화, 발전 ▶ e(out)+volve(roll)+ion

➕ election 선거　eliminate 제거하다　eminent 저명한

120

effort
[éfərt]

명 노력, 작업 ▶ ef(out)+fort(strong)

➕ eclipse (일/월)식　effective 효과적인　erupt 분출하다

121

exceed
[iksí:d]

동 능가하다, 초과하다 ▶ ex(out)+ceed(go)

➕ exaggerage 과장하다　execution 사형 집행　exploit 이용하다

122

non-verbal
[nɑnvə́:rbəl]

형 비언어적인 ▶ non(not)+verb(word)+al

➕ nonflammable 불연성의　non-renewable 재생불가능한

123

multiply
[mʌ́ltəplài]

동 증가하다, 배가시키다 ▶ multi(many)+ply(fold)

➕ multiple 다수의　multitude 다수　multilateral 다자간의

124

superficial
[sjù:pərfíʃəl]

형 피상적인 ▶ super(over)+fic(face)+ial

➕ superior 뛰어난　supervise 감독하다　supreme 최고의

125

belief
[bilí:f]

명 믿음, 신념 ▶ be(make)+lief(light)

➕ behave 행동하다　belong ~에 속하다　belittle 얕보다

PRACTICE

정답 및 해설 p.13

A 주어진 접두사에 어울리는 어근과 접미사를 골라 단어를 완성하고, 그 의미를 쓰시오.

		보기	보기	
1	con	-bol	ing	_____, _____
2	e	-sequent	tion	_____, _____
3	sym	-whelm	ate	_____, _____
4	co	-volu	ly	_____, _____
5	over	-oper	ic	_____, _____

B 밑줄 친 부분의 의미가 다른 하나를 고르시오.

1 ① antisocial   ② obstacle   ③ contrast   ④ embrace

2 ① overlook   ② superficial   ③ sustain   ④ survival

3 ① inherent   ② illogical   ③ non-verbal   ④ amoral

C 알맞은 단어를 〈보기〉에서 골라 빈칸을 채우시오.

〈보기〉 malfunction   illogical   exceed   alone   compromise

1 Holding me responsible for what the boss did is _____.

2 Costs of the modified construction plan could _____ $1 billion.

3 Both sellers and buyers need to be willing to _____ on the price.

4 Parents say that it may be nice to be _____ together without their kids.

5 The nuclear power plant may explode within a few days because of the cooler _____.

D 네모 안에서 문맥에 맞는 낱말로 가장 적절한 것을 고르시오.

1 Little does the internet or social media lead us to exclude / embrace truth or fact. For example, it used to take some effort to find Holocaust-denying pseudohistory; now it's one click away.

2 The green design movement incorporates the principles of sustainability in the design of consumer goods. This approach not only creates products from recycled materials but also designs the products with an eye to their eventual disposal / approval as well as their use.

적용독해

1

다음 글의 밑줄 친 부분 중, 문맥상 낱말의 쓰임이 적절하지 <u>않은</u> 것은? 고1 학평 기출

Social connections are so essential for our survival and well-being that we not only cooperate with others to build relationships, we also compete with others for friends. And often we do ① <u>both</u> at the same time. Take gossip. Through gossip, we bond with our friends, sharing interesting details. But at the same time, we are ② <u>creating</u> potential enemies in the targets of our gossip. Or consider rival holiday parties where people compete to see who will attend *their* party. We can even see this ③ <u>harmony</u> in social media as people compete for the most friends and followers. At the same time, competitive exclusion can also ④ <u>generate</u> cooperation. High school social clubs and country clubs use this formula to great effect: It is through ⑤ <u>selective</u> inclusion *and exclusion* that they produce loyalty and lasting social bonds.

2

다음 글의 밑줄 친 부분 중, 문맥상 낱말의 쓰임이 적절하지 <u>않은</u> 것은? 고1 학평 기출

School assignments have typically required that students work alone. This emphasis on ① <u>individual</u> productivity reflected an opinion that independence is a necessary factor for success. Having the ability to take care of oneself without depending on others was considered a ② <u>requirement</u> for everyone. Consequently, teachers in the past less often arranged group work or encouraged students to acquire teamwork skills. However, since the new millennium, businesses have experienced ③ <u>more</u> global competition that requires improved productivity. This situation has led employers to insist that newcomers to the labor market provide evidence of traditional independence but also ④ <u>interdependence</u> shown through teamwork skills. The challenge for educators is to ensure individual competence in basic skills while ⑤ <u>decreasing</u> learning opportunities that can enable students to also perform well in teams.

---

1 survival 생존　cooperate 협력하다　relationship 관계　compete 경쟁하다　bond 유대를 형성하다; 유대　enemy 적　attend 참석하다　exclusion 배제　generate 야기하다, 일으키다　formula 공식　inclusion 포함　loyalty 충성

2 typically 전형적으로　require 요구하다　emphasis 강조　reflect 반영하다　independence 독립성　necessary 필요한　depend 의존하다　arrange 마련하다　acquire 배우다, 습득하다　insist 요구하다　provide evidence 입증하다　ensure 보장하다　competence 능력　decrease 줄다, 감소하다

보어 2 (5형식)

① 주어＋동사＋목적어＋보어(명사)

make, call, name, elect, appoint, choose, 등
- **A** My daughter named her puppy '**Walnut**'.
- **B** Researchers call this response **the placebo effect**.
- **C** The president appointed him **Minister of Defense**.

② 주어＋동사＋목적어＋보어(형용사)

make, keep, find, consider, leave, 등
- **D** Playing basketball makes me **happy**.
- **E** She always keeps her room **clean**.
- **F** I found the book **covered** with dust.
- **G** We consider this issue **extremely tricky**.

③ 주어＋동사＋목적어＋보어(to부정사)

allow, expect, enable, inspire, encourage, advise, cause, 등
- **H** He allowed me **to enter** the house.
- **I** She encouraged him **to write** creatively.

PRACTICE

A 어법상 틀린 부분을 바르게 고쳐 쓰시오.

1 UNICEF considered this aid project helpfully for war orphans.
2 When we face a dangerous situation, our nose allows more air getting to the lungs.
3 Her insistence that she would give me amazing meals kept me comfortably.
4 In your desire to make others happily, you may pretend to be someone you are not.
5 Unfair demands on our teens are placed by those who expect all things being done well.

B 네모 안에서 어법에 맞는 표현으로 가장 적절한 것을 고르시오.

1 Any discussion of coevolution quickly runs into that / what philosophers call a "causality dilemma," a problem we recognize from the question, "Which came first, the chicken or the egg?"

2 It is an enormously difficult task for consumers to be able to sort through the information they find and make decisions. And what makes it overwhelming / overwhelmingly is that the number of sources of information which we are to base those decisions upon has exploded.

정답 및 해설 p.14

적용독해

1 다음 글의 밑줄 친 부분 중, 어법상 틀린 것은? 고1 학평 기출 응용

Impressionist paintings are probably most popular; it is an easily understood art which does not ask the viewer ① to work hard to understand the imagery. Impressionism is 'comfortable' to look at, with its summer scenes and bright colours appealing to the eye. It is ② important to remember, however, that its public found this new way of painting ③ challenging not only in the way that it was made but also in ④ what was shown. They had never seen such 'informal' paintings before. The edge of the canvas cut off the scene in an arbitrary way, as if snapped with a camera. The subject matter included modernization of the landscape; railways and factories. Artists never considered these subjects ⑤ appropriately before.

2 다음 글의 밑줄 친 부분 중, 어법상 틀린 것은? 고1 학평 기출 응용

Non-verbal communication is not a substitute for verbal communication. Rather, it should function as a supplement, making the richness of the content of the message that is being passed across ① enhanced. Non-verbal communication can be useful in situations where speaking may be impossible or inappropriate. ② Imagine you are in an uncomfortable position while talking to an individual. Non-verbal communication will help you ③ get the symbolic message across to him or her to give you some time off the conversation to be comfortable again. ④ What non-verbal communication does not substitute verbal communication but rather complements it, which enables non-verbal communicators ⑤ to express emotions and attitudes properly is its another advantage. Without the aid of non-verbal communication, there are several aspects of your nature and personality that will not be adequately expressed.

---

1 impressionist 인상주의 화가 popular 인기 있는, 유명한 imagery 형상 appeal 관심을 끌다 informal 격식에 얽매이지 않는 arbitrary 임의 적인 modernization 현대화 landscape 풍경 appropriate 적절한

2 communication 의사소통 substitute 대체물 verbal 언어적인 function 기능 supplement 보충 richness 풍부 inappropriate 부적절한 symbolic 상징적인 conversation 대화 complement 보완하다 advantage 장점 aid 도움 several 몇몇의 aspect 측면 nature 본성 personality 성격 adequately 적절하게 express 표현하다

05강 **45**

글의 요지

1 다음 글의 요지로 가장 적절한 것은? `고1 학평 기출`

Information is worthless if you never actually use it. Far too often, companies collect valuable customer information that ends up buried and never used. They must ensure their data is accessible for use at the appropriate times. For a hotel, one appropriate time for data usage is check-in at the front desk. I often check in at a hotel I've visited frequently, only for the people at the front desk to give no indication that they recognize me as a customer. The hotel must have stored a record of my visits, but they don't make that information accessible to the front desk clerks. They are missing a prime opportunity to utilize data to create a better experience focused on customer loyalty. Whether they have ten customers, ten thousand, or even ten million, the goal is the same: create a delightful customer experience that encourages loyalty.

① 기업 정보의 투명한 공개는 고객 만족도를 향상시킨다.
② 목표 고객층에 대한 분석은 기업의 이익 창출로 이어진다.
③ 고객 충성도를 높이기 위해 고객 정보가 활용될 필요가 있다.
④ 일관성 있는 호텔 서비스 제공을 통해 단골 고객을 확보할 수 있다.
⑤ 사생활 침해에 대한 우려로 고객 정보를 보관하는 데 어려움이 있다.

2 다음 글의 요지로 가장 적절한 것은? `고2 학평 기출 응용`

Have you ever heard of 'Hamlet Syndrome?' When you enter a store, what do you see? It is quite likely that you will see many options and choices. It doesn't matter whether you want to buy tea, coffee, jeans, or a phone. In all these situations, we are basically flooded with options from which we can choose. What will happen if we ask someone, whether online or offline, if he or she prefers having more alternatives or less? The majority of people will tell us that they prefer having more alternatives. This finding is interesting because, as science suggests, the more the options multiply, the harder our decision making process will be. The thing is that when the amount of options exceeds a certain level, our decision making will start to suffer.

---

1 worthless 가치 없는 collect 수집하다 end up 결국 (어떤 처지에) 처하게 되다 bury 묻다 accessible 접근 가능한 appropriate 적절한 usage 사용 indication 표시 utilize 활용하다 focus on ~에 초점을 맞추다 delightful 즐거운

① 공정한 거래는 경제 정의 실현에 기여한다.
② 신중한 선택으로 불필요한 소비를 줄일 수 있다.
③ 구매 방법에 따라 제품에 대한 만족도가 달라진다.
④ 선택의 폭이 넓어질수록 의사 결정은 더 어려워진다.
⑤ 생산 과정의 투명성 확보는 소비자의 권리를 증진시킨다.

3

다음 글의 요지로 가장 적절한 것은? 고1 학평 기출 응용

The neuroscientist Antonio Damasio studied people who were perfectly normal in every way except for brain injuries that damaged their emotional systems. As a result, they were unable to make decisions or function effectively in the world. While they could describe exactly how they should have been functioning, they couldn't determine where to live, what to eat, and what products to buy and use. This finding contradicts the common belief that decision making is the heart of rational, logical thought. But modern research shows that the affective system provides critical assistance to your decision making by helping you make rapid selections between good and bad, reducing the number of things to be considered.

① 뇌 부상은 정상적인 활동에 큰 장애가 된다.
② 정서적 안정감은 효과적인 결정에 영향을 준다.
③ 느낌과 감정은 매일의 의사 결정에 매우 중요하다.
④ 논리적인 사고와 의사 결정은 밀접한 관련이 있다.
⑤ 뇌를 최대한 활용하는 것이 현명한 판단에 도움이 된다.

---

2 enter 들어가다 quite 많은 flood 넘치다, 범람하다 alternative 선택 사항 multiply 늘리다 decision 결정 process 과정 exceed 넘다, 초과하다 certain 특정한 suffer 고통받다

3 neuroscientist 신경과학자 normal 정상인, 평범한 except for ~을 제외하고는 injury 부상 damage 손상을 주다 effectively 효과적으로 describe 설명하다, 묘사하다 exactly 정확하게 determine 결정하다 contradict 모순되다 common 보편적인 rational 이성적인 logical 논리적인 affective 정서적인 critical 결정적인 assistance 도움 reduce 줄이다

06강 어근 1

126
imbalanced
[imbǽlənst]

형 불균형인 ❯ im(not)+ba/bi(two)+lance(저울)+ed
⊕ combine 결합하다   binary 이진법의   binoculars 쌍안경

127
negotiate
[nigóuʃièit]

동 협상하다, 타협하다 ❯ neg(not)+oti(leisure)+ate
⊕ negative 부정적인   neglect 무시하다   negligence 태만

128
pesticide
[péstisàid]

명 살충제 ❯ pest(해충)+cide(kill)
⊕ herbicide 제초제   germicide 살균제   genocide 대학살

129
protect
[prətékt]

동 보호하다 ❯ pro(before)+tect(cover)
⊕ detect 탐지하다   architect 건축가

130
fix
[fiks]

동 고치다, 고정하다 ❯ fix(fasten) 명 fixture 고정(물), 설비
⊕ affix 접사, 붙이다   prefix 접두사   suffix 접미사

131
outperform
[àutpərfɔ́ːrm]

동 더 나은 성과를 내다 ❯ out(than)+per(utterly)+form(수행하다)
⊕ outdo 더 잘하다   outlive 더 오래 살다   outweigh 더 중요하다

132
reflect
[riflékt]

동 반사하다, 반영하다, 숙고하다 ❯ re(back)+flect(bend)
⊕ flexible 유연한   reflex 반사 작용   inflect 굴절시키다

133
inheritance
[inhéritəns]

명 상속, 계승 ❯ in(into)+herit(heir)+ance
⊕ heir 상속인   heritage 유산   heredity 유전, 세습

134
straighten
[stréitən]

동 바로잡다, 해결하다 ❯ straight(unbent)+en(make)
⊕ straight 곧은, 연속한   straightforward 솔직한

135
resist
[rizíst]

동 저항하다 ❯ re(against)+sist(stand)
⊕ assist 돕다   exist 존재하다   persist 지속하다

136
determine
[ditə́ːrmin]

동 결정하다 ❯ de(completely)+termine(limit)
⊕ terminate 종결하다   terminally ill 불치병에 걸린

137
preserve
[prizə́ːrv]

동 보존하다 ❯ pre(before)+serve(keep)
⊕ reserve 예약하다   observe 관찰하다   deserve 받을 만하다
conserve 보호하다   service 근무, 복무, 예배, 접대

138

instead
[instéd]

부 대신에 ▶ in(in)+stead(place)

➕ stead 대신, 대리　steady 꾸준한　steadfast 충실한

139

constant
[kánstənt]

형 끊임없는 ▶ con(with)+sta(stand)+ant

➕ instant 즉석의　distant 멀리 떨어진　stagnant 정체된

140

gracious
[gréiʃəs]

형 우아한, 친절한 ▶ grace(pleasing)+(i)ous

➕ disgrace 불명예　congratulate 축하하다　gratitude 감사

141

declare
[diklέər]

동 선포하다 ▶ de(down)+clare(clear)　명 declaration 선언

➕ clarify 명확히 밝히다　clarity (명확한) 설명　unclarity 애매함

142

reward
[riwɔ́:rd]

명 보상　동 보상하다 ▶ re(back)+ward/ware(watch)

➕ award 상, (상을) 수여하다　aware 알고 있는　beware 조심하다

143

acquire
[əkwáiər]

동 얻다, 습득하다 ▶ ac(to)+quire(ask)

➕ require 필요로 하다　inquire 묻다　request 요청하다

144

discover
[diskʌ́vər]

동 발견하다 ▶ dis(away)+cover(cover)

➕ rediscover 재발견하다　recover 회복하다　uncover 밝히다

145

prevent
[privént]

동 못하게 하다, 예방하다 ▶ pre(before)+vent(come)

➕ advent 출현, 도래　adventure 모험　avenue 대로(큰 도로)

146

ingest
[indʒést]

동 섭취하다, 받아들이다 ▶ in(into)+gest(carry)

➕ digestion 소화　suggestion 제안　congestion 혼잡

147

involve
[inválv]

동 포함하다, 관련시키다 ▶ in(in)+volve(roll)

➕ evolve 진화하다　revolve 회전하다　devolve 양도하다

148

compare
[kəmpέər]

동 비교하다, 비유하다 ▶ com(with)+pare(equal)

➕ prepare 준비하다　repair 수리하다　impair 손상시키다

149

explode
[iksplóud]

동 폭발하다 ▶ ex(out)+plode(clap)

➕ applaud 박수갈채를 보내다　plausible 그럴듯한

150

describe
[diskráib]

동 묘사하다, 기술하다 ▶ de(down)+scribe(write)

➕ prescribe 처방하다　subscribe 구독하다　inscribe 새기다

ascribe ~탓으로 돌리다　transcribe 필사하다, 베끼다

 PRACTICE

A 주어진 접두사와 연결하고, 그 단어와 의미를 각각 쓰시오.

	보기				보기	
1 de		_____ , _____	**6** a		_____ , _____
2 re		_____ , _____	**7** de		_____ , _____
3 ob	serve	_____ , _____	**8** in	scribe	_____ , _____
4 pre		_____ , _____	**9** sub		_____ , _____
5 con		_____ , _____	**10** pre		_____ , _____

B 빈칸에 들어갈 알맞은 표현을 고르시오.

1 Putting on a play _____ a lot of work.

① revolves   ② evolves   ③ involves   ④ devolves

2 Parents must never _____ their children with others.

① prepare   ② repair   ③ compare   ④ impair

3 The FDA said food additives are not that harmful for us to _____.

① invest   ② suggest   ③ congest   ④ ingest

4 Studies show females _____ males at every level from primary to college.

① prevent   ② outperform   ③ declare   ④ negociate

5 Accoding to Greek mythology, Pandora couldn't _____ the temptation to take a look in the box.

① assist   ② exist   ③ persist   ④ resist

C 네모 안에서 문맥에 맞는 낱말로 가장 적절한 것을 고르시오.

1 With no bureaucracy, little to lose, and a passion to prove themselves, when it comes to innovation / resistance , small teams consistently outperform larger organizations.

2 A frozen dinner labeled "75% fat free" seems more appealing / disappointing than it would with the label "25% fat," but the latter might make us reflect more about what we might be eating.

적용독해

정답 및 해설 p.17

1 다음 글의 밑줄 친 부분 중, 문맥상 낱말의 쓰임이 적절하지 <u>않은</u> 것은? 〔고1 학평 기출〕

Pests and diseases are part of nature. In the ideal system there is a natural balance between predators and pests. If the system is ① <u>imbalanced</u>, one population can increase because it is not being preyed upon by another. The aim of natural control is not to eradicate pests and diseases. It is to ② <u>restore</u> a natural balance between pest and predator and keep pests and diseases down to an ③ <u>acceptable</u> level. However, pesticides, another option to natural pest and disease control, do not solve the pest problem. In the past 50 years, pesticide use has ④ <u>increased</u> ten times while crop losses from pest damage have doubled. Here lies the reason why natural control is ⑤ <u>avoided</u> more than pesticide use.

* eradicate: 박멸하다

2 다음 글의 밑줄 친 부분 중, 문맥상 낱말의 쓰임이 적절하지 <u>않은</u> 것은? 〔고1 학평 기출〕

In Ontario, there is an old-growth forest near Temagami. Some people want to cut down the trees for lumber. Others want to keep it as it is: they believe it is ① <u>unique</u> and must be protected for coming generations. Many people are somewhere in the ② <u>middle</u>, wanting some use and some protection. Most people are in favor of using our resources wisely. They prefer practices that make our resources ③ <u>sustainable</u>. That is, we should use our resources wisely now and we will still have more for the future. We are all responsible for looking after the environment. We can learn from First Nations' people who have long known the importance of ④ <u>changing</u> the environment for future generations. What you inherited and live with will become the ⑤ <u>inheritance</u> of future generations.

* First Nations' people: 캐나다 원주민

---

1 pest 해충 predator 포식자 population 개체군 increase 증가하다 prey upon ~을 잡아먹다 aim 목적 restore 회복하다 acceptable 받아들일 수 있는 pesticide 살충제 crop loss 작물 손실 lie (어떤 상태로) 있다

2 old-growth forest 원시림 lumber 목재 protect 보호하다 generation 세대 in favor of ~에 찬성하여 sustainable 지속 가능한 responsible 책임이 있는 inherit 물려받다 inheritance 유산

보어 3 (5형식)

① 지각동사(see, hear, feel, watch, observe, notice 등)

지각동사	목적어	목적격 보어	목적어와 보어의 관계
		동사원형/현재분사	능동
		과거분사(p.p.)	수동

A I heard him **call** my name. / I heard my name **called**.

② 사역동사(make, have, let 등)

사역동사	목적어	목적격 보어	목적어와 보어의 관계
		동사원형	능동
		과거분사(p.p.)	수동

B I had her **wash** my car. / I had my car **washed**.

③ 준사역동사(get, help 등)

		목적격 보어	목적어와 보어의 관계
get	목적어	to부정사	능동
		과거분사(p.p.)	수동
help	목적어	(to) 동사원형	

C I got her **to clean** her room. / I will get the task **done** immediately.
D She helped me **(to) do** my homework.

PRACTICE

A 어법상 틀린 부분을 바르게 고쳐 쓰시오.

1 I heard someone to cry out in the garden.
2 We watched the boys played on the playground.
3 She made me to clean my room.
4 I will never let him did that again.
5 I got my car to fix at the repair shop.
6 He helped me passing the exam.

B 네모 안에서 어법에 맞는 표현으로 가장 적절한 것을 고르시오.

1 Instead of dropping objects off buildings, Galileo decided to roll balls down a ramp to figure out whether the same force that made things fall / to fall would make balls roll down a ramp.

2 Even though you may feel compelled to answer a ringing phone, don't let distractions interrupt / to interrupt your attentive listening to the speaker. Answering phone calls during a conversation is disrespectful.

적용독해

1

다음 글의 밑줄 친 부분 중, 어법상 <u>틀린</u> 것은? 고1 학평 기출 응용

When I was a young girl, my room was always a mess. My mother was always trying to make me ① <u>straighten</u> it up, telling me, "Go clean your room!" I resisted her whenever I heard her ② <u>nagging</u> at me. I hated to be told what to do. I was determined to have my room the way I wanted it. Whether I actually liked living in a messy room or not ③ <u>was</u> another subject altogether. I never stopped to think about the benefits of having a clean room. To me, it was more important to get things ④ <u>to do</u> in my own way. And my mother, like most other parents, did not help me ⑤ <u>realize</u> the benefits for myself. Instead, she insisted on lecturing me.

2

다음 글의 밑줄 친 부분 중, 어법상 <u>틀린</u> 것은? 고3 학평 기출

Coming home from work the other day, I saw a woman trying to turn onto the main street and ① <u>having</u> very little luck because of the constant stream of traffic. I slowed and allowed her to turn in front of me. I was feeling pretty ② <u>good</u> until, a couple of blocks later, she stopped to let a few more cars into the line, causing us both to miss the next light. I found myself completely ③ <u>irritated</u> with her. How dare she slow me down after I had so graciously let her ④ <u>enter</u> the traffic! As I was sitting there stewing, I realized how ridiculous I was being. Suddenly, a phrase I once read came floating into my mind: 'You must do him or her a kindness for inner reasons, not because someone is keeping score or because you will be punished if you don't.' I realized ⑤ <u>what</u> I had wanted a reward: If I do this nice thing for you, you (or someone else) will do an equally nice thing for me.

* stew: 안달하다

---

1 mess 엉망, 혼돈 **try to** ~하려고 노력하다 **straighten up** 정돈하다 **resist** 저항하다 **nag** 잔소리를 하다 **subject** 문제, 주제 **lecture** 잔소리하다, 강의하다

2 constant 지속적인 stream 흐름 traffic 차량, 교통(량) irritated 짜증 난 graciously 친절하게 ridiculous 어리석은 phrase 구절 float 떠오르다 reason 동기, 이유 punish 처벌하다 reward 보상 equally 똑같이, 동등하게

글의 주제

1 다음 글의 주제로 가장 적절한 것은? 고1 학평 기출 응용

What Hippocratic ideas are still in practice today? Even though Hippocrates lived nearly 2,500 years ago, many of his ideas sound very familiar today. He would inquire about the family health history to see if any relatives had suffered from similar diseases. He asked questions about the patient's home to see if his or her environment might be causing the illness. After he observed patients' eating habits, he discovered that diet played an important role in preventing disease. Hippocrates was the first to understand the physical illness caused by emotional stress. He even made suggestions on what we call bedside manner. He said physicians should pay as much attention to the comfort and welfare of the patient as to the disease itself.

① various fields of Western medicine
② common beliefs in Hippocrates' time
③ diagnoses and treatments of ancient times
④ preventive measures in traditional medicine
⑤ Hippocratic ideas remaining in today's medicine

2 다음 글의 주제로 가장 적절한 것은? 고1 학평 기출 응용

Science fiction involves much more than shiny robots and fantastical spaceships. In fact, many of the most outlandish pieces of science fiction have their basis in scientific facts. Because a great deal of science fiction is rooted in science, it can be used to bring literature out of the English classroom and into the science classroom. Not only does science fiction help students see scientific principles in action, but it also helps to develop their critical thinking and creative skills developed. As students read a science fiction text, they must connect the text with the scientific principles they have learned. Students can read a science fiction text and a non-fiction text covering similar ideas and acquire the ability of comparing and contrasting the two. Students can also build their

---

1 inquire 물어보다 relative 친척 suffer (질병을) 앓다 patient 환자 ingest 섭취하다 prevent 예방하다 bedside manner (의사가) 환자를 대하는 태도 physician 의사 welfare 행복, 복지

creative skills by seeing scientific principles used in a different way, possibly creating science fiction stories of their own or imagining new ways to apply the knowledge and skills they have learned.

* outlandish: 이상한, 기이한

① common themes in science fiction movies
② influence of science fiction on popular culture
③ examples of scientific principles in science fiction
④ historical development of the science fiction genre
⑤ benefits of using science fiction in the science classroom

3

다음 글의 주제로 가장 적절한 것은? 고1 학평 기출 응용

One day after the space shuttle *Challenger* exploded, Ulric Neisser asked a class of 106 students to write down exactly where they were when they heard the news. Two and a half years later, he asked them the same question. In that second interview, he observed that 25 percent of the students gave completely different accounts of where they were. Half had significant errors in their answers and less than 10 percent remembered with any real accuracy. Results such as these are part of the reason people make mistakes on the witness stand when they are asked months later to describe a crime they witnessed. Between 1989 and 2007, 201 prisoners in the United States were proven innocent on the basis of DNA evidence. Seventy-five percent of those prisoners had been declared guilty on the basis of mistaken eyewitness accounts.

① causes of major space mission failures
② inaccuracy of information recalled over time
③ importance of protecting witnesses from threats
④ factors that improve people's long-term memories
⑤ ways to collect DNA evidence in crime investigations

---

2 involve 포함하다 spaceship 우주선 a great deal of 많은 root 뿌리를 내리다 literature 문학 principle 원리 critical 비판적인 acquire 습득하다 compare 비교하다 contrast 대조하다 apply 적용하다

3 explode 폭발하다 notice 알아차리다 completely 완전히 significant 중대한 accuracy 정확성 witness stand 증인석 describe 묘사하다 crime 범죄 witness 목격하다 prisoner 수감자 prove 밝혀지다 innocent 무죄의 evidence 증거 declare 선언하다 guilty 유죄의 eyewitness 목격자 account 진술

07강 어근 2

151
administration
[ədmìnistréiʃən]

명 행정(부), 관리 ▶ ad(to)+minister(serve 봉사하다)+ation

➕ minister 장관, 목사, 집행하다　maladministration 실정

152
amount
[əmáunt]

명 양, 액수 동 (합계가) ~에 달하다 ▶ a(to)+mount(climb)

➕ surmount 극복하다　paramount 뛰어난　demount 내려오다

153
October
[ɑktóubər]

명 10월(로마에서는 March가 첫 달) ▶ octo(8)+ber

➕ octopus 문어　octagon 팔각형　octuplets 여덟 쌍둥이

154
represent
[rèprizént]

동 나타내다, 대표하다 ▶ re(again)+pre(before)+sent(be)

➕ present 주다, 선물　presentation 발표　representation 표현

155
indicate
[índəkèit]

동 나타내다, 시사하다 ▶ in(in)+dic(speak)+ate

➕ dedicate 헌정하다　addiction 중독　abdicate 포기하다

156
impact
[ímpækt]

명 영향, 충돌 ▶ im(into)+pact(strike) cf. pact/pack(fasten)

➕ compact 소형의　package 소포

157
probability
[prɑ̀bəbíləti]

명 확률, 가능성, 개연성 ▶ probe(prove)+able+ity

➕ probably 아마도　improbable 있을 것 같지 않은

158
remember
[rimémbər]

동 기억하다 ▶ re(again)+mem(mindful)+ber

➕ memorial 기념의　commemoration 추모　memorization 암기

159
outcome
[áutkʌ̀m]

명 결과 ▶ out(out)+come(come)

➕ income 수입　upcoming 다가오는　overcome 극복하다

160
activate
[ǽktəvèit]

동 활성화하다 ▶ act(do)+ive+ate

➕ active 활동적인　actually 실제로　proactive 주도적인

161
graduate
[grǽdʒəwèit]

동 졸업하다 ▶ grad(step)+(u)ate

➕ grade 등급, 학년　gradual 점진적인　degrade 격하시키다

162
sufficient
[səfíʃənt]

형 충분한 ▶ suf(under)+fic(make)+ent

➕ deficient 부족한　efficient 효율적인　proficient 능숙한

artificial 인공적인　beneficial 이로운

163

neglect
[niglékt]

동 무시하다, 방치하다　❯ neg(deny)+lect(choose)

⊕ elect 선출하다　intellect 지성　dialect 방언, 사투리

164

recognize
[rékəgnàiz]

동 인식하다, 인정하다　❯ re(again)+co(with)+gni(know)+ize

⊕ cognitive 인지의　agnosticism 불가지론

165

exert
[igzə́ːrt]

동 영향을 미치다, 행사하다　❯ ex(out)+sert(join)

⊕ insert 삽입하다　desert 버리다　assert 강력히 주장하다

166

signal
[sígnəl]

명 신호　동 예고하다　❯ sign(mark)+al

⊕ design 디자인, 계획　signature 서명　significant 중요한

167

statistics
[stətístiks]

명 통계(자료), 통계학　❯ status(stand)+istics

⊕ statue 동상　status 지위　stature 키, 신장

168

revolution
[rèvəljúːʃən]

명 혁명, 회전, 공전　❯ re(again)+volv(roll)+tion

⊕ revolt 폭동　involvement 연루　volume 부피, 한 권

169

domination
[dàmənéiʃən]

명 지배, 우세　❯ domin(rule)+ation

⊕ domain 영역　dominion 지배권　predominate 우세하다

170

manufacture
[mæ̀njəfǽktʃər]

명 제조　동 제조하다　❯ manu(hand)+fact(make)+ure

⊕ fact 사실　factor 요인　artifact 인공물, 인공 유물

171

autonomous
[ɔːtánəməs]

형 자율적인, 자치제의　❯ auto(self)+nom(rule, 규칙)+y+ous

⊕ economical 경제적인　ergonomic 인체 공학적인　astronomical 천문학적인

172

agriculture
[ǽgrəkʌ̀ltʃər]

명 농업　❯ agri(field)+culture(plow)

⊕ cultivate 경작하다　apiculture 양봉　pisciculture (어류) 양식

173

unfortunately
[ʌnfɔ́ːrtʃənitli]

부 불행히도　❯ un(not)+fortune(luck)+ate+ly

⊕ fortunately 다행히　misfortune 불운, 불행

174

innovation
[ìnəvéiʃən]

명 혁신　❯ in(into)+nov(new)+ation

⊕ novel 새로운　novice 초보자　supernova 초신성

175

transform
[trænsfɔ́ːrm]

동 변형하다　❯ trans(across)+form(형태, 제공하다)

⊕ reform 개혁하다　conform 순응하다　inform 알리다

　perform 수행하다, 공연하다　deformed 기형적인

PRACTICE

A 주어진 접두사를 연결하고, 그 단어와 의미를 각각 쓰시오.

	보기				보기	
1 in		_____, _____	**6** ef		_____, _____
2 re		_____, _____	**7** de		_____, _____
3 per	form	_____, _____	**8** suf	ficient	_____, _____
4 con		_____, _____	**9** arti	ficial	_____, _____
5 trans		_____, _____	**10** bene		_____, _____

B 빈칸에 들어갈 알맞은 표현을 고르시오.

1 She denied _____ her children in any way.

  ① selecting   ② electing   ③ collecting   ④ neglecting

2 The colonel _____ a point on the map with his finger.

  ① addicted   ② dedicated   ③ indicated   ④ predicted

3 The minister was accused of _____ influence on the judiciary.

  ① inserting   ② exerting   ③ asserting   ④ deserting

4 The newspaper office paid an _____ fine for the distorted reports.

  ① economical   ② autonomic   ③ astronomical   ④ ergonomic

5 The sergeant ordered the officers not to do anything without his _____.

  ① agriculture   ② manufacture   ③ graduation   ④ signal

C 네모 안에서 문맥에 맞는 낱말로 가장 적절한 것을 고르시오.

1 By the end of the industrial revolution, fashion was more readily available and affordable to all classes, and by now designers worked sparsely / predominately within factories and no longer designed for individuals but for mass markets.

2 As it is estimated that each kilogram of mercury taken out of the environment can lead to up to $12,500 worth of social, environmental, and human health benefits, investments in manufacturing / eliminating mercury are money well spent.

적용독해

1

다음 글의 밑줄 친 부분 중, 문맥상 낱말의 쓰임이 적절하지 <u>않은</u> 것은? **고1 학평 기출**

Under the right circumstances, groups are remarkably intelligent, and are often ① <u>smarter</u> than the smartest people in them. Even if most of the people within a group are not especially well-informed or rational, it can still reach a ② <u>collectively</u> wise decision. This is a good thing, since human beings are not perfectly designed decision makers. We generally have less information than we'd like. We have ③ <u>sufficient</u> foresight into the future. Instead of insisting on finding the best possible decision, we will often ④ <u>accept</u> one that seems good enough. And we often let emotion affect our judgement. Yet despite all these limitations, when our imperfect opinions are gathered in the right way, our collective intelligence is often ⑤ <u>excellent</u>.

2

다음 글의 밑줄 친 부분 중, 문맥상 낱말의 쓰임이 적절하지 <u>않은</u> 것은? **고2 학평 기출**

Getting an "F" means only that you failed a test — not that you failed your life. From now on, imagine that the letter "F" when used as a grade ① <u>represents</u> the word: *feedback*. An "F" is an indication that you didn't understand the material well enough. It's a message that you should do something ② <u>differently</u> before the next test. If you think of "F" as *feedback*, you can change your thinking and behavior in ways that ③ <u>prevent</u> your success. You can choose a new learning strategy. Getting meaningful feedback on your performance is a powerful strategy for learning *anything*. Tests are not the only ④ <u>source</u> of feedback. Make a habit of asking for feedback from your teachers, friends, and anyone else who knows you. Just determine what you want to ⑤ <u>improve</u> and ask, "How am I doing?"

---

1 circumstance 상황 remarkably 두드러지게 rational 합리적인 collectively 집단적으로 generally 일반적으로 sufficient 충분한 foresight 예지 instead of ~대신에 insist 고집하다, 우기다 judgement 판단 despite ~에도 불구하고 limitation 한계 gather 모으다
2 represent 나타내다, 의미하다 indication 표시, 지시 performance 수행, 일, 작업 prevent 막다 strategy 전략, 작전 source 원천, 근원 determine 결정하다

수동태 1(3형식/4형식)

① 3형식(주어+동사+목적어) 문장의 수동태

A Americans respect the Founding Fathers.
→ The Founding Fathers are respected (by Americans).
B She takes good care of her children.
→ Her children are taken good care of (by her).

② 3형식 문장의 목적어가 명사절인 경우

say, think, believe, expect, suppose 등
C People think that our brain activates the nerve.
→ It is thought that our brain activates the nerve.
→ Our brain is thought to activate the nerve.

③ 4형식(주어+동사+간접목적어+직접목적어) 문장의 수동태

give, tell, teach, send, show, remind, make, buy 등
D I gave my kid a cosmetic pouch.
→ My kid was given a cosmetic pouch (by me). (간접목적어가 주어)
→ A cosmetic pouch was given to my kid (by me). (직접목적어가 주어)

PRACTICE

A 밑줄 친 부분을 어법상 바르게 고쳐 쓰시오.

1 Lots of support and help <u>need</u> for a voluntary program to succeed.
2 The electric car can travel at 50 miles per hour and needs to <u>recharge</u> every 70 miles.
3 It <u>believes</u> that Benjamin Franklin was an outstanding inventor.
4 The amount of venture capital available in the market <u>expects</u> to decline this year.
5 The school promised to give us everything we needed, including uniforms and bags, but we just <u>gave</u> a stationery box.

B 네모 안에서 어법에 맞는 표현으로 가장 적절한 것을 고르시오.

1 Construction activities in seismically prone and hazardous areas that are vulnerable to different damaging effects of earthquakes are best avoiding / avoided . However, as such situations are often unavoidable, appropriate strengthening measures are required.

2 Engaging in Internet searches increases people's cognitive self-esteem: people who search the Internet for facts they didn't know and ask / are asked where they found the information often report that they had known it all along.

60

적용독해

1 다음 글의 밑줄 친 부분 중, 어법상 <u>틀린</u> 것은? 고1 학평 기출 응용

It's important to remember that good decisions can still lead to bad outcomes. Here is an example. Soon after I got out of school, I ① <u>was offered</u> a job. I wasn't sure that was a great fit for me. After carefully considering the opportunity, I decided to turn it down. I thought that I ② <u>would</u> be able to find another job that was a better match. Unfortunately, the economy soon grew worse quickly and I ③ <u>was spent</u> months looking for another job. I kicked myself for not taking that position, which started to look more and more ④ <u>appealing</u>. I had made a good decision which ⑤ <u>was based</u> upon all the information I had at the time, but in the short run, it didn't lead to a great outcome.

2 다음 글의 밑줄 친 부분 중, 어법상 <u>틀린</u> 것은? 고1 학평 기출

Alfred Chandler was Professor of Business History in the Graduate School of Business Administration, Harvard University. He was an economic historian ① <u>whose</u> work has centered on the study of business history and, in particular, administration. He long argued that this is a much ② <u>neglected</u> area in the study of recent history. His studies of big business have ③ <u>carried</u> out with grants from a number of sources including the Alfred P. Sloan Foundation. His work has been internationally recognized, his book *The Visible Hand* ④ <u>was awarded</u> the Pulitzer Prize for History and the Bancroft Prize in Oct., 1978. Chandler ⑤ <u>taught</u> business history at a variety of universities in the US and Europe.

---

1 outcome 결과, 성과   turn down ~을 거절하다   unfortunately 유감스럽게도, 불행하게도   kick oneself 자책하다   appealing 매력적인, 흥미를 끄는   in the short run 단기적인 관점에서 보면
2 Graduate School 대학원   Business Administration 경영학   administration 경영, 관리   argue 주장하다   neglect 간과하다   grant 지원금   internationally 국제적으로   award (상을) 수여하다, 주다   a variety of 다양한

글의 제목

1 다음 글의 제목으로 가장 적절한 것은? `고1 학평 기출`

Studies from cities all over the world show the importance of life and activity as an urban attraction. People gather where things are happening and seek the presence of other people. Faced with the choice of walking down an empty or a lively street, most people would choose the street with life and activity. The walk will be more interesting and feel safer. Events where we can watch people perform or play music attract many people to stay and watch. Studies of benches and chairs in city space show that the seats with the best view of city life are used far more frequently than those that do not offer a view of other people.

① The City's Greatest Attraction: People
② Leave the City, Live in the Country
③ Make More Parks in the City
④ Feeling Lonely in the Crowded Streets
⑤ Ancient Cities Full of Tourist Attractions

2 다음 글의 제목으로 가장 적절한 것은? `고2 학평 기출`

If you've ever visited a fortune-teller you probably came away amazed at the things they knew about you — things no one else could possibly have known. So it must be a supernatural power, right? Research into the fortune-telling business shows that fortune-tellers use a technique known as "cold reading," which can produce an accuracy of around 80 percent when "reading" a person you've never met. While it can appear magical to some people, it is simply a process based on the careful observation of body-language signals plus an understanding of human nature and a knowledge of probability statistics. It's a technique practiced by tarot-card readers, astrologers, and palm readers to gather information about a "client."

* cold reading: 사전 지식 없이 빠르게 알아차리는 것

---

1 life 생활, 일상, 활기 urban 도시의 attraction 매력 face 직면하다 lively 활기찬 perform 공연하다 frequently 자주 crowded 붐비는, 혼잡한 ancient 고대의 tourist attraction 관광 명소

① Don't Ignore Supernatural Things
② How Fortune-Tellers Know So Much
③ Why People Want Their Fortune Told
④ Nonverbal Signals Show Your Emotions
⑤ Your Future Depends on Your Willpower

3

다음 글의 제목으로 가장 적절한 것은? 고2 학평 기출

The realization of human domination over the environment began in the late 1700s with the industrial revolution. Advances in manufacturing transformed societies and economies while producing significant impacts on the environment. American society became structured on multiple industries' capitalistic goals as the development of the steam engine led to the mechanized production of goods in mass quantities. Rural agricultural communities with economies based on handmade goods and agriculture were abandoned for life in urban cities with large factories based on an economy of industrialized manufacturing. Innovations in the production of textiles, iron, and steel provided increased profits to private companies. Simultaneously, those industries exerted authority over the environment and began dumping hazardous by-products in public lands and waterways.

① Strategies for Industrial Innovations
② Urbanization: A Road to a Better Life
③ Industrial Development Hurt the Environment
④ Technology: A Key to Sustainable Development
⑤ The Driving Force of Capitalism Was Not Greed

---

2 fortune-teller 점술가 amazed 깜짝 놀란 supernatural 초자연적인 accuracy 정확성 magical 마법의 probability statistics 확률 통계 astrologer 점성가 palm reader 수상가(손금을 봐주는 사람)

3 realization 실현 domination 지배 industrial 산업의 revolution 혁명 advance 발달, 발전 manufacturing 제조(업) significant 중대한 structure 구축하다, 조직하다 multiple 여러 가지의, 많은, 다수의 capitalistic 자본주의적인 mechanize 기계화하다 mass quantity 대량 rural 시골의 agricultural 농업의 abandon 버리다 urban 도시의 textile 직물 private 사적인 simultaneously 동시에 exert 행사하다, 발휘하다 authority 권력 dump 내버리다 hazardous 유해한, 위험한

08강 어근 3

176
remedy
[rémidi]

명 치료(법) ▸ re(again)+med(cure)+y

➕ medicine 약, 의학　medic 위생병　meditate 명상하다

177
tension
[ténʃən]

명 긴장, 갈등 ▸ tens(stretch)+ion

➕ extension 확장, 연장　pretension 가식

178
forecast
[fɔ́ːrkæ̀st]

명 예보, 예측 ▸ fore(before)+cast(throw)

➕ broadcasting 방송　recast 재투표하다　downcast 의기소침한

179
defeat
[difíːt]

명 패배 동 패배시키다 ▸ de(against)+feat(make)

➕ feat 위업　feature 특징, 특색　counterfeit 위조하다

180
interact
[ìntərǽkt]

동 상호 작용하다 ▸ inter(between)+act(do)

➕ exact 정확한　react 반응하다　transact 거래하다

181
encourage
[inkə́ːridʒ]

동 고무시키다, 격려하다 ▸ en(make)+cour(heart)+age

➕ core 핵심　courage 용기　discourage 낙담시키다

182
location
[loukéiʃən]

명 위치, 장소 ▸ locat(place)+ion　locate 동 위치를 알아내다

➕ allocation 할당, 배당　dislocation 탈구

183
extraordinary
[ikstrɔ́ːrdənèri]

형 특별한, 뛰어난 ▸ extra(out)+ordin(order)+ary

➕ ordinary 일반적인　subordinate 종속적인　coordinate 조화시키다

184
sociology
[sòusiálədʒi]

명 사회학 ▸ socio(companion)+logy(study)

➕ society 사회　antisocial 반사회적인　associate 관련시키다

185
improve
[imprúːv]

동 개선하다, 향상시키다 ▸ im(into)+prove(입증하다)

➕ proof 증거　disprove 반증하다　approve 승인하다

186
summit
[sʌ́mit]

명 정상, 정상 회담 ▸ summa(highest)+it(go)

➕ sum 합계, 금액　summary 요약　summa cum laude 최우등

187
imply
[implái]

동 암시하다, 의미하다 ▸ im(in)+ply(fold)

➕ apply 지원하다　supply 공급하다　multiply 증가시키다

➕ reply 대답하다　comply 순응하다　employ 고용하다

188

expedition
[èkspidíʃən]

명 원정(대), 탐험(대)　❯ ex(out)+pedi(foot)+tion

➕ pedestrian 보행자　peddler 행상인　impediment 장애

189

psychologist
[saikálədʒist]

명 심리학자　❯ psycho(mind)+logy(study)+ist

➕ psychoanalyst 정신분석학자　psychiatrist 정신과 의사

190

advise
[ədváiz]

동 충고하다, 조언하다　❯ ad(to)+vise(look)

➕ revise 수정하다　supervise 감독하다　previous 이전의

191

result
[rizʌ́lt]

명 결과 동 결과로서 발생하다　❯ re(back)+sult(leap)

➕ insult 모욕　exult 기뻐 날뛰다　assault 폭행

192

admission
[ədmíʃən]

명 입장, 입학, 인정　❯ ad(to)+miss(send)+ion

➕ emission 방출　dismissal 해산　submission 제출, 굴복

193

attempt
[ətémpt]

동 시도하다 명 노력, 시도　❯ at(to)+tempt(try, test)

➕ tempt 유혹하다, ~할 마음이 들게 하다　temptation 유혹

194

assignment
[əsáinmənt]

명 과제, 할당된 임무　❯ as(to)+sign(mark)+ment

➕ sign 기호, 신호　resignation 사임　designation 지명

195

position
[pəzíʃən]

명 위치, 입장, 직책　❯ pose(put, place)+tion

➕ posture 자세, 포즈　disposal 처리　preposition 전치사

196

remain
[riméin]

동 계속 ~하다, 남아 있다　❯ re(back)+main(stay)

➕ remainder 나머지　permanent 영원한　immanent 내재하는

197

vividly
[vívidli]

부 생생하게, 선명하게　❯ viv/vit/vig(live)+id+ly

➕ vital 중요한, 활력있는　vigor 활력　revive 소생시키다

198

advocate
[ǽdvəkit]

명 옹호자 동 옹호하다　❯ ad(to)+voc(call)+ate

➕ vocation 직업　vocabulary 어휘　equivocal 애매한

199

precise
[prisáis]

형 정확한　❯ pre(before)+cise(cut)

➕ concise 간결한　decisive 단호한　scissors 가위

200

ecology
[ikálədʒi]

명 생태(학)　❯ eco(house)+logy(study)

➕ zoology 동물학　theology 신학　anthropology 인류학

➕ biology 생물학　geology 지질학　archaeology 고고학

PRACTICE

정답 및 해설 p.22

A 주어진 접두사를 연결하고, 그 단어와 의미를 각각 쓰시오.

1	ap		_____ , _____	6	bio		_____ , _____
2	im		_____ , _____	7	geo		_____ , _____
3	sup	보기 ply	_____ , _____	8	theo	보기 logy	_____ , _____
4	com		_____ , _____	9	socio		_____ , _____
5	multi		_____ , _____	10	psycho		_____ , _____

B 빈칸에 들어갈 알맞은 표현을 고르시오.

1 He ventured on a(n) _____ of the North Pole, never to return.

① peddler   ② pedestrian   ③ impediment   ④ expedition

2 Carbon dioxide is a result of the _____ of carbon and oxygen.

① enactment   ② interaction   ③ reaction   ④ transaction

3 _____ groups protested against the revised Antipollution Act.

① Theological   ② Geological   ③ Astronomical   ④ Ecological

4 There are some extremists who openly _____ violence.

① explore   ② advocate   ③ remedy   ④ remain

5 The IMF _____ that the economy of all but one OECD country will grow this year.

① interacts   ② defeats   ③ forecasts   ④ improves

C 네모 안에서 문맥에 맞는 낱말로 가장 적절한 것을 고르시오.

1 After observing the habits of a daily planning group and a monthly planning one, researchers discovered that monthly planners did better | similar / compared | to daily planners, in terms of improvements in study habits and attitudes, because they kept it up much longer.

2 Studies have found that along with rapid eye movement, our heart rates increase and our respiration is also elevated — although our bodies are kept | motionless / movable | and are basically paralyzed due to a nerve center in the brain.

66

적용독해

1 다음 글의 밑줄 친 부분 중, 문맥상 낱말의 쓰임이 적절하지 <u>않은</u> 것은? 고2 학평 기출

Do you know one of the best remedies for coping with family tension? Two words: "I'm sorry." It's amazing how ① <u>hard</u> some people find them to say. They think it implies weakness or defeat. Nothing of the kind. In fact, it is precisely the ② <u>opposite</u>. Another good way of relieving tension is a row! The sea is ever so much calmer after a storm. A row has another ③ <u>advantage</u>. When tempers are raised, unspoken truths usually come out. They may hurt a bit, especially at the time. Yet, at the end, you know each other a bit ④ <u>better</u>. Lastly, most of the tensions and quarrels between children are ⑤ <u>risky</u>. Even when they seem to be constant, wise parents don't worry too much.

* row: 말다툼

2 다음 글의 밑줄 친 부분 중, 문맥상 낱말의 쓰임이 적절하지 <u>않은</u> 것은? 고1 학평 기출

New technologies create new interactions and cultural rules. As a way to ① <u>encourage</u> TV viewing, social television systems now enable social interaction among TV viewers in different locations. These systems are known to build a greater sense of ② <u>connectedness</u> among TV-using friends. One field study focused on how five friends between the ages of 30-36 communicated while watching TV at their homes. The technology allowed them to ③ <u>see</u> which of the friends were watching TV and what they were watching. They chose how to communicate via social television — whether through voice chat or text chat. The study showed a strong ④ <u>preference</u> for text over voice. Users offered two key reasons for favoring text chat. First, text chat required less effort and attention, and was more ⑤ <u>unpleasant</u> than voice chat. Second, study participants viewed text chat as more polite.

---

1 remedy 처방 cope with ~에 대처하다 tension 갈등, 긴장 상태 amazing 놀라운 imply 의미하다, 암시하다 weakness 약함 defeat 패배 relieve (고통, 부담 따위를) 덜다 calm 잔잔한 temper 화, 짜증 unspoken 입 밖에 내지 않은 quarrel 싸움, 말다툼 constant 지속적인, 계속되는

2 interaction 상호 작용 encourage 부추기다 location 장소, 위치 connectedness 유대 field study 현장 연구 allow ~ to do ~가 …할 수 있게 하다 via ~을 통해 voice chat 음성 채팅 text chat 문자 채팅 preference 선호(도) offer 말하다, 제출하다 favor 선호하다 participant 참가자 polite 예의 바른, 공손한

수동태 2 (5형식)

① 5형식의 수동태

A The city council elected her its chairperson. (보어가 명사) ▶p.52
→ She was elected its chairperson (by the city council).

B Scientists found the assumption true. (보어가 형용사) ▶p.52
→ The assumption was found true (by scientists).

C The manager inspired his colleagues to do their best on the project. (보어가 to부정사) ▶p.52
→ His colleagues was inspired to do their best on the project (by the manager).

② 지각동사/사역동사의 수동태

D The experimenter saw lab rats eat the food. (보어가 동사원형)
→ Lab rats were seen <u>to eat</u> the food (by the experimenter).

E Parents often make their kids do the chores. (보어가 동사원형)
→ Their kids are often made <u>to do</u> the chores (by parents).

F A firefighter heard a child calling for help. (보어가 현재분사)
→ A child was heard calling for help (by a firefighter).

G She made her computer repaired. (보어가 과거분사)
→ Her computer was made (to be) repaired (by her).

PRACTICE

A 어법상 틀린 부분을 바르게 고쳐 쓰시오.

1 Cooking is an activity that defines Homo sapiens, who call "the cooking animal."
2 The butterfly moved its hindwings, while its antennae were kept motionlessly.
3 Any strategic benefit for attacking is not expected being gained.
4 Tourists are encouraged transit from the guided tour into the solo tour.
5 Salty and fatty food products are made taste better to the consumer.

B 네모 안에서 어법에 맞는 표현으로 가장 적절한 것을 고르시오.

1 Despite the abundant evidence that innovation has transformed almost everybody's lives for the better in innumerable ways, something new is often considered undesirable / undesirably .

2 Ironically, when we tell ourselves that we do not want to engage in behaviors that we are not legally allowed to do / doing our brains interpret this *don't* as a challenge to commit the illegal acts.

적용독해

1 다음 글의 밑줄 친 부분 중, 어법상 틀린 것은? 고2 학평 기출 응용

It was once considered amazing to reach the summit of Mount Everest. It was even a national honor ① <u>to have</u> a climber waving a national flag there. But now that almost 4,000 people have reached its summit, the achievement means less than it did a half century ago. In 1963, six people reached the top, but in the spring of 2012, the summit ② <u>was crowded</u> with more than 500 people. Then what makes it possible for so many people to reach the summit? They ③ <u>were enabled</u> to reach the summit by one important factor: improved weather forecasting. In the past, lack of information ④ <u>was led</u> expeditions to attempt the summit whenever their team members were ready. Today, all teams know exactly when the weather will ⑤ <u>be considered</u> perfect for climbing by hyper-accurate satellite forecasts, and they often go for the top on the same days.

2 다음 글의 밑줄 친 부분 중, 어법상 틀린 것은? 고3 학평 기출 응용

One of the greatest ways to cultivate a possibility mind-set is ① <u>to prompt</u> yourself to dream one size bigger than you normally do. Let's face it: Most people dream too small. Many try to make their dreams even smaller. In contrast, Henry Curtis advises, "Your plans should ② <u>be made</u> as fantastic as you like because twenty-five years from now, they will not seem so special. Make your plans ten times as ③ <u>great</u> as you first planned, and twenty-five years from now you will wonder why you did not make them fifty times as great." If you are motivated ④ <u>to dream</u> more expansively and to make your goals at least a step beyond what makes you comfortable, you will ⑤ <u>force</u> to grow. This will set you up to believe in greater possibilities.

---

1 summit 정상 honor 명예 forecast 예보하다; 예보 expedition 원정대 hyper-accurate 초정밀의 satellite 위성
2 cultivate (정신을) 계발하다, 발전시키다 mind-set 사고방식 prompt 자극하다 normally 평소대로 motivate ~에 동기(자극)를 주다
expansively 광대하게 beyond 너머

내용 일치

1

Vivian Malone Jones에 관한 다음 글의 내용과 일치하지 <u>않는</u> 것은? 고2 학평 기출

Vivian Malone Jones was the first African-American woman who entered the University of Alabama in 1963, along with fellow black student James Hood. Their entry resulted in then Governor George Wallace standing in the door of the university in an attempt to halt their admission. They entered the university but only after an agreement was reached between the White House and Wallace's aides. Ms. Jones further distinguished herself as the first African-American to graduate from the University of Alabama in 1965. She moved to Washington, DC and joined the U.S. Department of Justice as a staff member of its Voter Education Project. Following that assignment, she moved to Atlanta and took a position with the Environmental Protection Agency (EPA), where she was appointed director of civil rights and urban affairs. She retired in 1996 remaining active in civil rights organizations.

① Alabama 대학교에 들어간 최초의 흑인 여성이다.
② 대학 정문에서 입학을 저지당하기도 했다.
③ 1956년에 Alabama 대학교를 졸업했다.
④ Atlanta로 이주하여 EPA에서 근무했다.
⑤ 은퇴 후에도 인권 단체에서 활동했다.

2

Bessie Coleman에 관한 다음 글의 내용과 일치하지 <u>않는</u> 것은? 고1 학평 기출 응용

Bessie Coleman was born in Texas in 1892. When she was eleven, she was told that the Wright brothers had flown their first plane. Since that moment, she dreamed about the day she would soar through the sky. At the age of 23, Coleman moved to Chicago, where she worked at a restaurant to save money for flying lessons. However, she had to travel to Paris to take flying lessons because American flight schools at the time admitted neither women nor Black people. In 1921, she finally became the first Black woman to earn an international pilot's license. She also studied flying acrobatics in Europe and made her first appearance in an airshow in New York in 1922. The next generation was inspired to pursue their dreams of flying by this female pioneer of flight.

* flying acrobatics: 곡예 비행

---

1 **attempt** 시도 **halt** 중단시키다 **admission** 입학 **aide** 보좌관 **distinguish oneself** 이름을 떨치다 **assignment** 과제, 임무 **appoint** 임명하다 **civil rights** 인권 **organization** 단체

① 11살 때 Wright 형제의 첫 비행 소식을 들었다.

② 비행 수업을 듣기 위해 파리로 가야 했다.

③ 국제 조종사 면허를 딴 최초의 흑인 여성이 되었다.

④ 유럽에서 에어쇼에 첫 출현을 했다.

⑤ 다음 세대가 비행의 꿈을 추구하도록 영감을 주었다.

3

Janaki Ammal에 관한 다음 글의 내용과 일치하지 <u>않는</u> 것은? 고2 학평 기출 응용

Janaki Ammal, one of India's most extraordinary scientists, was born in 1897, and was expected to wed through an arranged marriage. Despite living at a time when literacy among women in India was less than one percent, she decided to reject tradition and attend college. In 1924, she went to the U.S. and eventually received a doctorate in botany and ecology from the University of Michigan. Ammal contributed to the development of the sweetest sugarcane variety in the world. She moved to England where she co-authored the *Chromosome Atlas of Cultivated Plants*, describing plant chromosome, vividly. Following a series of famines, she returned to India to help increase food production at the request of the Prime Minister. However, Ammal disagreed with the deforestation taking place in an effort to grow more food. She became an advocate for the preservation of native plants and successfully saved the Silent Valley from the construction of a hydroelectric dam.

① 관습을 따르지 않고 대학에 입학하기로 결심했다.

② 세계에서 가장 단 사탕수수 품종 개발에 기여했다.

③ *Chromosome Atlas of Cultivated Plants*를 공동 집필했다.

④ 식량 생산을 증가시키는 데 도움을 주기 위해 인도로 돌아갔다.

⑤ 수력 발전 댐의 건설로부터 Silent Valley를 지키는 데 실패했다.

---

2 soar 날아오르다 admit ~에게 입학을 허가하다 license 면허 acrobatics 곡예 pursue 추구하다 pioneer 개척자

3 extraordinary 유명한 arranged marriage 중매결혼 literacy 읽고 쓰는 능력 reject 거부하다 attend 입학하다 receive 받다 doctorate 박사 학위 botany 식물학 ecology 생태학 contribute to ~에 기여하다 sugarcane 사탕수수 variety 품종, 종류 co-author 공동 집필하다 chromosome 염색체 famine 기근 request 요청 deforestation 삼림 벌채 advocate 옹호자 hydroelectric 수력 전기의

09강 어근 4

201
demonstrate
[démənstrèit]

동 입증하다, 증명하다 ❯ de(utterly)+monstr(show)+ate
⊕ undemonstrated 논증되지 않은　remonstration 간언, 충고

202
accommodate
[əkámədèit]

동 수용하다 ❯ ac(to)+com(with)+mod(scale 척도)+ate
⊕ mode 형태, 방법　modern 현대의　modify 변경하다

203
institution
[ìnstitjú:ʃən]

명 (공공) 기관, 시설 ❯ in(into)+stit(stand)+ution
⊕ constitution 구성　substitution 대체　superstition 미신

204
predict
[pridíkt]

동 예측하다, 예언하다 ❯ pre(before)+dict(speak)
⊕ dictionary 사전　dictation 받아쓰기　contradict 반박하다

205
effective
[iféktiv]

형 효과적인 ❯ ef(out)+fect(make)+ive
⊕ defect 결점, 결함　infection 전염(병)　affection 애정

206
coexist
[kòuigzíst]

동 공존하다 ❯ co(with)+ex(out)+sist(stand)
⊕ insist 주장하다　subsist 연명하다　consistent 일관된

207
conversation
[kànvərséiʃən]

명 대화 ❯ con(with)+verse(turn)+ation
⊕ adversity 역경　diverse 다양한　reverse 반대의, 뒤의

208
illustrate
[íləstrèit]

동 설명하다, 예시하다 ❯ il(to)+lustr(light)+ate
⊕ illuminate 빛을 비추다　luxurious 사치스러운

209
capital
[kǽpitəl]

명 수도, 자본, 대문자 형 주요한 ❯ capit(head)+al
⊕ captain 선장, 주장　capitalism 자본주의　decapitation 참수

210
inclined
[inkláind]

형 경향이 있는, 기울어진 ❯ in(into)+cline(slope)+ed
⊕ decline 감소하다, 거절하다　recline 기대다, 뒤로 젖히다

211
motivate
[móutəvèit]

동 동기 부여하다 ❯ mot(move)+ive+ate
⊕ promotion 승진　remote 멀리 떨어진　emotion 감정, 정서

212
deception
[disépʃən]

명 사기, 기만 ❯ de(away)+cept(take)+ion
⊕ exception 예외　conception 생각　reception 수령, 환영회
⊕ perception 인식, 지각　interception 가로채기, 방해, 요격

213

profession
[prəféʃən]

명 (전문) 직업 ▶ pro(before)+fess(speak)+ion

⊕ professor 교수　confession 고백, 자백　professional 전문가

214

refuse
[rifjúːz]

동 거절하다, 거부하다 ▶ re(back)+fuse(pour)

⊕ confuse 혼동하다　transfuse 수혈하다　diffuse 발산하다

215

agent
[éidʒənt]

명 중개인, 요원, 행위자, 약제 ▶ ag(do)+ent

⊕ agenda 의제　agile 민첩한　agitate 선동하다

216

diminish
[dimíniʃ]

동 축소하다 ▶ di(away)+min(small)+ish

⊕ minimum 최소, 최저　miniature 축소 모형　minority 소수

217

astronomy
[əstránəmi]

명 천문학 ▶ astro(star)+nomy(study)

⊕ astronaut 우주비행사　disaster 재난　astrophysics 천체물리학

218

gravitation
[grævitéiʃən]

명 인력, 중력 ▶ grav(heavy)+(i)tate+ion

⊕ gravity 중력　aggravation 악화　grieve 몹시 슬퍼하다

219

complement
[kámpləmənt]

동 보완하다 명 보어 ▶ com(with)+ple(full)+ment

⊕ implement 시행하다　depletion 고갈, 감소

220

surface
[sə́ːrfis]

명 표면 동 수면 위로 오르다 ▶ sur(over)+face(면)

⊕ face 얼굴, 직면하다　preface 서문　efface 지우다

221

include
[inklúːd]

동 포함하다 ▶ in(in)+clude(close)

⊕ exclude 배제하다　enclose 동봉하다　disclose 공개하다

222

dependence
[dipéndəns]

명 의지, 의존 ▶ de(down)+pend(hang)+ence

⊕ suspend 매달다, 정지시키다　expend 지출하다, 소비하다

223

theme
[θiːm]

명 주제, 테마 ▶ theme(put, place)

⊕ hypothesis 가설　synthesis 합성, 종합　photosynthesis 광합성

224

central
[séntrəl]

형 중심의, 중앙의 ▶ centr(center)+al

⊕ concentrate 집중하다　eccentric 별난, 괴짜 같은

225

suspect
[səspékt]

동 의심하다 명 용의자 ▶ sus(under)+spect(look)

⊕ expect 기대하다　respect 존경하다　inspect 조사하다

⊕ aspect 측면, 양상　prospect 전망　perspective 관점

PRACTICE

A 주어진 접두사를 연결하고, 그 단어와 의미를 각각 쓰시오.

		보기				보기	
1	a		_____, _____	**6**	de		_____, _____
2	re		_____, _____	**7**	ex		_____, _____
3	in	spect	_____, _____	**8**	per	ception	_____, _____
4	sus		_____, _____	**9**	con		_____, _____
5	pro		_____, _____	**10**	inter		_____, _____

B 빈칸에 들어갈 알맞은 표현을 고르시오.

1 The pool and gym are _____ for hotel guests.

① inclusively   ② exclusively   ③ conclusively   ④ reclusively

2 I absolutely _____ to take part in anything illegal.

① refuse   ② confuse   ③ transfuse   ④ diffuse

3 Travel expenses vary _____ on when you travel.

① suspending   ② appending   ③ impending   ④ depending

4 The policy will have the _____ of creating jobs for local people.

① defect   ② affection   ③ effect   ④ infection

5 The ruling party's share of the vote _____ sharply due to the president's misrule.

① skyrocketed   ② accommodated   ③ diminished   ④ illustrated

C 네모 안에서 문맥에 맞는 낱말로 가장 적절한 것을 고르시오.

1 Conquerors have understood that knowledge is essential for dominating a territory, and rulers know that power cannot be executed without being well-informed / well-mannered — mortality tables, tax data, and the like are crucial to running an effective public administration.

2 A form of popular culture, sports songs (memorable and easily sung choruses in which fans can participate) can be said to display pleasure and emotional excess, in addition / contrast to the dominant culture, which tends to maintain 'respectable aesthetic distance and control'.

적용독해

1 다음 글의 밑줄 친 부분 중, 문맥상 낱말의 쓰임이 적절하지 <u>않은</u> 것은? 고2 학평 기출

The discovery that attitudes don't always reflect actions came as a great surprise. Richard LaPiere, a professor at Standford University, gave a powerful demonstration of the ① <u>disconnect</u> between attitude and behavior in the 1930s. He traveled around the US with some colleagues from China. At the time, many people in the US had a ② <u>negative</u> opinion of Chinese people. LaPiere wrote to hotels and restaurants along the route, asking whether they would ③ <u>accommodate</u> him and his Chinese guests. Of the 128 who wrote back, 92 percent told him that they would ④ <u>accept</u> to serve Chinese customers. But when he traveled around the country, visiting the same hotels and restaurants, the Chinese travelers were treated with courtesy in 249 out of 250 establishments. Remarkably, the powerful unfavorable attitudes didn't ⑤ <u>predict</u> actual behavior.

2 다음 글의 밑줄 친 부분 중, 문맥상 낱말의 쓰임이 적절하지 <u>않은</u> 것은? 고2 학평 기출

A story is only as believable as the storyteller. For story to be effective, trust must be established. Yes, trust. Whenever someone stops to listen to you, an element of ① <u>unspoken</u> trust exists. Your listener unconsciously trusts you to say something worthwhile to him, something that will not waste his time. The few minutes of attention he is giving you is ② <u>sacrificial</u>. He could choose to spend his time elsewhere, yet he has stopped to ③ <u>respect</u> your part in a conversation. This is where story comes in. Because a story illustrates points clearly and often bridges topics easily, trust can be established *quickly*, and recognizing this time element to story is essential to trust. ④ <u>Wasting</u> your listener's time is the capital letter at the beginning of your sentence — it leads the conversation into a sentence ⑤ <u>worth</u> listening to *if* trust is earned and not taken for granted.

---

1 reflect 반영하다 demonstration 증명 colleague 동료 negative 부정적인 accommodate 받아 주다, 들어주다 treat 응대하다
courtesy 호의, 예의 establishment 숙박업소 predict 예측하다
2 establish 확립하다 trust 신뢰 exist 존재하다 unconsciously 무의식적으로 worthwhile 가치 있는 sacrificial 희생의 elsewhere 다른
곳에 respect 존중하다 illustrate 설명하다 bridge 연결하다 recognize 인지하다 essential 필수적인 earn 얻다 take for granted 당
연한 일로 여기다

수동태 3 (수동태 시제)

① 조동사＋동사원형

> **A** Kids may think of the cloud as alive.
> → The cloud **may be thought** of as alive (by kids).

② 진행형 시제의 수동태

> **B** Workers are constructing the cathedral.
> → The cathedral **is being constructed** (by workers)

③ 완료시제의 수동태

> **C** Colonists have occupied the country for 200 years.
> → The country **has been occupied** for 200 years (by colonists).

④ 동명사/to부정사의 수동태

> **D** Some prey have their own tactics to avoid **being killed**.
> **E** Captors forced all of the dinosaurs **to be caged**.

PRACTICE

A 밑줄 친 부분을 어법에 맞게 고쳐 쓰시오.

1 Entries will judge on creativity, content, and effectiveness of delivery.
2 The swine escaped from the cages to avoid slaughtering.
3 I was being counseled people who wanted better jobs to show more initiative.
4 I think the garbage that has dumped in my driveway for the past week is yours.
5 Every sensation our body feels has to wait for the information to carry to the brain.

B 네모 안에서 어법에 맞는 표현으로 가장 적절한 것을 고르시오.

1 Erich Fromm proposes that humans are driven to transcend the state of merely having created / been created ; instead, humans seek to become the creators, the active shapers of their own destiny.

2 Bundle pricing is packaging together two or more products, usually complementary ones, to sell / be sold for a single price, which is usually considerably less than the sum of the prices of the individual products.

적용독해

1

다음 글의 밑줄 친 부분 중, 어법상 **틀린** 것은? 　고1 학평 기출 응용

Grateful people are inclined to make healthy decisions. Life and sports present many situations where critical and difficult decisions have to ① be made. Selfish people are not able to make decisions that would be considered ② soundly as confidently as grateful people are. This includes the decision to be self-motivated. Frustrated parents ask: "How do I motivate my child to do sports or continue in sports? Sometimes my child gets ③ discouraged and does not want to put the required effort into his or her sports? What can I, as a parent, do or say to help?" For kids or adults to ④ be motivated is difficult and almost impossible because they are centered on their own narrow selfish desires. However, kids and adults who live as grateful people are able to motivate ⑤ themselves. They also welcome suggestions from others, even parents.

2

다음 글의 밑줄 친 부분 중, 어법상 **틀린** 것은? 　고1 학평 기출

Suppose, on your wedding day, your best man delivers a heart-warming, moving toast that ① makes you cry. You later learn he didn't write it himself but bought it online. Then, would the toast mean less than it was at first, before you knew it ② was written by a paid professional? Most people would agree the bought wedding toast has less value than an authentic one. Although a bought toast might "work" in the sense of ③ being achieved its desired effect, that effect might depend on deception. That is, if you purchased a moving masterpiece of a toast online, you would probably ④ cover it up! If a bought toast depends for its effect on concealing its origin, that's a reason to suspect it's a corrupt version of the real thing. Wedding toasts are goods that can, in a sense, ⑤ be bought. But buying and selling them diminishes their value.

* toast: 축사

---

1 grateful 감사할 줄 아는　be inclined to ~하는 경향이 있다　present 제시하다　critical 중요한　selfish 이기적인　sound 건전한
self-motivated 스스로를 동기 유발시키는　frustrated 좌절한　discouraged 낙심한　be centered on ~에 집중하다　narrow 편협한
2 suppose 가정하다　best man 신랑 들러리　heart-warming 마음이 따뜻해지는　authentic 진짜의　depend on ~에 좌우되다　deception
기만　purchase 구입하다　masterpiece 걸작　conceal 감추다　suspect 의혹을 가지다　corrupt 타락한　diminish 떨어뜨리다

1 다음 빈칸에 들어갈 말로 가장 적절한 것을 고르시오. 고1 학평 기출

Jupiter is here _____. In the early hours of September 10, an astronomer in Oregon spotted a bright flash of light on Jupiter. Astronomers believe this brilliant burst to be an asteroid hitting the giant planet. Scientists say that the asteroid may have been headed for Earth, but instead, Jupiter took the blow. And this may not be the first time Jupiter has saved Earth from being hit. Jupiter has the strongest gravitational pull of any planet. The gravitational pull of Jupiter grabs passing asteroids and pulls them to its surface — and away from Earth. The impacts are leading scientists to study possible marks from asteroids on Jupiter. Chances of actually hitting Earth are very unlikely, but scientists keep a close watch on asteroids as there are so many of them in orbit.

* asteroid: 소행성

① to affect Earth's gravity
② to protect our little planet
③ to change the orbit of Earth
④ to prevent explosion of satellites
⑤ to provide us with alternative energy

2 다음 빈칸에 들어갈 말로 가장 적절한 것을 고르시오. 고1 학평 기출

Judgements about flavor are often influenced by predictions based on the _____ of the food. For example, strawberry-flavored foods would be expected to be red. However, if colored green, because of the association of green foods with flavors such as lime, it would be difficult to identify the flavor as strawberry unless it was very strong. Color intensity also affects flavor perception. A stronger color may cause perception of a stronger flavor in a product, even if the stronger color is simply due to the addition of more food coloring. Texture also can be misleading. A thicker product may be perceived as tasting richer or stronger simply because it is thicker, and not because the thickening agent affects the flavor of the food.

① origin
② recipe
③ nutrition
④ appearance
⑤ arrangement

----

1 Jupiter 목성 astronomer 천문학자 blow 충돌 gravitational pull 중력(의 끌어당김) surface 표면 orbit 궤도
2 judgement 판단 flavor 맛 association 연관성 intensity 강도 perception 인식 due to ~ 때문에 addition 첨가 texture 질감
misleading 오해하게 하는 thick 걸쭉한 thickening agent (액체의) 농후 재료

3

다음 빈칸에 들어갈 말로 가장 적절한 것을 고르시오. **고1 학평 기출 응용**

The best way in which innovation changes our lives is by _____. The main theme of human history is that we become steadily more specialized in what we produce, and steadily more diversified in what we consume: unstable self-sufficiency is being changed into safer mutual interdependence. By concentrating on serving other people's needs for forty hours a week — which we call a job — you can spend the other seventy-two hours (not counting fifty-six hours in bed) relying on the services provided to you by other people. Innovation has made it possible to work for a fraction of a second in order to be able to afford to turn on an electric lamp for an hour, providing the quantity of light that would have required a whole day's work if you had to make it yourself by collecting and refining sesame oil or lamb fat to burn in a simple lamp, as much of humanity did in the not so distant past.

① respecting the values of the old days
② enabling people to work for each other
③ providing opportunities to think creatively
④ satisfying customers with personalized services
⑤ introducing and commercializing unusual products

---

3 innovation 혁신 steadily 꾸준히 specialize 전문화하다 diversify 다양화하다 self-sufficiency 자급자족 mutual 서로의 interdependence 상호 의존 concentrate 집중하다 rely on 의지하다 a fraction of a second 아주 짧은 시간 afford ~의 여유가 있다 electric lamp 전등 quantity 양 refine 정제하다

10강 어근 5

226
ancestor
[ǽnsestər]

명 조상, 선조 ❯ ance/anti(before)+cess(go)+or
➕ ancient 고대의   antique 골동품   anticipate 기대하다

227
progress
[prəgrés]

명 진보, 발전 ❯ pro(before)+gress(go)
➕ aggression 공격   Congress 미국 의회   retrogress 퇴화하다

228
especially
[ispéʃəli]

부 특히, 더욱 ❯ e(out)+spec(look)+ially
➕ species 종   specimen 표본, 견본

229
remind
[rimáind]

동 상기시키다, 생각나게 하다 ❯ re(again)+mind(think)
➕ mindset 사고방식, 마음가짐   mentality 사고방식, 심리

230
method
[méθəd]

명 방법, 수단 ❯ meta(change)+(h)od(way)
➕ period 기간, 시대   episode 한 회, 한 편   exodus 대탈출

231
respond
[rispánd]

동 반응하다, 대응하다 ❯ re(back)+spond(promise)
➕ responsible 책임 있는   correspond 일치하다

232
empathy
[émpəθi]

명 공감, 감정 이입 ❯ em(in)+pathy(feeling)
➕ sympathy 동정, 연민   antipathy 반감   compassion 동정

233
relevant
[réləvənt]

형 관련된 ❯ re(back)+lev(lift)+ant
➕ relevance 연관   elevated 고상한   alleviate 경감하다   relieved 안심의

234
explore
[iksplɔ́ːr]

동 탐구하다, 탐험하다, 연구하다 ❯ ex(out)+plore(cry)
➕ deplore 한탄하다   implore 간청하다

235
avoid
[əvɔ́id]

동 피하다, 막다 ❯ a(away)+void/vacu(empty)
➕ void 공허감, 슬픔   vacuum 진공   evacuate 소개시키다

236
necessary
[nèsəséri]

형 필요한 ❯ ne(not)+cess(go)+ary
➕ accession 승낙, 취득   unprecedented 전례 없는

237
emit
[imít]

동 방출하다 ❯ e(out)+mit(send)
➕ submit 제출하다   permit 허용하다   admit 인정하다
➕ commit 저지르다   transmit 전송하다

238

account
[əkáunt]

동 설명하다, 차지하다 ❯ ac(to)+count(count)

➕ count 세다, 중요하다　accountant 회계사　discount 할인

239

similar
[símələr]

형 유사한 ❯ simil(like)+ar　similarity 명 유사(점)

➕ simile 직유　assimilate 동화하다　simultaneously 동시에

240

combine
[kəmbáin]

동 결합하다, 합치다 ❯ com(with)+bi(two)+ne

➕ biped 두발 동물　bilateral 쌍방간의　billion 십억

241

century
[séntʃəri]

명 세기 ❯ cent(hundred)+ury

➕ centenary 백 주년　centigrade 섭씨(= Celsius)

242

destruction
[distrʌ́kʃən]

명 파괴, 파멸 ❯ de(against)+struct(stand)+ion

➕ construction 건설　reconstruction 재건　obstruction 방해

243

intention
[inténʃən]

명 의도, 의사 ❯ in(in)+tend(stretch)+ion

➕ attend 참석하다　extend 확대하다　pretend ~체 하다

244

according
[əkɔ́:rdiŋ]

부 ~에 따라 ❯ ac(to)+cord(heart)+ing

➕ accord 일치, 조화　discord 불화　concord 조화, 일치

245

director
[diréktər]

명 감독, 이사, 소장 ❯ di(away)+rect(straight)+or

➕ correct 정정하다　erect 세우다　rectangle 직사각형

246

immediate
[imí:diət]

형 즉각적인 ❯ im(not)+medi(middle)+ate

➕ medium 매개체　intermediate 중급　mediate 중재하다

247

measure
[méʒər]

동 측정하다 명 대책, 조치 ❯ meas(gauge)+ure

➕ immeasurable 엄청난　immense 막대한　dimension 차원

248

outsource
[àutsɔ́:rs]

동 외주 제작하다, 위탁하다 ❯ out(out)+source(원천, 출처)

➕ resource 자원　insourcing 자체 제작

249

instruction
[instrʌ́kʃən]

명 지시, 강의, 설명서 ❯ in(in)+struct(stand)+ion

➕ industry 산업　instrument 도구　infrastructure 하부 구조

250

maintain
[meintéin]

동 유지하다, 주장하다 ❯ main(hand)+tain(hold)

➕ attain 달성하다　contain 포함하다　obtain 얻다, 획득하다

➕ retain 보유하다　sustain 지속하다　entertain 즐겁게 해 주다

PRACTICE

A   주어진 접두사를 연결하고, 그 단어와 의미를 각각 쓰시오.

1	e	_____, _____	**6**	at	_____, _____
2	ad	_____, _____	**7**	ob	_____, _____
3	com	_____, _____	**8**	re	_____, _____
4	per	_____, _____	**9**	sus	_____, _____
5	sub	_____, _____	**10**	main	_____, _____

보기: **mit**   보기: **tain**

B   빈칸에 들어갈 알맞은 표현을 고르시오.

1 The nurse weighed me and _____ my height.

① reminded   ② combined   ③ maintained   ④ measured

2 The Earth is being destroyed, all in the name of _____.

① aggression   ② retrogress   ③ progress   ④ congress

3 I didn't _____ for her to see the painting until it was finished.

① attend   ② extend   ③ pretend   ④ intend

4 All the pupils are _____ in the basics of road safety, like how to cross at the crosswalk.

① obstructed   ② destructed   ③ instructed   ④ constructed

5 The use of fossil fuels cannot be _____ due to the lack of renewable energy facilities.

① emitted   ② explored   ③ measured   ④ avoided

C   네모 안에서 문맥에 맞는 낱말로 가장 적절한 것을 고르시오.

1 If the nature of a thing is such that when removed from the environment in which it naturally occurs it alters radically, you will not figure out an accurate account of it by examining it within natural / laboratory conditions.

2 More recently there have been attempts to argue that unpaid work is volunteering / work because 'it is an activity that combines labour with raw materials to produce goods and services with enhanced economic value'.

적용독해

1 다음 글의 밑줄 친 부분 중, 문맥상 낱말의 쓰임이 적절하지 <u>않은</u> 것은? 고1 학평 기출

Many successful people tend to keep a good bedtime routine. They take the time just before bed to reflect on or write down three things that they are ① <u>thankful</u> for that happened during the day. Keeping a diary of things that they appreciate ② <u>reminds</u> them of the progress they made that day in any aspect of their lives. It serves as a key way to stay motivated, especially when they experience a ③ <u>success</u>. In such case, many people fall easily into the ④ <u>trap</u> of replaying negative situations from a hard day. But regardless of how badly their day went, successful people typically ⑤ <u>avoid</u> that trap of negative self-talk. That is because they know it will only create more stress.

2 다음 글의 밑줄 친 부분 중, 문맥상 낱말의 쓰임이 적절하지 <u>않은</u> 것은? 고3 학평 기출

Empathy is made possible by a special group of nerve cells called mirror neurons. These special cells enable us to ① <u>reflect</u> emotions. Mirror neurons were first discovered by Italian scientists who, while looking at the activity of individual nerve cells inside the brains of monkeys, noticed that neurons in the ② <u>same</u> area of the brain were activated whether the animals were performing a particular movement or simply observing another monkey perform the same action. It appeared as though the cells in the ③ <u>observer's</u> brain "mirrored" the activity in the performer's brain. A ④ <u>unfamiliar</u> phenomenon takes place when we watch someone experiencing an emotion and feel the same emotion in response. The same neural systems get ⑤ <u>activated</u> in a part of the insula, which is part of the mirror neuron system, and in the emotional brain areas associated with the observed emotion.

* insula: 뇌도(거울 뉴런 조직의 한 부분)

---

1 tend to ~하는 경향이 있다 bedtime 자기 전의 routine 습관, 일상 reflect on ~을 돌아보다 appreciate 감사하다 progress 발전 regardless of ~에 상관없이

2 empathy 공감 nerve 신경 cell 세포 activate 활성화하다 unfamiliar 생소한 phenomenon 현상 take place 발생하다 associated with ~와 관련된

접속사 1 (명사절)

1 명사절을 이끄는 「접속사 that + 완전한 절」

- **A** <u>That the book is based on a true story</u> is wrong. (주어)
- **B** His only fault is <u>that he has no fault</u>. (보어)
- **C** I know <u>that she wants to go there</u>. (목적어)

2 동격절

the fact/feeling/impression/rumor/idea/news/possibility/opinion 등 + that + 완전한 절: ~라는 사실/느낌/인상/소문/생각/뉴스/가능성/의견....)

- **D** Let's consider **the idea** <u>that your brain has a network of neurons</u>.

3 명사절을 이끄는 「접속사 if/whether + 완전한 절」

- **E** I wonder + Is he honest? → I wonder **whether/if** he is honest. (목적어)
- **F** I asked her + Do you like me? → I asked her **whether/if** she liked me.
- **G** Passing the exam depends on **whether** I study hard or not. (전치사의 목적어)
- **H** **Whether** he will succeed is not certain yet. (주어)
  = It is not certain yet **whether/if** he will pass the exam.
- **I** The question is **whether** he is right or wrong. (보어)

4 의문사가 이끄는 명사절: 의문문(의문사 + 동사 + 주어)을 명사절(의문사 + 주어 + 동사)로 전환

- **J** I don't know + Who is she? → I don't know **who she is**. (의문대명사)
- **K** She asked me + Where do you live? → She asked me **where I live**. (의문부사)

PRACTICE

A 밑줄 친 부분에서 틀린 것을 찾아 어법에 맞게 고쳐 쓰시오.

1 To never take a risk means <u>what you will never succeed</u>.

2 A god called Moinee came down to Tasmania to see <u>that the matter was</u>.

3 The would-be bride asked me <u>that I would accept the invitation</u>.

4 <u>The fact which the earth revolves the sun</u> surprised the religious community.

B 네모 안에서 어법에 맞는 표현으로 가장 적절한 것을 고르시오.

1 Griffin, who received a Ph.D. in zoology from Harvard University in 1942, demonstrated what / that bats emit high-frequency sounds with which they can locate objects as small as flying insects.

2 Because they challenge how we think inanimate objects and living things should behave, so curious are toys that appear to be alive that / whether many toys today exploit this principle to generate great sales.

적용독해

1　다음 글의 밑줄 친 부분 중, 어법상 **틀린** 것은?　고1 학평 기출 응용

Although there is usually a correct way of holding and playing musical instruments, the most important instruction to begin with is ① that they are not toys and that they must be looked after. ② Allowing children time to explore ways of handling and playing the instruments for themselves before showing them. ③ Whether they can find different ways to produce sounds is an important stage of musical exploration. Correct playing comes from the desire to find the most appropriate sound quality and ④ find the most comfortable playing position so that one can play with control over time. As instruments and music become more complex, learning appropriate playing techniques becomes ⑤ increasingly relevant.

2　다음 글의 밑줄 친 부분 중, 어법상 **틀린** 것은?　고1 학평 기출 응용

The human brain, it turns out, has shrunk in mass by about 10 percent since it peaked in size 15,000-30,000 years ago. One possible reason is ① that many thousands of years ago humans lived in a world of dangerous predators where they had to have their wits about them at all times to avoid ② being killed. Today, we have effectively domesticated ourselves and many of the tasks of survival — from avoiding immediate death to building shelters to obtaining food — has been outsourced to the wider society. We are smaller than our ancestors too, and it is a characteristic of domestic animals ③ that they are generally smaller than their wild cousins. Because brain size is not necessarily an indicator of human intelligence, ④ if we have smaller brains doesn't matter. It does matter ⑤ what our brains today are wired up differently, and perhaps more efficiently, than those of our ancestors.

1　musical instrument 악기　instruction 가르침, 지도　look after ~을 관리하다, ~을 돌보다　explore 탐구하다, 탐험하다　handle 다루다　produce 만들어 내다, 생산하다　stage 단계　desire 욕구, 욕망　appropriate 알맞은　quality 질, 품질　comfortable 편안한　complex 복잡한　relevant 유의미한, 관련된
2　shrink 줄어들다　mass 부피　peak 절정에 달하다　predator 포식자　wit 기지　domesticate 길들이다　immediate 즉각적인　shelter 은신처　obtain 얻다　outsource 위탁하다　ancestor 조상　wild 야생의　cousin 사촌　indicator 지표　be wired up 타고나다　perhaps 아마도

1 다음 빈칸에 들어갈 말로 가장 적절한 것은? 고1 학평 기출

To fight productivity-slowing energy burnout typical in offices during the day, a design firm in Amsterdam has recently introduced a new method for ensuring that its employees go home on time and rest. Every day promptly at 6 p.m., everyone's desks are raised to the ceiling by iron cables, and the space is then transformed into either a dance floor or yoga studio open for free to the community. The creative director of the firm, Sander Veenendaal, stated that this new measure has not only improved workers' lives, but helped to build up their brand as well. _____ is becoming a serious priority in offices around the world hoping to achieve similar results.

* burnout: (심신의) 소모

① Managing conflicts
② Enforced rest time
③ Enhanced cooperation
④ Individualized workspace
⑤ A flexible work schedule

2 다음 빈칸에 들어갈 말로 가장 적절한 것은? 고1 학평 기출

Houses in flames, crops stolen, and hasty graves for the dead. This was the legacy of Attila's Huns, sweeping across northern Italy and causing massive destruction to the remains of the Roman Empire. But they unintentionally left another, more positive legacy as well. Refugees from burning cities were desperate to find safe refuge. As things got worse, in the sixth century, more Roman citizens streamed to the wetlands to avoid the mass killings and destruction on the mainland. Over the next few centuries they transformed the tough surroundings into an architectural wonder: Venice! Built out of misfortune, Venice eventually turned into one of the richest and most beautiful cities in the world. Thus _____.

---

1 recently 최근에 method 방법 promptly 즉시 transform 바꾸다 creative director 광고 제작 감독 state 말하다 measure 정책 priority 우선순위

2 flame 불길 crop 농작물 hasty 급하게 grave 무덤 legacy 유산 destruction 파괴 remains 유물 unintentionally 의도치 않게 refugee 피난민 desperate 필사적인 stream 줄을 지어 이동하다 wetland 습지대 architectural 건축의

① harsh necessity can be the mother of glorious invention
② excessive greed can give rise to unexpected disasters
③ a good beginning does not always make a good ending
④ an ounce of prevention is well worth a pound of cure
⑤ humans are powerless before the forces of nature

3

다음 빈칸에 들어갈 말로 가장 적절한 것은? 고2 학평 기출

The biggest trap many family gardeners fall into is creating a garden that is too large. Even though you may have the best of intentions, over time a garden that is too large will become a maintenance nightmare. My family, like many others, eagerly planted large gardens only to cut back slowly on the time devoted to gardening. Sometime in September, we ended up with a garden full of overripened fruit and out-of-control, overgrown plants. This situation is not enjoyable for adult gardeners, let alone for children. Most children (and many adults) won't enjoy spending their warm sunny days tending an overgrown garden plot. When thinking about the size of your family garden, be _____. Plan the size according to the time your family can devote to the garden.

① diligent   ② ambitious   ③ realistic
④ challenging   ⑤ cooperative

---

3 trap 함정 intention 의도 maintenance 유지 nightmare 악몽 eagerly 열심히 cut back on ~을 줄이다 devote ~ to ... ~을 …에 바치다 end up 결국 ~에 이르게 되다 overripened 너무 익은 let alone ~은 말할 것도 없이 tend 돌보다 plot 밭뙈기, 작은 면적의 땅

11강

어근 6

251

equality
[ikwáləti]

몡 평등 ❯ equal(same)+ity

➕ inequality 불평등 equator 적도 adequate 적당한, 충분한

252

eliminate
[ilímənèit]

동 제거하다 ❯ e(out)+limin(threshold 문지방)+ate

➕ preliminary 예비의, 예선 subliminal 잠재의식의

253

achieve
[ətʃíːv]

동 이룩하다, 달성하다 ❯ ac(to)+chieve(head)

➕ chief 우두머리, 최고의 mischief 장난, 악영향

254

cave
[keiv]

몡 동굴 ❯ cave(empty, hollow) cf. cavern 큰 동굴

➕ cavity 충치 excavate 발굴하다 concave 오목한

255

nutrient
[njúːtriənt]

몡 영양분, 자양분 ❯ nutri(nourish)+ent

➕ nourish 양분을 주다 nutrition 영양(섭취) nurture 양육

256

conscious
[kánʃəs]

형 의식하는, 의식이 있는 ❯ con(with)+sci(know)+ous

➕ science 과학 subconscious 무의식의 conscience 양심

257

capture
[kǽptʃər]

동 사로잡다 ❯ capt(take)+ure

➕ captive 포로 captivate 마음을 사로잡다 escape 탈출하다

258

remove
[rimúːv]

동 제거하다 ❯ re(away)+move

➕ mobile 이동성이 있는 countermove 대응 방식, 반대 운동

259

sequence
[síːkwəns]

몡 서열, 순서, 연속 ❯ sequ(follow)+ence

➕ consequence 결과 subsequent 뒤이은 persuit 추구

260

subject
[səbdʒékt]

몡 주제, 과목, 주어, 피실험자 ❯ sub(under)+ject(throw)

➕ object 물건, 목적어 reject 거부하다 inject 주입하다

261

edit
[édit]

동 편집하다, 수정하다 ❯ e(out)+dit/don(give)

➕ add 더하다, 첨가하다 tradition 전통 donation 기부

262

access
[ǽksès]

몡 접근, 접속 ❯ ac(to)+cess(go)

➕ success 성공 succession 계승 excess 초과

➕ recess 휴식, 휴회 process 과정

263

invention
[invénʃən]

명 발명 ❯ in(in)+vent(come)+ion

⊕ venue 장소　revenue 세입, 수입　intervene 개입하다

264

inflate
[infléit]

동 부풀리다, 팽창시키다 ❯ in(in)+flate(blow)

⊕ deflation (통화)수축　stagflation 불경기와 인플레이션의 병존

265

repetition
[rèpətíʃən]

명 반복, 재발 ❯ re(again)+peti(seek)+tion

⊕ appetite 식욕　petition 청원(서)　perpetual 끊임없는

266

fraction
[frǽkʃən]

명 분수, 일부 ❯ frac(break)+tion

⊕ frail 허약한　fragile 깨지기 쉬운　fracture 골절

267

retain
[ritéin]

동 유지하다, 보유하다 ❯ re(back)+tain(hold)

⊕ abstain 절제하다　detain 구금하다　pertain 관련되다

268

explain
[ikspléin]

동 설명하다 ❯ ex(out)+plain(flat)

⊕ plain 분명한, 평원　planet 행성　plateau 고원

269

dialog
[dáiəlɔ̀(ː)g]

명 대화 ❯ dia(across)+log(speak)

⊕ apologize 사과하다　etymology 어원　epilogue 맺음말

270

audience
[ɔ́ːdiəns]

명 청중, 관객 ❯ audi(hear)+ence

⊕ audition 시연(심사)　inaudible 들을 수 없는　acoustic 음향의

271

section
[sékʃən]

명 부분, 구역, 절개 ❯ sect(cut)+ion

⊕ sector 부문　bisect 양분하다　Caesarean section 제왕절개

272

translate
[trænsléit]

동 번역하다, 해석하다 ❯ trans(across)+late(carry)

⊕ correlation 상관관계　dilate 팽창하다　superlative 최상의

273

comprehend
[kàmprihénd]

동 이해하다, 파악하다 ❯ com(with)+prehend/pris/prey(take)

⊕ apprehend 체포하다　predator 포식자　comprise 구성되다

274

cyclic
[sáiklik]

형 주기적인, 순환하는 ❯ cycle(circle)+ic

⊕ recycle 재생하다　circulate 순환하다　encircle 둘러싸다

275

transfer
[trænsfə́ːr]

동 이전하다, 이체하다 ❯ trans(across)+fer(carry)

⊕ infer 추론하다　offer 제공하다　suffer 겪다　defer 연기하다

⊕ prefer 선호하다　refer 언급하다　interfere 간섭하다

PRACTICE

A   주어진 접두사를 연결하고, 그 단어와 의미를 각각 쓰시오.

	보기			보기	
1 of		_____, _____	**6** ac		_____, _____
2 in		_____, _____	**7** ex		_____, _____
3 re	fer	_____, _____	**8** re	cess	_____, _____
4 pre		_____, _____	**9** suc		_____, _____
5 trans		_____, _____	**10** pro		_____, _____

B   빈칸에 들어갈 알맞은 표현을 고르시오.

1 The novel has been _____ into 10 languages.

   ① translated   ② correlated   ③ dilated   ④ elated

2 Finnish citizens are given full _____ of gender and opportunity.

   ① equator   ② adequacy   ③ equality   ④ inequality

3 A _____ of the subjects displayed aggressive behaviors after the experiment.

   ① dialog   ② nutrient   ③ reply   ④ fraction

4 These _____ boards and boats can make your summer holiday fantastic.

   ① intimate   ② removable   ③ inflatable   ④ subjective

5 Earthquakes can recur _____ around Circum-Pacific belt, also known as Ring of Fire.

   ① equally   ② cyclically   ③ accessibly   ④ consciously

C   네모 안에서 문맥에 맞는 낱말로 가장 적절한 것을 고르시오.

1 After lengthy discussions about the intention and construction of each film section ended, the composer roughed out and recorded musical passages for a scene or sequence, and then the director filmed these sections and edited them in accordance / discordance with the musical construction.

2 Although achieving the appropriate scientific ends is always the necessary goal of a study, protection of the rights and welfare of human participants must override / overestimate scientific efficiency.

적용독해

1 다음 글의 밑줄 친 부분 중, 문맥상 낱말의 쓰임이 적절하지 <u>않은</u> 것은? 고2 학평 기출

Dworkin suggests a classic argument for a certain kind of equality of opportunity. From Dworkin's view, justice requires that a person's fate be determined by things that are within that person's ① <u>control</u>, not by luck. If differences in well-being are determined by circumstances lying outside of an individual's control, they are ② <u>unjust</u>. According to this argument, inequality of well-being that is driven by differences in individual choices or tastes is ③ <u>acceptable</u>. But we should seek to ④ <u>eliminate</u> inequality of well-being that is driven by factors that are not an individual's responsibility and which prevent an individual from achieving what he or she values. We do so by ⑤ <u>neglecting</u> equality of opportunity or equality of access to fundamental resources.

2 다음 글의 밑줄 친 부분 중, 문맥상 낱말 의 쓰임이 적절하지 <u>않은</u> 것은? 고3 학평 기출

Life is rhythmic, cyclic, and always evolving. It's difficult not to ① <u>notice</u> repetition and renewal going on all around you. Just as darkness comes at the end of each day, so also comes the ② <u>dawn</u> to spread light across the land. Just as plants must die at the end of their life cycle, the seeds they have produced will emerge as new plants in the spring. Understanding the cyclical nature of life will ③ <u>reassure</u> you that difficult times won't last forever, and you will feel joy and happiness again. The rough times must be endured and taken as they come, but they are not ④ <u>temporary</u>, nor do they last forever. There will always be good times and bad, feasts and famines, hot summers and cold winters. Whenever you feel stuck in a dark cave, spiritually dry, or just plain gloomy, take time to remind yourself that ⑤ <u>change</u> is on its way.

---

1 classic 고전적인　equality 평등　justice 정의　fate 운명　unjust 불평등한　inequality 불평등　acceptable 허용 가능한　neglect 무시하다
fundamental 기본적인　resource 자원
2 rhythmic 주기적인　cyclic 순환하는　evolve 발전하다　repetition 반복　renewal 재생　spread 퍼뜨리다　emerge 나타나다　reassure 안심시키다　temporary 일시적인　famine 기근　stuck 움직일 수 없는　spiritually 정신적으로　remind 상기시키다

접속사 2 (부사절)

① 부사절을 이끄는 접속사의 종류

A	시간 접속사: when, while, before, since, as, until(till), as soon as 등
B	이유 접속사: because, since, as, for, in that, now that, in case 등
C	조건 접속사: if, unless, once, suppose, given (that), provided (that) 등
D	양보 접속사: though, although, even if, even though 등
E	기타 접속사: whereas(~하는 반면에 = while)

② 부사절의 접속사 + 완전한 절

A The police shot the criminal **when** he escaped from the jail.

B **Although** animals look different, they all have something in common.

C **If** you choose the safe option all of your life, you will never grow.

D The family gave the dog away **because** he got too big.

PRACTICE

A 알맞은 접속사를 보기에서 골라 빈칸을 채우시오.

> 〈보기〉   whereas   unless   while   in that   though

1 I had a relaxing picnic in the park _____ I was chatting with my loved ones.

2 The candidate had an advantage over the others _____ he could speak Spanish and Chinese.

3 He realized that _____ he attempted to get on the roof, all three would probably be in danger.

4 Carbon dioxide is widely considered to be a pollutant, _____ living things emit carbon dioxide when they breathe.

5 The indoor tree would grow more because it was protected and safe, _____ the outdoor tree had to cope with the elements.

B 네모 안에서 어법에 맞는 표현으로 가장 적절한 것을 고르시오.

1 The immense improvement in the yield of farming, as a result of innovations in mechanization, new varieties of fertilizer and pesticides, and genetic engineering, has banished famine from the face of the planet considerably and drastically reduced malnutrition, even during / while the human population has continued to expand.

2 Although / Despite burying your head in the sand and believing no news is good news is tempting, trust me, if customers are not complaining to you, then they are complaining to other people or they are just never using your business again.

적용독해

1 다음 글의 밑줄 친 부분 중, 어법상 틀린 것은? [고2 학평 기출 응용]

If there's one thing koalas are good at, it's sleeping. For a long time many scientists suspected that koalas were so lethargic ① underline{because} the compounds in eucalyptus leaves kept the cute little animals in a drugged-out state. But more recent research has shown that the leaves are simply so low in nutrients ② underline{that} koalas have almost no energy. Therefore they tend to move as little as possible — and when they do move, they often look ③ underline{as though} they're in slow motion. Koalas spend little time thinking ④ underline{despite} they rest sixteen to eighteen hours a day. In fact, they spend most of that time unconscious; their brains actually appear to have shrunk over the last few centuries. The koala is the only known animal ⑤ underline{whose} brain only fills half of its skull.

* lethargic: 무기력한

2 다음 글의 밑줄 친 부분 중, 어법상 틀린 것은? [고3 학평 기출 응용]

In 1909, Herbert Cecil Booth happened to be inside the Empire Music Hall ① underline{when} his interest was captured by a demonstration of a cleaning machine. The machine certainly stirred up dust, but it ultimately proved ineffective in collecting and removing it. Booth asked the man demonstrating the machine ② underline{whether} suction rather than pressure wouldn't work better. He indignantly replied ③ underline{that} suction had been tried on numerous occasions but didn't work. Booth's mind quickly went to work on the problem. Several days later, ④ underline{during} he was discussing his thoughts on the subject with friends, he attempted to illustrate his idea by unfolding his handkerchief, placing it on the velvet seat of his chair, placing his lips upon the handkerchief, and inhaling. ⑤ underline{As soon as} they saw the quantity of dust he had managed to draw out from the chair, Booth's friends were surprised. Booth patented his new invention that same year.

---

1 suspect 의심하다 compound 화합물, 혼합 성분 nutrient 영양분 as though 마치 ~처럼 unconscious 의식이 없는 shrink 줄어들다, 작아지다 skull 두개골

2 demonstration 시연 stir up 일으키다 ineffective 비효율적인 remove 제거하다 suction 흡입 pressure 압력 indignantly reply 화를 내며 답하다 discuss ~에 관하여 (서로) 이야기하다 illustrate 설명하다 unfold 펼치다 handkerchief 손수건 inhale (숨을) 들이마시다 draw out ~을 빼내다 patent 특허를 얻다

빈칸 추론 3

1 다음 빈칸에 들어갈 말로 가장 적절한 것은? 고1 학평 기출

Teachers at Stone Mountain State College (S.M.S.C.) give higher grades than teachers at other colleges in the state college system. More than one-third of the undergraduate grades awarded in the spring semester 2005 were A's, and only 1.1 percent were F's. The percentage of A's awarded to graduate students was even higher; almost two-thirds were A's. The students, of course, may be happy because they received high grades. However, evidence suggests that this trend is _____. When they applied to a graduate or professional school, they got disadvantages because the admission offices believed an A from S.M.S.C. is not equal to an A from other universities. Grade inflation, therefore, may hurt a student from S.M.S.C. who intends to apply to a graduate or professional school.

① decreasing the quality of higher education
② causing students to neglect their studies
③ attracting more foreign students
④ having negative consequences
⑤ spreading to other states

---

1 undergraduate 학부 semester 학기 evidence 증거 **suggest** 시사하다 **apply to** ~에 지원하다 **disadvantage** 불이익 **admission** 입학 inflation 인플레이션, (물가) 폭등 **intend to** ~할 의향이 있다

2 다음 빈칸에 들어갈 말로 가장 적절한 것은? 〔고2 학평 기출〕

Consider the "power" of a baseball bat. All the energy gained by the bat is supplied by the batter. The bat is just an instrument that helps send the ball on its way. If it does its job well, then we usually say that the bat is powerful. In physics terms, we should really describe the bat in terms of its efficiency. An efficient bat would be one that allows the batter to transfer the energy in his arms to the ball without _____ in the process. In fact, all bats are very inefficient in the sense that only a small fraction of the energy in the arms is given to the ball. Most of that energy is retained in the bat and in the arms as a result of the "follow through" after the bat strikes the ball.

① any friction to the ball   ② too much loss of energy
③ decrease of swing speed   ④ help from another instrument
⑤ enhancement of physical strength

3 다음 빈칸에 들어갈 말로 가장 적절한 것은? 〔고2 학평 기출〕

Most times a foreign language is spoken in film, subtitles are used to translate the dialogue for the viewer. However, there are occasions when foreign dialogue is left unsubtitled (and thus incomprehensible to most of the target audience). This is often done if the movie is seen mainly from the viewpoint of a particular character who does not speak the language. Such absence of subtitles allows the audience to feel a similar sense of incomprehension and alienation that the character feels. An example of this is seen in *Not Without My Daughter*. The Persian language dialogue spoken by the Iranian characters is not subtitled because the main character Betty Mahmoody does not speak Persian and the audience is _____.

① learning the language used in the film
② impressed by her language skills
③ attracted to her beautiful voice
④ participating in a heated debate
⑤ seeing the film from her viewpoint

---

2 supply 공급하다   instrument 도구   physics 물리학   describe 설명하다   efficiency 효율성   transfer 옮기다   fraction 부분, 일부   retain 보유하다

3 foreign 외국의   subtitle 자막(*v.* 자막을 넣다)   translate 통역하다   dialogue 대화   viewer 관객   occasion 경우   incomprehensible 이해할 수 없는   target audience 주요 대상 관객   mainly 주로   viewpoint 관점, 시각   particular 특정한   absence 부재   alienation 소외

12강 어근 7

276
adapt
[ədǽpt]

동 적응하다, 개조하다　❯ ad(to)+apt(adjust)
➕ apt 적절한　aptitude 적성　maladapted 부적응의

277
comfort
[kʌ́mfərt]

명 위로, 편안함　❯ com(with)+fort(strong)
➕ effort 노력, 활동　fortress 요새　fortify 강화하다

278
monotonous
[mənátənəs]

형 단조로운　❯ mono(one)+tone(어조)+ous
➕ monolog 독백　monarch 군주　monopoly 독점

279
invade
[invéid]

동 침입하다, 침해하다　❯ in(into)+vade(go)
➕ evade 피하다, 면하다　pervade 스며들다, 널리 퍼지다

280
forbid
[fərbíd]

동 금지하다　❯ for(not)+bid(ask)
➕ forget 잊다　forgive 용서하다　forbear 삼가다

281
literally
[lítərəli]

부 글자 그대로, 말 그대로　❯ liter(letter)+ally
➕ literary 문학의　illiterate 문맹의　literature 문학

282
define
[difáin]

동 규정하다, 정의를 내리다　❯ de(completely)+fine(end)
➕ refine 세련하다　confine 국한하다　infinite 무한한

283
separate
[sépərèit]

동 분리하다, 구분하다　❯ se(apart)+pare(prepare)+ate
➕ prepare 준비하다　repair 수리하다　apparatus 장치

284
assess
[əsés]

동 평가하다, 판단하다　❯ as(to)+sess(sit)
➕ settle 정착하다　session 학기　obsession 강박 관념

285
flourish
[flə́:riʃ]

동 번창하다, 성장하다　❯ flori/flour(꽃)+ish
➕ floral 꽃무늬의　florist 화초 재배가, 꽃집　flowery 화려한

286
aircraft
[ɛ́ərkræ̀ft]

명 항공기　❯ air+craft(make)
➕ craft 공예, 항공기　craftsmanship 솜씨, 장인 정신

287
express
[iksprés]

동 표현하다　❯ ex(out)+press(누르다)
➕ depress 우울하게 하다　impress 깊은 인상을 주다　compress 압축하다
➕ suppress 억제하다　oppress 억압하다

288

equation
[ikwéiʒən]

명 방정식 ❯ equa(equal)+tion

➕ equivalent 등가의   equivocal 모호한   equilibrium 평형, 균형

289

molecule
[málǝkjù:l]

명 분자 ❯ mole(mass)+cule(small)

➕ particulate 미립자   particle 입자   vehicle 차량

290

oxygen
[áksidʒən]

명 산소 ❯ oxy(acid)+gen(birth)

➕ nitrogen 질소   hydrogen 수소   antigen 항원

291

barometer
[bǝrámitǝr]

명 척도, 지표, 기압계 ❯ baro(weight)+meter(measure)

➕ meter 운율, 계량기   thermometer 온도계   symmetry 대칭

292

contribution
[kàntrǝbjú:ʃən]

명 기여, 공헌 ❯ con(with)+tribut(give)+ion

➕ distribution 분배, 공급, 분포   retribution 보복

293

medium
[mí:diǝm]

명 중간, 매(개)체, 수단 ❯ med(middle)+ium

➕ mean 평균, 중용   amid ~하는 가운데   Mesolith 중석기

294

creativity
[krì:eitívǝti]

명 창의성 ❯ create(make)+ive+ity

➕ increase 증가   decrease 감소   recruit 채용

295

concern
[kǝnsə́:rn]

명 관심(사), 우려, 걱정 ❯ con(with)+cern(seperate)

➕ discern 식별하다, 분간하다   unconcern 무관심, 태연함

296

firm
[fǝ:rm]

명 기업, 회사 형 확고한, 견고한 ❯ firm(strong)

➕ affirm 단언하다   confirm 확증하다   infirm 병약한

297

metabolism
[mǝtǽbǝlìzǝm]

명 신진대사 ❯ meta(change)+bol(throw)+ism

➕ metaphor 은유   metaphysics 형이상학   metamorphosis 변형

298

elongate
[iló:ŋgeit]

동 연장하다 ❯ e(out)+long(long)+ate

➕ prolong 장기화하다   longevity 수명, 장수   longitude 경도

299

resolve
[rizálv]

동 해결하다, 결심하다 ❯ re(back)+solve(loose)

➕ solution 해법   absolute 절대적인   resolute 단호한

300

conduct
[kándʌkt]

동 행동하다, 지휘하다, 전도하다 ❯ con(with)+duct(draw, lead)

➕ reduction 감소   production 생산   introduction 소개, 도입

➕ conduction 전도   abduction 유괴   deduction 연역법

PRACTICE

A 주어진 접두사를 연결하고, 그 단어와 의미를 각각 쓰시오.

	보기				보기	
1 de		_____, _____	**6** re		_____, _____
2 im		_____, _____	**7** ab		_____, _____
3 ex	press	_____, _____	**8** pro	duction	_____, _____
4 op		_____, _____	**9** con		_____, _____
5 com		_____, _____	**10** intro		_____, _____

B 빈칸에 들어갈 알맞은 표현을 고르시오.

1 Working is strictly _____ to Jews on the Sabbath.

① forgotten   ② forbidden   ③ forgiven   ④ forborne

2 The powers of the president are clearly _____ in the Constitution.

① confined   ② refined   ③ defined   ④ infinite

3 Korea has been _____ up to almost a thousand times by foreign troops.

① conducted   ② invaded   ③ assessed   ④ separated

4 One bus had a head-on _____ with another, resulting in over 20 casualties.

① collision   ② adaptation   ③ contribution   ④ elongation

5 The word "polygraph," which refers to a lie detector, _____ means "many writings."

① creatively   ② comfortably   ③ monotonously   ④ literally

C 네모 안에서 문맥에 맞는 낱말로 가장 적절한 것을 고르시오.

1 Because the art of storytelling involves finding good ways to express one's experiences in a way appropriate to the listener, good storytellers tell their experiences in such a way as to eliminate the dullest parts or improve / delete the dull parts by playing with the facts.

2 There are many risks of colliding with vehicles on the narrow road where students walk to school, so we ask that you expand / obstruct the school road for students' safety and comfort.

적용독해

1 다음 글의 밑줄 친 부분 중, 문맥상 낱말의 쓰임이 적절하지 <u>않은</u> 것은? 고1 학평 기출

We notice repetition among confusion, and the opposite: we notice a break in a repetitive pattern. But how do these arrangements make us feel? And what about "perfect" regularity and "perfect" chaos? Some repetition gives us a sense of ① security, in that we know what is coming next. We like some ② predictability. We arrange our lives in largely repetitive schedules. ③ Randomness, in organization or in events, is more challenging and more frightening for most of us. With "perfect" chaos we are ④ excited by having to adapt and react again and again. But "perfect" regularity is perhaps even more horrifying in its monotony than randomness is. It ⑤ implies a cold, unfeeling, mechanical quality. Such perfect order does not exist in nature; there are too many forces working against each other. Either extreme, therefore, feels threatening.

2 다음 글의 밑줄 친 부분 중, 문맥상 낱말의 쓰임이 적절하지 <u>않은</u> 것은? 고1 학평 기출

When the Muslims invaded southern Europe in the eighth century, they passed a law forbidding the sale of pork. This was done because the founder of the Muslim religion had declared pork to be unclean. This law, of course, didn't ① change the Europeans' love of pork, and there soon developed a black market for the meat. In ② secret transactions, usually conducted at night, farmers would sell to city dwellers pigs concealed in large bags. Occasionally, a dishonest farmer would ③ trick a buyer by selling a bag containing not a pig but a cat. If something went wrong and the bag came ④ open during the transaction, this literally "let the cat out of the bag" and this is why ⑤ keeping a secret is said to be "letting the cat out of the bag."

---

1 **repetition** 반복 **confusion** 혼돈 **opposite** 반대 **arrangement** 배열 **regularity** 규칙성 **chaos** 무질서 **security** 안정감 **predictability** 예측 가능성 **randomness** 임의성 **challenging** 힘든 **horrify** 끔찍하다 **monotony** 단조로움 **imply** 내포하다 **exist** 존재하다 **against** ~에 대항하여 **extreme** 극단 **threatening** 위협적인

2 **Muslim** 이슬람교의 **invade** 침략하다 **law** 법 **forbid** 금지하다 **sale** 판매 **founder** 창시자 **religion** 종교 **declare** 선언하다 **transaction** 거래 **conduct** 행하다, 행동하다 **city dweller** 도시 주민 **occasionally** 때때로, 가끔 **dishonest** 부정직한 **contain** 담고 있다 **let the cat out of the bag** 비밀을 폭로하다, 비밀을 누설하다

전치사

① 전치사의 종류

- 시간: in, at, on, before, after, until(till), for, during, from, since 등
- 장소/위치: in, at, on, beneath, over, above, under, below, behind 등
- 방향: to, toward, into, out of, along, around, across, through 등
- 기타: of, by, like, unlike, about, despite, without, notwithstanding 등
  cf. before, after, for, until(till), since: 전치사와 접속사 모두 사용 가능

② 전치사의 특징: 전치사＋목적어(명사/동명사/명사절)

A The sun was sinking **below the horizon**.

B **On arriving** at the airport, she ran toward the booth.

C This article provides a useful guide **on how often we should replace pillows**.

③ 주의해야 할 전치사: during, despite, because of, (al)though

D I went to the beach **during** my summer vacation. (전치사)

E I went on a tour **while** I stayed in New York. (접속사)

F He would play the piano **despite** his hearing problems. (전치사)

G He likes to help others **(al)though** he is not wealthy. (접속사)

PRACTICE

A 어법상 틀린 부분을 바르게 고쳐 쓰시오.

1 Volunteers get satisfaction from enrich their social network in the service of others.

2 The tools for analysis the information were not available until the early 1990s.

3 Digital rudeness usually takes place during someone else is talking to us.

4 The Okavango River never reaches the sea because of its water flows inland.

5 Despite people commonly believe that eight hours of sleep is ideal, the truth is it all depends on how you feel.

B 네모 안에서 어법에 맞는 표현으로 가장 적절한 것을 고르시오.

1 As most artists conform to the stylistic conventions of the era into which they are born, the history of perspective in Western painting matters │ because / because of │ what it reveals for the art of living.

2 The early-twentieth-century modernist writers put emphasis on apparent simplicity in prose and poetry by consciously │ avoidance / avoiding │ old-fashioned words, elaborate images, grammatical inversions, and sometimes even meter and rhyme.

적용독해

1 다음 글의 밑줄 친 부분 중, 어법상 **틀린** 것은? **고2 학평 기출 응용**

Commercial airplanes generally travel airways similar to roads, ① <u>although</u> they are not physical structures. Airways have fixed widths and defined altitudes, which separate traffic moving in opposite directions. Vertical separation of aircraft allows some flights to pass over airports ② <u>during</u> other processes occur below. Air travel usually covers long distances, with short periods of intense pilot activity at takeoff and landing and long periods of lower pilot activity ③ <u>while</u> in the air, the portion of the flight known as the "long haul." During the long-haul portion of a flight, pilots spend more time in assessing aircraft status than ④ <u>searching</u> out nearby planes. This is ⑤ <u>because</u> collisions between aircraft usually occur in the surrounding area of airports, while crashes due to aircraft malfunction tends to occur during long-haul flight.

* long haul: 장거리 비행

2 다음 글의 밑줄 친 부분 중, 어법상 **틀린** 것은? **고2 학평 기출 응용**

Scientists who have observed plants growing in the dark have found ① <u>that</u> they are vastly different in appearance, form, and function from those grown in the light. This is true even ② <u>when</u> the plants in the different light conditions are genetically identical and are grown under identical conditions of temperature, water, and nutrient level. Seedlings grown in the dark limit the amount of energy going to organs that do not function at full capacity in the dark, like cotyledons and roots, and instead initiate elongation of the seedling stem to propel the plant out of darkness. ③ <u>While</u> in full light, seedlings reduce the amount of energy they allocate to stem elongation. The energy is directed to expanding their leaves and ④ <u>develop</u> extensive root systems. This is a good example of phenotypic plasticity. The seedling adapts to distinct environmental conditions by ⑤ <u>modifying</u> its form and the underlying metabolic and biochemical processes.

* cotyledon: 떡잎 ** phenotypic plasticity: 표현형 적응성

---

1 commercial 민간의, 상업적인 airway 항로 structure 구조(물) fixed 고정된 width 폭 define 규정하다 opposite 반대의 vertical 상하의, 수직의 aircraft 항공기 (*pl.* aircraft) flight 비행(기), 항공편 intense 고강도의, 강렬한 takeoff 이륙 landing 착륙 assess 평가하다 collision 충돌 crash (비행기의) 추락 malfunction 오작동, 고장

2 vastly 상당히, 매우 appearance 외관 genetically 유전적으로 identical 동일한 temperature 온도 nutrient 영양소 capacity 능력 initiate 시작하다 elongation 연장 propel 나아가다 allocate 배분하다 direct 향하게 하다 expand 확장하다 extensive 광범위한 distinct 별개의 modify 바꾸다 underlying 근원적인 metabolic 신진대사 biochemical 생화학적인

무관한 문장

1 다음 글에서 전체 흐름과 관계 <u>없는</u> 문장은? [고1 학평 기출 응용]

Of the many forest plants that can cause poisoning, wild mushrooms may be among the most dangerous. ① This is because people sometimes confuse the poisonous and edible varieties, or they eat mushrooms without making a positive identification of the variety. ② Many people enjoy hunting wild species of mushrooms in the spring season, because they are excellent edible mushrooms and are highly prized. ③ However, some wild mushrooms are dangerous, leading people to lose their lives due to mushroom poisoning. ④ Growing a high-quality product at a reasonable cost is a key barometer of whether or not farming edible mushrooms for profit. ⑤ To be safe, a person must be able to identify edible mushrooms before eating any wild one.

2 다음 글에서 전체 흐름과 관계 <u>없는</u> 문장은? [고1 학평 기출 응용]

According to Marguerite La Caze, fashion contributes to our lives and provides a medium for us to develop and exhibit important social virtues. ① Fashion may be beautiful, innovative, and useful; we can display creativity and good taste in our fashion choices. ② And in dressing with taste and care, we represent both self-respect and a concern for the pleasure of others. ③ There is no doubt that fashion can be a source of interest and pleasure which links us to each other. ④ Although having developed first in Europe and America, today the fashion industry is an international and highly globalized industry. ⑤ That is, fashion provides a sociable aspect along with opportunities to imagine oneself differently — to try on different identities.

---

1 poisoning 중독, 음독 confuse 혼동하다 edible 식용의 variety 품종 positive 확실한 identification 확인 pressurize ~에 압력을 가하다 excellent 훌륭한 reasonable 합리적인 key 핵심적인 barometer 척도

2 contribute to ~에 기여하다 virtue 가치 taste 취향 dress 옷을 입다 concern 관심 industry 산업 sociable 사교적인 identity 정체성

3

다음 글에서 전체 흐름과 관계 <u>없는</u> 문장은? **고1 학평 기출 응용**

If you had to write a math equation, you probably wouldn't write, "Twenty-eight plus fourteen equals forty-two." It would take too long to write and it would be hard to read quickly. You would write, "28+14=42." ① Chemistry is the same way. ② Chemists have to write chemical equations all the time, and it would take too long to write and read if they had to spell everything out. ③ So this is the very reason for chemists using chemicals, just like we do every day. ④ A chemical formula lists all the elements that form each molecule and uses a small number to the bottom right of an element's symbol to stand for the number of atoms of that element. ⑤ For example, the chemical formula for water is H_2O, which tells us that a water molecule is made up of two hydrogen ("H" and "2") atoms and one oxygen ("O") atom.

---

3 math 수학 equation 등식, 방정식 probably 아마 chemistry 화학 all the time 항상 spell out ~을 상세히 다 쓰다 list 나열하다, 열거하다 element 원소, 요소 form 구성하다, 형성하다 bottom 아래(의) stand for ~을 나타내다, ~을 대표하다 be made up of ~으로 이루어지다 hydrogen 수소 oxygen 산소

13강 어근 8

301

criminal
[krímənəl]

형 형사상의, 범죄의 명 범죄자 ▶ crime(범죄)+al

➕ discriminate 차별하다 incriminate (죄를) 뒤집어씌우다

302

compound
[kəmpáund]

명 화합물 형 복합의 ▶ com(with)+pound(put)

➕ propound 제시하다 postpone 연기하다 opponent 맞상대

303

miracle
[mírəkl]

명 기적 ▶ mira(wonder)+cle

➕ admire 존경하다 marvelous 경탄할 만한 mirage 신기루

304

distort
[distɔ́:rt]

동 왜곡하다 ▶ dis(away)+tort(twist)

➕ extort 갈취하다 retort 대꾸하다 torrent 급류

305

allege
[əlédʒ]

동 (증거 없이) 주장하다 ▶ al(to)+lege(send)

➕ delegate 위임하다 legacy 유산 relegate 좌천시키다

306

universe
[júːnəvə̀:rs]

명 우주 ▶ uni(one)+verse(turn)

➕ unify 통합하다 unite 연합하다 unanimously 만장일치로

307

detail
[ditéil]

명 세부 사항 ▶ de(completely)+tail(cut)

➕ retail 소매 entail 수반하다 curtail 삭감하다

308

laborious
[ləbɔ́:riəs]

형 근면한, 부지런한 ▶ labor(노동)+ious

➕ collaborate 협력하다 elaborate 정교한 laboratory 실험실

309

invest
[invést]

동 투자하다 ▶ in(in)+vest(clothe)

➕ vest 조끼, 옷을 입다 divest 옷을 벗기다, 박탈하다

310

portable
[pɔ́:rtəbl]

형 휴대할 수 있는 ▶ port(carry)+able

➕ port 항구 import 수입하다 export 수출하다

311

generate
[dʒénərèit]

동 발생시키다, 생성하다 ▶ gener(birth)+ate

➕ gene 유전자 generous 관대한 ingenious 독창적인

312

dispel
[dispél]

동 떨쳐버리다 ▶ dis(away)+pel(push)

➕ expel 내쫓다, 추방하다 compel 강요하다 repel 격퇴하다

➕ propel 추진하다 appeal 호소하다

313

justify
[dʒʌ́stəfài]

동 정당화하다 ▶ just(right)+(i)fy

⊕ justice 정의   injustice 불의   maladjusted 부적응의

314

consume
[kənsjúːm]

동 소비하다, 섭취하다 ▶ con(with)+sume(take)

⊕ assume 생각하다   resume 다시 시작하다   presume 추정하다

315

voluntary
[váləntèri]

형 자발적인 ▶ volunt(free will)+ary

⊕ involuntary 본의 아닌   benevolent 자선적인   malevolent 악의적인

316

dehydration
[téritɔ̀ːri]

명 탈수 ▶ de(down)+hydra(water)+tion

⊕ hydrogen 수소   carbohydrate 탄수화물   hydrant 소화전

317

territory
[spisífik]

명 영토 ▶ terra(earth)+tory

⊕ Mediterranean 지중해   terrestrial 지구의   inter 매장하다

318

specific
[kleim]

형 구체적인 ▶ spec(look)+(i)fic

⊕ special 특별한   despise 경멸하다   skeptical 회의적인

319

claim
[kleim]

동 주장하다, 요구하다 명 요구, 주장, 청구권 ▶ claim(shout)

⊕ exclaim 소리치다   proclaim 선포하다   counterclaim 반소하다

320

provide
[prəváid]

동 제공하다, 공급하다 ▶ pro(before)+vide(look)

⊕ evidence 증거   individualism 개인주의   view 간주하다

321

automatically
[ɔ̀ːtəmǽtik(ə)li]

부 자동적으로 ▶ auto(self)+matic(moving)+ally

⊕ autograph 자필 서명   autonomy 자치   autobiography 자서전

322

alarm
[əlɑ́ːrm]

동 깜짝 놀라게 하다, 경종을 울리다 ▶ al(to)+arm(weapon)

⊕ armor 갑옷   rearmament 재무장   armistice 휴전

323

current
[kə́ːrənt]

형 현재의 명 해류 ▶ cur(run)+ent

⊕ occur 발생하다   recur 재발하다   excursion 야유회

324

habitat
[hǽbitæ̀t]

명 서식지 ▶ habit(have)+at

⊕ habit 습관   cohabit 동거하다   inhabit 거주하다

325

abstract
[ǽbstrækt]

형 추상적인 ▶ abs(away)+tract/tire(draw)

⊕ attract 끌어당기다   contract 수축하다   extract 추출하다

⊕ distract 산만하게 하다   retire 퇴직하다

PRACTICE

A 주어진 접두사를 연결하고, 그 단어와 의미를 각각 쓰시오.

		보기				보기
1	ex		_____ , _____	**6**	at		_____ , _____
2	re		_____ , _____	**7**	ex		_____ , _____
3	dis	**pel**	_____ , _____	**8**	con	**tract**	_____ , _____
4	com		_____ , _____	**9**	dis		_____ , _____
5	pro		_____ , _____	**10**	abs		_____ , _____

B 빈칸에 들어갈 알맞은 표현을 고르시오.

1 The benefits of learning English made it a(n) _____ language.

① adversary ② reversible ③ universal ④ conversational

2 Chinese _____ in Korean real estate totaled 2 trillion won last year.

① consumption ② alarm ③ investment ④ specification

3 An interesting fact about woodpeckers is that they prefer dead trees as their _____.

① territory ② habitat ③ universe ④ labor

4 Japan has often tried to _____ Korean history, offering a colonial view of past events.

① allege ② dispel ③ justify ④ distort

5 The company is having difficulty _____ semiconductors owing to the RE 100 regulation.

① drawing ② exporting ③ ejecting ④ reporting

C 네모 안에서 문맥에 맞는 낱말로 가장 적절한 것을 고르시오.

1 If there were two habitats, a rich one containing a lot of resources and a poor one containing few, and there were no territoriality or fighting, we would be free to destruct / exploit the richer habitat in order to achieve the higher pay-off.

2 If we had special glasses that gave us the power to see the odorous world the way that other organisms perceive it, we would encounter a world far different / similar from what we currently experience, such that we would see compounds being released into the air from leaves, bark, and roots.

적용독해

1 다음 글의 밑줄 친 부분 중, 문맥상 낱말의 쓰임이 적절하지 <u>않은</u> 것은? 고2 학평 기출

A lot of people find that physical movement can sometimes ① <u>dispel</u> negative feelings. If we are feeling negative, it can be very easy for us to stop wanting to stay ② <u>active</u> in our everyday life. This is why many people who suffer from depression are also found sleeping in and having no motivation to go outside or exercise. Unfortunately, this ③ <u>lack</u> of exercise can actually compound many negative emotions. Exercise and movement is a great way for us to start getting rid of negative energies. Many people find that when they are ④ <u>angry</u>, they go into a state where they want to exercise or clean. This is actually a very healthy and positive thing for you to do and a great way for you to begin to ⑤ <u>intensify</u> your negative emotions so that they no longer affect your life and harm your relationships.

2 다음 글의 밑줄 친 부분 중, 문맥상 낱말의 쓰임이 적절하지 <u>않은</u> 것은? 고2 학평 기출

Spine-tingling ghost stories are fun to tell if they are really scary, and even more so if you claim that they are true. People get a ① <u>thrill</u> from passing on those stories. The same applies to miracle stories. If a rumor of a miracle gets written down in a book, the rumor becomes hard to ② <u>believe</u>, especially if the book is ancient. If a rumor is ③ <u>old</u> enough, it starts to be called a "tradition" instead, and then people believe it all the more. This is rather odd because you might think they would realize that older rumors have had more time to get ④ <u>distorted</u> than younger rumors that are close in time to the alleged events themselves. Elvis Presley and Michael Jackson lived too ⑤ <u>recently</u> for traditions to have grown up, so not many people believe stories like "Elvis seen on Mars."

---

1 dispel 떨쳐버리다 **suffer** 앓다 **depression** 우울증 **motivation** 동기 **lack** 부족 **compound** 악화시키다 **get rid of** ~을 제거하다
intensify 격렬하게 하다 **deconstruct** 해체하다
2 spine-tingling 스릴 넘치는 **claim** 주장하다 **ancient** 옛날의 **distort** 왜곡하다 **alleged** (근거 없이) 주장된

to부정사 1(명사적/형용사적)

① 명사적 용법

A <u>**To play**</u> the piano is very difficult. (주어)

    = It is very difficult **to play** the piano. (가주어-진주어)

B Jane likes **to read** novels. (목적어)

C He finds it easy **to take** a walk every morning. (가목적어-진목적어)

D My job is <u>**to design**</u> computer programs. (주격 보어)

    cf. The coach encouraged us **to do** our best. (목적격 보어) ▶p.52

      (allow, advise, inspire, force, persuade, encourage, enable 등)

E I know <u>**how to speak**</u> English. (의문사 + to부정사)

② 형용사적 용법: 명사 + to부정사

F I have many <u>things **to do**</u> today.

G Mike has no <u>house **to live in**</u>.

PRACTICE

A 밑줄 친 부분을 어법에 맞게 고쳐 쓰시오.

1 <u>This</u> is impossible for him to swim across the river.

2 To go by bicycle is faster than <u>go</u> by bus.

3 The goal of the advertisement was <u>sell</u> more cars to women.

4 Each of us has the power <u>define</u> our own lives.

5 There is one sure way for lonely patients <u>to making</u> friends.

6 I will not allow my son <u>swimming</u> in the reservoir.

7 The nurse persuaded me <u>get</u> treatment.

B 네모 안에서 어법에 맞는 표현으로 가장 적절한 것을 고르시오.

1 The principle of humane treatment exerts an important constraint on the administration of criminal justice, a state-run process which has the potential to do very great harm to anybody and be / being justified.

2 The beliefs and behaviors of healthy parents provide psychological and social information to the children that function almost like food does for the body; in this case, the information automatically helps building / to build their personal realities and shape their behaviors.

적용독해

1 다음 글의 밑줄 친 부분 중, 어법상 <u>틀린</u> 것은? [고3 학평 기출]

Leonardo da Vinci was one of the most learned and well-rounded persons ever ① <u>to live</u>. The entire universe from the wing of a dragonfly to the birth of the earth was the playground of his curious intelligence. But did Leonardo have some mystical or innate gift of insight and invention, or ② <u>was</u> his brilliance learned and earned? Certainly he had an unusual mind and an uncanny ability ③ <u>to see</u> what others didn't see. But the six thousand pages of detailed notes and drawings present clear evidence of a diligent, curious student — a perpetual learner in laborious pursuit of wisdom who was constantly exploring, questioning, and testing. ④ <u>To expand</u> your mind is vital to being creative. Therefore, ⑤ <u>invest</u> regularly in learning opportunities is one of the greatest gifts you can give yourself.

* uncanny: 예리한

2 다음 글의 밑줄 친 부분 중, 어법상 <u>틀린</u> 것은? [고2 학평 기출 응용]

The old-fashioned method which fish samplers use is ① <u>to watch</u> fish near a dam and push a button each time a fish swims up the ladder. They also get to measure a fish occasionally, which involves capturing the fish in a tank that has had the oxygen sucked out of it and holding it captive until it stops ② <u>to move</u>. Once it's still, they can put a tape measure to it before returning it to a recuperation tank. Finally the fish gets tagged and released back to continue its journey. A more common method ③ <u>to capture</u> fish is electrofishing, which involves pulling an electric wire which is attached to a portable generator through a river. The fish are stunned and almost ④ <u>magically</u> drawn to the wire, at which point samplers catch them in a net and take them to a holding place to measure and ⑤ <u>weigh</u> them before returning them to the stream.

* recuperation: 회복

---

1 well-rounded 다재다능한 entire 전체의 dragonfly 잠자리 curious 호기심 있는 mystical 신비적인 innate 타고난 insight 통찰 brilliance 탁월함 earn 획득하다 certainly 분명히 unusual 비범한 diligent 부지런한 perpetual 끊임없는 laborious 부지런한 pursuit 추구 vital 필수적인 invest 투자하다

2 measure 측정하다 occasionally 종종, 가끔 capture 잡다, 포획하다 oxygen 산소 captive 포획 상태의 tag 꼬리표를 붙이다 release 풀어놓다 journey 여정 electrofishing 전류어로법 attach 부착하다 portable 휴대할 수 있는 generator 발전기 stun 기절시키다 weigh 무게를 달다

글의 순서

1

주어진 글 다음에 이어질 글의 순서로 가장 적절한 것은? `고1 학평 기출`

> It is said that in ancient Athens the followers of Plato gathered one day to ask themselves the following question: "What is a human being?"

(A) Holding it in his hand, he shouted "Look! I present you with a human being." After the stir had died down, the philosophers gathered again and improved their definition. A human being, they said, is featherless biped with broad nails.

(B) This curious story from the history of early philosophy shows the kinds of difficulties philosophers have sometimes been faced with when attempting to give abstract, general definitions of what it is to be human.

(C) After a great deal of thought, they came up with the following answer: "a human being is a featherless biped." Everybody seemed content with this definition until a philosopher burst into the lecture hall with a live featherless chicken.

① (A) – (C) – (B) ② (B) – (A) – (C) ③ (B) – (C) – (A)
④ (C) – (A) – (B) ⑤ (C) – (B) – (A)

2

주어진 글 다음에 이어질 글의 순서로 가장 적절한 것은? `고1 학평 기출`

> Memory has two types — implicit and explicit memory. When you learn things without really thinking about it, it's implicit memory or body memory. Knowing how to breathe when you were born is an implicit memory.

(A) Explicit memories, on the other hand, are the memories or the specific things that you consciously try to recall. You use explicit memory every day on a conscious level.

(B) No one taught this to you. Some of the things you've learned since childhood also become implicit memories. Implicit memories are imprinted in the brain's autonomic portion; that is why even after years of not riding a bike you still know how to ride.

---

1 **gather** 모이다 **stir** 소란 **die down** 줄어들다 **philosopher** 철학자 **improve** 개선하다 **definition** 정의 **biped** 두 발 동물 **broad** 넓은 **abstract** 추상적인 **content** 만족하는 **lecture hall** 강당

(C) Trying to find the keys, trying to remember when an event is supposed to take place, where it's going to be held, and with whom you are going. Explicit memories are the tasks you have written down on your calendar or planner.

① (A) – (C) – (B)　　　　② (B) – (A) – (C)　　　　③ (B) – (C) – (A)
④ (C) – (A) – (B)　　　　⑤ (C) – (B) – (A)

3

주어진 글 다음에 이어질 글의 순서로 가장 적절한 것은? 고2 학평 기출

> In April 1997, the U.S. Food and Drug Administration ruled that toothpaste manufacturers weren't adhering closely enough to voluntary safety guidelines. As a result, all toothpaste tubes now bear a scary-sounding warning.

(A) In the months following the new warning, toothpaste consumer lines fielded hundreds of questions from worried parents, and poison control centers were flooded with calls as well. They told parents the same thing: your child is fine and may vomit, or not.

(B) It was like this one: "Keep out of the reach of children under 6 years of age. If more than used for brushing is accidentally swallowed, get medical help or contact a poison control center right away."

(C) The only reason to see a doctor, however, is if the vomiting gets so serious that dehydration becomes an issue. That's right: you can eat your fill of delicious toothpaste and not come away with anything more serious than nausea and diarrhea.

① (A) – (C) – (B)　　　　② (B) – (A) – (C)　　　　③ (B) – (C) – (A)
④ (C) – (A) – (B)　　　　⑤ (C) – (B) – (A)

---

2 implicit 내재적인　explicit 외재적인　breathe 호흡하다　specific 특정한　recall 기억하다　conscious 의식적인　imprinted 각인된　autonomic 자율 신경의, 자동적인　suppose 개최하다

3 Food and Drug Administration(FDA) 식약청　rule 규정하다　manufacturer 제조업자　adhere (조약을) 지키다　voluntary 자발적인　bear 담고 있다　warning 경고문　field 처리하다　flood 넘치다　vomit 토하다　accidentally 우연히　swallow 삼키다　dehydration 탈수증　come away with 경험하다　nausea 메스꺼움　diarrhea 설사

14강 어근 9

326
innate
[inéit]

형 타고난, 선천적인 ● in(in)+nate(born)

⊕ native 원주민   prenatal 출생 전의   postnatal 산후의

327
persuade
[pərswéid]

동 설득하여 ~을 하게 하다 ● per(thoroughly)+suade(advice)

⊕ dissuade 설득하여 ~을 단념시키다

328
attribute
[ǽtrəbjùːt]

동 탓/덕분으로 돌리다 ● at(to)+tribute(give)

⊕ contribute 기여하다, 공헌하다   distribute 분배하다, 살포하다

329
causal
[kɔ́ːzəl]

형 인과 관계의 ● cause(원인, 이유)+al   casualty 명 인과 관계

⊕ excuse 변명   accuse 고발하다, 비난하다

330
announce
[ənáuns]

동 발표하다, 안내 방송하다 ● an(to)+nounce(speak)

⊕ pronounce 발음하다   denounce 규탄하다

331
contemporary
[kəntémpərèri]

형 현대의, 동시대의 ● con(with)+tempor(time, try)+ary

⊕ tempo 박자, 속도   temporary 일시적인, 임시의

332
accompany
[əkʌ́mpəni]

동 동행하다, 수반하다 ● ac(to)+com(with)+pan(bread)+y

⊕ company 회사, 친구, 손님   companion 동반자, 반려자

333
durable
[djú(ː)ərəbl]

형 내구성이 있는, 오래 가는 ● dur(last)+able

⊕ during ~(하는) 동안   endure 견디다   perdure 영속하다

334
ignore
[ignɔ́ːr]

동 무시하다 ● i(not)+gno(know)+re

⊕ ignorance 무지, 무시   diagnosis 진단   prognosis 예후

335
management
[mǽnidʒmənt]

명 경영, 관리 ● manu(hand)+age+ment

⊕ manner 방식   manure 거름   manuscript 원고

336
facilitate
[fəsílitèit]

동 용이하게 하다 ● facile(make easier)+ity+ate

⊕ facile 쉽고 용이한   facility 시설   faculty 재능

337
reject
[ridʒékt]

동 거절하다, 거부하다 ● re(back)+ject(throw)

⊕ object 반대하다   inject 주입하다   eject 방출하다

⊕ project 투사하다   subject ~를 받게 하다

338

exposure
[ikspóuʒər]

명 노출, 폭로 ▸ ex(out)+pose(put)+ure

⊕ oppose 반대하다　propose 제안하다　compose 작곡하다

339

regulation
[règjəléiʃən]

명 규제, 규정 ▸ regu/reig(rule)+lat(carry)+ion

⊕ regulate 규제하다　reign 통치 기간　sovereignty 주권

340

geography
[dʒiágrəfi]

명 지리(학) ▸ geo(earth)+graph(write)+y

⊕ geology 지질학　geometry 기하학　geothermal 지열의

341

influence
[ínfluəns]

명 영향 동 영향을 미치다 ▸ in(into)+flu(flow)+ence

⊕ fluent 유창한　fluid 액체　influenza 독감　influx 유입

342

photography
[fətágrəfi]

명 사진(술), 사진 촬영 ▸ photo(light)+graph(write)+y

⊕ photocopier 복사기　photosynthesis 광합성

343

biology
[baiálədʒi]

명 생물학 ▸ bio(life)+logy(study)

⊕ autobiography 자서전　symbiosis 공생

344

anniversary
[ænəvə́:rsəri]

명 기념일 ▸ anni/enni(year)+verse(turn)+ary

⊕ annually 매년　biennially 격년으로　centennial 백 주년

345

community
[kəmjú:nəti]

명 공동체, 지역사회 ▸ com(with)+mun(duty)+ity

⊕ communication 의사소통　commute 통근하다

346

democracy
[dimákrəsi]

명 민주주의 ▸ demo(people)+cracy(rule)

⊕ theocracy 신정　bureaucracy 관료제　autocracy 독재

347

pleasure
[pléʒər]

명 즐거움, 기쁨 ▸ please(즐겁게 하다)+ure

⊕ unpleasant 불쾌한　displeased 불쾌한　placid 차분한

348

cognitive
[kágnitiv]

형 인지의, 인식의 ▸ co(with)+gni(know)+tive

⊕ cognition 인지, 인식　recognition 인식, 인정

349

withstand
[wiðstǽnd]

동 저항하다, 견디다 ▸ with(against)+stand

⊕ withdraw 철수하다, 인출하다　withhold 보류하다

350

require
[rikwáiər]

동 요구하다 ▸ re(again)+quir/quest(seek)+e

⊕ inquire 문의하다　acquire 얻다, 인수하다　request 요청

⊕ conquer 정복하다　conquest 정복　requisite 필수 요건

PRACTICE

A 주어진 접두사를 연결하고, 그 단어와 의미를 각각 쓰시오.

	보기				보기
1 e		_____, _____	**6** ac		_____, _____
2 re		_____, _____	**7** re	quire (×3)	_____, _____
3 ob	ject	_____, _____	**8** in		_____, _____
4 in		_____, _____	**9** re	quest (×2)	_____, _____
5 sub		_____, _____	**10** con		_____, _____

B 빈칸에 들어갈 알맞은 표현을 고르시오.

1 Children under 10 must be _____ by an adult.

① required ② accompanied ③ attributed ④ facilitated

2 Government _____ of loan sharking should be tightened.

① rejection ② ignorance ③ announcement ④ regulation

3 People were shocked that the victim's parents _____ the death penalty.

① supposed ② composed ③ exposed ④ opposed

4 The _____ location of the villages has changed due to industrialization.

① geological ② geometric ③ geographical ④ geothermal

5 The company examined the _____ relationship between product quality and consumer satisfaction.

① cognitive ② influential ③ causal ④ contemporary

C 네모 안에서 문맥에 맞는 낱말로 가장 적절한 것을 고르시오.

1 Across hundreds of thousands of years, artistic endeavors may have been the playground of human cognition / ignorance , providing a safe arena for training our imaginative capacities and infusing them with a potent faculty for innovation.

2 To overcome death as the obstacle that was facilitating / hindering the evolution of human intelligence, our ancestral community played its ultimate trump card, which propelled our species forward, ahead of all others: namely, spoken and written language in words and math.

적용독해

1   다음 글의 밑줄 친 부분 중, 문맥상 낱말의 쓰임이 적절하지 <u>않은</u> 것은? `고1 학평 기출`

People are innately inclined to look for causes of events, to form explanations and stories. That is one reason storytelling is such a ① <u>persuasive</u> medium. Stories resonate with our experiences and provide examples of new instances. From our experiences and the stories of others we tend to form ② <u>generalizations</u> about the way people behave and things work. We attribute causes to events, and as long as these cause-and-effect ③ <u>pairings</u> make sense, we use them for understanding future events. Yet these causal attributions are often mistaken. Sometimes they implicate the ④ <u>wrong</u> causes, and for some things that happen, there is no single cause. Rather, there is a complex chain of events that all contribute to the result; if any one of the events would not have occurred, the result would be ⑤ <u>similar</u>. But even when there is no single causal act, that doesn't stop people from assigning one.

* resonate: 떠올리게 하다   ** implicate: 연관시키다

2   다음 글의 밑줄 친 부분 중, 문맥상 낱말의 쓰임이 적절하지 <u>않은</u> 것은? `고2 학평 기출`

Our culture is biased toward the fine arts — those creative products that have no function other than pleasure. Craft objects are less worthy; because they serve an everyday function, they're not purely ① <u>creative</u>. But this division is culturally and historically ② <u>relative</u>. Most contemporary high art began as some sort of craft. The composition and performance of what we now call "classical music" began as a form of craft music ③ <u>ignoring</u> required functions in the Catholic mass, or the specific entertainment needs of royal patrons. For example, chamber music really was designed to be performed in chambers — small intimate rooms in wealthy homes — often as ④ <u>background</u> music. The dances composed by famous composers from Bach to Chopin originally did indeed accompany dancing. But today, with the contexts and functions they were composed for ⑤ <u>gone</u>, we listen to these works as fine art.

----

1 innately 선천적으로   be inclined to ~하는 경향이 있다   persuasive 설득력 있는   instance 예, 사례   generalization 일반화   attribute 귀착하다   assign (원인 등을) ~에 돌리다

2 biased 편향된   fine arts 순수 예술   function 기능; 기능하다   other than ~ ~ 이외에, ~을 제외하고   craft 공예   division 구분, 분리   relative 상대적인, 관련 있는   contemporary 현대의, 현시대의   composition 작곡, 작문, 구성   mass 미사   entertainment 오락, 즐거움   patron 후원자   chamber 방, 실내   intimate 친밀한   compose 작곡하다   accompany 동반하다   context 맥락

to부정사 2(부사적)

1 부사적 용법

A He came **to see** his friend yesterday. (목적)
B She was surprised **to hear** the news. (원인)
C He must be a fool **to do** such a thing. (이유·판단의 근거)
D You would be foolish **to do** it. (조건)
E The boy grew up **to be** a great cop. (결과)
F He worked hard, **only to fail** in the entrance exam.
G He is rich **enough to buy** that car. (정도)
　= He is **so** rich **that** he can buy that car.
H That book was **too** difficult for me **to** understand. (too ~ to)
　= That book was **so** difficult **that** I **couldn't** understand it.

PRACTICE

A 다음 문장의 밑줄 친 to부정사의 용법에 해당하는 기호를 보기에서 골라 쓰시오.

〈보기〉　　N(명사적 용법)　　A(형용사적 용법)　　AD(부사적 용법)

1 The easiest and quickest way to calm an angry child is <u>to give</u> them food.
2 The applicant was mad <u>to say</u> such outrageous things during the interview.
3 When animals know what <u>to expect</u>, they can feel more confident and calm.
4 Whenever we feel annoyed, we turn to food <u>to make</u> ourselves feel better.
5 She is one of the first three students <u>to earn</u> a master's degree in fine arts.
6 It would take too long <u>to write</u>, and it would be hard to read quickly.
7 He is smart enough <u>to use</u> memory techniques when preparing for exams.

B 네모 안에서 어법에 맞는 표현으로 가장 적절한 것을 고르시오.

1 Posts that hold up signs and street lights need to be strong and durable enough to withstand winds, storms, and earthquakes. Every so often, though, these same posts need to break easily on impact │ to reduce / reducing │ damage and save lives.

2 │ Empowering / To empower │ everyone connected to the Internet to access both the collective wisdom and the pocket money of everyone else who connects to the Internet, crowdfunding can be viewed as the democratization of business financing.

적용독해

정답 및 해설 p.42

1 다음 글의 밑줄 친 부분 중, 어법상 틀린 것은? 고2 학평 기출

Most of us play it safe by putting our needs aside when faced with the possibility of feeling guilty or ① disappointing others. At work you may allow a complaining coworker to keep stealing your energy ② to avoid conflict — ending up hating your job. At home you may say yes to family members who give you a hard time to avoid their emotional rejection, only ③ to feel frustrated by the lack of quality time that you have for yourself. We work hard ④ to manage the perceptions of others, ignoring our own needs, and in the end we give up the very thing that will enable us ⑤ live meaningful lives.

2 다음 글의 밑줄 친 부분 중, 어법상 틀린 것은? 고3 학평 기출 응용

When you organize a party, a seminar, or any other kind of event, ① make sure you don't just get the people who already know each other clustering together. If you invite people to a meal, you can use place cards ② to facilitate successful networking. Organize games so that people sitting at each table can mix. When you announce, "The buffet is open," address the subject openly by saying, "Take this opportunity ③ to get to know new people." A lot of people find this an effective icebreaker to be able to start speaking to others. Don't be afraid of issuing name badges at large gatherings if people don't know each other. Get each person ④ write something typical but a bit mysterious on the badge. That is a nice way of making it possible for people ⑤ to start a conversation with people they don't know.

---

1 put aside ~을 제쳐두다　need 욕구　face 직면하다　guilty 죄책감을 느끼는　complaining 불평하는　coworker 직장 동료　conflict 마찰, 갈등　end up 결국 ~하게 되다　hate 싫어하다　emotional 정서적인, 감정적인　rejection 거부, 거절　frustrated 좌절한　quality 질 좋은　manage 관리하다　perception 인식　ignore 무시하다　in the end 결국
2 organize 조직하다　anniversary 기념일　cluster 모여들다　invite 초대하다　facilitate 용이하게 하다　announce 알리다　address 다루다　effective 효과적으로　icebreaker 서먹함을 풀어주는 것　issue 발급하다　gathering 모임, 집회　typical 전형적으로　mysterious 신비한

문장 위치

1 글의 흐름으로 보아, 주어진 문장이 들어가기에 가장 적절한 곳은? 고1 학평 기출 응용

> So skin cells, hair cells, and nail cells no longer produce new cells.

Do hair and fingernails continue to grow after a person dies? The short answer is no, though it may not seem that way to the casual observer. (①) That's because after death, the human body dehydrates, causing the skin to shrink, or become smaller. (②) This shrinking exposes the parts of the nails and hair that were once under the skin, causing them to appear longer than before. (③) According to biologists, fingernails grow about 0.1 millimeters a day, but in order to grow, they need glucose — a simple sugar that helps to power the body. (④) Once the body dies, there's no more glucose. (⑤) Moreover, a complex hormonal regulation directs the growth of hair and nails, none of which is possible once a person dies.

2 글의 흐름으로 보아, 주어진 문장이 들어가기에 가장 적절한 곳은? 고1 학평 기출

> Yet, attach a camera to them, and suddenly we can see so much more.

Photography has always played an important part in our understanding of how the universe works. (①) Although telescopes help us see far beyond the limits of the naked eye, on their own they are still limited. (②) Details are revealed that would otherwise be invisible. (③) Indeed, 19th century astronomers working with the first astronomical cameras were astonished to discover that outer space was much more crowded than they had thought. (④) Their first photographs of the night sky showed unknown stars and galaxies. (⑤) Once cameras were taken on board rockets and orbiting satellites, they saw the universe clearly for the first time.

---

1 casual 무심결의, 일상의 observer 관찰자 dehydrate 수분이 빠지다 shrink 줄다, 수축하다 expose 노출시키다 complex 복잡한 regulation 조절, 규제 direct 지휘하다, 이끌다

2 attach 부착하다 telescope 망원경 beyond 그 너머에 naked eye 육안 reveal 드러내다 astronomer 천문학자 astonish 깜짝 놀라게 하다 outer space 우주 crowded 복잡한 on board 승선한, 탑승한 orbiting 궤도를 선회하는 satellite 인공위성

3 글의 흐름으로 보아, 주어진 문장이 들어가기에 가장 적절한 곳은? 고1 학평 기출

> In return, the guest had duties to his host.

Geography influenced human relationships in Greece. Because the land made travel so difficult, the guest-host relationship was valued. (①) If a stranger, even a poor man, appeared at your door, it was your duty to be a good host, to give him a shelter and share your food with him. (②) "We do not sit at a table only to eat, but to eat together," said the Greek author Plutarch. (③) Dining was a sign of the human community and differentiated men from beasts. (④) These included not abusing his host's hospitality by staying too long, usually not more than three days. (⑤) A violation of this relationship by either side brought human and divine anger.

* divine: 신(神)의

---

3 duty 의무　host 주인　geography 지형, 지리　influence 영향을 주다　value 중요하게 여기다　shelter 거처, 숙소　author 저자　beast 짐승　abuse 악용하다　hospitality 환대　violation 위반

15강 어근 10

351
approach
[əpróutʃ]

동 접근하다, 다가가다 ❯ ap(to)+proach(near)

➕ unapproached 독보적인　reproach 비난　approximately 대략

352
manipulate
[mənípjulèit]

동 조작하다 ❯ manu(hand)+pul(fill)+ate

➕ manual 수동의　manifest 명백한　emancipate 해방시키다

353
headache
[hédèik]

명 두통 ❯ head+ache(pain)

➕ toothache 치통　stomachache 복통　backache 요통

354
principle
[prínsəpl]

명 원리, 원칙 ❯ prin/prim(first)+cip(take)+le

➕ principal 교장　primitive 원시의　priority 우선순위

355
circumstance
[sə́:rkəmstæ̀ns]

명 (주위) 환경 ❯ circum(around)+stance(stand)

➕ stance 자세, 입장　instance 예, 사례　substance 물질

356
compliment
[kámpləment]

명 칭찬, 찬사 ❯ com(with)+pli(fold)+ment

➕ applicant 지원자　implication 암시　duplication 복제

357
accomplish
[əkámpliʃ]

동 이룩하다, 성취하다 ❯ ac(to) com(with)+pli(fold)+sh

➕ explicit 분명한　implicit 내포된, 함축된　diploma 졸업장

358
defend
[difénd]

동 방어하다 ❯ de(away)+fend(strike)

➕ fence 담장　offend 감정을 해치다　fender bender 접촉 사고

359
prohibit
[prouhíbit]

동 금지하다 ❯ pro(before)+hibit(have)

➕ inhibit 방해하다　exhibit 전시하다

360
infant
[ínfənt]

명 유아 ❯ in(not)+fa(speak)+nt

➕ fable 우화　fabulous 멋진

361
adolescence
[æ̀dəlésəns]

명 청소년기, 사춘기 ❯ ad(to)+ol(grow)+escence(begin)

➕ abolish 폐지하다　adult 성인, 성체

362
inspire
[inspáiər]

동 영감을 주다, 고무하다 ❯ in(in)+spire(breath)

➕ aspire 열망하다　expire 만료되다　respire 호흡하다

➕ conspire 공모하다　perspire 땀을 흘리다　suspire 탄식하다

363

experience
[ikspí(:)əriəns]

명 경험 ▸ ex(out)+per(attempt)+ence

⊕ expert 전문가　　expertise 전문 지식　　experiment 실험

364

sensory
[sénsəri]

형 감각의 ▸ sense(감각)+ory

⊕ sensible 분별있는　　sensitive 민감한, 예민한　　resent 분개하다

365

possess
[pəzés]

동 소유하다 ▸ poss/pot(power)+sess(sit)

⊕ possible 가능한　　potential 가능성, 잠재력　　potent 강력한

366

attach
[ətǽtʃ]

동 부착하다 ▸ at(to)+tach(stake 말뚝)

⊕ detach 떼어내다　　attack 공격하다

367

contact
[kántækt]

명 접촉, 연락 ▸ con(with)+tact/tag/tang(touch)

⊕ contagion 전염　　intangible 무형의

368

critically
[krítikəli]

부 결정적으로, 매우 ▸ cri(separate)+tic+al+ly

⊕ critic 비평가　　crisis 위기　　criterion 기준　　hypocrisy 위선

369

distinct
[distíŋkt]

형 뚜렷한, 구별되는, 독특한 ▸ dis(away)+stinct(찌르다)

⊕ instinct 본능　　extinct 멸종된　　stimulate 자극하다

370

barrier
[bǽriər]

명 장애(물), 장벽 ▸ barr(stick 막대기)+ier

⊕ barren 불모의　　embarrass 당황하게 하다　　barrel 통

371

adhere
[ædhíər]

동 달라붙다, 고수하다 ▸ ad(to)+here(stick 붙다)

⊕ inherent 타고난　　coherent 일관성 있는　　hesitate 주저하다

372

tribe
[traib]

명 부족, 종족, 집단 ▸ tri(three)+be

⊕ triple 3중의　　tripod 삼각대　　trilingual 3개 국어를 하는

373

immigrate
[íməgrèit]

동 ~로 이민가다, 이주하다 ▸ im(into)+migr(move)+ate

⊕ migrating 철에 따라 이동하는　　emigrate ~(자국)에서 (타국)으로 이민가다

374

synonym
[sínənim]

명 동의어 ▸ syn(same)+nonym(name)

⊕ antonym 반의어　　anonymous 익명의　　unanimous 만장일치의

375

interrupt
[ìntərʌ́pt]

동 방해하다, 끼어들다 ▸ inter(between)+rupt(break)

⊕ abrupt 갑작스런　　disrupt 붕괴시키다　　erupt 분출하다

⊕ corrupt 부패한　　bankrupt 파산한

PRACTICE

A 주어진 접두사를 연결하고, 그 단어와 의미를 각각 쓰시오.

		보기					보기		
1	e		_____, _____	**6**	a		_____, _____
2	ab		_____, _____	**7**	in		_____, _____
3	cor	rupt	_____, _____	**8**	re	spire	_____, _____
4	dis		_____, _____	**9**	ex		_____, _____
5	inter		_____, _____	**10**	per		_____, _____

B 빈칸에 들어갈 알맞은 표현을 고르시오.

1 The words *kind*, *type*, and *sort* are _____.

① antonymous   ② unanimous   ③ anonymous   ④ synonymous

2 Taking photos is _____ in the gallery, let alone smoking.

① accomplished   ② attached   ③ prohibited   ④ interrupted

3 The country developed formidable weapons to _____ itself.

① contact   ② defend   ③ possess   ④ approach

4 The mechanic _____ the hi-tech machine skillfully with one hand.

① manufactured   ② menifested   ③ emancipated   ④ manipulated

5 Being compared to Reverend Martin Luthur King is a great _____ to me.

① complement   ② principle   ③ compliment   ④ barrier

C 네모 안에서 문맥에 맞는 낱말로 가장 적절한 것을 고르시오.

1 Color has not always been synonymous / antonymous with truth and reality. In the past, ancient Greek philosophers had a tendency to attack the use of color in painting because they considered color to be an ornament that obstructed the truth.

2 Adolescence is a stage of development in which teens have superb cognitive abilities and high rates of learning and memory, so these abilities give them a distinct advantage over adults, but because they are so ready to learn, they are also extremely vulnerable / alternative to learning the wrong things.

적용독해

1 다음 글의 밑줄 친 부분 중, 문맥상 낱말의 쓰임이 적절하지 <u>않은</u> 것은? 〔고1 학평 기출〕

Honesty is a fundamental part of every strong relationship. Use it to your advantage by being open with what you feel and giving a ① <u>truthful</u> opinion when asked. This approach can help you escape uncomfortable social situations and make friends with honest people. Follow this simple policy in life — never lie. When you ② <u>develop</u> a reputation for always telling the truth, you will enjoy strong relationships based on trust. It will also be more difficult to manipulate you. People who lie get into trouble when someone threatens to ③ <u>uncover</u> their lie. By living true to yourself, you'll ④ <u>avoid</u> a lot of headaches. Your relationships will also be free from the poison of lies and secrets. Don't be afraid to be honest with your friends, no matter how painful the truth is. In the long term, lies with good intentions ⑤ <u>comfort</u> people much more than telling the truth.

2 다음 글의 밑줄 친 부분 중, 문맥상 낱말의 쓰임이 적절하지 <u>않은</u> 것은? 〔고1 학평 기출 응용〕

The title of Thomas Friedman's 2005 book, *The World Is Flat*, was based on the belief that globalization would inevitably bring us closer together. It has done that, but it has also inspired us to build ① <u>barriers</u>. When faced with perceived threats — the financial crisis, terrorism, violent conflict, refugees and immigration, the increasing gap between rich and poor — people ② <u>adhere</u> more tightly to their own groups. One founder of a famous social media company believed social media would ③ <u>divide</u> us. In some respects it has, but it has simultaneously given voice and organizational ability to new cyber tribes, some of whom spend their time ④ <u>spreading</u> blame and division across the World Wide Web. There seem now to be as many tribes, and as much conflict between them, as there have ever been. Is it possible for these tribes to ⑤ <u>coexist</u> in a world where the concept of "us and them" remains?

---

1 fundamental 근본적인　to one's advantage ~에게 유리하게　truthful 정직한　approach 접근법　uncomfortable 불편한　social 사회적인　policy 방침, 정책　reputation 평판　get into trouble 곤경에 처하다　threaten to ~하겠다고 위협하다　uncover 폭로하다　avoid 피하다　no matter how 아무리 ~할지라도　in the long term 장기적으로 보면　good intentions 선의
2 globalization 세계화　inevitably 불가피하게, 필연적으로　inspire ~을 야기시키다　barrier 장벽　perceive 인지하다, 인식하다　threat 위협　financial crisis 금융 위기　violent 폭력적인　conflict 갈등, 분쟁　refugee 난민　respect 측면　simultaneously 동시에　organizational 조직적인　ability 능력　spread 뿌리다, 퍼뜨리다　blame 비난　division 분단, 분열　coexist 공존하다

to부정사 3
(to부정사 to와 전치사 to)

① to+동사원형

be able to (~할 수 있다)	be unable to (~할 수 없다)
be likely to (~할 것 같다)	be unlikely to (~할 것 같지 않다)
be willing to (기꺼이 ~하다)	be unwilling to (~하기를 꺼려 하다)
be going to (~할 예정이다)	be about to (막 ~하려 하다)
be sure to (반드시 ~하다)	make sure to (반드시 ~하다)
tend to (~하는 경향이 있다)	have a tendency to (~하는 경향이 있다)
be used to (~하는 데 사용 되다)	be reluctant to (마지못해 ~하다)

② 전치사 to+(동)명사

contribute to (~에 기여하다)	look forward to (~를 고대하다)
similar to (~와 유사한)	when it comes to (~에 관해서라면)
in addition to (~뿐만 아니라)	devote oneself to (~에 헌신하다)
be used to (~에 익숙하다)	be accustomed to (~에 익숙하다)
from A to B (A부터 B까지)	lead to (~를 이끌다/야기하다)
alternative to (~에 대한 대안)	vulnerable to (~에 취약한)

PRACTICE

A 어법상 틀린 부분을 바르게 고쳐 쓰시오.

1 Chimps are more likely to joining others for hunts.

2 Make sure to enjoying yourself, lest you miss such a rare opportunity.

3 This auditorium will be used to holding the 3-D video conference.

4 The social habits of monkeys range from deciding on rank to delouse each other.

5 Hemingway had devoted himself to provide people with more access to literature.

B 네모 안에서 어법에 맞는 표현으로 가장 적절한 것을 고르시오.

1 The federal government released a report in 2009 stating that the nation's air traffic control system was vulnerable to a cyber attack that could interrupt communication with pilots and alter the flight information used to distinguish / distinguishing aircraft as they approach an airport.

2 The serious problem of the algorithm is that an algorithm design firm might be under contract to design algorithms for a wide range of uses, from deciding which patients awaiting transplants are chosen to receive organs, to determine / determining which criminals facing sentencing should be given probation or the maximum sentence.

적용독해

1 다음 글의 밑줄 친 부분 중, 어법상 틀린 것은? 고2 학평 기출 응용

Although instances occur in which partners start their relationship by ① <u>telling</u> everything about themselves to each other, such instances are rare. In most cases, the amount of disclosure increases over time. We begin relationships by revealing relatively little about ourselves; then if our first bits of self-disclosure are well ② <u>received</u> and bring on similar responses from the other person, we're willing to ③ <u>reveal</u> more. This principle is critically important to remember. It would usually be a mistake to assume ④ <u>that</u> the way to build a strong relationship would be to reveal the most private details about yourself when first making contact with another person. Unless the circumstances are unique, such baring of your soul can often lead to ⑤ <u>scare</u> potential partners away rather than bring them closer.

* bare: 드러내다

2 다음 글의 밑줄 친 부분 중, 어법상 틀린 것은? 고1 학평 기출 응용

What could be wrong with the compliment "I'm so proud of you"? Plenty. Just as it is misguided to offer your child false praise, ① <u>it</u> is also a mistake to reward all of his accomplishments. Although rewards sound positive, they can be likely ② <u>to cause</u> negative consequences. It is because they can take away from the love of learning. If you consistently reward a child for her accomplishments, she starts to focus more on getting the reward than on ③ <u>what</u> she did to earn it. The focus of her excitement shifts from enjoying learning itself to ④ <u>please</u> you. If you applaud every time your child identifies a letter, she may become a praise lover who eventually ⑤ <u>becomes</u> less interested in learning the alphabet for its own sake than for hearing you applaud.

---

1 instance 사례 rare 드문 disclosure 숨김없이 털어놓는 이야기, 드러냄 reveal 드러내다 relatively 비교적 assume ~라고 생각하다 private 사적인 potential 가능성이 있는, 잠재적인

2 compliment 칭찬하다 misguided 잘못 판단된 praise 칭찬 accomplishment 성취 take away from ~을 감소시키다 focus 집중하다 shift 옮겨가다 applaud 박수를 치다 eventually 결국 for A's own sake A 자체를 위해서

글의 요약

1 다음 글의 내용을 한 문장으로 요약하고자 한다. 빈칸 (A), (B)에 들어갈 말로 가장 적절한 것은?

고1 학평 기출

Children are much more resistant to giving something to someone else than to helping them. One can observe this difference clearly in very young children. Even though one-and-a-half-year-olds will support each other in difficult situations, they are not willing to share their own toys with others. The little ones even defend their possessions with screams and, if necessary, blows. This is the daily experience of parents troubled by constant quarreling between toddlers. There was no word I heard more frequently than "Mine!" from my daughters when they were still in diapers.

⇩

Although very young children will _____(A)_____ each other in difficult situations, they are unwilling to _____(B)_____ their possessions.

	(A)	(B)		(A)	(B)
①	ignore	⋯⋯ share	②	help	⋯⋯ hide
③	ignore	⋯⋯ defend	④	meet	⋯⋯ hide
⑤	help	⋯⋯ share			

---

1 resistant 저항하는 be willing to 기꺼이 ~하다 possession 소유물 scream 소리침 if necessary 필요하면 blow 일격, 강타 constant 끊임없는 toddler (아장아장 걷는) 아기 frequently 자주 diaper 기저귀 ignore 무시하다

2 다음 글의 내용을 한 문장으로 요약하고자 한다. 빈칸 (A), (B)에 들어갈 말로 가장 적절한 것은?

More than 40 years ago, psychologist Sibylle Escalona carried out what has become a classic study of the play behaviors of 128 infants and their mothers. Her major finding was that, even if the infants had a large variety of toys to play with, the sensorimotor play of babies playing alone was less sustained than that of babies who had an adult to interact with. The mothers seemed to be skilled social directors. They tended to adapt the play activities to the immediate needs of children by varying their own activities in response to what the children were doing. For example, mothers would vary the rate at which they offered new play materials and introduce variations or increase the intensity of play when the children seemed to be losing interest. As a result, the mothers were able to sustain their children's interest in the various play activities and thereby increase the length of their attention spans.

* sensorimotor: 감각 운동의

⇩

In one study, it was found that the ____(A)____ role played by mothers helped infants to be ____(B)____ to their play activities for longer than those with limited access to adults.

	(A)		(B)		(A)		(B)
①	guiding	⋯⋯	attentive	②	guiding	⋯⋯	indifferent
③	creating	⋯⋯	restricted	④	sacrificing	⋯⋯	sensitive
⑤	sacrificing	⋯⋯	addicted				

---

2 carry out 수행하다　classic 고전적인　infant 유아　sustain 지속하다　interact 상호 작용하다　director 감독자　adapt 맞추다　immediate 즉각적인　variation 변화　intensity 강도　span (지속되는) 시간　attentive 주의 깊은　restricted 제한된

PART 2

16강 – 30강

16강 상업·광고

376
advertisement
[ædvərtáizmənt]

명 광고   advertise 동 광고하다
➕ commercial ad 상업 광고   leaflet 전단지   brochure 광고 책자

377
warranty
[wɔ́(:)rənti]

명 (품질) 보증(서), 담보(= mortgage)
a five-year warranty on a car 자동차의 5년 보증서

378
replacement
[ripléismənt]

명 대체(품), 교체, 대신할 사람   replace 동 대체하다
✔ 대체하다: change, substitute, alternate

379
entrepreneur
[à:ntrəprənə́:r]

명 기업가   entrepreneurial 형 기업가적인
✔ 기업가: businessman, enterpriser, industrialist

380
commerce
[kámə(:)rs]

명 상업   commercial 형 상업의, 상업적인
➕ exchange 교환   trade 교역, 거래   barter 물물교환

381
product
[prádəkt]

명 제품, 상품, 생산물   produce 동 생산하다
✔ 상품: goods, commodity, merchandise

382
corporation
[kɔ̀:rpəréiʃən]

명 회사, 기업   corporate 형 기업의
➕ startup 신생 기업   venture firm 벤처 기업   enterprise 기업

383
financial
[finǽnʃəl]

형 금융의, 재정적인   finance 명 금융, 재정
➕ monetary 통화의   fiscal 재정의   budgetary 예산의

384
cancel
[kǽnsəl]

동 취소하다   cancellation 명 취소
✔ 취소하다: call off, withdraw, revoke

385
contract
[kántrækt]

명 계약(서)   동 계약하다, 수축하다(= shrink)
✔ 협정: agreement, treaty, pact

386
skyrocket
[skáiràkit]

명 급상승하다, 급등하다(↔ nosedive 급락하다)
✔ 급등하다: rise sharply, soar, surge

387
competition
[kàmpitíʃən]

명 경쟁, 대회, 경기   compete 동 경쟁하다
Competition is heating up and sales are shrinking. 경쟁이 치열해지고 매출도 줄어들고 있다.

388
retail
[rí:tèil]

명 소매(↔ wholesale)　　부 소매값으로　　retailer 명 소매상

buy wholesale, not retail 소매가 아닌 도매로 사다

389
conflict
[kánflikt]

명 갈등, 분쟁, 상충, 대립　　동 상충하다, ~와 충돌하다

⊕ discord 갈등　　dispute 분쟁　　friction 마찰　　contradiction 상충

390
profit
[práfit]

명 이익, 수익, 이윤　　nonprofitable 형 비영리의

✓ 이익, 이로움: benefit, interest, good

391
inquiry
[inkwáiəri]

명 문의, 조사, 질문　　inquire 동 조사하다, 문의하다, 묻다

✓ 조사하다: investigate, examine, probe

392
shipment
[ʃípmənt]

명 화물, 운송, 배송　　ship 동 운송하다

✓ 화물: cargo, freight　　배송: delivery, transportation

393
purchase
[pə́:rtʃəs]

명 구입　　동 구입하다　　purchaser 동 구입자(=buyer)

make a purchase in bulk 대량 구매하다

394
appreciate
[əprí:ʃièit]

동 진가를 인정하다, 감사하다, 감상하다, 가치가 오르다

appreciation 명 감상, 감사, 가치 상승

395
inconvenience
[ìnkənví:njəns]

명 불편, 불편한 점　　inconvenient 형 불편한

cause inconvenience to others 남들에게 폐를 끼치다

396
complaint
[kəmpléint]

명 불평, 불만　　complain 동 불평하다

The most common complaint is about poor service. 가장 흔한 불평은 서비스가 안 좋다는 것이다.

397
demand
[dimǽnd]

명 수요, 요구　　동 요구하다

✓ 요구하다: require, call for, claim, ask

398
request
[rikwést]

동 요청하다, 요구하다　　명 요청, 간청

You can request a free copy of the leaflet. 무료 광고지를 한 부 신청할 수 있다.

399
client
[kláiənt]

명 고객, 의뢰인　　clientele 의뢰인, (단골) 고객, 환자

a campaign to attract new clients 신규 고객 유치 운동

400
payment
[péimənt]

명 지불(금), 대금, 지급(액), 상환

He has missed his debt payments for three months. 그는 3개월 동안 채무 상환을 연체했다.

PRACTICE

정답 및 해설 p.46

A 알맞은 단어를 〈보기〉에서 골라 빈칸을 채우시오.

> 〈보기〉   complain   contract   skyrocket   profits   commercial

1 I got a _____ with a major publisher.

2 Unemployment _____ed from five percent to fifteen percent.

3 This song was her biggest _____ success.

4 I'm going to _____ to the manager about the poor service.

5 The company's _____ were lower than expected.

B 빈칸에 들어갈 알맞은 표현을 고르시오.

1 If you have the time to help, we'd really _____ it.

① payment   ② complain   ③ finance   ④ appreciate

2 The concert was _____ed due to the bad weather.

① conflict   ② demand   ③ cancel   ④ retail

3 Last month they sold twice as many cars as their major _____.

① contracts   ② competitors   ③ demand   ④ profits

4 There is a five-year _____ on all smart TVs in the shop.

① replacement   ② enterprise   ③ warranty   ④ finance

5 We apologize for any _____ caused by the late departure of your flight.

① commerce   ② retail   ③ supply   ④ inconvenience

C 네모 안에서 문맥에 맞는 낱말로 가장 적절한 것을 고르시오.

1 Interruption marketing occurs when the customer receives indispensable / unrequested direct marketing messages, such as direct mail, emails, and text messages that are commonly referred to in negative terms, such as 'junk mail' and 'spam.'

2 A buffer gives us time to respond and adapt to any sudden moves by other cars. Similarly, we can reduce the conflict / compromise of doing the essentials in our work and lives simply by creating a buffer — by always being prepared for unexpected events.

적용독해

1 다음 글의 밑줄 친 부분 중, 문맥상 낱말의 쓰임이 적절하지 <u>않은</u> 것은? 고1 학평 기출 응용

Is the customer *always* right? When customers return a broken product to a famous company, which makes kitchen and bathroom fixtures, the company nearly always offers a ① <u>replacement</u> to maintain good customer relations. Still, "there are times you've got to say 'no,'" explains the warranty expert of the company, such as when a product is ② <u>undamaged</u> or has been abused. Entrepreneur Lauren Thorp, who owns an e-commerce company, says, "While the customer is 'always' right, sometimes you just have to ③ <u>admit</u> a customer's unreasonable demand." When Thorp has tried everything to resolve a complaint and ④ <u>realizes</u> that the customer will be dissatisfied no matter what, she ⑤ <u>returns</u> her attention to the rest of her customers, who she says are "the reason for my success."

2 다음 글의 밑줄 친 부분 중, 문맥상 낱말의 쓰임이 적절하지 <u>않은</u> 것은? 고2 학평 기출 응용

Today's consumers are not just looking for a good product at a fair price. They are looking beyond the product or service to the ethics of the company that supplies it. The shift in focus by consumers is ① <u>evident</u> in their concerns about the companies they purchase from. For example, there is growing interest in labor practices, environmental policies, and social responsibilities. As a result, companies are under more and more ② <u>pressure</u> to produce not only financial results, but also social and environmental change. Companies need to respond to the pressure because customers are ③ <u>voicing</u> their concerns in every way, from boycotting stores to suing companies. Some multinational companies have experienced the anger of ethical consumers in recent years, and have been forced to ④ <u>respond</u> quickly to protect their reputations and their existence as companies. This growing ⑤ <u>indifference</u> on ethical consumption is a trend that cannot be ignored.

* sue: 고소하다, 소송을 제기하다

---

1 fixture 설비, 비품 replacement 교체 maintain 유지하다 still 그럼에도 불구하고, 아직 warranty (상품 등의) 보증 entrepreneur 기업가 abuse 남용하다 e-commerce 전자 상거래 admit 수용하다 unreasonable 비합리적인, 말도 안되는 demand 요구, 요구하다

2 consumer 소비자 ethics 윤리 evident 분명한 concern 관심, 걱정 labor practices 노동 관행 policy 정책 responsibility 책임 financial result 재무 성과 voice 목소리를 내다 boycott 불매 동맹하다 multinational 다국적의 reputation 평판, 명성 trend 추세 ignore 무시하다

동명사 1

1 동명사의 역할

A **Taking** the subway is faster than driving a car. (주어)
B My hobby is **playing** computer games. (보어)
C I like **going** shopping at a mall. (타동사의 목적어)
D They are fond of **swimming** in the river. (전치사의 목적어)

2 동명사를 목적어로 취하는 동사

enjoy, finish, mind, avoid, give up, keep, postpone, consider, imagine 등
E I enjoyed **reading** the detective novel.
F Jane finished **doing** her homework.

3 to부정사를 목적어로 취하는 동사

want, hope, expect, decide, manage, refuse, fail, attempt, afford, force 등
G She refused **to give** testimony.
H The politician decided **to publish** a book about his life.

PRACTICE

A 어법상 틀린 부분을 바르게 고쳐 쓰시오.

1 People believed that touch newborns was not good for them because it would spread germs.
2 He noticed how skilled his father was at quickly application a quality coat of paint to a wall.
3 The physicians were forced recommending either surgery or radiation for their patients with lung cancer.
4 The younger people are when they start using a brand or product, the more likely they are to keep to use it for years to come.
5 The Hazda nomads of Tanzania spend around fourteen hours a week to collect food.

B 네모 안에서 어법에 맞는 표현으로 가장 적절한 것을 고르시오.

1 Despite the conventional wisdom of some management trainers that group brainstorming is an effective way of generation / generating impressive ideas, more objective research has recently suggested otherwise.
2 When approaching practical music making for the first time in the classroom, it is a good idea to avoid to use / using instruments altogether.

적용독해

1 다음 글의 밑줄 친 부분 중, 어법상 **틀린** 것은? 고2 학평 기출

The best thing I did as a manager was ① <u>making</u> every person in the company responsible for doing just one thing. I had started doing this just to simplify the task of ② <u>managing</u> people. But then I noticed a deeper result: defining roles reduced conflict. Most fights inside a company happen when colleagues compete for the same responsibilities. Startup companies face an especially high risk of this since job roles are fluid at the early stages. ③ <u>Eliminating</u> competition makes it easier for everyone to build the kinds of long-term relationships that transcend mere professionalism. More than that, internal peace is what enables a startup to survive at all. When a startup fails, we often imagine it ④ <u>surrendering</u> to predatory rivals in a competitive ecosystem. But every company is also its own ecosystem, and internal conflict makes it ⑤ <u>vulnerably</u> to outside threats.

* transcend: 초월하다

2 다음 글의 밑줄 친 부분 중, 어법상 **틀린** 것은? 고2 학평 기출

For companies interested in delighting customers, exceptional value and service become part of the overall company culture. For example, year after year, Pazano ranks at or near the top of the hospitality industry in terms of customer satisfaction. The company's passion for ① <u>satisfying</u> customers is summed up in its credo, which promises that its luxury hotels will deliver a truly memorable experience. Although a customer-centered firm seeks to deliver high customer satisfaction relative to competitors, it does not attempt ② <u>maximizing</u> customer satisfaction. A company can always increase customer satisfaction by lowering its price or ③ <u>increasing</u> its services. But this may result in lower profits. Thus, the purpose of marketing is ④ <u>generating</u> customer value profitably. This requires a very delicate balance: the marketer must continue ⑤ <u>creating</u> more customer value and satisfaction but not risk the company's profitability.

* credo: 신조

---

1 simplify 단순화하다 define 규정하다 conflict 갈등 colleague 동료 compete 경쟁하다 fluid 유동적인 professionalism 전문성 internal 내부의 surrender 굴복하다 vulnerably 취약하게

2 delight 즐겁게 하다 exceptional 뛰어난, 이례적인 overall 전반적인 hospitality industry (호텔, 식당 등의) 서비스업 satisfaction 만족 passion 열정 sum up 요약하다 customer-centered 고객 중심의 firm 기업, 회사 maximize 최대화하다 generate 창출하다, 만들어 내다 delicate 섬세한, 연약한

글의 목적

1 다음 글의 목적으로 가장 적절한 것은? 고1 학평 기출

Dear Mr. Stevens,

   This is a reply to your inquiry about the shipment status of the desk you purchased at our store on September 26. Unfortunately, the delivery of your desk will take longer than expected due to the damage that occurred during the shipment from the furniture manufacturer to our warehouse. We have ordered an exact replacement from the manufacturer, and we expect that delivery will take place within two weeks. As soon as the desk arrives, we will telephone you immediately and arrange a convenient delivery time. We regret the inconvenience this delay has caused you.

Sincerely,

Justin Upton

① 영업시간 변경을 공지하려고
② 고객 서비스 만족도를 조사하려고
③ 상품의 배송 지연에 대해 설명하려고
④ 구매한 상품의 환불 절차를 안내하려고
⑤ 배송된 상품의 파손에 대해 항의하려고

---

1 inquiry 문의 shipment 배송 warehouse 창고 replacement 대체품 immediately 즉시, 바로 convenient 편리한 regret 유감이다

2 다음 글의 목적으로 가장 적절한 것은? 고2 학평 기출

As a recent college graduate, I am very excited to move forward with my career in marketing and gain additional experience in a food sales environment specifically. I have heard wonderful things about your company and would love to join your team. While my prior experience has been in retail, I have always wanted to move in the direction of food sales. My volunteer experience has allowed me to work with people from all walks of life, and I know how much they appreciate your company's contributions to the local charity. If hired as a member of your Marketing Department, my goal would be to get new clients and to ensure that current customers continue to feel excited about their purchases.

① 식품 회사의 자원봉사 활동에 감사하려고
② 식품 회사의 신입 사원 모집에 지원하려고
③ 식품을 통한 구호 사업에 대해 설명하려고
④ 자선 단체에 대한 식품 지원을 요청하려고
⑤ 새로운 고객에게 회사의 식품을 홍보하려고

3 다음 글의 목적으로 가장 적절한 것은? 고2 학평 기출

We are concerned that we have not heard from you since we sent you the selections you chose when you joined the Club. As you know, the payment is always due when you receive your selections. Because we have not received the payment, we have suspended your membership privileges. Don't miss out on all the benefits your membership offers you: the widest selection of music, great discounts and more! Please return the bottom portion of this letter with your check in the enclosed envelope. Send us your payment today. Paying promptly will restore your membership to good standing.

① 지불해야 할 돈의 납부를 요청하려고
② 구매한 제품의 반품 방법을 알리려고
③ 회원의 자격 요건에 대해 안내하려고
④ 회원 자격이 회복되었음을 통보하려고
⑤ 회비를 인상하게 된 이유를 설명하려고

---

2 prior 이전의 retail 소매 volunteer 자원 봉사 appreciate 감사하다 contribution 공헌 department 부서 current 기존의
3 concerned 염려하는 due 기한이 된 suspend 일시적으로 중지하다 privilege 특혜 benefit 혜택 bottom 하부, 밑바닥 portion 부분
enclosed 동봉된 envelope 봉투 promptly 신속히 restore 회복시키다

17강

감정·태도·분위기

401
emotion
[imóuʃən]

명 감정, 정서   emotionless 형 감정이 없는   emotional 형 감정적인
➕ EQ 감성 지수(emotional quotient)

402
atmosphere
[ǽtməsfiər]

명 분위기, 대기   atmospheric 형 대기의, 분위기 있는
a homely/tense atmosphere 가정적인/긴장된 분위기

403
attitude
[ǽtitʃùːd]

명 태도, 자세   attitudinal 형 태도의
an attitude of humility 겸손한 태도

404
suspense
[səspéns]

명 긴장감, 보류   suspend 동 보류하다, 일시 정지시키다
➕ nervous 긴장되는   tense 긴장한   concerned 우려하는

405
relieved
[rilíːvd]

형 안심하는, 안도하는   relief 명 구조, 안도
a sigh of relief 안도의 한숨

406
sorrowful
[sárəfəl]

형 슬픈(=sad), 비탄에 잠긴(= grieved)   sorrow 명 슬픔
➕ mourning 애도하는   regretful 후회하는

407
passionate
[pǽʃənit]

형 열정적인(= enthusiastic), 관심이 많은(= interested)
✔ 열정: passion, enthusiasm, fervor

408
refreshed
[rəfréʃt]

형 상쾌한   refresh 동 상쾌하게 하다
➕ refreshing 새로운, 신선한   refreshment 다과

409
frightened
[fráitənd]

형 무서운, 공포에 질린   fright 명 두려움, 공포
✔ 무서운: scared, horrified, terrified

410
ashamed
[əʃéimd]

형 부끄러워하는(↔ proud)   shame 명 수치심, 창피
➕ embarrassed 당황한   humiliated 굴욕적인

411
gratitude
[grǽtitʃùːd]

명 감사, 고마움, 사의   ingratitude 명 배은망덕
✔ 감사하는: grateful, thankful, appreciative

412
boring
[bɔ́ːriŋ]

형 지루한, 따분한   boredom 명 지루함, 권태
I was bored with the tedious lecture. 나는 따분한 강의가 지루했다.

413

irritating
[íritèitiŋ]

형 짜증나게 하는, 자극하는　irritate 동 짜증나게 하다

✔ 불쾌한: upset, annoying, offensive

414

indifferent
[indífərənt]

형 무관심한, 무심한　indifference 명 무관심, 무심

➕ cold 냉담한　aloof 초연한　apathetic 무감각한

415

disappointed
[dìsəpɔ́intid]

형 실망한, 낙담한(= discouraged)　disappoint 동 실망시키다

➕ frustrated 좌절한　depressed 우울한

416

rage
[reidʒ]

명 분노, 격분　enrage 동 격분시키다

✔ 분노: anger, resentment, fury

417

shiver
[ʃívər]

동 덜덜 떨다(= quake)　shivering 형 떨고 있는

✔ 떨다, 떨리다: shake, tremble, quiver

418

festive
[féstiv]

형 축제(분위기)의, 흥겨운　sports fest(ival) 체육대회

➕ lively 활기찬　delightful 즐거운　cheerful 쾌활한

419

solemn
[sáləm]

형 엄숙한(= grave), 진지한(= serious)

➕ dignified 위엄 있는　frivolous 경박한

420

urgent
[ɔ́ːrdʒənt]

형 긴급한(= emergent), 다급한　urgency 명 위급, 긴급

✔ 임박한: impending, imminent, at hand

421

frantically
[fræn(t)ikəli]

부 미친 듯이　frantic 형 정신없는

➕ mad 화난, 미친　insane 미친, 정신 이상의

422

despise
[dispáiz]

동 경멸하다(= look down on), 멸시하다

➕ mock 조롱하다　laugh at ~를 비웃다

423

envious
[énviəs]

형 부러워하는, 시기하는　envy 동 부러워하다, 질투하다

➕ jealous 시기 질투하는　arrogant 거만한

424

thrifty
[θrífti]

형 검소한(= frugal)　thrift 명 검소, 검약

➕ greedy 욕심 많은　miserly, stingy 인색한

425

timid
[tímid]

형 소심한, 겁 많은　timidly 부 소심하게

➕ shy 수줍은, 부끄러운　cowardly 비겁한

PRACTICE

A

알맞은 단어를 〈보기〉에서 골라 빈칸을 채우시오.

〈보기〉	atmosphere	timid	attitude	envious	thrifty

1 The library has a relaxed _____.

2 The judge's _____ toward crimes touched me.

3 She was _____ of her sister's lovely hair.

4 The book changed the _____ boy into a more extroverted person.

5 Young children should be _____ with money.

B

빈칸에 들어갈 알맞은 표현을 고르시오.

1 The toddler is _____ of being left alone.

　① scary　　　② suspense　　　③ irrating　　　④ frightened

2 The movie was so _____ that I fell asleep.

　① impressive　　② boring　　　③ moved　　　④ despicable

3 That our team lost the game _____ us.

　① ashamed　　　② timid　　　③ suspended　　　④ disappointed

4 It's so _____ that the student never replies to my emails.

　① urgent　　　② irritating　　　③ annoyed　　　④ festive

5 The patient was _____ that all the tests were negative.

　① relieved　　　② thrifty　　　③ satisfying　　　④ jealous

C

네모 안에서 문맥에 맞는 낱말로 가장 적절한 것을 고르시오.

1 An advocate of free speech and religious toleration, Voltaire declared, " I may disapprove of what you say, but I will defend to the death your right to say it," a powerful defense of the idea that even views that you despise apply / deserve to be heard.

2 People unknowingly sabotage their own work when they try to undermine others, lest they become more successful, because the self doesn't know that resentment of another person's success booms / curtails one's own chances of success.

적용독해

1 다음 글의 밑줄 친 부분 중, 문맥상 낱말의 쓰임이 적절하지 <u>않은</u> 것은? [고2 학평 기출]

Suspense takes up a great share of our interest in life. A play or a novel is often robbed of much of its interest if you know the plot ① <u>beforehand</u>. We like to keep guessing as to the outcome. The circus acrobat employs this principle when he achieves a feat after purposely ② <u>failing</u> to perform it several times. Even the deliberate manner in which he arranges the opening scene ③ <u>increases</u> our expectation. In the last act of a play, a little circus dog balances a ball on its nose. One night when the dog ④ <u>hesitated</u> and worked with a long time before he would perform his feat, he got a lot more applause than when he did his trick at once. We not only like to wait, feeling ⑤ <u>relieved</u>, but we appreciate what we wait for.

2 다음 글의 밑줄 친 부분 중, 문맥상 낱말의 쓰임이 적절하지 <u>않은</u> 것은? [고2 학평 기출]

Sadness in our culture is often considered an unnecessary and undesirable emotion. Numerous self-help books promote the ① <u>benefits</u> of positive thinking and positive behaviors, assigning negative affect in general, and sadness in particular, to the category of "problem emotions" that need to be ② <u>eliminated</u>. Much of the psychology profession is employed in managing and relieving sadness. Yet some degree of sorrow and depression has been far more ③ <u>accepted</u> in previous historical ages than is the case today. From the classic philosophers through Shakespeare to the works of Chekhov, Ibsen, and the great novels of the 19th century, exploring the emotions of sadness, longing, and depression has long been considered ④ <u>destructive</u>. It is only recently that a thriving industry promoting positivity has managed to ⑤ <u>remove</u> this earlier and more balanced view of human affectivity.

---

1 suspense 긴장   take up 끌다, 차지하다   rob A of B A에게서 B를 강탈하다   acrobat 곡예사   employ 적용하다   expectation 기대하는 것   hesitate 머뭇거리다   appreciate 진가를 인정하다
2 unnecessary 불필요한   undesirable 바람직하지 않은   numerous 수많은   self-help book 자기 계발서   assign 지정하다   affect 감정, 정서   in general 일반적으로   profession 직업, 전문직   relieve 완화시키다   sorrow 슬픔   depression 우울   longing 갈망   destructive 파괴적인   thriving 번창하는   affectivity 정서

동명사 2

① 동명사/to부정사 사용에 주의해야 하는 동사

동사	동명사	to부정사
stop	~하는 것을 멈추다	~ 하기 위해 멈추다(부사적용법)
remember	(과거) ~했던 것을 기억하다	(미래) ~할 것을 기억하다
forget	(과거) ~했던 것을 잊다	(미래) ~할 것을 잊다
regret	~한 것을 후회하다	~하게 되어 유감이다
try	~를 시험 삼아 해보다	~하도록 노력하다

② 동명사/to부정사에 따라 달라지는 의미

- **A** He **stopped crossing** the street.
- **B** He **stopped to cross** the street.
- **C** I **remembered/forgot meeting** her yesterday.
- **D** I **remembered/forgot to meet** her tomorrow.
- **E** I **regret having** trusted the agent's words.
- **F** I **regret to say** that your wife had a car accident.
- **G** I **tried putting** on a pair of yellow shoes.
- **H** I **tried to pass** the exam.

PRACTICE

A 어법상 **틀린** 부분을 바르게 고쳐 쓰시오.

1 He stopped resting for a few minutes after running.

2 She remembers to see the BTS members in concert last year.

3 I will never forget to see the movie *Cinema Paradiso* when I was young.

4 He told me that he regretted to say harsh things to me last night.

5 Why don't you try to turn the computer off and on again?

B 네모 안에서 어법에 맞는 표현으로 가장 적절한 것을 고르시오.

1 When the defender feels understood by the blamer, and that they are on the same side, there's nothing to defend against anymore, and the defender stops to feel / feeling enraged and frustrated.

2 Meteorologists must always remember keeping / to keep records of data variations for precise weather predictions because wind speed and direction differ between weather stations in different landscapes.

적용독해

1 다음 글의 밑줄 친 부분 중, 어법상 **틀린** 것은? 고1 학평 기출 응용

My dad worked very late hours as a musician — until about three in the morning — so he slept late on weekends. As a result, we didn't have much of a relationship when I was young, other than him constantly nagging me to take care of chores like mowing the lawn and cutting the hedges whenever I forgot ① to do them. He was a responsible man dealing with an irresponsible kid. Memories of how we interacted seem funny to me today. For example, one time he told me ② to cut the grass and I decided ③ to do just the front yard and postpone ④ to do the back, but then it rained for a couple days and the backyard grass became so high I had to cut it with a sickle. That took so long that by the time I was finished, the front yard was too high to mow. Although I hated doing chores, I have always remembered ⑤ to mow the lawn since then.

* sickle: 낫

2 다음 글의 밑줄 친 부분 중, 어법상 **틀린** 것은? 고2 학평 기출 응용

When I was young, my parents worshipped medical doctors as if they were exceptional beings possessing godlike qualities. But I never dreamed of ① pursuing a career in medicine until I entered the hospital for a rare disease. I became a medical curiosity, attracting some of the area's top specialists to look in on me and ② review my case. As a patient, and a teenager eager ③ to return to college, I asked each doctor who examined me, "What caused my disease?" "How will you make me better?" The typical response was nonverbal. They shook their heads and walked out of my room. I remember ④ thinking to myself, "Well, I could do that." When it became clear to me that no doctor could answer my basic questions, I stopped ⑤ to ask them. Returning to college, I pursued medicine with a great passion.

---

1 nagging 잔소리하는 chore 허드렛일 mow the lawn 잔디를 깎다 hedge 울타리 덤불 postpone 미루다
2 worship 우러러보다, 숭배하다 exceptional 뛰어난, 특별한 possess (자격, 능력을) 지니다, 가지다 godlike 신과 같은 quality 재능, 속성, 특질 pursue 추구하다 medicine 의학 rare 희귀한 specialist 전문가 look in on ~을 방문하다 review 관찰하다, 정밀 검사하다 eager 간절히 바라는 typical 전형적인 nonverbal 비언어적인, 말을 쓰지 않는 passion 열정

심경

1

다음 글에 드러난 'I'의 심경으로 가장 적절한 것은? **고2 학평 기출 응용**

Hours later — when my back aches from sitting, my hair is styled and dry, and my almost invisible makeup has been applied — Ash tells me not to forget to change into my dress. We've been waiting until the last minute, afraid any refreshments I eat might accidentally fall onto it and stain it. There's only thirty minutes left until the show starts, and the nerves that have been torturing Ash seem to have escaped her, choosing a new victim in me. My palms are sweating, and I have butterflies in my stomach. Nearly all the models are ready, some of them already dressed in their nineteenth-century costumes. Ash tightens my corset.

① tense and nervous ② proud and confident

③ relieved and pleased ④ indifferent and bored

⑤ irritated and disappointed

---

1 ache 아프다 invisible 보이지 않는 refreshments 다과 accidentally 우연히 stain 얼룩지게 하다 nerve 초조함, 날카로운 신경 torture 괴롭히다 victim 희생자 palm 손바닥 sweat 땀이 나다 have butterflies in one's stomach 안절부절못하다 tighten 조이다

2 다음 글에 드러난 Dave의 심경 변화로 가장 적절한 것은? 고2 학평 기출 응용

Dave sat up on his surfboard and looked around. He was the last person in the water that afternoon. Suddenly something out toward the horizon caught his eye and his heart froze. It was every surfer's worst nightmare — the fin of a shark. He stopped relaxing, turned his board toward the beach, and started kicking his way to the shore. It was no more than 20 meters away! Shivering, he gripped his board tighter and tried to kick harder. 'I'm going to be okay,' he thought to himself. 'I need to let go of the fear.' Five minutes of terror that felt like a lifetime passed before he was on dry land again. Dave sat on the beach and caught his breath. His mind was at ease. He was safe. He let out a contented sigh as the sun started setting behind the waves.

* fin: 지느러미

① frighened → relieved
② indifferent → proud
③ amazed → horrified
④ hopeful → worried
⑤ ashamed → grateful

3 다음 글의 상황에 나타난 분위기로 가장 적절한 것은? 고2 학평 기출 응용

Meghan looked up and saw angry gray clouds rolling across the water. The storm had turned and was coming her way. She stood up and reached for her sandals. That's when she spotted her dog splashing around in the middle of the lake. At first she thought he was playing. She watched for a second or two, then realized her dog wasn't playing. He was trying to keep from going under. She regretted letting him play alone at the lake side. With her heart pounding like a trip-hammer, she ran into the water and started swimming toward the dog. Before she got to the dog, the rain started. She saw the dog, and seconds later he was gone. She pushed forward frantically, her arms reaching out in long strokes, her legs kicking harder and faster.

① grave and solemn
② tense and urgent
③ calm and peaceful
④ festive and lively
⑤ monotonous and boring

---

2 horizon 수평선, 지평선 shiver 떨다 grip 붙잡다 at ease 마음이 편안한 contented 만족한 set (해가) 지다
3 spot 발견하다 splash 물을 튀기다 regret 후회하다 pound 세게 치다 trip-hammer 스프링 해머, 기계 해머 frantically 미친 듯이
reach out (손 등을) 뻗다 stroke 차다, 치다

18강 사회 · 인간관계

426
society
[səsáiəti]

명 사회, 학회, 협회   social 형 사회의, 사회적인

➕ sociologist 사회학자   sociopathic 반사회적인   societal 사회의, 사회 활동의

427
charity
[tʃǽrəti]

명 자선, 자선 단체, 구호품   charitable 형 자선을 위한

➕ philanthropy 자비, 박애   salvation 구제

428
generous
[dʒénərəs]

형 관대한, 너그러운   generosity 명 관대함

➕ tolerant 관대한, 관용의   broad-minded 아량이 있는

429
loneliness
[lóunlinis]

명 외로움, 고독(= solitude)   lonely 형 외로운

a lonely and deserted island 인적 없는 무인도

430
personality
[pə̀rsənǽləti]

명 성격, 인성, 개성, 인격   personal 형 개인의, 개인적인

➕ character 성격, 인격   individuality 개성

431
fulfill
[fulfíl]

동 이행하다, 성취하다, 충족시키다   fulfillment 명 성취

✅ 성취/달성하다: achieve, accomplish, attain

432
compel
[kəmpél]

동 강요하다, 억지로 하게 하다   compelling 형 매력적인, 강력한

✅ 어쩔 수 없이 ~하다: be forced/compelled/obliged to

433
behavior
[bihéivjər]

명 행동, 행위   behavioral 형 행동의

✅ 행동: action, movement, conduct

434
feedback
[fíːdbæ̀k]

명 반응, 의견, 피드백

✅ 반응: response, reaction, reflex(반사 작용)

435
reinforce
[rìːinfɔ́ːrs]

동 강화하다, 보강하다   reinforcement 명 강화

reinforcement of patent rights 특허권 강화

436
ethnic
[éθnik]

형 인종의, 민족의   ethnicity 명 민족성

➕ race 인종   nation 민족(a people)

437
invaluable
[invǽljuəbl]

형 귀중한(↔ valueless), 소중한   valuables 명 귀중품

✅ 귀중한: precious, priceless, cherished

438

conventional
[kənvénʃənəl]

형 관습적인, 전통적인, 틀에 박힌　convention 명 관습, 집회

➕ customary 관례적인　traditional 전통적인　stereotypical 진부한

439

embark
[imbá:rk]

동 시작하다, 착수하다　embarkment 명 착수, 개시

✅ 시작/착수하다: begin, launch, commence

440

development
[divéləpmənt]

명 개발, 발전, 발달, 성장　develop 동 발달시키다, 개발하다

➕ creation 개발　advancement 발전　growth 성장

441

interpersonal
[ìntərpə́:rsənəl]

형 대인 간의　interpersonally 부 대인 간에, 상호 간에

➕ personal relations 대인 관계　intrapersonal 개인 내의

442

encounter
[inkáuntər]

동 만나다, 마주치다, 직면하다 명 마주침, 직면

✅ 직면하다: face, be faced with, confront, be confronted with

443

minority
[minɔ́(:)rəti]

명 소수(↔ majority), 소수 집단, 미성년　minor 형 작은 편의, 중요치 않은

✅ 일부의 : a portion of, a handful of, a fraction of

444

nurture
[nə́:rtʃər]

동 양육하다, 육성하다　nature and nurture 본성과 양육

✅ 양육하다: raise, bring up, rear

445

respective
[rispéktiv]

형 각각의　respectively 부 각각

➕ irrespective of ~와 관계없이(= regardless of)

446

mistrust
[mistrʌ́st]

명 불신(= distrust) 동 불신하다　trustworthy 형 신뢰할 수 있는

✅ 불신: disbelief, suspicion, discredit

447

self-esteem
[selfistí:m]

명 자존감, 자부심　esteem 동 존중하다, 존경하다

➕ self-confidence 자신감　self-conceit 자만심

448

obstacle
[ábstəkl]

명 장애(물), 방해, 난관

✅ 방해, 장애: obstruction, hindrance, impediment

449

colleague
[káli:g]

명 동료, 동업자　colleagueship 동료애

✅ 동료: coworker, peer, associate

450

instinctively
[instíŋktivli]

부 본능적으로(by instinct), 직관적으로　instinct 명 본능　instinctive 형 본능적인

✅ 타고난: inborn, innate, inherent, natural

PRACTICE

A   알맞은 단어를 〈보기〉에서 골라 빈칸을 채우시오.

> 〈보기〉   self-esteem   encounter   obstacle   colleague   minority

1 Fear of change is a(n)_____ to progress.

2 Her innovative idea was applauded by her _____s.

3 This brutal behavior was my first _____ with racism.

4 Only a(n)_____ of people were involved in the violent act.

5 His failure to enter the college led to a loss of _____.

B   빈칸에 들어갈 알맞은 표현을 고르시오.

1 UNICEF was established to _____ children around the globe.

  ① embark   ② nurture   ③ compell   ④ encounter

2 The handshake is a social _____ in western countries.

  ① encounter   ② convention   ③ mistrust   ④ obstacle

3 We hold a concert every year to raise money for _____.

  ① behavior   ② personality   ③ reinforcement   ④ charity

4 This school has students from many different _____ groups.

  ① instinct   ② lonely   ③ ethnic   ④ invaluable

5 'Energy from waste' accounted for twenty percent and fifteen percent of all energy sources in India and Butan, _____.

  ① generously   ② lonely   ③ intuitively   ④ respectively

C   네모 안에서 문맥에 맞는 낱말로 가장 적절한 것을 고르시오.

1 Claiming that cooking food doesn't do good, and that even children should be nurtured without medical intervention, Shelton was harshly criticized / supported by his contemporaries for advocating fasting over medical treatment.

  * fasting: 단식

2 All types of lying, when discovered, have indirect harmful effects, but these harmful effects might occasionally be outweighed by the benefits / drawbacks which arise from a lie. For example, lying to the seriously ill about their life expectancy might give them a chance of living longer.

적용독해

1 다음 글의 밑줄 친 부분 중, 문맥상 낱말의 쓰임이 적절하지 <u>않은</u> 것은? `고2 학평 기출`

Openness is important no matter what your business or venture. The *Charity Water* website ① <u>includes</u> a Google Map location and photographs of every well. When you look at the site, you can see what *Charity Water* is doing. Many people are ② <u>hesitant</u> to give to nonprofits, because they don't know where or how their money is actually going to be used. This is why it can be a good idea to get individuals or an organization to underwrite your operational costs. This way, all the donations you collect go straight to the people you are working to help — making your donors feel ③ <u>uncertain</u> their dollars are doing good things — and that only creates more generosity on their part. Being open also ④ <u>encourages</u> you to be responsible with the money you take in. If people are aware of where their money goes, you'll be ⑤ <u>less</u> likely to spend it on a fancy office or high salaries.

2 다음 글의 밑줄 친 부분 중, 문맥상 낱말의 쓰임이 적절하지 <u>않은</u> 것은? `고2 학평 기출`

We live in an age of constant interaction, and yet more of us are claiming we are "lonely" than ever before. Loneliness has nothing to do with how many people are physically around us, but has everything to do with our failure to ① <u>get</u> what we need from our relationships. Virtual personalities online and characters on television ② <u>fulfill</u> our natural emotional-needs artificially, and hence occupy the blurry margins in which our brains have ③ <u>difficulty</u> distinguishing real from unreal. The more we rely on these personalities and characters to get a sense of "connectedness," the more our brains encode them as ④ <u>"irrelevant."</u> This means our brains can be tricked, and the irony is that we are complicit in the deception. As need-driven animals, we seek out the paths of ⑤ <u>least</u> resistance to get what we need, and electronic immersion provides the most accessible, nonchemical path yet invented.

* complicit: 공범인, 공모한

---

1 no matter what 비록 무엇이 ~한다 하더라도   hesitant 망설이는   nonprofit 비영리 단체   underwrite (서명하여) 동의하다   operational 운용의   donation 기부금   donor 기부자   generosity 너그러움   fancy 멋진   salary 급여

2 virtual 가상의   fulfill 충족하다   artificially 인위적으로   hence 이런 이유로   occupy 차지하다   blurry 모호한, 불분명한   margin 영역   distinguish 구별하다   encode 인지하다, 암호로 하다   be complicit in ~에 연루된   deception 속임수   seek out 찾다, 탐색하다   resistance 저항   immersion 몰입   accessible 접근하기 쉬운

분사 1

① 분사

> **A** The man **who cooks / is cooking** the food at this restaurant is my father.
> → The man **cooking** the food at this restaurant is my father.
>
> **B** My friend gave me a book **which is written in English**.
> → My friend gave me a book **written** in English.

② 자주 출제되는 주요 표현

be filled with (~로 가득차다)	be involved in (~와 관련되다)
be located in / at (~에 위치하다)	be faced with (~에 직면하다)
be absorbed in (~에 몰두하다)	be covered with (~로 덮혀있다)
be known as (~로 알려져 있다)	be based on (~에 기반을 두고 있다)
be satisfied with (~에 만족하다)	be compared with (~와 비교하다)

③ 분사구문 ▶ p.92

> **C** When I heard the news, I was disappointed.
> → **(When) Hearing** the news, I was disappointed.
> → I was disappointed **when hearing** the news.
>
> **D** When I was motivated by my friend, I did well in school.
> → **(When) Motivated** by my friend, I did well in school.
> → I did well in school **when motivated** by my friend.

PRACTICE

A 어법상 틀린 부분을 바르게 고쳐 쓰시오.

1 A child was hit by a car while walked across the crosswalk.

2 When asking "Do you want to have a car?" he answered, "Yes."

3 Antarctica is a continent using entirely for peaceful purposes.

4 The farmers checked the tools and processes involving in growing vegetables.

5 Situating at an elevation of 1,350m, the city of Kathmandu enjoys a warm climate.

B 네모 안에서 어법에 맞는 표현으로 가장 적절한 것을 고르시오.

1 Appropriately naming / named the Baroque, meaning irregular or distorted, European painting in the 16th century largely focused on capturing motion, drama, action, and powerful emotion.

2 In the past when there were few sources of news, people could either expose themselves to mainstream news — where they would likely see beliefs different from their own expressing / expressed — or they could avoid news altogether.

적용독해

1 다음 글의 밑줄 친 부분 중, 어법상 틀린 것은? 고2 학평 기출 응용

The competition to sell manuscripts to publishers ① is fierce. I would estimate that less than one percent of the material ② sent to publishers is ever published. Since so much material is being written, publishers can be very selective. The material they choose to publish must have commercial value. When ③ well-written and free of errors, the material is more likely to be published. Any manuscript ④ contained factual errors can cause mistrust, standing little chance at being accepted for publication. However generous they are, most publishers will not want to waste time with writers ⑤ whose material contains too many mistakes.

2 다음 글의 밑줄 친 부분 중, 어법상 틀린 것은? 고1 학평 기출

Improved consumer water consciousness may be the cheapest way ① to save the most water, but it is not the only way consumers can contribute to water conservation. With technology ② progressing faster than ever before, there are plenty of devices that consumers can install in their homes to save more. More than 35 models of high-efficiency toilets are on the U.S. market today, some of which use less than 1.3 gallons per flush. ③ Starting at $200, these toilets are affordable and can help the average consumer save hundreds of gallons of water per year. Appliances officially ④ approving as most efficient are tagged with the Energy Star logo to alert the shopper. Washing machines with that rating use 18 to 25 gallons of water per load, ⑤ compared with older machines that use 40 gallons. High-efficiency dishwashers save even more water. These machines use up to 50 percent less water than older models.

---

1 competition 경쟁 manuscript 원고, 필사본 publisher 출판사, 출판업자 fierce 치열한 selective 선택적인, 선별적인 commercial 상업적인 stand little chance at ~의 가능성이 거의 없다
2 consciousness 의식 contribute to ~에 기여하다 conservation 보존 progress 진보하다 high-efficiency 고효율 flush (변기) 물내림 affordabale 가격이 알맞은 appliance 기기, 가전제품 approve 승인하다 alert 알리다 dishwasher 식기세척기

1 다음 글에서 필자가 주장하는 바로 가장 적절한 것은? 고1 학평 기출 응용

How do you encourage other people when they are changing their behavior? Suppose you see a friend who is on a diet and has been losing a lot of weight. It's tempting to tell her that she looks great and she must feel wonderful. It feels good for someone to hear positive comments, and this feedback will often be encouraging. However, if you end the discussion there, then the only feedback your friend is getting is about her progress toward an outcome. Instead, continue the discussion. Ask about what she is doing that has allowed her to be successful. What is she eating? Where is she working out? What are the lifestyle changes she has made? When focusing on the process of change rather than the outcome, the conversation reinforces the value of creating a sustainable process.

① 상대방의 감정을 고려하여 조언해야 한다.
② 토론 중에는 지나치게 공격적인 질문을 삼가야 한다.
③ 효과적인 다이어트를 위해 구체적인 계획을 세워야 한다.
④ 지속적인 성장을 위해서는 단점보다 장점에 집중해야 한다.
⑤ 행동을 바꾸려는 사람과는 과정에 초점을 두어 대화해야 한다.

2 다음 글에서 필자가 주장하는 바로 가장 적절한 것은? 고2 학평 기출 응용

Though we are marching toward a more global society, various ethnic groups traditionally do things quite differently, and a fresh perspective is valuable in creating an open-minded child. Measured by how many ideas they can come up with and by the resulting association skills, extensive multicultural experience makes kids more creative and allows them to capture unconventional ideas from other cultures to expand on their own ideas. As a parent, you should expose your children to other cultures as often as possible. If you can, travel with your child to other countries; live there if possible. If neither is possible, there are lots of things you can do at home, such as exploring local festivals, borrowing library books about other cultures, and cooking foods from different cultures at your house.

---

1 tempting 솔깃한 discussion 대화 progress 진전 outcome 결과 reinforce 강화하다 sustainable 지속 가능한

① 자녀가 전통문화를 자랑스럽게 여기게 해야 한다.
② 자녀가 주어진 문제를 깊이 있게 탐구하도록 이끌어야 한다.
③ 자녀가 다른 문화를 가능한 한 자주 접할 수 있게 해야 한다.
④ 창의성 발달을 위해 자녀의 실수에 대해 너그러워야 한다.
⑤ 경험한 것을 돌이켜 볼 시간을 자녀에게 주어야 한다.

3

다음 글에서 필자가 주장하는 바로 가장 적절한 것은? 고2 학평 기출

Without guidance from their teacher, students will not embark on a journey of personal development that recognizes the value of cooperation. Left to their own devices, they will instinctively become increasingly competitive with each other. They will be compelled to compare scores, reports, and feedback within the classroom environment — just as they do in the sporting arena. We don't need to teach our students about winners and losers. The playground and the media do that for them. However, we do need to teach them that there is more to life than winning and about the skills they need for successful cooperation. A group working together successfully requires individuals with a multitude of social skills, as well as a high level of interpersonal awareness. While some students inherently bring a natural understanding of these skills with them, they are always in the minority. To bring cooperation between peers into your classroom, you need to teach these skills consciously and carefully, and nurture them continuously throughout the school years.

① 학생의 참여가 활발한 수업 방법을 개발해야 한다.
② 학생에게 성공적인 협동을 위한 기술을 가르쳐야 한다.
③ 학생의 의견을 존중하는 학교 분위기를 조성해야 한다.
④ 학생의 전인적 발달을 위해 체육활동을 강화해야 한다.
⑤ 정보를 올바르게 선별하도록 미디어 교육을 실시해야 한다.

---

2 **march** 나아가다 **ethnic** 민족의 **traditionally** 전통적으로 **perspective** 관점 **measure** 측정하다 **association** 연상, 관련 **extensive** 광범위한 **capture** 포착하다, 붙잡다 **unconventional** 관습에 얽매이지 않은, 색다른 **expand** 확장하다 **expose** 접하게 하다 **at home** 국내에서 **explore** 탐방하다, 탐험하다
3 **embark on** ~에 착수하다 **cooperation** 협력 **instinctively** 본능적으로 **increasingly** 점점 더 **be compelled to** 하는 수 없이 ~하다 **multitude** 다양한 **interpersonal** 대인 간 **inherently** 선천적으로 **consciously** 의식적으로

19강 생활

451
crave
[kreiv]

동 갈망하다, 간절히 원하다   craving 명 갈망, 열망

✔ 갈망하다: desire, long, yearn

452
potentially
[pəténʃəli]

부 잠재적으로   potential 형 잠재적인 명 잠재력

Korea's potential growth rate 한국의 잠재 성장률

453
ingredient
[ingríːdiənt]

명 재료, 성분, 주요 내용

➕ element 요소   factor 요인   component 구성 요소

454
uniformity
[jùːnəfɔ́ːrməti]

명 획일(성), 한결같음   uniform 형 획일적인 명 제복, 교복

➕ biform 두 가지 형태의   multiform 다양한 형태의

455
install
[instɔ́ːl]

동 설치하다, 장착하다   installment 명 설치, 할부(금)

➕ set up 설치하다   equip 장착하다   furnish 갖추다

456
enhance
[inhǽns]

동 높이다, 향상하다, 강화하다   enhancement 명 향상, 강화

✔ 향상하다: improve, uplift, better, boost

457
modify
[mɑ́dəfài]

동 변경하다, 변형하다   modified 형 변형된

✔ 바꾸다: change, shift, alter, transform

458
loose
[luːs]

형 느슨한, 헐렁한, 풀려난 동 (매듭 등을) 풀다   loosen 동 느슨하게 하다, 완화하다

➕ loose a knot 매듭을 풀다   loosen a rope 밧줄을 느슨하게 하다

459
apparel
[əpǽrəl]

명 의복, 의류

✔ 의복, 의류: clothing, dress, attire, garment

460
solitary
[sɑ́litèri]

형 혼자의, 유일한, 외로운   solitude 명 고독

a lonely senior citizen's solitary death 독거노인의 고독사

461
frequent
[fri(ː)kwént]

형 빈번한, 잦은 동 자주 가다   frequency 명 빈발, 주파수

✔ 드문, 흔치 않은: infrequent, unusual, uncommon

462
electronic
[ilektrɑ́nik]

형 전자의, 전자공학의   electron 명 전자

➕ eletromagnetic 전자기의   electromotive 전동의   electrostatic 정전기의

463

condition
[kəndíʃən]

명 조건, 상태, 환경, 상태, 질병　동 조절하다
➕ conditional 조건부의　unconditionally 무조건으로

464

solid
[sálid]

형 고체의, 단단한, 확실한　solidify 동 굳어지다
➕ liquid 액체의　gaseous 기체의

465

virtue
[vɔ́ːrtʃuː]

명 미덕(↔ vice), 덕목　virtuous 형 도덕적인, 고결한
➕ virtuous cycle 선순환　vicious cycle 악순환

466

reckless
[réklis]

형 무모한, 무분별한(↔ sensible)　recklessly 부 무모하게
✅ 무모한: careless, thoughtless, inconsiderate

467

trait
[treit]

명 특징, 특성
✅ 특징, 특성: characteristic, feature, distinction, quality

468

deficient
[difíʃənt]

형 부족한(↔ sufficient), 결함 있는　deficiency 명 부족, 결함
✅ 부족한: short, wanting, lacking, insufficient

469

latest
[léitist]

형 최신의, 최근의　late-later-latest
✅ 최근에: recently, lately, of late

470

typical
[típikəl]

형 전형적인, 일반적인　typically 부 일반적으로, 전형적으로
✅ 일반적인: usual, general, normal

471

regularly
[régjələrli]

부 정기적으로, 규칙적으로(↔ irregularly)　regular 형 규칙적인, 정기적인
➕ regulate 규제하다, 조절하다　regularity 규칙성

472

comply
[kəmplái]

동 준수하다, 따르다, 순응하다　compliance 명 순응, 준수
✅ 준수하다: follow, observe, conform, abide by

473

conceal
[kənsíːl]

동 숨기다(↔ reveal), 감추다(= hide)　concealment 명 은닉
conceal the classified documents 기밀 문서를 숨기다

474

swear
[swɛər]

동 맹세하다, 욕하다　swear-swore-sworn
✅ 맹세: promise, pledge, oath, vow

475

mutual
[mjúːtʃuəl]

형 상호 간의(= reciprocal), 서로의　mutually 부 상호 간에
the principles of mutual trust and mutual respect 상호 신뢰와 존중의 원칙

PRACTICE

A   알맞은 단어를 〈보기〉에서 골라 빈칸을 채우시오.

> 〈보기〉   comply   modify   conceal   swear   mutually

1   The bomb was _____ed in the trash bin.

2   Students must _____ strictly with these instructions.

3   I _____ that I will get my revenge someday.

4   We can _____ the design to make it suitable for commercial production.

5   Politeness and truth are often _____ incompatible.

B   빈칸에 들어갈 알맞은 표현을 고르시오.

1   Hard work is a vital _____ for success.

    ① potencial   ② electronic   ③ ingredient   ④ frequency

2   Fashion designers _____(e)d simplicity because they hated medieval costume.

    ① crave   ② trait   ③ loose   ④ swear

3   We should avoid a diet _____ in calcium and protein.

    ① solid   ② solitary   ③ uniform   ④ deficient

4   People who visit a certain shop _____ are called 'frequent customers.'

    ① recklessly   ② similarly   ③ regularly   ④ comply

5   Always think before you act. Remember that patience is a _____.

    ① trait   ② virtue   ③ condition   ④ concealment

C   네모 안에서 문맥에 맞는 낱말로 가장 적절한 것을 고르시오.

1   Psychological studies of the *Kuleshov* effect have confirmed the impact of social context on emotion. For example, if a person smiles at you and then the smile turns into a neutral expression, that person will appear somewhat enhanced / disappointed .

2   Although gamblers and businesspeople crave again and again to recapture that high from winning so much money, the reality that sudden luck or success cannot be sustained / terminated makes them more prone to feeling depressed.

적용독해

1 다음 글의 밑줄 친 부분 중, 문맥상 낱말의 쓰임이 적절하지 <u>않은</u> 것은? 고1 학평 기출

It's no surprise that labels are becoming the "go to" place when people have questions about how food is ① <u>produced</u>. But new Cornell University research finds that consumers crave more information, especially for the potentially ② <u>harmful</u> ingredients that aren't included in the product. The laboratory study of 351 shoppers found consumers willing to pay a premium when a product label says "free of" something, but only if the package provides ③ <u>"negative"</u> information on whatever the product is "free of." For example, a food labeled "free" of a food dye will compel some consumers to buy that product. But even more people will buy that product if that same label ④ <u>excludes</u> information about the risks of ingesting such dyes. "When they get more information about ingredients, consumers are more ⑤ <u>confident</u> about their decisions and value the product more," Harry M. Kaiser, a Cornell professor, said.

2 다음 글의 밑줄 친 부분 중, 문맥상 낱말의 쓰임이 적절하지 <u>않은</u> 것은? 고3 학평 기출 응용

Girls usually agreed that wearing a uniform to school every day ① <u>reduced</u> their daily stresses. Not having to worry about what to wear meant one less decision to make every morning. Many of them also felt that the uniform ② <u>enhanced</u> school spirit and solidarity. They could feel like they belong to a community. Moreover, the uniforms ③ <u>eliminated</u> their individuality. Just ask the girls who wear it if you want to know a thousand and one ways to ④ <u>modify</u> a school uniform: ties can be worn loosely or tight, and skirts can be raised or lowered in any of a half-dozen ways. Then there are accessories — a gray region in the dress code, but an entire subcontinent in the world of women's apparel. There are a million ⑤ <u>options</u> in the domain of hairpins, watches, and bags alone.

---

1 **crave** 간절히 원하다 **potentially** 잠재적으로 **ingredient** 성분 **laboratory** 실험실 **premium** 초과액, 더 많은 비용 **dye** 염료 **compel** 강요하다 **exclude** 제외하다 **ingest** 섭취하다 **confident** 확신하는
2 **enhance** 향상시키다 **solidarity** 결속, 단결 **eliminate** 제거하다 **individuality** 개성 **modify** 수정하다, 변경하다 **gray** 불분명한 **subcontinent** 하위 영역 **apparel** 의복, 의상 **domain** 영역

분사 2

① 부대상황: 동시동작(∼하면서), 연속동작(그리고 ∼하다)

> **A** Jane entered the room, **while she smiled** at us.
> = Jane entered the room, **smiling** at us. (동시동작)
> **B** The train departed at five **and reached** Seoul at ten.
> = The train departed at five, **reaching** Seoul at ten. (연속동작)

② with 분사구문: with + 목적어 + 분사 (∼가 …하면서, ∼을 …인 채로)

> **C** She left the car on with the engine **running**. (with + 목적어 + 현재분사)
> **D** He sat all day long with his legs **crossed**. (with + 목적어 + 과거분사)

③ 감정 형용사: 감정을 불러일으키면 현재분사, 감정을 느끼면 과거분사

> surprise, excite, interest, delight, bore, satisfy, move, touch, embarrass, depress, please, irritate, frighten, frustrate, shock, impress, scare, disappoint, relieve, refresh, annoy 등
> **E** The movie was so **exciting**.
> **F** The spectators were so **excited** about the game.
> **G** Feeling envy and anger all the time is **exhausting**.
> **H** He looked **exhausted**, so I made him go to bed.

PRACTICE

A 밑줄 친 부분을 어법에 맞게 고쳐 쓰시오.

1 <u>Walk</u> around the museum, they listened to the guide's explanations.
2 The wild duck swims with its tail <u>holding</u> above the water.
3 Sparrows are <u>scary</u> of the machine mimicking the sound of eagles.
4 She stood there with tears <u>run</u> down her face.
5 It is not <u>surprised</u> that those who are good at music are good at languages as well.

B 네모 안에서 어법에 맞는 표현으로 가장 적절한 것을 고르시오.

1 The swarm phase of locusts, which are normally solitary, is triggered as their numbers build up, threatened / threatening their food supply. This is why they swarm — to search for food in a new location.

* locust: 메뚜기

2 Our own time is still largely under the influence of earlier electrical innovations, however dazzling / dazzled we may be of the electronic, computerized, and media wonders of the twenty-first century.

적용독해

1 다음 글의 밑줄 친 부분 중, 어법상 <u>틀린</u> 것은? [고3 학평 기출 응용]

Hairdressers are constantly servicing clients who come in with a picture clipped from a beauty magazine and tell the stylist, "This is the look I want — cut my hair like this." A stylist can just do the cut, ① <u>telling</u> the customer that she got exactly what she wanted. But a good stylist knows that what a customer thinks she wants is often not ② <u>what</u> she really wants. The "look" in that picture will frequently not be the "look" on this particular customer. Good stylists often tell customers that their job is not just to execute perfectly the cut they ③ <u>were asked</u> for. Of course, customers can be ④ <u>embarrassing</u> to hear that but soon they nod. That's because they come to understand that good stylists know ⑤ <u>how</u> the face and bone structure of the client, along with the condition of the hair would change the look from the client's chosen picture.

2 다음 글의 밑줄 친 부분 중, 어법상 <u>틀린</u> 것은? [고3 학평 기출 응용]

The observation ① <u>that</u> old windows are often thicker at the bottom than at the top is often offered as supporting evidence for the view that glass flows over a time scale of centuries. However, most experts are ② <u>unsatisfied</u> with this assumption; once solidified, glass does not flow anymore. The reason for the observation is that in the past, ③ <u>making</u> uniformly flat glass was almost impossible. The technique used to make panes of glass was to spin molten glass, ④ <u>creating</u> a round, mostly flat plate. This plate was then cut to fit a window. However, the edges of the disk became thicker as the glass spun. The glass would ⑤ <u>place</u> thicker side down for the sake of stability when installed in a window frame.

* molten: 녹은, 용해된

---

1 constantly 끊임없이 client 고객 clip 자르다, 오리다 frequently 종종 execute 실행하다 embarrassing 당황하게 만드는 nod 끄덕이다
2 observation 관찰 thick 두꺼운 bottom 밑바닥 evidence 증거 time scale 시간 척도 assumption 가정 solidify 굳게 하다
plate 판 stability 안정성 install 설치하다

함의 추론

1 밑줄 친 at the "sweet spot"이 다음 글에서 의미하는 바로 가장 적절한 것은? 고1 학평 기출 응용

For almost all things in life, there can be too much of a good thing. Even the best things in life aren't so great in excess. This concept has been discussed at least as far back as Aristotle. He argued that being virtuous means finding a balance. For example, people should be brave, but if someone is too brave they become reckless. People should be trusting, but if someone is too trusting, they are considered gullible. For each of these traits, it is best to avoid both deficiency and excess, living at the "sweet spot" that maximizes well-being. Aristotle's suggestion is that virtue is the midpoint, where someone is neither too generous nor too stingy, neither too afraid nor recklessly brave.

* excess: 과잉   ** gullible: 잘 속아 넘어가는

① at the time of a biased decision
② in the area of material richness
③ away from social pressure
④ in the middle of two extremes
⑤ at the moment of instant pleasure

2 밑줄 친 have that same scenario가 다음 글에서 의미하는 바로 가장 적절한 것은?

고1 학평 기출 응용

There are more than 700 million cell phones used in the US today and at least 140 million of those cell phone users will abandon their current phone for a new phone every 14-18 months. I'm not one of those people who just "must" have the latest phone. Actually, I use my cell phone until the battery no longer holds a good charge. At that point, it's time. So I figure I'll just get a replacement battery. But I'm told that battery is no longer made and the phone is no longer manufactured because there's newer technology and better features in the latest phones. That's a typical justification. The phone wasn't even that old; maybe a little over one year? I'm just one example. Can you imagine how many countless other people have that same scenario? It is not surprising that cell phones take the lead when it comes to "e-waste."

---

1 virtuous 미덕이 있는   reckless 무모한   deficiency 부족   maximize 극대화하다   generous 관대한   stingy 인색한

① have frequent trouble updating programs

② cannot afford new technology due to costs

③ spend a lot of money repairing their cell phones

④ are driven to change their still usable cell phones

⑤ are disappointed with newly launched phone models

3

밑줄 친 a "media diet"가 다음 글에서 의미하는 바로 가장 적절한 것은? 고2 학평 기출

The most dangerous threat to our ability to concentrate is not that we use our smartphone during working hours, but that we use it too irregularly. By checking our emails every now and then on the computer and our text messages here and there on our phone with no particular schedule or rhythm in mind, our brain loses its ability to effectively filter. The solution is to regulate your devices as if you were on a strict diet. When it comes to nutrition, sticking to a fixed time plan for breakfast, lunch, and dinner allows your metabolism to adjust, thereby causing less hunger during the in-between phases. Your belly will start to rumble around 12:30 p.m. each day, but that's okay because that's a good time to eat lunch. If something unexpected happens, you can add a snack every now and then to get fresh energy, but your metabolism will remain under control. It's the same with our brain when you put it on a "media diet."

* rumble: 우르르 울리다

① balancing the consumption of traditional and online media

② regulating the use of media devices with a set schedule

③ avoiding false nutritional information from the media

④ stimulating your brain with various media sources

⑤ separating yourself from toxic media contents

---

2 abandon 버리다 current 현재의 latest 최신의 replacement 교체 manufacture 제조하다 feature 기능 justification 정당화 take the lead 선두에 있다 when it comes to ~에 관해서라면

3 threat 위협 irregularly 불규칙적으로 regulate 조절하다 nutrition 영양 stick to ~를 고수하다 metabolism 신진대사 adjust 적응하다 thereby 그렇게 함으로써 phase 단계 belly 배 snack 간식

교육·학문

476
education
[èdʒukéiʃən]

명 교육, 훈련　　educate 동 교육하다, 훈련하다　　educated 형 교육받은
✅ 교육: training, instruction, schooling

477
curriculum
[kəríkjələm]

명 교과 과정　　extracurricular activity 방과 후 활동
Computer courses are included in the curriculum. 컴퓨터 강좌는 교육 과정에 포함되어 있다.

478
mindful
[máindfəl]

형 유의하는, 염두에 두는
be mindful of learning disabilities 학습 장애에 유의하다

479
satisfy
[sǽtisfài]

동 만족시키다, 충족시키다(≠dissatisfy)　　satisfaction 명 만족
✅ ~에 만족하다: be satisfied with, be content with, be pleased with

---

480
incorporate
[inkɔ́ːrpərèit]

동 포함하다, 통합하다　　incorporation 명 결합, 합병
✅ 통합하다: unify, combine, integrate, consolidate

481
calculate
[kǽlkjəlèit]

동 계산하다, 생각하다　　calculator 명 계산기
differential and integral calculus 미적분

482
grasp
[ɡræsp]

동 파악하다, 이해하다, 잡다(= grip)
✅ 파악하다: figure out, identify, comprehend

483
underlying
[ʌ́ndərlàiiŋ]

형 근본적인, 기저에 있는　　underlie 동 근본이 되다
✅ 근본적인: basic, fundamental, radical

484
devoted
[divóutid]

형 헌신적인, 전념하는　　devotion 명 헌신(commitment)
✅ ~에 전념하다: devote/commit/dedicate oneself to

485
quote
[kwout]

동 인용하다, 전하다　명 인용문(= quotation)
➕ quote (남의 말을 그대로) 인용　　cite (증거로서 사례를) 인용

486
humble
[hʌ́mbl]

형 겸손한(= modest), 초라한(= shabby)
➕ arrogant, haughty 오만한　　stubborn 완고한

487
superior
[sju(ː)píəriər]

형 우수한(↔ inferior)　　sense of superiority 우월감
✅ 라틴계 비교급: superior to, inferior to, prior to, prefer A to B

488

evaluate
[ivǽljuèit]

동 평가하다(= assess), 고려하다　　evaluation 명 평가, 감정

➕ overvaluation 과대평가　　undervaluation 과소평가

489

overlook
[òuvərlúk]

동 간과하다(= ignore), 내려다보다(= look down)

✅ look over, take in, break out → overlook, intake, outbreak

490

oriented
[ɔ́:rièntid]

형 ~ 지향적인, ~ 중심적인　　orientation 명 방향성, 취향

✅ the Orient 동양(*cf.* the Occident 서양)

491

refinement
[rifáinmənt]

명 세련, 개선, 정제, 순화　　refine 동 개선하다, 정제하다

refine the learning strategy 학습 전략을 개선하다

492

fundamental
[fʌ̀ndəméntəl]

형 기초적인, 근본적인　　fundamentally 부 근본적으로

seek fundamental solutions 근본적인 해법을 찾다

493

grade
[greid]

명 학년, 등급, 성적 동 등급을 매기다, 분류하다

➕ gradation 단계적 변화　　GPA 평점(grade point average)

494

policy
[pɑ́lisi]

명 정책, 방침

the present government's policy on education 현 정부의 교육 정책

495

standard
[stǽndərd]

명 기준, 표준 형 표준의　　substandard 형 표준 이하의

➕ standard 권위가 있는 기준　　criterion 판단의 기준

496

summarize
[sʌ́məràiz]

동 요약하다　　in summary 요약하면(= in brief, in short)

✅ 요약하다: sum up, abstract, abridge

497

institute
[ínstitʃùːt]

명 연구소, 학회, (전문) 대학 동 설치하다, 실시하다

➕ institute a lawsuit / a reform 소송을 제기하다 / 개혁을 실시하다

498

lecture
[léktʃər]

명 강의, 설교, 훈계 동 강의하다, 꾸짖다

✅ 강사: lecturer, instructor, teacher, trainer

499

discipline
[dísəplin]

명 규율, 훈련, 징계, 학과목 동 훈련하다, 징계하다　　disciplined 형 기강이 잡힌

✅ 훈련하다: train, drill, exercise

500

tuition
[tjuːíʃən]

명 학비, 수업료, (개인) 교습

➕ tuition / medical / admission / late / transfer fee 학비 / 의료비 / 입장료 / 연체료 / 이적료

PRACTICE

A 알맞은 단어를 〈보기〉에서 골라 빈칸을 채우시오.

〈보기〉	summary	discipline	tuition	mindful	Institute

1 College _____ is about $ 30,000 per year on average.

2 The educational authorities have to be _____ of their responsibilities.

3 This is the _____ of the main points of the scholar's lecture.

4 The Massachusetts _____ of Technology is in the state of Massachusetts.

5 The university merged two fields into a single _____.

B 빈칸에 들어갈 알맞은 표현을 고르시오.

1 I cannot _____ his mistake anymore.

   ① calculate   ② underlie   ③ overlook   ④ summarize

2 It is important to _____ whether this could happen again.

   ① satisfy   ② incorporate   ③ devote   ④ evaluate

3 Opposition to the government's educational _____ is growing.

   ① grades   ② summary   ③ policies   ④ devotion

4 Educators ought to remember the _____ principles of equal education.

   ① aware   ② fundamental   ③ humble   ④ corporate

5 I was impressed by Chomsky's _____ on GB theory.

   ① tuition   ② oriented   ③ disciplinary   ④ lecture

C 네모 안에서 문맥에 맞는 낱말로 가장 적절한 것을 고르시오.

1 If the goal is to figure out how best to cover a set curriculum — to fill students with necessary facts — then it might seem appropriate to try to maximize time on task in ways such as by suspending / assigning extra homework.

2 Mental rehearsal is such a prominent / trivial technique in sports training because whenever you perform a specific action your brain fires off in a very specific pattern, and whenever you *imagine* yourself performing this same action, your brain fires off in almost the same pattern.

적용독해

1 다음 글의 밑줄 친 부분 중, 문맥상 낱말의 쓰임이 적절하지 <u>않은</u> 것은? [고3 학평 기출]

Sometimes athletes need to be allowed to practice their skills on their own before they receive feedback. That way they can determine what is working and what isn't and can become more ① <u>mindful</u> of their strengths and weaknesses. If you attempt to provide assistance when athletes would prefer to practice on their own, you may be ② <u>wasting</u> a lot of time and breath. When athletes realize that their best efforts are producing ③ <u>satisfactory</u> outcomes, they are usually more motivated to hear what you have to say. In other words, athletes are responsive to assistance when they fail to achieve the outcome they were hoping for. A coach's challenge, then, is to remain patient until these and other types of ④ <u>teachable</u> moments arise. The reward for such ⑤ <u>patience</u> is athletes who are motivated to hear what you have to say and eager to incorporate your suggestions.

2 다음 글의 밑줄 친 부분 중, 문맥상 낱말의 쓰임이 적절하지 <u>않은</u> 것은? [고3 학평 기출]

In the 1970s, when schools began allowing students to use portable calculators, many parents ① <u>objected</u>. They worried that a reliance on the machines would weaken their children's grasp of mathematical concepts. The fears, subsequent studies showed, were largely ② <u>unneeded</u>. No longer forced to spend a lot of time on routine calculations, many students gained a deeper understanding of the principles underlying their exercises. Today, the story of the calculator is often used to support the argument that our growing dependence on online databases is ③ <u>disadvantageous</u>. In freeing us from the work of remembering, it's said, the Web allows us to devote more time to creative thought. The pocket calculator ④ <u>relieved</u> the pressure on our working memory, letting us use that critical short-term store for more abstract reasoning. The calculator, a powerful but highly specialized tool, turned out to be an ⑤ <u>aid</u> to our working memory.

---

1 athlete 운동선수 mindful ~에 유념하는 assistance 도움 outcome 성과, 결과 challenge 어려움 patient 참을성 있는 arise 생기다 eager 의욕 incorporate 통합시키다
2 reliance 의존성 subsequent 후속의, 뒤이은 routine 상례적인, 틀에 박힌 underlie ~의 기초가 되다 pocket 휴대용의, 소형의

대명사

① it의 쓰임

> A The college awards many scholarships to **its** students. (대명사) ▶p.198
>
> B **It** is natural that we get upset at the situation. (가주어)
>
> C We found **it** strange that the door was open. (가목적어)
>
> D **It** was during the earthquake that the building was destroyed. (it~that 강조)

② that의 쓰임

> E Janet told me **that** she would always help me. (접속사)
>
> F It was true **that** Hanna recently quit her job. (진주어)
>
> G She thought it unlikely **that** he would do all of these tasks. (진목적어)
>
> H Such a decision is based on the expectation **that** she will pass the exam. (동격)
>
> I It was a pair of sneakers **that** my daughter bought yesterday. (it~that 강조)
>
> J Look at the boys **that** are lying and reading on the lawn. (관계대명사)
>
> K The color of the wall goes well with **that** of the floor. (대명사) ▶p.198

PRACTICE

A 어법에 맞게 〈보기〉에서 골라 밑줄 친 부분을 바르게 고쳐 쓰시오. (반복 가능)

〈보기〉	it	that	those	what

1 I will do whatever it takes to be the best, however hard <u>one</u> may be.

2 <u>That</u> matters is that you read as much as you can.

3 One peculiar thing is the fact <u>which</u> this fish swims like a mermaid.

4 In spite of his denial, his playing skills are beyond <u>that</u> of an amateur.

5 The book is written in such simple language <u>what</u> we can easily get the author's meaning.

B 네모 안에서 어법에 맞는 표현으로 가장 적절한 것을 고르시오.

1 Kelly Crowe, a CBC News reporter quoting one epidemiologist, writes, "There is increasing concern ⎡which / that⎤ in modern research, false findings may be the majority or even the vast majority of published research claims."

2 The world's first complex writing form, Sumerian cuneiform, followed an evolutionary path moving from pictographic to ideographic representations, that is to say, from the depiction of objects to ⎡that / those⎤ of abstract notions, sometime around 3,500 BC.

* cuneiform: 설형 문자

적용독해

1 다음 글의 밑줄 친 부분 중, 어법상 **틀린** 것은? 고1 학평 기출

Although it is obvious that part of our assessment of food is its visual appearance, ① <u>it</u> is perhaps surprising how visual input can override taste and smell. People find ② <u>it</u> very difficult to correctly identify fruit-flavoured drinks if the colour is wrong, for instance an orange drink ③ <u>that</u> is coloured green. Perhaps even more striking is the experience of wine tasters. One study of Bordeaux University students of wine and wine making revealed ④ <u>what</u> they chose tasting notes appropriate for red wines, such as 'prune and chocolate', when they were given white wine coloured with a red dye. Experienced New Zealand wine experts were similarly tricked into thinking that the white wine Chardonnay was in fact a red wine, when ⑤ <u>it</u> had been coloured with a red dye.

* override: ~에 우선하다 ** prune: 자두

2 다음 글의 밑줄 친 부분 중, 어법상 **틀린** 것은? 고1 학평 기출 응용

Intellectual humility is admitting you are human and there are limits to the knowledge you have. It involves recognizing that you possess cognitive and personal biases, and ① <u>that</u> your brain tends to see things in such a way that your opinions and viewpoints are favored above others. ② <u>It</u> is being willing to work to overcome those biases in order to be more objective and make informed decisions. People who display intellectual humility are more likely to be receptive to the belief ③ <u>which</u> learning from others who think differently than they do is beneficial. They tend to be well-liked and respected by others because they make it clear ④ <u>that</u> they value what other people bring to the table. It is intellectually humble people ⑤ <u>that</u> want to learn more and are open to finding information from a variety of sources. They are not interested in trying to appear or feel superior to others.

---

1 assessment 평가 input 입력 tasting note 시음표 appropriate 적합한 dye 색소, 염료
2 intellectual 지적인, (뛰어난) 지성을 지닌 humility 겸손, 겸허 admit 인정하다, 허가하다 possess 보유하다, 가지다 receptive 잘 받아들이는, 수용하는 well-liked 매우 사랑을 받는, 호감을 산 humble 겸손한 superior 우수한

글의 요지

1

다음 글의 요지로 가장 적절한 것은? 고1 학평 기출 응용

A goal-oriented mind-set can create a "yo-yo" effect. Many runners work hard for months, but as soon as they cross the finish line, they stop training. The race is no longer there to motivate them. When all of your hard work is focused on a particular goal, what is left to push you forward after you achieve it? This is why many people find themselves returning to their old habits after accomplishing a goal. Although the purpose of setting goals is similar to that of building systems, in that both help you play more effectively, there is a key difference between the two. True long-term thinking is goal-less thinking. It's not about any single accomplishment. It is about the cycle of endless refinement and continuous improvement. Ultimately, it is your commitment to the process that will determine your progress.

① 발전은 한 번의 목표 성취가 아닌 지속적인 개선 과정에 의해 결정된다.
② 결승선을 통과하기 위해 장시간 노력해야 원하는 바를 얻을 수 있다.
③ 성공을 위해서는 구체적인 목표를 설정하는 것이 중요하다.
④ 지난 과정을 끊임없이 반복하는 것이 성공의 지름길이다.
⑤ 목표 지향적 성향이 강할수록 발전이 빠르게 이루어진다.

2

다음 글의 요지로 가장 적절한 것은? 고1 학평 기출

Learners function within complex developmental, cognitive, physical, social, and cultural systems. Research and theory from diverse fields have contributed to an evolving understanding that all learners grow and learn in culturally defined ways in culturally defined contexts. While humans share basic brain structures and processes, as well as fundamental experiences such as relationships with family, age-related stages, and many more, each of these phenomena is shaped by an individual's precise experiences. Learning does not happen in the same way for all people because cultural influences are influential from the beginning of life. These ideas about the intertwining of learning and culture have been supported by research on many aspects of learning and development.

* intertwine: 뒤얽히다

---

1 **goal-oriented** 목표 지향적인 **mind-set** 사고방식 **as soon as** ~하자마자 **no longer** 더 이상 ~ 아닌 **motivate** 동기를 주다 **push ~ forward** ~를 앞으로 밀고 나아가다 **accomplish** 성취하다 **purpose** 목적 **cycle** 순환 **refinement** 정제 **commitment** 전념 **progress** 발전, 진보

① 문화 다양성에 대한 체계적 연구가 필요하다.

② 개인의 문화적 경험이 학습에 영향을 끼친다.

③ 인간의 뇌 구조는 학습을 통해 복잡하게 진화했다.

④ 원만한 대인관계 형성은 건강한 성장의 토대가 된다.

⑤ 학습 발달 단계에 적합한 자극을 제공하는 것이 좋다.

3

다음 글의 요지로 가장 적절한 것은? **고1 학평 기출**

Rather than attempting to punish students with a low grade or mark in the hope it will encourage them to give greater effort in the future, teachers can better motivate students by considering their work as incomplete and then requiring additional effort. Teachers at Beachwood Middle School in Beachwood, Ohio, record students' grades as *A*, *B*, *C*, or *I* (Incomplete). Students who receive an *I* grade are required to do additional work in order to bring their performance up to an acceptable level. This policy is based on the belief that students perform at a failure level or submit failing work in large part because teachers accept it. The Beachwood teachers reason that if they no longer accept substandard work, students will not submit it. And with appropriate support, they believe students will continue to work until their performance is satisfactory.

① 학생에게 평가 결과를 공개하는 것은 학습 동기를 떨어뜨린다.

② 학생에게 추가 과제를 부여하는 것은 학업 부담을 가중시킨다.

③ 지속적인 보상은 학업 성취도에 장기적으로 부정적인 영향을 준다.

④ 학생의 자기주도적 학습 능력은 정서적으로 안정된 학습 환경에서 향상된다.

⑤ 학생의 과제가 일정 수준에 도달하도록 개선 기회를 주면 동기 부여에 도움이 된다.

---

2 complex 복잡한 diverse 다양한 defined 한정된 fundamental 기본적인 phenomenon 현상 (*pl.* phenomena) shape 형성하다 precise 정확한

3 incomplete 불완전한, 미완성의 additional 추가적인, 부가적인 acceptable 받아들일 수 있는 submit 제출하다 reason 추론하다, 생각하다 substandard 기준 이하의 appropriate 적절한 satisfactory 만족스러운

21강 역사·문화

501
uncertain
[ʌnsɔ́ːrtən]

형 불확실한(↔ certain)　　uncertainty 명 불확실성

✔ 애매한: vague, ambiguous, equivocal, hazy

502
drawback
[drɔ́ːbæk]

명 단점, 불리한 점, 결점

✔ 단점: weakness, shortcoming, demerit, flaw, downside

503
religion
[rilídʒən]

명 종교　　religious 형 종교의, 독실한(↔ irreligious)

➕ Christianity 기독교　　Buddhism 불교　　Islam 이슬람교

504
philosophy
[filásəfi]

명 철학, 사상, 이론　　philosopher 명 철학자

pure and applied philosophy 순수철학과 응용철학

505
forbear
[fɔ́ːrbɛ̀ər]

동 참다, 억제하다　　forbear–forbore–forborne

✔ 참다: bear, stand, endure, put up with

506
opponent
[əpóunənt]

명 반대자(↔ proponent), 상대, 적수　　oppose 동 반대하다

get rid of a political opponent 정적을 제거하다

507
term
[təːrm]

명 용어, 임기, 기간　　terms 명 조건, 말투, 비용

✔ 학기: term(일 년 3학기), semester (일 년 2학기)

508
realm
[relm]

명 영역, 범위, 분야

be considered a male realm 남성의 영역으로 인식되다

509
speculate
[spékjəlèit]

동 추측하다, (심사)숙고하다　　speculation 명 추측, 투기

✔ 숙고하다: reflect on, deliberate, ponder, contemplate

510
perspective
[pərspéktiv]

명 관점(= point of view), 시각, 전망

I have a different perspective. 나는 다른 관점을 가지고 있다.

511
outweigh
[àutwéi]

동 ~보다 뛰어나다, 능가하다

The positives outweigh the negatives. 긍정적인 것이 부정적인 것보다 낫다.

512
strife
[straif]

명 분쟁, 투쟁, 갈등　　strive 동 ~와 싸우다, 분투하다, 노력하다

➕ class strife/struggle 계급 투쟁　　hunger strike 단식 투쟁　　outdoor protest 장외 투쟁

513
context
[kántekst]

명 맥락, 문맥, 상황　contextual 형 맥락상의

grasp from the context 문맥으로 파악하다

514
incident
[ínsidənt]

명 사건(= event), 사고(= accident)　incidentally 부 우연히

➕ incidence 발생(률), 발병(률)　coincidence 우연의 일치

515
linguistic
[liŋgwístik]

형 언어의, 언어(학)적인　linguistics 명 언어학　linguist 명 언어학자

➕ bilingual 2개 언어를 할 수 있는　lingua franca 국제 공용어

516
explicitly
[iksplísitli]

부 명시적으로(↔ implicitly), 분명히　explicit 형 분명한

✅ 분명히: clearly, obviously, evidently, definitely

517
diffuse
[difjú:z]

동 퍼뜨리다, 발산하다　형 널리 퍼진

His fame is diffused throughout the school. 그의 명성은 학교에 널리 퍼져 있다.

518
confine
[kənfáin]

동 국한하다, 제한하다, 감금하다　confinement 명 감금

✅ 제한하다: limit, restrict, constrain

519
majority
[mədʒɔ́(:)rəti]

명 대부분(↔ minority), 과반수　major 형 주요한, 중대한, 대다수의

an absolute/overwhelming majority of 절대다수의

520
voyage
[vɔ́iidʒ]

명 항해, 여행　동 항해하다

Bon voyage/appetit! 즐거운 여행이 되시길/맛있게 식사하시길!

521
peculiar
[pikjú:ljər]

형 특이한, 독특한　peculiarity 명 특성, 특수성

peculiar institution 흑인 노예 제도(미국 남부에 특유한 제도)

522
characteristic
[kæriktərístik]

명 특징　형 특징적인, 특유한　character 명 성격, 기질, 특성

individual characteristics, individuality 개성

523
mold
[mould]

명 주형틀, 곰팡이　동 (틀에 넣어) 만들다

mold bronze into a statue 청동으로 동상을 만들다

524
prevail
[privéil]

동 만연하다, 우세하다　prevalent 형 만연한, 널리 퍼진

✅ 널리 퍼진: widespread, prevailing, widely diffused

525
interpret
[intə́:rprit]

동 해석하다, 통역/번역하다　interpretation 명 통역, 번역

interpret A as B A를 B로 해석/이해하다　interpret A into B A를 B로 통역/번역하다

PRACTICE

A   알맞은 단어를 〈보기〉에서 골라 빈칸을 채우시오.

> 〈보기〉   peculiar   uncertain   linguistic   prevalent   religious

1 I was _____ what he meant.

2 I've never met such a deeply _____ person like him.

3 Dr. Lee is interested in the _____ development of young children.

4 There was something rather _____ about her voice.

5 COVID-19 has been _____ in Europe this year.

B   빈칸에 들어갈 알맞은 표현을 고르시오.

1 I _____(e)d her silence as anger.

① diffuse   ② mold   ③ major   ④ interpret

2 The novel is based on a tragic historical _____.

① linguistic   ② incident   ③ drawback   ④ prevalent

3 The benefits of the surgery far _____ the risks without it.

① outweigh   ② confine   ③ speculate   ④ forbear

4 Philosophers must try not to see everything from a Western _____.

① speculation   ② majority   ③ perspective   ④ opponent

5 We _____(e)d our study on Korean culture to 10 cases.

① interpret   ② prevail   ③ diffuse   ④ confine

C   네모 안에서 문맥에 맞는 낱말로 가장 적절한 것을 고르시오.

1 Much of what we call political risk is in fact uncertainty, which resorts / applies to all types of political risks, from civil strife to tax evasion and regulatory changes.

2 Some characteristics of cities that must be maintained, even if the population decreases, are productivity and diversity as these are two key factors of improbability / sustainability .

적용독해

1 다음 글의 밑줄 친 부분 중, 문맥상 낱말의 쓰임이 적절하지 <u>않은</u> 것은? 고1 학평 기출

From the beginning of human history, people have asked questions about the world and their ① <u>place</u> within it. For early societies, the answers to the most basic questions were found in ② <u>religion</u>. Some people, however, found the traditional religious explanations inadequate, and they began to search for answers based on reason. This ③ <u>consistency</u> marked the birth of philosophy, and the first of the great thinkers that we know of was Thales of Miletus. He used reason to inquire into the nature of the universe, and encouraged others to do ④ <u>likewise</u>. He passed on to his followers not only his answers but also the process of thinking ⑤ <u>rationally</u>, together with an idea of what kind of explanations could be considered satisfactory.

2 다음 글의 밑줄 친 부분 중, 문맥상 낱말의 쓰임이 적절하지 <u>않은</u> 것은? 고2 학평 기출

The ancient Egyptians and Mesopotamians were the Western world's philosophical forebears. In their concept of the world, nature was not an ① <u>opponent</u> in life's struggles. Rather, man and nature were in the same boat, companions in the same story. Man thought of the natural world in the ② <u>same</u> terms as he thought of himself and other men. The natural world had thoughts, desires, and emotions, just like humans. Thus, the realms of man and nature were ③ <u>indistinguishable</u> and did not have to be understood in cognitively different ways. Natural phenomena were imagined in the same terms as human experience. These ancients of the Near East did ④ <u>neglect</u> the relation of cause and effect, but when speculating about it they came from a "who" rather than a "what" perspective. When the Nile rose, it was because the river ⑤ <u>wanted</u> to, not because it had rained.

---

1 religion 종교 inadequate 불충분한 reason 이성 consistency 일관성 philosophy 철학 inquire 탐구하다 likewise 이와 같이
rationally 이성적으로
2 forebear 선조 concept 개념 opponent 적, 경쟁자 companion 동반자 realm 영역 indistinguishable 불분명한 cognitively 인지
적으로 phenomena 현상들 neglect 무시하다 cause and effect 원인과 결과 speculate 숙고하다 perspective 관점

관계대명사

① 관계대명사의 역할: 접속사＋명사

A She is **a poet**. ＋ **She** writes poems in English.
→ She is a poet **and** she writes poems in English.
→ She is a poet **who** writes poems in English.

② 관계대명사의 특징: 선행사＋who/which/that＋불완전한 절

B A thief is someone **who** steals things. (주격 관계대명사)
C I have an American friend **whose** name is Mike. (소유격 관계대명사)
D Almost every student (**whom**) I know dislikes math. (목적격 관계대명사)
E English is the subject (**that/which**) I am most interested in.
→ English is the subject **in which** I am most interested. (X in that)

③ 관계대명사 what: 선행사(×)＋what＋불완전한 절

F **What** he says is different from **what** he does.
G The students didn't understand **what** their teacher said.

PRACTICE

A 밑줄 친 부분을 어법에 맞게 고쳐 쓰시오.

1 The obese people <u>whom</u> were sure of their success lost 10 kg more than self-doubters.

2 Kate, <u>who</u> hands were those of a person who'd worked hard, got what she wanted.

3 Adequate hydration improves cognitive function among adolescents, <u>that</u> is important for learning.

4 Believing <u>what</u> the road to success will be rocky leads to greater success.

5 The teacher asked his students <u>that</u> they thought their future would be like.

B 네모 안에서 어법에 맞는 표현으로 가장 적절한 것을 고르시오.

1 Claiming that emotions are vital for intelligent action, and that the benefits of having emotions outweigh the drawbacks, means adopting | that / what | Dylan Evans calls 'the positive view of emotion'.

2 Around 600 BC Herodotus was commissioned by the ancient Egyptian King Necho II to write about an exploratory voyage | which / in which | the king reportedly ordered a Phoenician expedition to sail clockwise around Africa, starting at the Red Sea and returning to the mouth of the Nile.

적용독해

1   다음 글의 밑줄 친 부분 중, 어법상 **틀린** 것은?   고2 학평 기출

An ambiguous term is one which has more than a single meaning and ① whose context does not clearly indicate which meaning is intended. For instance, a sign posted at a fork in a trail ② which reads "Bear To The Right" can be understood in two ways. The more probable meaning is that it is instructing hikers to take the right trail, not the left. But let us say that the ranger ③ who painted the sign meant to say just the opposite. He was trying to warn hikers against taking the right trail because there is a bear in the area ④ through which it passes. The ranger's language was therefore careless, and open to misinterpretation ⑤ what could have serious consequences. The only way to avoid linguistic ambiguity is to spell things out as explicitly as possible: "Keep left. Do not use trail to the right. Bears in the area."

2   다음 글의 밑줄 친 부분 중, 어법상 **틀린** 것은?   고2 학평 기출 응용

Language is one of the primary features ① that distinguishes humans from other animals. Many animals, including dolphins, whales, and birds, do indeed communicate with one another through patterned systems of sounds, scents, and other chemicals, or movements. Furthermore, some nonhuman primates have ② been taught to use sign language to communicate with humans. However, the complexity of human language, its ability to convey nuanced emotions and ideas, and its importance for our existence as social animals, set it apart from the communication systems ③ which are used by other animals. In many ways, language is the essence of culture. It provides the single most common variable ④ what different cultural groups are identified. Language not only facilitates the cultural diffusion of innovations; it also helps to shape the way ⑤ that we think about, perceive, and name our environment.

---

1 ambiguous 모호한   context 문맥   intend 의도하다   fork 갈림길   trail 오솔길   probable 가능성이 있는   instruct 알려주다   ranger 삼림 관리인   opposite 정반대   language 언어   misinterpretation 오역   consequence 결과   explicitly 명백하게

2 feature 특징   distinguish 구분하다   scent 냄새   primate 영장류   complexity 복잡성   nuanced 미묘한 차이가 있는   existence 존재   set apart 구분하다   essence 본질   variable 변수, 변인   identify 구별하다   facilitate 용이하게 하다   diffusion 확산   innovation 혁신   perceive 인지하다

글의 주제

1

다음 글의 주제로 가장 적절한 것은? 고1 학평 기출

Animals as well as humans engage in play activities. In animals, play has long been seen as a way of learning and practicing skills and behaviors that are necessary for future survival. In children, too, play has important functions during development. From its earliest beginnings in infancy, play is a way in which children learn about the world and their place in it. Children's play serves as a training ground for developing physical abilities — skills like walking, running, and jumping, which are necessary for everyday living. Play also allows children to try out and learn social behaviors and to acquire values and personality traits that will be important in adulthood. For example, they learn how to compete and cooperate with others, how to lead and follow, how to make decisions, and so on.

① necessity of trying out creative ideas
② roles of play in children's development
③ contrasts between human and animal play
④ effects of children's physical abilities on play
⑤ children's needs at various developmental stages

2

다음 글의 주제로 가장 적절한 것은? 고1 학평 기출 응용

Vegetarian eating is moving into the mainstream as more and more young adults say no to meat, poultry, and fish. According to the American Dietetic Association, "approximately planned vegetarian diets are healthful, are nutritionally adequate, and provide health benefits in the prevention and treatment of certain diseases." But health concerns are not the only reason that young adults give for changing their diets. Some make the choice out of concern for animal rights. When faced with the statistics that show the majority of animals raised as food live in confinement, many teens who protest those conditions give up meat. Others turn to vegetarianism to support the environment.

---

1 engage 참여하다 survival 생존 infancy 유아기 ground 토대 personality trait 성격 특성 adulthood 성인기 compete 경쟁하다
cooperate 협력하다

Meat production uses vast amounts of water, land, grain, and energy and creates problems with animal waste and resulting pollution.

① reasons why young people go for vegetarian diets
② ways to build healthy eating habits for teenagers
③ vegetables that help lower your risk of cancer
④ importance of maintaining a balanced diet
⑤ disadvantages of plant-based diets

3 다음 글의 주제로 가장 적절한 것은? 고2 학평 기출

It has long been held that the capacity for laughter is a peculiarly human characteristic. The witty Lucian of Samosata (2nd century A.D.) noted that the way to distinguish a man from a donkey is that one laughs and the other does not. In all societies humor is important not only in individual communication but also as a molding force of social groups, reinforcing their norms and regulating behavior. "Each particular time, each era, in fact each moment, has its own condition and themes for laughter because of the major preoccupations, concerns, interests, activities, relations, and mode prevailing at the time." The ultimate goal of anyone who studies another culture, such as ancient Greece, is to understand the people themselves who were more than the sum total of monuments, historical incidents, or social groupings. One way to approach this goal directly is to study the culture's humor. As Goethe aptly observed: "Men show their characters in nothing more clearly than in what they think laughable."

① typical process of cultural assimilation
② function of laughter in building friendship
③ educational need for intercultural competence
④ roles of humor in criticizing social problems
⑤ humor as a tool for understanding a culture

---

2 vegetarian 채식주의자 mainstream 주류 approximately 대략적으로 nutritionally 영양학적으로 adequate 적당한 concern 염려, 관심 statistics 통계 confinement 구금 grain 곡식 pollution 오염
3 capacity 능력 peculiarly 독특하게 mold 형성하다 reinforce 강화하다 norm 규범 regulate 규제하다 era 시대 theme 주제 preoccupation 사고 prevailing 널리 퍼진 ultimate 궁극적인 sum total 총합계 monument 유물 incident 사건 approach 접근하다 observe 언급하다

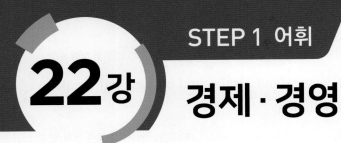
526

economy
[ikánəmi]

명 경제, 경기　　economic 형 경제의　economics 명 경제학

economical way to buy appliances 실속 있는 가전제품 구입법

527

mortgage
[mɔ́ːrɡidʒ]

명 주택 담보 대출　동 저당 잡히다

mortgage interest rates 모기지 금리

528

insurance
[inʃú(ː)ərəns]

명 보험, 보험금　　insure 동 보험에 가입하다

car/fire/travel insurance 차/화재/여행 보험

529

industrial
[indʌ́striəl]

형 산업의, 공업의　　industry 명 산업, 근면

Industrial/Glorious/French Revolution 산업/명예/프랑스 혁명

530

executive
[igzékjətiv]

명 임원, 중역, 이사　형 경영의, 행정의　　execute 동 실행하다, 집행하다, 처형하다

CEO 최고경영자(chief executive officer)

531

abundant
[əbʌ́ndənt]

형 풍부한, 많은　　abundance 명 풍부, 다수

✔ 풍부한: rich, plentiful, ample, affluent

532

choice
[tʃɔis]

명 선택, 선정　　choose 동 선택하다

✔ 선택하다: select, opt, elect(선거에서 뽑다), mischoose(잘못 선택하다)

533

prompt
[prɑmpt]

형 신속한, 즉석의　동 유발하다, 촉구하다　　promptly 부 신속히

✔ 신속하게: quickly, rapidly, swiftly, speedily

534

government
[ɡʌ́vərnmənt]

명 정부　　govern 동 지배하다　govennmental 형 정부의

national, state, and local government 국가, 주, 지방 정부

535

merge
[məːrdʒ]

동 합병하다　　merger 명 (사업체의) 합병

➕ immerge 가라앉다　　emerge 나타나다　　submerge 잠기다

536

unprecedented
[ʌnprésidèntid]

형 전례 없는　　precede 동 선행하다　precedent 명 선례, 전례

A is preceded by B A가 B를 뒤따르다(↔ A is followed by B)

537

share
[ʃɛər]

명 몫, 지분, 주식(= stock)　동 공유하다

I own ten shares of stock. 나는 10주의 주식을 가지고 있다.

178

538
principal
[prínsəpəl]

형 주요한, 주된 명 교장, 원금
✔ 주요한: main, major, key, central, chief, prime

539
specialize
[spéʃəlàiz]

동 전문으로 하다, 전공하다(= major)　specialty 명 전문, 특징
specialize in macroeconomics 거시경제학을 전공하다

540
joint
[dʒɔint]

형 공동의 명 관절
G7 Summit Joint Statement G7 정상 공동 성명

541
alternative
[ɔːltə́ːrnətiv]

명 대안, 대체(물) 형 대체의, 다른　alternate 동 대체하다
alternative energy and alternative fuel 대체 에너지와 대체 연료

542
liberate
[líbərèit]

동 해방하다, 자유롭게 하다　liberty 명 자유　liberation 명 해방
✔ 풀어 주다: free, release, acquit, emancipate

543
offset
[ɔ́(ː)fsét]

동 상쇄하다, 벌충하다 명 상쇄
ways to offset tax cuts for the rich 부자 감세를 상쇄할 방법

544
engage
[ingéidʒ]

동 관여하다, (관심) 끌다, 종사하다, 고용하다, 교전하다, 약혼하다
engagement 명 참여, 개입, 약속, 약혼, 교전.

545
devastate
[dévəstèit]

동 파괴하다, 황폐화시키다　devastating 형 파괴적인. 충격적인
✔ 파괴하다: break, destroy, destruct, demolish

546
fluctuate
[flʌ́ktʃuèit]

동 (수시로) 변동하다, 요동치다　fluctuating 형 변동을 거듭하는
fluctuate from day to day 매일매일 변하다

547
recruit
[rikrúːt]

동 채용하다, (신병을) 모집하다 명 신입사원, 신병
➕ beginner 초보자　newcomer 신입(생)　rookie 신참 선수

548
candidate
[kǽndidèit]

명 후보(자), 지원자, 수험생
a candidate for president 대통령 후보자　a candidate for an exam 시험 응시자

549
strategy
[strǽtidʒi]

명 전략, 방법, 계획　strategic 형 전략적인
lack of strategy and tactics 전략 전술의 부재

550
destiny
[déstəni]

명 운명(= fate), 숙명　destine 동 예정해 두다, ~을 운명짓다
tragic destiny 비극적 운명　by destiny 운명에 따라

PRACTICE

A 알맞은 단어를 〈보기〉에서 골라 빈칸을 채우시오.

| 〈보기〉 | recruit | liberate | specialize | engage | prompt |

1 Corporations have difficulty _____ing qualified staff.

2 Curiosity _____(e)d her to ask a few questions.

3 Chinese women were _____(e)d from the custom of foot-binding.

4 We need to _____ an attorney to negotiate on our behalf.

5 She _____(e)d in business administration at an Ivy League school.

B 빈칸에 들어갈 알맞은 표현을 고르시오.

1 Ladies and gentlemen, I present to you the Republican _____ for mayor.

① prompt   ② candidate   ③ mortgage   ④ government

2 Some rural schools have been _____(e)d to cut education costs nationwide.

① devastate   ② liberate   ③ merge   ④ recruit

3 Every single state has to formulate a(n) _____ for dealing with cyber crime.

① insurance   ② liberty   ③ offset   ④ strategy

4 This movie is a(n) _____ effort produced by Hollywood and Bollywood filmmakers.

① alternative   ② joint   ③ principal   ④ abundant

5 The _____ Revolution, which originated in the UK in the eighteenth century brought about many changes worldwide.

① Government   ② Knowledge   ③ Industrial   ④ Executive

C 네모 안에서 문맥에 맞는 낱말로 가장 적절한 것을 고르시오.

1 Regions Financial Corporation offers retail and commercial banking, trust, mortgage, and insurance products to customers in a network of more than 1,500 offices where the company tries to more fully serve the financial needs of its current customers, thereby missing / acquiring a larger share of each customer's financial business.

2 A theory of social psychology called *system justification theory* describes how people tend to see social, economic, and political systems as good, fair, and legitimate if they have succeeded / collapsed as a result of those systems.

적용독해

1 다음 글의 밑줄 친 부분 중, 문맥상 낱말의 쓰임이 적절하지 <u>않은</u> 것은? 　고2 학평 기출

The overabundance of options in today's marketplace gives you more freedom of choice. However, there may be a price to pay in terms of happiness. According to research by psychologists David Myers and Robert Lane, all this choice often makes people ① <u>depressed</u>. Researchers gave some shoppers 24 choices of jams to taste and others only 6 choices. Those who had ② <u>fewer</u> choices were happier with the tasting. Even more surprisingly, the ones with a smaller selection purchased jam 31% of the time, while those with a wider range of choices only purchased jam 3% of the time. The ironic thing about this is that people nearly always say they want ③ <u>more</u> choices. Yet, the more options they have, the more ④ <u>relieved</u> they become. Savvy restaurant owners provide fewer choices. This allows customers to feel more relaxed, ⑤ <u>prompting</u> them to choose easily and leave more satisfied with their choices.

*savvy: 사리에 밝은

2 다음 글의 밑줄 친 부분 중, 문맥상 낱말의 쓰임이 적절하지 <u>않은</u> 것은? 　고3 학평 기출

Financial markets have become more variable since exchange rates were freed in 1973 and authorities seem to have lost control over them. As a result, interest rates and exchange rates now ① <u>fluctuate</u> more rapidly than at any time. At the same time, companies' profit margins have been squeezed by the lowering of trade barriers and ② <u>increased</u> international competition. The result is that companies worldwide have been forced to learn to accept and deal with their financial ③ <u>hazard</u>. No longer can managers stick their heads in the sand and ④ <u>pretend</u> that because their firms make cars, or sell soap powders, they need only worry about this year's car or whether their new detergent washes whiter than Brand X. Many have found to their cost, ⑤ <u>acknowledging</u> interest-rate, currency or commodity risks can hurt a company just as badly as the failure of a new product.

---

1 overabundance 과잉　marketplace 시장　psychologist 심리학자　depressed 우울한　selection 선택 사항　purchase 구입하다　ironic 역설적이게도　relieved 안도하는　prompt 촉진하다
2 authorities 당국　fluctuate 요동치다　profit margin 이윤　barrier 장벽　hazard 위험, 위기　acknowledge 인정하다　currency 통화　commodity 상품

관계부사

① 관계부사의 기능: (선행사)＋관계부사＋완전한 절

A This is the house ＋ The famous actress lived in it.

B This is the house **(that / which)** the famous actress lived in.

＝This is the house **in which** the famous actress lived.

＝This is the house **where** the famous actress lived.

② 관계부사의 쓰임

C Do you remember the cafe **where** we first met? (장소)

D January is the month **when** the weather in Korea is the coldest. (시간)

E Tell me the reason **why** you were late for school. (이유)

③ 관계부사 how

F This is **the way (that/in which)** I can solve the problem.

＝This is **how** I can solve the problem.

G This is **the way how** I can solve the problem. (×)

PRACTICE

A 밑줄 친 부분을 어법에 맞게 고쳐 쓰시오.

1 She followed her daughter to the window that she could see the rainbow.

2 Some squirrels prefer habitats what the earth is soft and easy to dig in.

3 Ant colonies that have a "risk-taking" personality are more common in the north, where has a colder climate.

4 The E-book reading rates doubled in 2013, that the *Harry Potter* series was published.

5 His father let him carry a heavy backpack the way how "big people" do.

B 네모 안에서 어법에 맞는 표현으로 가장 적절한 것을 고르시오.

1 Under a capitalist social system, in which / where the government has no say in how dominant a company may become in its industry or how companies take over and merge with one another, dominance can only be achieved by becoming really good at what you're doing.

2 The unprecedented ability to measure time precisely found its most authoritarian expression in the factory clock in the eighteenth century, that / when it became a prime weapon of the Industrial Revolution.

적용독해

1 다음 글의 밑줄 친 부분 중, 어법상 틀린 것은? 고1 학평 기출 응용

The first underwater photographs were taken by an Englishman named William Thompson. In 1856, he waterproofed a simple box camera, attached it to a pole, and ① lowered it beneath the waves off the coast of southern England. During the 10-minute exposure, the camera slowly flooded with seawater, but the picture survived. This is ② how underwater photography was born. Near the surface, ③ where the water is clear and there is enough light, it is quite possible for an amateur photographer to take great shots with an inexpensive underwater camera. At greater depths ④ which it is dark and cold, photography is the principal way of exploring this mysterious deep-sea world, 95 percent of ⑤ which has never been seen before.

* exposure: 노출

2 다음 글의 밑줄 친 부분 중, 어법상 틀린 것은? 고2 학평 기출 응용

Trying to produce everything yourself would mean you are using your time and resources to produce many things ① for which you are a high-cost provider. This would translate into lower production and income. For example, even though most doctors might be good at record keeping and arranging appointments, it is generally in their interest to hire someone to perform these services. The time doctors use to keep records is time ② when they could have spent seeing patients. The opportunity cost of record keeping for doctors will be high because the time ③ that is spent with their patients is worth a lot. Thus, doctors will almost always find it ④ advantageous to hire someone else to keep and manage their records. Moreover, when the doctor specializes in the provision of physician services and ⑤ hires someone who has a comparative advantage in record keeping, costs will be lower and joint output larger than would otherwise be achievable.

---

1 waterproofed 방수의 attach 부착하다 pole 막대 exposure 노출 flood 차오르다 principal 주요한 explore 탐사하다
2 translate 해석되다 appointment 약속 keep records 기록하다 hire 고용하다 specialize 전문으로 하다 physician 의사
comparative advantage 비교 우위 output 결과물 otherwise 그렇지 않으면 achievable 달성할 수 있는

글의 제목

1 다음 글의 제목으로 가장 적절한 것은? 고1 학평 기출

Near an honesty box where people placed coffee fund contributions, researchers at Newcastle University in the UK alternately displayed images of eyes and of flowers. Each image was displayed for a week at a time. During all the weeks in which eyes were displayed, bigger contributions were made than during the weeks when flowers were displayed. Over the ten weeks of the study, contributions during the 'eyes weeks' were almost three times higher than those made during the 'flowers weeks.' It was suggested that 'the evolved psychology of cooperation is highly sensitive to subtle cues of being watched,' and that the findings may have implications for how to provide effective nudges toward socially beneficial outcomes.

* nudge: 넌지시 권하기

① Is Honesty the Best Policy?
② Flowers Work Better than Eyes
③ Contributions Can Increase Self-Respect
④ The More Watched, The Less Cooperative
⑤ Eyes: Secret Helper to Make Society Better

2 다음 글의 제목으로 가장 적절한 것은? 고1 학평 기출 응용

Only a generation or two ago, when mentioning the word algorithms would have drawn a blank from most people, there was no AI world and no worries about job loss. By contrast, our current generation now faces the loss of many traditional jobs in everything from art to healthcare in AI world. While some of these losses may be partly offset by the creation of new human jobs, others, such as doctors who focus on diagnosing known diseases and giving familiar treatments, will probably be replaced by AI doctors. But precisely because of that, there will be much more money to pay human doctors to do groundbreaking research and develop new medicines or surgical procedures. AI might help create new human jobs in another way. Instead of humans competing with AI, they could focus on servicing and using AI. For example, the replacement of human pilots by

---

1 contribution 기부(금) alternately 번갈아 evolved 진전된 sensitive 민감한 subtle 미묘한 implication 암시 beneficial 이익이 되는

drones has eliminated some jobs but created many new opportunities in maintenance, remote control, data analysis, and cyber security.

* offset: 상쇄하다

① What Makes Robots Smarter?

② Is AI Really a Threat to Your Job?

③ Watch Out! AI Can Read Your Mind

④ Future Jobs: Less Work, More Gains

⑤ Ongoing Challenges for AI Development

3

다음 글의 제목으로 가장 적절한 것은? 고2 학평 기출 응용

The free market has liberated people in a way that Marxism never could. What is more, as A. O. Hirschman, the Harvard economic historian, published his classic study *The Passions and the Interests*, where he showed the market was seen by Enlightenment thinkers Adam Smith, David Hume, and Montesquieu as a powerful solution to one of humanity's greatest traditional weaknesses: violence. When two nations meet, said Montesquieu, they can do one of two things: they can wage war or they can trade. If they wage war, both are likely to lose in the long run. If they trade, both will gain. That, of course, was the logic behind the establishment of the European Union: to lock together the destinies of its nations, especially France and Germany, in such a way that they would have an overwhelming interest not to wage war again as they had done to such devastating cost in the first half of the twentieth century.

* Marxism: 마르크스주의

① Trade War: A Reflection of Human's Innate Violence

② Free Market: Winning Together over Losing Together

③ New Economic Framework Stabilizes the Free Market

④ Violence Is the Invisible Hand That Disrupts Capitalism!

⑤ How Are Governments Involved in Controlling the Market?

---

2 mention 언급하다 draw a blank 반응을 얻지 못하다 diagnose 진단하다 precisely 정확히 groundbreaking 획기적인 surgical procedure 수술 절차 compete 경쟁하다 eliminate 제거하다 maintenance 정비 analysis 분석

3 liberate 자유롭게 하다 enlightenment 계몽 weakness 약점 violence 폭력 wage war 전쟁을 벌이다 gain 이득을 얻다 logic 논리 establishment 설립 lock 묶다 destiny 운명 overwhelming 저항할 수 없는 devastating 파괴적인

예술 · 문학

551
vitality
[vaitǽləti]

명 활력, 생명력　vital 형 중요한, 필수적인

give vitality to the art world 예술계에 활력을 불어넣다

552
improvise
[ímprəvàiz]

동 즉흥적으로 하다, 즉석에서 하다　improvisation 명 즉석에서 하기

Jazz bands improvise new melodies. 재즈 밴드들은 새로운 멜로디를 즉흥적으로 연주한다.

553
enthusiastic
[inθjùːziǽstik]

형 열정적인(= passionate), 열렬한　enthusiam 명 열정, 열광

excessive enthusiasm for the work 일에 대한 지나친 열정

554
compose
[kəmpóuz]

동 구성하다, 작곡하다, 창작하다　composition 명 작문, 작곡

✔ ~로 구성되다: be composed of, consist of, be made up of

555
proportion
[prəpɔ́ːrʃən]

명 비율, 비례

✔ 비율: rate, ratio, percentage

556
radical
[rǽdikəl]

형 급진적인, 과격한, 근본적인

radical reform and radical change 급진적 개혁과 급진적 변화

557
coordinate
[kouɔ́ːrdənèit]

동 조정하다, 조화를 이루다　형 동등한　명 좌표

We need to coordinate our schedules. 우리는 스케줄을 조율해야 한다.

558
exhibition
[èksəbíʃən]

명 전시(회)　exhibit 동 전시하다

✚ fair (전문) 전시회　expo(sition) 박람회

559
intrinsic
[intrínsik]

형 내적인, 내재적인(↔ extrinsic), 본질적인

✔ 내적인: inner, internal, implicit

560
discern
[disə́ːrn]

동 분간하다, 식별하다　discernible 형 분간할 수 있는

discern public and private matters 공과 사를 구별하다

561
illusion
[iljúːʒən]

명 착각, 환상, 환각　illusionary 형 환상의, 착각의

have an illusion 착각을 일으키다　under an illusion 착각 속에　optical illusion 착시

562
foundation
[faundéiʃən]

명 토대, 기반, 창설, 재단　found 동 설립하다

✔ 설립하다 found–founded–founded / 찾다 find–found–found

563

fame
[feim]

명 명성, 명예　famous 형 유명한　infamous 형 악명 높은

Hall of Fame 명예의 전당　good fame 호평

564

portray
[pɔːrtréi]

동 묘사하다, 그리다　portrayal 명 묘사, 연기

➕ portrait 초상화　watercolor 수채화　landscape 풍경화

565

embody
[imbádi]

동 구체화하다, 포함하다　embodiment 명 구현, 화신

embody creative ideas from the work 창의적인 생각을 작품에 나타내다

566

endeavor
[endévər]

명 노력, 시도 동 노력하다, 시도하다

➕ endeavor (계속적인) 노력　effort (목표 달성을 위한) 노력

567

enroll
[inróul]

동 등록하다, 입학하다　enrollment 명 등록, 입학

allow foreign students to enroll 외국인 학생들의 입학을 허용하다

568

literature
[lítərətʃùər]

명 문학, 문헌　literary 형 문학의

➕ poetry 시　essay 수필　play 희곡　novel 소설

569

tragic
[trǽdʒik]

형 비극적인　tragedy 명 비극

➕ comic 희극적인　romantic 낭만적인　classical 고전적인

570

prominent
[prámənənt]

형 유명한, 저명한, 두드러진　prominence 명 중요성, 명성

✔ 유명한, 저명한: well-known, noted, eminent

571

instrument
[ínstrəmənt]

명 도구, 기구, 악기　instrumental 형 수단이 되는

without instrumental accompaniment 무반주로

572

competent
[kámpitənt]

형 유능한, 능력 있는(↔ incompetent)　competence 명 능력

✔ 유능한: capable, talented, professional

573

reputation
[rèpjə(ː)téiʃən]

명 평판, 명성　reputable 형 평판이 좋은

have a good/bad reputation 평판이 좋다/나쁘다

574

author
[ɔ́ːθər]

명 저자, 작가(= writer)

➕ authoress 여류 작가　novelist 소설가　poet 시인

575

conceive
[kənsíːv]

동 생각하다, 상상하다, 구상하다　conception 명 구상, 이해, 개념

regard/think of/look upon/conceive A as B: A를 B라고 생각하다

PRACTICE

정답 및 해설 p.66

A   알맞은 단어를 〈보기〉에서 골라 빈칸을 채우시오.

> 〈보기〉   tragedy   reputation   author   portrait   foundation

1 Van Gogh's self-_____s reflect parts of his character.

2 The writer has a(n) _____ for writing a lot of fairytales.

3 It would be a(n) _____ if the amusement park had to close.

4 The _____ of *The Old Man and The Sea* is Ernest Hemingway.

5 Monet's style of painting became the _____ of impressionism.

B   빈칸에 들어갈 알맞은 표현을 고르시오.

1 She plans to _____ into college in the fall.

　① endeavor　　② discern　　③ enroll　　④ improvise

2 The artist drew the hands considerably out of _____.

　① instrument　　② reputation　　③ proportion　　④ exhibition

3 Passionate about reading many works of literature, he became a(n) _____ critic.

　① intrinsic　　② literary　　③ illusive　　④ tragic

4 Beethoven _____(e)d the *Moonlight* Sonata in 1801 and "*Für Elise*" in 1810.

　① enroll　　② exhibit　　③ found　　④ compose

5 Through this training, students will gain _____ in a variety of skills.

　① portrayal　　② author　　③ conceive　　④ competence

C   네모 안에서 문맥에 맞는 낱말로 가장 적절한 것을 고르시오.

1 Because our experiences make us feel alive and give us greater opportunities to grow, placing value on and investing in experiences provides us with a greater sense of insecurity / vitality .

2 Most business executives like to start with the big picture and then work out the details. That's the reason why so many of the best examples of improvised innovation take place inside / outside of formal organizations.

적용독해

1 다음 글의 밑줄 친 부분 중, 문맥상 낱말의 쓰임이 적절하지 <u>않은</u> 것은? `고1 학평 기출`

Music appeals powerfully to young children. Watch preschoolers' faces and bodies when they hear rhythm and sound — they light up and move ① <u>enthusiastically</u>. They communicate comfortably, express themselves creatively, and ② <u>let out</u> all sorts of thoughts and emotions as they interact with music. In a word, young children think music is a lot of ③ <u>fun</u>, so do all you can to make the most of the situation. Throw away your own ④ <u>willingness</u> and forget all your concerns about whether you are musically talented or whether you can sing or play an instrument. They don't matter when you are enjoying music with your child. Just follow his or her ⑤ <u>lead</u>, have fun, sing songs together, listen to different kinds of music, move, dance, and enjoy.

2 다음 글의 밑줄 친 부분 중, 문맥상 낱말의 쓰임이 적절하지 <u>않은</u> 것은? `고3 학평 기출`

Until the twentieth century, when composers began experimenting freely with form and design, classical music continued to ① <u>follow</u> basic rules relating to structure, not to mention harmony. There still was room for ② <u>individuality</u> — the great composers didn't follow the rules, but made the rules follow them — yet there was always a fundamental proportion and logic behind the design. Even after many of the rules were ③ <u>overturned</u> by radical concepts in more recent times, composers, more often than not, still organized their thoughts in ways that ④ <u>produced</u> an overall, unifying structure. That's one reason the atonal, incredibly complex works by Arnold Schönberg or Karlheinz Stockhausen, to name two twentieth-century Modernists, are nonetheless ⑤ <u>inaccessible</u>. The sounds might be very strange, but the results are still decidedly classical in terms of organization.

* atonal: 무조의, 장조나 단조 등의 조를 따르지 않는

---

1 appeal 호소하다 preschooler 취학 전의 아동 enthusiastically 열정적으로 express 표현하다 all sorts of 모든 종류의 willingness 기꺼이 하는 마음

2 composer 작곡가 experiment with ~을 실험하다 relating to ~와 관련 있는 structure 구조 not to mention ~은 말할 것도 없이 harmony 화음, 조화 fundamental 기본적인 proportion 비율, 균형 logic 논리 radical 급진적인 more often than not 대개, 자주 overall 전반적인 unifying 통일적인 incredibly 매우, 엄청나게 nonetheless 그럼에도 불구하고 decidedly 확실히 in terms of ~의 측면에서

수의 일치 1

1 단수 동사를 이끄는 주어

> **A** <u>One</u> of the concerns of parents with kids is safety. (단수 명사)
>
> **B** <u>Honesty</u> is the best policy. (셀 수 없는 명사)
>
> **C** <u>Protecting their human rights</u> really matters. (구)
>
> **D** <u>That she was sentenced to be guilty</u> is not true. (절)
>
> **E** <u>The burglar</u> who was caught yesterday is my neighbor. (단수 선행사–단수 명사)
>
> **F** <u>The number of exported cars</u> has steadily risen. (the number of + 명사)

2 복수 동사를 이끄는 주어

> **G** <u>The pyramids</u> built for the pharaohs of Egypt are tombs. (복수 명사)
>
> **H** <u>The employees</u> who work hard have to get paid well. (복수 선행사–복수 명사)
>
> **I** <u>The irresponsible</u> don't assess their roles frequently enough. (the + 형용사)
>
> **J** <u>A number of mountain lakes</u> are in Yosemite National Park. (a number of + 명사)

3 수식어(구/절)는 동사의 수에 영향을 미치지 않는다

> **K** The writer **born in New York** was raised by his grandmother. (분사구)
>
> **L** The common belief **that a double rainbow brings luck** is a myth. (동격절)

PRACTICE

A 어법상 틀린 부분을 바르게 고쳐 쓰시오.

1 The number of people who remains single has largely increased.

2 The fact that someone is interested in helping those people are beyond me.

3 The use of cameras and video cameras are not permitted here.

4 More important are the huge increase in parental concern about their children.

5 Humans have evolved rituals of eating, which has survived for thousands of years.

B 네모 안에서 어법에 맞는 표현으로 가장 적절한 것을 고르시오.

1 Activities which develop many of the coordination skills, aural sensitivity, responses to visual cues and symbols, and the musical understanding necessary to play an instrument is / are able to be established without instruments.

2 The idea that leaders *inherently* possess certain physical, intellectual, or personality traits that distinguish them from nonleaders seem / seems to be the foundational belief of the trait-based approach to leadership.

적용독해

1 다음 글의 밑줄 친 부분 중, 어법상 **틀린** 것은? `고1 학평 기출 응용`

When *Harry Potter and the Deathly Hallows*, the seventh and final volume of J. K. Rowling's fantasy series about the adventures of a boy wizard, ① <u>was</u> released in the United States in 2007, it sold 8.3 million copies in its first 24 hours on sale. ② <u>Isn't</u> the fact that twelve publishers declined to publish the first volume shocking? Although success is at least partly determined by intrinsic quality, it is also possible that what people come to like ③ <u>depends</u> very much on what they believe others like. In such a world, so simple ④ <u>is</u> the explanation for why a particular book becomes a hit: it sold well because lots of people bought it. Cultural artifacts such as books and movies can now 'snowball' in popularity in ways they could not a century ago, turning cultural commerce into a collection of difficult-to-predict, winner-take-all markets. Tiny differences in performance or product quality ⑤ <u>translates</u> into vast differences in payoff.

2 다음 글의 밑줄 친 부분 중, 어법상 **틀린** 것은? `고2 학평 기출 응용`

The reason why personal music players are common and people are listening to music through headphones a lot ① <u>seems</u> related to the fact that many of us are attracted to recorded music these days. Recording engineers and musicians have learned to create special effects that ② <u>tickle</u> our brains by exploiting neural circuits that evolved to discern important features of our auditory environment. These special effects are similar in principle to 3-D art, motion pictures, or visual illusions, none of which ③ <u>have</u> been around long enough for our brains to have evolved special mechanisms to perceive them. Rather, they leverage perceptual systems that ④ <u>are</u> in place to accomplish other things. Only because they use these neural circuits in novel ways ⑤ <u>is</u> 3-D art, motion pictures, and visual illusions found especially interesting. The same is true of the way that modern recordings are made.

* auditory: 청각의 ** leverage: 이용하다

---

1 volume (책의) 권, 책 wizard 마법사 decline 거절하다 intrinsic 자체의, 본질적인 depend on ~에 의존하다 artifact 가공물 popularity 인기 commerce 상업 payoff 수익, 이득

2 exploit 활용하다 neural 신경의 circuit 회로 evolve 진화하다 discern 분간하다 feature 특징 principle 원리 visual 시각의 mechanism 방법 perceive 인식하다 perceptual 지각의 novel 새로운

내용 일치

1

Lotte Laserstein에 관한 다음 글의 내용과 일치하지 <u>않는</u> 것은? `고2 학평 기출 응용`

Lotte Laserstein was born into a Jewish family in East Prussia. One of her relatives ran a private painting school, which allowed Lotte to learn painting and drawing at a young age. Later, she earned admission to the Berlin Academy of Arts and completed her master studies as one of the first women in the school. In 1928 her career skyrocketed as she gained widespread recognition, but after the seizure of power by the Nazi Party, the exhibition of her artwork was forbidden in Germany. In 1937 she emigrated to Sweden. She continued to work in Sweden but the fame she had enjoyed before was never recaptured. In her work, Lotte repeatedly portrayed Gertrud Rose, her closest friend. To Lotte, she embodied the type of the "New Woman" and was so represented.

① 어린 나이에 회화와 소묘를 배웠다.
② Berlin Academy of Arts에 입학 허가를 받았다.
③ 나치당의 권력 장악 이후 독일에서 작품 전시를 금지 당했다.
④ 이전에 누렸던 명성을 스웨덴에서 되찾았다.
⑤ 가장 가까운 친구인 Gertrud Rose를 그렸다.

2

Shah Rukh Khan에 관한 다음 글의 내용과 일치하지 <u>않는</u> 것은? `고2 학평 기출 응용`

Shah Rukh Khan is an Indian film actor and producer. Khan studied economics in college but spent much of his time at Delhi's Theatre Action Group, where he studied acting. He moved from Delhi to Mumbai to pursue a full-time career in Bollywood, which led him to great fame. Referred to in the media as the "King of Bollywood" or "King Khan," he has appeared in more than 80 Bollywood films. In 2007, Khan was awarded the rank of Officer of the Order of Arts and Letters for his contribution to cinema by the French government. He is regularly featured on lists of the most influential people in Indian culture, and in 2008, he was chosen as one of the 50 most powerful people in the world. Khan's philanthropic endeavors have provided health care and disaster relief, and he was honored with UNESCO's Pyramide con Marni award in 2011 for his support of children's education.

---

1 relative 친척 private 사적인 admission 입학 skyrocket 급상승하다, 급등하다 widespread 폭넓은 forbid 금지하다 portray 그리다
embody 구체화하다 represent 표현하다

① 인도의 영화배우이자 제작자이다.

② 대학에서 경제학을 공부했다.

③ 80편이 넘는 Bollywood 영화에 출연했다.

④ 2007년에 세계에서 가장 영향력 있는 50인 중 한 명으로 선정되었다.

⑤ 아동 교육에 대한 후원으로 2011년에 UNESCO에서 상을 받았다.

3

Ivan Turgenev에 관한 다음 글의 내용과 일치하지 <u>않는</u> 것은? `고3 학평 기출 응용`

Ivan Turgenev, the first Russian writer to be widely celebrated in the West, was born in Russia in 1818. He entered the University of Moscow in 1833, but before a year had passed he transferred to the University of St. Petersburg because of a family move. Later, he traveled to Germany, where he enrolled at the University of Berlin and studied philosophy for three years. Upon returning to St. Petersburg and failing to find an academic position, he began work as a public official there, but his interests turned more and more toward literature. After retiring from the service, he went to France. By the mid-1850s, he was spending as much time in Europe as in Russia. In August of 1860 in England, he conceived the idea for his *Fathers and Sons*; he finished the novel in July of 1861 in Russia. The book received a hostile reaction in Russia, but gained prominence in the Western world and has been a bestseller for a long time. He received an honorary degree from the University of Oxford in 1879.

① Moscow 대학 입학 후 St. Petersburg 대학으로 옮겼다.

② 독일에서 3년 동안 철학을 공부했다.

③ St. Petersburg에서 공무원으로 일한 적이 있다.

④ 소설 *Fathers and Sons*를 영국에서 완성했다.

⑤ Oxford 대학으로부터 명예 학위를 받았다.

---

2 **pursue** 수행하다　**referred to** ~라고 불리는　**be featured on** ~에 등장하다　**influential** 영향력 있는　**philanthropic** 박애(주의)의　**endeavor** 노력　**relief** 구호, 구조

3 **celebrate** 칭송하다　**transfer** 옮기다, 바꾸다　**enroll** 등록하다　**philosophy** 철학　**conceive** 생각하다　**hostile** 적대적인　**prominence** 명성　**honorary** 명예의　**degree** 학위

24강 자연

576
fertile
[fə́:rtəl]

형 비옥한, 다산의　fertility 명 비옥, 다산, 풍부
✅ 불모의 땅 : infertile/barren/sterile land

577
identify
[aidéntəfài]

동 확인하다, 식별하다, 동일시하다　identity 명 정체성
➕ ID 신분증(identification card)

578
latitude
[lǽtətjùːd]

명 위도　longitude 명 경도
seen at the extreme northern latitude 최고북위에서 관측되는

579
continent
[kántənənt]

명 대륙　continental 형 대륙의
➕ the African continent = the continent of Africa 아프리카 대륙

580
zoology
[zouálədʒi]

명 동물학　zoologist 명 동물학자　zoological 형 동물학의
Zoology is the scientific study of animals. 동물학은 동물에 관한 과학적인 연구이다.

581
density
[dénsəti]

명 밀도, 농도　dense 형 밀집한, 무성한
➕ population density 인구 밀도　traffic density 교통량

582
reproduce
[rìːprədjúːs]

동 번식하다, 복제하다, 재생하다　reproduction 명 번식, 복제, 재생
✅ 복제하다: copy, clone, duplicate, replicate

583
predator
[prédətər]

명 포식자(↔ prey), 포식동물　predatory 형 약탈하는
➕ herbivore 채식동물　carnivore 육식동물　omnivore 잡식동물

584
eradicate
[irǽdəkèit]

동 근절하다(= uproot, root out)　eradication 명 근절, 척결
eradicate illegality and corruption 부정부패를 척결하다

585
species
[spíːʃiːz]

명 종　The Origin of Species 종의 기원
✅ 종속과목강문계역: species-genus-family-order-class-phylum-kingdom-domain

586
mature
[mətjúər]

형 성숙한, 무르익은 동 성숙하다　maturity 명 성숙, 만기
➕ immature 미숙한　premature 조숙한

587
degenerate
[didʒénərèit]

동 악화하다, 퇴화하다, 전락하다 형 퇴폐적인, 타락한
The patient's health degenerated rapidly. 환자의 건강이 급속히 나빠졌다.

588

vegetation
[vèdʒitéiʃən]

명 초목, 식물　　vegetable 명 채소, 식물 인간

➕ vegetarian 채식주의자　　vegan 절대 채식주의자

589

mutation
[mju(ː)téiʃən]

명 돌연변이, 변이　　mutant 명 돌연변이종

cells affected by mutation 돌연변이에 영향을 받은 세포들

590

endanger
[indéindʒər]

동 위험에 빠뜨리다　　endangerment 명 멸종 위기의 상황

The lynx is an endangered species. 스라소니는 멸종위기종이다.

591

microscopic
[màikrəskápik]

형 아주 작은, 미시적인　　microscope 명 현미경

➕ telescope 망원경　　endoscope 내시경　　periscope 잠망경

592

distinguish
[distíŋgwiʃ]

동 구별하다, 구분하다　　distinct 형 구별되는, 독특한

Mules are genetically distinct. 노새는 유전적으로 구분된다.

593

fossil
[fásl]

명 화석, 낡은 사고/제도　　fossilized 형 화석화된

The coelacanth is a living fossil. 실러캔스는 살아있는 화석이다.

594

decompose
[dìːkəmpóuz]

동 분해되다, 부패하다(= decay)　　decomposition 명 분해, 부패

a mummy that remains undecomposed 썩지 않은 미라

595

dwell
[dwel]

동 거주하다, 서식하다　　dwell-dwelled/dwelt-dwelled/dwelt

✔ 살다: live, reside, inhabit

596

moist
[mɔist]

형 습한(= humid), 축축한, 촉촉한　　moisture 명 수분, 습기

➕ moist and damp 습하고 축축한　　hot and humid 고온다습한

597

component
[kəmpóunənt]

명 구성 요소, 성분, 부품　　componential 형 성분의

the components of a machine 기계 부품들

598

mammal
[mǽməl]

명 포유류, 포유동물　　mammalian 형 포유류의

➕ primate 영장류　　reptile 파충류　　amphibian 양서류

599

significant
[signífikənt]

형 중요한(↔ insignificant), 상당한　　signify 동 의미하다, 중요하다

✔ of+명사=형용사: of significance(중요한), of no use(쓸모없는)

600

segment
[segmént]

명 부문, 마디　동 나누다, 분할하다

The insect is segmented into head, chest, and abdomen. 곤충은 머리, 가슴, 배로 나뉜다.

PRACTICE

A 알맞은 단어를 〈보기〉에서 골라 빈칸을 채우시오.

〈보기〉	components	latitude	density	mammal	species

1 Monaco has extremely high population _____.

2 Various spider _____ are exhibited in the insect museum.

3 The bat is a flying _____ and the whale is a swimming one.

4 Lines of _____ are the imaginary horizontal lines of the earth.

5 The four _____ of soil include minerals, organic matter, water, and air.

B 빈칸에 들어갈 알맞은 표현을 고르시오.

1 The earth comprises five major oceans and seven _____.

　① fossils　　② continents　　③ predators　　④ species

2 Albinism is a kind of _____ causing the absence of pigment in the skin.

　① vegetation　　② density　　③ mutation　　④ fertility

3 The zookeeper _____(e)d each fish into two pieces to give to the seals.

　① decompose　　② mature　　③ segment　　④ reproduce

4 The results of the research are highly _____ for conserving the environment.

　① microscopic　　② componential　　③ moisturized　　④ significant

5 Organic farming strongly affects the future of the _____(e)d species.

　① degenerate　　② signify　　③ produce　　④ endanger

C 네모 안에서 문맥에 맞는 낱말로 가장 적절한 것을 고르시오.

1 As it is the latitude on the earth that largely determines the climate and length of the growing season, crops domesticated in one part of Eurasia can be transplanted across the continent with only minimal / maximal need for adaptation to the new location.

2 Zoologist John Krebs points out that deceptive signaling is, itself, an evolutionary adaptation, a trait that developed in our earliest animal ancestors, to gain survival and degenerative / reproductive benefits.

적용독해

정답 및 해설 p.69

1 다음 글의 밑줄 친 부분 중, 문맥상 낱말의 쓰임이 적절하지 <u>않은</u> 것은? 고1 학평 기출

Pests and diseases are part of nature. In the ideal system there is a natural ① <u>balance</u> between predators and pests. If the system is imbalanced, one population can ② <u>increase</u> because it is not being preyed upon by another. The aim of natural control is not to eradicate pests and diseases. It is to ③ <u>restore</u> a natural balance between pest and predator and keep pests and diseases down to an acceptable level. However, pesticides, another option to natural pest and disease control, do not ④ <u>solve</u> the pest problem. In the past 50 years, pesticide use has increased ten times while crop losses from pest damage have doubled. Here lies the reason why natural control is ⑤ <u>avoided</u> more than pesticide use.

* eradicate: 박멸하다

2 다음 글의 밑줄 친 부분 중, 문맥상 낱말의 쓰임이 적절하지 <u>않은</u> 것은? 고1 학평 기출

Some species use alarm calls to share information about potential predators. Their alarm calls seem to convey very ① <u>specific</u> information about the nature of the predator that has been detected as they become more mature. When a young vervet monkey ② <u>spots</u> a bird in the sky above it, it will give an alarm call. In this case a sort of "cough-cough" noise. At this stage, the call appears to be an innate possible-danger-above signal because it is given as a ③ <u>response</u> to any large flying object, dangerous or otherwise. But as the monkey matures, the range of stimuli that will trigger the call ④ <u>broadens</u>. Eventually the use of this alarm call will be restricted to those situations when an eagle is spotted in the skies above. Upon hearing the call the members of the group will scan the sky to locate the ⑤ <u>threat</u> and then make a dash for the cover provided by dense vegetation.

* innate: 타고난, 선천적인   ** vegetation: 초목, 식물

---

1 pest 해충   population 개체군   prey 잡아먹다   aim 목적   restore 회복하다   predator 포식자   pesticide 살충제
2 alarm 경계 신호   convey 전달하다   predator 포식자   detect 탐지하다   a sort of 일종의   mature 성숙하다   range 범위   stimulus 자극
trigger 유발하다   broaden 넓어지다   restrict 제한하다   spot 발견하다   locate 위치를 찾다   make a dash 돌진하다   dense 빽빽한

수의 일치 2

(1) 단수 대명사 it

A If my father says, **"You are good,"** **it** is a compliment to my talent.

B **The town** is rooted in **its** function as an important stop along the trading route.

C She was carrying **a newborn** and trying to take **it** to the hospital.

(2) 복수 대명사 they

D It's easy to forget that **our parents** often know better, but **they** do.

E The corporation trains **workers** to perform **their** jobs in a certain way.

F Our **emotions** are so diverse that we cannot always appreciate **them** properly.

(3) 지시대명사 that/those

G **The decrease rate** of the upper class was lower than **that** of the middle class.

H Reading lets us look beyond our own **lives**, letting us know **those** of others.

(4) 부정대명사 one/ones

I Out of all the other **desserts**, identify the **one** that you like best.

J We are more likely to know **popular people** than unpopular **ones**.

PRACTICE

A 어법상 틀린 부분을 바르게 고쳐 쓰시오.

1 As customers form routines around a product, they come to depend upon them and become less price-sensitive.

2 Things often seem at its worst just before they get better.

3 Korea has remained free of the disease in spite of their close location to these countries.

4 The difference between the number of group donors and those of individual donors was the largest in 2009.

5 Because his brother needed a football, he decided to obtain ones for him.

B 네모 안에서 어법에 맞는 표현으로 가장 적절한 것을 고르시오.

1 Imagine some mutation appears which makes animals spontaneously die at the age of 50. More than 99 percent of animals carrying this mutation will never experience its / their ill effects because they will die before it has a chance to act.

2 The technical and economic importance of the light and of the electrical system that surrounded it matches that / those of any other invention we could name, at least from the last two hundred years.

적용독해

1 다음 글의 밑줄 친 부분 중, 어법상 틀린 것은? 고2 학평 기출 응용

One of the keys to insects' successful survival in the open air lies in ① their outer covering — a hard waxy layer that helps prevent their tiny bodies from dehydrating. To take oxygen from the air, they use narrow breathing holes in the body-segments. These ② ones take in air passively and can be opened and closed as needed. Instead of blood ③ containing in vessels, they have free-flowing hemolymph, which helps keep their bodies ④ rigid, aids movement, and assists the transportation of nutrients and waste materials to the appropriate parts of the body. The nervous system is modular, which means each of the body segments has ⑤ its own individual and autonomous brain. Insect bodies are structured and function completely differently from our own.

* hemolymph: 헐림프   ** modular: 모듈식의(여러 개의 개별 단위로 되어 있는)

2 다음 글의 밑줄 친 부분 중, 어법상 틀린 것은? 고3 학평 기출

The lizards that climb walls and ceilings do not tend to fall off. But it is not because ① they have great suction — as a matter of fact, they are not really using ② them at all. Here is how the feet work: on the bottom are dozens and dozens of tiny grooves, which you can see if you have ever looked ③ closely at a lizard in a terrarium. On each of those little grooves you can see, there are dozens more that are not visible to the naked eye. And on each of those dozens of grooves ④ are hundreds, if not thousands, of hairlike bumps. Now, if you take a microscopic look at even the smoothest surface in their feet, you will see ⑤ it is covered with microscopic pits, bumps, and grooves.

* groove: 가늘고 길게 패인 곳

---

1 waxy 밀랍   dehydrate 탈수화시키다   oxygen 산소   body-segment 몸의 마디   passively 수동적으로   vessel 혈관   rigid 단단한   transportation 이동   nutrient 영양분   appropriate 적절한   individual 개별적인, 개개인의   autonomous 자율적인   structure 구조화하다

2 lizard 도마뱀   ceiling 천장   suction 흡착(력)   bottom 바닥   dozen 다수   terrarium 테라늄   naked eye 육안   hairlike 털 같은   bump 돌기   microscopic 현미경으로만 보이는, 현미경을 사용하는   smooth 매끄러운   pit 미세한 홈

1

다음 빈칸에 들어갈 말로 가장 적절한 것을 고르시오. 고1 학평 기출

Interestingly, in nature, _____. The distinction between predator and prey offers a clarifying example of this. The key feature that distinguishes predator species from prey species isn't the presence of claws or any other feature related to biological weaponry. The key feature is *the position of their eyes*. Predators evolved with eyes facing forward—which allows for binocular vision that offers accurate depth perception when pursuing prey. Prey, on the other hand, often have eyes facing outward, maximizing peripheral vision, which allows them to detect danger that may be approaching from any angle. Consistent with our place at the top of the food chain, humans have eyes that face forward. We have the ability to gauge depth and pursue our goals, but we can also miss important action on our periphery.

* depth perception: 거리 감각 **periphery: 주변

① eyes facing outward are linked with the success of hunting

② the more powerful species have a narrower field of vision

③ humans' eyes facing forward enable them to detect danger

④ eyesight is closely related to the extinction of weak species

⑤ animals use their eyesight to identify members of their species

2

다음 빈칸에 들어갈 말로 가장 적절한 것을 고르시오. 고1 학평 기출

As much as we can learn by examining fossils, it is important to remember that they seldom _____. Things only fossilize under certain sets of conditions. Modern insect communities are highly diverse in tropical forests, but the recent fossil record captures little of that diversity. Many creatures are consumed entirely or decompose rapidly when they die, so there may be no fossil record at all for important groups. It's a bit similar to a family photo album. Maybe when you were born your parents took lots of pictures, but over the years they took photographs occasionally,

---

1 **distinction** 차이, 구별 **clarify** 분명히 하다 **presence** 존재 **biological** 생물학적인 **weaponry** 무기 **forward** 앞쪽의 **binocular vision** 쌍안시, 양안시(두 눈으로 보는 것) **accurate** 정확한, 정밀한 **pursue** 쫓다, 추적하다 **outward** 바깥쪽의, 외부의 **maximize** 최대화하다 **detect** 감지하다, 찾아내다, 발견하다 **approach** 접근하다, 다가오다 **consistent with** ~와 일치하는 **food chain** 먹이 사슬 **be linked with** ~와 연결되어 있다, 관련이 있다 **eyesight** 시력, 시야 **extinction** 멸종

and sometimes they got busy and forgot to take pictures at all. Very few of us have a complete photo record of our life. Fossils are just like that. Sometimes you get very clear pictures of the past, while at other times there are big gaps, and you need to notice what they are.

*decompose: 부패하다

① tell the entire story
② require further study
③ teach us a wrong lesson
④ change their original traits
⑤ make room for imagination

3

다음 빈칸에 들어갈 말로 가장 적절한 것을 고르시오. [고1 학평 기출]

Scientists believe that the frogs' ancestors were water-dwelling, fishlike animals. The first frogs and their relatives gained the ability to come out on land and enjoy the opportunities for food and shelter there. But they _____. A frog's lungs do not work very well, and it gets part of its oxygen by breathing through its skin. But for this kind of "breathing" to work properly, the frog's skin must stay moist. And so the frog must remain near the water where it can take a dip every now and then to keep from drying out. Frogs must also lay their eggs in water, as their fishlike ancestors did. And eggs laid in the water must develop into water creatures, if they are to survive. For frogs, metamorphosis thus provides the bridge between the water-dwelling young tadpoles and the land-dwelling adults.

*metamorphosis: 탈바꿈 ** tadpole: 올챙이

① still kept many ties to the water
② had almost all the necessary organs
③ had to develop an appetite for new foods
④ often competed with land-dwelling species
⑤ suffered from rapid changes in temperature

---

2 fossil 화석 seldom 좀처럼 ~하지 않게 fossilize 화석화하다 certain 특정한, 확실한 diverse 다양한 tropical 열대의 capture 담아내다, 잡다 creature 생명체, 생물 consume 사로잡다, 소비하다 occasionally 가끔 complete 완전한 notice 인지하다, 주목하다
3 ancestor 조상 water-dwelling 물에 사는 fishlike 물고기와 같은 relative 친척 gain 얻다 opportunity 기회, 가능성 shelter 살 곳, 쉼터, 은신처 lung 폐 oxygen 산소 breathe 호흡하다 moist 촉촉한 take a dip (몸을) 잠깐 담그다, 잠깐 수영을 하다 every now and then 이따금 dry out 건조해지다 lay (알을) 낳다 land-dwelling 육지에 사는 adult 성체

과학

601 **withhold** [wiðhóuld]	图 보류하다, 억제하다, 밝히지 않다 ✅ 억제하다: hold back, contain, curb, suppress, inhibit
602 **consistently** [kənsístəntlē]	🔵 일관적으로(↔ inconsistently), 지속적으로 consistent 📄 한결같은, 일관된 consist of/in/with ~로 구성되다/~에 있다/~와 일치하다
603 **virtual** [və́:rtʃuəl]	📄 가상의, 실질적인 ➕ fictional 허구의 imaginary 가상의 fake 가짜의
604 **undo** [ʌndú:]	图 원상태로 돌리다, 원상 회복하다 What's done cannot be undone. 엎지른 물은 다시 담을 수 없다.
605 **domesticate** [dəméstəkèit]	图 길들이다, 가축화하다 domestic 📄 (동물이) 길든, 가정의, 국내의 how to domesticate wild dogs 들개를 가축화하는 법
606 **shrink** [ʃriŋk]	图 수축하다, 감소하다 shrinkage 📗 수축, 감소 ✅ 수축하다: contract, constrict, deflate
607 **phenomenon** [finámənàn]	📗 현상, 비범한 사람 pl. phenomena A rainbow is a natural phenomenon. 무지개는 자연현상이다.
608 **marvel** [má:rvəl]	📗 경이로움 图 놀라다, 경탄하다 marvelous 📄 경이로운 ✅ 경이로운: amazing, incredible, phenomenal
609 **authority** [əθɔ́:rəti]	📗 권위, 권한, 당국 authorize 图 권한을 부여하다 school/health/French authorities 학교/보건/프랑스 당국
610 **skeptical** [sképtikəl]	图 회의적인, 미심쩍은 skeptic 📗 회의론자 voice skepticism over ~에 대해 회의적인 목소리를 내다
611 **artificial** [à:rtəfíʃəl]	图 인공의, 인위적인 artificially 🔵 인위적으로 artificial satellite/intelligence/insemination 인공 위성/지능/수정
612 **scale** [skeil]	📗 규모, 등급, 척도, 비늘 图 (기준에 따라) 평가하다 a strong earthquake of the sixth degree on the seismic scale 진도 6의 강진

613

probe
[proub]

동 조사하다, 탐사하다　명 조사, 우주 탐사선

send a space probe for lunar probe 달 탐사용 탐사선을 보내다

614

friction
[fríkʃən]

명 마찰, 불화, 갈등

diplomatic/intra-party/commercial friction 외교적/당내/통상 마찰

615

simplify
[símpləfài]

동 단순화하다, 간소화하다　simplicity 명 단순함, 소박함

simplify one's explanation 설명을 평이하게 하다

616

essence
[ésəns]

명 본질, 핵심, 정수　essential 형 필수적인

Objectivity is the essence of science. 객관성은 과학의 본질이다.

617

conclude
[kənklú:d]

동 결론짓다, 종결하다, 체결하다　conclusion 명 결론, 결말

reach a conclusion 결론에 도달하다　jump to conclusions 속단하다

618

reliable
[riláiəbl]

형 신뢰할 만한(↔ unreliable), 신빙성 있는, 의지할 수 있는

rely 동 의지하다　reliance 명 의존　reliability 명 신뢰도

619

genetics
[dʒənétiks]

명 유전학, 유전적 요인　genetic 형 유전의, 유전학의　gene 명 유전자

dominant/recessive gene 우성/열성 (유전)인자

620

initiate
[iníʃièit]

동 시작하다, 일으키다　initiative 명 (새로운) 계획, 주도권

initiate a new business 새 사업을 시작하다

621

fatal
[féitəl]

형 치명적인(= deadly)　fate 명 운명

receive a fatal injury 치명상을 입다

622

expertise
[èkspəːrtíːz]

명 전문성, 전문 지식, 전문 기술　expert 명 전문가

areas of special expertise 특수 전문 분야

623

gadget
[gǽdʒit]

명 기기, 장치　gadgetry 명 기구류, 기계 장치

⊕ machinery 기계류　jewelry 보석류　weaponry 무기류

624

procedure
[prəsíːdʒər]

명 절차, 과정, 방식　proceed 동 진행하다

Installing a computer is a simple procedure. 컴퓨터를 설치하는 것은 간단한 절차입니다.

625

vacuum
[vǽkjuəm]

명 진공, 공백, 진공청소기　동 진공청소기로 청소하다

His death has left a vacuum in us. 그의 죽음은 우리에게 공백(감)을 남겼다.

PRACTICE

A 알맞은 단어를 〈보기〉에서 골라 빈칸을 채우시오.

| 〈보기〉 | undo | consistently | conclude | domesticate | withhold |

1 The jury _____(e)d that the accused was not guilty.

2 He has _____ denied the allegations during the investigation.

3 There's no way of _____ing the damage to his reputation.

4 Approximately 4,000 BCE, llamas were _____(e)d by the Incas.

5 The owner decided to _____ payment until they completed the work.

B 빈칸에 들어갈 알맞은 표현을 고르시오.

1 Air is sucked out of the waste pipe, creating a _____.

① fate   ② scale   ③ vacuum   ④ gadget

2 The police have no right to _____ into my personal life.

① rely   ② initiate   ③ marvel   ④ probe

3 The _____ for dealing with complaints needs to be simplified.

① friction   ② authority   ③ phenomenon   ④ procedure

4 Exposure to radioactivity is _____ to children and young women.

① genetic   ② fatal   ③ reliable   ④ virtual

5 Thanks to her engineering _____, she was designated as a laboratory director.

① shrinkage   ② expertise   ③ skepticism   ④ essence

C 네모 안에서 문맥에 맞는 낱말로 가장 적절한 것을 고르시오.

1 It is possible to remove an individual's willingness to do something by consistently providing rewards for the action for some time and then encouraging / withholding them.

2 While a physical newspaper requires huge printing presses and a distribution network linking trucks, shops, and ultimately newspaper sellers, in the marvelously digital world a single person can communicate with the whole world with the aid of a single computer and without / despite requiring a single tree to be cut down.

적용독해

1   다음 글의 밑줄 친 부분 중, 문맥상 낱말의 쓰임이 적절하지 <u>않은</u> 것은?   고1 학평 기출

Recent research suggests that evolving humans' relationship with dogs changed the structure of both species' brains. One of the various physical changes caused by ① <u>domestication</u> is a reduction in the size of the brain: 16 percent for horses, 34 percent for pigs, and 10 to 30 percent for dogs. This is because once humans started to take care of these animals, they ② <u>no longer</u> needed various brain functions in order to survive. Animals who were fed and protected by humans did not need many of the skills required by their wild ancestors and ③ <u>lost</u> the parts of the brain related to those capacities. A ④ <u>similar</u> process occurred for humans, who seem to have been domesticated by wolves. About 10,000 years ago, when the role of dogs was firmly established in most human societies, the human brain also ⑤ <u>expanded</u> by about 10 percent.

2   다음 글의 밑줄 친 부분 중, 문맥상 낱말의 쓰임이 적절하지 <u>않은</u> 것은?   고2 학평 기출 응용

A phenomenon in social psychology, the Pratfall Effect states that an individual's perceived attractiveness increases or decreases after he or she makes a mistake — depending on the individual's ① <u>perceived</u> competence. As celebrities are generally considered to be competent individuals, and often even presented as flawless or perfect in certain aspects, committing blunders will make one's humanness ② <u>endearing</u> to others. Basically, those who never make mistakes are perceived as being ③ <u>more</u> attractive and "likable" than those who do occasionally. Perfection, or the attribution of that quality to individuals, creates a perceived ④ <u>distance</u> that the general public cannot relate to — making those who never make mistakes perceived as being less attractive or likable. However, this can also have the ⑤ <u>opposite</u> effect — if a perceived average or less than average competent person makes a mistake, he or she will be less attractive and likable to others.

* blunder: 부주의하거나 어리석은 실수

---

1 relationship 관계 structure 구조 domestication 사육 reduction 감소 take care of ~을 돌보다 ancestor 조상 relate 관련시키다 capacity 능력 occur 나타나다 domesticate 길들이다 firmly 굳게, 확실히 establish 확립하다
2 phenomenon 현상 psychology 심리학 perceive 인지하다 attractiveness 매력 competence 능력, 재능 generally 일반적으로 flawless 흠이 없는, 완벽한 commit 저지르다 endearing 사랑을 받는, 사랑스러운 occasional 이따금, 가끔의, 때때로 attribution 속성

대동사와 접속사(병렬 구조)

(1) 대동사(일반동사 → do, be 동사 → be 동사)

> **A** Don't use your heart **to solve** the problem, use your brain **to do** it.
>
> **B** Lobsters <u>were so expensive</u>, but they <u>aren't</u> nowadays.

(2) so+대동사+주어(~도 그렇다), nor/neither+대동사+주어(~도 그렇지 않다)

> **C** As civilizations **developed**, so **did** fashions.
>
> **D** Ambulances **are** equipped with a siren device, and so **are** police cars.
>
> **E** She didn't **appreciate** his contribution nor **did** her friends.
>
> **F** He **is** not very empathetic and neither **is** his wife.

(3) 접속사의 종류와 병렬 구조

> 등위접속사: and, or, but 등
>
> **G** Mom would scrub, mop, and dust everything.
>
> 상관접속사: not A but B. both A and B. either A or B. neither A nor B, not only A but (also) B, 등
>
> **H** This book is not only useful but also amusing.
>
> (종속접속사 : 명사절 접속사 ▶p.84, 부사절 접속사 ▶p.92)

PRACTICE

A 어법상 틀린 부분을 바르게 고쳐 쓰시오.

1 Animals communicate with body language, just as humans are.

2 Recently I noticed that my kids weren't as well-behaved as they used to do.

3 Sodas with caffeine take water from the body and so are other drinks with caffeine.

4 In an emergency, you have to open the doors yourself by pushing a button or depress a lever.

5 Teachers should learn not only what to teach and how to teach.

B 네모 안에서 어법에 맞는 표현으로 가장 적절한 것을 고르시오.

1 Losing weight is hard because people usually think they burned a larger number of calories than they actually were / did and undo exercise by eating a lot of food.

2 I would like to ask for a refund of the price difference between an item offered in your retail store and the same item I bought from your website, which I believe would be a better solution to packing up this electronic gadget and ship / shipping it back to you for a full refund.

적용독해

1 다음 글의 밑줄 친 부분 중, 어법상 **틀린** 것은? [고3 학평 기출 응용]

Albert Einstein talked about what influenced his life as a scientist. He remembered seeing a pocket compass when he was five years old and ① marveling that the needle always pointed north. In that moment, Einstein recalled, he "felt something ② deeply hidden behind things." Around the age of six, Einstein began studying the violin. When after several years he recognized the mathematical structure of music, the violin became a lifelong friend of ③ his. When Einstein was ten, his family enrolled him in the Luitpold Gymnasium, where he developed a suspicion of authority that many other students ④ didn't. The trait served Einstein well later in life as a scientist. His habit of skepticism made it ⑤ easily to question many long-standing scientific assumptions.

2 다음 글의 밑줄 친 부분 중, 어법상 **틀린** 것은? [고1 학평 기출 응용]

You may have seen headlines in the news about some of the things machines powered by artificial intelligence can do. However, if you were to consider all the tasks ① that AI-powered machines could actually perform, it would be quite mind-blowing! One of the key features of artificial intelligence is that it enables machines to learn new things rather than ② requires programming specific or new tasks. Therefore, the core difference between computers of the future and ③ those of the past is that future computers will be able to learn and self-improve. In the near future, smart virtual assistants will know more about you than your closest friends and family members ④ are. Can you imagine how that might change our lives? These kinds of changes are exactly why it is so important ⑤ to recognize the implications that new technologies will have for our world.

---

1 compass 나침반 marvel 놀라다 recall 회상하다 hidden 숨겨진 mathematical 수학적인 enroll 등록하다 suspicion 의심 authority 권위 trait 특성 skepticism 회의론 assumption 가설

2 consider 고려하다, 생각하다 task 작업, 업무 perform 수행하다 mind-blowing 놀라운 feature 특징 specific 특화된, 특정한 core 핵심적인 self-improve 스스로 개선하다 virtual 가상의 assistant 비서, 보조원 recognize 인식하다, 인지하다 implication 영향, 함축, 암시

빈칸 추론 2

1 다음 빈칸에 들어갈 말로 가장 적절한 것을 고르시오. 고1 학평 기출

If you ask a physicist how long it would take a marble to fall from the top of a ten-story building, he will likely answer the question by assuming that the marble falls in a vacuum. In reality, the building is surrounded by air, which applies friction to the falling marble and slows it down. Yet the physicist will point out that the friction on the marble is so small that its effect is negligible. Assuming the marble falls in a vacuum simplifies the problem without substantially affecting the answer. Economists make assumptions for the same reason: Assumptions can simplify the complex world and make it easier to understand. To study the effects of international trade, for example, we might assume that the world consists of only two countries and that each country produces only two goods. By doing so, we can _____. Thus, we are in a better position to understand international trade in the complex world.

* negligible: 무시할 수 있는

① prevent violations of consumer rights
② understand the value of cultural diversity
③ guarantee the safety of experimenters in labs
④ focus our thinking on the essence of the problem
⑤ realize the differences between physics and economics

2 다음 빈칸에 들어갈 말로 가장 적절한 것을 고르시오. 고1 학평 기출 응용

When reading another scientist's findings, think critically about the experiment. Ask yourself: Were observations recorded during or after the experiment? Do the conclusions make sense? Can the results be repeated? Are the sources of information reliable? You should also ask if the scientist or group conducting the experiment was unbiased. The reason you should do this is to see if you have any special interest in the outcome of the experiment. For example, if a drug company pays for an experiment to test how well one of its new products works, there is a special interest involved: The drug company profits

---

1 physicist 물리학자 marble 구슬 vacuum 진공 상태 friction 마찰 point out 지적하다 simplify 단순화하다 substantially 상당히, 많이 affect 영향을 주다 consist of 구성되다

if the experiment shows that its product is effective. Therefore, the experimenters aren't
_____. They might ensure the conclusion is positive and benefits the
drug company. When assessing results, think about any biases that may be present!

① inventive
② objective
③ untrustworthy
④ unreliable
⑤ decisive

3
다음 빈칸에 들어갈 말로 가장 적절한 것을 고르시오. 고2 학평 기출 응용

The growing field of genetics is showing us what many scientists have suspected for years — foods can immediately influence the genetic blueprint. This information helps us better understand that genes are under our control and not something we must obey. Consider identical twins; both individuals are given the same genes. In mid-life, one twin develops cancer, and the other lives a long healthy life without cancer. A specific gene instructed one twin to develop cancer, but in the other the same gene did not. One possibility is that the healthy twin had a diet that turned off the cancer gene — the same gene that instructed the other person to get sick. For many years, scientists have recognized other environmental factors, such as chemical toxins (tobacco for example), can contribute to cancer through their actions on genes. The notion that _____ is relatively new.

① identical twins have the same genetic makeup
② our preference for food is influenced by genes
③ balanced diet is essential for our mental health
④ genetic engineering can cure some fatal diseases
⑤ food has a specific influence on gene expression

---

2 findings 발견, 결과 critically 비판적으로 observation 관찰 conclusion 결론, 결과 make sense 이치에 맞다 reliable 신뢰할 만한 conduct 수행하다 unbiased 치우치지 않은 outcome 결과 work 작동하다, 효과가 있다 involved 관련된 profit 이익을 보다 objective 객관적인, 목표 assess 평가하다 bias 편향, 치우침 present 존재하는
3 genetics 유전학 suspect 의구심을 가지다 genetic blueprint 유전자 청사진, 게놈 지도 identical twin 일란성 쌍둥이 mid-life 중년 instruct 명령하다, 지시하다 possibility 가능성 turn off ~을 차단하다, ~을 끄다 recognize 인정하다, 인지하다 toxin 독소 contribute to ~의 원인이 되다, ~에 기여하다 relatively 비교적 preference 선호(도) cure 치료하다 fatal 치명적인

26강 환경

626
environment
[inváiərənmənt]

명 환경, 상황　environmental 형 환경의

✅ 환경: surroundings, circumstances

627
uphold
[ʌphóuld]

동 수호하다, 옹호하다, 확정하다

✅ (약속·법·질서 등을) 지키다: keep, obey, follow

628
climate
[kláimit]

명 기후, 기후대, 풍토　climatic 형 기후의

temperate/tropical/frigid climate 온대/열대/한대 기후

629
marine
[mərí:n]

형 해양의, 해상의 명 해병대원　maritime 형 바다의, 해양의

marine pollution/transportation/corps 해양오염/해운/해병대

630
ecosystem
[ékousìstəm]

명 생태계　ecology 명 생태학　eco-friendly 형 친환경적인

A water dam threatens the ecosystem. 댐은 생태계를 위협한다.

631
acute
[əkjú:t]

형 예리한(↔ blunt), 급성의(↔ chronic), 심한

✅ (감각·판단 등이) 예리한: keen, sharp

632
disturbance
[distə́:rbəns]

명 장애, 방해, 교란　disturb 동 방해하다

Alien species disturb the ecosystem. 외래종은 생태계를 교란한다.

633
disaster
[dizǽstər]

명 재난, 재해　disastrous 형 큰 피해를 초래하는

✅ 재난: accident, catastrophe, calamity

634
variation
[vɛ̀əriéiʃən]

명 변화/변동, 변형/변이, 차이　variable 명 변수

variation trend of rainfall 강우량의 변동 추이

635
toxic
[táksik]

형 유독한, 독성이 있는　toxin 명 독소

Toxic gases sprayed everywhere. 유독 가스가 사방으로 뿜어져 나왔다.

636
concentration
[kànsəntréiʃən]

명 집중, 농도　concentrate 동 집중하다, 농축되다

concentration toward the metropolitan area 대도시로의 집중

637
capacity
[kəpǽsəti]

명 능력, 용량, 수용력　capacious 형 (용량이) 큰

This room has a seating capacity of 10. 이 방은 10인의 좌석이 있다.

638

trigger
[trígər]

동 유발하다, 촉발시키다　명 방아쇠, 자극

trigger a rise in the wheat price 밀 가격의 인상을 유발하다

639

tropic
[trɑ́pik]

명 열대지방(= the tropics), 회귀선　tropical 형 열대의

Tropic of Cancer and Tropic of Capricorn 북회귀선과 남회귀선

640

degrade
[digréid]

동 저하하다, 퇴화하다, 격하시키다　degradation 명 분해, 저하, 오염

➕ biodegradable 생물 분해성의　photodegradable 광분해성의

641

particle
[pɑ́ːrtikl]

명 입자, 작은 조각　particulate 명 미립자

➕ dust particles and respiratory diseases 먼지 입자와 호흡기질환

642

extinction
[ikstíŋkʃən]

명 멸종, 소멸　extinct 형 멸종된　extinguish 동 진화하다

go extinct / sour / insane 멸종되다 / 상하다 / 실성하다

643

captive
[kǽptiv]

명 포로(↔ captor), 포획된 동물　형 포획된

➕ capture 잡다, 포착하다　captivate 마음을 사로잡다

644

tremendous
[triméndəs]

형 엄청난(= huge), 대단한, 거대한

have a tremendous effect on ~에 엄청난 영향을 미치다

645

threat
[θret]

명 위협, 위협하는 것　threaten 동 위협하다

threaten the natural environment 자연환경을 위협하다

646

organism
[ɔ́ːrgənìzəm]

명 생물, 생명체, 유기체

living organisms in the Antarctic 남극의 생명체

647

crisis
[krɑ́isəs]

명 위기, 사태

✔ sis(단수) → ses(복수) : crises, oases, bases, analyses

648

thrive
[θraiv]

동 번창하다, 번성하다(= flourish)　thrifty 형 절약하는, 무성하게 자라는

thrive / decline for three generations 3대가 번창하다 / 망하다

649

pollute
[pəljúːt]

동 오염시키다　polluted 형 오염된　pollution 명 오염, 공해

✔ 오염: contamination, degradation

650

counterpart
[káuntərpɑ̀ːrt]

명 상대, 상대방, 관계자

The president met his French counterpart. 대통령은 프랑스측 상대를 만났다.

PRACTICE

정답 및 해설 p.75

A 알맞은 단어를 〈보기〉에서 골라 빈칸을 채우시오.

> 〈보기〉   pollution   thrive   ecosystem   counterpart   extinction

1 Biodiversity is also important in marine _____(e)s.

2 Illegal fishing threatened minke whales with _____.

3 European summits discussed RE 100 with their Asian _____(e)s.

4 Most plants _____ best in sunny and watery conditions.

5 The _____ of our rivers by factories and farms is increasingly serious.

B 빈칸에 들어갈 알맞은 표현을 고르시오.

1 Pollution in the ocean poses a _____ to fish.

① particle   ② threat   ③ capacity   ④ variation

2 Due to a nuclear accident, Fukushima was declared a _____ area.

① variation   ② capacity   ③ climate   ④ disaster

3 The space for children to play in should be _____ friendly.

① tremendously   ② tropically   ③ environmentally   ④ acutely

4 All countries are responsible for _____ing international law.

① threaten   ② trigger   ③ disturb   ④ uphold

5 In August, many people were stung by jellyfish during _____ activities.

① acute   ② capable   ③ crisis   ④ marine

C 네모 안에서 문맥에 맞는 낱말로 가장 적절한 것을 고르시오.

1 How people behave often depends on what others do. For example, if most of my fellow citizens did not pay their green tax, there would be strong pressure for an amnesty for such offenders, which would increase / decrease my incentive to pay my environmental taxes too.

2 Climate-driven disturbances are affecting the world's coastal marine ecosystems more frequently and with greater intensity, but there are also many instances where marine ecosystems show remarkable deterioration / resilience to acute climatic events.

적용독해

1 다음 글의 밑줄 친 부분 중, 문맥상 낱말의 쓰임이 적절하지 <u>않은</u> 것은? **고1 학평 기출**

Detailed study over the past two or three decades is showing that the complex forms of natural systems are essential to their functioning. The attempt to ① <u>straighten</u> rivers and give them regular cross-sections is perhaps the most disastrous example of this form-and-function relationship. The natural river has a very ② <u>irregular</u> form: it curves a lot, spills across floodplains, and leaks into wetlands, giving it an ever-changing and incredibly complex shoreline. This allows the river to ③ <u>prevent</u> variations in water level and speed. Pushing the river into tidy geometry ④ <u>destroys</u> functional capacity and results in disasters like the Mississippi floods of 1927 and 1993 and, more recently, the unnatural disaster of Hurricane Katrina. A $50 billion plan to "let the river loose" in Louisiana recognizes that the ⑤ <u>controlled</u> Mississippi is washing away twenty-four square miles of that state annually.

* geometry: 기하학

2 다음 글의 밑줄 친 부분 중, 문맥상 낱말의 쓰임이 적절하지 <u>않은</u> 것은? **고3 학평 기출**

Not many years ago, schoolchildren were taught that carbon dioxide is the naturally occurring lifeblood of plants, just as oxygen is ours. Today, children are more likely to think of carbon dioxide as a ① <u>poison</u>. That's because the amount of carbon dioxide in the atmosphere has ② <u>increased</u> substantially over the past one hundred years, from about 280 parts per million to 380. But what people don't know is that the carbon dioxide level some 80 million years ago — back when our mammalian ancestors were evolving — was at least 1,000 parts per million. In fact, that is the ③ <u>concentration</u> of carbon dioxide you regularly breathe if you work in a new energy-efficient office building, for that is the level established by the engineering group that sets standards for heating and ventilation systems. So not only is carbon dioxide plainly not ④ <u>nontoxic</u>, but changes in carbon dioxide levels don't necessarily mirror human activity. Nor has atmospheric carbon dioxide necessarily been the ⑤ <u>trigger</u> for global warming historically.

---

1 detailed 상세한   cross-section 횡단면   spill 넘치다   floodplain 범람원   leak 새다   shoreline 강가   square mile 제곱마일
2 carbon dioxide 이산화탄소   occur 발생하다   lifeblood 생명   atmosphere 대기   substantially 상당히, 많이   ancestor 조상   concentration 농도   establish 설정하다   ventilation 환기

가정법 1

① 가정법 과거: 현재 사실의 반대(~한다면, …할 텐데)

> If + S + 과거동사~, S + would/could/should/might + 동사원형
>
> **A** If I **had** enough money, I **would go** around the world.
>   = As I don't have enough money, I can't go around the world.

② 가정법 과거완료: 과거 사실의 반대(~했다면, …했을 텐데)

> If + S + had p.p.~, S + would/could/should/might + have p.p.
>
> **B** If he **had studied** harder, he **could have succeeded**.
>   = As he didn't study harder, he couldn't succeed.

③ 명사를 이끄는 가정법 과거(~가 없다면, …할 텐데)

> If it were not for
> Were it not for + 명사, S + would/could/should/might + 동사원형
>
> **C** If it **were not** for water, we **wouldn't be** alive.

④ 명사를 이끄는 가정법 과거완료(~가 없었다면, …했을 텐데)

> If it had not been for
> Had it not been for + 명사, S + would/could/should/might + have p.p.
>
> **D** If it **had not been** for his help, I **couldn't have finished** it.

PRACTICE

A 밑줄 친 부분을 어법에 맞게 고쳐 쓰시오.

1 If they <u>lose</u> their jobs, they would not be able to survive.

2 If you had turned a light toward Mars that day, it would <u>reach</u> it in 3 minutes.

3 <u>Have</u> we not been so tired, we would have gone out in the morning.

4 If it were not for you, my life <u>will</u> be meaningless.

5 Had it not been for the WWF's help, whales might <u>become</u> extinct.

B 네모 안에서 어법에 맞는 표현으로 가장 적절한 것을 고르시오.

1 If the obese individual who has successfully gone through disease screening procedures and has gotten medical treatment for a diagnosed condition is / were lured back to his high caloric diet, he would be as much of a failure as if he never had been sold on the need to lose and control his weight.

2 In the past, humans in the tropics didn't know that pathogen density is much higher in the tropics than it is in temperate and cold climates. If they had learned that when they interacted with other groups that tended to get sick, they would stop / have stopped doing it.

* pathogen: 병원균

1 다음 글의 밑줄 친 부분 중, 어법상 틀린 것은? 〔고1 학평 기출 응용〕

Plastic is extremely slow to degrade and tends to float, which allows ① it to travel in ocean currents for thousands of miles. Most plastics break down into smaller and smaller pieces when exposed to ultraviolet (UV) light, ② forming microplastics. These microplastics are very difficult to measure once they are small enough to pass through the nets typically used to collect ③ them. Their impacts on the marine environment and food webs are still poorly understood. These tiny particles are known to be eaten by various animals and to get into the food chain. Because most of the plastic particles in the ocean ④ is so small, there is no practical way to clean up the ocean. We would have to filter enormous amounts of water if we ⑤ wanted to collect a relatively large amount of plastic.

* degrade: 분해되다

2 다음 글의 밑줄 친 부분 중, 어법상 틀린 것은? 〔고1 학평 기출 응용〕

For species approaching extinction, zoos can act as a last chance for survival. Recovery programs are established to coordinate the efforts of field conservationists and wildlife authorities. As populations of those species diminish ① it is not unusual for zoos to start captive breeding programs. If it were not for captive breeding programs, there ② would have been no way to protect against extinction. In some cases captive-bred individuals may be released back into the wild, supplementing wild populations. This is most successful in situations ③ where individuals are at greatest threat during a particular life stage. For example, turtle eggs may be removed from high-risk locations until after they hatch. This may increase the number of turtles that ④ survive to adulthood. If crocodile programs hadn't also been successful in protecting eggs and hatchlings, such tremendous hatchlings would not ⑤ have been released once they were better equipped to protect themselves.

* captive breeding: 포획 사육   ** hatch: 부화하다

---

1 extremely 매우 ocean current 해류 break down 분해되다 expose 노출시키다 tiny 아주 작은 particle 입자, 조각 relatively 비교적
2 extinction 멸종 recovery 회복 coordinate 통합하다 authority 당국 diminish 감소하다 unusual 드문 against ~에 맞서 release 방생하다, 풀어놓다 supplement 보충하다 tremendous 많은 equip 갖추다

빈칸 추론 3

1 다음 빈칸에 들어갈 말로 가장 적절한 것을 고르시오. `고1 학평 기출 응용`

Some deep-sea organisms are known to use bioluminescence as a lure, to attract prey with a little glow imitating the movements of their favorite fish, or like fireflies, as a sexual attractant to find mates. While there are many possible evolutionary theories for the survival value of bioluminescence, one of the most fascinating is to _____. The color of almost all bioluminescent molecules is blue-green, the same color as the ocean above. By self-glowing blue-green, the creatures no longer cast a shadow or create a silhouette, especially when viewed from below against the brighter waters above. Rather, by glowing themselves, they can blend into the sparkles, reflections, and scattered blue-green glow of sunlight or moonlight. If they didn't make their light, their goal of being un-seen would not be attained.

* bioluminescence: 생물 발광   ** lure: 가짜 미끼

① send a signal for help
② threaten enemies nearby
③ lift the veil of hidden prey
④ create a cloak of invisibility
⑤ serve as a navigation system

2 다음 빈칸에 들어갈 말로 가장 적절한 것을 고르시오. `고1 학평 기출 응용`

Researchers are working on a project that asks coastal towns how they are preparing for rising sea levels. Some towns have risk assessments; some towns even have a plan. But it's a rare town that is actually carrying out a plan. One reason we've failed to act on climate change is the common belief that _____. For decades, climate change was a prediction about the future. If scientists had not talked about it in the future tense, they would have coped with climate change better. Unfortunately, this became a habit in that even today many scientists still use the future tense, even though we know that a climate crisis is ongoing. Scientists also often focus on regions most

---

1 **organism** 유기체, 생물   **lure** 가짜 미끼   **imitate** 모방하다   **attractant** 유인 물질   **fascinate** 흥미를 끌다   **molecule** 분자   **above** 위쪽에   **silhouette** 실루엣   **below** 아래에   **blend** 섞다   **reflection** 반사   **attain** (목적을) 이루다, 달성하다

affected by the crisis, such as Bangladesh or the West Antarctic Ice Sheet, which for most Americans are physically remote.

① it is not related to science
② it is far away in time and space
③ energy efficiency matters the most
④ careful planning can fix the problem
⑤ it is too late to prevent it from happening

3 다음 빈칸에 들어갈 말로 가장 적절한 것을 고르시오. 고1 학평 기출 응용

Our homes aren't just ecosystems, they're unique ones, hosting species that are adapted to indoor environments and pushing evolution in new directions. Indoor microbes, insects, and rats have all evolved the ability to survive our chemical attacks, developing resistance to antibacterials, insecticides, and poisons. German cockroaches are known to have developed a distaste for glucose, which is commonly used as bait in roach traps. Had it not been for this adaptation, some indoor insects, which have fewer opportunities to feed than their outdoor counterparts, couldn't have developed the ability to survive when food is limited. Dunn and other ecologists have suggested that more species will _____ as the planet becomes more developed and more urban. Over a long enough time period, indoor living could drive our evolution, too. Perhaps my indoorsy self represents the future of humanity.

* glucose: 포도당 ** bait: 미끼

① produce chemicals to protect themselves
② become extinct with the destroyed habitats
③ evolve the traits they need to thrive indoors
④ compete with outside organisms to find their prey
⑤ break the boundaries between wildlife and humans

----

2 coastal 해안가의 prepare 대비하다 assessment 평가 climate 기후 prediction 예측 tense 시제 crisis 위기 region 지역 West Antarctic Ice Sheet 서남극 빙상 remote 먼, 먼 곳의

3 host 수용하다 adapt 적응하다 indoor 실내의 microbe 미생물 insect 곤충 chemical 화학적 antibacterials 항균제 insecticides 살충제 cockroach 바퀴벌레 distaste 혐오감 roach 바퀴벌레

27강 건강 · 의료

651
medicine
[médisin]

명 의학, 약품(= medication)   medical 형 의학의, 의료의
✔ 약: drug, remedy, cure, pill, tablet(정제), capsule(캡슐)

652
potassium
[pətǽsiəm]

명 칼륨   cf. potassium/sodium chloride 염화칼륨/염화나트륨
Bananas are potassium-rich. 바나나는 칼륨이 풍부하다.

653
absorb
[əbsɔ́:rb]

동 흡수하다(= soak), 감안하다   absorption 명 흡수, 몰두
be absorbed into blood 혈액 내에 흡수되다

654
elastic
[ilǽstik]

형 탄력 있는, 신축적인   elasticity 명 탄성
Collagen keeps your skin elastic. 콜라겐은 피부 탄력을 유지시킨다.

655
practice
[prǽktis]

동 연습하다, 훈련하다, 개업하다 명 관행, 연습, 실습, 개업
a medical practitioner 개업 의사

656
deliberately
[dilíbəritli]

부 의도적으로, 고의로   deliberate 형 의도적인 동 숙고하다
✔ 의도적으로: intentionally, by intention, on purpose

657
epidemic
[èpidémik]

명 전염병, 유행병   epidemically 부 유행병처럼
➕ food poisoning 식중독   hand, foot, and mouth disease 수족구병

658
disorder
[disɔ́:rdər]

명 질환, 장애, 무질서(↔ order)   disorderly 형 무질서한
✔ 질병: disease, condition, illness, malady

659
release
[rilí:s]

동 발표하다, 개봉하다, 출시하다, 방출하다, 석방하다, 면제하다
➕ release date 출시일, 개봉일, 발매일

660
organ
[ɔ́:rgən]

명 장기, 기관   organic 형 유기의, 유기적인   organism 명 유기체, 생물
➕ five viscera 오장(liver, heart, spleen, lung, kidney)

661
circulate
[sə́:rkjəlèit]

동 순환하다, 유통되다, 퍼지다   circulation 명 순환
➕ circulatory system 순환계

662
deprive
[dipráiv]

동 빼앗다, 박탈하다   deprivation 명 박탈
deprive/rob/strip/relieve A of B: A에게서 B를 빼앗다/강탈하다/박탈하다/없애다

663
mediate
[míːdièit]

동 중재하다, 조정하다　　mediator 명 중재자

mediate between both parties 양측을 중재하다

664
treatment
[tríːtmənt]

명 치료, 처리, 대우　　treat 동 치료하다, 처리하다, 대우하다

receive emergency treatment 응급 조치를 받다

665
surgical
[sɔ́ːrdʒikəl]

형 외과의, 수술의　　surgery 명 외과, 수술　　surgeon 명 외과의사

⊕ surgical knife 메스　　plaster cast 깁스

666
pharmacy
[fáːrməsi]

명 약국, 약품, 약학　　pharmaceutical 형 제약의, 약학의

college of pharmacy / medicine 약대 / 의대

667
mortal
[mɔ́ːrtəl]

형 죽음을 면할 수 없는(↔ immortal) 명 인간

⊕ mortality rate 사망률　　mortuary 영안실

668
risky
[ríski]

형 위험한　　risk 명 위험

✔ 위험: danger, hazard, peril, jeopardy

669
optimistic
[ùptəmístik]

형 낙관적인, 낙천적인　　optimism 명 낙관론, 낙천주의

⊕ pessimism 비관론　　nihilism 허무주의　　egoism 이기주의

670
addiction
[ədíkʃən]

명 중독　　addict 동 중독되다

addicted to online games 온라인 게임에 중독된

671
sanitary
[sǽnitèri]

형 위생의, 위생적인　　sanitation 명 위생

⊕ hygiene 위생　　dental hygienist 치위생사

672
obese
[oubíːs]

형 비만의　　obesity 명 비만

⊕ fat 뚱뚱한　　overweight 과체중의　　chubby 통통한

673
diagnose
[dáiəgnòus]

동 진단하다, 진단을 내리다　　diagnosis 명 진단

misdiagnose my disease as TB 내 질병을 결핵으로 오진하다

674
vessel
[vésəl]

명 (혈)관, 선박(= boat)

⊕ artery 동맥　　vein 정맥　　capillary 모세 혈관

675
transplant
[trænsplǽnt]

동 이식하다 명 이식

⊕ organ / hair transplant 장기 / 모발 이식　　dental / breast implant 치아 이식 / 가슴 성형

PRACTICE

A 알맞은 단어를 〈보기〉에서 골라 빈칸을 채우시오.

| 〈보기〉 | deliberate | risky | optimistic | elastic | sanitary |

1 Doctors say that it's too _____ to try and operate.

2 Over time, a rubber band will become less and less _____.

3 It is believed that a(n) _____ attitude leads to the release of serotonin.

4 The governor's speech enraged many citizens, but it wasn't _____.

5 The municipal authorities used a rating system to improve _____ conditions in restaurants.

B 빈칸에 들어갈 알맞은 표현을 고르시오.

1 If the brain is _____(e)d of oxygen, it stops working.

① addict　　　② mediate　　　③ release　　　④ deprive

2 The patient was wrongly _____(e)d with lung cancer.

① absorb　　　② deprive　　　③ diagnose　　　④ circulate

3 The number of the clinically _____ has increased in the younger generation.

① medical　　　② obese　　　③ elastic　　　④ surgical

4 Hardening of the blood _____ can cause diabetes or high blood pressure.

① treatment　　　② organ　　　③ vessel　　　④ medicine

5 The doors and windows should be open often to allow the air to _____.

① mediate　　　② absorb　　　③ release　　　④ circulate

C 네모 안에서 문맥에 맞는 낱말로 가장 적절한 것을 고르시오.

1 The ability to perform heart transplants was linked to the development of respirators, which could save many lives, but not all those whose hearts kept beating ever recovered any other significant functions. In some cases, their brains had ceased / adhered to function altogether.

2 By dismissing non-Western scientific paradigms as inferior at best and inaccurate at worst, the most rigid members of the conventional medical research community try to take / counter the threat that alternative therapies and research pose to their work, their well-being, and their worldviews.

1 다음 글의 밑줄 친 부분 중, 문맥상 낱말의 쓰임이 적절하지 <u>않은</u> 것은? `고1 학평 기출 응용`

What if fertilizers that prevent the uptake of nutrients into the plant and lead to the ① <u>reduction</u> of minerals in our food were not used? What if the use of pesticides that kill off beneficial bacteria, earthworms, and bugs in the soil that create many of the essential nutrients in the first place were ② <u>prohibited</u>? Fertilizing crops with nitrogen and potassium has led to declines in magnesium, zinc, iron and iodine. For example, there has been on average about a 30% decline in the magnesium content of wheat. This is partly due to potassium being a blocker against magnesium ③ <u>release</u> by plants. Lower magnesium levels in soil also occur with acidic soils and around 70% of the farmland on earth is now acidic. Thus, the overall characteristics of soil determine the ④ <u>accumulation</u> of minerals in plants. Indeed, nowadays our soil is less healthy and so are the plants ⑤ <u>grown</u> on it.

* pesticide: 살충제

2 다음 글의 밑줄 친 부분 중, 문맥상 낱말의 쓰임이 적절하지 <u>않은</u> 것은? `고3 학평 기출 응용`

The old maxim "I'll sleep when I'm dead" is unfortunate. If you adopted this mind-set, you would be dead sooner and the quality of that life would be ① <u>worse</u>. The elastic band of sleep deprivation can stretch only so far before it snaps. Sadly, human beings are in fact the only species that will deliberately deprive themselves of sleep without ② <u>legitimate</u> gain. Every component of wellness, and countless seams of societal fabric, are being ③ <u>eroded</u> by our costly state of sleep neglect: human and financial alike. So much so that the World Health Organization (WHO) has now declared a sleep loss epidemic throughout industrialized nations. It is no ④ <u>coincidence</u> that countries where sleep time has declined most dramatically over the past century, such as the US, the UK, Japan, and South Korea, and several in Western Europe, are also those suffering the greatest ⑤ <u>decline</u> in rates of physical diseases and mental disorders.

---

1 fertilizer 비료 uptake 흡수 reduction 감소 beneficial 이로운 soil 토양 prohibit 금지하다 nitrogen 질소 potassium 칼륨 decline 감소하다 zinc 아연 iodine 요오드 on average 평균적으로 wheat 밀 acidic 산성의 accumulation 축적 indeed 실제로
2 maxim 격언, 금언 unfortunate 유감스러운 mind-set 사고방식 elastic 고무로 된, 탄력 있는 deprivation 부족, 박탈 stretch 늘어나다 snap 툭 끊어지다 deliberately 의도적으로 legitimate 합당한 component (구성) 요소 wellness 건강 seam 이음매, 접합선 fabric (사회의) 구조, 직물 erode 약화시키다, 침식하다 so much so that ~할 정도이다 declare 선포하다 epidemic 유행병, 급속한 유행 coincidence 우연의 일치 mental disorder 정신 질환

가정법 2

(1) otherwise 가정법

> **A** Laziness **is** a bad trait in people who **could otherwise be** successful. (가정법 과거)
>
> **B** Thankfully, she **gave** me blankets, **otherwise** I **would have frozen** to death. (가정법 과거완료)

(2) wish 가정법

> **C** I **wish** I **had** a movie ticket now. (가정법 과거)
>
> **D** I **wish** I **had studied** harder when young. (가정법 과거완료)

(3) 기타 가정법

> **E** She talks **as if** she **were** a judge. (as if 가정법)
>
> **F** She talks **as though** she **had witnessed** the accident. (as though 가정법)
>
> **G** **What** (would happen) **if** you **had** triplets? (what if 가정법)

(4) 당위동사＋(that)＋S＋(should)＋동사원형: ~해야 한다고 …하다

> suggest, propose, insist, require, demand, advise, recommend, order 등
>
> **H** The doctor **recommended** that the patient (should) **avoid** sugary food. (당위성)
>
> *cf.* They **insisted** that the accident **had taken** place on the crosswalk. (단순 사실 전달)

PRACTICE

A 밑줄 친 부분을 어법에 맞게 고쳐 쓰시오.

1 Refrigerants preserve large amounts of food that might otherwise <u>have spoiled</u>.

2 I had to run at full speed toward the bus stop, otherwise, I would <u>miss</u> the bus.

3 I'm so upset whenever she lies to me. I wish she would no longer <u>have lied</u>.

4 I wish he <u>studied</u> hard in his school days.

5 The judge ordered that the criminal <u>was</u> sentenced to life imprisonment.

B 네모 안에서 어법에 맞는 표현으로 가장 적절한 것을 고르시오.

1 The state can regulate the private sector in order to account for the external costs companies would otherwise ⎡impose / have imposed⎤ on the public, such as pollution, and it can invest in public goods with little market potential, such as basic scientific research or the development of drugs.

2 Set up in 1965, the Harvard Brain Death Committee recommended that the absence of all "discernible central nervous system activity" ⎡be / is⎤ a new criterion for death, and the recommendation began a new era of medicine since its adoption in almost every country.

적용독해

1 다음 글의 밑줄 친 부분 중, 어법상 **틀린** 것은? 고1 학평 기출 응용

Bad lighting can increase stress on your eyes, as can light that is too bright, or light that shines directly into your eyes. Fluorescent lighting can also be tiring ① <u>as</u> is a flashlight in the dark. What you may not appreciate is ② <u>that</u> the quality of light may also be important. Most people are happiest in bright sunshine, which would otherwise not ③ <u>give</u> us a feeling of emotional well-being if not for the associated release of chemicals in the body. Artificial light, which typically contains only a few wavelengths of light, ④ <u>do</u> not seem to have the same effect on mood that sunlight has. To find the effect of light on improving the quality of your working environment, experts advise that you ⑤ <u>experiment</u> with working by a window or using full spectrum bulbs in your desk lamp.

* fluorescent lighting: 형광등

2 다음 글의 밑줄 친 부분 중, 어법상 **틀린** 것은? 고1 학평 기출 응용

It is widely believed that certain herbs somehow magically improve the work of certain organs, and "cure" specific diseases as a result. Such statements are unscientific and groundless. Sometimes herbs appear to work, since they tend to increase your blood circulation in an aggressive attempt by your body to eliminate them from your system. A temporary feeling of a high makes it ① <u>seem</u> as if your health condition has improved. Also, herbs can have a placebo effect, just like any other method, thus helping you feel better. Whatever the case, it is your body ② <u>that</u> has the intelligence to regain health, and not the herbs. How ③ <u>could</u> herbs have the intelligence needed to direct your body into getting healthier? That is impossible. ④ <u>Trying</u> to imagine how herbs might come into your body and intelligently fix your problems, and you will see how impossible it seems. Otherwise, it ⑤ <u>would mean</u> that herbs are more intelligent than the human body, which is truly hard to believe.

* placebo effect: 위약 효과

---

1 directly 직접적으로　appreciate 알고 있다　release 분비　artificial 인공의　wavelength 파장　expert 전문가　bulb 전구
2 certain 어떤, 특정한　organ 장기　cure 고치다, 치료하다　specific 특정한　statement 진술　groundless 근거 없는　circulation 순환
aggressive 공격적인　eliminate 제거하다　temporary 일시적으로　regain 되찾다　direct 어떤 방향으로 향하게 하다　imagine 상상하다

무관한 문장

1 다음 글에서 전체 흐름과 관계 없는 문장은? 고2 학평 기출 응용

In general, there are two major styles of practice when it comes to medicine. In the past, the relationship between the doctors and patients was mostly paternalistic. ① In this type of relationship, the doctor told what needed to be done, and the patient followed it without asking a lot of questions, even though patients wished to ask more. ② As this style of medicine that allows only for one-way communication slowly goes out of favor with the general public, the other style of medical practice (the informative style) is gradually taking hold as the more common type of doctor-patient relationship. ③ Many researchers insist that this paternalistic style be introduced to effectively improve care for patients. ④ The doctor's task in this case is not to tell what to do but to educate the patient about various treatment options. ⑤ Ultimately, the doctor allows his patients to reach an informed decision about their own health conditions.

* paternalistic: 가부장적인

2 다음 글에서 전체 흐름과 관계 없는 문장은? 고2 학평 기출 응용

Nurses hold a pivotal position in the mental health care structure and are placed at the centre of the communication network, partly because of their high degree of contact with patients, but also because they have well-developed relationships with other professionals. ① Because of this, nurses play a crucial role in interdisciplinary communication. ② They have a mediating role between the various groups of professionals and the patient and carer. ③ Mental healthcare professionals are legally bound to protect the privacy of their patients, so they may be, rather than unwilling, unable to talk about care needs. ④ This involves translating communication between groups into language that is acceptable and comprehensible to people who have different ways of understanding mental health problems. ⑤ This is a highly sensitive and skilled task, requiring that a nurse have a high level of attention to alternative views and a high level of understanding of communication.

---

1 practice 진료, 의사의 의료 행위, 개업 medicine 의료, 의학 relationship 관계 patient 환자 out of favor with ~의 총애를 잃은, ~의 눈 밖에 난 take hold 정착되다 ultimately 최종적으로

2 pivotal 중추적인 structure 체계 centre 중심 degree 정도 contact 접촉 crucial 중요한 interdisciplinary 학제 간의(여러 학문 분야가 관련된) mediate 중개하다 legally 법적으로 be bound to (법·의무상) ~해야 하다 privacy 사생활 unwilling 비자발적인, 꺼리는 translate ~을 번역하다 comprehensible 이해 가능한 sensitive 민감한

3

다음 글에서 전체 흐름과 관계 <u>없는</u> 문장은? `고2 학평 기출 응용`

From the earliest times, healthcare services have been recognized to have two equal aspects, namely clinical care and public healthcare. ① In classical Greek mythology, the god of medicine, Asklepios, had two daughters, Hygiea and Panacea: The former was the goddess of preventive health and wellness, or hygiene, and the latter the goddess of treatment and curing. ② In modern times, the societal ascendancy of medical professionalism has caused treatment of sick patients to overshadow those preventive healthcare services provided by the less heroic figures of sanitary engineers, biologists, and governmental public health officers. ③ Nevertheless, the quality of health that human populations enjoy is attributable less to surgical dexterity, innovative pharmaceutical products, and bioengineered devices than to the availability of public sanitation, sewage management, and services which control the pollution of the air, drinking water, urban noise. ④ Public healthcare services focus mainly on treatment and surgery after disease, which would otherwise not reduce high mortality rate. ⑤ The human right to the highest attainable standard of health depends on public healthcare services no less than on the skills and equipment of doctors and hospitals.

* ascendancy: 우세 ** dexterity: 기민함

---

3 mythology 신화 the former 전자 hygiene 위생 the latter 후자 treatment 치료 overshadow 가리다 sanitary 위생의 governmental 정부의 nevertheless 그럼에도 불구하고 attributable ~에 기인하는 surgical 수술의 pharmaceutical 제약의 bioengineered 생체공학적 availability 이용 가능성 sewage 하수 mortality rate 사망률 attainable 달성 가능한 standard 수준 depend on ~에 달려있다 equipment 장비

28강 정치·법

676

investigate
[invéstəgèit]

동 조사하다, 수사하다 investigation 명 조사, 연구, 수사
✔ 연구자: examiner, researcher, surveyor, investigator

677

tariff
[tǽrif]

명 관세 eliminate import tariffs 수입 관세를 철폐하다
➕ tax-free (부가가치세의) 면세 duty-free (모든 세금의) 면세

678

disperse
[dispə́:rs]

동 해산시키다(= scatter), 보급하다, 퍼뜨리다
The crowd slowly began to disperse. 군중은 서서히 흩어지기 시작했다.

679

violate
[váiəlèit]

동 위반하다, 침해하다 violation 명 위반, 침해
break/violate/breach the law 법을 어기다

680

security
[sikjú(:)ərəti]

명 안전, 안정, 안보, 보안 secure 형 안전한 동 보장하다
➕ the UN Security Council 유엔 안전보장 이사회

681

alliance
[əláiəns]

명 동맹, 연합, 협력 ally 동 동맹하다
The Allied Forces bombarded Germany. 연합군은 독일을 폭격했다.

682

temporary
[témpərèri]

형 일시적인(↔ permanent), 임시의 temporize 동 시간을 끌다, 임시 변동하다
The action is just a temporary solution. 그 조치는 임시방편이다.

683

exploit
[iksplɔ́it]

동 활용하다, 착취하다 exploitation 명 개발, 착취
✔ 활용하다: use, make use of, utilize, avail oneself of

684

compensate
[kámpənsèit]

동 보상하다(= make up for), 보완하다 compensation 명 보상
compensate/criticize A for B B 때문에 A에게 보상하다/비난하다

685

legally
[lí:gəli]

부 법적으로, 합법적으로(↔ illegally) legal 형 (합)법적인
be legally responsible for ~에 대해 법적으로 책임이 있다

686

poverty
[pávərti]

명 가난, 빈곤 poor 형 가난한, 빈곤한
➕ poverty-ridden 가난에 찌든 impoverish 가난하게 만들다

687

state
[steit]

명 국가, 주, 상태 동 진술하다, 말하다
Australia consists of six states and two territories. 호주는 6개의 주와 2개의 준주로 이루어져 있다.

688

distribute
[distríbju(:)t]

동 분배하다, 유통시키다   distribution 명 분배, 유통, 분포

distribute magazines to subscribers 잡지를 구독자에게 발송하다

689

geopolitical
[dʒì:oupəlítikəl]

형 지정학적인   geopolitics 명 지정학

➕ geo-economic 지리 경제학적인   geostrategic 지정학에 기초한 전략적인

690

isolation
[àisəléiʃən]

명 소외, 고립   isolated 형 고립된, 격리된

political and economic isolation 정치·경제적 소외

691

occupation
[àkjəpéiʃən]

명 직업, 점유, 점령   occupy 동 차지하다, 점령하다

Japan's 35-year forced occupation 일본의 35년 강점

692

pursue
[pərsjú:]

동 추구하다, 추진하다, 뒤쫓다   pursuit 명 추구, 추격

pursue money rather than happiness 행복보다 돈을 추구하다

693

discriminate
[diskrímənèit]

동 차별하다, 구별하다   discrimination 명 차별, 식별

discriminate/distinguish/differentiate A from B A와 B를 구별하다

694

dictator
[díkteitər]

명 독재자   dictatorial 형 독재의 dictate 동 (권위를 가지고) 명령하다, 받아쓰게 하다

✅ 독재: dictatorship, tyranny, autocracy, despotism

695

prejudice
[prédʒədis]

명 편견, 선입관   prejudiced 형 편견을 가진

prejudice against foreign residents 외국인 거주민에 대한 편견

696

censor
[sénsər]

동 검열하다, 금지하다 명 검열   censorship 명 검열 (제도)

domino effect of censoring journalists 언론인 검열의 도미노 효과

697

intervene
[ìntərví:n]

동 개입하다, 간섭하다   intervention 명 개입, 간섭

intervene in the financial market 금융 시장에 개입하다

698

neutral
[njú:trəl]

형 중립의, 중간의   neutralize 동 중화하다

keep politically neutral 정치적 중립을 지키다

699

statement
[stéitmənt]

명 진술, 성명(서), 표명   state 동 진술하다, 성명을 발표하다

make/issue/release a statement 발표하다, 표명하다

700

hierarchy
[háiərà:rki]

명 계층제, 위계   hierarchical 형 위계질서의

Almost all ancient societies were hierarchical. 거의 모든 고대사회는 계급제 사회였다.

PRACTICE

정답 및 해설 p.80

A 알맞은 단어를 〈보기〉에서 골라 빈칸을 채우시오.

> 〈보기〉   violate   exploit   distribute   pursue   censor

1 Police _____(e)d the gunman into an abandoned building.

2 Clothes and blankets have been _____(e)d to the refugees.

3 Reporters _____ themselves when they are oppressed by a regime.

4 If laborers don't know the Labor Standard Act, they can be _____(e)d.

5 The owner made his subordinate _____ tax laws to finance his business.

B 빈칸에 들어갈 알맞은 표현을 고르시오.

1 US military _____ caused the country to collapse.

  ① statement   ② intervention   ③ distribution   ④ hierarchy

2 Korea serves as a _____ hub connecting China with Japan.

  ① investigation   ② dictatorial   ③ geopolitical   ④ moderate

3 The Swiss government avoids war to stay officially _____.

  ① isolation   ② temporary   ③ neutral   ④ poor

4 The minister has plans to make ID carrying a _____ requirement.

  ① violating   ② dispersed   ③ intervene   ④ legal

5 Japan is a nation that has been closely _____ with the United States.

  ① neutral   ② pursued   ③ allied   ④ secure

C 네모 안에서 문맥에 맞는 낱말로 가장 적절한 것을 고르시오.

1 Because political scientists saw the international arena as a security competition among different states, states could gain much / little by cooperating with each other — except in temporary military alliances or security agreements that could fall apart at a moment's notice.

2 Even though he was imprisoned due to undermining the contemporary religious optimism about the universe and insulting powerful aristocrats and many of his books were censored, none of this stopped him from tolerating / challenging the prejudice and pretensions of those around him.

적용독해

1 다음 글의 밑줄 친 부분 중, 문맥상 낱말의 쓰임이 적절하지 <u>않은</u> 것은? 고2 학평 기출

Historical evidence points to workers being exploited by employers in the ① <u>absence</u> of appropriate laws or governmental intervention. This means that workers are not always compensated for their ② <u>contributions</u>, for their increased productivity, as economic theory would suggest. Employers will be able to exploit workers if they are not legally ③ <u>controlled</u>. Thus, the minimum wage laws may be the only way to prevent many employees from working at wages that are ④ <u>above</u> the poverty line. This point of view means that minimum wage laws are a source of correcting for existing market failure, ⑤ <u>enhancing</u> the power of markets to create efficient results.

2 다음 글의 밑줄 친 부분 중, 문맥상 낱말의 쓰임이 적절하지 <u>않은</u> 것은? 고2 학평 기출

Allowing people to influence each other reduces the ① <u>precision</u> of a group's estimate. To derive the most useful information from multiple sources of evidence, you should always try to make these sources ② <u>independent</u> of each other. This rule is part of good investigatory procedure. When there are multiple witnesses to an event, they are not allowed to ③ <u>discuss</u> it before giving their testimony. The goal is not only to prevent collusion by hostile witnesses, it is also to prevent witnesses from influencing each other. Witnesses who exchange their experiences will tend to make similar errors in their testimony, ④ <u>improving</u> the total value of the information they provide. The standard practice of ⑤ <u>open</u> discussion gives too much weight to the opinions of those who speak early and confidently, causing others to line up behind them.

* testimony: 증언 ** collusion: 공모, 담합

---

1 exploit 착취하다 absence 부재 appropriate 적절한 intervention 개입 compensate ~에 보상하다 contribution 기여
minimum wage 최저임금 poverty line 빈곤선(생계 유지에 필요한 최저 소득 기준) exist 현존하다 enhance 강화하다

2 influence ~에게 영향을 미치다 precision 정확도 estimate 평가 derive 끌어내다 independent 독립적인 investigatory 수사
procedure 절차 witness 목격자 discuss 의논하다 hostile 적대적인 exchange 교환하다 confidently 자신감 있게 line up 줄을 서다

강조 · 도치 · 생략

① 강조

A She **does drink** more than ten cups of coffee a day. (동사 강조)

B The cook said he made this delicious dish **himself**. (재귀대명사 강조)

C It was **the firefighter** that rescued the infant yesterday. (it 주어 that 강조)

D It was **the infant** that the firefighter rescued yesterday. (it 목적어 that 강조)

E It was **yesterday** that the firefighter rescued the infant. (it 부사 that 강조)

② 도치

F **Not until the morning** did she heard the news. (부정어)

G **Only after jogging for months** can we run a marathon. (only 부사구/절)

H **Enclosed** in the envelope is an important document. (2형식의 보어)

I **Down the street** stands the world's tallest building. (장소 부사구)

③ 생략

J Whoever wants to go home can **do** so. (대동사)

K You may call me if you would like **to**. (대부정사)

L The politician used to be shy when **she was** young. (주어 + be동사)

PRACTICE

A 어법상 틀린 부분을 바르게 고쳐 쓰시오.

1 The turtle ship does already exist 180 years before the war campaigns of 1592.

2 She participated in the K-pop dancing & singing contest himself.

3 Never before this great triumph has been achieved in the history of this world.

4 Creatures in water don't fight gravity as much as birds in the air are.

5 The Great Wall of China was made as massively as the pyramid did in Egypt.

B 네모 안에서 어법에 맞는 표현으로 가장 적절한 것을 고르시오.

1 The conventional view of what the state should do to foster innovation is that it is only by getting out of the way that / how governments can facilitate the economic dynamism of the private sector.

2 Whereas taxes, subsidies, tariffs, and regulations often serve to protect existing large corporations in the marketplace under a statist social system, a capitalist society doesn't have rights-violating taxes, tariffs, subsidies, or regulations favoring anybody nor it has / does it have antitrust laws.

적용독해

1

다음 글의 밑줄 친 부분 중, 어법상 **틀린** 것은? 고2 학평 기출 응용

Debating is as old as language itself and has taken many forms throughout human history. In ancient Rome, so critical ① <u>was</u> debate in the Senate that it greatly affected the conduct of civil society and the justice system. In Greece, it was before citizen juries composed of hundreds of Athenians ② <u>that</u> advocates for policy changes would routinely make their cases. In India, not only ③ <u>was</u> debate used to settle religious controversies, but it was also a very popular form of entertainment. Indian kings sponsored great debating contests, ④ <u>offer</u> prizes for the winners. China has its own ancient and distinguished tradition of debate. Beginning in the 2nd Century A.D., Taoist and Confucian scholars engaged in a practice known as 'pure talk' ⑤ <u>where</u> they debated spiritual and philosophical issues before audiences in contests that might last for a day and a night.

2

다음 글의 밑줄 친 부분 중, 어법상 **틀린** 것은? 고2 학평 기출 응용

Every farmer knows that the hard part is getting the field ① <u>prepared</u>. Inserting seeds and watching them grow ② <u>is</u> easy. In the case of science and industry, the community prepares the field, yet society tends to give all the credit to the individual who happens to plant a successful seed. Planting a seed does not necessarily require overwhelming intelligence; creating an environment that allows seeds to prosper ③ <u>is</u>. We need to give more credit to the community in science, politics, business, and daily life. It was Martin Luther King Jr. ④ <u>that</u> had this great strength: the ability to inspire people to work together to achieve, against all odds, revolutionary changes in society's perception of race and in the fairness of the law. But to really understand what he accomplished ⑤ <u>does</u> require looking beyond the man. Instead of treating him as the manifestation of everything great, we should appreciate his role in allowing America to show that it can be great.

* manifestation: 표명

---

1 debating 토론 throughout 내내 critical 중요한 Senate (고대 로마의) 원로원 conduct 경영 justice 사법 jury 배심원단 compose 구성하다 advocate 옹호자 policy 정책 controversy 논란 entertainment 오락 sponsor 후원하다 distinguished 훌륭한 Taoist 도교의 Confucian 유교의 scholar 학자 engage 참여하다 philosophical 철학적인
2 insert 심다 credit 공로 prosper 번성하다 politics 정치 fairness 공정성 accomplish 성취하다 treat ~으로 간주하다, 여기다

글의 순서

1

주어진 글 다음에 이어질 글의 순서로 가장 적절한 것을 고르시오. [고2 학평 기출 응용]

> *Power distance* is the term used to refer to how widely an unequal distribution of power is accepted by the members of a culture. It relates to the degree to which the less powerful members of a society accept their inequality in power and consider it the norm.

(A) In these cultures, there is more fluidity within the social hierarchy, and it is relatively easy for individuals to move up the social hierarchy based on their individual efforts and achievements.

(B) In contrast, in cultures with low acceptance of power distance (e.g., Finland, Norway, New Zealand, and Israel), people believe inequality should be minimal, and it is only as one of convenience that a hierarchical division is accepted.

(C) In cultures with high acceptance of power distance (e.g., India, Brazil, Greece, Mexico, and the Philippines), people are not viewed as equals, and everyone has a clearly defined or allocated place in the social hierarchy.

① (A) – (C) – (B)　　　② (B) – (A) – (C)　　　③ (B) – (C) – (A)
④ (C) – (A) – (B)　　　⑤ (C) – (B) – (A)

2

주어진 글 다음에 이어질 글의 순서로 가장 적절한 것을 고르시오. [고1 학평 기출 응용]

> Some people believe that the social sciences are falling behind the natural sciences.

(A) Even if social scientists discover the procedures that could reasonably be followed to achieve social improvement, seldom are they in a position to control social action. For that matter, even dictators find that there are limits to their power to change society.

---

1 **distance** 거리 **term** 용어 **refer to** 나타내다 **distribution** 분배 **relate to** ~와 관계가 있다 **norm** 규범 **fluidity** 유동성 **relatively** 상대적으로 **acceptance** 수용 **define** 규정하다 **allocate** 할당하다 **hierarchy** 계층
2 **fall behind** ~에 뒤떨어지다 **reasonably** 마땅히 **seldom** 좀처럼 ~않는 **dictator** 독재자 **maintain** 주장하다 **eliminate** 제거하다 **evil** 악 **racial** 인종의 **discrimination** 차별 **crime** 범죄 **limitation** 한계 **solution** 해결책

(B) They maintain that not only does social science have no exact laws, but it also has failed to eliminate great social evils such as racial discrimination, crime, poverty, and war. They suggest that social scientists have failed to accomplish what might reasonably have been expected of them.

(C) Never are such critics aware of the real nature of social science and of its special problems and basic limitations. For example, they forget that the solution to a social problem requires the ability to influence people on top of knowledge.

① (A) – (C) – (B)   ② (B) – (A) – (C)   ③ (B) – (C) – (A)
④ (C) – (A) – (B)   ⑤ (C) – (B) – (A)

3

주어진 글 다음에 이어질 글의 순서로 가장 적절한 것을 고르시오. 고2 학평 기출 응용

> When trying to sustain an independent ethos, cultures face a problem of critical mass. No single individual, acting on his or her own, can produce an ethos.

(A) They manage this feat through a combination of trade, to support their way of life, and geographic isolation. The Inuit occupy remote territory, removed from major population centers of Canada. If cross-cultural contact were to become sufficiently close, the Inuit ethos would disappear.

(B) Rather, an ethos results from the interdependent acts of many individuals. This cluster of produced meaning may require some degree of insulation from larger and wealthier outside forces. The Canadian Inuit maintain their own ethos, even though they number no more than twenty-four thousand.

(C) Hardly do distinct cultural groups of similar size, in the long run, persist in downtown Toronto, Canada, where they come in contact with many outside influences and pursue essentially Western paths for their lives.

* ethos: 민족(사회) 정신   ** insulation: 단절

① (A) – (C) – (B)   ② (B) – (A) – (C)   ③ (B) – (C) – (A)
④ (C) – (A) – (B)   ⑤ (C) – (B) – (A)

---

3 sustain 유지하다   critical mass 결정적 질량(임계 질량)   feat 업적   combination 조합   geographic 지리적인   isolation 고립   occupy 차지하다   remote 인가에서 떨어진, 먼   territory 영토   sufficiently 충분히   interdependent 상호의존적인   cluster 군집   wealthy 부유한   maintain 유지하다   distinct 다른   persist 지속되다   pursue 추구하다

사고 · 판단

701
morality
[mərǽləti]

명 도덕성(↔ immorality)　　moral 형 도덕의, 도덕적인
worldly morality vs. religious morality 세속적 도덕 대 종교적 도덕

702
ethical
[éθikəl]

형 윤리적인(↔ unethical), 윤리의, 도덕의　　ethics 명 윤리(학)
ethical and moral implications 윤리적, 도덕적 함의

703
estimate
[éstəmèit]

동 추정하다, 어림잡다, 견적을 내다　명 견적(액), 평가
estimate real-estate holdings 부동산의 가치를 추정하다

704
remark
[rimά:rk]

동 언급하다, 말하다　명 발언　　remarkable 형 주목할 만한
absurd/insulting/shocking remarks 터무니없는/모욕적인/폭탄 발언

705
judgement
[dʒʌ́dʒmənt]

명 판단　　judge 동 판단하다, 심사하다 명 판사, 심사위원
➕ judge from ~에 의해 판단하다　　judge by ~을 기준으로 판단하다

706
valid
[vǽlid]

형 유효한(↔ invalid), 타당한　　validity 명 타당성
➕ invalidate 무효로 하다　　validation 검증, 정당성

707
bias
[báiəs]

명 편견, 편향　　biased 형 편향된, 차별적인
racially and sexually biased 인종적 성별적 편견이 있는

708
stereotype
[stériətàip]

명 고정 관념　동 정형화하다
gender role stereotype 성별 역할에 대한 고정 관념

709
paradigm
[pǽrədàim]

명 패러다임, 사고방식, 인식의 틀
old/bygone/the first paradigm 낡은/과거의/최초의 패러다임

710
unique
[juːníːk]

형 독특한(↔ common), 유일한(= sole), 고유의
uniquely Arabic characteristics 아랍에만 있는 특징

711
categorize
[kǽtəgəràiz]

동 분류하다, 범주화하다　　category 명 범주, 부문
✔ 분류하다: classify, group, sort

712
deduction
[didʌ́kʃən]

명 추론, 공제, 연역법　　deduce 동 추론하다, 연역하다
Deduction is a way of extending your knowledge. 연역법은 당신의 지식을 확장하는 방법이다.

713
generalize
[dʒénərəlàiz]

동 일반화하다　　generally 부 일반적으로

⊕ overgeneralization 과잉일반화　　undergeneralization 과소일반화

714
refute
[rifjú:t]

동 반박하다, 논박하다　　refutable 형 반박의 여지가 있는

✅ 반박하다: retort, contradict, rebut, disprove

715
argument
[á:rgjumənt]

명 논쟁, 말다툼　　argue 동 언쟁을 하다, 주장하다

✅ 논쟁: controversy, dispute

716
convince
[kənvíns]

동 설득하다, 납득시키다, 확신시키다　　conviction 명 신념, 확신, 유죄 판결

convince the skeptical lawmakers 회의적인 국회의원을 설득하다

717
objective
[əbdʒéktiv]

명 목적, 목표　형 객관적인

⊕ objection 반대　　objectivity 객관성　　objectification 객관화

718
reasoning
[rí:zəniŋ]

명 추론, 논리, 이성　　reason 명 이유, 이성 동 추론하다, 판단하다

✅ 추론하다: infer, deduce, reason, extrapolate

719
accurate
[ǽkjərit]

형 정확한(↔ inaccurate), 정밀한, 올바른(= correct)　　accuracy 명 정확, 정확도

inaccurate statistics 부정확한 통계

720
evidence
[évidəns]

명 증거, 흔적 동 증거가 되다　　evident 형 명백한, 분명한

evidence against the hypothesis 그 가설에 반하는 증거

721
intuition
[ìntjuːíʃən]

명 직관, 직감　　intuitive 형 직관적인

AI has no ethical intuition. 인공 지능은 윤리적 직관력이 없다.

722
analyze
[ǽnəlàiz]

동 분석하다, 조사하다　analytic 형 분석적인　analysis 명 분석

The results must be analyzed in detail. 결과를 자세히 분석해야 한다.

723
insight
[ínsàit]

명 통찰력, 식견　　insightful 형 통찰력이 있는

show insight on life and death 삶과 죽음에 대한 통찰력을 보여 주다

724
assumption
[əsʌ́mpʃən]

명 가정, 추측　　assume 동 생각하다, 가정하다, 추측하다

Lots of evidence supports this assumption. 많은 증거가 이 가정을 뒷받침한다.

725
enlighten
[inláitən]

동 계몽하다, 설명하다　　enlightment 명 계몽, 이해

the dangerous idea that the elite enlighten the people 엘리트가 사람들을 계몽한다는 위험한 생각

PRACTICE

A   알맞은 단어를 〈보기〉에서 골라 빈칸을 채우시오.

〈보기〉   insight   enlightenment   stereotypes   categories   evidence

1 At present we have no _____ of life on other planets.

2 A priest in Belgium first showed _____ into how the universe began.

3 Feminists are people who don't conform to existing gender _____.

4 Evidence is divided into two _____: objective and circumstantial.

5 *V narod* was a rural _____ movement for the eradication of illiteracy in the 1930s.

B   빈칸에 들어갈 알맞은 표현을 고르시오.

1 It is legally and _____ wrong for lawyers to leak their clients' information.
  ① evidently   ② inaccurately   ③ validly   ④ ethically

2 Psychologists think that women's _____ is more accurate than men's.
  ① intuition   ② uniqueness   ③ enlightenment   ④ convince

3 Experts insisted on expanding existing tax _____ to revive domestic spending.
  ① reason   ② validity   ③ deductions   ④ remarks

4 Lawmakers presented low voter turnout as the _____ behind the proposal.
  ① accuracy   ② reasoning   ③ morality   ④ estimate

5 A public-opinion poll is not the most _____ method of determining the voters' opinions.
  ① objective   ② immortal   ③ argumentative   ④ categorizing

C   네모 안에서 문맥에 맞는 낱말로 가장 적절한 것을 고르시오.

1 Even if lying doesn't have any harmful effects in a particular case, it is still morally and ethically wrong because, if discovered, lying ⏐ strengthens / weakens ⏐ the general practice of truth-telling on which human communication relies.

2 Why we often feel that others are paying more attention to us than they really are can be explained by the spotlight effect, which involves seeing ourselves at center stage, thus intuitively ⏐ overestimating / underestimating ⏐ the extent to which others' attention is aimed at us.

적용독해

1 다음 글의 밑줄 친 부분 중, 문맥상 낱말의 쓰임이 적절하지 <u>않은</u> 것은? 〔고2 학평 기출〕

Sometimes our judgments of ourselves are unreasonably ① <u>negative</u>. This is especially true for people with low self-esteem. Several studies have shown that such people tend to ② <u>magnify</u> the importance of their failures. They often ③ <u>underestimate</u> their abilities. And when they get negative feedback, such as a bad evaluation at work or a disrespectful remark from someone they know, they are likely to believe that it ④ <u>inaccurately</u> reflects their self-worth. People with low self-esteem also have a higher-than-average risk of being depressed. This ⑤ <u>hurts</u> not only an individual's mental and emotional well-being but also his or her physical health and the quality of his or her social relationships.

2 다음 글의 밑줄 친 부분 중, 문맥상 낱말의 쓰임이 적절하지 <u>않은</u> 것은? 〔고1 학평 기출〕

You've probably heard the expression, "First impressions matter a lot." Life really doesn't give many people a ① <u>second</u> chance to make a good first impression. It has been determined that it takes only a few seconds for anyone to ② <u>assess</u> another individual. This is very noticeable in recruitment processes, where top recruiters can predict the direction of their eventual decision on any candidate within a few seconds of introducing themselves. So, a candidate's CV may 'speak' knowledge and competence, but their appearance and introduction may ③ <u>tell</u> of a lack of coordination, fear, and poor interpersonal skills. In this way, quick judgements are not only relevant in employment matters; they are ④ <u>equally</u> applicable in love and relationship matters too. On a date with a wonderful somebody who you've painstakingly tracked down for months, subtle things like bad breath or wrinkled clothes may ⑤ <u>double</u> your noble efforts.

* CV: 이력서(curriculum vitae)

---

1 unreasonably 터무니없이　self-esteem 자존감　magnify 확대하다　underestimate 과소평가하다　evaluation 평가　disrespectful 무례한　remark 말, 언급　reflect 반영하다, 나타내다　self-worth 자존감　higher-than-average 평균보다 높은　quality 질

2 expression 표현　impression 인상　assess 평가하다　noticeable 두드러진　recruitment 채용　candidate 지원자　competence 능력　lack 부족　coordination 신체 조정 능력　interpersonal 대인 관계에 관련된　judgement 판단　relevant 관련된　applicable 적용되는　painstakingly 공들여　track down 찾다　subtle 미묘한　wrinkle 주름이 지다　noble 숭고한, 고귀한

형용사와 부사

① 형용사의 쓰임

> A I have two very **cute** hamsters and a **creepy** snake. (명사 수식)
> B Successful people are **eager** to do their own work. (2형식의 보어) ▶p.36
> C We did our part by keeping our rooms **neat**. (5형식의 보어) ▶p.44

② 형태가 같은 형용사와 부사

	early	late	hard	only	long	fast	well
형용사	이른	늦은	근면한	유일한	긴	빠른	건강한
부사	일찍	늦게	열심히	오직	오래	빨리	잘

③ (부사)+완전한 절

> D He works **very hard** at his new job.
> E The child prodigy was **extremely** eager to solve the riddle.
> F He and she speak both English and German **fluently**.
> G The church **annually** gives its members calendars.

④ 의미가 다른 부사

late(늦게)	lately(최근에)	hard(열심히)	hardly(거의 ~ 않는)
near(가까이)	nearly(거의)	free(무료로)	freely(자유롭게)
high(높게)	highly(매우)	pretty(꽤)	prettily(예쁘게)
deep(깊게)	deeply(매우)	close(근처에)	closely(자세하게)

PRACTICE

A 어법상 틀린 부분을 바르게 고쳐 쓰시오.

1 When you make a list of every goal you have, be as specifically as possible.
2 Scientists considered some scenes of the movie unscientifically.
3 Not until we lose our health do we become keen aware of its importance.
4 Students found it hardly to read the book full of technical terms.
5 As a genius composer, Schubert wrote music as free as one would write a friendly letter.

B 네모 안에서 어법에 맞는 표현으로 가장 적절한 것을 고르시오.

1 Putting humans at risk if the study design does not permit a reasonable expectation of valid findings is never ethical, which means so many people don't consider the statement "Good science is good ethics" true / truly .

2 Whether the modern thinkers proceeded according to the logic of deduction or through the analysis of empirical data, the modern scientific method they developed entire / entirely consists in testing theories according to reason and in light of the available evidence.

적용독해

1

다음 글의 밑줄 친 부분 중, 어법상 <u>틀린</u> 것은? [고1 학평 기출]

The belief that humans have morality and animals don't is such a longstanding assumption that it could well be called a habit of mind, and bad habits, as we all know, are ① <u>extremely</u> hard to break. A lot of people have caved in to this assumption because it is ② <u>easier</u> to deny morality to animals than to deal with the complex effects of the possibility that animals have moral behavior. The historical tendency, framed in the outdated dualism of us versus them, ③ <u>is</u> strong enough to make a lot of people cling to the status quo. Denial of who animals are ④ <u>convenient</u> allows for maintaining false stereotypes about the cognitive and emotional capacities of animals. Clearly a major paradigm shift is ⑤ <u>needed</u>, because the lazy acceptance of habits of mind has a strong influence on how animals are understood and treated.

* dualism: 이원론(二元論) ** status quo: 현재 상태

2

다음 글의 밑줄 친 부분 중, 어법상 <u>틀린</u> 것은? [고3 학평 기출]

Driving is, for most of us, what psychologists call an overlearned activity. It is something we are so well practiced at that we are able to do it without much conscious thought. That makes our life ① <u>easier</u>, and it is how we become ② <u>skillfully</u> at things. Think of an expert tennis player. A serve is a complex maneuver with many different components, but the ③ <u>better</u> we become at it, the less we think of each individual step. One of the interesting things about learning and attention is that once something becomes automated, it gets ④ <u>executed</u> in a rapid string of events. If you try to pay attention, you screw it up. This is why the best hitters in baseball do not ⑤ <u>necessarily</u> make the best hitting coaches.

---

1 morality 도덕성 longstanding 오래된 assumption 가정 cave 굴복하다 deny 부정하다 deal with 다루다 complex 복잡한 tendency 경향 outdate 시대에 뒤처진 cling to ~을 고수하다 convenient 편리한 stereotype 고정 관념 paradigm 패러다임 shift 전환 lazy 안일한

2 practice 훈련하다 conscious 의식적인 maneuver 기술, 조작 component 구성 요소 automate 자동화하다 execute 실행하다 rapid 빠른 in string of 일련의 screw up 망치다

문장 위치

1 글의 흐름으로 보아, 주어진 문장이 들어가기에 가장 적절한 곳을 고르시오. 고2 학평 기출

> But the necessary and useful instinct to generalize can distort our world view.

Everyone automatically categorizes and generalizes all the time. Unconsciously. It is not a question of being prejudiced or enlightened. Categories are absolutely necessary for us to function. (①) They give structure to our thoughts. (②) Imagine if we saw every item and every scenario as truly unique — we would not even have a language to describe the world around us. (③) It can make us mistakenly group together things, or people, or countries that are actually very different. (④) It can make us assume everything or everyone in one category is similar. (⑤) And, maybe, most unfortunate of all, it can make us jump to conclusions about a whole category based on a few, or even just one, unusual example.

---

1 instinct 본능 generalize 일반화하다 distort (사실을) 왜곡하다 categorize (개개의 범주로) 분류하다 unconsciously 무의식적으로 prejudiced 편견을 가진 enlightened 계몽된 function (정상적으로) 활동하다 group together ~을 하나로 묶다 jump to conclusions 성급하게 결론을 내리다

2 글의 흐름으로 보아, 주어진 문장이 들어가기에 가장 적절한 곳을 고르시오. 고2 학평 기출

> If it did, we can move on and make an objective and informed decision.

Since we know we can't completely eliminate our biases, we need to try to limit the harmful impacts they can have on the objectivity and rationality of our decisions and judgments. (①)It is important that we are aware when one of our cognitive biases is activated and make a conscious choice to overcome that bias. (②) We need to be aware of the impact the bias has on our decision making process and our life. (③) Then we can choose an appropriate de-biasing strategy to combat it. (④) After we have implemented a strategy, we should check in again to see if it worked in the way we had hoped. (⑤) If it didn't, we can try the same strategy again or implement a new one until we are ready to make a rational judgment.

3 글의 흐름으로 보아, 주어진 문장이 들어가기에 가장 적절한 곳을 고르시오. 고2 학평 기출 응용

> Another possibility is that neither argument is refuted, because both have a degree of reason on their side.

One benefit of reasons and arguments is that they can foster humility. If two people disagree without arguing, all they do is yell at each other. In contrast, if both sides give arguments that articulate reasons for their positions, then new possibilities open up. (①) One of the arguments gets refuted — that is, it is shown to fail. (②) In that case, the person who depended on the refuted argument learns that he needs to change his view, which is one way to achieve humility — on one side at least. (③) Even if neither person involved is convinced by the other's argument, both can still come to appreciate the opposing view. (④) They also realize that, even if they have some truth, they do not have the whole truth. (⑤) They can gain humility when they recognize and appreciate the reasons against their own view.

* humility: 겸손   ** articulate: 분명히 말하다

---

2 objective 객관적인 completely 완전히 bias 편견 harmful 해로운 rationality 합리성 overcome 극복하다 strategy 전략 combat 싸우다 implement 실행하다 rational 이성적인

3 refute 반박하다 foster 기르다 yell 고함치다 depend on ~에 의존하다 convince 설득하다 appreciate 이해하다 oppose 반대하다

연구 · 실험

726
experiment
[ikspérəmənt]

명 실험, 시도 동 실험하다   experimental 형 실험의
experimental group and control group 실험군과 대조군

727
finding
[fáɪndɪŋ]

명 연구 결과, 조사 결과
the key findings from these studies 이 연구들의 주요 결과

728
numerous
[njúːmərəs]

형 수많은(= innumerable)   numerical 형 수적인, 숫자상의
✔ 수많은: countless, uncountable, immeasurable

729
support
[səpɔ́ːrt]

동 지원하다, 지지하다, 뒷받침하다 명 지지, 부양   supporting 형 지지하는
evidence supporting the hypothesis 가설을 뒷받침하는 증거

730
verify
[vérəfài]

동 검증하다, 사실임을 입증하다   verification 명 확인, 입증, 증거
in a complete and verifiable manner 완벽하고 검증 가능한 방식으로

731
falsify
[fɔ́ːlsəfài]

동 왜곡하다, 거짓임을 증명하다   falsification 명 위조, 조작
deliberately falsify the fact 사실을 고의로 왜곡하다

732
criterion
[kraɪtí(ː)əriən]

명 기준(= standard), 조건(= condition)   pl. criteria
✔ -on(단수) → -a(복수): phenomenon → phenomena(현상)

733
external
[ikstə́ːrnəl]

형 외부의(↔ internal), 대외적인 명 외부, 외모
✔ 외부의: outer, exterior, extrinsic

734
challenge
[tʃǽlindʒ]

명 도전, 어려움, 난제 동 도전하다
the biggest challenge 가장 큰 난제

735
hypothesis
[haɪpáθɪsis]

명 가설, 가정   pl. hypotheses   hypothesize 동 가정하다
✔ sis(단수) → ses(복수): thesis → theses(논문)   parenthesis → parentheses (괄호)

736
recall
[rikɔ́ːl]

동 회상하다, 기억하다, 회수하다
✔ 회상하다: look back, recollect, reminisce

737
match
[mætʃ]

명 경기, 시합 동 어울리다, 필적하다
No one matches him in speed. 속도 면에서는 아무도 그와 견줄 사람이 없다.

738

reveal
[riví:l]

동 드러내다, 밝히다 　 revelation 명 공개, 폭로

The researcher revealed the findings. 연구자는 결과를 공개했다.

739

randomly
[rǽndəmli]

부 무작위로, 임의로 　 random 형 무작위의, 되는대로의

✅ at+명사 = 부사: at random(함부로), at will(마음대로)

740

participant
[pɑ:rtísəpənt]

명 참가자, 피실험자(= subject) 　 participate 동 참여하다

✅ ~에 참가/참여하다: take part in, attend, be involved in

741

index
[índeks]

명 지수, 지표, 색인

price / discomfort / misery index 물가지수 / 불쾌지수 / 고통지수

742

additional
[ədíʃənəl]

형 추가의, 또 다른 　 addition 명 추가(물), 부가, 덧셈 　 add 동 추가하다, 합하다

the latest device with additional functionality 추가 기능을 갖춘 최신 기기

743

research
[risə́:rtʃ]

명 연구, 조사 동 조사하다

➕ R&D 연구 개발(research and development)

744

guarantee
[gæ̀rəntí:]

동 보장하다, 보증하다 명 보증, 약속

guarantee online anonymity 인터넷 익명성을 보장하다

745

pretend
[priténd]

동 ~인 체하다, 가장하다 　 pretension 명 가식

pretend to grasp technical terms 전문 용어를 이해하는 척하다

746

reverse
[rivə́:rs]

형 반대의, 거꾸로 된 동 바꾸다, 뒤집다 　 reversal 명 반전, 뒤바뀜, 역전

The government reversed the situation. 정부는 상황을 반전시켰다.

747

correlation
[kɔ̀(:)rəléiʃən]

명 상관관계 　 correlate 동 연관성이 있다

correlation between A and B A와 B의 상관관계

748

imitate
[ímitèit]

동 모방하다(= mimic), 흉내내다 　 imitation 명 모방

Imitation is the mother of innovation. 모방은 혁신의 어머니다.

749

stimulus
[stímjələs]

명 자극, 부양책 pl. stimuli 　 stimulate 동 자극하다

✅ us(단수) → i(복수): fungus → fungi(균류) 　 alumnus → alumni(동창생)

750

sacrifice
[sǽkrəfàis]

명 희생, 제물 동 희생하다, 제물로 바치다

Madame Curie sacrificed her life for research. 퀴리 부인은 연구에 일생을 바쳤다.

PRACTICE

정답 및 해설 p.86

A   알맞은 단어를 〈보기〉에서 골라 빈칸을 채우시오.

〈보기〉	pretend	randomly	imitate	reveal	correlation

1 The criminal refused to _____ his intentions.

2 Jury candidates should be selected _____ for a guarantee of fairness.

3 Vegetarian products that _____ meat are increasingly popular.

4 Researchers asked one group to _____ not to notice the scene.

5 Dr. Lee proved the _____ between education and the inheritance of wealth.

B   빈칸에 들어갈 알맞은 표현을 고르시오.

1 Please call or text us for _____ information.

   ① reverse   ② correlation   ③ pretension   ④ additional

2 An inspiring teacher _____(e)s creativity in students.

   ① imitate   ② stimulate   ③ sacrifice   ④ recall

3 It will take years to _____ the damage done by pollution.

   ① guarantee   ② experiment   ③ reverse   ④ participate

4 They need to _____ their theory through experiments.

   ① add   ② recall   ③ pretend   ④ verify

5 No experimenter has ever _____(e)d his achievements in molecular biology.

   ① participate   ② match   ③ pretend   ④ index

C   네모 안에서 문맥에 맞는 낱말로 가장 적절한 것을 고르시오.

1 It raises much less reactance to tell people what to do than to tell them what not to do. Therefore, advocating action should lead to | lower / higher | compliance than prohibiting action.

2 Some beginning researchers mistakenly believe that a good hypothesis is one that is guaranteed to be right. However, if we already know your hypothesis is true before you test it, | testing / denying | your hypothesis won't tell us anything new.

적용독해

1 다음 글의 밑줄 친 부분 중, 문맥상 낱말의 쓰임이 적절하지 <u>않은</u> 것은? 고1 학평 기출

When we *don't* want to believe a certain claim, we ask ourselves, "*Must* I believe it?" Then we search for contrary evidence, and if we find a single reason to ① <u>doubt</u> the claim, we can dismiss the claim. Psychologists now have numerous findings on "motivated reasoning," showing the many ② <u>tricks</u> people use to reach the conclusions they want to reach. When subjects are told that an intelligence test gave them a low score, they choose to read articles ③ <u>supporting</u> the validity of IQ tests. When people read a (fictitious) scientific study reporting heavy caffeine consumption is ④ <u>associated</u> with an increased risk of breast cancer, women who are heavy coffee drinkers find ⑤ <u>more</u> errors in the study than do less caffeinated women.

* fictitious: 가상의

2 다음 글의 밑줄 친 부분 중, 문맥상 낱말의 쓰임이 적절하지 <u>않은</u> 것은? 고2 학평 기출

Most beliefs — but not all — are open to tests of verification. This means that beliefs can be tested to see if they are correct or false. Beliefs can be verified or falsified with objective criteria ① <u>external</u> to the person. There are people who believe the Earth is flat and not a sphere. Because we have ② <u>objective</u> evidence that the Earth is in fact a sphere, the flat Earth belief can be shown to be false. Also, the belief that it will rain tomorrow can be tested for truth by ③ <u>waiting</u> until tomorrow and seeing whether it rains or not. However, some types of beliefs cannot be tested for truth because we cannot get external evidence in our ④ <u>lifetimes</u> (such as a belief that the Earth will stop spinning on its axis by the year 9999 or that there is life on a planet 100-million light-years away). Also, meta-physical beliefs (such as the existence and nature of a god) present considerable ⑤ <u>usefulness</u> in generating evidence that everyone is willing to use as a truth criterion.

* verification: 검증, 확인   ** falsify: 거짓임을 입증하다

----

1 dismiss 버리다 numerous 많은 conclusion 결론 subject 실험 대상자 article 기사 validity 타당성[도] consumption 섭취
be associated with ~와 관련된 breast cancer 유방암
2 correct 옳은 objective 객관적인 criterion 기준 external 외부의 sphere 구 axis 축 meta-physical 형이상적 considerable 상당한

비교 구문

① 원급: 「as 형용사/부사의 원급 as」 ~만큼 …한/하게

A This house is twice **as big as** that one.
B This stick is **not as(so) long as** that one.

② 비교급: 「형용사/부사의 비교급+than」 ~보다 더 …한/하게

C He behaved **better than** usual.
D His car is **more expensive than** mine.
E Her illness is getting **much more** serious. (비교급 강조 : much, even, far, a lot)
F **The longer** he walked, **the more** refreshed he felt. (the 비교급, the 비교급)

③ 최상급: 「the 형용사/부사의 최상급」 가장 …한/하게

G Joe is **the smallest** of all the students.
H What is **the most interesting** book you've ever read?

④ 불규칙 형태

원급	비교급	최상급	원급	비교급	최상급
good/well	better	best	bad/ill	worse	worst
many/much	more	most	little	less	least
late(시간)	later	latest	late(순서)	latter	last

PRACTICE

A 밑줄 친 부분을 어법에 맞게 고쳐 쓰시오.

1 More of us are claiming we are greedier <u>as</u> ever before.
2 The ad revenue of cable TV became <u>better</u> than twice that of radio in the first half year.
3 The more often coworkers work together, the <u>best</u> an organization performs.
4 Close reading enables kids to explore books <u>very</u> more deeply than surface-level reading.
5 As need-driven animals, we seek out the paths of <u>worst</u> resistance to get what we need.

B 네모 안에서 어법에 맞는 표현으로 가장 적절한 것을 고르시오.

1 Although hunting and gathering may be less productive and may generate far lower energy yields than farming, over longer periods of time farming societies were │ very / much │ more likely to suffer severe, existentially threatening famines than hunter-gatherers.

2 Even though touching our own faces seems to serve no special purpose, the research showed that the higher the rate of a subject's self-touching was in response to exposure to unpleasant noises, the │ more / most │ focused the individual remained.

적용독해

1

다음 글의 밑줄 친 부분 중, 어법상 **틀린** 것은? 고2 학평 기출

Traditionally, most ecologists assumed that community stability — the ability of a community to withstand environmental disturbances — ① is a consequence of community complexity. That is, a community with considerable species richness may function ② better and be more stable than a community with less species richness. According to this view, the greater the species richness, the ③ least critically important any single species should be. With many possible interactions within the community, it is unlikely that any single disturbance could affect enough components of the system to make a significant difference in ④ its functioning. Evidence for this hypothesis includes the fact ⑤ that destructive outbreaks of pests are more common in cultivated fields, which are low — diversity communities, than in natural communities with greater species richness.

* community: 군집, 군락

2

다음 글의 밑줄 친 부분 중, 어법상 **틀린** 것은? 고3 학평 기출

Older adults often take longer to make a decision than young adults ① do. But that does not mean they are any less sharp. According to research at Ohio State University, the slower response time of older adults has ② more to do with prizing accuracy over speed. In the study, published recently in the *Journal of Experimental Psychology: General*, college-age students and adults aged 60 to 90 performed timed tests of word recognition and recall. All participants were equally accurate, but the older group responded ③ far more slowly. When the researchers encouraged them to work faster, however, they were able to match the youngsters' speed without ④ significantly sacrificing accuracy. "In many simple tasks, the elderly take longer mainly because they decide to require more evidence to make their decision," says co-author Roger Ratcliff. When an older mind faces a task that ⑤ require speed, he says, a conscious effort to work faster can often do the trick.

---

1 assume 추정하다 withstand 견디다 disturbance 교란 richness 풍부도 hypothesis 가설 outbreak 발생 pest 해충
cultivated field 경작지 diversity 다양성

2 sharp 똑똑한 have to do with ~와 관련이 있는 prize 중요하게 여기다 accuracy 정확성 recognition 인지, 인식 recall 기억
match 따라잡다, 일치하다 conscious 의식적인

1 다음 글의 내용을 한 문장으로 요약하고자 한다. 빈칸 (A), (B)에 들어갈 말로 가장 적절한 것은?

고1 학평 기출 응용

In a study, psychologist Laurence Steinberg divided 306 people into three age groups: young adolescents, with a mean age of 14; older adolescents, with a mean age of 19; and adults, aged 24 and older. Subjects played a computerized driving game in which the player must avoid crashing into a wall that appears, without warning, on the roadway. Steinberg randomly assigned some participants to play alone or with two same-age peers looking on. Older adolescents scored about 50 percent higher on an index of risky driving when their peers were in the room. When other young teens were around, early adolescents drove twice as recklessly as when they played alone. In contrast, adults behaved in similar ways regardless of whether they were on their own or observed by others.

* recklessly: 무모하게

⇩

The _____(A)_____ of peers makes adolescents, but not adults, more likely to _____(B)_____ .

	(A)		(B)		(A)		(B)
①	presence	·····	take risks	②	presence	·····	behave cautiously
③	indifference	·····	perform poorly	④	absence	·····	enjoy adventures
⑤	absence	·····	act independently				

---

1 divide 나누다　adolescent 청소년　mean age 평균 연령　crash 충돌, 충돌하다　peer 또래　index 지수　regardless of ~에 상관없이

2

다음 글의 내용을 한 문장으로 요약하고자 한다. 빈칸 (A), (B)에 들어갈 말로 가장 적절한 것은?

고1 학평 기출 응용

An experiment on a teaching environment was conducted, where fifth and sixth graders were assigned to interact on a topic. With one group, the discussion was led in a way that built an agreement. With the second group, the discussion was designed to produce disagreements about the right answer. Students who easily reached an agreement were less interested in the topic, studied less, and were less likely to visit the library to get additional information. The most noticeable difference, though, was revealed when teachers showed a special film about the discussion topic — during lunch time! Only 18% of the agreement group missed lunch time to see the film, but 45% of the disagreement group stayed for the film. The thirst to fill a knowledge gap — to find out who was right within the group — can be much more powerful than the thirst for slides and jungle gyms.

⇩

According to the experiment above, students' interest in a topic ___(A)___ when they are encouraged to ___(B)___.

	(A)		(B)			(A)		(B)
①	increases	......	differ		②	increases	......	approve
③	increases	......	cooperate		④	decreases	......	participate
⑤	decreases	......	argue					

---

2 **conduct** 행동하다 **assign** 부여하다 **noticeable** 눈에 띄는 **reveal** 나타나다 **thirst** 열망 **gap** 차이

INDEX

WORD INDEX

지은이

김경태

현 남성고등학교 교사

The 상승 〈어법·어휘+유형편〉

펴 낸 이   주민홍
펴 낸 곳   서울특별시 마포구 월드컵북로 396(상암동) 누리꿈스퀘어 비즈니스타워 10층
            ㈜NE능률 (우편번호 03925)
펴 낸 날   2024년 1월 5일 초판 제1쇄 발행

전   화   02 2014 7114
팩   스   02 3142 0356
홈 페 이 지   www.neungyule.com
등 록 번 호   제1-68호
I S B N   979-11-253-4359-2
정   가   18,000원

NE 능률

고객센터

교재 내용 문의 : contact.nebooks.co.kr (별도의 가입 절차 없이 작성 가능)
제품 구매, 교환, 불량, 반품 문의 : 02-2014-7114
☎ 전화문의는 본사 업무시간 중에만 가능합니다.

NE능률 교재 MAP

수능

아래 교재 MAP을 참고하여 본인의 현재 혹은 목표 수준에 따라 교재를 선택하세요.
NE능률 교재들과 함께 영어실력을 쑥쑥~ 올려보세요!
MP3 등 교재 부가 학습 서비스 및 자세한 교재 정보는 www.nebooks.co.kr 에서 확인하세요.

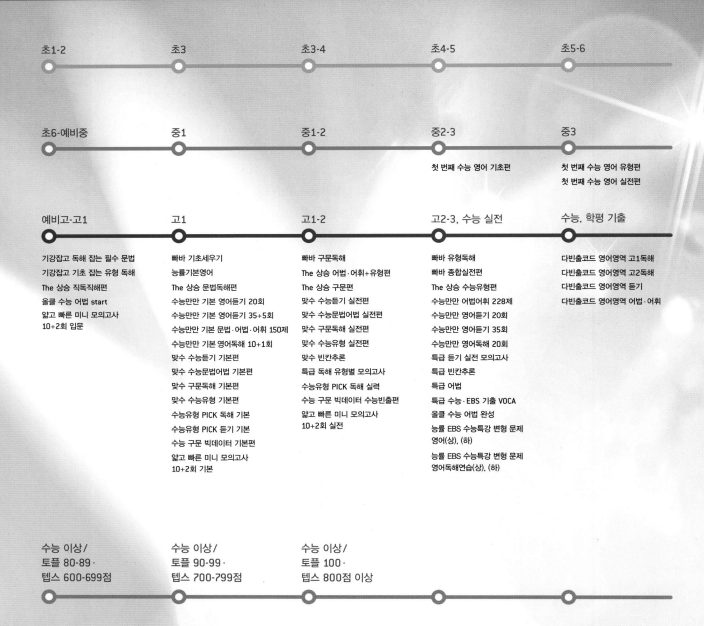

| 초1-2 | 초3 | 초3-4 | 초4-5 | 초5-6 |

| 초6-예비중 | 중1 | 중1-2 | 중2-3 | 중3 |

중2-3
첫 번째 수능 영어 기초편

중3
첫 번째 수능 영어 유형편
첫 번째 수능 영어 실전편

| 예비고-고1 | 고1 | 고1-2 | 고2-3, 수능 실전 | 수능, 학평 기출 |

예비고-고1
기강잡고 독해 잡는 필수 문법
기강잡고 기초 잡는 유형 독해
The 상승 직독직해편
올클 수능 어법 start
얇고 빠른 미니 모의고사
10+2회 입문

고1
빠바 기초세우기
능률기본영어
The 상승 문법독해편
수능만만 기본 영어듣기 20회
수능만만 기본 영어듣기 35+5회
수능만만 기본 문법·어법·어휘 150제
수능만만 기본 영어독해 10+1회
맞수 수능듣기 기본편
맞수 수능문법어법 기본편
맞수 구문독해 기본편
맞수 수능유형 기본편
수능유형 PICK 독해 기본
수능유형 PICK 듣기 기본
수능 구문 빅데이터 기본편
얇고 빠른 미니 모의고사
10+2회 기본

고1-2
빠바 구문독해
The 상승 어법·어휘+유형편
The 상승 구문편
맞수 수능듣기 실전편
맞수 수능문법어법 실전편
맞수 구문독해 실전편
맞수 수능유형 실전편
맞수 빈칸추론
특급 독해 유형별 모의고사
수능유형 PICK 독해 실력
수능 구문 빅데이터 수능빈출편
얇고 빠른 미니 모의고사
10+2회 실전

고2-3, 수능 실전
빠바 유형독해
빠바 종합실전편
The 상승 수능유형편
수능만만 어법어휘 228제
수능만만 영어듣기 20회
수능만만 영어듣기 35회
수능만만 영어독해 20회
특급 듣기 실전 모의고사
특급 빈칸추론
특급 어법
특급 수능·EBS 기출 VOCA
올클 수능 어법 완성
능률 EBS 수능특강 변형 문제
영어(상), (하)
능률 EBS 수능특강 변형 문제
영어독해연습(상), (하)

수능, 학평 기출
다빈출코드 영어영역 고1독해
다빈출코드 영어영역 고2독해
다빈출코드 영어영역 듣기
다빈출코드 영어영역 어법·어휘

수능 이상/
토플 80-89·
텝스 600-699점

수능 이상/
토플 90-99·
텝스 700-799점

수능 이상/
토플 100·
텝스 800점 이상

The 상승

독해 기본기에서
수능 실전 대비까지 The 상승

**어법·어휘
+ 유형편**

정답 및 해설

NE 능률

The 상승

독해 기본기에서
수능 실전 대비까지 The 상승

**어법 · 어휘
+ 유형편**

정답 및 해설

PRACTICE
p.10

A	1 shortage	2 likelihood	3 connection
	4 proposal	5 emphasis	6 purify
	7 visualize	8 weaken	9 beautify
	10 originate		
B	1 ① 2 ④ 3 ④ 4 ① 5 ④		
C	1 visualize	2 employ	

A

1 short+age (부족)　2 likely(→ i)+hood (가능성)
3 connect+ion (연결)　4 propos(e)+al (제안)
5 emphasis (강조)　6 pure(→ i)+fy (순화시키다)
7 visual+ize (시각화하다)　8 weak+en (약화시키다)
9 beauty(→ i)+fy (미화하다)　10 origin+ate (유래하다)

B

1 영화감독은 폭력을 미화할 의도는 없었다고 말했다.
2 북미 원주민들은 다양한 용도로 불을 사용했다.
3 결정이라는 것은 옳지 않으면서 이성적일 수 있고 이성적이지 않으면서도 옳을 수 있다.
4 만약 당신이 승진을 원한다면, 다른 직원들과의 관계를 강화시켜라.
5 저녁 파티에 초대받는 것은 우리로 하여금 초대한 사람을 다른 행사에 초대해야 한다는 압박감을 갖도록 한다.

C

1 코치들이 실제 경주나 대회를 앞두고 운동선수들에게 경기를 미리 (머릿속으로) 그려보도록 하는 기법은 마음으로 보게 되면 몸도 당연히 따라간다는 개념에서 유래했다.
2 에콰도르 정부는 열대 우림에 위치한 유전의 보호를 강조했는데, 이는 자신들의 자원을 보호하면서 기후 변화에 맞서 싸우기 위해 사용할 수 있는 대담한 아이디어로 간주되었다.

적용독해
p.11

1 ④	2 ④

1 ④

해석 사람들이 똑같은 매일, 매주, 매달 그리고 계절 리듬을 공유할

때, 그들 간의 관계는 더욱 빠르게 형성되고 더욱 강한 상태를 유지한다. 사람들은 서로를 더욱 깊이 신뢰하게 되고 협력도 더 쉬워진다. 결국, 그들은 빈번하게 똑같은 일을 하고 똑같은 문제들을 함께 해결한다. 사실, 몇몇 조직들은 강한 결속력을 유지하고 공유된 사고방식을 강화시키기 위해 정기 스탠딩 회의를 이용한다. 한 식품 회사의 최고 경영자는 그의 팀과 함께 매일 하는 간단한 회의에 대해 말한다. "빈번함이 만들어 내는 리듬은 관계가 약화되도록(→ 강화되도록) 하고, 개인의 습관이 이해되게 하고, 스트레스 원인들도 확인되게 한다. 이 모든 것은 팀의 구성원들이 자신의 역할 뿐만 아니라 그들이 어떻게 서로가 서로에게서 최상의 것을 얻어낼 수 있는지를 이해하도록 도와준다."라고 그는 말했다.

문제풀이 만나고 일하고 사고방식을 공유하는 것을 더 빈번히 할수록 사람들 간의 관계는 더 빠르고 강하게 형성되며 신뢰와 협력에도 도움이 된다고 했으므로 ④ weaken은 strengthen 등으로 고쳐야 한다.

구문분석

[6행] The rhythm [that frequency generates] allows [relationships to strengthen, personal habits to be understood, and stressors to be identified].
(S / O1 / O.C.1 / O2 / O.C.2 / O3 / O.C.3)

▶ 첫 번째 [ ]는 주어 The rhythm을 수식하는 주격 관계대명사절이다. 두 번째 [ ]는 5형식 문장 「allow+O+to-v」의 구조에서 목적어와 보어(to-v)가 A, B, and C 방식의 병렬로 연결되어 있다.

2 ④

해석 당신이 높이 올라갈수록 대기 속의 산소의 양은 감소한다. 저지대 사람들이 고지대 지역을 방문할 때, 고산병을 겪을 가능성은 높다. 다시 말해서 산소의 부족이 그들을 피곤하고 아프며 어지러운 증세를 느끼게 만드는 것이다. 고지대에 살고 있는 사람들은 그들의 몸이 산소의 부족에 적응되어 있기 때문에 정상적으로 호흡할 수 있다. 고지대에 사는 운동선수들이 저지대에서 뛰어난 기량을 발휘하는 것도 같은 이유이다. 산악인들이 높은 봉우리를 오르려고 할 때 그들은 어느 지점까지 오르고 며칠을 쉬어 줌으로써 고산병에 걸린다(→ (을) 피한다). 이것은 그들이 훨씬 높은 곳을 오르기 전에 몸이 산소의 부족에 적응할 시간을 준다.

문제풀이 산악인들이 높은 산에 오를 때 고지대에 적응하려고 간격을 두고 오르다가 쉬는 방법을 통해 고산병에 걸리지 않는다는 내용이므로 ④ get은 avoid 등으로 고쳐야 한다.

구문분석

[4행] People [living in high altitudes] are able to breathe normally [because their bodies have become used to the shortage of oxygen].
(S / V)

▶ 첫 번째 [ ]는 주어 People을 수식하는 현재분사구이며, 두 번째 [ ]는 이유를 나타내는 접속사 because로 시작하는 부사절을 나타낸다.

PRACTICE
p.12

A　1　Beautify → Beautifying / To beautify
　　2　He → That he
　　3　That → What
　　4　know → to know
　　5　repeating → repeat
B　1　to find　2　to say　3　think

A

1　집을 아름답게 하면 삶의 질이 향상된다. ▶ 명사구 주어
2　그가 그런 실수를 저질렀다는 것은 사실이 아니다. ▶ 명사절 주어
3　내게 부족한 것은 지혜이다. ▶ 관계대명사+불완전한 절
4　그녀의 나이를 아는 것은 중요하지 않다. ▶ 가주어–진주어 구문
5　개선하고 싶다면, 배우고 있는 것을 반복해라. ▶ 명령문

B

1　일부 지역 사회가 석탄 생산의 감소로부터 고통을 받고 있기 때문에 탄소 섬유를 생산하기 위해 석탄을 이용하는 경제적인 방법을 찾는 것은 그들의 노력을 활성하시키는 데 도움을 줄 것이다. ▶ it ~ to-v 가주어–진주어 구문
2　훨씬 더 좋은 것은, "다른 사람들이 당신의 응답만큼 유용한 응답을 제공하도록 돕기 위해, 당신과 다른 사람이 서로에 대한 몇 가지 질문에 대답했다고 그들에게 말해 주세요."라고 말하는 것이다. ▶ 2형식 문장(S+be-v+S.C.)의 도치문(S.C.+be-v+S)
3　구입을 고려하고 있는 그 구매품이 당신에게 단기적 혜택만을 줄 것임이 명확해진다면, 대신에 당신이 구매할 수 있는, 당신에게 장기적 혜택을 제공해 줄 경험에 대해 생각해 보라. ▶ 접속사 if로 시작하는 부사절, 동사원형으로 시작하는 주절(명령문)로 이루어진 문장

적용독해
p.13

1　⑤　2　③

1　⑤

해석 당신은 당신의 강점과 약점에 대하여 스스로에게 정직한가? 스스로에 대해 확실히 알고 당신의 약점이 무엇인지를 파악하는 것은 중요하다. 당신의 문제에 있어 스스로의 역할을 받아들이는 것은 해결책도 당신 안에 있다는 것을 이해함을 의미한다. 당신이 특정 분야에 약점이 있다는 것을 안다는 것은 당신이 배워서 상황을 개선하기 위해 스스로 해야만 할 것들을 행하는데 도움이 될 것이다. 당신의 사회적 이미지가 형편없다는 사실은 또한 당신이 스스로를 들여다보고

그것을 개선하기 위해 필요한 조치를 취하는데 도움이 될 것이다. 오늘 당장. 당신은 삶에 대응하는 방법을 선택할 능력이 있다. 오늘 당장 모든 변명을 끝내기로 결심하고, 일어나는 일에 대해 스스로에게 거짓말하는 것을 멈춰라. 성장의 시작은 당신이 자신의 선택에 대한 책임을 스스로 받아들이기 시작할 때 일어난다.

문제풀이 ⑤ 콤마 앞부분에 동사와 주어가 없는 상태이고, and 이후에는 stop이라는 명령문이므로 「명령문, and 명령문」이 되도록 Deciding을 동사 Decide로 고쳐야 한다.
① it ~ to-v 가주어–진주어 구문
② 동명사 주어
③ to부정사 주어
④ that절 주어

2　③

해석 무언가를 평가하기 위한 인식의 틀이 없는 평가 방식은 없다. 다음의 예를 생각해 보라. 대학생들이 위험에 처한 150명을 구할 수 있는 수백만 달러의 안전 대책을 지지하는지에 대해 질문을 받았다. 150명은 많은가 적은가? 그런데 무엇과 비교해서? 다른 대학생들은 위험에 처한 150명 중에 98퍼센트를 구할 수 있는 안전 대책을 지지하는 것이 더 나은지에 대해 질문을 받았다. 안전 대책이 150명을 구할 것이라는 이야기를 들은 학생들보다 이 학생들이 자신들이 들었던 대책에 대해 더 호의적이었다. 명백히, 150명 중 98퍼센트보다는 150명을 구하는 것이 더 낫지만, 98퍼센트를 구하는 대책이 분명히 비용 효과가 커 보인다. 98퍼센트라는 수치는 150명이라는 수치 자체가 주지 못하는 인식의 틀을 학생들에게 제공해 준다. 안전에 지출된 비용이 분별 있는 결정으로 보일지는 비교의 상황에 달려 있다. 안전 대책이 150명 중 98퍼센트를 구할 것이라는 이야기를 들었을 때, 150명과 150명의 98퍼센트 사이에서 인식의 틀이 만들어진다.

문제풀이 ③ 본동사 is의 주어 역할을 할 수 있어야 하므로 save를 동명사(saving) 또는 to부정사(to save)로 고쳐야 한다.
① 동사원형으로 시작하는 명령문
② it ~ to-v 가주어–진주어 구문
④ 수의 일치(단수명사 a measure가 주어이므로 단수동사 seems)
▶ p.190
⑤ whether절 주어

STEP 3 유형 **글의 목적**

1　①　2　②　3　①

1　①

해석 친애하는 Coling 씨께.
제 이름은 Susan Harris이며 Lockwood 고등학교 학생들을 대신하여 말씀드립니다. 우리 학교의 많은 학생들은 Lockwood 지역의 청년 실업 문제에 관한 프로젝트를 수행해 왔습니다. 4월 16일에 학교 강당에서 열리는 특별 발표회에 여러분들을 초대합니다. 발표회에서 학생들은 우리 지역에 있는 청년들을 위한 고용 기회를 만들어 내

기 위한 다양한 의견을 제안할 것입니다. 지역 사회의 저명인사 중 한 분으로서 귀하께서 참석해 주신다면 영광일 것입니다. 그곳에서 귀하를 뵐 수 있기를 기대합니다.

Susan Harris 드림

문제풀이 학생들이 프로젝트를 준비하여 개최하는 발표회에 참석하기를 요청하는 글이므로 ①이 가장 적절하다.

2 ②

해석 우리 호텔에 머물러 주셔서 감사합니다. 1976년에 호텔을 개업한 이래로 우리는 에너지 소비와 낭비를 줄임으로써 우리 지구를 보호하는 것에 헌신해 왔습니다. 지구를 보호하려는 노력으로, 우리는 새로운 정책을 채택했고, 여러분의 도움을 필요로 합니다. 만약 여러분이 문에 Eco 카드를 걸어 두시면, 우리는 여러분의 침대 시트와 베갯잇 그리고 잠옷을 교체하지 않을 것입니다. 또한, 컵이 씻길 필요가 없다면, 우리는 컵을 그대로 둘 것입니다. 여러분의 협조에 대한 보답으로 우리는 여러분을 대신하여 National Forest Restoration Project에 기부할 것입니다. 우리의 친환경 정책에 대한 여러분의 협조에 감사드립니다.

문제풀이 호텔이 환경 보호를 위해 취하는 여러 조치에 협조해 주기를 고객들에게 요청하는 글이므로 ②가 가장 적절하다.

구문분석

> [1행] [Since our hotel was opened in 1976], we have
> <u>S</u>
> <u>been committed</u> **to protecting** our planet [by reducing
> <u>V</u>
> our energy consumption and waste].
> ▶ '~하는 데 헌신하다'라는 의미의 commit oneself to는 수동태 형태가 현재완료시제와 결합하였으며 to는 전치사이므로 뒤에 (동) 명사가 온다. 첫 번째 [ ]는 '~이후로'라는 의미의 Since를 사용한 부사절이며, 두 번째 [ ]는 전치사 by가 이끄는 전치사구이다.

3 ①

해석 여러분은 지금까지 살았던 가장 위대한 사람들의 성공 비결을 배울 수 있다. 유명한 사람들의 삶이 전기에 기록되어 있어서 쉽게 읽고 연구할 수 있다. 위대한 정부 지도자, 사업가, 인도주의자들의 삶이 거기에 있다. 성공과 승리에 관하여 읽게 될 것이다. 또한 챔피언들이 승리하기까지 얼마나 많이 패배하는지도 알게 될 것이다. 전기를 읽으며, 자신이 그 위대한 사람들과 별로 다르지 않다는 놀라운 결론에 이르게 될지도 모른다. "그래, 나도 할 수 있다."라는 결론을 내릴 수도 있다. 자신의 삶을 의미 있게 만들 수 있다. 전기가 그 길을 안내하는 데 도움이 된다. 도서관이나 서점에 가거나 인터넷을 찾아보기만 하면 된다.

문제풀이 위대한 사람들의 성공 비결을 배우려면 그들의 전기를 읽어야 한다는 조언이므로 ①이 가장 적절하다.

구문분석

> [4행] You will also learn [**how many times** champions
> <u>S'</u>
> lose on their way to winning].
> <u>V'</u>
> ▶ [ ]는 「S+V+O(의문사절)」로 된 3형식 문장이며 명사의 기능을 하는 의문사절은 「의문사+S+V」의 어순이다.

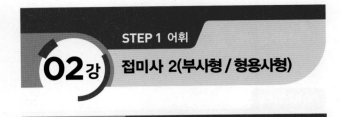

STEP 1 어휘

02강 접미사 2(부사형 / 형용사형)

PRACTICE
p.18

A
1 selfish 2 silently 3 lengthy
4 elementary 5 surrounding 6 hostile
7 forward 8 doubtful 9 humanoid
10 otherwise

B 1 ③ 2 ③ 3 ③ 4 ② 5 ②

C 1 hostile 2 lengthy

A

1 self+ish (이기적인) 2 silent+ly (조용히)
3 length+y (긴, 오랜) 4 element+ary (기본의)
5 surround+ing (둘러싸고 있는) 6 host+ile (적대적인)
7 for+ward (앞으로) 8 doubt+ful (의심스러운)
9 human+oid (인간 모양의) 10 other+wise (그렇지 않다면)

B

1 당신의 연구 제안서는 연구 목표에 대한 긴 논의가 포함되어야 한다.
2 준비위원회는 장례식 준비로 분주한 상태이다.
3 당신의 성공은 당신이 얼마나 폭넓게 공부를 하였느냐에 주로 좌우된다.
4 출판 연도를 고려했을 때, 그 책들은 최상의 상태이다.
5 우리가 어떤 행동을 반복할 때마다 무언가 새로운 것을 배우게 된다는 것은 의심할 여지가 없다.

C

1 자신의 작품들을 통해서 셰익스피어와 같은 작가들은 모든 등장인물이 끊임없이 가면을 쓰고 있다는 것을 암시하고 있다: 연극 *Othello* 속 Iago와 같은 악역들은 그들의 <u>적대적</u> 의도를 친근한 미소 뒤에 숨길 수 있다.
2 자신이 발명한 재봉틀의 특허권을 Isaac Singer가 도용했다는 사실을 알았을 때, Elias Howe는 Singer를 법정에 세우고 20년이라는 <u>오랜</u> 법정 공방 끝에 특허권 사용료를 받아낼 수 있었다.

적용독해
p.19

1 ③ 2 ④

1 ③

해석 물 위로 떠오르기 위해서, 물고기는 자신의 총 밀도를 낮춰야 하는데, 대부분의 물고기는 부레를 통해 그렇게 한다. 물고기는 주변 물에서 모은 산소로 자신의 부레를 채운다. 부레가 채워지면 그것은 팽창한다. 그 후, 물고기의 부피는 커지지만 무게는 크게 증가하지 않는다. 이것은 물고기의 밀도가 낮아졌음을 의미하고, 따라서 물고기는 더 큰 부력을 경험하게 된다. 마침내 부레가 완전히 팽창되었을 때, 물고기는 부피가 최소치(→ 최대치)가 되고 수면으로 떠오른다. 대부분의 물고기는 이런 방법으로 부상하지만 전부 그런 것은 아니다. 일부 물고기 종은 평생을 바다 밑바닥에서 움직이며 살아가기 때문에 부레가 필요 없다. 다른 물고기들은 앞으로 헤엄치면서 뜨거나 가라앉는다.

문제풀이 부레가 완전히 팽팽해질 때까지 산소를 채우면 물고기의 부피는 최대치가 되어 수면으로 떠오른다고 했으므로 ③ minimum은 maximum 등으로 고쳐야 한다.

구문분석

[7행] Some species don't need a swim bladder [because they spend all their lives moving along the ocean floor].
V   O'   O.C.'
▶ [ ]는 이유의 접속사 because로 시작하는 부사절이며, 그 부사절 속에 '[시간을] …하며 지내다'라는 의미의 「spend+O+(in) 현재분사」가 쓰였다.

2 ④

해석 어떻게 들리는지 들어 보기 위해서 여러분 자신의 에세이를 큰소리로 읽는 것이 도움이 될 수 있고, 때때로 다른 누군가가 그것을 읽는 것을 듣는 것이 훨씬 더 이로울 수 있다. 어느 쪽의 읽기든 그렇게 하지 않을 경우에 당신이 조용히 편집할 때 알아채지 못할지도 모르는 것들을 듣는 데 도움이 될 것이다. 하지만 누군가가 당신에게 읽어 주도록 하는 것이 불편하거나, 그것을 요청할 수 있는 누군가가 없다면, 컴퓨터가 여러분의 에세이를 여러분에게 읽어 주도록 할 수 있다. 물론, 그것은 완전히 똑같은 것은 아니고, 컴퓨터는 여러분에게 어떤 것이 '맞는 것처럼 들리지' 않을 때 이를 말해 주지 않을 것이다. 컴퓨터는 또한 어색한 것들에 대해서 더듬거리지도 않을 것이며, 그저 끝까지 계속해 나갈 것이다. 하지만 컴퓨터가 여러분의 글을 읽는 것을 듣는 것은 여러분이 그것을 직접 읽는 것과는 매우 유사한(→ 다른) 경험이다. 여러분이 그것을 시도해 본 적이 없다면, 이전에 알아채지 못했던 수정, 편집 및 교정이 필요한 부분들을 알아차리게 된다는 것을 알게 될 것이다.

문제풀이 컴퓨터가 글을 읽어 주는 것은 수정, 편집 및 교정에 있어서 우리가 직접 읽는 것보다 더 도움이 된다는 내용이므로 ④ similar는 different 등으로 고쳐야 한다.

구문분석

[2행] Either reading will help you to hear things that [you might otherwise not notice] when editing silently.
▶ [ ]는 otherwise 가정법 과거 구문이며, '그렇지 않으면 ~하는'의 의미이며, 「조동사의 과거형+otherwise+동사원형」의 구조이다.

PRACTICE
p.20

A	
	1 → is / was
	2 → who suffer / suffering
	3 → that are designed / designed
	4 → include
	5 → had
B	1 degraded 2 starting

A

1 내가 어제 산 그 사전은 초등학생용이다. ▶ 문장의 본동사 자리
2 괴롭힘으로 고통 받는 학생들의 수가 증가하고 있다. ▶ 본동사(is)가 있으므로 관계대명사절이나 현재분사 자리(「주격 관계대명사+be-v」 생략 가능)
3 인간의 행동을 모방하도록 설계된 휴머노이드 로봇은 널리 사용된다. ▶ 본동사(are)가 있으므로 관계대명사절이나 과거분사 자리(「주격 관계대명사+be-v」 생략 가능)
4 그녀는 불필요한 정보가 포함된 메시지를 보내지 않는다. ▶ 「선행사+주격 관계대명사+동사」
5 내가 집에 도착하자마자 내 폰이 없어진 사실을 깨달았다. ▶ 「no sooner+had+S+p.p.+than+S+과거동사」

B

1 남아프리카 공화국에서 외래 식물의 도입은 자연 식물 군락을 교란하고 피폐하게 하는 결과를 가져왔는데, 남아프리카 공화국의 서부 지역으로 도입된 호주 관목이 그 지역에서 풍부한 종의 핀보스 식물 군락을 퇴화시켰다. ▶ 문장의 본동사
2 1960년대 중반에 시작된 차량 및 도로에 관한 안전 법규를 폭넓게 도입함에 따라, 연간 주행 마일 수가 거의 300% 증가했음에도 불구하고, 고속도로 사망자 수는 1966년 대략 51,000명에서 2000년 42,000명으로 감소하였다. ▶ 문장의 본동사(led)가 있으므로 laws를 수식하는 현재분사 자리

적용독해
p.21

1 ④   2 ②

1 ④

해석 1970년대 중반에 어떤 과학자들이 미국에 있는 두 군데의 제조 공장 근로자들을 관찰했다. 안타깝게도 두 공장 모두 문을 닫기로 되어 있었다. 평균적으로 각자의 공장에서 20년 동안 근무하고 있었던 직원들은 대비할 겨를도 없이 실직을 당할 참이었다. 이 노동자들을 추적한 과학자들이 발견한 것은 그들이 실직 이후의 그 몇 주 동안보

다 공장이 문을 닫기 전에 몸이 아픈 날이 더 많았다는 것이었다. 자신의 직업 상실을 예상한 것에 의해 야기된 불안감은 그들의 건강과 안녕에 피해를 입혔다. 역설적이게도, 일단 실직이 되자 그 노동자들은 더 건강해졌다. 그것은 일자리가 없다면 삶이 어떻게 될 것인가에 대한 불확실성이 제거되었기 때문이었다. 불안감은 줄어들었고, 장차 일어날 수도 있는 일에 대해 그저 걱정만 하기보다는 관심이 새로운 일자리를 찾는 데로 돌려졌다.

문제풀이 ④ 부사절의 동사 자리이므로 주어 the uncertainty의 수와 시제에 맞게 being을 was로 고쳐야 한다.
① 본동사(were)가 있으므로 주어를 수식하는 현재분사
② 문장의 본동사
③ 문장의 본동사
⑤ 비교구문을 이용한 병렬 구조(to finding ~ rather than worrying) ▶ p.206

2 ②

해석 운동 영양학이 매우 새로운 학문 분야이긴 하지만, 선수들의 운동 기량을 향상할 수 있게 하는 음식에 관한 충고는 늘 존재해 왔다. 고대 그리스의 한 운동선수는 컨디션을 향상하기 위해 말린 무화과를 먹었다고 전해진다. 1908년 올림픽에서 마라톤 선수들은 기량을 향상하기 위하여 코냑을 마셨다는 보고가 있다. 1970년대에 스포츠계를 놀라게 한 십 대 달리기 천재인 Mary Decker는 경주 전날 밤 스파게티 한 접시를 먹었다고 말했다. 그러한 관행은 그것의 실제적인 이득 혹은 자신의 운동 분야에서 탁월한 능력을 보인 개인들이 인식한 이득 때문에 운동선수들에게 권고될 수도 있다. 분명 마라톤 중에 술을 마시는 것과 같은 이러한 관행 중 일부는 더 이상 추천되지 않지만, 경기 전날 밤의 고탄수화물 식사와 같은 다른 관행은 세월의 검증을 견뎌냈다.

문제풀이 ② 본동사(reported)가 있으므로 surprised를 주어를 수식하는 계속적 용법의 관계대명사절(who surprised)로 바꿔야 한다.
▶ p.174
① that절의 동사
③ 선행사+주격 관계대명사+동사 ▶ p.174
④ 문장의 본동사
⑤ 수일 일치 ▶ p.190

STEP 3 유형 **심경**

pp.22~23

1 ④   2 ①   3 ⑤

1 ④

해석 시합이 끝난 지 한 시간이 넘어서 내가 특별히 중압감을 느낄 필요가 없다. 나는 심신이 피곤해서 편안하게 쉬면서 차가운 음료를 즐기기 위해 앉아 있다. 그러나 어떤 이유에선지, 나는 신경을 끌 수가 없다. 마음속으로 나는 내가 내렸던 모든 결정을 검토해 본다. 나는 다른 심판들이 내가 했던 것에 대해 어떻게 생각할지 특히 궁금하다. 내가 했던 실수가 걱정이 되고, 관중들의 이의가 여전히 나의 귓속에서 맴돌고 있다. 나는 계속 나 자신에게 말을 한다. "게임은 잊어.",

"동료들과 나는 모든 사안에 동의했어.", "전반적으로, 나는 잘해냈어." 그러나 아무리 걱정을 털어내려고 해도 여전히 걱정이 된다.

문제풀이 시간이 갈수록 심판이 내 실수에 대해 어떻게 생각할지 신경이 쓰이고 걱정이 된다는 내용이므로 정답은 ④이다.

구문분석

[5행] I am concerned [about having made] mistakes.
▶ [ ]는 「전치사+목적어(동명사)」로 목적어가 단순동명사(making) 대신에 완료동명사(having made)로 쓰인 이유는 실수를 한 행동이 문장의 시제(am)보다 이전에 발생했기 때문이다.

2 ①

해석 Garnet은 촛불들을 불어서 끄고 누웠다. 심지어 홑이불 한 장조차 너무 더운 날이었다. 그녀는 땀을 흘리면서 비를 가져오지 않는 공허한 천둥소리를 들으면서 그곳에 누워 있었고, "나는 이 가뭄이 끝났으면 좋겠어."라고 속삭였다. 그날 밤늦게, Garnet은 그녀가 기다려 온 무언가가 곧 일어날 것 같은 기분이 들었다. 그녀는 귀를 기울이며 가만히 누워 있었다. 그 천둥은 더 큰 소리를 내면서 다시 우르르 울렸다. 그러고 나서 천천히, 하나하나씩, 마치 누군가가 지붕에 동전을 떨어뜨리는 것처럼 빗방울이 떨어졌다. Garnet은 희망에 차서 숨죽였다. 그 소리가 잠시 멈췄다. "멈추지 마! 제발!" 그녀는 속삭였다. 그런 다음 그 비는 세차고 요란하게 세상에 쏟아졌다. Garnet은 침대 밖으로 뛰쳐나와 창문으로 달려갔다. 그녀는 기쁨에 차서 소리쳤다. "비가 쏟아진다!" 그녀는 그 뇌우가 선물처럼 느껴졌다.

문제풀이 가뭄이 끝나기를 간절히 바라고 있었는데 마침내 비가 오자 기뻐 흥분한다는 내용이므로 정답은 ①이다.

구문분석

[2행] I wish [(that) the drought would end].
▶ I wish 가정법 과거 문장으로 「(that)+주어+조동사의 과거형+동사원형」으로 이루어져 있으며 '가뭄이 끝나면 좋으련만/좋을 텐데'로 해석한다.

[3행] Late in the night, Garnet had a feeling [that something {she had been waiting for} was about to happen].
▶ [ ]는 명사절 접속사 that이 이끌며 a feeling과 동격을 나타낸다. { }는 선행사 something을 수식하는 목적격 관계대명사가 생략된 관계사절이다.

3 ⑤

해석 Rowe는 거의 아무도 탐험하지 않은 장소에 있는 것을 좋아하기 때문에 그는 동굴을 발견하고 기쁨에 폴짝 뛴다. 동굴 입구에서 그는 나중에 그의 새로운 모험을 뽐내기 위해 휴대폰으로 사진을 계속 찍는다. 동굴 입구로부터 몇 미터 떨어진 바위에 멈추어서, 그는 얼음 동굴의 빛나는 광경을 본다. 그는 얼음으로 된 벽을 만지기 위해 손을 뻗으면서 "믿을 수 없을 정도로 아름답군!"이라고 말한다. 갑자기 그는 발을 헛디뎌 어둠 속으로 미끄러져 들어간다. 그는 위를 올려다보고 대략 20미터 위에 있는 틈의 빛을 본다. '전화로 도움을 요청해야

지.'라고 그는 생각한다. 하지만 그는 이렇게 깊은 지하에서는 (통화) 서비스가 되지 않는다는 것을 깨닫는다. 그는 위로 올라가려고 하지만 올라갈 수 없다. 그는 "거기 누구 있나요?"라고 외친다. 응답이 없다.

문제풀이 동굴을 발견한 흥분감이 이내 발을 헛디뎌 지하에 갇힌 후 전화마저 이용할 수 없는 절망감으로 바뀌었으므로 정답은 ⑤이다.

구문분석

[4행] He says, "Incredibly beautiful!" [stretching his hand out to touch the icy wall].
▶ [ ]는 부사절(as he is stretching...)이 분사구문으로 전환된 현재분사구로 동시동작을 의미하는 부대상황이다.

PRACTICE
p.26

A	1 accumulate	2 abnormal	3 device
	4 observe	5 interstellar	6 deny
	7 afford	8 retire	9 telescope
	10 undergo		
B	1 ④	2 ③	3 ①
C	1 impress	2 undergo	3 anticipate
	4 adequate	5 abnormal	
D	1 impressive	2 postpone	

A

1 ac(to)+cumulate: 축적하다
2 ab(away)+normal: 비정상적인
3 de(apart)+vice: 장치
4 ob(to, against)+serve: 관찰하다
5 inter(between)+stellar: (행)성간의
6 de(completely)+ny: 부정하다
7 af(to)+ford: ~할 여유가 있다
8 re(back)+tire: 퇴직하다
9 tele(far from)+scope: 망원경
10 under(beneath)+go: 겪다

B

1 im(not)+possible
2 in(not)+convenient
3 ab(away)+normal

C

1 선생님은 그의 능력에 깊은 인상을 받았다.
2 그 나라는 금융 위기를 겪고 있다.
3 그 여정은 우리가 예상한 것보다 더 오래 걸렸다.
4 이 컴퓨터는 프로 게이머들에게는 적합하지 않다.
5 인터뷰 전에 긴장하는 것은 비정상적이지 않다.

D

1 광고 전문가들은 역대 가장 기억에 남고 효과적인 광고들은 인상적인 줄거리(스토리라인)를 포함하고 있기 때문에 우리가 기억하는 광고들이 우리를 이야기 속으로 끌어들이려 한다는 것을 알게 되었다.
2 예정된 휴식들은 자기 강화의 전략적인 방법이 됨으로써 순조롭게 일이 진행되도록 하는 반면, 미리 계획되지 않은 휴식들은 마치 '자

유 시간'이 있다고 느끼게 만듦으로써 일정을 <u>미루게</u> 되는 기회를 제공하기 때문에 목표에서 벗어나게 한다.

적용독해

p.27

1 ③   2 ④

---

1 ③

해석 모든 사람은 세상 물정에 매우 밝지만, 학교에서는 부진한 어떤 젊은이를 알고 있다. 우리는 삶에서 많은 것에 대해 매우 똑똑한 사람이 그 똑똑함을 학업에 적용할 수 없는 것처럼 보이는 것이 낭비라고 생각한다. 우리가 깨닫지 못하는 것은 학교나 대학이 그러한 세상 물정에 밝은 사람들을 끌어들여 그들을 뛰어난 학업으로 안내해 줄 기회를 놓치는 잘못을 하고 있을지도 모른다는 것이다. 또한 우리는 왜 학교와 대학이 세상 물정에 밝은 사람들의 지적 잠재력을 <u>알아차리는지(→ 간과하는지)</u>에 대한 주요한 이유 중 하나를 고려하지 않는다. 말하자면 우리는 이러한 세상 물정에 밝은 사람들을 반지성적인 근심거리와 연관시킨다는 사실이다. 우리는 교육받은 삶, 지성인의 삶을 우리가 본질적으로 중요하며 학문적이라고 고려하는 과목과 교과서에 지나치게 좁게 연관시킨다.

문제풀이 학교 성적은 부진하지만 세상 물정에 밝은 사람들을 반지성적이며 학업에는 적응을 못할 거라는 선입견이 그들의 잠재력을 간과하게 만드는 요인이라는 내용이므로 ③ notice는 overlook 등으로 고쳐야 한다.

구문분석

[2행] We think [(that) **it** is a waste {**that** one who is so intelligent about so many things in life seems unable to apply that intelligence to academic work}].
▶ 「S+V+O」의 3형식 문장이며, [ ]는 명사절의 접속사 that이 생략된 목적절이다. { }는 목적절 속에서 가주어(it)−진주어(that절)의 that절을 가리킨다.

2 ④

해석 사람들은 삶이 나아질수록 더 높은 기대감을 지닌다. 하지만 기대감이 더 높아질수록 만족감을 느끼기는 더욱 어려워진다. 우리들은 기대감을 통제함으로써 삶에서 느끼는 만족감을 향상시킬 수 있다. 적절한 기대감은 많은 경험들을 즐거운 놀라움이 되도록 하는 여지를 남긴다. 과제는 적절한 기대감을 가지는 방법을 찾는 것이다. 이것을 위한 한 방법은 멋진 경험들을 드문 상태로 유지하는 것이다. 당신이 무엇이든 살 여유가 있더라도, 특별한 행사를 위해 훌륭한 와인을 아껴 두어라. 품위 있는 실크 블라우스를 특별한 즐거움이 되게 하라. 이것은 당신의 욕구를 <u>받아들이는(→ 억제하는)</u> 행동처럼 보일 수도 있지만, 내 생각은 그렇지 않다. 반대로, 그것은 당신이 즐거움을 계속해서 경험할 수 있도록 보장해 주는 방법이다. 멋진 와인과 멋진 블라우스가 당신을 기분 좋게 만들지 못한다면 무슨 의미가 있겠는가?

문제풀이 기대감을 통제함으로써 삶의 만족감을 향상시킬 수 있는데 그 과정이 우리의 욕구를 억제하는 것처럼 보일 수 있다는 내용이므

로 ④ accepting은 denying 등으로 고쳐야 한다.

구문분석

[6행] [No matter what you can afford], <u>save</u> <u>great wine</u>
                                          V   O
for upcoming special occasions.
▶ 「부사절+명령문」으로 된 문장으로, [ ]는 「no matter+what 관계대명사절」로 이루어져 있다. '무엇이든 ~하더라도'의 의미인 no matter what은 복합관계대명사 whatever로 바꾸어 쓸 수 있다.

STEP 2 어법 목적어

PRACTICE

p.28

A 1 to do   2 to cross
      3 eating   4 to do
      5 becoming   6 embarrassing
      7 to speak   8 to write
      9 themselves   10 itself
B 1 that   2 to make

A

1 그 여자는 규칙적인 운동을 하기로 계획했다. ▶ plan+to-v
2 나는 강을 건너려고 시도했다. ▶ attempt+to-v
3 Jane은 아침 식사를 마쳤다. ▶ finish+v-ing
4 그는 부상을 당한 후에 그 일을 하는데 어려움을 겪었다.
  ▶ struggle+to-v
5 그들은 교사가 되는 것에 대해 이야기했다. ▶ 전치사+v-ing
6 그 계획은 우리로 하여금 그 아이를 당황하게 하지 않으면서 도울 수 있도록 했다. ▶ 전치사+v-ing
7 위원회는 그의 제안을 받아들이지 않을 것이다. ▶ what+불완전한 구조
8 그는 영어로 이메일을 쓰는 것이 어렵다고 생각했다. ▶ 가목적어−진목적어 구문
9 돌고래는 서로를 모방하는데 있어 스스로를 제한하지 않는다.
  ▶ 주어와 목적어가 같아 재귀대명사 필요
10 자신의 독을 사용하여 그 물고기는 포식자로부터 자신을 보호한다. ▶ 주어와 목적어가 같아 재귀대명사 필요

B

1 연구에 따르면 많은 기생 생물들은 자신들이 옮겨질 수 있도록 그들의 숙주로 하여금 다른 잠재적인 숙주를 공격하거나, 죽임을 당하게 하고 잡아먹히도록 만든다. ▶ 명사절 접속사 that+완전한 절
2 Dudley 동물원을 방문하는 대부분의 방문객들은 매표소가 붐빌 수 있으니 동물원 웹사이트에 접속하여 예매를 하는 것이 편리하다고 생각한다. ▶ 가목적어−진목적어 구문

1 ③   2 ④

1 ②   2 ⑤   3 ②

1 ③

해석 그가 그것을 해낸 첫 번째 사람은 아닐지라도 네덜란드의 안경알 제작자 Hans Lippershey는 1608년에 한 개의 관 양쪽 끝에 두 개의 렌즈를 붙여 '소형 망원경'을 만든 것에 대해 인정을 받고 있다. 심지어 그때도, 두 개의 렌즈가 가까운 풍향계를 더 크게 보이도록 한다는 것을 발견한 사람은 Lippershey가 아니라 그의 아이들이었다. 그 렌즈들은 매우 강한 것이 아니었기 때문에 이런 초기 도구들은 장난감에 지나지 않았다. 소형 망원경을 하늘로 향하게 한 첫 번째 사람은 Galileo Galilei라는 이름을 가진 이탈리아 수학자이자 교수였다. 네덜란드의 소형 망원경에 대해 듣고 자기만의 소형 망원경을 만들기 시작했던 Galileo는 그 장치가 군대와 선원들에게 얼마나 유용할지를 즉시 깨달았다. 나중에 망원경이라 불리게 된, 더욱 개선된 소형 망원경들을 만들면서 Galileo는 망원경을 행성간 공간으로 향하게 했다.

문제풀이 ③ 문장에 본동사가 없으므로 to be를 was로 고쳐야 한다.
① for(전치사)+putting과 병렬되는 것으로 creating 앞에 for가 생략
② 명사절 접속사 that
④ 명사절 역할의 의문사절로 「의문사+S+V」 구조
⑤ 「decide+to-v」 ▶ p.134

2 ④

해석 우주의 불가사의한 것들에 관한 답을 찾는 많은 방법이 있고, 과학은 이러한 것들 중 단지 하나이다. 그러나 과학은 독특하다. 추측하는 대신에 과학자들은 그들의 생각이 사실인지 거짓인지 증명하도록 고안된 체계를 따른다. 그들은 그들의 이론과 결론을 끊임없이 재검토하고 시험한다. 기존의 생각들은 과학자들이 설명할 수 없는 새로운 정보를 찾을 때 대체된다. 누군가가 발견을 하면, 다른 사람들은 그들 자신의 연구에서 그 정보를 사용하기 전에 그것을 주의 깊게 검토한다. 더 이전의 발견들에 새로운 지식을 쌓아가는 이러한 방법은 과학자들이 그들의 실수를 바로잡는 것을 보장한다. 과학적 지식으로 무장해서, 사람들은 우리가 사는 방식을 변화시키는 도구와 기기를 만들고, 그것은 우리의 삶을 훨씬 더 쉽고 나아지게 만든다.

문제풀이 ④ 선행사가 없고 완전한 절이 이어지므로 what을 명사절 접속사 that으로 바꿔야 한다. ▶ p.84
① 「전치사+v-ing」
② 명사절 접속사 if(~인지 아닌지)
③ 단수 명사 a discovery를 가리키는 목적격 대명사 ▶ p.166
⑤ 선행사 machines에 맞는 주격 관계대명사 뒤의 복수 동사
▶ p.174

1 ②

해석 (어떤 일을) 미루게 될 때, 어떻게 하면 그 버릇으로부터, 그날 하루의 가장 힘든 일을 해내도록 바뀔까? 나는 "개구리를 먹어라(싫은 일을 먼저 해라)!"고 말한다. 그 생각은 Mark Twain의 말을 인용한 것이다: "하루 중, 아침에 살아있는 개구리를 제일 먼저 먹어라, 그러면 그 이후에는 그보다 더 나쁜 어떤 일도 여러분에게 일어나지 않을 것이다." 매일 아침, 가장 하기 싫지만 해야 하는 일들의 항목을 처리하는데 전념하라, 그리고 다른 어떤 것들보다 먼저 그 일을 하라. 아침 시간은 특히, 여러분의 정신을 산만하게 하는 것들이 적고 근무 시간 동안 쌓이는 스트레스가 없는 시간대이기 때문에, 글쓰기와 같은 창의적인 일들을 하기 위해 생산적이어야 할, 가장 이상적인 시간대이다. 꺼려지는 일에 제일 먼저 뛰어드는 동안, 그 장애물을 마침내 극복하고 여러분 앞에 온전한 하루가 남았을 때 얼마나 기분이 좋을지를 상상해 보라.

문제풀이 필자는 사람들이 보통은 어렵고 힘든 일을 미루는 경향이 있지만 차라리 아침에 먼저 해결하면 훨씬 도움이 된다고 주장하고 있다.

구문분석

> [1행] [Engaged in procrastination], how do you move **[from being** stuck **to doing** the day's most difficult tasks]?
> ▶ 첫 번째 [ ]는 When you are engaged in procrastination을 분사구문으로 전환한 경우이다. 두 번째 [ ]는 from A to B의 전치사구로 「전치사+v-ing」로 나타내고 있다.

2 ⑤

해석 대부분의 사람들은 자신의 역할을 충분히 자주 평가하지 않아서 차선의 상황에 안주하며 머물러야 하는 것보다 더 오래 여러 해 동안 그들의 위치에 머무른다. 그것이 옳은지 아닌지를 평가하기 전에 여러분이 하나의 역할에 머물러야 하는 시간의 양에 관한 마법의 숫자는 없다. 그러나 얼마나 자주 그러는지에 대해 생각하는 것은 이치에 맞다. 일부 사람들은 매일 혹은 매주 자신의 삶을 재조정하며 끊임없이 삶을 최적화시킨다. 다른 사람들은 여러 해를 기다리고 나서야 자신이 희망했던 곳과는 결국 떨어진 곳에 있다는 사실을 알아차리게 된다. 여러분이 문제를 해결하기 위한 방법을 찾으면서 여러분의 상황을 더 자주 평가하면 할수록 일들이 잘 되어 가고 있는 위치에 있는 자신을 더 많이 발견하게 될 가능성이 있다.

문제풀이 필자는 문제 해결 노력과 함께 자신의 상황을 더 자주 평가하고 재조정하면서 삶을 최적화시킬 수 있어야 발전할 수 있다고 주장하고 있다.

구문분석

[6행] **The more frequently** you assess your situation, [looking for ways to fix problems], **the more likely** you are to find yourself in a position [where things are going well].

▶「The 비교급 ~, the 비교급 ~」 구문으로 '~하면 할수록, 더 ~하다'라는 의미를 갖는다. 첫 번째 [ ]는 동시상황을 나타내는 분사구문을 나타내고 있으며, 두 번째 [ ]는 선행사 a position 을 수식하는 관계부사구이다.

3 ②

해석 The Pumpkin Plan의 작가인 Mike Michalowicz는 코미디언들이 최고의 대중 연설가라고 주장한다. 예를 들어, 코미디언들은 청중들의 주의를 한 시간 이상 끌어야 하고, 공연을 하는 동안 쉬지도 못하고, 청중들과 질의응답을 하면서 상호 작용을 할 수도 없다. 그들은 또한 그들이 청중들을 끊임없이 웃길 것이라고 예상된다. 그리고 청중들이 화면을 보려고 애쓰는 것이 아니라 자신들을 바라보기를 원하기 때문에, 발표를 위한 소프트웨어 프로그램조차 사용하지 않는다. 이러한 사실들은 당신이 공연을 잘하는 무대 위의 코미디언이 되어야 한다는 뜻은 아니다. 당신은 심지어 농담을 할 필요도 없다. 그러나 당신의 발표 기술을 향상시키기 위해서는 코미디언이 사용하는 테크닉을 관찰하고, 당신의 연설에 그것들을 활용하라.

문제풀이 필자는 연설이나 발표를 할 때 코미디언들이 공연에서 사용하는 기법과 방식을 본받아 활용하면 훌륭한 연설이나 발표가 될 수 있다고 주장하고 있다.

구문분석

[6행] These facts don't mean [(that) you need to be a comedian on stage {to perform well}].

▶[ ]는 동사 mean의 목적절로 쓰인 that 명사절로 접속사 that이 생략된 것이며, { }는 앞의 명사 a comedian을 수식하는 형용사적 용법의 to부정사구이다.

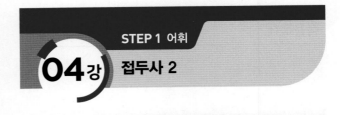

PRACTICE   p.34

A	1 select	2 diverse	3 diameter
	4 hemisphere	5 transmit	6 perceive
	7 output	8 present	9 downside
	10 supernatural		
B	1 ②	2 ③	3 ③
C	1 downsides	2 diverse	
	3 inevitable	4 agree	
	5 subtle		
D	1 by-product	2 specialized	

A

1 se(apart)+lect: 선별하다
2 di(away)+verse: 다양한
3 dia(across)+meter: 직경
4 hemi(half)+sphere: 반구
5 trans(across)+mit: 전송하다
6 per(completely)+ceive: 인지하다
7 out(out)+put: 산출
8 pre(before)+sent: 현재의
9 down(down)+side: 단점
10 super(over)+natural: 초자연적인

B

1 per(completely)+ceive
2 dis(away)+connected
3 post(after)+pone

C

1 일찍 결혼하는 것은 장단점이 있다.
2 그들은 스포츠에서 공학에 이르기까지 다양한 화제에 대해 이야기했다.
3 갈등은 때로 불가피할 수도 있지만, 노력을 통해 종종 피할 수도 있다.
4 대부분의 과학자들은 지구 온난화가 심각한 문제라는 데 동의한다.
5 얼굴 표정은 아주 미묘해서 정확히 알기 어렵다.

D

1 나무에서 떨어지는 산출물인 도토리는 그것을 먹는 다람쥐에게 중요한 투입물이다. 그 맛있는 식사의 부산물인 다람쥐 배설물은 그

것을 섭취하는 미생물에게 중요한 투입물이다.
2 인간의 뇌(대략 1.5kg, 1,500cc, 직경 15cm)가 비슷한 크기의 다른 포유류에 비해 아주 큰 이유는 큰 뇌가 개인들이 다른 사람들과 상호 작용을 할 필요가 있는 큰 집단에서 일반적으로 발생하는 문제들을 다루는 데 <u>전문화되어</u> 있다는 것이다.

적용독해

1 ④   2 ③

---

1 ④

해석 창의력은 우리가 일반적으로 인간만이 유일하게 가지고 있다고 간주하는 능력이다. 인류 역사를 통틀어, 우리는 지구상에서 가장 창의적인 존재였다. 새는 둥지를 틀 수 있고, 개미는 개미탑을 쌓을 수 있지만, 지구상의 어떤 다른 종도 우리 인간이 보여 주는 창의력 수준에 가까이 도달하지는 못한다. 하지만, 불과 지난 10년 만에 우리는 로봇 개발처럼, 컴퓨터로 놀라운 것을 할 수 있는 능력을 습득하였다. 2010년대의 인공 지능의 몰락(→ 급속한 발전)으로, 컴퓨터는, 몇 가지를 언급하자면, 이제 얼굴을 인식하고, 언어를 번역하고, 여러분을 대신해 전화를 받고, 시를 쓸 수 있으며 세계에서 가장 복잡한 보드게임에서 선수들을 이길 수 있다. 갑작스럽게, 우리는 우리의 창의력이 경쟁할 상대가 없지 않게 되는 가능성에 직면해야 할 것이다.

문제풀이 예전에는 인간이 가장 창의적인 존재였지만, 인공 지능으로 무장한 컴퓨터가 새로운 경쟁 상대로 급속도로 등장하는 가능성에 직면해야 한다는 내용이므로 ④ setback은 boom 등으로 고쳐야 한다.

구문분석

[1행] Creativity is a skill [(that) we usually consider uniquely human].
    O.C.
▶ [ ]는 원래 5형식 문장 we consider a skill uniquely human에서 a skill (that) we consider uniquely human으로 목적어 였던 a skill을 선행사로 하는 목적격 관계대명사절이 되었다.

---

2 ③

해석 나는 어느 여름날 저녁 스페인의 한 식당 밖에 앉아 저녁 식사를 기다리고 있었다. 주방의 향기가 나의 미뢰를 자극했다. 곧 먹게 될 내 음식은, 너무 작아 눈으로 볼 수는 없지만 코로는 감지되는, 대기 중을 떠다니는 분자의 형태로 내게 오고 있었다. 고대 그리스인들에게 이런 식으로 원자의 개념이 최초로 떠올랐는데, 빵 굽는 냄새는 그들에게 작은 빵 입자가 눈에 보이지 않게 존재한다는 생각이 들게 했다. 날씨의 순환이 이 생각이 틀렸음을 입증했다(→ (생각)을 강화했다). 지면 위 물웅덩이는 점차 말라 사라지고, 그런 다음 나중에 비가 되어 떨어진다. 수증기로 변하여 구름을 형성하고 땅으로 떨어지는 물 입자가 존재하는 게 틀림없고, 그래서 그 작은 입자들이 너무 작아 눈에 보이지 않더라도 그 물은 보존된다고 그들은 추론했다. 스페인

에서의 나의 파에야가 원자 이론에 대한 공로를 인정받기에는 4천 년이나 너무 늦게 내게 영감을 주었다.

문제풀이 고대 그리스인들이 냄새를 통해 눈에 보이지 않는 빵 입자가 존재하고 날씨의 순환을 통해 눈에 보이지 않는 물 입자가 존재한다고 추론했다는 내용을 통해 알 수 있듯이 ③ disproved는 reinforced 등으로 고쳐야 한다.

구문분석

[3행] My future meal was coming to me in the form of <u>molecules</u> [(which were) drifting through the atmosphere, too small for my eyes to see but detected by my nose].
▶ [ ]는 분사 drifting과 too samll, 그리고 detected 앞에 「주격 관계대명사+be-v」가 각각 생략되어 병렬을 이루는 분사구이다.

STEP 2 어법   보어 1(2형식)

PRACTICE

A
1 importantly → important
2 healthily → healthy
3 personally → personal
4 extinction → extinct
5 thirstily → thirsty

B
1 possible   2 effective

A

1 아침 식사는 하루 세끼 중 가장 중요하다. ▶「be-v+형용사 보어」
2 규칙적인 운동은 여러분의 신체를 건강하게 유지하도록 한다는 점을 명심해라. ▶「2형식 동사 keep+형용사 보어」
3 과거 10년 동안 지도 제작의 상당한 변화는 지도 제작이 개인적인 것으로 되었다는 점이다. ▶「2형식 동사 become+형용사 보어」
4 세계 곳곳에서 수천 종의 생물이 조용히 멸종되고 있다. ▶「2형식 동사 go+형용사 보어」
5 여러분의 뇌가 쪼그라들고 있기 때문에 여러분의 몸을 절대 갈증 나게 만들지 마라. ▶「2형식 동사 get+형용사 보어」

B

1 사람이 자신의 행동에 대한 결과를 다른 방식으로 해석하는 것이 가능하다. 이것은 필연적으로 자신의 미래 동기 부여와 행동에 영향을 미치게 된다. ▶「be-v+형용사 보어」
2 털가죽은 몸에 밀착되지 않기 때문에 더 많은 공기가 몸과 옷 사이에 들어올수록 그것은 공기의 단열층을 피부와 가까이에 있도록 가둬 두는 데 덜 효과적이다. ▶「be-v+형용사 보어」

정답 및 해설 **11**

1 ④   2 ②

1 ④

해석 운동하는 동안 편안함을 제공하기 위해 의류가 비쌀 필요는 없다. 기온과 운동하고 있을 환경 조건에 적절한 의류를 선택하라. 따뜻한 환경에서는 수분을 흡수하거나 배출할 수 있는 기능을 가진 옷이 몸에서 열을 발산하는 데 도움이 된다. 반면, 땀을 흘리는 것을 피하고 쾌적한 상태를 유지하기 위해 체온을 조절하려면 겹겹이 입어서 추운 환경에 대처하는 것이 최선이다. 쌀쌀한 날씨에 하는 운동에 적절한 의류는 따뜻한 느낌을 주어 운동 경험을 향상시킬 수 있다.

문제풀이 ④ 2형식 동사 remain 뒤에 형용사 보어가 와야 하므로 comfortably를 comfortable로 고쳐야 한다.
① 형용사구가 명사 clothing을 뒤에서 수식
② 「be-v+형용사 보어」
③ 「be-v+형용사의 최상급(good – better – best)」
⑤ 「2형식 동사 feel+형용사 보어」

2 ②

해석 각 종의 동물들은 서로 다른 범주의 냄새를 감지할 수 있다. 어떤 종도 그것이 살고 있는 환경에 존재하는 모든 분자를 감지할 수는 없는데, 우리는 냄새를 맡을 수 없지만 몇몇 다른 동물들은 냄새를 맡을 수 있는 몇 가지 것들이 있고, 그 반대의 경우도 있다. 어떤 냄새를 맡을 수 있는 능력이나 그것이 얼마나 좋은 느낌을 주는지와 관련된 개체들 사이의 차이 역시 존재한다. 예를 들어, 어떤 사람들은 미국에서 고수(cilantro)라고 알려진 고수(coriander)의 맛을 좋아하는 반면, 다른 사람들은 그것이 비누 맛이 나고 불쾌하다고 여긴다. 이러한 결과에는 우리의 후각을 조절하는 유전자 차이로 인한 내재된 유전적 요소가 있다. 궁극적으로, 특정 종에 의해 감지된 냄새들의 집합 그리고 그 냄새가 어떻게 인식되는가는 그 동물의 생태에 달려 있을 것이다. 이를 통해 각 종과 관련된 냄새의 원천을 찾고 그에 따라 반응하는 것이 가능해 진다.

문제풀이 ② 2형식 동사 seem이 있으므로 pleasantly를 pleasant로 고쳐야 한다.
① 「be-v+형용사 보어」
③ 「5형식 동사 find+목적어+형용사 보어」 ▶ p.44
④ 「의문사+주어+동사」인 의문사절의 주어 역할 ▶ p.84
⑤ 「be-v+형용사 보어」

STEP 3 유형   함의 추론

1 ③   2 ④   3 ⑤

1 ③

해석 기술은 의문의 여지가 있는 이점을 지니고 있다. 우리는 정확한

정보만 사용해서 의사 결정 과정을 간소하게 하는 것에 맞추어 너무 많은 정보를 조절해야 한다. 인터넷은 어떤 문제에 대해서도 너무 많은 무료 정보를 이용 가능하게 만들어서 우리는 어떤 결정을 하기 위해서 그 모든 정보를 고려해야 한다고 생각한다. 그래서 우리는 계속 인터넷에서 답을 검색한다. 이것이 우리가 개인적, 사업적, 혹은 다른 결정을 하려고 애쓸 때, 전조등 불빛에 노출된 사슴처럼, 우리를 정보에 눈 멀게 만든다. 오늘날 어떤 일에 있어서 성공하기 위해서, 우리는 눈 먼 사람들의 세계에서는 한 눈으로 보는 사람이 불가능해 보이는 일을 이룰 수 있다는 것을 명심해야 한다. 한 눈으로 보는 사람은 어떤 분석이든 단순하게 하는 것의 힘을 이해하고, 직관이라는 한 눈을 사용할 때 의사 결정자가 될 것이다.

문제풀이 정보의 홍수라는 현대 사회의 특징 때문에 의사 결정이 어렵지만 직관을 사용하면 효율적인 의사 결정을 할 수 있다는 내용으로 정보의 홍수로 인한 의사 결정의 어려움을 정보에 눈 먼 상태로 나타낸 것이므로 정답은 ③이다.
① 다른 사람들의 생각을 수용하기 꺼려 하게
② 무료 정보에 접근할 수 없게
③ 너무나 많은 정보 때문에 의사 결정을 할 수 없게
④ 이용 가능한 정보의 부족에 무관심하게
⑤ 의사 결정에 기꺼이 위험을 무릅쓰게

구문분석

[6행] [To be successful in anything today], we have to keep in mind [that {in the land of the blind}, a one-eyed person can accomplish the seemingly impossible].
▶ 첫 번째 [ ]는 목적을 나타내는 부사적용법의 to부정사구이며, 두 번째 [ ]는 동사구 keep in mind의 목적어로 명사절의 접속사 that이 이끄는 목적절이다. { }는 that절 속에서 삽입된 부사구이다.

2 ④

해석 실효성 있는, 효과적인 몸짓 언어는 개별 전달 신호의 합계 이상이다. 사람들이 사전식 접근법과 같은 기계적 암기로부터 의사 전달을 할 때, 그들은 더 큰 그림, 즉 사회적 인식의 모든 다양한 측면을 보지 못하게 된다. 대신, 그들은 팔짱을 낀 사람을 보고 "과묵하고, 화가 난" 것으로 생각한다. 그들은 미소를 보고 "행복한" 것으로 생각한다. 그들은 다른 사람들에게 "누가 윗사람인가"를 보여 주기 위해 세게 악수를 한다. 몸짓 언어 사전을 읽어서 몸짓 언어를 사용하려고 하는 것은 프랑스어 사전을 읽어서 프랑스어를 말하려고 하는 것과 같다. (의미 구성의) 요소들이 실효성 없는 혼란 상태로 분리되어 버리는 경향이 있다. 당신의 행동은 로봇처럼 어색해 보인다; 당신의 몸짓 언어 신호는 서로 단절된다. 당신의 몸짓 언어가 잘못 전달되었기 때문에 결국에는 당신이 마음을 끌려고 하는 바로 그 사람들을 혼란스럽게 하는 결과를 초래한다.

문제풀이 사회적 인식의 모든 다양한 측면을 보지 못하고 몸짓 언어를 사용하게 되면 의사소통에 지장을 줄 수 있다는 내용이므로 정답은 ④이다.
① 사회적 맥락에서 몸짓 언어를 배움으로써
② 몸짓 언어와 프랑스어를 비교하여

③ 몸짓 언어 전문가의 도움으로
④ 사회적 측면을 이해하지 않고
⑤ 사람들이 모국어를 배우는 방식으로

구문분석

> [9행] You **end up confusing** the very people [(that)
> you're trying to attract].
> ▶「end up+v-ing」로 동사구 end up은 동명사를 목적어로 취
> 하며, '결국 ~하게 되다'의 의미이다. [ ]는 목적어 the very
> people를 수식하는 목적격 관계대명사절로 관계대명사 that이
> 생략된 형태이다.

3 ⑤

해석 신체는 문제를 축적하는 경향이 있으며, 그것은 흔히 하나의 작
고 사소해 보이는 불균형에서 시작한다. 이 문제는 또 다른 미묘한 불
균형을 유발하고, 그것이 또 다른 불균형을, 그리고 그 다음에 몇 개
의 더 많은 불균형을 유발한다. 결국 여러분은 어떤 증상을 갖게 된
다. 그것은 마치 일련의 도미노를 한 줄로 세워 놓는 것과 같다. 여
러분은 첫 번째 도미노를 쓰러뜨리기만 하면 되는데, 그러면 많은 다
른 것들도 또한 쓰러질 것이다. 마지막 도미노를 쓰러뜨린 것은 무엇
인가? 분명히, 그것은 그것의 바로 앞에 있던 것이나, 그것 앞의 앞에
있던 것이 아니라, 첫 번째 도미노이다. 신체도 같은 방식으로 작동한
다. 최초의 문제는 흔히 눈에 띄지 않는다. 뒤쪽의 '도미노' 중 몇 개
가 쓰러지고 나서야 비로소 좀 더 분명한 단서와 증상이 나타난다. 결
국 여러분은 두통, 피로, 또는 우울증, 심지어 질병까지도 얻게 된다.
마지막 도미노는 목적지가 아니다. 여러분이 최종 결과인 증상만을
치료하려 한다면, 그 문제의 원인은 해결되지 않는다. 최초의 도미노
가 원인, 즉 가장 중요한 문제이다.

문제풀이 최종 결과인 증상은 최초의 사소해 보였던 불균형이 도미노
효과를 일으킨 것이므로 근본적인 해결이 중요하다는 내용이므로 정
답은 ⑤이다.
① 질병을 치료하는 데 정해진 순서는 없다.
② 사소한 건강 문제는 저절로 해결된다.
③ 여러분은 나이를 먹어가면서 점점 더 무기력해진다.
④ 아무리 늦어도 최종 결과인 증상을 치료할 수 있다.
⑤ 최종 증상은 최초의 사소한 문제에서 생겨난다.

구문분석

> [7행] **It**'s not until some of the later "dominoes" fall
> **that** more obvious clues and symptoms appear.
> ▶ 원래 문장은 Not until do some of the later "dominoes"
> fall more obvious clues and symptoms appear.이며, 이를
> it ~ that 강조구문으로 바뀐 경우이다.

PRACTICE
p.42

A	1	consequently, 결과적으로, 그 결과로
	2	evolution, 진화, 발전
	3	symbolic, 상징적인
	4	cooperate, 협력하다, 협조하다
	5	overwhelming, 압도적인, 매우 힘든
B	1 ④	2 ③ 3 ①
C	1 illogical	2 exceed
	3 compromise	4 alone
	5 malfunction	
D	1 embrace	2 disposal

A

1 con+sequent+ly (결과적으로)
2 e+volu+tion (진화)
3 sym+bol+ic (상징적인)
4 co+oper+ate (협력하다)
5 over+whelm+ing (압도적인)

B

1 em의 의미는 in, into이고 나머지는 의미가 against이다.
2 sus의 의미는 under이고 나머지는 의미가 over이다.
3 in의 의미는 in이고 나머지는 의미가 not이다.

C

1 상관이 한 일을 내가 책임진다는 것은 이치에 맞지 않다.
2 변경된 공사안대로의 비용은 10억 달러를 초과할 수도 있다.
3 판매자와 구매자 모두 가격에 대해 타협할 의향이 있어야 한다.
4 부모들은 아이들 없이 둘만 있는 시간을 보내는 것이 좋을 수도 있
다고 말한다.
5 원자력 발전소는 냉각기가 고장났기 때문에 후 며칠 내에 폭발할
수도 있다.

D

1 인터넷이나 소셜 미디어가 진실이나 사실을 포용하게 하지 않는다.
예를 들어, 나치의 유대인 대학살을 부정하는 가짜 역사를 찾으려
면 예전에는 어느 정도의 노력이 필요했으나, 이제 클릭 한 번이면
된다.
2 친환경 디자인 운동은 지속 가능성 원칙을 소비재 디자인에 포함
시킨다. 이런 접근법은 재활용 재료로부터 상품들을 만들어낼 뿐만

아니라, 그것들의 사용은 물론 마지막 처분도 고려하여 상품을 디자인한다.

적용독해
p.43

1 ③   2 ⑤

1 ③

해석 사회적 관계는 우리의 생존과 웰빙을 위해 매우 필수적이어서 우리는 관계를 형성하기 위해 다른 사람과 협력할 뿐만 아니라, 친구를 얻기 위해 다른 사람과 경쟁하기도 한다. 그리고 자주 우리는 동시에 둘 다를 한다. 가십을 생각해 보자. 가십을 통해 우리는 친구들과 흥미로운 세부사항을 공유하면서 유대를 형성한다. 그러나 동시에 우리는 가십의 대상들 중에서 잠재적인 적을 만들어낸다. 또는 누가 '그들의' 파티에 참석할 것인지를 알아보기 위해 경쟁하는 라이벌 관계의 휴일 파티를 생각해 보라. 우리는 심지어 소셜 미디어에서도 사람들이 가장 많은 친구들과 팔로워들을 얻기 위해 경쟁할 때 이러한 조화를(→ 긴장감을) 볼 수 있다. 동시에 경쟁적 배제는 또한 협력도 만들어낼 수 있다. 고등학교 친목 동아리와 컨트리 클럽은 이러한 공식을 사용하여 큰 효과를 발휘한다. 그들이 충성과 지속적인 사회적 유대를 형성하는 것은 선택적인 포함 '그리고 배제'를 통해서이다.

문제풀이 사회적 관계는 협력 관계이기도 하지만 긴장감을 유발하는 경쟁 관계이며, 경쟁적 배제와 협력은 상호 보완 관계라는 내용이므로 harmony가 아니라 tension 등으로 고쳐야 한다.

구문분석

[9행] **It is** [through selective inclusion *and exclusion*] **that** they produce loyalty and lasting social bonds.
▶ [ ]는 it ~ that 강조구문의 강조 대상을 나타내고 있다.

2 ⑤

해석 학교 과제는 전형적으로 학생들이 혼자 하도록 요구해 왔다. 이러한 개별 생산성의 강조는 독립성이 성공의 필수 요인이라는 의견을 반영했던 것이다. 타인에게 의존하지 않고 자신을 관리하는 능력을 가지는 것이 모든 사람에게 요구되는 것으로 간주되었다. 따라서, 과거의 교사들은 모둠 활동이나 학생들이 팀워크 기술을 배우는 것을 덜 권장했다. 그러나, 뉴 밀레니엄 시대 이후, 기업들은 향상된 생산성을 요구하는 더 많은 국제적 경쟁을 경험하고 있다. 이러한 상황은 고용주들로 하여금 노동 시장의 초입자들이 전통적인 독립성뿐만 아니라 팀워크 기술을 통해 보여지는 상호 의존성도 입증해야 한다고 요구하도록 만들었다. 교육자의 도전 과제는 기본적인 기술에서의 개별 능력을 보장하는 동시에 학생들이 팀에서 잘 수행할 수 있도록 하는 학습 기회를 줄여 주는(→ 늘려 주는) 것이다.

문제풀이 과거와는 달리 기업에서처럼 학교에서도 학생들의 개별 능력을 보장해 줌과 동시에 팀워크 기술을 신장시킬 기회를 늘려 줘야 한다는 내용이므로 ⑤ decreasing은 adding 등으로 고쳐야 한다.

구문분석

[1행] School assignments **have** typically required [that students (should) **work** alone].
▶ [ ]는 「당위의 동사(충고, 주장, 요구, 제안, 명령 등)+that+S+(should)+동사원형」의 형태로 쓰였으며, 이 문장에서는 have required가 있으므로 '~을 해야 한다고 요구해 왔다'로 해석한다.

✎ STEP 2 어법   보어 2(5형식)

PRACTICE
p.44

A   1 helpfully → helpful
        2 getting → to get
        3 comfortably → comfortable
        4 happily → happy
        5 being → to be
B   1 what   2 overwhelming

A

1 UNICEF는 이 원조 프로젝트가 전쟁고아들에게 도움이 될거라 생각했다. ▶ 「consider+O+형용사 보어」
2 위험한 상황에 직면하면 우리의 코는 더 많은 공기가 폐로 들어갈 수 있도록 해 준다. ▶ 「allow+O+to-v」
3 나에게 맛있는 식사를 해 주겠다는 그녀의 주장은 나를 편안하게 해 줬다. ▶ 「keep+O+형용사 보어」
4 다른 사람을 기쁘게 하려는 욕망으로 당신은 당신이 아닌 다른 사람인 척 할 수 있다. ▶ 「make+O+형용사 보어」
5 우리의 청소년들에게 부당한 요구를 하는 것은 모든 것이 잘 될 것이라고 기대하는 사람들에 의해 발생합니다. ▶ 「expect+O+to-v」

B

1 공진화(共進化)에 대한 어떠한 논의도 철학자들이 '인과관계 딜레마'라고 부르는 것, 즉 '어느 것이 먼저인가, 닭인가 아니면 달걀인가?'라는 질문에서 우리가 인식하는 문제에 곧 부딪힌다.
▶ 「what+S+5형식 동사(call)+목적격 보어」
2 소비자들이 자신이 찾은 정보를 자세히 살펴보고 결정을 내릴 수 있는 것은 매우 힘든 과업이다. 그리고 그것을 매우 힘든 것으로 만드는 것은 우리가 결정을 내리는 데 근거가 되는 정보 원천의 수가 폭발적으로 증가해 왔다는 것이다. ▶ 「what+5형식 동사(make)+O+형용사 보어」

적용독해
p.45

1 ⑤   2 ④

1 ⑤

해석 인상주의 화가의 그림은 아마도 가장 인기가 있다. 그것은 보는 사람에게 그 형상을 이해하기 위해 열심히 노력할 것을 요구하지 않는 쉽게 이해되는 예술이다. 인상주의는 보기에 '편하고', 여름의 장면과 밝은 색깔은 눈길을 끈다. 그러나 이 새로운 그림 방식은 그것이 만들어지는 방법뿐 아니라, 보이는 것에 있어서도 대중들에게 도전적이었다는 것을 기억하는 것이 중요하다. 그들은 이전에 그렇게 '형식에 구애받지 않는' 그림을 본 적이 결코 없었다. 캔버스의 가장자리는 마치 카메라로 스냅 사진을 찍는 것처럼, 임의적으로 장면을 잘랐다. 그 소재는 기찻길과 공장과 같은 풍경의 현대화를 포함했다. 이전에는 이러한 대상이 결코 화가들에게 적절하다고 여겨지지 않았다.

문제풀이 ⑤ 「consider+O+형용사 보어」의 형식을 취하므로 appropriately를 appropriate로 고쳐야 한다.
① 「ask+O+to-v」
② 「be-v+형용사 보어」 ▶ p.36
③ 「find+O+형용사 보어」
④ 불완전한 구조가 이어지며 선행사가 없는 관계대명사 what
▶ p.174

2 ④

해석 비언어적 의사소통은 언어적 의사소통의 대체물이 아니다. 오히려 그것은 전달되고 있는 메시지 내용의 풍부함을 강화시키도록 해 주며, 보충으로서 기능해야 한다. 비언어적 의사소통은 말하기가 불가능하거나 부적절한 상황에서 유용할 수 있다. 여러분이 어떤 개인과 이야기하는 동안 불편한 입장에 있다고 상상해 보라. 비언어적 의사소통은 다시 편안해지도록 대화에서 잠깐 벗어날 시간을 여러분에게 달라는 상징적인 메시지를 여러분이 그 사람에게 건네도록 도와줄 것이다. 비언어적 의사소통이 언어적 의사소통을 대체하는 것이 아니라 오히려 그것을 보완하여, 비언어적 의사소통자가 감정과 태도를 적절하게 표현할 수 있도록 한다는 것은 또 다른 장점이다. 비언어적 의사소통의 도움이 없다면 적절하게 표현되지 못할 여러분의 본성과 성격의 여러 측면들이 있다.

문제풀이 ④ 뒤에 완전한 구조가 이어지므로 What을 주어 역할의 명사절 접속사 That으로 고쳐야 한다.
① 「make+O+형용사 보어(과거분사)」
② 동사원형으로 시작하는 명령문 ▶ p.12
③ 「help+O+(to) 동사원형」 ▶ p.52
⑤ 「enable+O+to-v」

STEP 3 유형 **글의 요지**
pp.46~47

1 ③　2 ④　3 ③

1 ③

해석 만약 여러분이 결코 정보를 실제로 사용하지 않는다면 그것은 가치가 없다. 너무나 자주 기업들은 결국에는 묻히고 절대로 사용되지 않는 귀중한 고객 정보를 수집한다. 그들은 그들의 정보가 적절한 때의 사용을 위해 접근 가능하도록 보장해야 한다. 호텔의 경우, 정보 사용을 위한 하나의 적절한 때는 프런트 데스크의 체크인이다. 나는 내가 자주 방문했던 호텔에 종종 체크인하는데 결국 프런트 데스크에 있는 사람들이 나를 고객으로 알아차린다는 표시를 보여 주지 않는다. 그 호텔은 내 방문 기록을 저장하고 있음이 분명하지만 그들은 그 정보가 프런트 데스크 직원들에게 접근 가능하도록 해 주지 않는다. 그들은 고객 충성도에 초점을 맞춘 더 나은 경험을 만들 수 있도록 정보를 활용할 최적의 기회를 놓치고 있다. 그들이 열 명, 만 명 혹은 심지어 천만 명의 고객을 가지고 있든 목표는 동일하다. 즉, 충성도를 높이는 즐거운 고객 경험을 만들어 내라.

문제풀이 수집한 고객 정보는 적절한 때에 고객을 위해 사용할 수 있어야 고객 충성도를 높일 수 있다는 내용이므로 ③이 정답이다.

구문분석

[2행] They must ensure [(that) their data is accessible for use at the appropriate times].
▶ [ ]는 동사 ensure의 목적절로 명사절의 접속사 that이 생략된 형태이다.

[7행] They are missing a prime opportunity [**to utilize** data] [**to create** a better experience focused on customer loyalty].
▶ 첫 번째 [ ]는 앞의 명사 opportunity를 수식하는 형용사적 용법의 to부정사구이며, 두 번째 [ ]는 목적을 나타내는 부사적 용법의 to부정사구이다.

2 ④

해석 당신은 Hamlet Syndrome에 대해 들어 본 적이 있는가? 당신이 상점에 들어갈 때, 무엇을 보게 되는가? 당신은 많은 선택 사항들과 선택지를 보게 될 것이다. 당신이 차, 커피, 청바지 혹은 전화기를 사고 싶어 하는가의 여부는 중요하지 않다. 이러한 모든 상황 속에서, 우리는 기본적으로 우리가 고를 수 있는 선택 사항들로 넘쳐나게 된다. 만약, 온라인이든 오프라인이든, 우리가 누군가에게 더 많은 선택 사항을 선호하는지 더 적은 선택 사항을 선호하는지를 묻는다면, 무슨 일이 일어날까? 대다수의 사람들은 그들이 더 많은 선택 사항을 갖는 것을 선호한다고 우리에게 말할 것이다. 이러한 발견은 흥미로운데 왜냐하면, 과학이 보여 주듯이, 선택의 폭이 늘어날수록, 우리의 의사 결정 과정은 더 어려워질 것이기 때문이다. 중요한 점은 선택 사항의 양이 일정 수준을 넘어서면, 우리의 의사 결정이 고통스러워지기 시작할 것이라는 점이다.

문제풀이 물건을 구매할 때 더 많은 선택 사항을 선호한다고 대부분의 사람들은 말하지만, 실제로 선택 사항이 많아지면 의사 결정이 더 어려워진다는 내용이므로 정답은 ④이다.

구문분석

[2행] **It** doesn't matter [**whether** you want to buy tea, coffee, jeans, or a phone].
▶ 가주어-진주어 구문으로 대체로 It ~ that 구문이 쓰이지만 여기서는 진주어절로 that절 대신에 [ ]처럼 whether절이 사용되었다.

3 ③

해석 신경과학자인 Antonio Damasio는 감정 체계에 손상을 입힌 뇌 부상을 제외하고 모든 면에서 완벽하게 정상인 사람들을 연구했다. 결과적으로, 그들은 세상 속에서 효과적으로 결정을 내리거나 기능할 수 없었다. 그들은 자신들이 어떻게 기능하고 있어야 했는지 정확하게 설명할 수는 있었지만, 어디에 살고, 무엇을 먹고, 어떤 제품을 사서 사용할지는 결정할 수가 없었다. 이러한 연구 결과는 의사 결정이 이성적이고 논리적인 사고의 핵심이라는 보편적 믿음에 반한다. 그러나 최신 연구는 정서적 체계가 여러분이 좋고 나쁜 것 사이에서 빨리 선택하도록 돕고, 고려해야 할 것들의 수를 줄여 주면서 여러분의 의사 결정에 결정적인 도움을 준다는 것을 보여 준다.

문제풀이 의사 결정이 이성적인 사고의 핵심이라는 예전의 생각과는 달리 정서적 체계가 의사 결정에 결정적인 도움을 준다는 연구 결과에 대한 언급을 통해 ③이 정답임을 알 수 있다.

구문분석

[1행] he neuroscientist Antonio Damasio studied <u>people</u> [who were perfectly normal in every way except for <u>brain injuries</u> {that damaged their emotional systems}].
▶ [　]는 선행사 people을 수식하는 주격 관계대명사절이며, {　}는 선행사 brain injuries를 수식하는 주격 관계대명사절을 나타낸다.

PRACTICE
p.50

A
1 deserve, ~를 받을 만하다
2 reserve, 예약하다 　 3 observe, 관찰하다
4 preserve, 보존하다 　 5 conserve, 보호하다
6 ascribe, ~탓으로 돌리다
7 describe, 묘사하다 　 8 inscribe, 새기다
9 subscribe, 구독하다
10 prescribe, 처방하다

B
1 ③ 　 2 ③ 　 3 ④ 　 4 ② 　 5 ④

C
1 innovation 　 2 appealing

A

1 de+serve(keep): ~를 받을 만 하다
2 re+serve(keep): 예약하다
3 ob+serve(keep): 관찰하다
4 pre+serve(keep): 보존하다
5 con+serve(keep): 보호하다
6 a+scribe(write): ~탓으로 돌리다
7 de+scribe(write): 묘사하다
8 in+scribe(write): 새기다
9 sub+scribe(write): 구독하다
10 pre+scribe(write): 처방하다

B

1 연극 한 편을 무대에 올리는 것은 많은 노력을 <u>수반한다</u>.
2 부모는 절대 자신의 아이와 남의 아이를 <u>비교해서는</u> 안된다.
3 (미국) 식약청은 식품 첨가물은 우리가 <u>섭취하기에</u> 그렇게 해롭지는 않다고 말했다.
4 연구 결과에 따르면 초등학교에서 대학까지 모든 단계에서 여자는 남자보다 더 <u>뛰어나다</u>.
5 그리스 신화에 따르면, 판도라는 상자를 열어 보고 싶은 유혹을 <u>이겨내지</u> 못했다.

C

1 관료주의가 없고, 잃을 것도 별로 없으며, 자신들을 입증하고자 하는 열정을 갖고 있어서, <u>혁신</u>에 관한 한, 소집단은 더 큰 조직보다 일관되게 더 높은 기량을 발휘한다.
2 "무지방 75%" 표시를 붙인 냉동식품은 "지방 25%" 표시를 붙였을 때보다 더 <u>매력적으로</u> 보일 것이다. 그러나 후자의 것이 우리가 먹게 될 것에 대해 더 많이 숙고하게 할 수도 있다.

적용독해

1 ⑤   2 ④

1 ⑤

해석 해충과 질병은 자연의 일부이다. 이상적인 체계에서는 포식자와 해충 간에 자연적으로 균형이 잡힌다. 만약 그 체계가 불균형을 이루면, 한 개체군은 다른 개체군에 의해 잡아먹히지 않기 때문에 개체 수가 증가할 수 있다. 자연 통제의 목적은 해충과 질병을 완전히 없애는 것이 아니다. 그것은 해충과 포식자 사이의 자연의 균형을 회복하고 해충과 질병을 적정 수준까지 낮추는 것이다. 하지만 해충과 질병에 대한 자연적인 통제의 또 다른 대안으로 사용되는 살충제는 해충 문제를 해결하지 못한다. 지난 50년 동안 살충제 사용은 10배 증가한 반면, 해충의 피해로 인한 곡식의 손실은 두 배가 되었다. 자연 통제가 살충제 사용보다 더 기피되는 (→ 선택되는) 이유가 여기에 있다.

문제풀이 자연 통제의 대안으로 사용되는 살충제는 해충 문제의 해법이 되지 못해서 자연 통제가 더 선호된다는 내용이므로 ⑤ avoided는 chosen 등으로 고쳐야 한다.

구문분석

[7행] In the past 50 years, pesticide use has increased ten times [while crop losses {from pest damage} have doubled].
▶ [ ]는 역접의 의미를 갖는 접속사 while을 사용한 부사절이며, { }는 부사절의 주어 crop losses를 수식하는 전치사구이다.

2 ④

해석 Ontario 주, Temagami 지역 근처에 원시림이 있다. 어떤 사람들은 목재용으로 그 나무들을 베려고 한다. 다른 사람들은 그것을 그 상태 그대로 지키고 싶어 한다. 그들은 그것이 독특하고 다음 세대를 위해 보호되어야 한다고 믿고 있다. 많은 사람들은 일부 나무는 사용하고 일부 나무는 보호하기를 원하면서, 중간적 입장에 있다. 대부분의 사람들은 우리의 자원을 현명하게 사용하는 것을 찬성한다. 그들은 우리의 자원을 지속 가능하게 만드는 관행을 선호한다. 즉, 우리는 현재 우리의 자원을 현명하게 사용해야 하고 그러면 우리는 미래를 위해 여전히 더 많은 자원을 가지게 될 것이다. 우리 모두는 환경을 돌볼 책임이 있다. 우리는 미래 세대를 위해 환경을 바꾸는(→ 보존하는) 것의 중요성을 오랫동안 인식해 왔던 캐나다 원주민으로부터 배울 수 있다. 당신이 물려받았고 지금 더불어 살아가고 있는 것이 미래 세대의 유산이 될 것이다.

문제풀이 일부 나무는 사용하고 일부 나무는 보호하면서 자원을 지속 가능하게 만들어 미래 세대에 유산으로 남겨 주는 캐나다 원주민으로부터 배워야 한다는 내용이므로 ④ changing은 preserving 등으로 고쳐야 한다.

구문분석

[5행] They prefer practices [that make our resources sustainable].
▶ [ ]는 「practices+주격 관계대명사+5형식 동사(make)+O+형용사 보어」로 이루어져 있다.

STEP 2 어법 보어 3(5형식)

PRACTICE
p.52

A 1 to cry → cry / crying
   2 played → play / playing
   3 to clean → clean
   4 did → do
   5 to fix → fixed
   6 passing → (to) pass

B 1 fall   2 interrupt

A

1 나는 누군가가 정원에서 소리치는 것을 들었다. ▶「지각동사+목적어+동사원형/현재분사」
2 우리는 아이들이 운동장에서 노는 것을 지켜봤다. ▶「지각동사+목적어+동사원형/현재분사」
3 그녀는 내가 방을 청소하도록 시켰다. ▶「사역동사+목적어+동사원형」
4 나는 그가 그것을 다시 하도록 허락하지 않을 것이다. ▶「사역동사+목적어+동사원형」
5 나는 수리 공장에서 내 차를 수리하도록 했다. ▶「get+목적어+과거분사(수동 의미)」
6 그는 내가 시험에 합격하도록 도움을 줬다. ▶「help+목적어+(to) 동사원형」

B

1 건물에서 물체들을 떨어뜨리는 것 대신에, Galileo는 물건들을 떨어지게 만들었던 똑같은 힘이 경사로에서 공들이 굴러 내려가게 만드는 지를 알기 위해 경사로 아래로 공들을 굴리기로 했다.
   ▶「make+목적어+동사원형」
2 전화벨이 울리면 전화를 받아야 한다고 느낄지라도, 집중을 방해하는 것들이 화자의 말을 여러분이 주의 깊게 듣는 것을 방해하게 두지 마라. 대화 중에 전화를 받는 것은 무례한 일이다. ▶「let+목적어+동사원형」

정답 및 해설 17

적용독해

1 ④   2 ⑤

---

1 ④

해석 내가 어린 소녀였을 때, 내 방은 항상 엉망이었다. 어머니는 "가서 방 치워!"라고 나에게 말씀하시며 내가 방을 정돈하게 하려고 항상 노력하셨다. 나는 엄마가 잔소리하는 소리를 들을 때마다 어머니에게 저항했다. 나는 무엇을 하라고 말을 듣는 것이 싫었다. 나는 단호히 내가 원하는 방식으로 방을 두었다. 내가 어질러진 방에서 지내는 것을 좋아하느냐 아니냐는 전적으로 다른 문제였다. 나는 깨끗한 방을 갖는 것의 이점들에 대해 멈추어서 생각해 본 적이 결코 없었다. 나에게는, 내 방식대로 하는 것이 더 중요했다. 그리고 대부분의 다른 부모님들처럼, 어머니는 내가 그 이점들을 혼자 힘으로 깨닫도록 하지 않았다. 대신에 그녀는 나에게 잔소리를 하겠다고 고집하셨다.

문제풀이 ④ 준사역동사 get은 목적어 뒤에 to부정사나 과거분사가 올 수 있는데 목적어와 보어가 수동 관계이므로 과거분사 done이 와야 한다.
① 「사역동사＋목적어＋동사원형」
② 「지각동사＋목적어＋v-ing」
③ 주어가 whether 명사절이므로 동사는 단수형 ▶ p.190
⑤ 「help＋목적어＋(to)동사원형」

2 ⑤

해석 며칠 전 퇴근하면서 나는 어떤 여자가 큰 길로 들어오려고 애쓰는데 계속되는 차량 흐름 때문에 기회가 별로 없는 것을 봤다. 나는 속도를 줄이고 그녀가 내 앞에 들어오게 해 주었다. 나는 기분이 꽤 좋았는데, 그 후 두어 블록 간 후에 그녀가 몇 대의 차를 끼워 주려고 차를 멈추는 바람에 우리 둘 다 다음 신호를 놓치게 되었다. 나는 그녀에게 완전히 짜증 났다. 내가 그렇게 친절하게 그녀가 들어오게 해 주었는데 어떻게 감히 그녀가 나를 느리게 가게 한단 말인가! 내가 안달하면서 (자동차에) 앉아 있을 때 나는 내 자신이 참으로 어리석게 굴고 있다는 사실을 깨달았다. 불현듯 언젠가 읽었던 문구 하나가 마음속에 떠올랐다. '누군가 점수를 매기고 있기 때문이거나, 하지 않으면 처벌을 받기 때문이 아니라 내적 동기로 사람들에게 친절을 베풀어야 한다.' 나는 내가 보상을 원하고 있다는 사실을 깨달았다. 내가 당신에게 이런 친절을 베푼다면 당신(또는 어떤 다른 사람)이 나에게 그만한 친절을 베풀 것이라는 생각이었다.

문제풀이 ⑤ 동사 realized의 목적절이며, 뒤에 완전한 절이 이어지므로 명사절의 접속사 that이 쓰여야 한다.
① 「지각동사＋목적어＋현재분사 and 현재분사」
② 「2형식 동사 feel＋형용사 보어」 ▶ p.36
③ 「5형식 동사 find＋목적어＋형용사 보어」 ▶ p.44
④ 「사역동사＋목적어＋동사원형」

STEP 3 유형   글의 주제

1 ⑤   2 ⑤   3 ②

1 ⑤

해석 오늘날 어떤 Hippocrates의 견해가 여전히 실행되고 있을까? 비록 Hippocrates가 거의 2,500년 전에 살았을지라도 그의 견해 중 많은 것들이 오늘날에도 아주 친숙하게 들린다. 그는 친척 중 누군가가 비슷한 질병을 앓았었는지를 알아보기 위해 가족 병력에 대해 물어보곤 했다. 그는 환자의 환경이 그 질병을 야기하는지를 알아보기 위해 환자의 가정에 관해서 질문했었다. 그는 환자들의 식습관을 관찰한 후, 식습관이 질병을 예방하는 데 중요한 역할을 한다는 것을 발견했다. Hippocrates는 정서적 스트레스로 인해 야기된 신체적 질병을 이해한 최초의 사람이었다. 그는 심지어 의사가 환자를 대하는 태도라고 일컫는 것에 관해서도 제안을 했다. 그는 의사가 질병 자체만큼 환자의 안락함과 행복에도 많은 관심을 기울여야 한다고 말했다.

문제풀이 질병을 해결하기 위한 Hippocrates의 혜안이 지금 시대에도 실행되고 있다는 내용이므로 ⑤가 가장 적절하다.
① 서양 의학의 다양한 분야
② Hippocrates 시대의 통념들
③ 고대의 진단과 치료
④ 전통 의학의 예방 조치
⑤ 현대 의학에 남아있는 Hippocrates 사상

구문분석

[2행] He would inquire about the family health history
　　　 S　V
to see [if any relatives had suffered from similar
　　　　　　 S'　　　 V'
diseases].
▶ [　]는 접속사 if로 시작하는 동사 see의 목적절을 나타내며, 주절의 시제가 과거일 때 그 보다 먼저 일어난 일을 언급하므로 과거완료시제(had p.p.)가 쓰였다.

2 ⑤

해석 공상 과학 소설은 반짝이는 로봇과 환상적인 우주선 그 이상의 더 많은 것을 포함한다. 실제로, 대부분의 많은 기이한 공상 과학 소설 작품들은 과학적 사실에 기초를 둔다. 많은 공상 과학 소설이 과학에 기초를 두고 있기 때문에 그것은 문학을 영어 교실에서 끌어내어 과학 교실로 가져오기 위해 사용될 수 있다. 공상 과학 소설은 학생들이 과학적 원리들이 실제로 쓰이는 것을 볼 수 있도록 도움을 줄 뿐만 아니라 또한 학생들의 비판적 사고와 창의적 기술을 길러 주는 데에 도움을 준다. 학생들은 공상 과학 소설의 글을 읽으면서 그들이 배운 과학적 원리와 그 글을 연결시켜야만 한다. 학생들은 비슷한 개념을 다루는 공상 과학 소설의 글과 논픽션의 글을 읽고, 그 둘을 비교하고 대조할 수 있는 능력을 습득할 수 있다. 또한 학생들은 아마도 자기가 직접 과학 소설 이야기를 창조하거나 그들이 배운 지식과 기술을 적용하는 새로운 방법들을 상상하면서 다양한 방식으로 사용된 과학적 원리를 봄으로써 창의적 기술을 기를 수 있다.

문제풀이 공상 과학 소설은 과학에 기초를 두고 있기 때문에 과학 수업에서 여러 도움이 될 수 있다는 내용으로서 주제로는 ⑤가 가장 적절하다.

① 공상 과학 영화에 담긴 공통 주제
② 공상 과학 소설이 유행하는 문화에 미친 영향
③ 공상 과학 소설의 과학적 원리에 대한 사례
④ 공상 과학 소설 장르의 역사적 발전
⑤ 과학 수업에서 공상 과학 소설을 활용하는 이점

구문분석

[4행] **Not only** <u>does</u> <u>science fiction</u> help students see
 　　　　　　V　　　　S
scientific principles in action.
▶ 원래 Science fiction not only helps였으나 not only의 강조를 위해 문두에 오면 주어와 동사는 도치된다.

3 ②

해석 우주왕복선 Challenger호가 폭발한 후 어느 날, Ulric Neisser가 한 학급의 106명 학생들에게 그들이 그 소식을 들었을 때 정확히 어디에 있었는지를 써 달라고 요청했다. 2년 반 후, 그는 그들에게 똑같은 질문을 했다. 그 두 번째 면담에서 그는 학생들 중 25퍼센트는 그들이 어디에 있었는지에 대해 완전히 다르게 설명한다는 사실을 지켜보았다. 절반은 그들의 답변에 있어서 중대한 오류를 범했고 10퍼센트 미만이 어느 정도라도 실질적인 정확성을 가지고 기억했다. 이와 같은 결과는 사람들이 자신이 목격한 범죄를 묘사해 달라고 몇 달 후 요청받았을 때 증인석에서 실수를 저지르는 이유의 일부이다. 1989년과 2007년 사이, 미국에서는 201명의 수감자들이 DNA 증거에 기초하여 무죄라고 밝혀졌다. 이러한 수감자들 중 75퍼센트가 잘못된 목격자 진술에 기초하여 유죄로 판결을 받았었다.

문제풀이 시간이 흐를수록 우리의 기억이 부정확해진다는 연구 결과와 사례에 대한 글로서 주제로는 ②가 가장 적절하다.

① 우주 탐사 임무 실패의 주요 원인
② 시간이 지나면서 회상되는 기억의 부정확성
③ 증인을 위협으로부터 보호하는 것의 중요성
④ 사람들의 장기 기억을 향상시키는 요인들
⑤ 범죄 수사에서 DNA 증거를 수집하는 방법

구문분석

[1행] Ulric Neisser <u>asked</u> <u>a class of 106 students</u> <u>to</u>
 　　　　　　　　　 V　　　　　O
<u>write down</u> exactly [where they were {when they
 　O.C.
heard the news}].
▶ 이 문장은 「ask+O+to-v」의 구조를 갖는 5형식 문장으로 목적격 보어에 to부정사구가 왔다. write down의 목적어로 쓰인 [　]는 의문사 where로 시작하는 의문사절이며 {　}는 접속사 when으로 시작하는 시간의 부사절이다.

PRACTICE

p.58

A
1 inform, 알리다　2 reform, 개혁하다
3 perform, 수행하다　4 conform, 순응하다
5 transform, 변형하다　6 efficient, 효율적인
7 deficient, 부족한　8 sufficient, 충분한
9 artificial, 인공적인　10 beneficial, 이로운

B　1 ④　2 ③　3 ②　4 ③　5 ④

C　1 predominately　2 eliminating

A

1 in+form(형태, 제공하다): 알리다
2 re+form(형태, 제공하다): 개혁하다
3 per+form(형태, 제공하다): 수행하다
4 con+form(형태, 제공하다): 순응하다
5 trans+form(형태, 제공하다): 변형하다
6 ef+fic(make)+ent: 효율적인
7 de+fic(make)+ent: 부족한
8 suf+fic(make)+ent: 충분한
9 arti+fic(make)+al: 인공적인
10 bene+fic(make)+al: 이로운

B

1 그녀는 어떤 식으로든 아이들을 방치했다는 혐의를 부인했다.
2 대령은 손가락으로 지도상의 한 지점을 가리켰다.
3 그 장관은 사법부에 영향력을 행사했다는 혐의로 고소당했다.
4 그 신문사는 왜곡 보도로 천문학적인 벌금을 냈다.
5 경위는 신호가 있을 때까지 아무것도 하지 말라고 경찰들에게 명령했다.

C

1 산업혁명이 끝나갈 무렵, 패션은 모든 계층에게 더욱 쉽게 이용할 수 있고 구매 가능하게 되었으며, 그 쯤에 디자이너들은 주로 공장에서 일했고 더 이상 개인을 위해서가 아닌 대량 판매 시장을 위해서 디자인했다.
2 환경에서 1킬로그램씩 제거된 수은은 12,500 달러에 달하는 사회적, 환경적 그리고 인간 건강상의 혜택으로 이어질 수 있다고 추정되기 때문에, 수은을 제거하는 데 이루어진 투자는 잘 쓰인 자금이다.

1 ③　　2 ③

1 ③

해석 적절한 상황 하에서 집단들은 두드러지게 현명하고, 종종 집단 내 가장 똑똑한 사람들보다 더 똑똑하다. 비록 집단 내 대부분의 사람들이 특별히 박식하거나 합리적이지 않을지라도 집단적으로 현명한 결정에 이를 수 있다. 이것은 인간이 완벽하게 설계된 의사 결정자가 아니기 때문에 좋은 것이다. 우리는 일반적으로 우리가 원하는 것보다 적은 정보를 가지고 있다. 우리는 미래에 대한 충분한(→ 제한된) 예지력을 가지고 있다. 최선의 가능한 결정을 찾는 것을 고집하는 대신에 우리는 종종 충분히 좋아 보이는 것을 받아들인다. 그리고 우리는 감정이 우리의 판단에 영향을 미치게 한다. 하지만 이러한 모든 한계에도 불구하고 우리의 불완전한 의견들이 적절한 방식으로 모아질 때, 우리의 집단 지능은 종종 뛰어나다.

문제풀이 우리의 예지력이나 감정이 판단과 의사 결정에 있어 나름의 한계가 있기 때문에 개개인들의 총화인 집단 지성이 더 나을 수 있다는 내용이므로 ③ sufficient는 limited 등으로 고쳐야 한다.

구문분석

> [6행] [Instead of insisting on finding the best possible decision], we will often accept one [that seems good enough].
> ▶ 첫 번째 [ ]는 「Instead of+v-ing」로 시작하는 부사구이고, 두 번째 [ ]는 선행사 one을 수식하는 주격 관계대명사절이다. one은 decision의 부정대명사이다.

2 ③

해석 'F'를 받았다는 것은 단지 시험에서 낙제했다는 것을 의미할 뿐이지 인생에서 낙제했다는 것을 의미하는 것이 아니다. 지금부터, 등급으로 사용될 때 문자 'F'는 단어 feedback(피드백)을 나타낸다고 생각하라. 'F'는 자료를 충분히 이해하지 못했다는 하나의 표시이다. 그것은 다음 시험 전에 무엇인가를 다르게 해야 한다는 메시지이다. 'F'를 피드백으로 생각하면, 성공을 가로막는(→ 촉진하는) 방식으로 사고와 행동을 변화시킬 수 있다. 새로운 학습 전략을 선택할 수 있다. 수행한 일에 의미 있는 피드백을 받는다는 것은 '무엇인가'를 배우기 위한 강력한 전략이다. 시험은 피드백의 유일한 원천이 아니다. 선생님, 친구 그리고 당신을 알고 있는 누군가에게 피드백을 요청하는 습관을 들여라. 그저 향상시키고자 하는 것을 결정하고, "제가 어떻게 하죠?"라고 질문하라.

문제풀이 'F'를 '낙제'가 아니라 '피드백'이라고 생각을 바꾸고 주변 사람들에게 피드백을 요청하는 방식으로 사고와 행동을 변화시키면 성공할 수 있다는 내용으로 ③ prevent는 promote 등으로 고쳐야 한다.

구문분석

> [4행] It's a message [that you should do something differently before the next test].
> ▶ [ ]는 명사절의 접속사 that이 이끌며 a message와 동격절을 나타낸다.

STEP 2 어법 　수동태 1(3형식 / 4형식)

PRACTICE
p.60

A　1 → are needed　　2 → be recharged
　　3 → is believed　　4 → is expected
　　5 → were given

B　1 avoided　　2 are asked

A

1 자원봉사 프로그램이 성공하려면 많은 지지와 도움이 요구된다.
▶ 동사 need의 목적어가 주어로 온 수동형
2 전기 자동차는 시속 50마일로 운행하기 때문에 70마일마다 충전될 필요가 있다. ▶ to recharge의 수동태
3 Benjamin Franklin이 훌륭한 발명가였다라고 사람들은 생각한다. ▶ 목적어가 절인 경우(People believe that...)의 수동태
4 올해는 시장에서 이용 가능한 벤처 자금의 규모가 줄어들 것으로 예상된다. ▶ It is expected that the amount of venture capital shows a steeper decline this year.의 단문화
5 학교는 교복과 가방을 포함하여 우리가 필요한 모든 것을 주겠다고 약속했지만, 우리는 문구 한 상자만 받았다. ▶ 간접목적어를 주어로 한 수동태

B

1 다양한 피해를 주는 지진의 영향에 취약한, 지진이 발생하기 쉽고 위험한 지역에서의 건설 활동은 피하는 것이 가장 좋다. 그러나 이와 같은 상황은 불가피한 경우가 많기 때문에 적절한 강화 조치가 필요하다. ▶ 타동사 avoid의 목적어가 없으므로 수동태 필요
2 인터넷 검색을 하는 것이 사람들의 인지적 자존감을 강화한다: 자신이 몰랐던 사실을 인터넷에서 검색한 다음 나중에 어디에서 그 정보를 찾았는지에 대해 질문받는 사람들은 자주 자신이 그 정보를 (검색 이전부터) 내내 알고 있었다고 말한다. ▶「people(간접목적어)+who(주격 관계대명사)+be asked+직접목적어」

적용독해

p.61

1 ③   2 ③

1 ③

해석 좋은 결정을 내린다 해도 나쁜 결과가 올 수 있음을 기억하는 것은 중요하다. 여기 한 가지 사례가 있다. 내가 학교를 졸업하자 곧 일자리를 제안 받았다. 그것이 나에게 아주 잘 맞는 것인지 확신이 없었다. 나는 그 기회에 대해 곰곰이 생각해 본 후, 그 제안을 거절하기로 마음먹었다. 나는 더 잘 맞는 다른 일자리를 찾을 수 있을 것이라고 생각했다. 유감스럽게도, 경제는 곧 빠르게 나빠졌고, 나는 다른 일자리를 찾기 위해 수 개월을 보냈다. 나는 그 일자리를 선택하지 않은 것에 대해 자책했고, (거절한) 그 일자리는 점점 더 매력적으로 보이기 시작했다. 나는 그 당시에 가진 모든 정보에 기초하여 좋은 결정을 내렸지만, 단기적인 관점에서 보면 그것은 그다지 좋은 결과를 가져온 것은 아니었다.

문제풀이 ③ 「spend+O(시간)+v-ing」이므로 능동의 spent가 되어야 한다.

① 간접목적어를 주어로 한 4형식 문장의 수동태
② 주절의 동사가 과거이므로 종속절의 동사도 과거(시제 일치)
④ 「2형식 동사 look+형용사 보어」 ▶ p.36
⑤ 「base+O+(up)on」의 수동태

2 ③

해석 Alfred Chandler는 하버드 대학 경영 대학원의 경영사 교수였다. 그는 경영 사학자였으며 그의 연구는 경영사 그리고 특히 경영 관리 연구에 집중되어 왔다. 그는 이것이 최근 역사 연구에서 대단히 간과된 영역이라고 오랫동안 주장했다. 대기업에 대한 그의 연구들은 Alfred P. Sloan 재단을 포함한 수많은 기관으로부터 지원된 연구비로 진행되어 왔다. 그의 연구는 국제적으로 인정받아 왔고, 그의 저서인 『보이는 손』은 1978년 10월에 퓰리처 역사상과 뱅크로프트 상을 수상하게 되었다. Chandler는 미국과 유럽의 다양한 대학에서 경영사를 가르쳤다.

문제풀이 ③ carry의 목적어가 주어로 된 수동태 문장이므로 been carried가 되어야 한다.

① 소유격 관계대명사(선행사+whose+명사) ▶ p.174
② neglected가 명사 area를 수식하는 과거분사형 형용사 ▶ p.150
④ 간접목적어를 주어로 한 4형식 문장의 수동태
⑤ 3형식 능동태 문장

pp.62~63

STEP 3 유형   글의 제목

1 ①   2 ②   3 ③

1 ①

해석 전 세계의 도시에서 행해진 연구들은 도시의 매력으로서의 생활

과 활동의 중요성을 보여 준다. 사람들은 무언가 일이 일어나고 있는 곳에 모이고 다른 사람들의 존재를 찾는다. 텅 빈 거리 혹은 활기찬 거리에서 걷기라는 선택에 직면하면, 대부분의 사람들은 생활과 활동으로 가득한 거리를 선택할 것이다. 걷는 그 길이 더 흥미로울 것이고 더 안전하게 느껴질 것이다. 사람들이 공연을 하거나 음악을 연주하는 것을 볼 수 있는 행사는 많은 사람들을 끌어들여 머무르면서 구경하게 한다. 도시 공간의 벤치와 의자에 대한 연구들은 다른 사람들을 볼 수 없는 자리보다 도시의 생활을 가장 잘 볼 수 있는 자리가 훨씬 더 자주 이용된다는 것을 보여 준다.

문제풀이 사람들의 생활과 활동으로 가득한 곳이 사람들의 마음을 끌고 도시의 매력으로 작용한다는 내용이므로 ①이 가장 적절하다.

① 도시의 가장 큰 매력: 사람
② 도시를 떠나 시골에 살라
③ 도시에 더 많은 공원을 만들라
④ 붐비는 거리에서 외로움을 느끼는 것
⑤ 관광 명소로 가득한 고대 도시들

구문분석

[6행] Studies of benches and chairs in city space show
      S   V
[that the seats with the best view of city life are used
far more frequently than those {that do not offer a
                          ↑_____|
view of other people}].

▶ [ ]는 이 문장의 동사인 show의 목적절로 명사절의 접속사 that이 이끌고 있다. { }는 앞의 선행사 those를 수식하는 주격 관계대명사절이다. those는 복수명사 seats를 대신하는 대명사이다.

2 ②

해석 점술가를 찾아가 본 적이 있다면 여러분은 아마 그들이 여러분에 대해 알고 있는 것, 즉 다른 사람이라면 도저히 알 수 없었을 것을 알고 있는 것에 깜짝 놀라면서 자리를 떴을 것이다. 그럼 그것이 초능력임에 틀림없다, 그렇지 않은가? 점술업에 대한 조사는 점술가가 "사전 지식 없이 빠르게 알아차리는 것"으로 알려진 기술을 사용한다고 보여 주는데, 그것(그 기술)은 결코 만난 적이 없는 사람을 "읽어 낼" 때 80퍼센트 정도의 정확성을 이끌어 낼 수 있다. 몇몇 사람들에게 마법인 것처럼 보일 수 있지만, 그것은 인간 본성에 대한 이해와 확률 통계에 대한 지식뿐만 아니라 몸짓 언어 신호에 대한 주의 깊은 관찰에 기초를 둔 과정에 불과하다. 그것은 "고객"에 관한 정보를 모으기 위해 타로 카드 점술가, 점성가 그리고 수상가에 의해 행해지는 기술이다.

문제풀이 점술가들은 초능력을 가진 존재가 아니라 그들만의 여러 기술을 사용하여 상당히 정확하게 예측한다는 내용이므로 ②가 가장 적절하다.

① 초자연적인 것들을 무시하지 마라
② 점술가들이 어떻게 그렇게 많이 아는가
③ 사람들이 왜 점을 보기를 원하는가
④ 비언어적인 신호들은 감정을 보여 준다
⑤ 미래는 의지력에 달려 있다

구문분석

[3행] Research into the fortune-telling business shows ―V―
[that fortune-tellers use a technique {known as "cold reading}," {which can produce an accuracy of around 80 percent when "reading" a person you've never met}].

▶ [ ]는 동사 shows의 목적절을 나타내며, 첫 번째 { }는 a technique를 수식하는 과거분사구이다. 두 번째 { }는 계속적 용법의 관계대명사절로 which는 a technique를 가리킨다.

3 ③

해석 환경에 대한 인간의 지배의 실현은 1700년대 후반 산업 혁명과 함께 시작되었다. 제조업의 발달은 사회와 경제를 변화시키면서 환경에 중대한 영향을 미쳤다. 증기 기관의 발달이 기계화를 통한 상품의 대량 생산으로 이어지면서 미국 사회는 여러 산업의 자본주의적 목표에 따라 구축되었다. 수제 상품과 농업에 기반을 둔 경제를 가진 시골의 농업 사회는 산업화된 제조업 경제를 기반으로 한 대규모 공장이 있는 도시에서의 삶을 위해 버려졌다. 직물, 철, 철강 생산의 혁신은 사기업의 이윤을 증대시켰다. 동시에, 그런 산업들은 환경에 권력을 행사하였고 공공 토지와 수로에 유해한 부산물을 내버리기 시작했다.

문제풀이 산업 발달이 사회와 경제를 변화시키면서 환경에 부정적인 영향을 미쳤다는 내용이므로 ③이 가장 적절하다.
① 산업 혁신을 위한 전략
② 도시화: 더 나은 삶으로 가는 길
③ 산업 발달이 환경을 해쳤다
④ 기술: 지속 가능한 발전의 열쇠
⑤ 자본주의의 원동력은 탐욕이 아니었다

구문분석

[5행] Rural agricultural communities with economies ――S――
[based on handmade goods and agriculture] were ―――――――――――――――――――――――――― ―V―
abandoned for life in urban cities with large factories [based on an economy of industrialized manufacturing].

▶ 첫 번째 [ ]는 economies를 수식하는 과거분사구이며, 두 번째 [ ]는 urban cities를 수식하는 과거분사구이다.

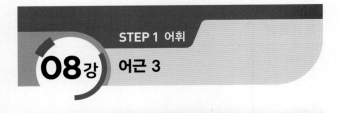

STEP 1 어휘

08강 어근 3

PRACTICE
p.66

A
1 apply, 적용하다   2 imply, 의미하다
3 supply, 공급하다   4 comply, 순응하다
5 multiply, 증가시키다   6 biology, 생물학
7 geology, 지질학   8 theology, 신학
9 sociology, 사회학
10 psychology, 심리학

B   1 ④   2 ②   3 ④   4 ②   5 ③

C   1 compared   2 motionless

A

1 ap+ply(fold): 적용하다
2 im+ply(fold): 의미하다
3 sup+ply(fold): 공급하다
4 com+ply(fold): 순응하다
5 multi+ply(fold): 증가시키다
6 bio+logy(study): 생물학
7 geo+logy(study): 지질학
8 theo+logy(study): 신학
9 socio+logy(study): 사회학
10 psycho+logy(study): 심리학

B

1 그는 북극 탐험을 감행했으나 결국 돌아오지 못했다.
2 이산화탄소는 탄소와 산소가 상호 작용한 결과이다.
3 환경 단체들은 개정된 오염방지법에 대해 항의 시위를 벌였다.
4 폭력을 공공연히 옹호하는 일부 극단주의자들이 있다.
5 IMF는 올해 OECD 국가 중 한 개 국가를 제외하고 모두 경제가 성장할 거라고 예측한다.

C

1 연구자들은 일별로 계획을 세우는 집단과 월별로 계획을 세우는 집단의 습관을 관찰한 후, 월별로 계획을 세운 집단은 훨씬 더 오랫동안 꾸준히 계속해 나갔기 때문에 일별로 계획을 세운 집단과 비교했을 때 학습 습관과 태도의 향상이라는 측면에서 더 뛰어났다.
2 연구들은 우리의 몸은 뇌의 신경 중추 때문에 움직이지 않고 기본적으로 마비되지만, 급속 안구 운동과 함께 우리의 심장 박동이 증가하고 우리의 호흡 또한 높아진다는 것을 발견했다.

적용독해

p.67

1 ⑤   2 ⑤

1 ⑤

해석 가족 간의 갈등에 대처하는 데 가장 좋은 처방 중 하나를 아는 가? 'I'm sorry.'라는 두 단어이다. 몇몇 사람들이 그 말을 하는 것을 얼마나 어려워하는지 놀랍다. 그들은 그것이 약함이나 패배를 의미한다고 생각한다. 전혀 그렇지 않다. 사실, 정확하게 반대이다. 갈등을 덜어 주는 또 다른 좋은 방법은 말다툼이다. 바다는 폭풍 후에 훨씬 더 잔잔해진다. 말다툼은 또 다른 이점을 갖고 있다. 화가 날 때, 입 밖에 내지 않은 진실이 일반적으로 나오게 된다. 그것들은 특히 그 순간에 약간 감정을 상하게 할 수도 있다. 그러나 끝에 가서는 서로를 조금 더 잘 알게 된다. 마지막으로 아이들 간의 갈등과 싸움의 대부분은 위험한(→ 자연스러운) 것이다. 그것들이 지속적인 것처럼 보일 때조차, 현명한 부모는 지나치게 걱정하지 않는다.

문제풀이 말다툼은 갈등을 해결하는 데 있어 사과보다 더 큰 이점이 있으며, 그래서 부모는 아이들의 갈등을 자연스러운 것으로 크게 신경 쓰지 않는다는 내용이므로 ⑤ risky를 natural 등으로 고쳐야 한다.

구문분석

[2행] **It**'s amazing [**how** hard some people <u>find</u> <u>them</u> <u>to</u> <u>say</u>].
   V   O   S.C.

▶ 가주어–진주어 구문으로 가주어는 It이며, [ ]가 진주어를 나타내는 부분으로 의문사 how로 시작하는 의문사절이다. 진주어절 속의 동사 find는 목적격보어로 to부정사를 취한다.

2 ⑤

해석 새로운 기술은 새로운 상호 작용과 문화적 규칙을 만든다. TV 시청을 부추기는 방법으로 이제 소셜 텔레비전 시스템은 서로 다른 장소에 있는 TV 시청자들 사이의 사회적 상호 작용을 가능하게 한다. 이런 시스템들은 TV를 이용하는 친구들 사이에 더 큰 유대감을 만드는 것으로 알려져 있다. 한 현장 연구는 30세에서 36세 사이의 다섯 명의 친구들이 자기들의 집에서 TV를 보면서 어떻게 의사소통하는지에 초점을 두었다. 그 기술은 그들이 친구들 중 어떤 이가 TV를 보고 있는지와 그들이 무엇을 보고 있는지를 알 수 있게 했다. 그들은 소셜 텔레비전을 통해 의사소통하는 방법, 즉 음성 채팅을 할 것인지 혹은 문자 채팅을 할 것인지를 선택했다. 그 연구는 음성 채팅보다는 문자 채팅에 대한 선호도가 강하다는 것을 보여 주었다. 이용자들은 문자 채팅을 선호하는 두 가지 주요한 이유를 말했다. 우선, 문자 채팅은 수고와 집중을 덜 필요로 했고 음성 채팅보다 더 재미없었다(→ 재미있었다). 둘째, 연구 참여자들은 문자 채팅을 더 예의 바른 것으로 여겼다.

문제풀이 소셜 텔레비전으로 의사소통을 할 때 사람들은 문자 채팅에 대한 선호도가 높았다는 이유로 재미있었다는 것과 예의 바른 것을 들었다는 내용이므로 ⑤ unpleasant는 enjoyable 등으로 고쳐야 한다.

구문분석

[5행] The technology <u>allowed</u> <u>them</u> <u>to see</u> [**which** of
           V   O   O.C.
the friends were watching TV and **what** they were watching].

▶ 이 문장은 5형식으로 「allow+O+to-v」의 구조이다. 목적격보어로 쓰인 to부정사구 to see의 목적어인 which 의문사절과 what 의문사절이 and로 병렬되고 있다.

STEP 2 어법   수동태 2(5형식)

PRACTICE

p.68

A   **1** call → are called
     2 motionlessly → motionless
     3 being gained → to be gained
     4 transit → to transit
     5 taste → to taste

B   **1** undesirable   **2** to do

A

1 요리는 호모 사피엔스를 규정하는 활동인데, 그래서 호모 사피엔스는 '요리를 하는 동물'로 부른다. ▶ 선행사+주격 관계대명사+be called+명사 보어
2 그 나비는 더듬이는 가만히 둔 채 뒷날개를 움직였다. ▶ 「keep+O+형용사 보어」의 수동태
3 공격을 함으로써 얻을 수 있는 어떤 전략적 이득을 기대할 수 없다. ▶ 「expect+O+to-v」의 수동태
4 관광객들은 가이드가 있는 여행으로부터 혼자 하는 여행으로 옮겨 가도록 장려된다. ▶ 「encourage+O+to-v」의 수동태
5 소비자들의 입맛에 더 맞도록 짜고 기름진 음식들이 만들어진다. ▶ 「사역동사 make+O+동사원형」의 수동태

B

1 혁신이 무수한 방식으로 거의 모든 사람의 삶을 더욱 나은 쪽으로 바꿔 왔다는 많은 증거에도 불구하고, 어떤 새로운 것은 종종 바람직하지 않은 것으로 여겨진다. ▶ 「consider+O+형용사 보어」의 수동태
2 아이러니하게도, 우리가 우리의 뇌가 법적으로 허용되지 않는 행동을 하고 싶지 않다고 스스로에게 말할 때, 우리의 뇌는 이 '않다'를 불법적인 행동을 저지르기 위한 도전으로 해석한다. ▶ 「allow+O+to-v」의 수동태

1 ④   2 ⑤

1 ④

해석 에베레스트산 정상에 도달하는 것은 한때 놀라운 것으로 여겨졌었다. 그곳에서 국기를 흔드는 등반가를 갖는 것은 심지어 국가적 명예였다. 그러나 거의 4,000명이 그곳의 정상에 도달했기 때문에, 그 업적은 반세기 전보다 의미하는 바가 더 적어졌다. 1963년에 6명이 정상에 도달했지만, 2012년 봄에 정상에는 500명 이상의 사람들로 붐볐다. 그렇다면 그렇게 많은 사람들이 정상에 도달하는 것을 가능하게 하는 것은 무엇인가? 많은 사람들이 정상에 도달할 수 있게 해 준 한 가지 중요한 요인 즉 향상된 일기 예보에 의해서였다. 과거에 정보의 부족은 원정대들이 그들의 팀 구성원들이 준비가 될 때마다 정상(등정)을 시도하게 했다. 오늘날 모든 팀들은 초정밀 위성 예보에 의해 등반을 위한 날씨가 언제 완벽할지를 정확하게 알며, 그들은 자주 같은 날에 정상을 향해 간다.

문제풀이 ④ 동사의 목적어가 있으므로 was led를 능동의 led로 바꿔야 한다.
① 가주어-진주어 구문 ▶ p.12
② 동사 crowd의 목적어가 주어가 된 수동태
③ 「enable+O+to-v」의 수동태
⑤ 「consider+O+형용사 보어」의 수동태

구문분석

[5행] Then what <u>makes</u> <u>it</u> <u>possible</u> for so many people
     V   O   O.C.
[to reach the summit]?
▶ 「make+O+형용사 보어」의 구조로 it은 가목적어이며 [ ]이 진목적어 역할을 하는 to부정사구이다. for so many people은 to reach의 의미상 주어이다.

2 ⑤

해석 실현 가능하다는 사고방식을 계발하는 가장 좋은 방법 중 하나는 평소에 꾸는 것보다 조금 더 큰 꿈을 꾸도록 당신 자신을 자극하는 것이다. 현실을 보면 대부분의 사람들은 꿈을 너무 작게 꾼다. 많은 사람들이 그들의 꿈을 더 작게 만들기 위해 노력한다. 이와는 대조적으로 Henry Curtis는 "지금부터 25년이 지나면 당신의 계획은 아주 특별하게 보이지 않을 것이기 때문에 원하는 대로 당신의 계획을 환상적으로 만들어라. 당신이 최초 계획했던 것보다 10배 더 크게 당신의 계획을 세워라. 그러면 지금부터 25년 후에 당신은 왜 50배 더 크게 만들지 않았을까 생각할 것이다"라고 조언한다. 당신이 더 광대하게 꿈을 꾸고 당신을 편안하게 해 주는 것보다 한 단계 위로 목표를 정하도록 동기부여 된다면, 당신은 성장할 수밖에 없을 것이다. 이것이 당신이 보다 더 큰 가능성을 믿도록 할 것이다.

문제풀이 ⑤ 「force+O+to-v」의 수동태로 force를 be forced로 바꿔야 한다.
① 주격 보어 역할의 to부정사구 ▶ p.36
② 「make+O+형용사 보어」의 수동태

③ 「make+O+형용사 보어」
④ 「motivate+O+to-v」의 수동태

구문분석

[1행] One of the greatest <u>ways</u> [to cultivate a possibility
   S
mind-set] <u>is</u> [to prompt yourself {to dream one size
     V   S.C.
bigger than you normally do}].
▶ 첫 번째 [ ]는 명사 ways를 수식하는 형용사적 용법의 to부정사구이며, 두 번째 [ ]는 주격 보어 역할의 명사적 용법의 to부정사구이다. { }는 '~하기 위해'라는 의미의 목적을 나타내는 부사적 용법의 to부정사구이다.

1 ③   2 ④   3 ⑤

1 ③

해석 Vivian Malone Jones는 동료 흑인 학생인 James Hood와 함께 1963년에 Alabama 대학교에 들어간 최초의 아프리카계 미국인 여성이었다. 그들의 입학은 당시 주지사였던 George Wallace가 그들의 입학을 저지하기 위해 대학 정문에 서 있게 만들었다. 백악관과 Wallace의 보좌관들 사이에 합의가 있은 후에야 그들은 입학했다. Ms. Jones는 1965년에 Alabama 대학교를 졸업한 최초의 아프리카계 미국인으로 더욱 이름을 떨쳤다. 그녀는 Washington DC로 옮겨 the U.S. Department of Justice에서 Voter Education Project의 직원으로 일했다. 그 임무에 이어서 그녀는 Atlanta로 옮겨 Environmental Protection Agency (EPA)에서 근무했는데, 그곳에서 그녀는 인권과 도시 관련 업무의 책임자로 임명되었다. 그녀는 1996년에 은퇴했고, 인권 단체에서 여전히 활동했다.

문제풀이 Vivian Malone Jones는 1965년에 대학을 졸업했다고 했으므로 ③이 일치하지 않는다.

구문분석

[2행] Their entry resulted [**in** then Governor George
Wallace **standing** in the door of the university in an
attempt to halt their admission].
▶ [ ]는 전치사구로서 전치사 뒤에는 명사(구) 또는 동명사가 와야 한다. 여기서는 standing이라는 동명사가 왔고 앞에 있는 Governor George Wallace는 standing의 의미상 주어이다.

2 ④

해석 Bessie Coleman은 1892년에 텍사스에서 태어났다. 그녀가 11살이었을 때 그녀는 Wright 형제가 그들의 첫 비행을 했다는 것을 들었다. 그때부터 그녀는 자신이 하늘을 높이 날아오르는 그날을 꿈꿨다. 23살 때 Coleman은 시카고로 이사했고 그곳에서 비행 수업을 위한 돈을 모으기 위해 식당에서 일했다. 그러나 그 당시 미국 비행 학교가 여성이나 흑인의 입학을 허가하지 않았기 때문에 그녀는 비행 수업을 듣기 위해 파리로 가야 했다. 1921년에 그녀는 마침내 국제 조종사 면허를 딴 최초의 흑인 여성이 되었다. 그녀는 또한 유럽에서 곡예비행을 공부했고 1922년에 뉴욕의 에어쇼에 그녀의 첫 출현을 했다. 이 여성 비행 개척자에 의해 다음 세대가 그들의 비행의 꿈을 추구하도록 영감을 받았다.

문제풀이 유럽에서 곡예비행을 공부했고 뉴욕의 에어쇼에 첫 출현을 했다고 했으므로 ④가 일치하지 않는다.

구문분석

> [3행] At the age of 23, Coleman moved to Chicago, [where she worked at a restaurant {to save money for flying lessons}].
> ▶ [ ]는 앞에 있는 Chicago를 가리키는 관계부사 where가 사용된 계속적 용법의 관계부사절이다. { }는 목적의 의미를 갖는 부사적 용법의 to부정사구이다.

3 ⑤

해석 인도의 가장 유명한 과학자 중 한 명인 Janaki Ammal은 1897년에 태어났고, 중매를 통해 결혼할 것으로 기대되었다. 인도 여성들의 식자율이 1%보다 낮았던 시기에 살았음에도 불구하고, 그녀는 관습을 따르지 않고 대학에 입학하기로 결심했다. 1924년에 그녀는 미국으로 갔고 마침내 Michigan 대학에서 식물학과 생태학 박사 학위를 받았다. Ammal은 세계에서 가장 단 사탕수수 품종 개발에 기여했다. 그녀는 영국으로 건너가 그곳에서 *Chromosome Atlas of Cultivated Plants*를 공동 집필하며 식물의 염색체를 생생하게 묘사했다. 연이은 기근이 있은 후, 그녀는 수상의 요청으로 식량 생산을 증가시키는 데 도움을 주기 위해 인도로 돌아갔다. 그러나 Ammal은 더 많은 식량을 재배하기 위한 노력으로써 삼림 벌채가 일어나는 것에 동의하지 않았다. 그녀는 토종 식물 보존에 대한 옹호자가 되었고, 수력 발전 댐의 건설로부터 Silent Valley를 성공적으로 지켰다.

문제풀이 수력 발전 댐의 건설로부터 Silent Valley를 성공적으로 지켰다고 했으므로 ⑤가 일치하지 않는다.

구문분석

> [9행] Ammal disagreed with the deforestation [taking place in an effort {**to grow** more food}].
> ▶ [ ]는 the deforestation을 수식하는 현재분사구이다. { }는 앞에 있는 an effort를 수식하는 형용사적 용법의 to부정사구이다.

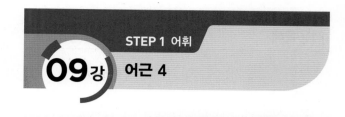
PRACTICE
p.74

A　1 aspect, 측면　2 respect, 존경하다
　　3 inspect, 조사하다　4 suspect, 의심하다
　　5 prospect, 전망　6 deception, 기만
　　7 exception, 예외　8 perception, 인식
　　9 conception, 생각
　　10 interception, 가로채기

B　1 ②　2 ①　3 ④　4 ③　5 ③

C　1 well-informed　2 contrast

A

1 a+spect(look): 측면
2 re+spect(look): 존경하다
3 in+spect(look): 조사하다
4 sus+spect(look): 의심하다
5 pro+spect(look): 전망
6 de+cept(take)+ion: 기만
7 ex+cept(take)+ion: 예외
8 per+cept(take)+ion: 인식
9 con+cept(take)+ion: 생각
10 inter+cept(take)+ion: 가로채기

B

1 수영장과 헬스장은 호텔 고객 전용입니다.
2 나는 불법적인 일이라면 무슨 일이든 절대 참여하지 않는다.
3 여행 경비는 여행 시기에 따라 달라진다.
4 그 정책은 지역 주민을 위한 일자리 창출에 영향을 미칠 것이다.
5 대통령의 실정으로 여당의 득표율은 급감했다.

C

1 정복자들은 지식이 영토를 지배하는 데 필수적이라는 것을 이해해 왔고 통치자들은 권력이 충분한 정보가 없이는 이행될 수 없다는 것, 즉 사망률 표, 세금 자료 그리고 그와 같은 것들이 효과적인 공공 행정을 운영하는 데 중요하다는 것을 알고 있다.
2 대중문화의 한 형태인 sports songs(팬들이 참여할 수 있는 외우기 쉽고 부르기 쉬운 합창)는 '품위 있는 미적 거리와 통제'를 유지하는 경향이 있는 지배적인 문화와는 대조적으로, 즐거움과 감정적 과잉을 보여 준다고 말할 수 있다.

1 ④   2 ④

1 ④

해석 태도가 항상 행위를 반영하지 않는다는 것을 발견한 것은 매우 놀랍다. Stanford 대학의 교수인 Richard LaPiere는 1930년대에 태도와 행위가 무관함에 대한 강력한 증명을 내놓았다. 그는 중국에서 온 몇몇 동료와 미국을 여행했다. 그 당시에, 많은 미국 사람들은 중국인에 대해서 부정적인 견해를 갖고 있었다. LaPiere는 여행 일정에 있는 호텔과 식당에, 그와 그의 중국인 손님들을 받아 줄 수 있는지를 묻는 편지를 썼다. 답장을 보내온 128개의 업소 중에서, 92퍼센트가 그에게 중국인 손님들을 받겠다(→ 거부하겠다)는 응답을 했다. 그러나, 그가 전국을 여행하며, (편지를 보냈던) 같은 호텔과 식당을 방문했을 때, 250개 중 249개 업소가 중국인 여행객들을 호의적으로 응대했다. 놀랍게도, 강하게 비우호적이었던 태도는 실제 행동을 예측 해내지 못했다.

문제풀이 태도와 행위가 무관한지에 대한 연구 조사에서 중국인에 대해 부정적이었던 태도와는 달리 호텔과 식당에서는 압도적으로 중국인 손님을 거부하지 않겠다고 했고 실제로 호의적으로 응대했으므로 ④ accept는 refuse 등으로 고쳐야 한다.

구문분석

[1행] The discovery [that attitudes don't always reflect actions] came as a great surprise.

▶ [ ]는 명사절의 접속사 that이 이끌어 주어 The discovery와 동격절을 이루고 있다.

2 ④

해석 이야기는 오직 이야기하는 사람만큼 믿을 만하다. 이야기가 효과적이려면 신뢰가 확립되어야 한다. 그렇다. 신뢰다. 누군가가 여러분의 말을 듣기 위해 멈출 때마다, 무언의 신뢰라는 요소가 존재한다. 여러분의 이야기를 듣는 사람은 여러분이 가치 있는 어떤 것, 즉 그의 시간을 낭비하지 않을 어떤 것을 그에게 말할 것이라고 무의식적으로 신뢰한다. 그가 여러분에게 주는 몇 분간의 관심은 희생적이다. 그는 다른 어딘가에 자신의 시간을 보내는 걸 선택할 수 있었지만, 그는 대화에서 여러분의 파트를 존중하기 위해 멈추었다. 이것이 이야기가 들어오는 곳이다. 이야기가 요점을 분명하게 설명하고, 종종 주제들을 쉽게 연결하기 때문에 신뢰가 '빨리' 확립될 수 있으며, 이러한 이야기의 시간적 요소를 인지하는 것이 신뢰에 필수적이다. 여러분의 이야기를 듣는 사람의 시간을 허비하는(→ 존중하는) 것이 여러분의 문장 맨 앞의 대문자(시작점)이다. '만약' 신뢰가 얻어지고 당연하게 여겨지지 않는다면 그것은 대화를 들을 만한 가치가 있는 문장으로 이끈다.

문제풀이 누군가의 이야기를 듣기 위해 멈춘다는 것은 이야기하는 사람이 시간을 낭비하지 않을 거라는 신뢰가 확립되었다는 의미이며, 이야기를 하는 사람은 이야기를 듣는 사람의 시간을 존중한다는 신뢰

를 얻어야 한다는 내용이므로 ④ Wasting은 Respecting 등으로 고쳐야 한다.

구문분석

[4행] The few minutes of attention [(that) he is giving you] is sacrificial.

▶ [ ]는 이 문장의 주어인 attention을 수식하는 목적격 관계대명사절로 관계대명사가 생략되었다.

STEP 2 어법   **수동태 3(수동태 시제)**

A   1 → will be judged

      2 → being slaughtered

      3 → was counseling

      4 → has been dumped

      5 → to be carried

B   1 been created   2 be sold

A

1 출품작들은 창의성, 내용 그리고 전달의 효과성을 기준으로 평가될 것입니다. ▶ 주어가 동사 judge의 목적어이므로 수동태
2 돼지들은 도살당하는 것을 피해 우리에서 도망쳤다. ▶ 주어가 동사 slaughter의 목적어이므로 수동태
3 나는 더 많은 진취성을 보여 줄 수 있는 더 좋은 직업을 원한 사람들과 상담하고 있었다. ▶ 동사 counsel의 목적어가 있으므로 능동태
4 제 생각에는 지난주 내내 우리 집 진입로에 엎질러져 있던 쓰레기통이 귀하의 쓰레기통인 것 같습니다. ▶ 주어 the garbage가 동사 dump의 목적어이므로 수동태
5 우리 몸이 느끼는 모든 감각은 그 정보가 뇌에 전달되기까지 기다려야 한다. ▶ 의미상 주어 the information이 동사 carry의 목적이므로 수동태

B

1 Erich Fromm은 인간은 단지 창조된 상태를 넘어서도록 이끌리지만 대신에 창조자 즉 자신의 운명을 만드는 적극적인 행위자가 되려고 노력하는 존재라고 제안한다. ▶ 의미상 주어가 humans로 동사 create의 목적이므로 수동태
2 묶음 가격이란 대개 보완적인 제품 두 개 이상의 제품을 단일 가격에 판매되도록 함께 포장하는 것인데, 그것(단일 가격)은 일반적으로 개별 제품 가격의 합계보다 상당히 더 저렴하다. ▶ 의미상 주어가 two or more products로 동사 sell의 목적어이므로 수동태

적용독해

1 ②　2 ③

STEP 3 유형　빈칸 추론 1

1 ②　2 ④　3 ②

1 ②

해석 감사할 줄 아는 사람들은 건전한 결정을 내리는 경향이 있다. 인생과 스포츠는 중요하고 어려운 결정이 내려져야 하는 많은 상황들을 제시한다. 이기적인 사람들은 감사할 줄 아는 사람들만큼 건전할 것으로 여겨지는 결정을 내리지 못한다. 이것은 스스로를 동기 유발시키는 결정을 포함한다. 좌절한 부모는 묻는다. "어떻게 내가 아이에게 스포츠를 하거나 스포츠를 계속하도록 동기를 부여해야 할까? 때때로 내 아이가 낙심하여 스포츠에 필요한 노력을 기울이려 하지 않는 것은 아닐까? 부모로서 돕기 위해 내가 무엇을 하거나 말해야 하지?" 자기들만의 편협한 이기적인 욕구에 집중하기 때문에 아이들 또는 어른들이 동기 유발되는 것은 어렵고 거의 불가능한 일이다. 그러나 감사할 줄 아는 사람들로서 살아가는 아이들과 어른들은 스스로를 동기 유발시킬 수 있다. 그들은 또한 다른 사람들 심지어 부모들로부터의 제안을 환영한다.

문제풀이 ② 「consider+O+형용사 보어」의 수동태이므로 형용사가 되도록 soundly를 sound로 고쳐야 한다.
① 타동사 make의 목적어가 없으므로 수동태
③ 분사의 주어가 감정을 느끼면 과거분사 ▶ p.158
④ 타동사 motivate의 목적어가 없으므로 수동태
⑤ 주어와 목적어가 동일하면 목적어에 재귀대명사 ▶ p.28

2 ③

해석 당신의 결혼식 날 당신의 신랑 들러리가 당신을 울게 만드는 마음을 따뜻하게 하고, 감동적인 축사를 한다고 가정해 보자. 나중에 그가 스스로 축사를 쓴 것이 아니라 온라인에서 그것을 샀다는 것을 알게 된다. 그러면 당신은 그것이 보수를 받은 전문가에 의해 쓰였다는 것을 알기 전인 처음에 그 축사가 의미했던 때보다 축사의 의미가 덜하다는 것인가? 대부분의 사람들은 구매한 축사가 진짜 축사보다 가치가 덜하다는 데 동의를 한다. 비록 구매한 축사가 그것에 기대된 결과를 이룬다는 점에서 "효과가 있"지라도 그 효과는 기만에 좌우될지도 모른다. 즉 만약 당신이 온라인에서 감동적인 걸작인 축사를 구입한다면 당신은 아마도 그것을 감출 것이다! 만약, 구입한 축사가 그것의 출처를 감추는 것에 그것의 효과가 좌우된다면, 그것이 진품의 타락한 변형이라는 의혹을 가지는 이유이다. 결혼 축사는 어떤 점에서 구매될 수 있는 상품이다. 그러나 그것들을 사고파는 것은 그것의 가치를 떨어뜨린다.

문제풀이 ③ 타동사 achieve의 목적어가 있는 능동태 문장이므로 being achieved를 achieving으로 고쳐야 한다.
① 선행사+주격 관계대명사+동사 ▶ p.174
② 타동사 write의 목적어가 없으므로 수동태
④ 타동사 cover의 목적어가 있으므로 능동태
⑤ 타동사 buy의 목적어가 없으므로 수동태

1 ②

해석 목성은 우리의 작은 행성(지구)을 보호하기 위해 여기에 있다. 9월 10일 새벽에 Oregon 주의 한 천문학자는 목성 표면에서 밝은 광채를 관측했다. 천문학자들은 이 화려한 폭발은 소행성이 그 거대한 행성(목성)에 부딪친 것으로 믿는다. 과학자들은 소행성이 지구를 향하고 있었을 것이나 목성이 그 충돌을 대신했다고 말한다. 그리고 목성이 충돌로부터 지구를 구한 것은 이번이 처음은 아닐지도 모른다. 목성은 어떤 행성보다 가장 강력한 중력(의 끌어당김)을 가지고 있다. 목성의 중력은 지나가는 소행성을 잡아당겨 그것들을 자신의 표면으로 끌어당긴다 — 즉, 지구로부터 멀어지도록. 그 영향은 과학자들이 소행성으로 인해 생긴 것으로 추측되는 목성 위의 흔적을 연구하게 하고 있다. 실제로 (소행성이) 지구에 부딪칠 가능성은 희박하지만 과학자들은 궤도를 돌고 있는 소행성이 매우 많기 때문에 그것들을 주시하고 있다.

문제풀이 목성의 강력한 중력이 소행성을 끌어당겨 소행성이 지구와 충돌하지 않도록 한다는 내용의 글이므로 빈칸에는 ② '우리의 작은 행성을 보호하기 위해'가 들어가는 것이 가장 적절하다.
① 지구의 중력에 영향을 미치기 위해
③ 지구의 궤도를 바꾸기 위해
④ 위성의 폭발을 막기 위해
⑤ 우리에게 대체 에너지를 제공하기 위해

구문분석

[2행] Astronomers believe this brilliant burst to be an asteroid [hitting the giant planet].
　V　　O　　O.C.
▶ 이 문장은 「believe+O+to-v」의 구조로 동사 believe는 to부정사를 목적격 보어로 취한다. [ ]는 an asteroid를 수식하는 현재분사구이다.

2 ④

해석 맛에 대한 판단은 흔히 음식의 겉모습에 기초한 예측에 의해 영향을 받는다. 예를 들어, 딸기 맛이 나는 음식들은 빨간색일 것으로 기대된다. 그러나 녹색으로 칠해진다면, 라임과 같은 맛을 가진 녹색 음식의 연관성 때문에, 그것이 매우 강하지 않는 한 그 맛을 딸기로 알아보기 어려울 것이다. 색의 강도 또한 맛의 인식에 영향을 준다. 더 강한 색깔이 나는 것이 단순히 더 많은 식용 색소의 첨가 때문일지라도, 더 강한 색깔이 식품에서의 더 강한 맛의 지각을 유발할 수도 있다. 질감 역시 오해하게 할 수 있다. 더 걸쭉한 음식은 농후 재료가 음식의 맛에 영향을 주기 때문이 아니라 단순히 그것이 더 걸쭉하기 때문에 맛이 더 풍부하거나 강하다고 인식될 수도 있다.

문제풀이 음식의 색과 그 색의 강도가 맛에 대한 판단과 인식에 영향을 준다는 내용의 글이므로 빈칸에는 ④ '겉모습'이 들어가는 것이 가장 적절하다.

① 기원   ② 요리법
③ 영양   ⑤ 배열

구문분석

[7행] A thicker product may [be perceived as] tasting richer or stronger.
▶ 3형식 능동태 문장으로 「주어+perceive+A+as+B」의 구조에서 수동태로 전환하면 [ ]과 같이 「A+be perceived+as+B」로 전환된다.

3 ②

해석 혁신이 우리의 삶을 바꾸는 최고의 방법은 사람들이 서로를 위해 일할 수 있도록 함으로써이다. 인류 역사의 주요한 주제는 우리가 생산하는 데 꾸준히 더 전문화되고 소비하는 데 꾸준히 더 다양화되는 것이다. 즉, 불안정한 자급자족에서 더 안전한 서로 간의 상호 의존으로 옮겨 간다는 것이다. 일주일에 40시간 동안 사람들의 필요를 충족시키는 것, 즉 우리가 직업이라고 부르는 것에 집중함으로써, 여러분은 다른 사람들에 의해 여러분에게 제공되는 서비스에 의지하여 나머지 72시간(잠자는 56시간은 계산에 넣지 않고)을 보낼 수 있다. 혁신은 전등을 한 시간 동안 켜는 여유를 가질 수 있게 하기 위해 아주 짧은 시간 동안 일하는 것을 가능하게 했고, 그것(혁신)은 만약 여러분이 그리 멀지 않은 과거에 많은 인류가 했던 것처럼 단순한 등을 켜기 위해 참기름이나 양의 지방을 모으고 정제함으로써 그것(빛)을 스스로 만들어야 했다면 하루 종일의 노동을 필요로 했었을 빛의 양을 제공했다.

문제풀이 인류의 역사는 자급자족의 불안정성에서 분업화의 상호 의존으로 바뀌면서 발전해 왔다는 내용의 글이므로 빈칸에는 ② '사람들이 서로를 위해 일할 수 있도록'이 들어가는 것이 가장 적절하다.
① 옛 시절의 가치를 존중하도록
③ 창의적으로 사고할 기회를 주도록
④ 맞춤화된 서비스로 고객을 만족시키도록
⑤ 특별한 제품을 도입하고 판매하도록

구문분석

[7행] Innovation has made **it** possible [**to work** for a
             <u>has made</u> <u>it</u>
             V   O   O.C.
fraction of a second].
▶ 이 문장의 목적어로 사용된 it은 가목적어로 [ ]가 진목적어구인 to부정사구이다.

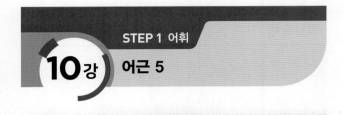

PRACTICE   p.82

A   1 emit, 방출하다   2 admit, 인정하다
      3 commit, 저지르다   4 permit, 허용하다
      5 submit, 제출하다   6 attain, 달성하다
      7 obtain, 얻다   8 retain, 보유하다
      9 sustain, 지탱하다   10 maintain, 유지하다
B   1 ④   2 ③   3 ④   4 ③   5 ④
C   1 laboratory   2 work

A

1 e+mit(send): 방출하다
2 ad+mit(send): 인정하다
3 com+mit(send): 저지르다
4 per+mit(send): 허용하다
5 sub+mit(send): 제출하다
6 at+tain(hold): 달성하다
7 ob+tain(hold): 얻다
8 re+tain(hold): 보유하다
9 sus+tain(hold): 지탱하다
10 main+tain(hold): 유지하다

B

1 간호사가 내 몸무게를 재고 키를 <u>측정했다</u>.
2 지구는 발전이라는 이름 하에 계속 파괴되고 있다.
3 나는 그림이 완성될 때까지 그녀가 볼 수 없도록 할 <u>생각이었다</u>.
4 모든 학생들은 횡단보도 건너는 법 같은 도로 안전의 기본에 대해 <u>교육받는다</u>.
5 재생 에너지 시설의 부족으로 화석 연료의 사용을 <u>피할 수 없다</u>.

C

1 사물의 본질이 그것(사물)이 자연스럽게 발생하는 환경으로부터 동떨어져 있을 때 그것(사물의 본질)이 근본적으로 변하는 그런 것이라면, 여러분은 <u>실험실</u> 환경 안에서 조사하는 것으로 그것(사물의 본질)에 대한 정확한 설명을 찾아내지 못할 것이다.
2 최근에 '그것(무급 노동)이 향상된 경제적 가치를 지닌 재화와 서비스를 생산하기 위해 노동과 원자재를 결합하는 활동이기' 때문에 무급 노동이 <u>일</u>이라고 주장하는 시도가 있어 왔다.

1 ③　　**2** ④

1 ③

해석 많은 성공적인 사람들은 취침 전에 하는 좋은 습관을 가지는 경향이 있다. 그들은 잠들기 직전, 낮 동안에 일어났던 고마운 세 가지 일들에 대해 돌아보거나 적어 보는 시간을 가진다. 감사하는 일들에 대해 일기를 쓰는 것은 삶의 어떠한 측면에서든 그것들이 그날 이룬 발전을 떠올리게 한다. 그것은 특히 그들이 성공을(→ 어려움을) 경험할 때 동기를 유지하도록 해 주는 핵심적인 역할을 한다. 그러한 경우, 많은 사람들은 힘든 하루로부터 오는 부정적인 장면들을 되풀이해 떠올리는 덫에 쉽게 빠진다. 그러나 그날 하루가 얼마나 힘들었는지 관계없이, 성공적인 사람들은 대개 부정적인 자기 대화의 덫을 피한다. 왜냐하면 그것이 더 많은 스트레스를 유발할 뿐이라는 것을 그들이 알기 때문이다.

문제풀이 성공한 사람들은 자기 전에 그날에 있었던 뿌듯했던 일들을 돌아보는 좋은 습관이 있으며, 이 습관은 어려움을 경험할 때 동기를 유지하도록 해 준다는 내용이므로 ③ success는 hardship 등으로 고쳐야 한다.

구문분석

[3행] Keeping a diary of things [that they appreciate] reminds them of the progress [they made that day in any aspect of their lives].

▶ 이 문장의 주어는 동명사 Keeping으로 시작하는 동명사구이므로 동사는 단수 동사 reminds가 되었다. 첫 번째 [ ]는 명사 things를 수식하는 목적격 관계대명사절이다. 3형식 remind A of B는 'A에게 B를 떠올리게 하다'의 의미이고, 두 번째 [ ]는 B에 해당하는 the progress를 수식하는 목적격 관계대명사이다.

2 ④

해석 공감은 거울 뉴런이라 불리는 특별한 신경 세포 그룹에 의해 가능해진다. 이러한 특별한 세포들은 우리가 감정을 반영할 수 있도록 해 준다. 거울 뉴런은 이탈리아 과학자들에 의해 처음 발견되었는데, 그들은 원숭이 뇌 속의 개별 신경 세포의 활동을 보면서, 그 동물들이 특정한 행동을 하든지 또는 단지 다른 원숭이가 똑같은 행동을 하는 것을 관찰하든지 간에 뇌의 똑같은 부분의 뉴런이 활성화된다는 것을 알아차렸다. 그것은 마치 관찰자의 뇌세포들이 행위자의 뇌의 행동을 "반영"하는 것처럼 보였다. 우리가 어떤 사람이 감정을 겪는 것을 보고 그에 반응해서 똑같은 감정을 느낄 때 낯선(→ 비슷한) 현상이 발생한다. 똑같은 신경 조직이 거울 뉴런 조직의 한 부분인 뇌도의 한 영역과 관찰된 감정과 관련이 있는 감정 뇌 영역에서 활성화된다.

문제풀이 우리 뇌에 있는 거울 뉴런은 어떤 다른 사람이 감정을 겪는 것을 보면 활성화되어 우리도 유사한 감정을 느끼는 공감이 가능해진다는 내용이므로 ④ unfamiliar를 similar 등으로 고쳐야 한다.

구문분석

[1행] Empathy **is made possible** by a special group of nerve cells [called mirror neurons].

▶ 「make+O+형용사 보어(possible)」의 구조였던 문장을 목적어 Empathy를 주어로 옮긴 수동태 구문이다. [ ]는 nerve cells를 수식하는 과거분사구이다.

STEP 2 어법　접속사 1(명사절)

PRACTICE   p.84

A　1 what → that
　　2 that → what
　　3 that → whether/if
　　4 which → that
B　1 that　2 that

A

1 위험을 전혀 무릅쓰지 않는 것은 결코 성공하지 못할 것임을 의미한다. ▶ 명사절 접속사 that+완전한 절
2 Moinee라고 불리는 신이 무엇이 문제인지를 알아보고자 Tasmania로 내려왔다. ▶ 의문대명사 what+불완전한 절
3 그 예비 신부는 나에게 초대를 수락할지 아닐지를 물었다. ▶ 명사절 접속사 whether/if(~인지 아닌지)
4 지구가 공전한다는 사실은 종교계를 놀라게 했다. ▶ 동격절 접속사 that+완전한 절

B

1 1942년에 Harvard University에서 동물학 박사 학위를 받은 Griffin은 박쥐가 날아다니는 곤충만큼 작은 사물들의 위치를 파악할 수 있게 하는 고주파음을 발사한다는 것을 증명했다. ▶ 명사절 접속사 that + 완전한 절
2 우리가 생각하는 무생물과 생물의 행동 방식을 거스르기 때문에 살아 있는 듯 보이는 장난감은 많은 호기심을 불러일으켜서 오늘날 많은 장난감이 이 원리를 이용해 큰 판매를 낸다. ▶ so ~ that 구문

---

1 ②　　**2** ⑤

1 ②

해석 비록 악기를 잡고 연주하는 정확한 방법이 대체로 있다고 해도 우선적으로 가장 중요한 가르침은 악기가 장난감이 아니라는 것과 악기를 관리해야 한다는 것이다. 아이들에게 (악기를 직접 다루고 연주하는) 방법을 알려 주기 전에 악기를 직접 다루고 연주하는 방법을 탐구할 시간을 주어라. 아이들이 소리를 만들어 내는 여러 가지 방법을 찾을 수 있는지 없는지는 음악적 탐구의 중요한 단계이다. 정확한 연주는 가장 알맞은 음질을 찾고 오랜 시간 동안 잘 다루면서 연주할 수 있도록 가장 편안한 연주 자세를 찾으려는 욕구에서 나온다. 악기와 음악이 더 복잡해짐에 따라, 알맞은 연주 기술을 알게 되는 것은 점점 더 유의미해진다.

문제풀이 ② 문장의 동사가 없으므로 동명사 Allowing이 아니라 동사 Allow로 시작하는 명령문이 되어야 한다. ▶ p.12
① 보어 역할의 완전한 절이 이어지는 명사절 접속사 that
③ 주어 역할의 완전한 절이 이어지는 명사절 접속사 whether
④ 병렬 구조(to find ~ and find ~) ▶ p.206
⑤ 형용사를 수식하는 부사 ▶ p.238

2 ⑤

해석 인간의 뇌는 15,000년에서 30,000년 전 크기가 정점에 도달한 이래 부피가 약 10퍼센트만큼 줄어들었다는 것이 밝혀졌다. 한 가지 가능한 이유는 수천 년 전에 인간은 죽임을 당하는 것을 피하기 위해 항상 그들(위험한 포식자)에 대한 자신들의 기지를 발휘했어야 하는 위험한 포식자의 세계에서 살았다는 것이다. 오늘날, 우리는 우리 자신을 효율적으로 길들여 왔고 생존의 많은 과업이 — 즉각적인 죽음을 피하는 것부터 은신처를 짓는 일과 음식을 얻어 내는 일까지 — 더 넓은 사회로 위탁되어 왔다. 우리는 우리의 조상보다 더 작기도 한데, 가축이 그들의 야생 사촌보다 일반적으로 더 작다는 것은 가축의 한 특징이다. 뇌 크기가 반드시 인간의 지능의 지표는 아니기 때문에, 우리가 더 작은 뇌를 가지고 있는지 아닌지는 중요하지 않다. 오늘날 우리의 뇌가 다르게, 그리고 우리 조상들의 그것들보다 아마도 더 효율적으로 타고났다는 사실이 중요하다.

문제풀이 ⑤ 완전한 절이 이어지고 진주어 역할의 명사절이 되도록 what이 아니라 명사절 접속사 that이 되어야 한다.
① 보어 역할의 명사절 접속사 that
②「avoid+동명사」 ▶ p.134
③ it ~ that 가주어-진주어
④ 주어 역할의 명사절 접속사 if

STEP 3 유형 **빈칸 추론 2**

1 ②   2 ①   3 ③

---

1 ②

해석 낮 동안 사무실에서 전형적으로 생산성이 저하되는 에너지 소모와 싸우기 위해 Amsterdam에 있는 한 디자인 회사는 회사 직원들이 정시에 퇴근하여 휴식을 취하는 것을 보장하는 새로운 방법을 최근에 도입했다. 매일 정각 오후 6시에, 모든 사람들의 책상이 강철 케이블에 의해 천장까지 올라가면, 그때 그 공간은 지역 사회에 무료로

개방되는 무도회장 또는 요가 스튜디오로 바뀐다. 그 회사의 광고 제작 감독인 Sander Veenendaal은 이 새로운 정책은 직원들의 삶을 개선시킬 뿐만 아니라 그들의 브랜드를 더 높이는 데 도움이 되었다고 말했다. 강요된 휴식 시간은 비슷한 결과를 얻고자 바라는 전 세계의 사무실에서 중요한 우선순위가 되고 있다.

문제풀이 한 디자인 회사가 직원들이 정시에 퇴근하여 휴식을 취하도록 하는 강제 정책을 시행하여 회사와 직원들 모두에도 도움이 되었으며 이 정책이 널리 퍼졌다는 내용의 글이므로 빈칸에는 ② '강요된 휴식 시간은'이 가장 적절하다.
① 갈등을 관리하는 것은
③ 향상된 협동은
④ 개별화된 작업 공간은
⑤ 유연한 근무 시간제는

구문분석

[1행] [To fight productivity-slowing energy burnout typical in offices during the day], a design firm in Amsterdam has recently introduced a new method [for ensuring {that its employees go home on time and rest}].
▶ 첫 번째 [ ]는 목적을 나타내는 부사적 용법의 to부정사구이다. 두 번째 [ ]는 「전치사+(동)명사구」를 나타낸다. { }는 ensuring의 목적절로 명사절의 접속사 that이 이끌고 있다.

2 ①

해석 불길에 휩싸인 집들, 약탈당한 농작물들, 죽은 사람들을 위한 급하게 만든 무덤들. 이것은 북이탈리아를 휩쓸고 로마 제국 유물에 대량 파괴를 일으킨 Attila의 훈족들의 유산이었다. 그러나 그들은 의도치 않게 또 다른, 더 긍정적인 유산 또한 남겼다. 불타는 도시들을 떠나는 피난민들은 안전한 피난처를 찾기 위해 필사적이었다. 6세기에 상황이 더 악화되면서, 더 많은 로마 시민들은 본토에서의 대량 살상과 파괴를 피하기 위해 습지대로 줄을 지어 이동했다. 그 다음 수 세기에 걸쳐 그들은 그 힘든 환경을 건축의 경이로움으로 변화시켰다. 바로 Venice였다! 불행으로부터 지어진 Venice는 결국 세계에서 가장 풍요롭고 아름다운 도시들 중의 하나로 바뀌었다. 이와 같이 가혹한 필요가 영광스러운 발명의 어머니가 될 수 있다.

문제풀이 훈족의 침입으로 피난민들은 척박한 습지대 베니스로 이주한 후 베니스를 세계적인 도시로 변화시켰다는 내용의 글이므로 빈칸에는 ① '가혹한 필요가 영광스러운 발명의 어머니가 될 수 있다'가 가장 적절하다.
② 과도한 탐욕은 예상치 못한 참사를 야기할 수 있다
③ 시작이 좋다고 항상 끝이 좋은 것은 아니다
④ 1온스의 예방은 1파운드의 치료만큼의 가치가 있다
⑤ 인간은 대자연의 힘 앞에 무기력하다

구문분석

[1행] This was the legacy of Attila's Huns, [**sweeping** across northern Italy and **causing** massive destruction to the remains of the Roman Empire].

▶[ ]는 who swept ~ and who caused ~라는 계속적 용법의 주격 관계대명사절에 해당하는 분사구문 2개가 「sweeping ~ and causing ~」으로 병렬되고 있다.

3 ③

해석 가족 정원을 가꾸는 많은 사람들이 빠져드는 가장 큰 함정은 너무 큰 정원을 만드는 것이다. 비록 의도가 아무리 좋을지라도, 시간이 지나면서 너무 큰 정원은 그 유지에 있어 악몽이 될 것이다. 다른 많은 사람들과 마찬가지로 우리 가족도 식물들을 심어 큰 정원을 열심히 만들어 나갔지만 결국에는 정원 가꾸기에 들이는 시간을 서서히 줄이게 되었다. 9월 언제쯤인가 마침내 우리의 정원은 너무 익은 과일과 통제 할 수 없게 된 과도하게 자란 식물들로 가득 차게 되었다. 이 상황은 아이들은 말할 것도 없이 정원을 가꾸는 성인들에게도 즐겁지 않은 일이다. 대부분 아이들(그리고 많은 성인들)이 햇살이 비치는 더운 날을 (식물들이) 과도하게 자란 정원 밭뙈기를 돌보며 지내는 것을 즐기지 않을 것이다. 여러분의 가족 정원의 크기에 대해 생각할 때는 현실적이 되라. 여러분의 가족이 정원에 들일 수 있는 시간에 맞추어 (정원의) 크기를 계획하라.

문제풀이 정원이 너무 크면 유지하는 데 어려움을 겪기 때문에 현실적인 측면에서 정원의 크기를 계획하라는 내용의 글이므로 빈칸에는 ③ '현실적'이 가장 적절하다.
① 근면한　　　② 야심 찬
④ 도전적　　　⑤ 협동적

구문분석

[3행] My family, like many others, eagerly planted large gardens [**only to cut** back slowly on the time {devoted to gardening}].
　S   V
　O
▶[ ]는 「only+to-v」로 to부정사의 부사적 용법(결과)이며, '결국 ~하다'의 의미이다.

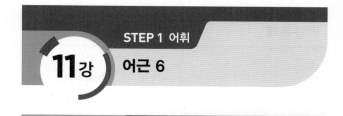

PRACTICE
p.90

A			
	1 offer, 제안하다	2 infer, 추론하다	
	3 refer, 가리키다	4 prefer, 선호하다	
	5 transfer, 옮기다	6 access, 접근	
	7 excess, 초과	8 recess, 휴식	
	9 success, 성공	10 process, 과정	
B	1 ① 　 2 ③ 　 3 ④ 　 4 ③ 　 5 ②		
C	1 accordance 　 2 override		

A

1 of+fer(carry): 제안하다
2 in+fer(carry): 추론하다
3 re+fer(carry): 가리키다
4 pre+fer(carry): 선호하다
5 trans+fer(carry): 옮기다
6 ac+cess(go): 접근
7 ex+cess(go): 초과
8 re+cess(go): 휴식
9 suc+cess(go): 성공
10 pro+cess(go): 과정

B

1 그 소설은 열 개 국어로 번역되었다.
2 핀란드 시민들은 성별과 기회에 있어 완전한 평등을 누린다.
3 피실험자 중 일부가 실험이 끝난 후 공격적인 행동을 보였다.
4 (공기 주입으로) 부풀게 할 수 있는 이 보드와 보트는 여러분의 여름휴가를 환상적이게 할 수 있습니다.
5 '불의 고리'라고도 알려진 환태평양 조산대 주변에서는 지진이 주기적으로 재발할 수 있다.

C

1 영화의 각 섹션의 의도와 구성에 대한 긴 논의가 끝난 후, 작곡가는 한 장면이나 연속된 장면에 맞는 악절에 대한 계획을 대략적으로 세운 다음 녹음을 했고, 그런 다음 감독은 이 섹션을 촬영하고 음악적 구성에 맞추어서 그것을 편집했다.
2 비록 적절한 과학적 목적을 달성하는 것이 항상 연구의 필수 목표일지라도 인간 참가자의 권리와 복지 보호가 과학적 효율성보다 더 우선되어야만 한다.

1 ⑤   **2** ④

1 ⑤

해석 Dworkin은 어떤 한 종류의 기회의 평등에 관한 고전적 주장을 제시한다. Dworkin의 관점에서 정의는 한 사람의 운명이 운이 아닌 그 사람의 통제 내에 있는 것들에 의해 결정되는 것을 요구한다. 행복에 있어서의 차이가 개인의 통제 밖에 있는 환경에 의해 결정된다면, 그 차이는 불공평하다. 이 주장에 따르면, 개인의 선택이나 취향의 차이에 의해 만들어진 행복의 불평등은 허용 가능하다. 그러나 우리는 개인의 책임이 아니면서 개인 자신이 중요하게 여기는 것을 성취하지 못하게 막는 요소에 의해 만들어지는 행복의 불평등을 제거하기 위해 노력해야 한다. 우리는 기회의 평등 또는 기본적인 자원에의 접근의 평등을 무시함으로써(→ 보장함으로써) 그렇게 한다.

문제풀이 행복의 여부가 개인의 통제 밖에 있는 환경에 의해 결정된다면 이는 불공정한 것으로, 모두에게 기회의 평등이 보장되어야 한다는 주장이므로 ⑤ neglecting을 ensuring 등으로 고쳐야 한다.

구문분석

[6행] But we should seek to eliminate inequality of well-being that is driven by factors [**that** are not an individual's responsibility and **which** prevent an individual from achieving what he or she values].
▶ [ ]는 선행사 factors를 수식하는 주격 관계대명사절 2개가 and로 병렬되고 있는 구조이다.

2 ④

해석 삶은 주기적이고 순환하고 항상 발전하고 있다. 반복과 재생이 여러분 주위에서 일어나고 있다는 것을 알아차리지 못하기란 어려운 일이다. 하루의 끝에 어둠이 오는 것과 마찬가지로, 땅 곳곳에 빛을 퍼뜨리기 위해 새벽이 온다. 삶의 주기가 끝날 때 식물이 죽어야만 하는 것과 마찬가지로, 식물이 생산한 씨앗은 봄에 새로운 식물로 나타날 것이다. 삶의 순환의 본질을 이해하면 어려운 시기가 영원히 지속되지는 않으며, 여러분은 다시 기쁨과 행복을 느낄 것이라고 안심하게 될 것이다. 여러분은 힘든 시간이 오면 견디고 받아들여야 하지만, 힘든 시간은 일시적인(→ 불변하는) 것이 아니며 영원히 지속되지도 않는다. 좋은 때와 나쁜 때, 잔치와 기근, 무더운 여름과 추운 겨울은 항상 있을 것이다. 컴컴한 동굴 속에서 옴짝달싹 못 하고 정신적으로 메말라 있고 또는 전적으로 우울하다고 느낄 때마다, 시간을 가지고 변화가 진행되고 있다는 것을 여러분 자신에게 상기시켜라.

문제풀이 삶은 순환하며 발전하고 있기 때문에 어려운 시기는 영원하지 않다는 것을 유념하라는 내용이므로 ④ temporary를 constant 등으로 고쳐야 한다.

구문분석

[5행] Understanding the cyclical nature of life will
     S

reassure you [that difficult times won't last forever,
   V   I.O.   D.O.
and you will feel joy and happiness again].

▶ 이 문장의 주어는 동명사 Understanding으로 시작하는 명사구이다. [ ]는 「reassure+I.O.+D.O(that절)」의 구조에서 직접목적어에 해당하는 that절을 가리키며, '~에게 …이라고 말하여 안심시키다'의 의미이다.

STEP 2 어법   접속사 2(부사절)

PRACTICE   p.92

A   1 while   2 in that   3 unless
       4 though   5 whereas

B   1 while   2 Although

A

1 나는 공원에서 사랑하는 이들과 함께 이야기를 나누며 편안하게 소풍을 즐겼다.

2 그 지원자는 스페인어와 중국어를 할 수 있다는 점에서 다른 지원자들보다 유리했다.

3 자신이 지붕으로 올라서려는 시도를 하지 않는다면 아마도 셋 다 위험에 처할 수도 있다는 것을 그는 깨달았다.

4 살아 있는 생명체가 숨을 쉴 때 이산화탄소를 방출함에도 불구하고, 이산화탄소는 오염 물질로 널리 간주 된다.

5 집 밖의 나무는 악천후를 이겨내야 하는 반면에, 실내의 나무는 보호를 받아 안전하기 때문에 실내의 나무가 더 잘 자랄 것이다.

B

1 기계화, 새로운 종류의 비료와 살충제, 유전 공학에서의 혁신의 결과인 농업 생산량의 엄청난 향상은, 심지어 인구가 계속 팽창하는 동안에도, 지구상에서 기근을 상당히 몰아냈고 영양실조를 대폭 줄였다. ▶ 접속사 while+완전한 절

2 비록 문제를 직시하려고 하지 않고 무소식이 희소식이라고 믿는 것이 솔깃할 수 있지만, 내 말을 믿어라, 만약 고객들이 여러분에게 불만 사항을 제기하지 않는다면 그들은 다른 사람에게 불만을 제기하거나 다시는 여러분의 기업을 이용하지 않고 있는 것이다.
▶ 접속사 although+완전한 절

1 ④   **2** ④

1 ④

해석 코알라가 잘하는 것이 한 가지 있다면, 그것은 자는 것이다. 오랫동안 많은 과학자들은 유칼립투스 잎 속의 화합물이 그 작고 귀여운 동물들을 몽롱한 상태로 만들어서 코알라들이 그렇게도 무기력한 상태에 있는 것이라고 의심했다. 그러나 더 최근의 연구는 그 잎들이 단순히 영양분이 너무나도 적기 때문에 코알라가 거의 에너지가 없는 것임을 보여 주었다. 그래서 코알라들은 가능한 한 적게 움직이는 경향이 있다. 그리고 그것들이 실제로 움직일 때에는, 흔히 그것들은 마치 슬로 모션으로 움직이는 것처럼 보인다. 그것들은 하루에 16시간에서 18시간 동안 휴식을 취하지만 코알라는 생각을 하는 데에 시간을 거의 사용하지 않는다. 사실, 코알라는 의식이 없는 상태로 그 시간의 대부분을 보낸다; 그것들의 뇌는 실제로 지난 몇 세기 동안 크기가 줄어든 것처럼 보인다. 코알라는 뇌가 겨우 두개골의 절반을 채운다고 알려진 유일한 동물이다.

문제풀이 ④ 완전한 절이 이어지므로 전치사 despite를 접속사 (al)though로 고쳐야 한다.
① 완전한 절이 이어지는 접속사 because
② 「so ~ that+절」
③ 「접속사 as though+절」
⑤ 「선행사+소유격 관계대명사+명사」 ▶ p.174

2 ④

해석 1909년, Herbert Cecil Booth는 우연히 Empire Music Hall 안에 있었는데, 그때 청소기 시연이 그의 흥미를 끌었다. 그 기계는 분명히 먼지를 일으키긴 했으나 결국 먼지를 모으고 제거하는 데는 비효율적임이 밝혀졌다. Booth는 그 기계를 시연하는 사람에게 압력이 아니라 흡입이 더 효과가 있지는 않을지 물어보았다. 그는 흡입도 여러 차례 시험해 봤지만 효과가 없었다고 화를 내며 대답했다. Booth의 마음은 재빨리 그 문제의 연구에 착수하였다. 며칠 뒤에 그 주제에 관해 친구들과 자신의 생각을 말하면서 그는 손수건을 펼쳐서 의자의 벨벳으로 된 앉는 부분에 놓고는 그 손수건에 입술을 대어 숨을 들이쉼으로써 자신의 생각을 실제로 보여주려고 했다. Booth의 친구들은 그 의자에서 빨려 나온 먼지의 양에 놀랐다. Booth는 그 해에 새로운 발명품의 특허를 얻었다.

문제풀이 ④ 완전한 절이 이어지므로 전치사 during을 접속사 while로 고쳐야 한다.
① 「접속사 when+절」
② 「접속사 whether+절」
③ 「접속사 that+절」
⑤ 「접속사 as soon as+절」

STEP 3 유형 **빈칸 추론 3** pp.94~95

1 ④   2 ②   3 ⑤

1 ④

해석 Stone Mountain State College의 교사들이 주립대학 체제의 다른 대학 교사들보다 더 높은 점수를 주고 있다. 2005년 봄학기에 부여된 학부 성적의 1/3이상이 A였고, 1.1 퍼센트만이 F였다. 대

학원 학생들에게 부여된 A의 비율은 심지어 더 높았다; 거의 2/3가 A였다. 물론, 학생들은 높은 성적을 받아 기쁠지도 모른다. 그러나, 증거는 이런 경향이 부정적인 결과를 갖고 있다고 시사한다. 그들이 대학원이나 전문학교에 지원할 때, 입학처들은 S.M.S.C.에서의 A가 다른 대학에서의 A와 같지 않다고 믿기 때문에 그들은 불이익을 받는다. 그러므로, 성적 인플레이션은 대학원이나 전문학교에 지원할 의향이 있는 S.M.S.C.의 학생들에게 고통을 줄지 모른다.

문제풀이 성적 인플레이션은 학생들에게는 기쁨을 줄 수도 있지만 상급 학교에 진학할 때 불이익이 될 수도 있음을 알려 주는 내용의 글이므로 빈칸에는 ④ '부정적인 결과를 갖고'가 가장 적절하다.
① 고등 교육의 질을 낮추고
② 학생들이 공부를 무시하게끔 하고
③ 더 많은 외국 학생들을 유치하려
⑤ 다른 주로 확산시키고

구문분석

[2행] <u>More than one-third</u> of <u>the undergraduate grades</u> [awarded in the spring semester 2005] <u>were</u> A's.
▶ 이 문장의 주어는 More that one-third이고 동사는 뒤에 있는 were이다. [ ]는 the undergraduate grades를 수식하는 과거분사구이다.

2 ②

해석 야구 배트의 "힘"을 생각해 보아라. 배트에 의해서 얻어진 모든 에너지는 타자에 의해 공급된다. 배트는 단지 공을 제 방향으로 보내도록 도와주는 도구이다. 배트가 그 일을 잘 해낸다면, 우리는 보통 그 배트가 강력하다고 말한다. 물리학 용어로, 우리는 실제로 그것의 효율성의 관점에서 배트를 설명해야 한다. 효율적인 배트란 그 과정에서 너무 많은 에너지의 손실 없이 타자로 하여금 그의 팔의 에너지를 공으로 전달하게 해 주는 배트일 것이다. 사실, 팔의 에너지의 단지 적은 부분이 공에 주어진다는 점에서 모든 배트는 매우 비효율적이다. 배트가 공을 친 후에 "팔을 끝까지 뻗어 주는 동작(follow through)"의 결과로 그 에너지의 대부분은 배트와 팔에 남아 있게 된다.

문제풀이 배트를 휘둘러 공을 칠 때의 물리학적 원리는 공에 전해지는 팔의 에너지는 적게 하고 팔을 뻗어 주는 동작의 결과로 그 에너지의 대부분은 배트와 팔에 남아 있게 된다는 내용의 글이므로 빈칸에는 ② '너무 많은 에너지의 손실'이 들어가야 가장 적절하다.
① 공에 가해지는 어떠한 마찰
③ 스윙 속도의 감소
④ 다른 도구로부터의 도움
⑤ 물리적 힘의 강화

구문분석

[4행] An efficient bat would be <u>one</u> [that allows the batter to transfer the energy in his arms to the ball]
▶ [ ]는 선행사 one을 수식하는 주격 관계대명사절이며, one은 a bat을 가리키는 대명사이다.

3 ⑤

해석 영화에서 외국어가 사용되는 대부분의 경우 관객을 위해 대화를 통역하려고 자막이 사용된다. 하지만 외국어 대화가 자막 없이 (그리하여 대부분의 주요 대상 관객이 이해하지 못하게) 처리되는 경우가 있다. 영화가 그 언어를 할 줄 모르는 특정한 등장인물의 관점에서 주로 보여지는 경우에 흔히 이렇게 처리된다. 그러한 자막의 부재는 관객이 그 등장인물이 느끼는 것과 비슷한 몰이해와 소외의 감정을 느끼게 한다. 이것의 한 예를 *Not Without My Daughter*에서 볼 수 있다. 주인공 Betty Mahmoody가 페르시아어를 하지 못하기 때문에 이란인 등장인물들이 하는 페르시아어 대화에는 자막이 없으며, 관객은 <u>그녀의 시각에서 영화를 보고 있게 된다</u>.

문제풀이 우리가 모르는 외국어가 사용되는 영화에 자막 없이 처리되는 경우(그 언어를 할 줄 모르는 특정한 등장인물의 관점에서 주로 보여지는 경우)가 있는데, 관객은 그 등장인물이 느끼는 것과 비슷한 몰이해와 신의의 감정을 느끼게 된다는 내용의 글이므로 빈칸에는 ⑤ '그녀의 시각에서 영화를 보고 있게 된다'가 들어가는 것이 가장 적절하다.
① 영화에서 사용되는 언어를 배우게 된다.
② 그녀의 언어 능력에 감탄하게 된다.
③ 그녀의 아름다운 목소리에 끌리게 된다.
④ 열띤 논쟁에 참여하게 된다.

구문분석

[2행] there are <u>occasions</u> [when foreign dialogue is left unsubtitled (and thus difficult to understand to most of the target audience)].
▶ [ ]는 선행사 occasions를 수식하는 관계부사절이다.

PRACTICE
p.98

A 1 depress, 낙담시키다
2 impress, 깊은 인상을 주다
3 express, 표현하다   4 oppress, 억압하다
5 compress, 압착하다   6 reduction, 감소
7 abduction, 유괴   8 production, 생산
9 conduction, 전도
10 introduction, 소개, 도입

B 1 ②   2 ③   3 ②   4 ①   5 ④

C 1 improve   2 expand

A

1 de+press(누르다): 낙담시키다
2 im+press(누르다): 깊은 인상을 주다
3 ex+press(누르다): 표현하다
4 op+press(누르다): 억압하다
5 com+press(누르다): 압착하다
6 re+duct(draw, lead)+ion: 감소
7 ab+duct(draw, lead)+ion: 유괴
8 pro+duct(draw, lead)+ion: 생산
9 con+duct(draw, lead)+ion: 전도
10 intro+duct(draw, lead)+ion: 소개, 도입

B

1 유태인들은 안식일에 일하는 것이 엄격히 <u>금지된다</u>.
2 대통령의 권한은 헌법에 분명히 <u>규정되어</u> 있다.
3 한국은 지금까지 거의 천 번 정도 외국 군대의 <u>침략을</u> 받았다.
4 버스가 다른 버스와 <u>정면충돌</u>해서, 20명 이상의 사상자가 발생했다.
5 polygraph라는 단어는 <u>문자 그대로</u> '많은 글'을 의미하며 거짓말 탐지기를 가리킨다.

C

1 이야기하기 기술은 자신의 경험을 청자에게 적합한 방식으로 표현하는 좋은 방법을 찾는 것을 포함하기 때문에, 훌륭한 스토리텔러는 가장 지루한 부분을 없애 버리거나 사실을 활용하여 지루한 부분을 <u>개선하는</u> 것과 같은 방식으로 자신의 경험을 말한다.
2 학생들이 걸어서 등교하는 좁은 도로에서는 차량과 충돌할 위험이 많으므로, 우리는 학생들의 안전과 편안함을 위해 등하굣길을 <u>확장</u>해 주기를 요청한다.

적용독해

1 ④ 2 ⑤

1 ④

해석 우리는 혼돈 속에서 반복을 알아차리고 그 반대, 즉 반복적인 패턴에서의 단절을 알아차린다. 그러나 이러한 배열들이 우리로 하여금 어떻게 느끼도록 만들까? 그리고 '완전한' 규칙성과 '완전한' 무질서는 어떨까? 어느 정도의 반복은 우리가 다음에 무엇이 올지 안다는 점에서 우리에게 안정감을 준다. 우리는 어느 정도의 예측 가능성을 좋아한다. 우리는 대체로 반복적인 스케줄 속에 우리 생활을 배열한다. 조직에서 또는 행사에서 임의성은 우리 대부분에게 더 힘들고 더 무섭다. '완전한' 무질서로 인해 우리는 몇 번이고 적응하고 대응해야만 하는 것에 흥미진진해 한다(→ 좌절한다). 그러나 '완전한' 규칙성은 아마도 그것의 단조로움에 있어서 임의성보다 훨씬 더 끔찍할 것이다. 그것은 차갑고 냉혹하며 기계 같은 특성을 내포한다. 그러한 완전한 질서가 자연에는 존재하지 않으며 서로 대항하여 작용하는 힘이 너무 많다. 그러므로 어느 한쪽의 극단은 위협적으로 느껴진다.

문제풀이 우리는 어느 정도의 반복적 패턴으로 인한 어느 정도의 예측 가능성을 좋아하지만, 양극단 즉 완전한 무질서는 우리를 좌절시키고 완전한 규칙성은 끔찍함을 경험하게 할 것이라는 내용이므로 ④ excited는 frustrated 등으로 고쳐야 한다.

구문분석

[3행] Some repetition gives us a sense of security, [in
　　　　S　　　　　V　I.O.　　D.O.
that we know what is coming next].
▶ 간접목적어와 직접목적어를 수반하는 수여동사 give가 사용된 문장이며, [ ]는 '~이라는 점에서'라는 의미의 부사절이다.

2 ⑤

해석 이슬람교도들이 8세기에 남부 유럽을 침략했을 때, 그들은 돼지고기의 판매를 금지하는 법을 통과시켰다. 이슬람교의 창시자가 돼지고기는 깨끗하지 않다고 선언했었기 때문에 이것이 이루어졌다. 물론이 법이 돼지고기에 대한 유럽 사람들의 애정을 바꾸지는 못했고 곧고기를 위한 암시장이 발달했다. 대개 밤에 행해졌던 비밀스런 거래속에서 농부들은 도시 주민들에게 큰 가방에 숨겨진 돼지를 팔고는했다. 때때로 정직하지 못한 농부는 돼지가 아닌 고양이가 담긴 가방을 팔아서 구매자들을 속이고는 했다. 만약 어떤 것이 잘못되어서 거래 중에 가방이 열리게 되면 이것은 글자 그대로 "고양이가 가방 밖으로 나가게 하는 것"이다. 그래서 이러한 이유로 비밀을 유지하는(→ 폭로하는) 것을 "고양이를 가방 밖으로 나가게 한다."라고 말한다.

문제풀이 암시장에서 가방에 돼지를 숨겨 팔던 시절에 고양이를 돼지로 속여 파는 경우가 있었는데, 실수로 고양이가 가방에서 탈출하는 상황이 발생한 데서 유래한 비밀 폭로와 관련된 표현을 소개하는 내용이므로 ⑤ keeping은 revealing 등으로 고쳐야 한다.

구문분석

[8행] ... this is [why keeping a secret is said to be "letting the cat out of the bag"]
▶ [ ]는 의문사 why를 통해 이유를 나타내는 명사절이며, why 뒷부분은 원래 people say that keeping a secret is "letting the cat out of the bag"의 수동태이다.

STEP 2 어법 　전치사

PRACTICE

A 　1 enrich → enriching
　　 　2 analysis → analyzing
　　 　3 during → while
　　 　4 because of → because
　　 　5 Despite → Though/Although/Even though

B 　1 because of 　2 avoiding

A

1 자원봉사자들은 다른 사람들을 위해 봉사하면서 자신들의 사회적 관계망을 풍부하게 하는 데서 만족감을 느낀다. ▶「전치사(from)+v-ing」
2 정보를 분석하기 위한 도구들은 1990년대 초반까지 이용할 수 없었다. ▶「전치사(for)+v-ing+목적어」
3 디지털 무례함은 대개 상대방이 우리에게 얘기하는 동안에 발생한다. ▶「접속사 while+완전한 절」
4 Okavango River는 Botswana에서 그 강물이 내륙에서 흐르기 때문에 바다에 이르지 못한다. ▶「접속사 because+완전한 절」
5 사람들은 8시간의 수면이 이상적이라고 흔히들 생각하지만, 사실은 여러분이 어떻게 느끼느냐에 전적으로 달려있다. ▶ 접속사 Though/Although/Even though+완전한 절

B

1 대부분 예술가가 자신이 태어난 시대의 양식적 관습에 순응하기 때문에, 서양화에서 원근법의 역사는 그것이 삶의 기술에 대해 드러내는 것 때문에 중요하다. ▶「전치사(because of)+명사(절)」
2 오래된 낱말, 정교한 비유, 문법적 도치, 그리고 때때로 운율과 각운조차 의식적으로 피함으로써 20세기 초반 근대주의 작가들은 산문과 시에서의 명백한 단순성을 강조하였다. ▶「전치사(by)+v-ing」

적용독해

1 ② 　2 ④

1 ②

해석 일반적으로 민간 항공기는 물리적 구조물은 아니지만 도로와 유사한 항로로 운항한다. 항로에는 고정된 폭과 규정된 고도가 있으며, 그것들이 반대 방향으로 움직이는 통행을 분리한다. 항공기 간에 상하 간격을 둠으로써 아래에서 다른 과정이 이루어지는 동안 일부 비행기가 공항 위를 통과할 수 있게 된다. 항공 여행은 보통 장거리에 걸치며, 이륙과 착륙 시 짧은 시간의 고강도 조종사 활동과, '장거리 비행'이라고 알려진 비행 부분인, 공중에 있는 동안 긴 시간의 저강도 조종사 활동이 있다. 비행에서 장거리 비행 부분 동안 조종사들은 근처의 비행기를 탐색하는 것보다 항공기 상태를 평가하는 데 더 많은 시간을 보낸다. 이는 항공기 간의 충돌은 대개 공항 주변 지역에서 발생하는 반면 항공기 오작동으로 인한 추락은 장거리 비행 중에 발생하는 경향이 있기 때문이다.

문제풀이 ② 완전한 절이 이어지므로 전치사 during을 접속사 while로 고쳐야 한다.
① 접속사(although)+완전한 절
③ 접속사(while)+(주어+be 동사)+전치사구(in the air)
④ 전치사(in)+assessing ~ than searching ~ : 병렬
⑤ 접속사(because)+완전한 절

2 ④

해석 어둠 속에서 식물이 자라는 것을 관찰해 온 과학자들은 그것들이 빛 속에서 길러진 것들과 외관, 형태 그리고 기능에서 상당히 다르다는 것을 발견해 왔다. 이것은 다른 빛 조건에 있는 식물들이 유전적으로 동일하고 온도, 물 그리고 영양소 수준의 동일한 조건에서 길러질 때에도 적용된다. 어둠 속에서 길러진 묘목은 떡잎이나 뿌리처럼, 어둠 속에서 완전한 능력으로 기능하지 않는 기관으로 가는 에너지의 양을 제한하고, 대신 그 식물을 어둠에서 벗어나 나아가게 하기 위하여 묘목 줄기의 연장을 시작한다. 충분한 빛을 쬐는 동안 묘목은 그것들이 줄기 연장에 배분하는 에너지의 양을 줄인다. 그 에너지는 그것들의 잎을 확장하고 광범위한 근계(根系)를 발달시키는 데로 향한다. 이것이 표현형 적응성의 좋은 예이다. 묘목은 그것의 형태와 근원적인 신진대사 및 생화학적 과정을 바꿈으로써 별개의 환경 조건에 적응한다.

문제풀이 ④ 전치사(to) 뒤에 동명사 expanding과 and로 병렬 연결되어야 하므로 develop을 developing으로 고쳐야 한다.
① 명사절의 접속사(that)+완전한 절
② 부사절의 접속사(when)+완전한 절
③ 접속사(while)+(주어+be 동사)+전치사구
⑤ 전치사(by)+동명사+목적어

STEP 3 유형 무관한 문장

pp.102~103

1 ④   2 ④   3 ③

1 ④

해석 중독을 일으킬 수 있는 많은 산림 식물 중에서 야생 버섯은 가장 위험한 것들 중의 하나이다. 이는 사람들이 종종 독성이 있는 품종과

먹을 수 있는 품종을 혼동하거나 혹은 품종에 대해 확실한 확인을 하지 않고 버섯을 먹기 때문이다. 야생 버섯 종들이 훌륭한 식용 버섯이고 매우 귀하게 여겨지기 때문에 많은 사람들이 봄에 야생 버섯 종을 찾아다니기를 즐긴다. 그러나 몇몇 야생 버섯은 위험해서 그 독성으로 사람들의 목숨을 잃게 한다. (합리적인 비용으로 높은 품질의 상품을 재배하는 것이 이윤을 위해 식용 버섯을 기르느냐 아니냐를 결정하는 핵심적인 척도이다.) 안전을 위해서 사람들은 야생 버섯을 먹기 전에 식용 버섯을 식별할 수 있어야 한다.

문제풀이 식용 버섯과 독버섯을 잘 식별해야 한다는 내용의 글이므로, 이윤을 위해 버섯 재배를 한다고 언급한 ④는 글의 흐름과 무관하다.

구문분석

[1행] [Of the many forest plants {that can cause poisoning}], wild mushrooms may be among the most dangerous.
S / V
▶ [ ]는 '~ 중에서'라는 의미의 전치사 Of로 시작하는 부사구이며, { }는 forest plants를 수식하는 주격 관계대명사절이다.

2 ④

해석 Marguerite La Caze에 따르면, 패션은 우리의 삶에 기여하고 우리가 중요한 사회적 가치를 개발하고 나타내는 수단을 제공한다. 패션은 아름다울 수 있고, 혁신적일 수 있으며, 유용할 수 있다. 우리는 패션을 선택하는데 있어서 창의성과 좋은 취향을 드러낼 수 있다. 그리고 취향과 관심에 따라 옷을 입을 때, 우리는 자아 존중과 타인의 즐거움에 대한 관심 모두를 보여 준다. 의심할 여지없이, 패션은 우리와 타인을 연결해 주는 흥미와 즐거움의 원천이 될 수 있다. (패션 산업은 유럽과 미국에서 처음 발달했지만, 오늘날에는 국제적이고 매우 세계화된 산업이 되었다.) 다시 말해, 패션은 자신을 다르게 상상하는, 즉, 다른 정체성을 시도하는 기회와 더불어 친교적인 측면을 제공한다.

문제풀이 패션이 주는 여러 이점을 설명하는 글이므로, 패션 산업에 관해 언급한 ④는 글의 흐름과 무관하다.

구문분석

[5행] There is no doubt [that fashion can be a source of interest and pleasure {which links us to each other}].
▶ [ ]는 접속사 that이 이끄는 명사절로 doubt와 의미상 동격절이며, { }는 앞에 있는 a source를 가리키는 주격 관계대명사절이다.

3 ③

해석 만일 여러분이 수학 등식을 써야 한다면, 여러분은 아마 '스물여덟 더하기 열 넷은 마흔 둘과 같다.'라고 쓰지 않을 것이다. 그것은 쓰는 데 너무 오래 걸리고 빨리 읽기가 어려울 것이다. 여러분은 '28 + 14 = 42'라고 쓸 것이다. 화학도 마찬가지이다. 화학자들은 항상 화학 방정식을 써야 하고, 만약 그들이 모든 것을 상세히 다 써야 한다면 쓰고 읽는 데 너무 오래 걸릴 것이다. (그래서 바로 이런 이유 때문에 우리가 매일 화학 약품을 사용하는 것처럼 화학자가 화학 약

품을 사용한다.) 화학식은 각 분자를 구성하는 모든 원소를 나열하고 그 원소의 원자 수를 나타내기 위해 원소 기호의 오른쪽 아래에 작은 숫자를 사용한다. 예를 들어, 물의 화학식은 H_2O이다. 그것은 우리에게 하나의 물 분자는 두 개의 수소 원자('H'와 '2')와 하나의 산소 원자('O')로 이루어져 있다는 것을 말해 준다.

문제풀이 수학 등식이나 화학 방정식을 상세히 다 쓸 때의 단점을 설명하는 글이므로, 우리와 화학자가 화학 약품을 쓰는 이유를 언급한 ③은 글의 흐름과 무관하다.

구문분석

[6행] A chemical formula lists all the elements [that form each molecule] and uses a small number to the bottom right of an element's symbol [**to stand** for the number of atoms of that element].

▶ 이 문장은 주어 A chemical formula에 동사 2개 lists와 uses가 and로 병렬되는 문장이다. 첫 번째 [ ]는 the elements를 수식하는 주격 관계대명사절이며, 두 번째 [ ]는 목적을 나타내는 부사적 용법의 to부정사구이다.

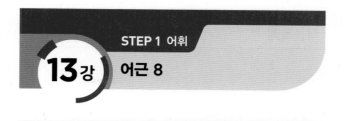

PRACTICE

p.106

A
1 expel, 내쫓다   2 repel, 격퇴하다
3 dispel, 떨쳐버리다   4 compel, 강요하다
5 propel, 추진하다   6 attract, 매료시키다
7 extract, 추출하다   8 contract, 수축하다
9 distract, 산만하게 하다
10 abstract, 추상적인

B
1 ③   2 ③   3 ②   4 ④   5 ②

C
1 exploit   2 different

A

1 ex+pel(push): 내쫓다
2 re+pel(push): 격퇴하다
3 dis+pel(push): 떨쳐버리다
4 com+pel(push): 강요하다
5 pro+pel(push): 추진하다
6 at+tract(draw): 매료시키다
7 ex+tract(draw): 추출하다
8 con+tract(draw): 수축하다
9 dis+tract(draw): 산만하게 하다
10 abs+tract(draw): 추상적인

B

1 영어 배우기의 장점으로 영어가 국제어가 되었다는 것이다.
2 한국 부동산에 대한 중국인의 투자는 작년에 총 2조원에 달했다.
3 딱따구리에 관한 흥미로운 사실은 그들이 서식지로 죽은 나무를 더 좋아한다는 것입니다.
4 일본은 종종 과거 사건에 대한 식민지적 시각을 제공하면서 한국 역사를 왜곡하려고 노력해 왔다.
5 그 회사는 RE 100 규제 때문에 반도체를 수출하는 데 어려움을 겪고 있다.

C

1 많은 자원을 보유한 풍족한 서식지와 자원을 거의 보유하지 못한 부족한 서식지, 두 개의 서식지가 있고, 영토권이나 싸움이 없다면, 우리는 더 높은 이익을 얻도록 더 풍족한 서식지를 자유롭게 이용할 것이다.
2 우리가 다른 유기체가 지각하는 방식으로 냄새로 가득한 세상을 보는 능력을 주는 특수 안경을 끼고 있다면, 나뭇잎, 나무껍질, 뿌리로부터 화합물이 대기 중으로 방출되고 있는 것을 볼 수 있는 우리가 현재 경험하는 바와 아주 다른 세상과 마주칠 것이다.

적용독해

p.107

1 ⑤   2 ②

1 ⑤

해석 많은 사람은 신체 움직임이 때때로 부정적인 감정들을 떨쳐버릴 수 있음을 발견한다. 만약 우리가 부정적으로 느끼고 있다면, 우리가 일상생활에서 활동적인 상태이고 싶어 하는 것을 멈추기가 매우 쉬울 수 있다. 이것이 또한 우울증을 겪는 많은 사람이 계속 잠을 자고, 외출을 하거나 운동을 하려는 동기가 없는 것으로 발견되는 이유이다. 불행히도, 이러한 운동의 부족이 실제로 많은 부정적인 감정을 악화시킬 수 있다. 운동과 움직임은 우리가 부정적인 에너지를 제거하기 시작하는 훌륭한 방법이다. 많은 사람은 자신들이 화날 때 그들이 운동을 하거나 청소를 하고 싶은 상태가 된다는 점을 깨닫는다. 이것은 사실상 여러분이 하는 매우 건강하고 긍정적인 일이며, 그것(부정적인 감정)들이 더 이상 여러분의 삶에 영향을 미치지 않고 관계를 해치지 않도록 여러분이 자신의 부정적인 감정들을 강화하기(→ 해체하기) 시작하는 훌륭한 방법이다.

문제풀이 부정적인 감정은 우리의 활동을 위축시키고, 이는 다시 부정적인 감정을 악화시킬 수 있지만, 운동과 움직임은 부정적인 감정을 없애는 좋은 방법이라는 내용이므로 ⑤ intensify는 deconstruct 등으로 고쳐야 한다.

구문분석

[8행] This is actually a very healthy and positive thing [for you to do]] and a great way [for you to begin] to intensify your negative emotions

▶ 첫 번째, 두 번째 [ ] 모두 「for+의미상 주어+to-v」의 구조인 to부정사구가 명사를 수식하는 형용사적 용법으로 for you는 to부정사의 의미상의 주어이다.

2 ②

해석 스릴 넘치는 유령 이야기는 정말 무섭다면 들려주기에 재밌고, 만약 당신이 그 이야기가 사실이라고 주장하면 훨씬 더 그렇다. 사람들은 그런 이야기를 전달하는 것으로부터 스릴을 느낀다. 이것은 기적 이야기에도 동일하게 적용된다. 만약 기적에 대한 소문이 어떤 책에 쓰여 진다면, 특히 그 책이 먼 옛날의 것이라면, 그 소문은 믿기(→ 의문을 제기하기) 힘들어진다. 만약 소문이 충분히 오래된 것이라면, 그것은 대신 '전통'으로 불리기 시작하고, 그러고 나서 사람들은 그것을 한결 더 믿는다. 이것은 다소 이상한데, 그 이유는 그들이 (근거 없이) 주장된 사건 그 자체에 시간상 가까운 최근의 소문보다 오래된 소문이 왜곡될 시간이 더 있다는 점을 깨달을 것이라고 당신이 생각할 수 있기 때문이다. Elvis Presley와 Michael Jackson은 전통이 생겨나기에는 너무 최근에 살아서 "Elvis가 화성에서 목격되었다"와 같은 이야기를 믿는 사람이 많지 않다.

문제풀이 오래된 소문은 근거가 충분하지 않음에도 사람들은 의문을 제기하지 않고 믿는 경향이 있다는 내용이므로 ② believe는 challenge 등으로 고쳐야 한다.

구문분석

[1행] Spine-tingling ghost stories are fun [to tell] [if they are really scary], and even more so [if you claim that they are true].

▶ 첫 번째 [ ]는 보어로 쓰인 형용사 fun을 수식하는 부사적용법의 to부정사구이고, 두 번째, 세 번째 [ ]는 모두 조건을 나타내는 if 부사절이다. so는 앞에 있는 fun to tell의 의미를 나타낸다.

STEP 2 어법   to부정사 1 (명사적 / 형용사적)

PRACTICE

p.108

A 1 → It   2 → to go
   3 → to sell   4 → to define
   5 → to make   6 → to swim
   7 → to get

B 1 be   2 to build

A

1 그가 헤엄쳐서 강을 건너는 것은 불가능하다. ▶ it ~ to 가주어 진주어 구문
2 자전거 타고 가는 것이 버스를 타고 가는 것보다 더 빠르다. ▶ 비교 구문을 이용한 명사적 용법의 병렬
3 그 광고의 목적은 여성들에게 더 많은 차를 파는 것이었다. ▶ to부정사의 명사적 용법
4 우리 각자는 우리의 삶을 결정할 수 있는 힘이 있다. ▶ to부정사의 형용사적 용법
5 외로운 환자들이 친구를 사귈 수 있는 한 가지 확실한 방법이 있다. ▶ to부정사의 형용사적 용법
6 나는 아들이 저수지에서 수영하는 것을 허용하지 않을 것이다.
  ▶ 「allow+O+to-v」
7 간호사는 치료를 받도록 나를 설득했다. ▶ 「persuade+O+to-v」

B

1 인도적 대우의 원칙은 형사법 집행에 중요한 제약을 가하는데, 이는 누구에게나 매우 큰 피해를 주고 정당화 될 가능성을 가진 국가 운영 과정이다. ▶ 명사(potential)를 수식하는 to부정사의 병렬 구조(to do ~ and be ~)
2 건강한 부모들의 믿음과 행동은 음식이 신체에서 하는 것과 거의 똑같이 기능하는 심리적 정보와 사회적 정보를 아이들에게 제공하는데, 이 경우에는 그 정보가 자동적으로 아이들의 개인적 현실을 만들어 내고 그들의 행동을 형성하는 것을 돕는다.
  ▶ 「help+to-v」

적용독해
p.109

1 ⑤ 2 ②

1 ⑤

해석 Leonardo da Vinci는 지금껏 살았던 사람 가운데 가장 박식하고 다재다능한 사람 중 한 명이었다. 잠자리 날개부터 지구의 탄생에 이르기까지 전 우주는 그의 호기심 많은 지성의 놀이터였다. 그러나 Leonardo는 신비하거나 타고난 통찰과 발명의 어떤 재능을 가지고 있었는가, 아니면 그의 탁월함이 학습되고 획득된 것인가? 분명 그는 비범한 정신과 다른 사람들이 보지 못하는 것을 보는 예리한 능력을 가지고 있었다. 하지만 6천 쪽의 자세한 메모와 그림은 부지런하고 호기심 많은 학생 즉, 부지런히 지식을 추구하는 가운데, 끊임없이 탐구하고, 의문을 제기하고, 시험하는 끊임없는 학습자에 대한 분명한 증거를 보여 준다. 여러분의 지성을 넓히는 것은 창의적으로 되는 것에 필수적이다. 그러므로 학습 기회에 자주 투자하는 것은 여러분이 자신에게 줄 수 있는 가장 멋진 선물 가운데 하나이다.

문제풀이 ⑤ 동사 is가 있어 문장의 주어가 필요한 자리이므로 invest를 to invest로 고쳐야 한다.
① to부정사의 형용사적 용법
② 병렬 구조(일반동사의 의문문 or be동사의 의문문) ▶ p.206
③ to부정사의 형용사적 용법
④ to부정사의 명사적 용법

2 ②

해석 Fish samplers가 사용하는 예전 방법은 댐 근처에서 물고기를 보고 물고기가 물고기 수로 위로 뛰어오를 때마다 버튼을 누르는 것이다. 또한 그들은 종종 물고기를 측정했는데 이 작업은 산소가 제거된 탱크 안에 물고기를 잡아두고 물고기가 움직임을 멈출 때까지 포획 상태로 놔두는 것을 포함한다. 일단 물고기가 잠잠해지면 그들은 회복 탱크에 물고기를 되돌려 놓기 전에 물고기의 길이를 측정한다. 마지막으로 물고기는 꼬리표가 붙여져서 그것의 여정을 지속할 수 있도록 수로 위로 다시 풀려나게 된다. 물고기를 잡는 더 흔한 방법은 전류어로법인데, 이 방법은 강을 가로질러서 휴대할 수 있는 발전기에 부착된 전선을 당기는 일을 포함한다. 그 물고기들은 기절하고 거의 신기하게 전선으로 끌려온다. 그리고 그 순간 samplers는 그물에 물고기를 잡아 시냇물로 물고기를 되돌려 보내기 전 길이를 재고 무게를 달아보기 위해 임시 보관 장소에 옮겨놓는다.

문제풀이 ② '~하는 것을 멈추다'라는 의미의 「stop+v-ing」이 되도록 to move를 moving으로 고쳐야 한다. ▶ p.142
① to부정사의 명사적 용법
③ to부정사의 형용사적 용법
④ drawn을 수식하는 부사 ▶ p.238
⑤ 부사적 용법으로 쓰인 to부정사의 병렬 구조(to measure and weigh) ▶ p.116

STEP 3 유형 글의 순서

1 ④ 2 ② 3 ②

1 ④

해석 고대 아테네에서 플라톤의 추종자들이 어느 날 모여서 다음과 같은 질문을 스스로에게 했다고 한다. "인간이란 무엇인가?" (C) 많은 생각을 한 후에, 그들은 다음과 같은 답을 생각해냈다. "인간은 깃털 없는 두 발 동물이다." 모든 사람은 한 철학자가 살아 있는 깃털 없는 닭을 가지고 강당으로 불쑥 들어올 때까지는 이 정의에 만족하는 것처럼 보였다. (A) 그것을 손에 들고, 그는 "보시오! 내가 여러분들에게 인간을 보여 주겠소."라고 외쳤다. 소란이 잠잠해진 후에, 철학자들은 다시 모여서 그들의 정의를 개선했다. 그들은 인간이 넓은 발톱을 가진 깃털 없는 두 발 동물이라고 말했다. (B) 초기 철학의 역사에서 나오는 이 흥미로운 이야기는 인간이라는 것이 무엇인가에 대한 추상적이고 일반적인 정의를 내리려고 할 때, 철학자들이 때때로 직면했던 어려움의 종류들을 보여 준다.

문제풀이 철학자들이 인간이란 무엇인가라는 질문에 관한 내용의 주어진 글 다음에, 그들이 그 질문에 대한 답을 생각해내자 한 철학자가 깃털 없는 닭을 가지고 강당으로 들어온다는 내용의 (C)가 오고, 철학자들이 기존의 정의를 개선하는 내용의 (A)에 이어, 이 이야기가 인간에 대한 정의를 내릴 때 철학자들이 가졌던 어려움을 보여 준다는 내용의 (B)로 이어지는 것이 자연스럽다.

구문분석

[1행] It is said [that {in ancient Athens} the followers
                                                          S
of Plato gathered one day {**to ask** themselves the
         V
following question: "What is a human being?"}]
▶ [ ]는 가주어 It에 대한 진주어절로 명사절의 접속사 that이 이끌고 있다. 첫 번째 { }는 삽입된 부사구이고, 두 번째 { }는 목적을 나타내는 부사적 용법의 to부정사구이다.

2 ②

해석 기억은 두 가지 종류가 있다. 내재적 기억과 외재적 기억이다. 여러분이 무언가에 대해서 진정으로 생각하지 않고서 그것을 배울 때, 그것은 내재적 기억 혹은 신체 기억이다. 태어났을 때 호흡하는 법을 아는 것은 내재적 기억이다. (B) 아무도 여러분에게 이것을 가르쳐 주지 않았다. 또한 어릴 적부터 여러분이 배운 것 중 일부는 내재적 기억들이 된다. 내재적 기억들은 뇌의 자율 신경 부분에 각인된다. 그것은 자전거를 수년 동안 타지 않고서도 여전히 자전거 타는 법을 알고 있는 이유이다. (A) 반면에 외재적 기억들은 여러분이 의식적으로 기억하려고 노력하는 기억들 혹은 특정한 것들이다. 여러분은 매일 의식적 차원에서 외재적 기억을 사용한다. (C) 열쇠를 찾기 위해 노력하는 것, 행사가 언제 개최되는지, 어디서 그것이 개최되는지, 그리고 누구와 함께 그 행사에 가야 하는지 기억하려고 노력하는 것. 외재적 기억들은 여러분이 여러분의 달력이나 일정표에 적어 왔던 과업들이다.

문제풀이 두 가지 종류의 기억 중 내재적 기억이 있다는 내용의 주어진 글 다음에, 내재적 기억에 대한 부연 설명을 하는 (B)가 오고, 내재적 기억과 구별되는 외재적 기억을 설명하는 (A) 이후에, 외재적 기억의 사례를 들어 주는 내용의 (C)로 이어지는 것이 자연스럽다.

구문분석

[2행] Knowing [how to breathe {when you were born}] is an implicit memory.

▶ 이 문장의 주어는 동명사 Knowing으로 시작하는 동명사구이고 동사는 is이다. [ ]는 「의문사+to-v(명사적 용법)」로 동사 know의 목적어이며, { }는 때를 나타내는 부사절이다.

3 ②

해석 1997년 4월 미국 식약청은 치약 제조업자들이 자발적인 안전 지침을 충분히 철저하게 지키지 않는다고 규정했다. 그 결과, 지금 모든 치약 튜브는 끔찍하게 들리는 경고문을 담고 있다. (B) 그것은 이런 것이었다: "6세 이하 아이들의 손이 닿지 않는 곳에 두시오. 만약 양치질을 위해 사용되는 양 이상을 우연히 삼킨다면 그 즉시 의학적인 도움을 얻거나 유독물 관리 센터로 연락하시오." (A) 그 새로운 경고문이 실린 다음 몇 달 안에 치약 회사 고객 센터들은 걱정하는 부모로부터 온 수 백 개의 질문을 처리했고 유독물 관리 센터들 또한 전화 통화가 넘쳐났다. 그들은 부모들에게 같은 말을 했다: 당신의 아이는 괜찮다. 그리고 구토를 할 수도 있고 하지 않을 수도 있다. (C) 하지만 의사에게 진찰을 받는 유일한 이유는 구토가 너무 심각해져서 탈수증이 문제가 되는 경우이다. 그렇다: 당신은 맛있는 치약을 양껏 먹을 수 있고, 기껏해야 메스꺼움과 설사에 걸릴 뿐이다.

문제풀이 미국 식약청의 덕택으로 현재의 모든 치약에는 경고문이 있다는 주어진 글 다음에, 그 경고문의 내용을 구체적으로 알려 주는 (B)가 오고, 그 경고문으로 인해 발생한 상황의 사례를 제시하는 (A)가 온 후, 치약을 많이 먹어도 끔찍한 일이 발생하지 않는다는 결론의 (C)로 이어지는 것이 자연스럽다.

구문분석

[11행] The only reason [to see a doctor], however, is [if the vomiting gets so serious that dehydration becomes an issue].

▶ 첫 번째 [ ]는 주어 reason을 수식하는 형용사적 용법의 to부정사구이다. 두 번째 [ ]는 주격 보어 역할을 하는 명사절의 접속사 if가 이끄는 명사절이다. 이때 if는 '~인 경우'라는 의미이다.

PRACTICE
p.114

A
1 eject, 방출하다　2 reject, 거부하다
3 object, 반대하다　4 inject, 주입하다
5 subject, ~를 받게 하다　6 acquire, 얻다
7 require, 요구하다　8 inquire, 묻다
9 request, 요청하다　10 conquest, 정복

B　1 ②　2 ④　3 ④　4 ③　5 ③

C　1 cognition　2 hindering

A

1 e+ject(throw): 방출하다
2 re+ject(throw): 거부하다
3 ob+ject(throw): 반대하다
4 in+ject(throw): 주입하다
5 sub+ject(throw): ~를 받게 하다
6 ac+quir(seek)+e: 얻다
7 re+quir(seek)+e: 요구하다
8 in+quir(seek)+e: 묻다
9 re+quest(seek): 요청하다
10 con+quest(seek): 정복

B

1 10세 미만의 아동은 성인과 동반해야 합니다.
2 고리 사채업에 대한 정부 규제가 강화되어야 한다.
3 희생자의 부모가 사형 제도를 반대했다는 사실에 사람들은 놀랐다.
4 산업화로 인해 촌락의 지리적 위치가 변해 왔다.
5 그 회사는 상품의 질과 소비자 만족도 간의 인과 관계를 조사했다.

C

1 수십만 년에 걸쳐, 예술적 노력은 우리의 상상력을 양성하고 혁신을 위한 강력한 능력을 불어넣기 위한 안전한 활동 무대를 제공하는, 인간 인지의 놀이터였을지도 모른다.
2 인간 지능의 진화를 방해했었던 장애물로서의 죽음을 극복하기 위해, 우리 조상들의 공동체는 우리 종족을 다른 모든 것들을 능가하여 앞으로 나아가게 했던 궁극적인 비장의 카드를 사용했는데, 즉, 말과 수학에서의 언문이다.

1 ⑤   **2** ③

1 ⑤

해석 사람들은 선천적으로 사건의 원인을 찾는, 즉, 설명과 이야기를 구성하려는 경향이 있다. 그것이 스토리텔링이 그토록 설득력 있는 수단인 한 가지 이유이다. 이야기는 우리의 경험을 떠올리게 하고 새로운 경우의 사례를 제공한다. 우리의 경험과 다른 이들의 이야기로부터 우리는 사람들이 행동하고 상황이 작동하는 방식에 관해 일반화하려는 경향이 있다. 우리는 사건에 원인을 귀착시키고 이러한 원인과 결과 쌍이 이치에 맞는 한, 그것을 미래의 사건을 이해하는 데 사용한다. 하지만 이러한 인과 관계의 귀착은 종종 잘못되기도 한다. 때때로 그것은 잘못된 원인을 연관시키기도 하고 발생하는 어떤 일에 대해서는 단 하나의 원인만 있지 않기도 하다. 오히려 그 결과에 모두가 원인이 되는 복잡한 일련의 사건들이 있다. 만일 사건들 중에 어느 하나라도 발생하지 않았었다면, 결과는 <u>유사할(→ 다를)</u> 것이다. 하지만 원인이 되는 행동이 단 하나만 있지 않을 때조차도, 그것이 사람들로 하여금 하나의 원인이 되는 행동의 탓으로 돌리는 것을 막지는 못한다.

문제풀이 특정 결과를 유발하는 원인이 여러 개일 수 있어서 그 중 어느 하나라도 발생하지 않으면 결과는 달라질 텐데 사람들은 하나의 원인이 되는 행동으로 귀착하려는 경향이 있다는 내용이므로 ⑤ similar는 different 등으로 고쳐야 한다.

구문분석

[9행] **if** any one of the events <u>would not have occurred</u>,
                                  V
the result <u>would be</u> similar.
          V
▶ 이 문장은 혼합 가정문으로 if절은 가정법 과거완료(would+have p.p.)이고, 주절은 가정법 과거(would+동사원형)로 이루어져 있으며, '(과거에)~했더라면, (현재에)~할 텐데'라는 의미이다.

2 ③

해석 우리의 문화는 순수 예술 — 즐거움 외에는 어떤 기능도 가지고 있지 않은 창조적 생산물 — 쪽으로 편향되어 있다. 공예품은 덜 가치가 있다; 그것들은 일상의 기능을 제공하기 때문에 그것들은 순수하게 창의적이지 않다. 하지만 이러한 구분은 문화적으로 역사적으로 상대적이다. 대부분의 현대의 고급 예술은 일종의 공예로써 시작했다. 우리가 오늘날 "고전 음악"이라고 부르는 것의 작곡과 연주는 가톨릭 미사에서 요구되어지는 기능 또는 왕실 후원자의 특정한 오락적 요구를 <u>무시하는(→ 충족시키는)</u> 공예 음악의 형태로 시작했다. 예를 들면, 실내악은 실제로 방들 — 부유한 가정의 작고 친밀한 방들 — 에서 종종 배경 음악으로 연주되도록 설계되었다. Bach에서 Chopin에 이르는 유명한 작곡가들에 의해서 작곡되어진 춤곡들은 원래는 사실상 춤을 동반했다. 하지만 오늘날, 그들이 작곡되어진 맥락과 기능들이 사라진 채로, 우리는 이러한 작품들을 순수 예술로 듣는다.

문제풀이 고전 음악은 당시 특정한 오락적 요구를 충족하려는 공예 음악의 형태였는데, 오늘날 우리는 그러한 맥락과 기능을 도외시한 채 순수 예술로 음미한다는 내용이므로 ③ ignoring은 satisfying 등으로 고쳐야 한다.

구문분석

[9행] <u>The dances</u> [composed by famous composers
      S
from Bach to Chopin] originally <u>did</u> indeed
                                V
<u>accompany</u> dancing.
  V
▶ [ ]는 주어 The dances를 수식하는 과거분사구이며, 이 문장의 동사는 did accompany로 여기 did는 강조 do동사의 과거형이다.

STEP 2 어법   to부정사 2(부사적)

PRACTICE   p.116

A   **1** N   **2** AD   **3** N   **4** AD   **5** A
      6 AD   **7** AD

B   **1** to reduce   **2** Empowering

A

1 화난 아이를 진정시키는 가장 쉽고 가장 빠른 방법은 음식을 주는 것이다. ▶ 명사적 용법(보어 자리)
2 지원자는 면접에서 말도 안 되는 말을 해서 화가 났다. ▶ 부사적 용법(원인)
3 기대할 수 있는 것이 무엇인지 알고 있을 때, 동물은 자신감과 차분함을 더 많이 느낄 수 있다. ▶ 명사적 용법(의문사+to부정사)
4 우리가 짜증이 날 때마다, 우리 자신의 기분을 더 좋게 만들기 위해 음식에 의존한다. ▶ 부사적 용법(목적)
5 그녀는 순수 미술 석사 학위를 취득한 첫 세 명의 학생들 중 한 명이다. ▶ 명사를 수식하는 형용사적 용법
6 그것은 쓰는 데 너무 오래 걸리고 빨리 읽기가 어려울 것이다.
▶ 부사적 용법(too ~ to)
7 그는 시험공부를 할 때 암기 기법을 사용할 정도로 똑똑하다.
▶ 부사적 용법(정도)

B

1 표지판, 가로등을 지탱하는 기둥들은 바람, 폭풍, 지진을 견딜 수 있을 만큼 튼튼하고 내구성이 있어야 한다. 그러나 종종, 이 동일한 기둥들은 피해를 줄이고 생명을 구하기 위해 충격에 쉽게 부서질 필요가 있다. ▶ 목적의 부사적 용법
2 인터넷에 연결된 모든 사람이 인터넷에 접속하는 모든 사람의 집단 지혜와 적은 돈에 다가갈 수 있게 해 주기 때문에, 크라우드 펀딩은 기업 자금 조달의 민주화로 여겨질 수 있다. ▶ Because it empowers...의 분사구문

1 ⑤　　**2** ④

1 ⑤　　2 ②　　3 ④

1 ⑤

해석 우리 대부분은 죄책감을 느끼거나 다른 사람들이 실망하게 할 수 있는 가능성에 직면했을 때 우리의 욕구를 제쳐둠으로써 위험을 무릅쓰지 않는다. 직장에서 마찰을 피하려고 여러분은 불평하는 직장 동료가 계속 여러분의 에너지를 빼앗아 가는 것을 허용하여 결국 여러분 자신의 직장을 싫어하게 될 지도 모른다. 집에서는 여러분을 힘들게 하는 가족 구성원들이 정서적으로 거절당한다는 느낌을 갖지 않도록 하기 위하여 그들에게 '그래'라고 말해 결국 여러분 자신을 위한 양질의 시간의 부족으로 좌절하게 될지도 모른다. 우리는 자신의 욕구를 무시한 채로 다른 사람들의 (우리에 대한) 인식을 관리하기 위해 열심히 노력하고, 결국 자신이 의미 있는 삶을 살도록 해 줄 바로 그것을 포기한다.

문제풀이 ⑤ 「5형식 동사 enable+O+to-v」이므로 live를 to live로 고쳐야 한다. ▶ p.44
① 병렬 구조(of feeling ~ or disappointing ~) ▶ p.206
② 부사적 용법(목적)
③ 부사적 용법(결과)
④ 부사적 용법(목적)

2 ④

해석 당신이 파티, 세미나, 또는 기타 다른 종류의 행사를 조직할 때, 이미 서로 알고 있는 사람들끼리만 모여 있지 않도록 해라. 만약 당신이 사람들을 식사에 초대한다면, 성공적인 관계 형성을 용이하게 하기 위해 좌석표를 이용할 수 있다. 각 테이블에 앉아 있는 사람들이 섞일 수 있도록 게임을 조직해라. 당신이 "뷔페 만찬이 시작됩니다"라고 알릴 때, "이 기회를 새로운 사람들을 알 수 있는 기회로 삼으세요"라고 말함으로써 이 주제를 공개적으로 다뤄라. 많은 사람들은 이것이 다른 사람들에게 이야기를 시작할 수 있도록 효과적으로 서먹함을 풀어 주는 것임을 알게 된다. 큰 모임에서 사람들이 서로를 잘 모른다면 이름표를 발급하는 것을 주저하지 마라. 각각의 사람들에게 이름표에 전형적이지만 약간 신비로운 것을 쓰도록 해라. 그것은 사람들이 모르는 사람들과 대화를 시작하는 것을 가능하게 만드는 좋은 방법이다.

문제풀이 ④ 「5형식 동사 get+O+to-v」이므로 write를 to write로 고쳐야 한다. ▶ p.52
① 동사원형으로 시작하는 명령문 ▶ p.12
② 부사적 용법(목적)
③ 명사를 수식하는 형용사적 용법
⑤ it ~ to 가목적어-진목적어(명사적 용법)

1 ⑤

해석 사람이 죽은 후에 머리카락과 손톱은 계속해서 자랄까? 무심코 보는 사람에게는 그것은 그렇게 보이지 않을 수도 있지만, 간단한 대답은 '아니다'이다. 그것은 죽음 후에 인간 몸에 수분이 빠지면서 피부가 수축되게 또는 더 작아지게 만들기 때문이다. 이러한 수축은 한때 피부 아래에 있었던 손톱과 머리카락의 일부를 노출시키고 그것들이 이전보다 길어 보이게 만든다. 생물학자들에 따르면, 손톱은 하루에 약 0.1mm씩 자라지만 그것이 자라기 위해서는 신체에 힘을 주도록 도와주는 단당인 글루코오스가 필요하다. 일단 몸이 죽으면 더 이상 글루코오스는 없다. 따라서 피부 세포, 머리카락 세포, 손톱 세포는 더 이상 새로운 세포를 만들어 내지 않는다. 더욱이, 복잡한 호르몬 조절 시스템은 머리카락과 손톱의 성장을 지휘하지만 일단 사람이 죽게 되면 이 모든 것이 불가능하다.

문제풀이 우리 몸이 죽으면 글루코오스가 없으므로 새로운 세포를 더 이상 만들어 낼 수 없다는 문장은 ⑤ 앞의 손톱과 머리카락이 자라려면 글루코오스가 필요하다는 내용과 연결사 moreover를 통해 사람이 죽으면 머리카락과 손톱의 성장 모두가 불가능하다는 내용의 앞인 ⑤에 들어가는 것이 가장 적절하다.

구문분석

[3행] That's because after death, the human body dehydrates, [causing the skin to shrink, or become smaller].
▶ [ ]는 연속 동작을 의미하는 부대상황의 분사구문이다.

2 ②

해석 사진술은 우주가 어떻게 작용하는지를 우리가 이해하는데 있어서 항상 중요한 역할을 해왔다. 비록 망원경이 우리가 육안의 한계를 넘어 멀리까지 볼 수 있도록 도와줄지라도, 망원경 그 자체만으로는 여전히 한계가 있다. 그러나, 카메라를 망원경에 부착하면 갑자기 우리는 훨씬 더 많은 것을 볼 수 있다. 그러지 않으면 볼 수 없을 세부 사항들이 드러난다. 최초 천문 카메라로 작업을 한 19세기 천문학자들은 그들이 생각했던 것보다 우주가 훨씬 더 복잡하다는 것을 발견하고 정말로 깜짝 놀랐다. 최초의 밤하늘 사진들은 알려지지 않은 별들과 은하계들을 보여 주었다. 카메라가 로켓이나 궤도 위성에 부착되었을 때, 우주가 처음으로 뚜렷하게 보였다.

문제풀이 역접의 접속사 Yet으로 시작하여 망원경을 부착하면 더 많은 것을 볼 수 있다는 주어진 문장은 ② 앞의 망원경이 육안의 한계를 넘어서지만 여전히 한계가 있다는 내용과 세부적인 사항들을 볼 수 있게 되었다는 내용 사이인 ②에 들어가는 것이 가장 적절하다.

구문분석

[5행] Indeed, 19th century <u>astronomers</u> [working with
                       S
the first astronomical cameras] <u>were</u> astonished [**to**
                                    V
discover {**that** outer space was much more crowded
than they had thought}].

▶ 첫 번째 [ ]는 주어 astronomers를 수식하는 현재분사구이
고, 이 문장의 동사는 were가 된다. 두 번째 [ ]는 원인을 나타내
는 부사적 용법의 to부정사구이며, { }는 동사 discover의 목적
절로 명사절의 접속사 that이 이끄는 명사절을 나타낸다.

3 ④

해석 그리스에서는 지형이 인간 관계에 영향을 미쳤다. 그 땅이 이동
을 매우 어렵게 만들었기 때문에 손님과 주인의 관계는 중요하게 여
겨졌다. 어떤 낯선 이가, 가난한 사람이라도, 문 앞에 나타나면 선한
주인이 되어 그에게 거처를 주고 그와 음식을 나누는 것이 의무였다.
"우리는 먹기만 하려고 식탁에 앉는 것이 아니라 함께 먹으려고 식탁
에 앉는다."라고 그리스의 작가인 Plutarch가 썼다. 식사를 하는 것
은 인간 사회의 표식이고 인간을 짐승과 구별했다. 답례로 손님은 주
인에게 의무가 있었다. 이런 의무에는, 보통 사흘을 넘지 않아야 하는
데 너무 오래 머물러서 주인의 환대를 악용하지 않는 것이 포함되었
다. 어느 편이든 이 관계를 위반하는 것은 인간과 신의 분노를 가져왔
다.

문제풀이 답례로 손님이 주인에게 해야 할 의무가 있다는 주어진 문
장은 ④ 앞의 그리스에서는 지형 때문에 사람들의 이동이 어려워서
낯선 이라도 집을 방문하면 주인은 음식과 잠자리를 제공하는 것이
의무라고 하며 집주인의 의무를 언급하는 내용과 ④ 뒤에 손님의 의
무 사례를 언급하고 있는 내용 사이인 ④에 들어가는 것이 가장 적절
하다.

구문분석

[3행] [If a stranger, even a poor man, appeared at your
door], **it** was your duty [**to be** a good host, **to give** him
a shelter and (**to**) **share** your food with him].

▶ 첫 번째 [ ]는 접속사 If로 시작하는 조건을 나타내는 부사절이
며, 두 번째 [ ]는 가주어 it에 대한 진주어 to부정사구 3개가 병
렬되어 나타나고 있다.

PRACTICE
p.122

A 1 erupt, 분출하다 2 abrupt, 갑작스런
   3 corrupt, 부패한 4 disrupt, 붕괴시키다
   5 interrupt, 방해하다 6 aspire, 열망하다
   7 inspire, 고무시키다 8 respire, 호흡하다
   9 expire, 만료되다 10 perspire, 땀을 흘리다

B 1 ④ 2 ③ 3 ② 4 ④ 5 ③

C 1 synonymous 2 vulnerable

A

1 e+rupt(break): 분출하다
2 ab+rupt(break): 갑작스런
3 cor+rupt(break): 부패한
4 dis+rupt(break): 붕괴시키다
5 inter+rupt(break): 방해하다
6 a+spire(breath): 열망하다
7 in+spire(breath): 고무시키다
8 re+spire(breath): 호흡하다
9 ex+spire(breath): 만료되다
10 per+spire(breath): 땀을 흘리다

B

1 kind, type, sort는 모두 <u>동의어</u>이다.
2 미술관 내에서는 흡연은 말할 것도 없이 사진 촬영도 금지되어 있다.
3 그 나라는 <u>스스로를 방어하기</u> 위해 가공할 무기를 개발했다.
4 정비사는 첨단 기계를 한 손으로 능숙하게 <u>조작했다</u>.
5 마틴 루터 킹 목사님과 비교된다는 것은 나에게는 큰 <u>찬사</u>이다.

C

1 색이 항상 진실과 실제와 <u>동의어</u>였던 것은 아니다. 옛날 고대 그리
  스 철학자들은 색을 진실을 가리는 장식으로 여겼기 때문에 그림에
  서의 색의 사용을 맹비난하는 경향이 있었다.
2 청소년기는 십 대들이 매우 뛰어난 인지적 능력과 높은 학습 및 기
  억 속도를 지니는 발달 단계여서, 이런 능력은 그들에게 성인에 비
  해 두드러진 장점을 주지만, 그들은 학습을 할 준비가 매우 잘 되어
  있기 때문에 잘못된 것을 학습하기도 대단히 <u>쉽다</u>.

적용독해
p.123

1 ⑤ 2 ③

1 ⑤

해석 정직은 모든 굳건한 관계의 근본적인 부분이다. 자신이 느끼는 것에 대해 솔직하게 말하고, 질문을 받았을 때 정직한 의견을 줌으로써 그것을 여러분에게 유리하게 사용하라. 이 접근법은 여러분이 불편한 사회적 상황에서 벗어나고 정직한 사람들과 친구가 될 수 있도록 도와줄 수 있다. 삶에서 다음과 같은 분명한 방침을 따르라. 절대로 거짓말을 하지 말라. 항상 진실만을 말한다는 평판이 쌓이면, 여러분은 신뢰를 바탕으로 굳건한 관계를 누릴 것이다. (누군가가) 여러분을 조종하는 것도 더 어려워질 것이다. 거짓말을 하는 사람은 자신의 거짓말을 폭로하겠다고 누군가가 위협하면 곤경에 처하게 된다. 자신에게 진실하게 삶으로써, 여러분은 많은 골칫거리를 피할 것이다. 또한 여러분의 관계에는 거짓과 비밀이라는 해악이 없을 것이다. 진실이 아무리 고통스러울지라도 친구들에게 정직하게 대하는 것을 두려워하지 말라. 장기적으로 보면, 선의의 거짓말은 진실을 말하는 것보다 사람들에게 훨씬 더 많이 위안을 준다(→ 상처를 준다).

문제풀이 정직한 태도를 유지하면 우리가 얻는 이점이 많으므로 선의의 거짓말도 하지 않는 것이 중요하다는 내용이므로 ⑤ comfort는 hurt 등으로 고쳐야 한다.

구문분석

[9행] Don't be afraid to be honest with your friends, [**no matter how** painful the truth is].
▶ [ ]는 양보의 부사절로 no matter how는 however와 바꿔 쓸 수 있으며 '아무리 ~할지라도'의 의미이다.

2 ③

해석 Thomas Friedman의 2005년 저서의 제목인 'The World Is Flat'은 세계화가 필연적으로 우리를 더 가깝게 만들 것이라는 믿음에 근거하였다. 그것은 그렇게 해 왔지만 또한 우리가 장벽을 쌓도록 해왔다. 금융 위기, 테러 행위, 폭력적 분쟁, 난민과 이민자, 증가하는 빈부 격차 같은 인지된 위협들에 직면할 때, 사람들은 자신의 집단에 더 단단히 달라붙는다. 한 유명 소셜 미디어 회사 설립자는 소셜 미디어가 우리를 분열시킬(→ 결합시킬) 것이라고 믿었다. 어떤 면에서는 그래 왔지만 그것은 동시에 새로운 사이버 부족들에게 목소리와 조직력을 부여해 왔고, 이들 중 일부는 자신의 시간을 월드 와이드 웹(World Wide Web)에서 비난과 분열을 퍼뜨리는 데 시간을 보낸다. 지금까지 그래 온 만큼이나 현재 많은 부족들, 그리고 그들 사이의 많은 분쟁이 존재하는 것처럼 보인다. '우리와 그들'이라는 개념이 남아있는 세계에서 이러한 부족들이 공존하는 것이 가능할까?

문제풀이 세계화가 우리를 더 가깝게 만들기도 했지만 동시에 장벽을 쌓도록 해 왔듯이, 소셜 미디어도 어떤 면에서는 우리를 결합시키기도 하지만 역시 동시에 우리를 분열시키기도 한다는 내용이므로 ③ divide를 unite 등으로 고쳐야 한다.

구문분석

[1행] The title of Thomas Friedman's 2005 book, *The World Is Flat*, was based on the belief [that globalization would inevitably bring us closer together].

▶ The title of Thomas Friedman's 2005 book와 The World Is Flat는 동격이다. [ ]는 the belief와 동격절로 명사절의 접속사 that이 이끌고 있다.

STEP 2 어법 — to부정사 3 (to부정사 to와 전치사 to)

PRACTICE p.124

A
1 joining → join
2 enjoying → enjoy
3 holding → hold
4 delouse → delousing
5 provide → providing

B
1 distinguish   2 determining

A

1 침팬지들은 사냥을 위해 다른 침팬지들에 더 합류하는 경향이 더 많다. ▶ be likely to+동사원형
2 그렇게 드문 기회를 놓치지 않도록 꼭 인생을 즐기며 살아라. ▶ make sure to+동사원형
3 3차원 화상 회의를 열기 위해 이 강당이 사용될 것이다. ▶ be used to+동사원형 : ~하는 데 사용되다
4 원숭이의 사회적 습성은 서열을 정하는 것부터 상대방의 이를 잡아 주는 것까지 다양하다. ▶ from A to B
5 Hemingway는 사람들이 문학을 더 많이 접하도록 하는데 전념했다. ▶ devote oneself to+(동)명사

B

1 2009년에 연방 정부는 국가의 항공 교통 관제 시스템이 조종사들과의 통신을 방해하고 항공기가 공항에 접근할 때 항공기를 구별하는 데 사용되는 비행 정보를 변경할 수 있는 사이버 공격에 취약하다고 기술한 보고서를 내놓았다. ▶ 「be used to+동사원형」: ~하는 데 사용되다
2 알고리즘의 심각한 문제는 한 알고리즘 설계 회사가, 이식을 기다리는 어느 환자가 장기를 받도록 선택될지 결정하는 것부터 선고에 직면한 어느 범죄자가 집행 유예 또는 최고형을 받아야 하는지 결정하는 것까지의, 광범위한 용도를 위해 알고리즘을 설계하도록 계약을 체결할지도 모른다는 것이다. ▶ from A to B

적용독해 p.125

1 ⑤   2 ④

1 ⑤

해석 파트너들이 자신에 관한 모든 것을 서로에게 말함으로써 관계를 시작하는 사례도 일어나기는 하지만, 그러한 사례는 드물다. 대부분의 경우에, 털어놓는 이야기의 양은 시간이 지나면서 증가한다. 우리는 자신에 대해 비교적 거의 드러내지 않음으로써 관계를 시작하고, 그런 뒤 우리가 처음에 조금 털어놓은 자신에 관한 이야기가 잘 받아들여지고 상대방으로부터도 비슷한 반응을 불러온다면, 우리는 더 많은 것을 드러내기를 기꺼이 한다. 이러한 원칙을 기억하는 것이 아주 중요하다. 다른 사람과 처음 교제할 때 확고한 관계를 형성하는 방법이 자신에 관한 가장 사적인 세부 사항을 드러내는 것이라고 여기는 것은 대개 잘못된 생각일 것이다. 상황이 독특하지 않다면, 그런 식으로 여러분의 마음을 드러내는 것은 파트너가 될 가능성이 있는 사람들을 더 가까이 다가오게 하기보다는 놀라게 하여 쫓아버릴 가능성이 있다.

문제풀이 ⑤ lead to 뒤에는 (동)명사가 와야 하므로 scare를 scaring으로 고쳐야 한다.
① 「전치사+v-ing」
② 타동사 receive의 목적어가 없으므로 수동태 ▶ p.60
③ 「be willing to+동사원형」
④ 명사절인 목적절 ▶ p.28

2 ④

해석 "나는 네가 참 자랑스러워."라는 칭찬에 있어 잘못된 점이 무엇일까? 많다. 자녀에게 거짓된 칭찬을 하는 것이 잘못된 판단이듯, 자녀의 모든 성취에 대해 보상하는 것 또한 실수이다. 보상이 긍정적으로 들리기는 하지만, 그것은 종종 부정적인 결과로 이끌어 준다. 이는 그것이 배움의 즐거움을 감소시킬 수 있기 때문이다. 만약 당신이 자녀의 성취에 대해 지속적으로 보상을 해 준다면, 당신의 자녀는 보상을 얻기 위해 하는 일 자체 보다는 보상을 얻는 것에 좀 더 집중하기 시작한다. 자녀의 즐거움의 초점이 배움 그 자체를 즐기는 것에서 당신을 기쁘게 하는 것으로 옮겨 간다. 만약 당신이 자녀가 글자를 알아볼 때마다 박수를 쳐 준다면, 자녀는 결국 당신이 칭찬하는 것을 듣기 위해서 알파벳 배우기에 관심을 갖기보다 알파벳 그 자체를 배우는 것에 흥미를 덜 갖게 되는 칭찬 애호가가 될 수도 있다.

문제풀이 ④ from A to B 구문의 from과 to는 모두 전치사여서 A와 B 모두 (동)명사가 와야 하므로 please를 pleasing으로 고쳐야 한다.
① it은 가주어−진주어 구문의 가주어
② 「be likely to+동사원형」
③ 「전치사+명사절(what+불완전한 절)」 ▶ p.100
⑤ 「선행사+주격 관계대명사+동사」 ▶ p.174

STEP 3 유형 **글의 요약**   pp.126~127

1 ⑤   2 ①

1 ⑤

해석 아이들은 다른 사람을 돕는 것보다는 무언가를 주는 것에 훨씬

더 저항한다. 우리는 아주 어린 아이들에게서 이러한 차이점을 확실히 관찰할 수 있다. 1년 6개월 된 아기들은 어려운 상황에서는 서로 도와주려 하지만, 그들 자신의 장난감은 다른 아기들과 기꺼이 공유하려 하지 않는다. 그 어린 아기들은 심지어 자신의 소유물을 소리를 지르면서 필요하면 주먹을 날리며 지킨다. 이것은 (걸음마를 배우는) 아기들 사이의 끊임없는 싸움으로 문제를 겪고 있는 부모들의 일상적인 경험이다. 내 딸들이 기저귀를 차고 있을 때조차 그들에게서 "내거야!"라는 말보다 더 자주 들었던 말은 없었다.
→ 아주 어린 아이들은 어려운 상황에서 서로를 (A) 도와주려고는 하지만, 그들은 자신의 소유물은 기꺼이 (B) 공유하려 하지 않는다.

문제풀이 어린 아기들은 어려운 상황에서 서로 도움을 주는 것에 저항감은 별로 없지만, 그들의 소유물을 주거나 공유하는 것에는 저항감이 심하다는 내용의 글이다.

구문분석

[5행] This is the daily experience of parents [troubled {by constant **quarreling** between toddlers}].
▶ [ ]는 선행사 parents를 수식하는 과거분사구이며, { }는 「전치사+(동)명사구」의 전치사구를 나타내고 있다.

2 ①

해석 40년도 더 전에, 심리학자 Sibylle Escalona는 128명의 유아들과 그 엄마들의 놀이 행동에 관한 고전적인 연구가 된 것을 실행했다. 그녀의 주요한 발견은 유아들이 가지고 놀 수 있는 많은 다양한 장난감을 가지고 있더라도, 혼자서 노는 아기들의 감각 운동 놀이가 상호 작용할 어른이 있었던 아이들보다 덜 지속되었다는 것이었다. 엄마들은 노련한 사회적 감독자처럼 보였다. 그들은 아이들이 하고 있었던 것에 반응하여 자기 자신들의 활동을 달리함으로써 놀이 활동을 아이들의 즉각적인 필요에 맞추는 경향이 있었다. 예를 들어 엄마들은 새로운 놀이 재료를 내놓는 속도를 달리했으며, 아이들이 흥미를 잃는 것처럼 보일 때는 변화를 주거나 놀이의 강도를 높이기도 했다. 그 결과 엄마들은 다양한 놀이 활동에 대한 아이들의 흥미를 유지할 수 있었으며 그에 의해 아이들의 주의 집중 시간도 늘릴 수 있었다.
→ 한 연구에서 엄마가 수행한 (A) 안내하는 역할은 유아들이 어른에 대한 접촉이 제한적이었던 유아들보다 더 오래 그들의 놀이 활동에 (B) 집중하도록 도왔다는 것이 발견되었다.

문제풀이 아기들이 놀이 활동을 할 때, 혼자 노는 아기들보다 엄마가 주도하는 놀이에 참여하는 아기들이 흥미 유지와 집중 시간에 더 큰 영향을 받는다는 연구 결과를 제시하는 글이다.

구문분석

[1행] More than 40 years ago, psychologist Sibylle Escalona carried out [**what** has become a classic study of the play behaviors of 128 infants and their mothers].
▶ [ ]는 문장의 동사구 carried out의 목적절로 선행사를 필요로 하지 않는 관계대명사 what이 쓰인 명사절이다.

정답 및 해설 **45**

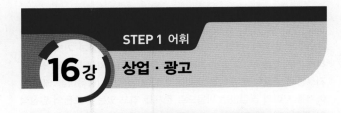

STEP 1 어휘
16강
상업 · 광고

PRACTICE
p.132

A	1 contract 2 skyrocket 3 commercial
	4 complain 5 profits
B	1 ④ 2 ③ 3 ② 4 ③ 5 ④
C	1 unrequested 2 conflict

A
1 나는 대형 출판사와 <u>계약</u>을 맺었다.
2 실업률이 5퍼센트에서 15퍼센트로 <u>급등</u>했다.
3 이 노래는 그녀의 최대 <u>상업적</u>인 성공작이었다.
4 나는 형편없는 서비스에 대해 매니저에게 <u>항의</u>를 해야겠다.
5 그 회사의 <u>수익</u>은 예상보다 낮았다.

B
1 시간을 내어 도와주신다면, 정말 <u>고맙겠</u>습니다.
2 콘서트가 악천후로 <u>취소</u>되었다.
3 지난달 그들은 주요 <u>경쟁사</u>보다 두 배나 많은 차를 판매했다.
4 그 가게에서 판매되는 모든 스마트 TV의 <u>보증 기간</u>은 5년입니다.
5 비행기의 출발 지연으로 <u>불편</u>을 끼친 점을 사과드립니다.

C
1 <u>끼어들기</u> 마케팅은 고객이 흔히 '정크 메일'과 '스팸'이라는 부정적인 용어로 일컬어지는 광고용 우편물, 이메일, 그리고 문자메시지와 같이 요구하지 <u>않은</u> 직접적인 마케팅 메시지를 받을 때 발생한다.
2 완충 지대는 우리에게 다른 차들의 갑작스러운 움직임에 반응하고 적응할 시간을 준다. 마찬가지로, 우리는 단지 완충 지대 ― 항상 예상치 못한 사건에 대비하는 것 ― 를 만듦으로써 우리의 일과 삶에서 필수적인 일을 할 때의 <u>갈등</u>을 줄일 수 있다.

적용독해
p.133

1 ③ 2 ⑤

1 ③
해석 고객은 항상 옳은가? 주방과 욕실 설비를 만드는 한 유명한 회사에 고객들이 고장 난 제품을 반품할 때 그 회사는 좋은 고객 관계를 유지하기 위해 거의 항상 대체품을 제공한다. 그럼에도, 그 회사의 상품 보증 전문가는 상품이 멀쩡하거나 남용되었을 때와 같이, "'안 돼요.'라고 말을 해야 할 때가 있다."고 설명한다. 전자 상거래 회사를

소유한 기업가 Lauren Thorp는 "고객이 '항상' 옳지만, 때로는 당신이 고객의 불합리한 요구를 <u>수용(→ 거절)</u>해야만 한다."고 말한다. Thorp가 고객의 불만을 해결하기 위해 최선을 다해왔는데 그 고객이 어떠한 경우에도 만족하지 않을 것이란 사실을 깨달을 때, 그녀는 자신의 주의를 나머지 다른 고객들에게 돌리는데, 그 고객들은 "내 성공의 이유"라고 그녀는 말한다.

문제풀이 고객의 불만을 해결하기 위해 최선을 다해야 하지만 때로는 고객의 불합리한 요구를 거절해야 할 때도 있다는 내용이므로 ③ admit는 reject 등으로 고쳐야 한다.

구문분석

[7행] When Thorp <u>**has tried**</u> everything to resolve
a complaint and <u>**realizes**</u> [that the customer will be
dissatisfied no matter what], <u>she</u> <u>returns</u> <u>her attention</u>
to the rest of her customers, [who (she says) are "the
reason for my success."]

▶ When이 이끄는 절은 no matter what까지이며 동사는 has tried와 realizes로 병렬 구조이다. 첫 번째 [ ]는 realizes의 목적어로 접속사 that이 이끌고 있으며 두 번째 [ ]는 customers를 수식하는 계속적 용법의 주격 관계대명사절이다. ( )는 삽입절이다.

2 ⑤
해석 오늘날의 소비자들은 적정한 가격의 괜찮은 제품을 찾고 있는 것만이 아니다. 그들은 제품이나 서비스를 넘어서 그것을 제공하는 기업의 윤리까지 살펴보고 있다. 소비자들에 의한 주안점의 전환은 그들이 물건을 구매하는 기업에 대한 관심에서 분명히 드러난다. 예를 들면, 노동 관행, 환경 정책, 그리고 사회적 책임에 대한 관심이 커져 가고 있다. 이에 따라 기업들은 재무적 성과뿐만 아니라 사회적, 환경적 변화를 끌어내야 하는 압박감을 점점 더 많이 받고 있다. 기업은 그 압력에 대응할 필요가 있는데, 고객들이 그들의 관심사를 상점에 대한 불매 동맹하기에서부터 기업에 대한 고소에 이르기까지 모든 방법으로 목소리를 내고 있기 때문이다. 몇몇 다국적 기업은 최근 윤리적 소비자의 분노를 겪었으며, 평판과 기업으로서의 존재를 보호하기 위해 재빨리 반응하도록 강요받아 왔다. 윤리적 소비에 대한 이런 커지는 <u>무관심(→ 중요성)</u>은 무시될 수 없는 추세이다.

문제풀이 소비자들이 제품의 품질뿐만 아니라 해당 기업의 윤리적 책임에 대한 관심도 더 두는 추세여서 윤리적 소비의 중요성이 무시될 수 없다는 내용이므로 ⑤ indifference는 emphasis 등으로 고쳐야 한다.

구문분석

[7행] <u>Companies</u> <u>need</u> to respond to the pressure
because customers are voicing their concerns in every
way, [**from** boycotting stores **to** suing companies].

▶ [ ]에서 전치사구 「from A to B」는 'A에서 B까지'라는 뜻으로 every way와 동격이며, from과 to는 모두 전치사이므로 A와 B에는 (동)명사가 와야 한다.

PRACTICE

p.134

A　1 touch → touching
　　2 application → applying
　　3 recommending → to recommend
　　4 to use → using
　　5 to collect → collecting

B　1 generating　　2 using

A

1 사람들은 세균을 퍼트릴 수 있어서 신생아를 만지는 것은 좋지 않다고 믿었다. ▶ that절의 동명사 주어
2 그는 그의 아버지가 벽에 양질의 페인트를 재빠르게 바르는데 얼마나 능숙한지 알게 되었다. ▶「전치사+v-ing+O」
3 내과 의사들은 자신의 폐암 환자들에게 수술이나 방사선 치료 둘 중에서 하나를 권하는 것을 강요받았다. ▶「force+to-v」
4 사람들이 상표나 상품을 사용하기 시작하는 시기가 어리면 어릴수록, 그들은 미래에 그것을 계속 사용할 가능성이 높아진다.
　▶「keep+v-ing」
5 탄자니아의 Hazda 유목민들은 식량을 채집하는데 일주일에 14시간 정도를 소비한다. ▶「spend+시간/돈+v-ing」

B

1 일부 경영 관리 강사들은 일반적인 통념으로서 집단 브레인스토밍이 놀라운 아이디어를 만들어내는 효과적인 방법이라고 하지만 최근 더 객관적인 연구는 이와 다르게 제안하고 있다. ▶「전치사+v-ing+O」
2 처음으로 교실에서 실제 음악을 만들어 내는 일에 접근할 때 악기 사용을 완전히 피하는 것이 좋은 생각이다. ▶「avoid+v-ing」

적용독해

p.135

1 ⑤　2 ②

1 ⑤

해석 내가 관리자로서 가장 잘한 일은 회사의 모든 사람들이 한 가지 일을 하는 것에만 책임을 지도록 만든 것이었다. 나는 단지 사람들을 관리하는 업무를 단순화하기 위해 이렇게 하기 시작했다. 하지만 그 이후 나는 더 의미 있는 결과를 알게 되었다. 역할을 정해 주는 것이 갈등을 줄여 준다는 것이다. 대부분의 회사 내부의 다툼은 동료들이 같은 임무를 두고 경쟁할 때 발생한다. 신생 기업들은 초기 단계에서 업무의 역할들이 유동적이기 때문에 이럴 위험이 특히 높다. 경쟁

을 없애는 것은 모든 사람들이 단순한 전문성을 초월하는 종류의 장기적인 관계를 구축하는 것을 더 수월하게 만든다. 그 이상으로, 내부적인 평화는 신생 기업이 어쨌든 살아남는 것을 가능케 하는 것이다. 신생 기업이 실패할 때, 우리는 종종 그 기업이 경쟁적인 생태계에서 경쟁 관계에 있는 포식자에게 굴복했다고 생각한다. 그러나 모든 회사는 또한 그 자체가 생태계이며 내부의 갈등은 그 회사가 외부의 위협에 취약하도록 만든다.

문제풀이 ⑤ 5형식 동사 make의 목적격 보어 자리는 형용사가 들어가야 하므로 vulnerably를 형용사 vulnerable로 고쳐야 한다.
① 보어 자리에 동명사
②「전치사+v-ing」
③ 주어 자리에 동명사
④「imagine+O+v-ing」

2 ②

해석 고객들을 즐겁게 하는 데 관심이 있는 기업들에게, 뛰어난 가치와 서비스는 기업 문화 전반의 일부가 된다. 예를 들어, 해마다, 고객 만족이라는 측면에서 Pazano는 서비스업 중 최상위 또는 상위권을 차지한다. 고객을 만족시키기 위한 그 기업의 열정은 그것의 신조에 요약되어 있고, 이는 그 기업의 고급 호텔이 진정으로 기억될 만한 경험을 제공할 것을 약속한다. 고객 중심 기업은 경쟁사 대비 높은 고객 만족을 제공하고자 하지만, 그것은 고객 만족을 최대화하려고 하지는 않는다. 기업은 가격을 낮추거나 서비스를 증진시킴으로써 고객 만족을 항상 높일 수 있다. 하지만 이것은 더 낮은 이윤으로 이어질지도 모른다. 따라서, 마케팅의 목적은 수익을 내면서 고객 가치를 창출하는 것이다. 이것은 매우 미묘한 균형을 필요로 한다: 마케팅 담당자는 더 많은 고객 가치와 만족을 계속해서 창출해야 하지만 회사의 이윤창출을 위협해서는 안된다.

문제풀이 ② attempt는 to부정사를 목적어로 취하므로 maximizing을 to maximize로 고쳐야 한다.
①「전치사+v-ing」
③ 병렬구조: by lowering or increasing ▶ p.206
④ 보어 자리에 동명사
⑤「continue+v-ing」

구문분석

[3행] The company's passion for satisfying customers
　　　　　　S
is summed up in its credo, [**which** promises {that
　　V
its luxury hotels will deliver a truly memorable
　　　　S′　　　　　V′
experience}].
　　O′
▶ [ ]는 주격 관계대명사의 계속적인 용법이며 관계절 안에서
{ }의 that은 명사절 접속사로 동사 promises의 목적절이다.

1 ③　2 ②　3 ①

1 ③

해석 Stevens 씨께,

이것은 당신이 9월 26일 우리 가게에서 구매한 책상의 배송 상황 문의에 대한 회신입니다. 불행히도, 당신의 책상 배송이 가구 제조 업체에서 우리 창고로 배송되는 동안 발생한 파손 때문에 예상된 것보다 더 오래 걸릴 것입니다. 우리는 제조 업체로부터 똑같은 대체품을 주문했고, 그 배송이 2주 안에 이뤄질 것으로 예상합니다. 우리는 그 책상이 도착하자마자 당신에게 바로 전화해서 편리한 배송 시간을 정할 것입니다. 우리는 이 지연이 당신에게 일으킨 불편에 대해 유감으로 생각합니다.

진심을 담아,

Justin Upton 드림

문제풀이 배송하려던 제품이 파손되어 대체품을 주문했지만 지연되고 있음을 알리는 글이므로 정답은 ③이다.

구문분석

[2행] Unfortunately, the delivery of your desk will take
         $\underset{S}{}$ $\underset{V}{}$
longer than expected **due to** the damage [that occurred
during the shipment from the furniture manufacturer
to our warehouse.]
► 「due to+명사」는 '~ 때문에'라는 뜻이며 [ ]는 선행사 damage를 수식하는 주격 관계대명사절이다.

2 ②

해석 최근에 대학을 졸업한 사람으로서, 저는 마케팅 직종으로 옮겨 구체적으로 식품 판매 분야에 대한 추가적인 경험을 할 수 있게 되어 기쁩니다. 당신의 회사에 대한 놀라운 일들에 대해 들었고, 당신의 팀에 합류하기를 바라 왔습니다. 저의 이전 경험들이 주로 소매업에 관한 것이었지만, 저는 항상 식품 판매 분야로 옮기고 싶었습니다. 저의 자원 봉사 경험은 모든 삶의 분야의 사람들과 함께 일할 수 있도록 해주었고, 지역 자선 단체에 대한 당신 회사의 공헌에 대해 그들이 얼마나 많이 감사하는지를 저는 알고 있습니다. 만약 당신 회사의 마케팅 부서 일원으로서 고용이 된다면, 저의 목표는 새로운 고객을 만들고, 기존의 고객들이 그들의 구매에 대해서 계속 즐거워 할 수 있도록 확신시키는 것입니다.

문제풀이 근무하고 싶은 회사에 채용을 요청하는 글이므로 정답은 ②이다.

구문분석

[7행] [If hired as a member of your Marketing
Department], my goal would be **to get** new clients
and **to ensure** [that current customers continue to feel
excited about their purchases.]
► 첫 번째 [ ]는 가정법 과거 문장으로 부사절 If I were hired... 에서 「S+be동사」가 생략되고 「접속사 if+과거분사」만이 남은 형태이다. 주절의 to get과 to ensure는 보어 역할의 to부정사구로 and로 병렬 구조를 이루고 있으며 두 번째 [ ]는 ensure의 목적절로 쓰였다.

3 ①

해석 저희는 귀하가 클럽에 가입할 때 선택하셨던 제품을 보내드린 이후로 귀하로부터 답변을 듣지 못해 염려하고 있습니다. 아시는 바와 같이, 제품을 받으시면 항상 지불 기한이 된 것입니다. 저희가 아직 돈을 받지 않았기 때문에, 귀하의 회원 자격 특혜를 일시적으로 중지하였습니다. 가장 다양하게 선택할 수 있는 음악들, 큰 폭의 할인 등 귀하의 회원 자격이 제공하는 모든 혜택들을 놓치지 마십시오! 이 편지의 아랫부분을 귀하의 수표와 함께 동봉된 봉투에 넣어 다시 보내 주십시오. 저희에게 오늘 대금을 보내 주십시오. 신속히 지불해 주시면 귀하의 회원 자격이 정상으로 회복될 것입니다.

문제풀이 제품에 대한 지불기한이 되었는데도 대금을 납부하지 않아 회원 자격이 일시 중지되었으니 바로 대금을 보내달라는 글이므로 정답은 ①이다.

구문분석

[4행] Don't miss out on **all the benefits** [your
membership **offers you**].
► [ ]는 목적격 관계대명사 that/which가 생략된 관계대명사절이다. 4형식 동사 offer는 「offer+I.O.+D.O.」 순이어야 하는데 「I.O.+(목적격 관계대명사)+S+V+D.O.」로 전환된 형태이다.

PRACTICE
p.140

A	**1** atmosphere	**2** attitude	**3** envious
	4 timid	**5** thrifty	
B	**1** ④ **2** ② **3** ④ **4** ② **5** ①		
C	**1** deserve	**2** curtails	

A

1 그 도서관은 편안한 분위기로 조성되어 있다.
2 범죄에 대한 판사의 태도에 나는 감동했다.
3 그녀는 여동생의 탐스러운 머릿결을 부러워했다.
4 그 책은 소심한 소년을 좀 더 외향적인 아이로 변모시켰다.
5 어린이들은 돈을 절약해서 써야 한다.

B

1 걸음마를 뗀 그 아이는 혼자 남겨지는 것을 무서워한다.
2 영화가 너무 지루해서 나는 잠이 들었다.
3 우리 팀이 경기에서 졌다는 사실이 우리를 실망시켰다.
4 그 학생이 내가 보낸 이메일에 전혀 답장을 보내지 않는 것은 무척 짜증나게 한다.
5 그 환자는 모든 검사 결과가 음성이라는 것에 안도했다.

C

1 언론의 자유와 종교적 관용의 옹호자인 Voltaire는 "나는 여러분이 하는 말을 싫어하지만, 그것을 말할 여러분의 권리를 목숨을 걸고 옹호할 것이다"라고 말했는데, 그것은 여러분이 경멸하는 의견조차도 들을 자격이 있다는 생각에 대한 강력한 변론이었다.
2 사람들은 다른 사람들이 더 성공하지 못하도록 그들을 깎아 내리려 할 때 자신도 모르게 자신의 일을 방해하게 되는데, 이는 다른 사람의 성공에 대해 분개하면 여러분 자신의 성공 기회가 줄어든다는 것을 자아는 알지 못하기 때문이다.

적용독해
p.141

1 ⑤   2 ④

1 ⑤

해석 긴장감은 인생에서 우리 흥미의 많은 부분을 차지한다. 만일 우리가 연극이나 소설의 줄거리를 미리 안다면 많은 흥미를 종종 잃는다. 우리는 결과에 관해서 추측을 지속하고 싶어 한다. 서커스 곡예사는 그가 여러 번의 고의적인 실패 이후에 자신의 연기를 성공할 때 이 원칙을 적용한다. 심지어 그가 앞선 연기에서 했었던 그러한 고의적인 태도조차도 우리의 기대를 증가시킨다. 연기의 마지막 장에서 작은 곡예를 하는 개가 코에 공을 올리는 연기를 한다. 어느 날 밤 그 개는 연기를 성공하기 전에 주저하고 오랫동안 시도를 했을 때, 그 개는 한 번에 기술을 보여 주었을 때보다 훨씬 더 많은 박수갈채를 받았다. 우리는 편안한(→ 긴장된) 마음으로 기다리기를 좋아할 뿐만 아니라 우리가 기다린 것의 진가를 인정할 줄도 안다.

문제풀이 줄거리나 결과를 미리 알게 되면 흥미를 잃기 때문에 우리는 긴장감을 유지하며 결과를 기다리기를 좋아한다는 내용이므로 ⑤ relieved는 nervous 등으로 고쳐야 한다.

구문분석

[4행] [Even the deliberate manner {in which he arranges the opening scene}] increases our expectation.
▶ [ ]가 문장의 주어부이고 increases가 동사이다. { }는 「전치사+관계대명사」로 the deliberate manner를 수식하는 관계대명사절이다.

2 ④

해석 우리 문화에서 슬픔은 종종 불필요하고 바람직하지 않은 감정으로 여겨진다. 수많은 자기 계발서들은 일반적으로는 부정적인 감정, 특히 슬픔을 제거될 필요가 있는 '문제적 감정'의 범주로 지정하면서 긍정적 사고와 긍정적 행동의 장점을 장려한다. 다수의 심리학 직종이 슬픔을 관리하고 완화시키는 일에 활용된다. 그러나 어느 정도의 슬픔과 우울은 현재의 경우에서보다 이전의 역사적 시대에서 훨씬 더 수용되어 왔다. 고대 철학자로부터 Shakespeare를 거쳐 Chekhov, Ibsen, 그리고 19세기의 위대한 소설에 이르기까지 슬픔, 갈망, 그리고 우울이라는 감정을 탐험하는 것은 파괴적인(→ 도움이 되는) 것으로 오랫동안 여겨져 왔다. 긍정성을 장려하는 번창하는 산업이 인간 정서에 대한 이전의 더 균형적인 이러한 관점을 가까스로 없앤 것은 불과 최근에 이르러서였다.

문제풀이 슬픔이나 우울은 부정적인 감정으로 여겨지지만 실제로 이러한 감정들은 예전부터 도움이 된다는 것을 알고 있었다는 내용이므로 ④ destructive는 instructive 등으로 고쳐야 한다.

구문분석

[9행] **It is** only recently **that** a thriving industry [promoting positivity] has managed to remove this earlier and more balanced view of human affectivity.
▶ 「it is ~ that」는 강조구문으로 부사구인 only recently를 강조하고 있다. [ ]는 앞의 주어 a thriving industry를 수식하는 현재분사구이다.

PRACTICE
p.142

A　1　resting → to rest

　　2　to see → seeing

　　3　to see → seeing

　　4　to say → saying

　　5　to turn → turning

B　1　feeling　　2　to keep

A

1　그는 달리기를 하고 나서 몇 분 쉬려고 멈췄다. ▶ stop to-v (~ 하려고 하던 일을 멈추다)

2　그녀는 작년에 콘서트에서 방탄소년단을 본 것을 기억하고 있다. ▶ remember v-ing (과거의 일을 기억하다)

3　나는 어렸을 적 영화 '시네마 천국'을 본 것을 잊지 못할 것이다. ▶ forget v-ing (과거의 일을 잊다)

4　그는 어젯밤에 나에게 심한 말을 한 것을 후회했다고 나에게 말했다. ▶ regret v-ing (과거의 일을 후회하다)

5　컴퓨터를 껐다가 다시 켜 보는 게 어때? ▶ try v-ing (시험 삼아 한 번 해보다)

B

1　방어자가 자신이 비난자에 의해 이해받고 있으며 서로가 같은 편이라고 느낄 때 방어할 것은 아무것도 없게 되고, 방어자는 분노감과 좌절감을 더 이상 느끼지 않게 된다. ▶ stop v-ing (하던 일/ 것을 멈추다)

2　풍속과 방향은 다른 지형들의 기상 관측소마다 다르기 때문에 기상학자들은 정확한 기상 예측을 위해 데이터 변동을 계속 기록해야 한다는 것을 항상 기억해야 한다. ▶ remember to-v (미래의 일을 기억하다)

적용독해
p.143

1　④　　2　⑤

1　④

해석 나의 아버지는 음악가로 매우 늦게, 대략 새벽 3시까지 일했고, 그래서 아버지는 주말마다 늦잠을 잤다. 그 결과, 내가 해야 할 것들을 잊어버릴 때마다 아버지가 잔디 깎기와 울타리 덤불 자르기처럼 내가 싫어했던 허드렛일을 돌보라고 계속 나에게 잔소리한 것을 제외하고는 내가 어렸을 때 우리는 많은 관계를 가지지 못했다. 그는 무책임한 아이를 다루는 책임감 있는 사람이었다. 우리가 소통했던 방식에 대한 기억들이 현재 나에게는 우스워 보인다. 예를 들어, 한번은 아버지가 나에게 잔디를 깎으라고 말했고, 나는 앞뜰만 하기로 하고 뒤뜰을 하는 것은 미루기로 결심했으나, 그러고 나서 며칠 동안 비가 내렸고 뒤뜰의 잔디가 너무 길게 자라서 나는 그것을 낫으로 베어내야만 했다. 그 일은 너무 오래 걸려서 내가 끝냈을 때쯤에는 앞뜰의 잔디가 깎기에 너무 자라버렸다. 허드렛일을 하는 것을 무척 싫어했지만, 그때 이후로 잔디 깎는 일을 항상 기억하고 있었다.

문제풀이 ④ postpone은 목적어로 동명사를 취하므로 to do를 doing으로 고쳐야 한다.

① 「forget+to-v(미래의 일을 잊다)」

② 5형식 동사 「tell+O+O.C.(to-v)」 ▶ p.44

③ 「decide+to-v」

⑤ 「remember+to-v(미래의 일을 기억하다)」

2　⑤

해석 내가 어릴 때 부모님은 의사들이 마치 신과 같은 재능을 지닌 뛰어난 존재인 것처럼 우러러보았다. 그러나 나는 희귀병으로 병원에 입원하고 나서야 의학에서의 직업을 추구할 것을 꿈꾸게 되었다. 나는 그 분야 최고의 몇몇 전문의들이 나를 방문하여 사례를 관찰하도록 이끄는 의학적 호기심의 대상이 되었다. 환자로서, 그리고 대학으로 돌아가기를 간절히 바라는 십 대로서, 나는 나를 진찰하는 의사마다 물었다. "무엇이 제 병의 원인인가요?" "어떻게 저를 낫게 해주실 건가요?" 전형적인 반응은 비언어적인 것이었다. 그들은 머리를 가로저으며 내 방을 나갔다. 나는 "음, 내가 그쯤은 할 수 있을 거야."라고 속으로 생각했던 것이 기억난다. 어떤 의사도 나의 기본적인 질문에 대답할 수 없다는 것이 내게 분명해졌을 때, 나는 의사들에게 더 이상 질문하지 않았다. 대학에 돌아와서 나는 매우 열정적으로 의학을 추구하게 되었다.

문제풀이 ⑤ 문맥상 stop v-ing(하고 있는 것을 멈추다)이므로 to ask를 asking으로 고쳐야 한다.

① 「전치사+(동)명사」 ▶ p.100

② 병렬 구조(to look and review) ▶ p.206

③ 「eager to+동사원형」 ▶ p.124

④ 「remember+v-ing(과거의 일을 기억하다)」

1　①　　2　①　　3　②

1　①

해석 몇 시간 후에, 앉아 있어서 허리가 아프고, 머리는 모양이 잡혀서 마르고, 거의 보이지 않는 화장을 했을 때, Ash는 나에게 드레스로 갈아입는 걸 잊지 말라고 말한다. 내가 먹는 다과가 우연히 드레스에 떨어져 얼룩지게 할까 두려워 우리는 마지막 순간까지 기다리고 있었다. 쇼가 시작될 때까지 30분밖에 남지 않았고 Ash를 괴롭히던 초조함이 그녀에게서 빠져나와 새로운 희생자로 나를 선택한 것 같다. 내 손바닥에서 땀이 나고, 나는 안절부절못한다. 거의 모든 모델이 준비가 되었고, 일부 모델은 이미 19세기 복장을 입고 있다. Ash가 내 코르셋을 조인다.

문제풀이 곧 시작될 쇼를 위해 준비하며 기다리는 동안 안절부절 긴장하는 모습을 묘사하고 있으므로 정답은 ①이다.

구문분석

[5행] ... and <u>the nerves</u> [that have been torturing Ash]
　　　　S ↑＿＿＿＿＿

<u>seem</u> to have escaped her, [choosing a new victim in
V

me.]

▶ 첫 번째 [ ]는 주격 관계대명사절로 주어 the nerves를 수식하고 있고 동사는 seem이다. 두 번째 [ ]는 〈부대상황〉을 나타내는 분사구문이다.

2 ①

해석 Dave는 그의 서핑보드 위에 앉아 주변을 둘러 보았다. 그는 그날 오후 물에 있는 마지막 사람이었다. 갑자기 수평선 위로 무언가가 그의 눈을 사로잡았고 그의 심장은 얼어붙었다. 그것은 모든 서퍼들의 최악의 악몽이었다 — 상어의 지느러미. 그는 휴식을 멈추고 보드를 해변 쪽으로 돌렸고 해안가 쪽으로 발차기를 시작했다. 그것은 단지 20미터 떨어져 있었다! 떨면서, 그는 그의 보드를 더 단단히 붙잡고 더 강하게 발차기를 시도했다. '나는 괜찮을 거야.' 그는 마음속으로 생각했다. '나는 공포를 떨쳐낼 필요가 있어.' 그가 육지에 다시 도착하기 전에 한평생처럼 느껴졌던 공포의 5분이 지나갔다. Dave는 해변에 앉아 숨을 내쉬었다. 그의 마음은 이제 편안해졌다. 그는 안전했다. 그는 태양이 파도 뒤로 지기 시작할 때 만족스러운 한숨을 내쉬었다.

문제풀이 서핑보드 위에 앉아 있던 중에 상어가 나타나자 두려움에 떨며 해변으로 도망친 후 안도의 한숨을 쉬는 모습을 묘사하고 있으므로 정답은 ①이다.

구문분석

[6행] <u>Five minutes of terror</u> [that **felt like** a lifetime]
　　　　S ＿＿＿＿＿↑

<u>passed</u> before he was on dry land again.
V

▶ [ ]는 주어 Five minutes of terror를 수식하는 주격 관계대명사절이고 「feel like ~」는 '~처럼 느끼다'라는 의미이다.

3 ②

해석 Meghan은 고개를 들어 성난 회색 구름이 물 위로 밀려오는 것을 보았다. 폭풍이 방향을 바꿔서 그녀 쪽으로 다가오고 있었다. 그녀는 일어나서 그녀의 샌들을 향해 손을 뻗었다. 그때 그녀는 호수 한가운데에서 첨벙거리고 있는 자신의 개를 발견했다. 처음에 그녀는 그녀의 개가 놀고 있다고 생각했다. 그녀는 1, 2초 정도 지켜봤고, 그러고 나서 그 개가 놀고 있는 것이 아니라는 것을 깨달았다. 그는 가라앉지 않으려고 애쓰고 있었다. 그녀는 호숫가에서 개가 혼자 놀게 한 것을 후회했다. 심장이 스프링 해머처럼 쿵쾅거리며 그녀는 물속으로 뛰어 들어가 그 개를 향해 헤엄치기 시작했다. 그녀가 그 개에 도달하기 전에, 비가 내리기 시작했다. 그녀는 개를 보았고, 그리고

몇 초 후에 그 개가 사라졌다. 그녀는 팔을 길게 뻗고, 다리를 더욱 힘차고 빠르게 차면서 미친 듯이 앞으로 나아갔다.

문제풀이 태풍이 다가오고 있는 와중에 물에 빠져 허우적거리는 개를 발견하고 구하러 가는 모습을 묘사하고 있으므로 정답은 ②이다.

구문분석

[1행] Meghan <u>looked</u> up and <u>saw</u> <u>angry gray clouds</u>
　　　　　　V1　　　　　　V2　　　　O

<u>rolling across the water.</u>
　O.C.

▶ and 다음은 「지각동사+O+O.C.」 구문으로 see의 목적격 보어로 현재분사 rolling이 쓰인 5형식 문장이다.

[6행] [**With** <u>her heart</u> pounding like a trip-hammer],
　　　　　　　O

she <u>**ran**</u> into the water and <u>**started**</u> swimming toward
　　V1　　　　　　　　　　　V2

the dog.

▶ [ ]는 〈부대상황〉을 나타내는 「with+O+현재분사」로 목적어와 분사와의 관계가 능동 관계이므로 현재분사(pounding)가 쓰였다. 「start+v-ing」는 '~하기 시작하다'라는 의미로 start는 동명사를 목적어로 하는 동사이다.

PRACTICE
p.148

A	1 obstacle	2 colleague	3 encounter
	4 minority	5 self-esteem	
B	1 ② 2 ② 3 ④ 4 ③ 5 ④		
C	1 criticized	2 benefits	

A

1 변화에 대한 두려움은 발전의 걸림돌이다.
2 그녀의 혁신적인 생각에 동료들은 박수갈채를 보냈다.
3 이러한 잔인한 행동은 내가 처음 접한 인종 차별이었다.
4 오직 소수의 사람들만이 그 폭력 사태에 연루되었다.
5 대학 입시의 실패는 그의 자존감 상실로 이어졌다.

B

1 유니세프는 전 세계 아이들을 양육하기 위해 설립되었다.
2 악수는 서구 국가에서 사회적 관습이었다.
3 우리는 자선기금을 모으기 위해 매년 콘서트를 연다.
4 이 학교에는 다양한 인종 출신의 학생들이 다니고 있다.
5 '폐기물 에너지화' 비율은 인도와 부탄에서 각각 20퍼센트와 15퍼센트를 차지했다.

C

1 음식을 요리하는 것은 도움이 안 되며, 아이들조차 의술의 개입 없이 양육되어야 한다고 주장한 Shelton은 의학적인 치료보다 단식을 옹호한다는 이유로 동시대 사람들로부터 심한 비난을 받았다.
2 모든 거짓말은 밝혀졌을 때 간접적인 해로운 영향을 미치게 되지만, 가끔 이러한 해로운 영향들이 어떤 거짓말에서 발생한 이로움보다 적을 수도 있다. 예를 들어, 심각하게 아픈 사람들에게 그들의 수명에 대해 거짓말하는 것은 그들에게 더 오래 살 기회를 줄 수도 있다.

적용독해
p.149

1 ③   2 ④

1 ③

해석 당신의 사업이 무엇이든지 간에 개방성이 중요하다. *Charity Water* 웹사이트는 Google Map 위치 기능과 모든 우물의 사진을 담고 있다. 당신이 그 사이트를 볼 때, 당신은 *Charity Water*가 하고 있는 일을 볼 수 있다. 많은 사람들은 그들의 돈이 실제로 어디에 서 혹은 어떻게 사용되는지를 알 수 없기 때문에 비영리 단체에 기부하는 것을 망설인다. 이것은 개인이나 단체가 당신의 운용 자금을 서명하여 동의하게 하는 것이 좋은 이유이다. 이런 식으로, 당신이 거둔 모든 기부금들은 당신이 돕고 있는 사람들에게 곧장 가게 되고, 이것은 기부자들로 하여금 기부금이 좋은 일을 하고 있다는 것을 불확실 (→ 확실)하게 해준다. 또한 기부자들은 더 아량을 베풀게 된다. 개방적으로 된다는 것은 또한 당신이 받는 돈에 대해서 책임감을 느끼도록 만들어 준다. 만약에 사람들이 그들의 돈의 흐름을 알게 된다면 당신은 멋진 사무실이나 높은 급여에 그 돈을 쓰게 될 가능성이 덜 할 것이다.

문제풀이 우리가 낸 기부금의 사용 현황을 명확히 알게 된다면 비영리 단체와 우리 모두에게 확실히 도움이 될 거라는 내용이므로 ③ uncertain은 certain 등으로 고쳐야 한다.

구문분석

> [5행] This is [why **it** can be a good idea **to get** individuals or an organization to underwrite your operational costs.]
> ▶ [ ]는 의문사 why가 이끄는 주격 보어 역할의 명사절이다. why절 속에 it ~ to부정사의 가주어-진주어 구문이 사용되었고, '~에게 …을 시키다'라는 의미로 사용되는 5형식 동사 get은 「get+O+O.C.(to-v)」의 구조를 가진다.

2 ④

해석 우리는 끊임없는 상호 작용의 시대에 살고 있지만, 우리 중 더 많은 이들이 어느 때보다도 '외롭다'고 주장하고 있다. 외로움은 우리 주변에 물리적으로 얼마나 많은 사람이 있는지와 관련 있는 것이 아니라, 우리가 인간관계로부터 필요로 하는 것을 획득하지 못하는 것과 전적으로 관련이 있다. 온라인의 가상 인물과 텔레비전 속의 등장인물이 우리 본연의 정서적 욕구를 인위적으로 충족하여, 뇌가 현실과 비현실을 잘 구분하지 못하는 불분명한 영역을 차지하게 된다. 우리가 '유대감'을 얻기 위해 이러한 가상 인물과 등장인물에게 더욱 의존할수록, 우리의 뇌는 더욱 더 그것들을 '관련없는(→ 관련된)' 것으로 인지한다. 이것은 우리의 뇌가 속을 수 있음을 의미하고, 아이러니한 것은 우리가 그 속임수의 공범이라는 사실이다. 욕구에 이끌리는 동물로서 우리는 우리가 필요로 하는 것을 얻기 위해서 저항이 가장 적은 경로를 탐색하고, 전자기기에 대한 몰입은 이제까지 발명된 가장 접근하기 쉽고 비화학적인 경로를 제공한다.

문제풀이 인간관계로부터 필요로 하는 것을 얻지 못해 외로움을 느끼는 현대인들이 가상 현실에 의존하게 되고 우리 뇌는 그것을 현실이라고 인지하게 된다는 내용이므로 ④ irrelevant는 relevant 등으로 고쳐야 한다.

구문분석

> [6행] **The more** we rely on these personalities and characters {**to get** a sense of "connectedness}," **the more** our brains encode them as "relevant."
> ▶ 「the+비교급 ~, the+비교급 …」 구문은 '~하면 할수록 더 …하다'의 의미이다. { }에서 to get은 목적을 나타내는 부사적 용법의 to부정사이다.

A 1 walked → walking
      2 asking → asked
      3 using → used
      4 involving → involved
      5 Situating → Situated

B 1 named   2 expressed

A

1 한 아이가 횡단보도를 건너다가 차에 치였다. ▶ 분사의 주어가 동작을 하면 현재분사
2 '차를 갖고 싶니?'라고 질문을 받자 그는 '그래.'라고 대답했다.
   ▶ 분사의 주어가 동작을 당하면 과거분사
3 남극은 전적으로 평화적인 목적으로 사용되는 대륙이다. ▶ 분사의 주어가 동작을 당하면 과거분사
4 농부들은 야채 재배와 관련된 도구와 과정을 점검했다. ▶ 분사의 주어가 동작을 당하면 과거분사
5 해발 1,350미터에 위치한 카트만두시는 온화한 날씨를 누린다.
   ▶ be situated at: ~에 위치하고 있다

B

1 불규칙적이거나 왜곡되었다는 뜻의 바로크라고 적절하게 이름 붙여진 16세기 유럽의 화법은 움직임, 극적임, 행동, 그리고 강력한 감정을 포착하는 데 주로 초점을 두었다. ▶ 분사의 주어가 동작을 당하면 과거분사
2 뉴스의 공급처가 얼마 없었던 과거에는, 사람들이 표현된 그들 자신의 것과 다른 신념을 보게 될 수도 있는 주류 뉴스에 노출되거나 혹은 뉴스를 전적으로 피할 수 있었다. ▶ 분사의 주어가 동작을 당하면 과거분사

적용독해   p.151

   1 ④   2 ④

1 ④

해석 출판사에 원고를 팔려는 경쟁은 치열하다. 출판사에 보내진 자료 중 1% 미만이 출판되는 것으로 나는 추산한다. 아주 많은 자료가 작성되고 있어, 출판사는 매우 선택적일 수 있다. 그들이 출판을 위해 선택하는 자료는 상업적 가치를 지니고 있어야 한다. 자료가 잘 작성되어 있고 오류가 없을 때 출판될 가능성이 더 있다. 사실 오류를 포함하는 어떤 원고도 불신을 유발하기 때문에, 출판을 위해 받아들여질 가능성이 거의 없다. 아무리 너그럽다 할지라도, 대부분의 출판사

는 자료에 너무 많은 오류를 포함하고 있는 집필자와 시간을 낭비하려 하지 않을 것이다.

문제풀이 ④ 분사의 주어가 동작을 하면 현재분사가 쓰여야 하므로 contained를 containing으로 고쳐야 한다.
① The competition+단수 동사 ▶ p.190
② 분사의 주어가 동작을 당하면 과거분사
③ 분사의 주어가 동작을 당하면 과거분사
⑤ 「선행사+소유격 관계대명사+명사」 ▶ p.174

2 ④

해석 물에 대한 향상된 소비자 의식이 가장 많은 물을 절약하는 가장 저렴한 방법일지 모르지만, 그것이 소비자들이 물 보존에 기여할 수 있는 유일한 방법은 아니다. 기술이 이전보다 더 빠르게 진보하면서, 소비자들이 물을 더 절약하기 위해 자신의 가정에 설치할 수 있는 많은 장치들이 있다. 35개가 넘는 고효율 변기 모델이 오늘날 미국 시장에 있으며, 그것들 중 일부는 물을 내릴 때마다 1.3갤런 미만을 사용한다. 200달러에서 시작하는 이 변기들은 가격이 적당하고 일반 소비자가 일 년에 수백 갤런의 물을 절약하는데 도움이 될 수 있다. 가장 효율이 높다고 공식적으로 승인된 기기들은 소비자가 알 수 있게 Energy Star 로고가 붙어 있다. 그런 등급의 세탁기들은 40갤런을 사용하는 구형 제품에 비해, 1회 세탁 시 18에서 25갤런의 물을 사용한다. 고효율 식기 세척기는 훨씬 더 많은 물을 절약한다. 이런 기계들은 구형 모델보다 물을 50퍼센트까지 덜 사용한다.

문제풀이 ④ 분사의 주어가 동작을 당하면 과거분사가 쓰여야 하므로 approving을 approved로 고쳐야 한다.
① to부정사의 형용사적 용법 ▶ p.108
② 분사의 주어가 동작을 하면 현재분사(with+O+분사구문)
▶ p.158
③ 분사의 주어가 동작을 하면 현재분사
⑤ 분사의 주어가 동작을 당하면 과거분사

1 ⑤

해석 당신은 다른 사람들이 그들의 행동을 바꾸려고 하고 있을 때 어떻게 그들을 격려하는가? 다이어트 중이며 몸무게가 많이 줄고 있는 한 친구를 당신이 만난다고 가정해 보자. 그녀가 멋져 보이고 기분이 정말 좋겠다고 그녀에게 말하고 싶을 것이다. 누구든 긍정적인 말을 듣는 것은 기분이 좋고 이런 피드백은 종종 고무적일 것이다. 그러나 만약 당신이 거기서 대화를 끝낸다면, 당신의 친구가 받게 되는 유일한 피드백은 결과를 향한 그녀의 진전에 대한 것뿐이다. 대신, 그 대화를 계속해라. 그녀의 성공을 가능케 한 어떤 것을 하고 있는지 물어라. 그녀가 무엇을 먹고 있는가? 그녀가 어디서 운동을 하고 있는가? 그녀가 만들어 낸 생활양식의 변화는 무엇인가? 결과보다 변화의 과정에 초점을 맞출 때, 대화는 지속 가능한 과정을 만들어 내는 가치를 강화시킨다.

문제풀이 필자는 사람들이 행동을 바꾸려고 할 때 긍정적인 피드백과 함께 구체적인 변화의 과정에 초점을 맞추어야 한다고 주장하고 있다.

구문분석

[6행] Ask about [**what** she is doing {**that** has allowed her to be successful.}]
O O.C.

▶ 첫 번째 [ ]는 전치사 about의 목적어인 간접의문문으로 「의문사+S+V」의 어순으로 쓰였다. 「allow+O+O.C.」는 '~가 …하게 하다'의 의미이다. { }는 what을 선행사로 하는 주격 관계대명사절이다.

2 ③

해석 우리는 더 글로벌한 사회로 나아가고 있지만, 다양한 민족 집단들은 전통적으로 상당히 다르게 일을 하고 있어, 개방적인 아이를 만드는 데 새로운 관점이 가치가 있다. 얼마나 많은 생각을 떠올릴 수 있는지와 그 결과로 도출된 연상 능력으로 측정되는, 광범위한 다문화 경험은 아이를 더 창의적으로 만들고 아이 자신의 생각을 확장하기 위해 다른 문화로부터 관습에 얽매이지 않는 생각을 그들이 포착할 수 있게 한다. 부모로서 가능한 한 자주 자녀가 다른 문화를 접하게 해야 한다. 할 수 있다면 자녀와 다른 나라로 여행하고, 가능하면 거기서 살라. 둘 다 가능하지 않은 경우에는 지역 축제 탐방하기와 다른 문화에 대한 도서관 책 빌리기, 집에서 다른 문화의 음식 요리하기와 같이 국내에서 할 수 있는 일이 많다.

문제풀이 필자는 글로벌한 사회에서 아이를 개방적인 사고를 갖게 하려면 다른 문화를 최대한 접하게 해야 한다고 주장하고 있다.

구문분석

[4행] ... extensive multicultural experience [**makes**
S V1
kids **more creative**] and [**allows** them **to capture**
O1 O.C.1 V2 O2 O.C.2
unconventional ideas from other cultures {to expand on their own ideas}].

▶ '~를 …하게 만들다'라는 의미인 「make+O+O.C.」와 '~가 …하게 하다'의 의미인 「allow+O+O.C.」가 and로 연결된 병렬구조이다. make는 목적격 보어로 형용사를 취했고 allow는 목적격보어로 to부정사가 쓰였다. { }는 목적을 나타내는 부사적 용법의 to부정사구이다.

3 ②

해석 선생님의 지도 없이는 학생들은 협력의 가치를 인정하는 개인적 발달의 여정에 나서지 않을 것이다. 하고 싶은 대로 내버려 두면, 그들은 본능적으로 서로 점점 더 경쟁적이 될 것이다. 그들은 스포츠 경기장에서와 마찬가지로 교실 환경 내의 점수, 성적표, 피드백을 비교하지 않을 수 없을 것이다. 우리는 학생들에게 승자와 패자에 대해 가르칠 필요가 없다. 운동장과 미디어가 그들을 위해 그렇게 하는 것이다. 하지만, 우리는 그들에게 승리하는 것보다 삶에 더 많은 것이 있다는 것과 성공적인 협력을 위해 그들이 필요로 하는 기술에 대해 가르쳐 줄 필요가 있다. 성공적으로 함께 일하는 그룹은 고도의 대인 의식뿐만 아니라 다양한 사회적 기술을 가진 개인들을 필요로 한다. 일

부 학생들은 본래 이러한 기술에 대한 자연스러운 이해를 가지고 있지만, 그들은 항상 소수이다. 당신의 교실에 또래들 사이의 협력을 이루도록 하기 위해서, 당신은 의식적이고 주의 깊게 이러한 기술들을 가르쳐야 하고, 학창 시절 내내 계속해서 그것들을 육성해야 한다.

문제풀이 필자는 교사가 학생들에게 승패를 강조하기 보다는 성공적인 협력에 필요한 기술을 가르쳐야 한다고 주장하고 있다.

구문분석

[8행] **A group** [working together successfully]
S
requires individuals with a multitude of social skills,
V O1
as well as a high level of interpersonal awareness.
O2

▶ 「A as well as B」는 'B뿐만 아니라 A도'의 의미로 목적어 2개가 병렬되고 있다. [ ]는 A group을 수식하는 현재분사구이다.

STEP 1 어휘

19강 생활

PRACTICE
p.156

A	1 conceal 2 comply 3 swear
	4 modify 5 mutually
B	1 ③ 2 ① 3 ④ 4 ③ 5 ②
C	1 disappointed 2 sustained

A

1 폭탄이 쓰레기통에 숨겨져 있었다.
2 학생들은 이 지침을 엄격히 따라야만 한다.
3 나는 언젠가 복수할 것을 맹세한다.
4 우리는 상업적 생산에 맞도록 디자인을 바꿀 수 있다.
5 정중함과 진실은 종종 상호 간에 양립하기 어렵다.

B

1 노력은 성공에 필수적인 요소이다.
2 패션 디자이너들은 중세의 복장을 싫어해서 단순함을 추구했다.
3 우리는 칼슘과 단백질이 부족한 식단을 피해야 한다.
4 특정 업소에 정기적으로 방문하는 사람들은 단골손님이라 불린다.
5 행동하기 전에 항상 생각하라. 인내는 미덕이라는 것을 명심해라.

C

1 'Kuleshov' 효과에 대한 심리학적 연구들은 사회적 상황이 감정에 미치는 영향을 확증했다. 예를 들어, 만약 어떤 사람이 여러분에게 미소를 지은 다음 그 미소가 감정이 드러나지 않는 표정으로 바뀌면, 그 사람이 다소 실망한 것처럼 보일 것이다.
2 비록 도박꾼들과 사업가들이 그렇게 많은 돈을 얻을 때의 그 황홀감을 계속해서 되찾고자 갈망하지만, 갑작스런 행운이나 성공이 지속될 수 없는 현실은 그들로 하여금 우울감을 더 느끼게 하기 쉽다.

적용독해
p.157

1 ④	2 ③

1 ④

해석 사람들이 식품이 어떻게 생산되는지 의문을 가질 때, 라벨이 "정보를 얻을 수 있는" 곳이 되고 있다는 것은 놀랄 일이 아니다. Cornell University의 최근 연구는 소비자들이 특히 제품에 포함되어 있지 않은 잠재적으로 유해한 성분들에 대한 더 많은 정보를 간절히 필요로 한다는 것을 알게 되었다. 351명의 소비자를 대상으로 한 이 실험 연구는 제품 라벨에 무언가가 "들어있지 않은"이라고 쓰여 있을 때 소비자들은 더 많은 비용을 기꺼이 지불하지만, 그것은 그 식품에 "들어있지 않은" 어떤 것에 대한 "부정적인" 정보가 제공될 때에만 그렇다는 것을 발견하였다. 예를 들면, 식용 염료가 들어있지 않다고 표기된 식품은 일부 소비자들로 하여금 그 식품을 구매할 수밖에 없도록 한다. 그러나 그것과 동일한 라벨이 그러한 염료를 섭취하는 위험에 대한 정보를 배제한다면(→ 포함한다면) 훨씬 더 많은 사람들이 그 식품을 구매할 것이다. "소비자들이 성분들에 대한 더 많은 정보를 얻게 될 때, 그들은 자신의 구매 결정에 대해 더 확신하게 되고 그 식품에 더 많은 가치를 부여하게 된다"라고 Cornell 대학의 교수인 Harry M. Kaiser가 말했다.

문제풀이 사람들은 식품을 구매할 때 라벨에 부정적인 정보가 있는 식품을 선호하며 특히 성분의 위험성을 알려 주는 정보가 있다면 더욱 그러하다는 내용이므로 ④ excludes는 includes 등으로 고쳐야 한다.

구문분석

[4행] The laboratory study of 351 shoppers **found**
　　　　S　　　　　　　　　　　　　　　　　V
consumers **willing** to pay a premium when a product
　　O　　　　O.C.
label says "free of" something, ...
▶ 「find+O+O.C.」의 5형식 문장은 '~이 …하다고 알다'라는 의미로 목적어와 목적격 보어가 능동 관계이므로 목적격 보어로 현재분사가 쓰였다.

2 ③

해석 여학생들은 대개 매일 등교할 때 교복을 착용하는 것이 일상의 스트레스를 감소시킨다는 사실에 동의했다. 무엇을 입을지에 대해 걱정하지 않아도 되는 것이 매일 아침 내려야 할 결정 한 가지가 줄어드는 것을 의미했다. 그 중 많은 아이들은 또한 교복이 애교심과 결속력을 향상시킨다고 느꼈다. 그들은 같은 공동체에 속해 있는 느낌을 가질 수 있었던 것이다. 게다가 교복은 그들의 개성을 없애버렸다(→ 유지했다). 교복을 바꿀 수 있는 천 한 가지의 방법을 알기를 원한다면 교복을 입은 여학생들에게 물어보기만 하면 된다. 넥타이는 느슨히 혹은 바짝 죄어서 입을 수 있다. 치마는 여섯 가지 중 어느 방식으로든 올리거나 내릴 수 있다. 그리고 복장 규정에서는 불분명한 영역이지만 여성의 복식 분야에서는 완전한 하나의 하위 영역인 액세서리가 있다. 머리 핀, 손목시계 그리고 가방 영역에서도 수많은 선택 사항이 있다.

문제풀이 여학생들이 교복을 착용하는 것이 여러 이점이 있으며 특히 여러 선택 사항을 활용하여 자신만의 개성을 유지할 수 있다는 내용이므로 ③ eliminated는 maintained 또는 didn't eliminate 등으로 고쳐야 한다.

구문분석

[2행] [**Not** having to worry about what to wear] **meant**
　　　　　　　　　　　　　　　　　　　S　　　　　　　V
one less decision {to make every morning}.
　　　　　O　↑_____|
▶ [ ]는 동명사구 주어인데 부정어 not은 동명사 앞에 온다.
{ }에서 to make는 decision을 수식하는 형용사적 용법(~할/~하는)의 to부정사구이다.

PRACTICE
p.158

A	1 Walking	2 held	3 scared
	4 running	5 surprising	
B	1 threatening	2 dazzled	

A

1 그들은 박물관을 돌아다니며 가이드의 설명을 들었다. ▶ 부대상황(연속동작)

2 야생 오리는 꼬리를 물 위로 들고 수영한다. ▶ 「with+O+과거분사」

3 참새들은 독수리 소리를 흉내내는 기계를 무서워한다. ▶ 분사의 주어가 감정을 느끼면 과거분사

4 그녀는 눈물을 흘리면서 그곳에 서 있었다. ▶ 「with+O+현재분사」

5 음악을 잘하는 사람들이 언어도 잘한다는 사실은 놀라운 일이 아니다. ▶ 명사절 주어가 감정을 불러일으킴

B

1 보통은 외톨이인 메뚜기 떼는 그 수가 늘어남에 따라 식량 공급을 위협한다. 이것이 바로 그들이 떼를 지어 다니는 이유이다 - 새로운 장소에서 먹이를 찾기 위해서 말이다. ▶ 부대상황(연속동작)

2 우리가 21세기의 전자, 전산화 그리고 미디어의 경이에 아무리 감탄할지라도 우리 자신의 시대는 여전히 대체로 초창기 전기 혁신의 영향 아래에 있다. ▶ 분사의 주어가 감정을 느끼면 과거분사

적용독해
p.159

1 ④　　2 ⑤

1 ④

해석 미용사는 미용 잡지에서 오려낸 사진을 들고 "이것이 내가 원하는 모습이에요. 이렇게 머리를 잘라 주세요."라고 말하는 고객들을 끊임없이 맞이한다. 미용사는 그냥 머리를 자르고, 고객이 원하는 바대로 되었다고 말할 수 있다. 그러나 훌륭한 미용사는 고객이 원한다고 생각하는 것이 흔히 그녀가 진짜로 원하는 것이 아니라는 것을 알고 있다. 그 사진 속의 '모습'은 그 특정 고객에게 어울리는 '모습'이 아닌 경우가 많다. 훌륭한 미용사는 그들의 일은 자신들이 요구받은 대로 단지 완벽하게 머리를 자르는 것만이 아니라는 것을 종종 고객들에게 말한다. 물론 고객들은 그 말을 듣고 당황해 하지만 곧 고개를 끄덕인다. 훌륭한 미용사는 고객의 얼굴과 (머리의) 골격, 머릿결의 상태가 고객이 선택한 사진에서 어떻게 변화시킬지를 알고 있다는 것을 그들은 이해하게 되기 때문이다.

문제풀이 ④ 분사의 주어가 감정을 느끼면 과거분사가 와야 하므로

embarrassing을 embarrassed로 고쳐야 한다.
① 부대상황(동시동작)
② 선행사가 없으며 what 뒤에는 불완전한 절 ▶ p.174
③ ask의 목적어가 없으므로 수동태 ▶ p.60
⑤ 목적어로서 의문사절 「의문사+S+V」 ▶ p.84

2 ⑤

해석 오래된 창을 보면 종종 윗부분보다 아랫부분이 더 두꺼운데 이것이 유리가 여러 세기 동안에 걸쳐서 흘러내린다는 견해를 뒷받침하는 중요한 증거로 제출되는 경우가 많다. 그러나 대부분의 전문가들은 이런 가정을 달가워하지 않는다. 일단 굳어지면 유리는 더 이상 흐르지 않는다. 그렇게 보이는 이유는 과거에는 고르게 평평한 유리를 만드는 것이 거의 불가능했기 때문이다. 유리창을 만드는 데 사용된 기술은 용해된 유리를 빠른 속도로 회전시켜 둥글고 가급적 평평한 판유리를 만드는 것이었다. 그리고 이 판유리는 창문에 맞게 절단되었다. 그러나 그 원판의 가장자리는 유리가 회전할 때 점점 더 두꺼워졌다. 창틀에 설치될 때, 그 유리는 안정성을 위해서 두꺼운 쪽을 아래로 하여 끼워졌다.

문제풀이 ⑤ 타동사 place의 목적어가 없어 수동태 문장이 되어야 하므로 place를 be placed로 고쳐야 한다. ▶ p.60
① 동격절 접속사 that ▶ p.166
② 분사의 주어가 감정을 느끼면 과거분사
③ that절 속의 동명사 주어 ▶ p.134
④ 부대상황(연속동작)

1 ④　　2 ④　　3 ②

1 ④

해석 인생의 거의 모든 것에는, 좋은 것에도 지나침이 있을 수 있다. 심지어 인생에서 최상의 것도 지나치면 그리 좋지 않다. 이 개념은 적어도 아리스토텔레스 시대만큼 오래전부터 논의되어 왔다. 그는 미덕이 있다는 것은 균형을 찾는 것을 의미한다고 주장했다. 예를 들어, 사람들은 용감해져야 하지만, 만약 어떤 사람이 너무 용감하다면 그 사람은 무모해진다. 사람들은 (타인을) 신뢰해야 하지만, 만약 어떤 사람이 (타인을) 너무 신뢰한다면 그들은 잘 속아 넘어가는 사람으로 여겨진다. 이러한 각각의 특성에 있어, 부족과 과잉 둘 다를 피하고 행복을 극대화하는 "sweet spot"에 머무르는 것이 최상이다. 아리스토텔레스는 미덕은 너무 관대하지도 너무 인색하지도, 너무 두려워하지도 너무 무모하게 용감하지도 않은 중간 지점에 있다고 말한다.

문제풀이 좋은 것도 지나치면 좋지 않을 수 있으니 부족과 과잉을 피하는 중용의 미덕을 겸비하자는 내용이므로 정답은 ④이다.
① 편향된 결정의 시기에
② 물질적으로 풍요로운 지역에
③ 사회적 압력으로부터 멀게
④ 양극단의 중간 지점에
⑤ 일시적인 쾌락의 순간에

[7행] Aristotle's suggestion is [that virtue is the
S   V   S.C.
midpoint, {where someone is **neither** too generous
nor too stingy, **neither** too afraid **nor** recklessly
brave}].
▶ [ ]는 문장의 주격 보어 부분이다. { }는 쉼표 다음에 관계
부사 where을 써서 the midpoint에 대해 부연 설명하고 있다.
「neither A nor B」는 'A도 아니고 B도 아닌'의 의미이다.

2 ④

해석 오늘날 미국에서 사용되는 휴대전화가 7억 개가 넘고 이 휴대전
화 사용자들 중 적어도 1억 4천만 명은 새 휴대전화를 위해 14–18
개월마다 그들의 현재 휴대전화를 버릴 것이다. 나는 최신 휴대전화
를 '반드시' 가져야 하는 그런 사람들 중 한 명은 아니다. 사실 나는
배터리가 더 이상 충전이 잘 되지 않을 때까지 내 휴대전화를 사용한
다. 그때라면 때가 된 것이다. 그래서 나는 그저 교체용 배터리를 사
야겠다고 생각한다. 그러나 나는 그 배터리가 더 이상 만들어지지 않
고, 최신 휴대전화에 더 새로운 기술과 더 나은 기능들이 있기 때문
에 그 휴대전화는 더 이상 제조되지 않는다고 듣게 된다. 그것이 전형
적인 정당화이다. 그 휴대전화는 심지어 그렇게 오래되지 않았다. 아
마도 1년 좀 넘게? 나는 단지 한 사례일 뿐이다. 얼마나 수많은 다른
사람들이 이와 똑같은 시나리오를 갖는지 당신은 상상할 수 있는가?
'전자 쓰레기'에 대해서는, 휴대전화가 선두에 있다는 것은 놀랍지 않다.

문제풀이 많은 사람들이 자신의 휴대폰이 구입한지 얼마 되지 않았음
에도 최신 모델로 교체하기 때문에 전자 쓰레기가 넘쳐난다는 내용이
므로 정답은 ④이다.
① 프로그램을 업데이트하는 데 자주 어려움을 겪는다
② 비용 때문에 신기술을 이용할 수 없다
③ 많은 돈을 휴대폰 수리에 쓴다
④ 여전히 사용 가능한 휴대폰을 교체하게 된다
⑤ 새로 출시된 휴대폰 모델에 실망한다

구문분석

[1행] There are more than 700 million cell phones [**used**
in the US today] and ...
▶ [ ]는 「주격 관계대명사+be동사」인 'which are'가 생략되고
과거분사형만 남아서 cell phones를 수식하는 과거분사구이다.

3 ②

해석 우리의 집중하는 능력에 있어 가장 위험한 위협은 우리가 근무
시간 동안 스마트폰을 사용하는 것이 아니라 우리가 그것을 지나치
게 불규칙적으로 사용하는 것이다. 특별한 일정이나 규칙성을 염두에
두지 않은 채 이따금 컴퓨터로 우리의 이메일을 확인하고 우리의 전
화로 문자 메시지를 여기저기에서 확인함으로써 우리의 뇌는 효과적
으로 여과하는 그것의 능력을 잃는다. 해결책은 마치 여러분이 엄격
한 다이어트 중에 있는 것처럼 여러분의 기기를 조절하는 것이다. 영
양에 관해서라면 아침, 점심 그리고 저녁 식사를 위한 정해진 시간 계
획을 고수하는 것이 여러분의 신진대사가 적응하도록 하고 그렇게 함

으로써 중간 단계 동안 허기를 덜 유발한다. 여러분의 배는 매일 오후
12시 반쯤 우르르 울리기 시작할 것이지만 그때는 점심을 먹기에 좋
은 시간이기 때문에 괜찮다. 만약 예기치 않은 무언가가 일어난다면
여러분은 활기를 얻기 위해 이따금 간식을 추가할 수 있지만 여러분
의 신진대사는 계속 통제된 상태로 있을 것이다. 여러분이 그것(뇌)을
'미디어 다이어트' 상태로 두었을 때 우리의 뇌도 마찬가지이다.

문제풀이 전자기기의 불규칙적 사용이 우리의 집중력을 떨어뜨리므
로 사용 시간 계획을 세우고 엄격히 고수해야 한다는 내용이므로 정
답은 ②이다.
① 전통 미디어와 온라인 미디어 소비의 균형
② 미디어 장치의 사용을 정해진 일정에 맞게 조절하기
③ 미디어로부터 영양가 없는 정보를 피하기
④ 다양한 미디어 원천으로 뇌를 자극하기
⑤ 유해한 미디어 콘텐츠로부터 자신을 분리하기

구문분석

[1행] The most dangerous threat to our ability [to
S
concentrate] is [**not** {that we use our smartphone during
V
working hours,} **but** {that we use it too irregularly}].
▶ 첫 번째 [ ]는 명사 ability를 수식하는 형용사적 용법의 to부
정사구이다. 두 번째 [ ]는 'A가 아니라 B다'라는 의미의 「not A
but B」 구문이 각각의 A와 B에 that절이 쓰인 문장이다.

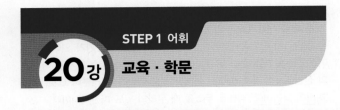

PRACTICE
p.164

A   1 tuition   2 mindful   3 summary
    4 Institute   5 discipline

B   1 ③   2 ④   3 ③   4 ②   5 ④

C   1 assigning   2 prominent

A

1 대학 학비는 연평균 약 3만 달러이다.
2 교육 당국은 그들의 책임을 염두에 두어야 한다.
3 이것이 그 학자의 강연 내용을 요점만 추려 요약한 것이다.
4 매사추세츠 공과대학은 매사추세츠주에 있다.
5 그 대학은 두 분야를 하나의 학문 분야로 통합했다.

B

1 나는 더 이상 그의 잘못을 간과할 수 없다.
2 이것이 또 일어날지를 평가하는 것은 중요하다.
3 정부의 교육 정책에 대한 반대가 커지고 있다.
4 교육자들은 평등 교육의 근본적 원리를 명심해야 한다.
5 나는 GB 이론에 대한 Chomsky의 강연을 듣고 감명받았다.

C

1 만약 목표가 학생들에게 필요한 사실로 가득 채울 정해진 교육 과정을 다루는 가장 좋은 방법을 알아내는 것이라면 추가 숙제를 부여하는 것과 같은 방식으로 과제에 들이는 시간을 최대화하려고 애쓰는 게 적절해 보일 수도 있다.
2 심리적 연습이 스포츠 훈련에서 그렇게 중요한 기술이 되는 것은 여러분이 특정한 행동을 수행할 때마다 뇌는 아주 특정한 방식으로 발화하고 여러분이 스스로 이 같은 행동을 수행하는 것을 '상상할' 때마다, 뇌는 거의 같은 방식으로 발화하기 때문이다.

적용독해
p.165

1 ③   2 ③

1 ③

해석 운동선수들은 피드백을 받기 전에 때로는 자신의 기술을 혼자서 연습하도록 허용될 필요가 있다. 그렇게 하면 그들은 무엇이 효과가 있고 무엇이 효과가 없는지를 결정할 수 있고, 그들의 강점과 약점에 더 주의를 기울일 수 있게 된다. 운동선수들이 혼자서 훈련하기를 선호할 때 도움을 주려고 시도한다면 여러분은 많은 시간과 말을 낭비하게 될지도 모른다. 운동선수들은 자신들이 최선을 다한 노력이 만족할 만한(→ 불만족스러운) 성과를 내고 있음을 깨달을 때, 대개 여러분이 말하고자 하는 것을 듣고자 하는 동기를 더 많이 부여받는다. 다시 말하면, 운동선수들은 그들이 바라는 성과를 달성하지 못할 때, 도움에 반응을 보인다. 그렇다면 코치에게 어려운 것은 이러한 그리고 다른 종류의 가르칠만한 순간이 생길 때까지 참고 기다리는 것이다. 그러한 인내심에 대한 보상은 여러분이 말하고자 하는 것을 듣고자 하는 동기부여가 되어있고 여러분의 조언을 받아들일 의욕을 보이는 선수들이다.

문제풀이 운동선수들이 코치의 피드백을 받기 전에 혼자서 연습하는 시간을 가진 후 자신의 성과가 불만족스러우면 코치의 도움을 받고 싶은 동기 부여가 되므로 코치는 그때까지 인내하라는 내용이므로 ③ satisfactory는 unsatisfactory 등으로 고쳐야 한다.

구문분석

[5행] When athletes realize [**that** their best efforts are producing unsatisfactory outcomes], they are usually more motivated to hear [**what** you have to say.]
▶ 첫 번째 [ ]는 접속사 that이 realize의 목적어인 명사절을 이끌고 있고 두 번째 [ ]는 선행사를 포함하는 관계대명사 what절이 쓰여 '~하는 것을'이라고 해석한다. to hear은 목적을 나타내는 부사적 용법의 to부정사이다.

2 ③

해석 1970년대에 학생들이 휴대용 계산기를 사용하도록 학교가 허락하기 시작했을 때, 많은 학부모들이 반대했다. 그들은 기계에 대한 의존성이 자녀들의 수학적 개념에 대한 이해력을 약화시킬 것이라고 걱정했다. 그런 우려가 대체로 불필요한 것이었음을 후속 연구가 보여 주었다. 더 이상 상례적인 계산에 많은 시간을 소모하지 않게 되어서, 많은 학생들은 그들의 연습 문제에 기초가 되는 원리에 대해 더 깊이 이해하게 되었다. 오늘날, 계산기에 관한 그 이야기는 온라인 데이터베이스에 대한 의존성 증가가 해가 되는(→ 도움이 되는) 것이라는 주장을 뒷받침하기 위해 종종 사용된다. 인터넷은 기억하는 일로부터 우리를 자유롭게 해서 우리가 창조적인 생각에 더 많은 시간을 바치도록 해준다고들 한다. 휴대용 계산기는 우리의 작동 기억에 대한 부담을 덜어주었고, 우리가 그 중요한 단기 저장소를 더 추상적인 추론을 위해 사용하도록 해주었다. 강력하지만 매우 전문화된 도구인 계산기는 우리의 작동 기억에 보조 도구라는 것이 판명되었다.

문제풀이 통념과는 달리 기계 장치는 우리가 창조적인 생각에 더 많은 시간을 들이도록 하는 데 도움이 된다는 내용이므로 ③ disadvantageous는 beneficial, advantageous 등으로 고쳐야 한다.

구문분석

[9행] The pocket calculator relieved the pressure on our working memory, [**letting** us **use** that critical short-term store for more abstract reasoning]
▶ [ ]는 〈부대상황〉을 나타내는 분사구문으로 주어 the pocket

calculator와 능동의 관계에 있으므로 현재분사형을 쓴다.
「let+O+O.C.」는 '~을 …하게 하다'라는 5형식 문장이며 let은
목적격 보어로 동사원형을 취한다.

PRACTICE
p.166

A　1 it　2 What　3 that
　　　4 those　5 that
B　1 that　2 that

A

1 그것이 아무리 어려울지라도 최고가 되기 위해 무엇이든 할 것이
다. ▶ it = whatever ~ best
2 중요한 것은 가능한 한 독서를 많이 해야 한다는 것이다. ▶ 선행
사가 없으며 what 뒤에 주어가 없는 불완전한 절
3 한 가지 특이한 점은 이 물고기가 인어처럼 헤엄친다는 사실이다.
▶ 동격절의 접속사는 that
4 그가 부인하고 있지만, 그의 경기 실력은 아마추어 실력 이상이다.
▶ those = skills
5 그 책은 아주 쉬운 언어로 쓰여 있어서 우리는 쉽게 저자의 뜻을
알 수 있다. ▶ 접속사 that+완전한 절

B

1 CBC News 기자인 Kelly Crowe는 한 전염병학자의 말을 인용
하며 "현대 연구에서 잘못된 결과는 게재된 연구 주장의 다수 또
는 심지어 대다수일 수도 있다는 증가하는 염려가 있다."라고 쓰고
있다. ▶ 동격절의 접속사는 that
2 세계 최초의 복잡한 쓰기 형태인 수메르 설형 문자는 기원전
3,500년경에 그림 문자에서 표의 문자적 표현으로, 즉 사물의 묘
사에서 추상적 개념의 그것(묘사)으로 나아가며 진화적 경로를 따
라갔다. ▶ that = depiction

적용독해
p.167

1 ④　2 ③

1 ④

해석 비록 음식에 대한 우리 평가의 일부가 음식의 시각적 외관인 것
은 분명하지만, 어떻게 시각적인 입력 정보가 맛과 냄새에 우선할 수
있는가는 놀라울 것이다. 만약 예를 들어 초록색 빛깔의 오렌지 음
료와 같이 색깔이 잘못되어 있다면, 사람들은 과일 맛이 나는 음료
를 정확하게 식별하는 것이 매우 어렵다는 것을 알게 된다. 포도주 맛

을 감정하는 사람들의 경험은 훨씬 더 놀라울 것이다. 포도주와 포도
주 제조에 관해 공부하는 Bordeaux University 학생들을 대상으로
한 연구는 그들이 붉은색 색소로 물들인 백포도주를 받았을 때, '자두
와 초콜릿'과 같은 적포도주에 적합한 시음표를 선택했다는 것을 보
여 주었다. 숙련된 뉴질랜드 포도주 전문가들도 마찬가지로 백포도주
Chardonnay를 붉은색 색소로 물들였을 때, 속아서 그것이 실제로
적포도주라고 생각하게 되었다.

문제풀이 ④ reveal의 목적어를 이끄는 명사절의 접속사를 찾는 문제
로 접속사 뒤에 완전한 절이 오므로 what을 that으로 고쳐야 한다.
① 가주어-진주어(how) 구문의 가주어
② 가목적어-진목적어 구문의 가목적어
③ 「선행사+주격 관계대명사+불완전한 절」 ▶ p.174
⑤ 단수 대명사 it(= the white wine)

2 ③

해석 지적 겸손이란 여러분이 인간이고 여러분이 가진 지식에 한계가
있다는 것을 인정하는 것이다. 여러분이 인지적이고 개인적인 편견을
가지고 있고, 여러분의 두뇌가 자신의 의견과 관점이 다른 것보다 선
호되는 방식으로 사물을 바라보는 경향이 있다고 인정하는 것을 포함
한다. 이것은 더 객관적이고 정보에 근거한 결정들을 내리기 위해 그
러한 편견들을 극복하고자 기꺼이 노력하는 것이다. 지적 겸손을 보
이는 사람들은 자신이 생각하는 것과 다르게 생각하는 다른 사람들
에게 배우는 것이 도움이 된다는 믿음에 더 수용적일 것이다. 그들은
다른 사람들이 제시하는 것을 존중한다는 것을 분명히 하기 때문에
다른 사람들에게 호감을 사고 존경받는 경향이 있다. 더 많은 것을 배
우고 싶어 하고 다양한 출처로부터 정보를 찾는 것에 개방적인 사람
들은 지적으로 겸손한 사람들이다. 그들은 다른 사람들보다 우월하게
보이거나 느끼려고 애쓰는 데 관심이 없다.

문제풀이 ③ 동격절의 접속사이므로 which를 that으로 고쳐야 한다.
① 「명사절 접속사 that+완전한 절」
② 단수 대명사 it (= intellectual humility)
④ 가목적어-진목적어 구문
⑤ it ~ that 강조구문 ▶ p.230

1 ①　2 ②　3 ⑤

1 ①

해석 목표 지향적인 사고방식은 "요요" 효과를 낼 수 있다. 많은 달리
기 선수들이 몇 달 동안 열심히 연습하지만, 결승선을 통과하는 순간
훈련을 중단한다. 그 경기는 더 이상 그들에게 동기를 주지 않는다.
당신이 애쓰는 모든 일이 특정한 목표에 집중될 때, 당신이 그것을 성
취한 후에 당신을 앞으로 밀고 나갈 수 있는 것은 무엇인가? 이것이
많은 사람들이 목표를 성취한 후 옛 습관으로 되돌아가는 자신을 발
견하는 이유다. 목표를 설정하는 목적이 시스템을 구축하는 그것과
비슷하지만, 두 가지 모두 보다 효과적으로 게임을 할 수 있도록 도와
준다는 점에서 두 가지 사이에는 핵심적인 차이가 있다. 진정한 장기

적 사고는 목표 지향적이지 않은 사고이다. 그것은 어떤 하나의 성취에 관한 것이 아니다. 그것은 끝없는 정제와 지속적인 개선의 순환에 관한 것이다. 궁극적으로, 당신의 발전을 결정짓는 것은 그 과정에 당신이 전념하는 것이다.

문제풀이 진정한 장기적인 사고는 지속적인 정제와 개선의 과정이므로 이 과정에 전념하는 것이 발전을 결정짓는다 내용이므로 ①이 정답이다.

구문분석

> [9행] Ultimately, **it is** <u>your commitment to the process</u> _S **that** <u>will determine</u> <u>your progress</u>.
> _V _O
> ▶ it is ~ that 강조구문으로 문장의 주어인 your commitment to the process를 강조하고 있다.

2 ②

해석 학습자들은 복잡한 발달적, 인지적, 신체적, 사회적, 그리고 문화적 체계 안에서 기능한다. 다양한 분야에서의 연구와 이론은 모든 학습자들이 문화적으로 한정된 맥락 안에서 문화적으로 한정된 방식으로 성장하고 배운다는 점에 대한 이해를 점차 발전시키는 데 기여해 왔다. 인간은 가족과의 관계, 나이와 관련된 단계, 그리고 더 많은 것들과 같은 기본적인 경험뿐만 아니라 기본적인 뇌 구조와 처리 과정을 공유하지만, 각각의 이러한 현상은 개인의 정확한 경험에 의해 형성된다. 학습은 문화적 영향이 인생의 시작부터 영향력이 있기 때문에 모든 사람들에게 똑같은 방식으로 일어나지는 않는다. 학습과 문화의 뒤얽힘에 관한 이러한 생각은 학습과 발달의 많은 측면에 대한 연구에 의해 지지되어 왔다.

문제풀이 학습과 발달은 개개인이 경험하는 한정된 문화적 맥락 안에서 한정된 방식으로 영향을 받는다는 내용이므로 정답은 ②이다.

구문분석

> [8행] **These ideas** [about the intertwining of learning _S and culture] <u>have been supported</u> by research on many _V aspects of learning and development.
> ▶ [ ]는 핵심 주어 these ideas를 수식하는 전치사구이며 핵심 주어는 복수(ideas)이므로 동사는 복수 동사(have)가 되어야 한다.

3 ⑤

해석 학생이 미래에 더 많은 노력을 기울이게 하고 싶은 바람에서 낮은 등급이나 점수로 학생을 벌주려고 하기보다는, 그들의 과제가 미완성이라고 여기고 추가적인 노력을 요구함으로써 교사는 학생에게 동기 부여를 더 잘할 수 있다. Ohio주 Beachwood의 Beachwood 중학교 교사는 학생의 등급을 *A*, *B*, *C* 또는 *I* (미완성)로 기록한다. *I* 등급을 받은 학생은 자신의 과제 수행을 수용 가능한 (기준에 맞는) 수준까지 끌어올리기 위해서 추가적인 과제를 하도록 요구받는다. 이런 방침은 학생이 낙제 수준으로 수행하거나 낙제 과제를 제출하는 것이 대체로 교사가 그것을 받아들이기 때문이라는 믿음에 근거한다. Beachwood의 교사는 만약 그들이 더 이상 기준 이하의 과제를 받아들이지 않는다면, 학생이 그것을 제출하지 않을 것

이라고 생각한다. 그리고 학생들은 적절한 도움을 받아서 자신의 과제 수행이 만족스러울 때까지 계속 노력할 것이라고 그들은 믿는다.

문제풀이 교사가 학생에게 동기를 부여하는 방법 중의 하나는 처벌보다는 추가적인 노력을 할 기회를 주면 된다는 내용이므로 ⑤가 정답임을 알 수 있다.

구문분석

> [6행] This policy is based on the belief [that students
> <u>perform</u> at a failure level or <u>submit</u> failing work in
> _{V1´} _{V2´}
> large part {because teachers accept it}].
> ▶ [ ]는 the belief와 동격으로 명사절의 접속사 that이 이끌고 있다. that절 속에 주어는 students로 동사 2개가 등위접속사 or로 병렬되고 있다. { }는 이유의 부사절이다.

PRACTICE
p.172

A 1 uncertain 2 religious 3 linguistic
　　4 peculiar 5 prevalent
B 1 ④ 2 ② 3 ① 4 ③ 5 ④
C 1 applies 2 sustainability

A

1 나는 그가 의미하는 바를 <u>정확히</u> 알지 못했다.
2 나는 그처럼 <u>종교적</u> 신념이 투철한 사람을 만난 적이 없다.
3 Dr. Lee는 어린 아이들의 <u>언어</u> 발달에 관심이 있다.
4 그녀의 목소리에 다소 <u>이상한</u> 점이 있었다.
5 코로나가 올해 유럽에서 <u>유행했다</u>.

B

1 나는 그녀의 침묵을 화난 것으로 <u>해석했다</u>.
2 그 소설은 비극적인 역사적 사건을 <u>바탕으로 하고</u> 있다.
3 수술을 했을 때의 이점이 안 했을 때의 위험을 훨씬 <u>능가한다</u>.
4 철학자들은 모든 것을 서구적 <u>관점에서</u> 보지 않도록 노력해야 한다.
5 우리는 한국 문화에 대한 연구를 10가지 사례로 <u>한정했다</u>.

C

1 우리가 정치적 리스크라고 부르는 것의 많은 부분은 사실 불확실성
　인데, 이것은 내란에서부터 세금 포탈, 규제상의 변화에 이르기까지
　모든 유형의 정치적 리스크에 <u>적용된다</u>.
2 비록 인구가 줄어들더라도 반드시 유지되어야만 하는 도시의 특성
　으로는 생산성과 다양성인데, 이는 <u>지속 가능성</u>의 두 가지 핵심 요
　소이기 때문이다.

적용독해
p.173

1 ③　　2 ④

1 ③

해석 인류 역사의 시작부터, 사람들은 세상과 그 세상 속에 있는 그들의 장소에 관하여 질문해 왔다. 초기 사회에 있어, 가장 기초적 의문에 대한 대답은 종교에서 발견되었다. 그러나 몇몇 사람들은 그 전통적인 종교적 설명이 충분하지 않다는 것을 알게 되었고, 이성에 근거하여 답을 찾기 시작하였다. 이러한 일관성(→ 변화)은 철학의 탄생을 보여 주었고, 우리가 아는 위대한 사상가들 중 첫 번째 사람은 Miletus의 Thales였다. 그는 우주의 본질을 탐구하기 위해 이성을

사용하였고, 다른 사람들도 이와 같이 하도록 권장하였다. 그는 자신의 추종자들에게 자신의 대답뿐만 아니라 어떤 종류의 설명이 만족스러운 것으로 여겨질 수 있는가에 대한 생각과 함께 이성적으로 생각하는 과정도 전했다.

문제풀이 의문의 대답을 종교에서 찾던 방식이 이성에서 찾는 방식으로 바뀌었고 Thales를 예로 들고 있으므로 ③ consistency는 shift 등으로 고쳐야 한다.

구문분석

> [6행] He <u>used</u> <u>reason</u> [to inquire into the nature of the
> 　　　　　V1　　O
> universe], and **encouraged** others **to do** likewise.
> 　　　　　　　　　　V2　　　O　　　O.C.
> ▶ [ ]는 목적의 부사적 용법의 to부정사구이다. 「encourage
> +O+O.C.」는 '~가 …하도록 장려하다'의 의미로 encourage
> 는 목적격 보어로 to부정사를 취한다. do는 앞에 나오는 'inquire
> into the nature of the universe'를 의미하는 대동사이다.

2 ④

해석 고대 이집트와 메소포타미아 사람들은 서구 사회의 철학적 선조였다. 세계에 대한 그들의 개념에서, 자연이 삶의 투쟁 안에서 적은 아니었다. 오히려, 인간과 자연은 같은 처지에 있는, 같은 이야기 속에 있는 동반자였다. 인간은 자신 그리고 다른 사람들을 생각하는 것과 같은 방식으로 자연 세계를 생각했다. 자연 세계는 인간들처럼 생각, 욕구 그리고 감정을 가지고 있었다. 그러므로 인간과 자연의 영역은 구분이 불분명했으며 인지적으로 다른 방식으로 이해될 필요는 없었다. 자연 현상들은 인간 경험과 똑같은 방식으로 상상되었다. 이러한 근동 지역의 고대인들은 인과 관계를 <u>무시(→ 인식)</u>하고는 있었지만, 그것에 대해서 숙고할 때에는 '무엇'의 관점보다는 '누구'의 관점에서 접근했다. 나일강이 불어났을 때, 그것은 그 강이 원했기 때문이지 비가 왔기 때문은 아니었다.

문제풀이 인간과 자연을 명확히 구분하지 않고 인과 관계를 '누구'의 관점에서 접근했던 고대 이집트와 메소포타미아인들의 사고방식이 서구 철학에 영향을 미쳤다는 내용이므로 ④ neglect는 recognize 등으로 고쳐야 한다.

구문분석

> [4행] Man **thought of** the natural world in the same
> terms **as** he thought of himself and other men.
> ▶ 「think of A as B」구문이며 'A를 B라 생각하다'의 의미이다.

STEP 2 어법 관계대명사

PRACTICE
p.174

A 1 who 2 whose 3 which
　　4 that 5 what
B 1 what 2 in which

A

1 자신의 성공을 확신했던 비만인들이 회의론자들보다 10킬로그램을 더 감량했다. ▶ 「선행사+주격 관계대명사+동사」

2 열심히 일한 사람의 손이었던 Kate는 자신이 원했던 것을 얻었다. ▶ 「선행사+소유격 관계대명사+명사」

3 적절한 수분을 유지한다는 것은 청소년들의 인지 기능을 높여 줄 수 있으며, 이것은 학습에 중요하다. ▶ comma 뒤에 관계대명사 that은 틀림

4 성공을 향한 길이 험난할 것이라고 믿는 것은 더 커다란 성공으로 이어진다. ▶ 「명사절 접속사+완전한 절」

5 선생님은 학생들에게 그들의 미래가 어떨지를 물었다. ▶ 4형식 문장: 「S+V+I.O.(his students)+D.O.(선행사가 없으며 what 뒤에 불완전한 절)」

B

1 감정이 지적 행동에 지극히 중요하고 감정을 지니는 것의 이점이 단점을 능가한다고 주장하는 것은 Dylan Evans가 '감정에 대한 긍정적인 관점'이라고 부르는 것을 받아들이는 것을 의미한다. ▶ 선행사가 없으며 what 뒤에 목적어가 없는 불완전한 절

2 Herodotus는 기원전 600년경 고대 이집트 왕 Necho 2세에 의해 탐험 항해에 대해 기록하도록 의뢰를 받았는데, 페니키아 원정대에게 홍해에서 출발해 나일강 하구로 돌아오도록 아프리카 주위를 시계 방향으로 항해하라고 명령했다고 한다. ▶ 「선행사+전치사+관계대명사+완전한 절」

적용독해
p.175

1 ⑤ **2** ④

---

1 ⑤

해석 모호한 용어란 하나 이상의 의미를 가지고 있으면서 어떤 의미가 의도되었는지를 그 문맥이 명확하게 보여 주지 못하는 용어이다. 예를 들어, 어떤 산길에 난 갈림길에 세워진 "Bear To The Right"이라는 문구의 표지판은 두 가지 방식으로 이해될 수 있다. 좀 더 가능성 있어 보이는 의미는 그 표지판이 등산객들에게 왼쪽 말고 오른쪽 길로 가라고 알려주고 있다는 것이다. 그러나 그 표지판을 만든 삼림 관리인이 정반대로 말하려 했다고 가정해 보자. 그는 등산객들에게 그 길이 통과하는 지역에 곰이 한 마리 있기 때문에 오른쪽 길로 가지 말라고 경고하고 있던 것이다. 따라서 그 삼림 관리인의 표현은 부주의하였고, 심각한 결과를 가져올 수도 있었던 오역의 가능성도 열려 있었다. 언어적 모호함을 피하는 유일한 길은 가능한 한 명백하게 자세히 설명하는 것이다. "왼쪽으로 가시오. 오른쪽 길로는 가지 마시오. 곰이 있는 지역입니다."

문제풀이 ⑤ 선행사가 있으며 주격 관계대명사 뒤에 불완전한 절이 이어지므로 what을 that이나 which로 고쳐야 한다.
① 「선행사+소유격 관계대명사+명사」
② 「선행사+주격 관계대명사+불완전한 절」
③ 「선행사+주격 관계대명사+불완전한 절」
④ 「선행사+전치사+관계대명사+완전한 절」

---

2 ④

해석 언어는 인간을 다른 동물과 구분하는 주요한 특징 중 하나이다. 돌고래, 고래, 그리고 새를 포함한 많은 동물들이 소리, 냄새, 그리고 다른 화학물질의 패턴이 있는 체계, 또는 움직임을 통해 실제로 서로 의사소통을 한다. 게다가, 인간이 아닌 어떤 영장류는 인간과 의사소통을 하기 위해 손짓을 사용하도록 가르침을 받아왔다. 하지만 인간 언어의 복잡성, 미묘한 차이가 있는 감정과 생각을 전달하는 그것의 능력, 그리고 사회적 동물로서 우리의 존재에 있어서의 그것의 중요성은 그것을 다른 동물들이 사용하는 의사소통 체계와 구분 짓는다. 여러 가지 면에서 언어는 문화의 본질이다. 그것은 다른 문화 집단들이 구별되게 하는 단 하나의 가장 보편적인 변인을 제공한다. 언어는 혁신의 문화적 확산을 촉진할 뿐 아니라, 그것은 또한 우리가 환경에 대하여 생각하고, 인지하고, 이름을 붙이는 방식을 형성하도록 돕는다.

문제풀이 ④ 선행사가 있으며 완전한 절이 이어지므로 what을 「전치사+관계대명사(by which)」로 고쳐야 한다. ▶ p.182
① 「선행사+주격 관계대명사+불완전한 절」
② 타동사 teach의 목적어가 없으므로 수동태 ▶ p.60
③ 「선행사+주격 관계대명사+불완전한 절」
⑤ the way와 how는 같이 쓸 수 없음 ▶ p.182

STEP 3 유형 글의 주제
p.176~177

1 ② **2** ① **3** ⑤

---

1 ②

해석 인간뿐만 아니라 동물도 놀이 활동에 참여한다. 동물에게 있어 놀이는 오랫동안 미래 생존에 필요한 기술과 행동을 학습하고 연마하는 방식으로 여겨져 왔다. 아이들에게 있어서도 놀이는 발달하는 동안 중요한 기능을 한다. 유아기의 가장 초기부터, 놀이는 아이들이 세상과 그 안에서의 그들의 위치에 대해 배우는 방식이다. 아이들의 놀이는 신체능력 — 매일의 삶에 필요한 걷기, 달리기, 그리고 점프하기와 같은 기술을 발달시키기 위한 훈련의 토대로서 역할을 한다. 놀이는 또한 아이들이 사회적 행동을 시도하고 배우며, 성인기에 중요할 가치와 성격적 특성을 습득하도록 한다. 예를 들어, 그들은 다른 사람들과 경쟁하고 협력하는 방식, 이끌고 따르는 방식, 결정하는 방식 등을 배운다.

문제풀이 놀이는 아이들이 신체 능력, 사회화, 그리고 성인기에 필요한 가치를 배우는 활동이라는 내용이므로 ②가 정답임을 알 수 있다.
① 창의적인 아이디어를 시도할 필요성
② 아동의 발달에 있어 놀이의 역할
③ 인간의 놀이와 동물의 놀이 간의 비교
④ 아동의 신체 활동이 놀이에 미치는 영향
⑤ 다양한 발달 단계에 따른 아동의 욕구

구문분석

> [3행] [From its earliest beginnings in infancy], play is **a way** [in which children learn about the world and their place in it.]

▶ 첫 번째 [ ]는 전치사 From의 부사구이며, 두 번째 [ ]는 선행사가 a way인 관계부사절로 선행사가 a way이고 완전한 절이 이어지므로 in which가 쓰였다.

2 ①

해석 채식은 점점 더 많은 젊은이들이 고기, 가금류, 생선에 반대함에 따라 주류가 되어가고 있다. American Dietetic Association에 따르면, 대략적으로 계획된 채식 식단이 건강에 좋고, 영양학적으로도 적당하고, 특정한 질병을 예방하고 치료하는 데 건강상의 이점을 제공한다. 그러나 건강에 대한 염려들이 젊은이들이 그들의 식단을 바꾸려고 하는 유일한 이유는 아니다. 몇몇은 동물의 권리에 대한 관심 때문에 선택한다. 음식으로 길러지는 대다수의 동물들이 갇혀서 산다는 것을 보여 주는 통계 자료를 볼 때, 그러한 상황에 저항하는 많은 십 대들은 고기를 포기한다. 다른 이들은 환경을 지지하기 위해 채식주의자가 된다. 고기를 생산하는 것은 거대한 양의 물, 땅, 곡식과 에너지를 사용하고 가축에서 나오는 쓰레기와 그에 따른 오염과 같은 문제들을 만들어 낸다.

문제풀이 채식 식단이 확산되는 여러 이유를 설명하는 내용이므로 ① 이 정답이다.
① 젊은 세대가 채식 식단을 선호하는 이유
② 십 대가 건강한 식습관을 형성할 수 있는 방법
③ 암의 위험을 낮춰 주는 채소들
④ 균형 있는 식단을 유지하는 것의 중요성
⑤ 채식 식단의 단점

구문분석

[6행] When faced with the statistics [that show {(that) the majority of animals raised as food live in confinement}], many teens [who protest those conditions] give up meat.

▶ 첫 번째 [ ]는 선행사 the statistics를 수식하는 주격 관계대명사절이고, { }는 동사 show의 목적절로 명사절의 접속사 that이 생략되어 있다. 두 번째 [ ]는 주어 many teens를 수식하는 주격 관계대명사절이다.

3 ⑤

해석 웃음의 능력은 인간의 독특한 특징이라고 오랫동안 여겨져 왔다. (기원후 2세기) Samosata의 재치 있는 Lucian이 인간을 당나귀와 구별하는 방법으로 한쪽은 웃고 다른 한쪽은 그렇지 않다는 것을 지적했다. 모든 사회에서 유머는 규범을 강화하고 행동을 규제하면서, 개인적인 의사소통에서 뿐만 아니라 사회적 그룹들을 형성하는 힘으로서도 중요하다. "그 당시에 널리 퍼져있는 주된 사고, 관심사, 흥미, 활동, 관계, 그리고 방식 때문에 각각 특정한 시간, 각각의 시대, 사실상 각각의 순간은 웃음에 대한 그 자체의 조건과 주제를 가지고 있다." 고대 그리스와 같은 다른 문화를 연구하는 누군가의 궁극적인 목표는 유물들, 역사적 사건들, 혹은 사회적 집단화의 총합계 이상이었던 사람들 그 자체를 이해하는 것이다. 이 목표에 직접적으로 접근하는 한 가지 방법은 그 문화의 유머를 연구하는 것이다. Goethe가

적절하게 언급한 대로 "그들이 무엇을 웃기다고 생각하는지 만큼 사람의 특성을 명확히 보여 주는 것도 없다."

문제풀이 유머는 특정 사회의 주된 사고방식, 관계, 활동 등 모든 영역의 총합이므로 사람들 그 자체를 이해하기 위해서는 그들이 속한 문화의 유머를 살펴봐야 한다는 내용이므로 ⑤가 정답임을 알 수 있다.
① 문화 동화의 전형적인 과정
② 우정을 맺는 데 있어 웃음의 기능
③ 다문화 능력의 교육적 필요성
④ 사회 문제를 비판하는 데 있어 유머의 역할
⑤ 문화를 이해할 수 있는 도구로서의 유머

구문분석

[2행] ... noted that the way to **distinguish** a man **from** a donkey is [that one laughs and the other does not.]
= a man   = a donkey

▶ 「distinguish A from B」는 'A를 B와 구별하다'의 의미이다. to distinguish는 명사 way를 수식하는 형용사적 용법의 to부정사이다. [ ]는 that이 이끄는 주격 보어절이다. the other does not 뒤에는 laugh가 생략되었다.

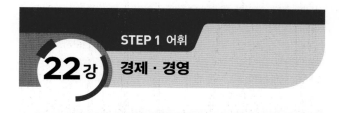

STEP 1 어휘

22강 경제 · 경영

PRACTICE   p.180

A	1 recruit	2 prompt	3 liberate
	4 engage	5 specialize	
B	1 ②	2 ③	3 ④	4 ②	5 ③
C	1 acquiring	2 succeeded	

A

1 기업들은 자격을 갖춘 직원들을 채용하는 데 어려움을 겪고 있다.
2 호기심은 그녀가 몇 가지 질문을 하도록 촉진시켰다.
3 중국 여인들은 전족이라는 악습으로부터 해방되었다.
4 우리를 대신해서 협상할 변호사를 고용할 필요가 있다.
5 그녀는 아이비리그 대학에서 경영학을 전공했다.

B

1 신사, 숙녀 여러분, 공화당 시장 후보를 소개해 드리겠습니다.
2 전국적으로 비용을 줄이기 위해 농촌 학교 중 일부가 통합되고 있다.
3 모든 주는 빠짐없이 사이버 범죄 대응 전략을 수립해야 한다.
4 이 영화는 할리우드와 발리우드 영화제작사들이 함께 제작한 합작품이다.

5 18세기 영국에서 시작된 <u>산업혁명</u>은 전 세계에 많은 변화를 가져다주었다.

C

1 Regions Financial Corporation은 1,500개가 넘는 지사의 네트워크에서 고객들에게 소매 및 상업 은행업, 신탁, 담보 대출, 그리고 보험 상품을 제공하며, 이를 통해 그 회사는 그것의 현재 고객들의 금융적 요구를 더 완벽히 충족시키려고 노력하며, 그것에 의해 각 고객의 금융 거래에서 더 큰 점유율을 획득한다.

2 '체제 정당화 이론'이라 불리는 사회 심리학의 한 분야는 만약 사람들이 그러한 체제의 결과로 성공했다면 어떻게 그들이 사회적, 경제적, 정치적 체제들을 좋고, 공정하며, 옳은 것으로 여기는 경향이 있는지를 설명한다.

적용독해
p.181

1 ④   2 ⑤

1 ④

해석 오늘날 시장에서 선택 항목의 과잉은 당신에게 더 많은 선택의 자유를 준다. 그러나 행복의 관점에서 치러야 할 대가가 있을지도 모른다. 심리학자 David Myers와 Robert Lane의 연구에 따르면 모든 이러한 선택은 자주 사람들을 우울하게 만든다. 연구자들이 어떤 쇼핑객들에게는 24개의 잼을 맛보게 했고 다른 사람들에게는 오직 6개만 맛보게 했다. 더 적은 선택 항목을 가진 사람들이 맛볼 때 더 행복했다. 훨씬 더 놀랍게도, 더 넓은 범위의 선택 사항을 가진 사람들 중 오직 그 당시 3%만이 잼을 구매한 반면, 더 적은 선택 사항을 가진 사람들 중에서는 그 당시 31%가 잼을 구매했다. 아이러니한 점은 사람들이 거의 항상 더 많은 선택 항목을 원한다고 말한다는 것이다. 그러나 그들이 더 많은 선택 항목을 가질수록 그들은 더 안도한다(→ 마비된다). 사리에 밝은 레스토랑 사장들은 더 적은 선택 항목을 제공한다. 이것은 고객들이 더 편안함을 느끼게 하고, 그들이 쉽게 선택하여 그 선택에 더 만족하도록 촉진한다.

문제풀이 사람들은 선택 항목이 많을수록 좋다고 말하지만 실제로는 의사 결정과 행복이라는 측면에서 그렇지 않다는 내용이므로 ④ relieved는 paralyzed 등으로 고쳐야 한다.

구문분석

> [10행] This **allows** customers **to feel** more relaxed, [**prompting** them **to choose** easily and (to) **leave** more satisfied with their choices.]
> ▶「allow+O+O.C.(to부정사)」 구문은 '~가 …하게 하다'의 의미이고 「prompt+O+O.C.(to부정사)」 구문은 '~가 …하게 촉진하다'라는 의미로 allow와 prompt는 목적격 보어로 to부정사를 취한다. [ ]는 연속 동작을 의미하는 분사구문인데 prompt의 목적격 보어가 to choose와 (to) leave가 접속사 and에 병렬 연결되었다.

2 ⑤

해석 1973년 환율 자율화 이후에 금융 시장들은 점점 변동성이 심해져 왔고 당국은 그에 대한 통제력을 상실해 온 것처럼 보인다. 그 결과로 이자율과 환율은 현재 어느 때보다 빠르게 요동치고 있다. 동시에, 무역 장벽의 완화와 증가하는 국제 경쟁으로 회사들의 이윤은 줄어들고 있다. 그 결과 전 세계 회사들은 그들의 재정 위기를 받아들이고 해결하는 법을 배워야 하는 상황에 처해 왔다. 관리자들은 더 이상 이 상황을 모른 척 외면할 수 없고, 그들의 회사가 차를 생산하거나 비누가루를 팔기 때문에 올해의 차에 대해 걱정하거나 새로운 세제가 브랜드 X보다 더 하얗게 세탁하는지에 대해서만 걱정할 필요가 있다는 태도는 취할 수 없다. 많은 회사들이 이자율, 통화, 상품 위기를 인정하는(→ 무시하는) 것이 새로운 상품의 실패만큼이나 그들의 회사에 타격을 줄 수 있다는 것을 대가를 치르고 나서야 알게 되었다.

문제풀이 환율 자율화로 인한 요동치는 이자율, 완화된 무역 장벽, 그리고 심화된 국제 경쟁이 기업들의 재정 위기를 초래하였으며 이러한 위기를 무시하면 회사에 큰 타격이 된다는 내용이므로 ⑤ acknowledging은 disregarding 등으로 고쳐야 한다.

구문분석

> [6행] No longer **can** managers **stick** their heads in the sand and **pretend** [that because their firms make cars, or sell soap powders, they need only worry about this year's car or whether their new detergent washes whiter than Brand X.]
> ▶ 부정어구인 no longer가 문두에 나와 「부정어구+조동사+S+V」의 어순으로 도치되었다. 본동사는 stick과 pretend가 접속사 and로 병렬 연결되었다. [ ]는 pretend의 목적어절이다.

STEP 2 어법 관계부사

PRACTICE
p.182

A　**1** where　**2** where　**3** which
　　　4 when　**5** that

B　**1** in which　**2** when

A

1 그녀는 무지개를 볼 수 있는 창으로 딸을 따라갔다. ▶「선행사+관계부사+완전한 절」

2 일부 다람쥐는 땅이 부드럽고 파기 쉬운 서식지를 선호한다.
▶「선행사+관계부사+완전한 절」: habitats where the earth is soft and easy to dig in = habitats where it is soft and easy to dig in the earth

3 '위험을 감수하는' 습성을 지닌 개미 군락은 기후가 더 추운 북쪽에서 훨씬 더 흔하다. ▶「선행사+관계대명사+불완전한 절」

4 전자책을 읽은 비율은 2013년에는 두 배로 증가했는데, 그때 '해리 포터' 시리즈가 출간되었다. ▶「선행사＋관계부사＋완전한 절」

5 그의 아버지는 그에게 '어른들'이 하는 것처럼 무거운 배낭을 메게 했다. ▶ the way와 how는 같이 쓸 수 없음

B

1 정부가 기업이 그것의 산업에서 얼마나 우위를 점하게 될지, 또는 어떻게 기업들이 서로 인수하고 합병하는지에 관해 발언권이 없는 자본주의 사회 체제하에서, 우위는 여러분이 하고 있는 것에 정말 능숙해짐으로써 오직 얻어질 수 있다. ▶「전치사＋관계대명사＋완전한 절」

2 시간을 정확하게 측정하는 이러한 전례 없는 능력은 18세기에 공장 시계에서 그것의 가장 권위적인 모습으로 나타났고, 18세기에 그것은 산업혁명의 주요 무기가 되었다. ▶「선행사＋관계부사＋완전한 절」

적용독해
p.183

1 ④ 2 ②

1 ④

해석 최초의 수중 사진은 William Thompson이라는 영국인에 의해 촬영되었다. 1856년에 그는 간단한 상자형 카메라를 방수 처리하고 막대에 부착하여 남부 England 연안의 바닷속으로 내려 보냈다. 10분간의 노출 동안 카메라에 서서히 바닷물이 차올랐지만 사진은 온전했다. 이것이 수중 사진술이 탄생한 방식이다. 물이 맑고 충분한 빛이 있는 수면 근처에서는 아마추어 사진작가가 저렴한 수중 카메라로 멋진 사진을 찍을 가능성이 상당히 높다. 어둡고 차가운 더 깊은 곳에서는 사진술이 신비로운 심해의 세계를 탐험하는 주요한 방법이며, 그곳의 95%는 예전에는 전혀 볼 수 없었다.

문제풀이 ④ 관계부사 뒤에 완전한 절이 오므로 which를 where로 고쳐야 한다.
① 병렬구조 : waterproofed, attached, and lowered ▶ p.206
②「관계부사＋완전한 절」
③「선행사＋관계부사＋완전한 절」
⑤「선행사＋관계대명사＋불완전한 절」

2 ②

해석 모든 것을 당신 스스로 생산하려고 노력하는 것은 당신이 고비용 공급자가 되는 많은 것들을 생산하기 위해 당신의 시간과 자원을 사용하고 있다는 것을 의미한다. 이것은 더 낮은 생산과 수입으로 해석될 수 있다. 예를 들면, 비록 대부분의 의사가 자료 기록과 진료 예약을 잡는 데 능숙할지라도, 이러한 서비스를 수행하기 위해 누군가를 고용하는 것은 일반적으로 그들에게 이익이 된다. 기록을 하기 위해 의사가 사용하는 시간은 그들이 환자를 진료하면서 보낼 수 있었던 시간이다. 그들이 환자와 보내게 되는 시간은 많은 가치를 가지기 때문에 의사들에게 자료 기록을 하는 기회비용은 높을 것이다. 따라서 의사는 자료 기록을 하고 그것을 관리하기 위해 누군가 다른 사람

을 고용하는 것이 이득이라는 것을 거의 항상 알게 될 것이다. 더군다나 의사가 진료 제공을 전문으로 하고, 자료 기록에 비교 우위를 가지고 있는 사람을 고용하면, 그렇게 하지 않으면 얻을 수 있는 것보다 그 비용은 더 낮아질 것이고 공동의 결과물이 더 커질 것이다.

문제풀이 ② 선행사＋관계부사 뒤에 불완전한 절(spend＋목적어＋~ing 구문에서 목적어가 없는)이 왔으므로 관계부사 when을 관계대명사 that이나 which로 고쳐야 한다.
①「선행사＋전치사＋관계대명사＋완전한 절」
③「선행사＋관계대명사＋불완전한 절」
④「find＋가목적어＋O.C.(형용사)＋진목적어(to-v)」 ▶ p.44
⑤ 병렬구조: 단수동사(specializes) and 단수동사(hires)

STEP 3 유형 글의 제목
pp.184~185

1 ⑤ 2 ② 3 ②

1 ⑤

해석 사람들이 커피 값을 기부하는 양심 상자 가까이에, 영국 Newcastle University의 연구자들은 사람의 눈 이미지와 꽃 이미지를 번갈아 가며 놓아두었다. 각각의 이미지는 일주일씩 놓여 있었다. 꽃 이미지가 놓여 있던 주들보다 눈 이미지가 놓여 있던 모든 주에 사람들이 더 많은 기부를 했다. 연구가 이루어진 10주 동안, '눈 주간'의 기부금이 '꽃 주간'의 기부금보다 거의 세 배나 많았다. 이 실험은 '진전된 협력 심리가 누군가가 지켜보고 있다는 미묘한 신호에 아주 민감하다'는 것과 이 연구 결과가 사회적으로 이익이 되는 성과를 내게끔 어떻게 효과적으로 넌지시 권할 것인가를 암시한다고 말했다.

문제풀이 기부에 관한 한 실험에서 꽃 이미지보다 사람의 눈 이미지가 있는 기간에 더 많은 기부금이 모였다는 결과가 나왔고, 이는 누군가가 지켜보고 있다는 미묘한 심리가 작용한 결과라는 내용이므로 ⑤가 정답이다.
① 정직이 최상의 정책일까?
② 꽃은 눈보다 더 낫다
③ 기여는 자존감을 높일 수 있다
④ 사람이 많으면 협동심은 떨어진다
⑤ 눈: 사회를 더 좋게 만드는 은밀한 기여자

구문분석

[5행] Over the ten weeks of the study, contributions [during the 'eyes weeks'] were almost **three times higher than** those [made during the 'flowers weeks.']
▶ 첫 번째 [ ]는 주어 contributions를 수식하는 전치사구이며, 「배수사(twice, three times, four times ...)＋비교급＋than」은 '~보다 몇 배 더 …한'의 의미이다. 두 번째 [ ]는 선행사 those를 수식하는 과거분사구이다. those는 앞에 사용된 명사 contributions를 가리킨다.

2 ②

해석 '알고리즘'이라는 단어를 언급하는 것은 대부분의 사람들로부터 아무 반응을 얻지 못했던 한 세대 혹은 두 세대 전만 해도, AI 세상도 없었고 직업 소실 걱정도 없었다. 대조적으로 우리의 현세대는 이제 인공지능 세계에서 예술부터 의료 이르는 모든 것에서 많은 전통적인 직업의 상실에 직면해 있다. 이러한 상실 중 일부는 새로운 직업의 창출로 부분적으로 상쇄될 수 있지만, 알려진 질병을 진단하고 친숙한 치료를 제공하는 데 집중하는 의사와 같은 사람들은 아마도 인공지능 의사들로 대체될 것이다. 그러나 정확히 그것 때문에, 획기적인 연구를 하고 새로운 약이나 수술 절차를 개발하도록 인간 의사에게 지급할 돈이 훨씬 더 많을 것이다. AI는 또 다른 방식으로 인간의 새로운 직업을 만드는 것을 도울지도 모른다. 인간이 AI와 경쟁하는 대신에, 그들은 AI를 정비하고 활용하는 것에 집중할 수 있다. 예를 들어, 드론에 의한 인간 조종사의 대체는 몇몇 직업을 없애 왔지만, 정비, 원격 조종, 데이터 분석, 그리고 사이버 보안에 있어서 많은 새로운 기회를 만들어 왔다.

문제풀이 AI로 인해 여러 분야에서 전통적인 직업이 사라지지만 AI로 인해 새로운 직업과 기회가 생겨난다는 내용이므로 ②가 정답임을 알 수 있다.

① 무엇이 로봇을 더 똑똑하게 만드는가?
② AI는 여러분의 직업에 정말로 위협일까?
③ 조심하라! AI는 여러분의 마음을 읽을 수 있다
④ 미래의 직업: 일은 더 적게, 수입은 더 많게
⑤ AI 개발의 지속적인 어려움

구문분석

[10행] For example, <u>the replacement</u> of human pilots
　　　　　　　　　　　　　　S
by drones <u>has eliminated</u> some jobs but <u>(has) created</u>
　　　　　　　V1　　　　　　　　　　　　　　　V2
many new opportunities ....
▶ 이 문장의 주어는 the placement이므로 동사는 단수동사 has가 된다. 동사 has eliminated와 created는 등위접속사 but으로 병렬되고 있으며 created 앞에는 has가 생략되었다.

3 ②

해석 자유 시장은 마르크스주의가 결코 할 수 없었던 방식으로 사람들을 자유롭게 해 왔다. 게다가 하버드 대학 경제 역사학자인 A. O. Hirschman이 자신의 대표적 연구서인 'The Passions and the Interests'을 출간했는데, 이 책에서 시장은 계몽주의 사상가들인 Adam Smith, David Hume 그리고 Montesquieu에 의해 인류의 가장 큰 전통적 약점들 중 하나인 폭력에 대한 강력한 해결책으로 여겨졌다고 말했다. Montesquieu가 말했던 바로는 두 국가가 만날 때 그들은 두 가지 중 하나를 할 수 있는데, 즉 그들은 전쟁을 벌이거나 거래를 할 수 있다. 만약 그들이 전쟁을 벌인다면, 둘 다 장기적으로 손해를 볼 가능성이 있다. 만약 그들이 거래를 한다면, 둘 다 이득을 얻을 것이다. 물론 그것이 유럽 연합의 설립 이면에 있는 논리였다. 즉 그것의 국가들, 특히 프랑스와 독일의 운명을 한데 묶었는데 그렇게 함으로써 그들이 20세기 전반에 너무나도 파괴적인 대가를 치르며 그랬던 것처럼 다시는 전쟁을 벌이지 않도록 그들은 저항할 수 없는 이해관계를 가졌을 것이다.

문제풀이 폭력에 대한 강력한 해결책을 제시한 책을 소개하며 두 국가가 전쟁을 벌이면 모두 손해를 보지만 거래를 하면 모두 이득을 얻는 이해관계가 있다는 내용이므로 ②가 정답이다.

① 무역 전쟁: 인간의 타고난 폭력성의 반영
② 자유 시장: 동반 몰락보다는 원윈 전략
③ 새로운 경제 체제는 자유 시장을 안정화시킨다
④ 폭력은 자본주의를 붕괴시키는 보이지 않는 손이다
⑤ 정부는 시장을 통제하는 데 있어 어떻게 관여하는가?

구문분석

[10행] ... **as** they **had done** to such devastating cost in the first half of the twentieth century.
▶ 접속사 as는 '~하는 것처럼'의 의미이고 had done은 had waged war의 뜻으로 앞에서 나온 단어의 반복을 피하려고 대동사를 썼다.

STEP 1 어휘
23강 예술·문학

PRACTICE　　　　　　　　　　　p.188

A	1 portrait	2 reputation	3 tragedy
	4 author	5 foundation	
B	1 ③	2 ③	3 ②	4 ④	5 ④
C	1 vitality	2 outside	

A

1 Van Gogh의 자화상은 그의 캐릭터의 일부를 반영하고 있다.
2 그 작가는 동화책을 많이 쓰는 것으로 평판을 얻고 있다.
3 놀이동산이 문을 닫아야 한다면 매우 안타까운 일이 될 것이다.
4 '노인과 바다'의 저자는 Ernest Hemingway이다.
5 Monet의 화풍은 인상주의의 토대가 되었다.

B

1 그녀는 가을에 대학에 입학할 계획이다.
2 그 화가는 상당히 균형(비율)이 안 맞는 크기로 손을 그렸다.
3 많은 문학 작품을 읽는 데 열정적이었던 그는 문학 비평가가 되었다.
4 Beethoven은 1801년에 '월광소나타'를, 1810년에 '엘리제를 위하여'를 작곡했다.
5 이 교육을 통해서 학생들은 다양한 기술에 관한 능력을 얻게 될 것이다.

C

1 우리의 경험은 우리가 살아있음을 느끼게 해 주고 우리에게 성장할 더 큰 기회를 주기 때문에, 경험에 가치를 두고 투자하는 것은 우리에게 더 큰 생동감을 준다.

2 대부분의 기업 관리자들은 큰 그림에서 시작하고 그 다음에 세부 사항을 해결하는 것을 좋아한다. 그런 이유 때문에 즉흥적 혁신의 가장 좋은 여러 사례는 공식적 조직 <u>밖에서</u> 일어난다.

적용독해

1 ④   2 ⑤

1 ④

해석 음악은 어린 아이들에게 강력하게 호소한다. 취학 전 아동들이 리듬과 소리를 들을 때 그들의 얼굴과 몸을 보라 ― 얼굴은 환해지고, 몸은 열심히, 열정적으로 움직인다. 그들은 음악과 상호 작용할 때 편안하게 소통하고 창의적으로 스스로를 표현하며 모든 종류의 사고와 감정을 표출한다. 한마디로 말해 어린 아이들은 음악을 매우 재미있게 생각한다. 그러므로 이 상황을 최대한 활용하기 위해 당신이 할 수 있는 모든 것을 해라. 기꺼이 하고 싶은 마음을(→ 주저함을) 버리고 당신이 음악적으로 재능이 있는지 혹은 노래를 할 수 있고 악기를 연주할 수 있는지에 대한 걱정들을 모두 잊어라. 당신이 아이와 음악을 즐길 때 그것들은 문제 되지 않는다. 그저 아이들이 이끄는 대로 따르고, 즐기고, 함께 노래하고, 다양한 종류의 음악을 듣고, 몸을 움직이고, 춤추고, 즐겨라.

문제풀이 취학 전 아동들에게 음악이 미치는 영향은 아주 긍정적이므로 부모가 아이들의 음악에 대한 반응을 최대한 활용하기 위해 주저하지 말고 할 수 있는 모든 것을 해야 한다는 내용이므로 ④ willingness는 hesitation 등으로 고쳐야 한다.

구문분석

[2행] They [communicate comfortably,] [express
        V1   V2
themselves creatively,] and [let out all sorts of
                                  V3
thoughts and emotions] **as** they interact with music.
▶ 세 개의 [ ]는 동사 communicate, express, let이 and로 병렬 연결되어 있고 '~할 때'라는 접속사 as의 부사절이 이어지고 있다.

2 ⑤

해석 작곡가들이 형식과 디자인을 자유롭게 실험하기 시작했던 20세기에 이를 때까지, 고전 음악은 화음은 말할 것도 없이, 구조와 관련 있는 기본적인 규칙들을 계속 따랐다. 여전히 개성을 발휘할 여지는 있었지만(위대한 작곡가들은 규칙을 따르지 않고, 규칙이 그들을 따르도록 만들었다), 디자인 이면에는 항상 기본적인 비율과 논리가 있었다. 많은 규칙이 더 최근 들어 급진적인 개념에 의해 뒤집어진 이후에도, 대개 작곡가들은 전체적이고 통일적인 구조를 생산해내는 방식으로 여전히 자신들의 생각을 구성했다. 그것이 20세기 모더니즘 작곡가 두 명을 예로 들면, Arnold Schönberg나 Karlheinz Stockhausen에 의해 작곡된 무조(無調)의 매우 복잡한 작품들이 그럼에도 불구하고 <u>접근할 수 없는(→ 접근 가능한)</u> 한 가지 이유이다. 그 소리는 매우 이상할지 모르지만, 그 결과는 여전히 구성의 측면에서 분명히 고전적이다.

문제풀이 고전음악 작곡가들은 항상 기본적인 비율과 논리를 따르려 했고 이후 여러 변화가 있었으며 아주 복잡한 작품들이 등장했음에도 접근 가능했던 이유는 구성의 측면에서 여전히 고전적이었기 때문이라는 내용이므로 ⑤ inaccessible는 approachable 등으로 고쳐야 한다.

구문분석

[5행] **Even after** many of the rules were overturned
by radical concepts in more recent times, **composers**,
                                              S
{more often than not}, still **organized their thoughts**
                              V   O
in ways [that produced an overall, unifying structure.]
▶ Even after는 '~한 이후에도'라는 의미의 〈시간〉의 부사절을 이끄는 접속사이고, { }에서 「more often than not」은 '대개, 자주'라는 의미의 삽입구이다. [ ]는 ways를 수식하는 주격 관계대명사절이다.

STEP 2 어법 수의 일치 1

PRACTICE

A 1 remains → remain
   2 are → is
   3 are → is
   4 are → is
   5 has → have
B 1 are   2 seems

A

1 결혼하지 않고 혼자 사는 사람들의 수가 엄청나게 증가했다.
▶ 「선행사 people+주격 관계대명사+복수 동사」
2 누군가가 그런 사람들을 돕는데 관심이 있다는 사실은 나는 상상할 수 없는 정도이다. ▶ S=The fact – 단수 동사
3 여기서는 카메라와 비디오 카메라의 사용이 허용되지 않습니다.
▶ S=The use – 단수 동사
4 더 중요한 것은 자녀에 대한 부모의 관심이 엄청나게 크다는 것이다. ▶ 2형식 도치문: 「S.C.+V+S」, S=the huge increase
5 인간은 뭔가를 먹는 의식을 발전시켜 왔는데, 이는 수천 년간 사라지지 않고 지속되었다. ▶ 「선행사 rituals+주격 관계대명사+복수 동사」

B

1 조정 능력, 청각적 감수성, 시각적 신호와 기호에 대한 반응 그리고 악기 연주에 필요한 음악적 이해의 많은 부분을 발달시키는 활동은 모두 악기 없이 자리 잡을 수 있다. ▶ S=Activities – 복수 동사

정답 및 해설 **67**

2 지도자는 그들을 지도자가 아닌 사람과 구별해 주는 특정한 신체적, 지적, 혹은 성격적 특성을 '선천적으로' 가지고 있다는 생각은 리더십에 대한 특성 기반 접근법의 기초적인 믿음인 것처럼 보인다. ▶ S=The idea(동격절 주어) – 단수 동사

적용독해   p.191

1 ⑤   2 ⑤

1 ⑤

해석 소년 마법사의 모험에 관한 J. K. Rowling의 판타지 시리즈 중 일곱 번째이자 마지막 권인 '해리포터와 죽음의 성물'이 2007년 미국에 출간되었을 때, 그것은 판매가 시작되고 첫 24시간 안에 8백 30만 부가 팔렸다. 열두 명의 출판업자가 그 첫 번째 책을 출판하기를 거절했다는 사실은 충격적이지 않은가? 성공이 적어도 자체의 질에 의해 부분적으로 결정되지만, 사람들이 좋아하게 되는 것은 다른 사람들이 좋아한다고 자신들이 믿는 것에 매우 많이 결정되는 일도 가능하다. 이런 세상에서 왜 특정한 책이 성공작이 되는지에 대한 설명은 아주 간단하다. 많은 사람들이 샀기 때문에 그것이 잘 팔렸다. 책과 영화 같은 문화적 가공물은 이제 한 세기 전에는 그럴 수 없었던 방식으로 인기가 '눈덩이처럼 불어날' 수 있고, 문화 상업을 예측하기 어려운 승자 독식 시장들의 집합체로 변모시킨다. 흥행성이나 상품의 질에서 작은 차이는 수익에서 엄청난 차이로 바뀐다.

문제풀이 ⑤ 주어가 복수 명사(Tiny differences)이므로 translates를 복수 동사 translate로 고쳐야 한다.
① 「도서명 주어+단수 동사」
② 2형식 의문문: 「단수 동사+동격절 S+C」
③ 「관계사절 S+단수 동사」
④ 2형식 도치문: 「C+단수 동사+S(the explanation)」 ▶ p.230

2 ⑤

해석 개인용 음악 플레이어가 흔하고 사람들이 헤드폰으로 음악을 많이 듣는 이유는 요즘 우리 중 그렇게나 많은 사람이 녹음된 음악에 끌린다는 사실과 관련이 있어 보인다. 녹음 엔지니어와 음악가는 우리 청각 환경의 중요한 특징들을 분간하도록 진화한 신경회로를 이용함으로써 우리의 뇌를 자극하는 특수 효과를 만들어 내는 것을 배웠다. 이러한 특수 효과들은 원리상 3-D 아트, 모션 픽처, 또는 착시와 비슷하지만, 그것들 중에 어느 것도 우리의 뇌가 그것들을 인식하기 위한 특수한 방법을 진화시킬 만큼 충분히 오랫동안 주변에 존재하지는 않았다. 오히려 그것들은 다른 것들을 성취하기 위해 자리 잡고 있는 인식 체계를 이용한다. 오로지 그것들이 이러한 신경회로를 새로운 방식으로 사용하기 때문에 3-D 아트, 모션 픽처, 그리고 착시는 특히 흥미롭다고 여겨진다. 동일한 것이 현대의 녹음된 음악이 만들어지는 방법에도 적용된다.

문제풀이 ⑤ 「Only because 부사절+복수 동사+복수 명사 주어」로 이루어진 도치문이며 주어가 복수 명사이므로 is를 are로 고쳐야 한다.
▶ p.230
① 「주어 The reason+단수 동사」

---

② 「선행사 special effects+주격 관계대명사+복수 동사」
③ 「선행사 3-D art, motion pictures, or visual illusions+주격 관계대명사+복수 동사」
④ 「선행사 perceptual systems+주격 관계대명사+복수 동사」

STEP 3 유형   내용 일치

1 ④   2 ④   3 ④

1 ④

해석 Lotte Laserstein은 동프로이센의 유대인 가정에서 태어났다. 그녀의 친척 중 한 명은 사립 미술 학교를 운영했는데, 이것은 Lotte가 어린 나이에 회화와 소묘를 배우도록 해주었다. 나중에, 그녀는 Berlin Academy of Arts에 입학 허가를 받았고 그 학교에서 최초의 여성 중 한 명으로 석사 과정을 마쳤다. 그녀는 폭넓은 인정을 받으며 1928년에 그녀의 경력은 급부상했지만, 나치당의 권력 장악 이후, 독일에서 그녀의 작품 전시는 금지 되었다. 1937년에 그녀는 스웨덴으로 이주했다. 그녀는 스웨덴에서 계속 활동했지만 그녀가 이전에 누렸던 명성을 결코 되찾지 못했다. 자신의 작품에서 Lotte는 자신의 가장 가까운 친구인 Gertrud Rose를 반복해서 그렸다. Lotte에게 그녀는 '신여성'의 유형을 구체화했고 그렇게 표현되었다.

문제풀이 스페인에서 계속 활동을 했지만 이전에 누렸던 명성을 되찾지는 못했다고 했으므로 정답은 ④이다.

구문분석

[1행] One of her relatives ran a private painting school,

[which **allowed** Lotte **to learn** painting and drawing
         V   O   O.C.

at a young age.]
▶ [ ]는 a private painting school을 부연 설명하는 계속적 용법의 주격 관계대명사절이다. 「allow+O+O.C.」는 '~가 …하게 하다'의 의미로 목적격 보어로는 to부정사를 취한다. learn은 동명사를 목적어로 취하는 동사이다.

2 ④

해석 Shah Rukh Khan은 인도의 영화배우이자 제작자이다. Khan은 대학에서 경제학을 공부했지만 Delhi의 Theatre Action Group에서 많은 시간을 보냈고, 그곳에서 연기를 공부했다. Bollywood에서 전업으로 일을 하기 위해 Delhi에서 Mumbai로 이주했고, 이는 그에게 큰 명성을 가져다주었다. "King of Bollywood" 또는 "King Khan"으로 매체에서 불렸던 그는 80편이 넘는 Bollywood 영화에 출연했다. 2007년에 프랑스 정부는 영화에 대한 공로로 Khan에게 the Order of Arts and Letters를 수여하였다. 그는 정기적으로 인도 문화에서 가장 영향력 있는 인물들 목록에 등재되며, 2008년에는 세계에서 가장 영향력 있는 50인 중 한 명으로 선정되었다. Khan의 박애주의적인 노력은 의료 서비스와 재난 구호를 제공해 왔으며, 그는 2011년에 아동 교육에 대한 후원으로 UNESCO에서 Pyramide con Marni 상을 받았다.

문제풀이 세계에서 가장 영향력 있는 50인 중 한 명으로 선정된 것은 2008년이라고 했으므로 정답은 ④이다.

구문분석

[4행] [**Referred to** in the media **as** the "King of Bollywood" or "King Khan,"] he has appeared in more than 80 Bollywood films.
▶ [ ]는 수동 분사구문으로 부사절의 주어와 주절의 주어가 같아 「접속사+S+be동사」가 모두 생략되고 referred to만 남은 형태이다. 「refer to A as B」는 'A를 B라고 부르다'라는 의미이다.

3 ④

해석 서양에서 널리 칭송받는 최초의 러시아 작가인 Ivan Turgenev는 1818년에 러시아에서 태어났다. 그는 1833년에 Moscow 대학에 입학하였으나, 일 년이 지나기도 전에 가족의 이사 때문에 St. Petersburg 대학교로 옮겼다. 나중에 그는 독일로 여행을 갔고 그곳에서 Berlin 대학에 등록하여 3년 동안 철학을 공부했다. St. Petersburg로 돌아와 교직을 구하는 데 실패하자 그곳에서 공무원으로서 일하기 시작했으나 그의 관심은 점점 더 문학으로 향했다. 공직에서 은퇴한 후, 그는 프랑스로 갔다. 1850년대 중반 무렵에 그는 러시아에 있었던 것만큼 많은 시간을 유럽에서 보내고 있었다. 1860년 8월에 영국에서 그는 자신의 *Fathers and Sons*에 대한 아이디어를 구상했고, 그 소설을 러시아에서 1861년 7월에 완성했다. 그 책은 러시아에서 적대적인 반응을 얻었지만 서구 세계에서는 명성을 얻었고 오랫동안 베스트셀러가 되어 왔다. 그는 1879년에 Oxford 대학으로부터 명예 학위를 받았다.

문제풀이 소설 *Fathers and Sons* 대한 구상은 영국에서 했고 러시아에서 완성했다고 했으므로 정답은 ④이다.

구문분석

[4행] Later, he traveled to Germany, [where he enrolled
             V1   ↑_____|
at the University of Berlin] and studied philosophy for
                                    V2
three years.
▶ [ ]는 Germany를 부연 설명하는 관계부사절이고 관계부사절 뒤에 완전한 절이 와야 한다.

STEP 1 어휘

24강 **자연**

PRACTICE p.196

A	1 density	2 species	3 mammal
	4 latitude	5 components	
B	1 ②	2 ③	3 ③	4 ④	5 ④
C	1 minimal	2 reproductive	

A

1 모나코는 인구 밀도가 매우 높다.
2 다양한 거미종들이 곤충박물관에 전시되어 있다.
3 박쥐는 날 수 있는 포유류이고 고래는 헤엄치는 포유류이다.
4 위도선은 지구상에 있는 가상의 수평선이다.
5 토양의 4대 성분으로는 무기물, 유기물, 물, 그리고 공기이다.

B

1 지구는 5대양 7대륙으로 이루어져 있다.
2 백색증은 피부에 색소가 없는 일종의 돌연변이이다.
3 물개에게 주려고 사육사는 각각의 생선을 두 조각으로 잘랐다.
4 그 연구 결과는 생태 보전 대책 수립에 아주 중요하다.
5 유기 농업은 멸종위기종의 미래와 밀접한 관련이 있다.

C

1 바로 그 지구의 위도가 기후와 성장 계절의 길이를 주로 결정하기 때문에, 유라시아의 한 지역에서 재배된 농작물들은 새로운 장소에의 적응에 대한 단지 최소한의 필요만 지닌 채 대륙을 가로질러 이식될 수 있다.
2 동물학자인 John Krebs는 기만적인 신호 보내기가 그 자체로 진화적 적응, 즉 생존과 번식의 이득을 얻기 위해 우리의 가장 초기의 동물 조상에서 발달했던 특성이라고 지적한다.

적용독해 p.197

1 ⑤	2 ④

1 ⑤

해석 해충과 질병은 자연의 일부이다. 이상적인 체계에서는 포식자와 해충 간에 자연적으로 균형이 잡힌다. 만약 그 체계가 불균형을 이루면, 한 개체군은 다른 개체군에 의해 잡아먹히지 않기 때문에 개체 수가 증가할 수 있다. 자연 통제의 목적은 해충과 질병을 완전히 없애는 것이 아니다. 그것은 해충과 포식자 사이의 자연의 균형을 회복하고 해충과 질병을 적정 수준까지 낮추는 것이다. 하지만 해충과 질병에 대한 자연적인 통제의 또 다른 대안으로 사용되는 살충제는 해충 문제를 해결하지 못한다. 지난 50년 동안 살충제 사용은 10배 증가한 반면, 해충의 피해로 인한 곡식의 손실은 두 배가 되었다. 자연 통제가 살충제 사용보다 더 피하여지는(→ 선택되는) 이유가 여기에 있다.

문제풀이 해충과 질병도 자연의 일부이므로 인위적인 통제보다는 자연 통제가 도움이 된다는 내용이므로 ⑤ avoided는 chosen 등으로 바꿔야 한다.

구문분석

[8행] **Here lies the reason** [why natural control is
　　　　부사　　V　　　S　　　↑___|
chosen more than pesticide use.]
▶ 부사 Here(여기에)이 문두에 오면서 주어와 동사가 도치되었다. [ ]는 the reason을 수식하는 관계부사절이다. 관계부사 why 다음에 완전한 절이 뒤따른다.

2 ④

해석 어떤 종들은 잠재적 포식자에 대한 정보를 공유하는 경계 신호를 사용한다. 그들이 더욱 성숙해짐에 따라 그들의 경계 신호는 탐지되어 온 포식자의 특성에 대해 매우 구체적인 정보를 전달하는 것 같다. 어린 버빗 원숭이가 자신의 위쪽 하늘에 있는 새 한 마리를 보면 경계 신호를 보낼 것이다. 이 경우에는 일종의 '콜록 콜록' 소리이다. 이 단계에서 위험하든 그렇지 않든, 그것은 어떤 커다란 비행 물체에 대한 반응으로 주어지는 것이므로 위쪽의 잠재적 위험에 대한 타고난 신호로 보인다. 그러나 원숭이가 성숙해가면서 신호를 유발하는 자극의 범위가 넓어진다(→ 좁아진다). 결국 이 경계 신호의 사용은 위쪽 하늘에 독수리가 보이는 그런 상황에 제한될 것이다. 그 신호를 듣자마자 집단의 구성원들은 위협적인 존재의 위치를 찾기 위해 하늘을 훑어보고 나서 빽빽한 초목에 의해 제공되는 은신처를 향해 돌진해 갈 것이다.

문제풀이 잠재적 포식자에 대한 정보를 공유하는 경계 신호를 사용하는 종들이 있는데 이들은 성숙해 가면서 어렸을 때보다 더 구체적인 정보를 전달한다는 내용이므로 ④ broadens는 narrows 등으로 바꿔야 한다.

구문분석

[1행] **Their alarm calls seem** to convey very specific
　　　　　　　S　　　　　V
information about the nature of the predator [that has
　　　　　　　　　　　　　　　　　　↑___|
been detected] {**as** they become more mature.}
▶ [ ]는 the predator를 수식하는 주격 관계대명사절이다. { }는 '~함에 따라서'의 의미인 접속사 as가 이끄는 〈시간〉의 부사절이다.

STEP 2 어법　**수의 일치 2**

PRACTICE　　　　　　　　　p.198

A　　1　them → it
　　　　2　its → their
　　　　3　their → its
　　　　4　those → that
　　　　5　ones → one

B　　1　its　　2　that

A

1 고객들이 한 제품에 대한 습관을 형성하면, 그들은 그것에 의존하게 되고 가격에 덜 민감해진다. ▶ it(a product)
2 상황은 종종 더 좋아지기 직전에 최악인 것처럼 보인다.
▶ their(things)
3 한국은 이런 국가들과 지리적으로 가까웠지만 그 질병으로부터 자유로웠다. ▶ its(Korea)
4 단체 헌혈자의 수와 개인 헌혈자의 수 사이의 차이는 2009년에 가장 컸다. ▶ that(the number)
5 그의 동생이 축구공을 필요로 해서, 그를 위해 축구공 하나를 꼭 얻으리라 결심했다. ▶ one(a football)

B

1 동물들을 50살의 나이에 저절로 죽게 만드는 어떤 돌연변이가 나타난다고 상상해 보라. 이 돌연변이를 지닌 99퍼센트보다 많은 동물들은 그것이 작용할 기회를 갖기 전에 그것들이 죽을 것이기 때문에 결코 그것의 부작용을 경험하지 못할 것이다. ▶ its(this mutation)
2 전깃불과 그 주변을 둘러싸고 있는 전기 시스템의 기술적, 경제적 중요성은 적어도 지난 200년 이래 우리가 열거할 수 있는 다른 어떤 발명품의 기술적, 경제적 중요성에 필적한다. ▶ that (technical and economic importance)

적용독해　　　　　　　　　p.199

1 ③　　2 ②

---

1 ③

해석 야외에서 곤충의 성공적인 생존의 열쇠 중 하나는 그들의 작은 몸이 탈수가 되는 것을 막도록 돕는 단단한 밀랍 같은 층인 외피에 있다. 그들은 공기로부터 산소를 흡수하기 위해 몸의 마디에 있는 좁은 호흡구들을 사용하는데, 이들은 공기를 수동적으로 흡입하고 필요로 할 때 열리고 닫힐 수 있다. 혈관 내 담긴 피 대신 그들은 자유롭게 흐르는 혈림프를 갖고 있는데, 이는 그들의 몸이 단단하게 유지되도록 돕고 움직임을 거들고 영양분과 노폐물이 적절한 몸의 부위로 이동하는 것을 도와준다. 신경 체계가 모듈식으로 되어 있는데, 각각의 몸의 마디가 그 자체의 개별적이고 자율적인 뇌를 갖고 있다는 의미이다. 곤충의 몸은 우리의 몸과는 완전히 다르게 구조화되어 있고 기

능하다.

문제풀이 ③ 꾸며 주는 명사 blood와 수동의 관계에 있으므로 containing이 아니라 contained가 되어야 한다. blood which is contained in vessels에서 주격 관계대명사와 be 동사가 생략된 경우이다. ▶ p.150
① their(insects)
② ones(breathing holes)
④ 5형식 동사 「keep+O+O.C.」 ▶ p.44
⑤ its(each segment)

2 ②

해석 벽과 천장을 오르는 도마뱀은 좀처럼 떨어지지 않는다. 그러나 이것은 도마뱀이 엄청난 흡착력이 있어서가 아니다. 실제로 도마뱀은 흡착력을 전혀 사용하지 않는다. 도마뱀의 다리는 이런 식으로 움직인다: 테라륨 속에 들어 있는 도마뱀을 자세히 관찰해 보면 발바닥에 수많은 매우 작은 주름(가늘고 길게 패인 곳)이 있는 것을 볼 수 있다. 여러분이 볼 수 있는 각각의 그 작은 주름에는 육안으로 보이지 않는 수십 개의 주름이 더 있다. 그리고 그 수십 개의 주름마다 수천 개는 아니지만 수백 개의 털같이 생긴 돌기(강모)가 있다. 이제, 현미경으로 살펴보면 발바닥의 가장 매끄러운 표면조차 그것이 미세한 홈, 강모, 주름 등으로 덮여 있음을 볼 수 있다.

문제풀이 ② suction을 가리키므로 them이 아니라 it으로 바꿔야 한다.
① they(lizards)
③ 「1형식 완전한 절+부사」 ▶ p.238
④ 도치 「전치사구+복수 동사+복수 명사 주어」 ▶ p.230
⑤ it(surface)

STEP 3 유형 **빈칸 추론 1** pp.200~201

1 ②   2 ①   3 ①

1 ②

해석 흥미롭게도 자연에서 더 강한 종은 더 좁은 시야를 가지고 있다. 포식자와 피식자의 대비는 이에 대한 분명한 예를 제공한다. 포식자 종과 피식자 종을 구별하는 주요 특징은 발톱이나 생물학적 무기와 관련된 어떤 다른 특징의 존재가 아니다. 중요한 특징은 '눈의 위치'이다. 포식자는 앞쪽을 향하고 있는 눈을 가지도록 진화하였고, 이것은 사냥감을 쫓을 때 정확한 거리 감각을 제공하는 양안시(兩眼視)를 허용한다. 반면에 피식자는 대체로 주변 시야를 최대화하는 바깥쪽을 향하는 눈을 가지고 있으며, 이것은 어떤 각도에서도 접근하고 있을지 모르는 위험을 그들이 감지할 수 있게 한다. 먹이가 사슬의 꼭대기에 있는 우리의 위치와 일치하여, 인간은 앞쪽을 향하는 눈을 가지고 있다. 우리는 거리를 측정하고 목표물들을 추적할 수 있는 능력을 갖추고 있지만, 또한 우리 주변의 중요한 행동을 놓칠 수도 있다.

문제풀이 정확한 거리 감각을 위해 포식자는 양안시를, 주변을 최대한 감시하기 위해 피식자는 주변시를 허용하도록 진화해 왔다는 내용의 글이므로 빈칸에는 ② '더 강한 종은 더 좁은 시야를 가지고 있다'가 들어가는 것이 가장 적절하다.

① 바깥쪽으로 향해 있는 눈은 사냥의 성공과 연관이 있다
③ 앞쪽으로 향해 있는 인간의 눈은 위험을 감지하게 해 준다
④ 시력은 약한 종의 멸종과 밀접한 관련이 있다
⑤ 동물들은 같은 종의 구성원들을 식별하기 위해 시야를 활용한다

구문분석

[6행] **Prey**, on the other hand, often **have** eyes facing
     S   V
outward, **maximizing** peripheral vision, [which allows
them to detect danger {that may be approaching from
any angle}].
▶ 문장의 주어는 prey, 동사는 have이다. prey는 셀 수 없는 명사이고 단수/복수 동사 모두 가능하다. maximizing은 《부대 상황》을 나타내는 분사구문이다. [ ]는 계속적 용법의 주격 관계대명사절이며, danger를 수식하는 { }는 주격 관계대명사절이다.

2 ①

해석 우리가 화석을 조사하며 알 수 있는 것만큼이나 그것들이 좀처럼 완전한 이야기를 전달하지 않는다는 것을 기억하는 것이 중요하다. 생물들은 일련의 특정 조건하에서만 화석화된다. 현대 곤충 군집들은 열대 우림 지역에서 매우 다양하지만, 최근 화석 기록은 그 다양성을 거의 담아내지 않는다. 많은 생명체는 죽을 때 완전히 먹히거나 급속히 부패해서 중요한 집단에 관한 화석 기록이 전혀 존재하지 않을 수도 있다. 그것은 가족 사진첩과도 약간 비슷하다. 아마도 여러분이 태어났을 때 여러분의 부모님은 사진을 많이 찍었겠지만, 시간이 흐르면서 그들은 가끔 사진을 찍었고, 때로는 바빠져서 사진 찍는 것을 아예 잊어버렸을지도 모른다. 우리 중 우리 인생의 완전한 사진 기록을 가진 사람은 거의 없다. 화석이 바로 그것과 같다. 때때로 여러분은 과거에 대한 매우 명확한 그림을 가지지만 다른 때에는 큰 공백들이 존재하고, 여러분은 그것들이 무엇인지를 인지할 필요가 있다.

문제풀이 특정 조건하에서만 생물은 화석화가 되므로 화석 기록은 한계와 공백이 생길 수밖에 없다는 내용의 글이므로 빈칸에는 ① '완전한 이야기를 전달하지'가 들어가는 것이 가장 적절하다.
② 추가 연구를 필요로 하지   ③ 우리에게 잘못된 교훈을 가르치지
④ 원래의 특성을 변화시키지   ⑤ 상상력의 여지를 주지

구문분석

[1행] **As much as** we can learn **by** examining fossils,
it is important **to remember** [that they seldom tell the entire story.]
▶ 「as much as~」는 '~만큼 많이'라는 의미이고 「by+v-ing」는 '~함으로써'의 뜻이다. it는 가주어이고 to부정사가 진주어인데 진주어인 to remember의 목적어는 접속사 that으로 연결된 [ ] 부분이다.

3 ①

해석 과학자들은 개구리의 조상이 물에 사는, 물고기 같은 동물이었다고 믿는다. 최초의 개구리와 그들의 친척은 육지로 나와 그곳에서 먹을 것과 살 곳에 대한 기회를 누릴 수 있는 능력을 얻었다. 하지만 개구리는 여전히 물과의 여러 인연을 유지했다. 개구리의 폐는 그다

지 기능을 잘하지 않고, 개구리는 피부를 통해 호흡함으로써 산소를 일부 얻는다. 하지만 이런 종류의 '호흡'이 제대로 이뤄지기 위해서는, 개구리의 피부가 촉촉하게 유지되어야 한다. 그래서 개구리는 건조해지는 것을 막기 위해 이따금 몸을 잠깐 담글 수 있는 물의 근처에 있어야 한다. 물고기 같은 조상들이 그랬던 것처럼, 개구리 역시 물속에 알을 낳아야 한다. 그리고 물속에 낳은 알이 살아남으려면, 물에 사는 생물로 발달해야 한다. 따라서, 개구리에게 있어서 탈바꿈은 물에 사는 어린 올챙이와 육지에 사는 성체를 이어주는 다리를 제공한다.

문제풀이 개구리의 조상은 물속에 살았지만 양서류로 진화하면서 올챙이와 성체로 구분된다는 내용의 글이므로 빈칸에는 ① '여전히 물과의 여러 인연을 유지했다'가 들어가는 것이 가장 적절하다.
② 필요한 거의 모든 기관을 가지고 있었다
③ 새로운 음식에 대한 입맛을 개발해야 했다
④ 종종 육지에 서식하는 종들과 경쟁했다
⑤ 급속한 기후 변화로 고통을 겪었다

구문분석

[5행] And so the frog must remain <u>near the water</u> [where it can take a dip every now and then to **keep from** dry**ing** out.]
▶ [ ]는 near the water를 선행사로 하는 관계부사절이다. 「every now and then」은 '때때로, 가끔'이라는 의미이고 「keep +from+v-ing」는 '~하는 것을 막다'라는 의미이다.

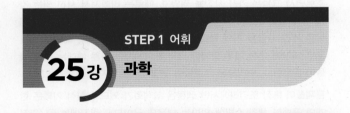

STEP 1 어휘

25강 과학

PRACTICE
p.204

A	1 conclude	2 consistently	3 undo
	4 domesticate	5 withhold	
B	1 ③ 2 ④ 3 ④ 4 ② 5 ②		
C	1 withholding	2 without	

A
1 배심원은 피고가 무죄라고 결론 내렸다.
2 조사 기간 내내 그는 일관되게 혐의를 부인했다.
3 그의 명성에 가해진 손상을 회복할 방법이 없다.
4 기원전 4천 년경 잉카인들은 라마를 길들였다.
5 건물주는 그들이 공사를 마칠 때까지 공사 대금 지급을 보류하기로 결정했다.

B
1 공기가 배기관을 통해 빠져나가면서 진공 상태가 된다.

2 경찰은 내 사생활을 캐물을 권한이 없다.
3 민원 처리 절차가 간소화될 필요가 있다.
4 방사능에 노출되는 것은 아이들과 젊은 여성들에게 치명적이다.
5 공학에 관한 전문 지식 덕분에 그녀는 연구소 소장으로 지명되었다.

C
1 행동에 대한 보상을 일정 기간 일관되게 제공한 후, 그것을 보류함으로써 무언가를 기꺼이 하고자 하는 개인의 마음을 없애는 것이 가능하다.
2 물리적 신문이 거대한 인쇄기와 트럭, 상점, 그리고 궁극적으로 신문 판매자들을 연결하는 유통망을 요구하는 반면에, 놀라울 정도로 디지털화된 세계에서 한 사람은 컴퓨터 한 대의 도움으로 그리고 한 그루의 나무도 베어질 필요 없이 전 세계와 소통할 수 있기 때문이다.

적용독해
p.205

1 ⑤   2 ③

1 ⑤

해석 최근의 연구는 진화하는 인간의 개와의 관계가 두 종 모두의 뇌 구조를 바꿨다는 것을 시사한다. 사육으로 인해 야기된 다양한 신체적 변화들 중 하나는 뇌 크기의 감소인데, 말은 16%, 돼지는 34% 그리고 개는 10에서 30% 감소했다. 이는 일단 인간이 이 동물들을 돌보기 시작하면서 그것들이 생존하기 위해 다양한 뇌 기능을 더는 필요로 하지 않았기 때문이다. 인간이 먹이를 주고 보호해 주는 동물들은 그것들의 야생 조상들에 의해 요구된 기술 중 많은 것들을 필요로 하지 않았고 그러한 능력들과 관련된 뇌의 부분들을 잃어버렸다. 유사한 과정이 인간에게 나타났는데, 그들은 늑대에 의해 길들여진 것으로 보인다. 약 만 년 전, 개의 역할이 대부분 인간 사회에서 확실하게 정해졌을 때, 인간의 뇌도 약 10% 커졌다(→ 줄어들었다).

문제풀이 가축화된 동물들은 야생의 조상들보다 뇌 크기가 감소했으며 인간 역시 가축화된 개에 의해 길들여져서 뇌가 줄어들었다는 내용이므로 ⑤ expanded는 shrank 등으로 바꿔야 한다.

구문분석

[6행] <u>Animals</u> [who were fed and protected by humans] **did not need** many of <u>the skills</u> [required by their wild ancestors] and **lost** the parts of the brain [related to those capacities].
▶ 첫 번째 [ ]는 주격 관계대명사절로 선행사 Animals를 수식하고 있다. 문장의 동사는 did not need와 lost가 and로 병렬 구조를 이루고 있다. 두 번째, 세 번째 [ ]는 required와 related 앞에 각각 〈관계대명사+be-v〉가 생략된 과거분사구로 '요구된'과 '관련된'의 의미이다.

2 ③

해석 사회 심리학의 한 현상인 Pratfall Effect는 한 개인의 인지된 매력도가 그 또는 그녀가 실수를 한 후에 그 사람의 인지된 능력에 따라 증가 또는 감소한다고 말한다. 유명 인사들은 일반적으로 능력 있는 사람들로 여겨지고 특정한 측면에서 종종 흠이 없고 완벽하다고도 보이기 때문에, 실수를 저지르는 것은 그 사람의 인간미를 다른 사람들에게 사랑을 받도록 만들 것이다. 기본적으로 실수를 전혀 저지르지 않는 사람들은 이따금 그러는 사람에 비해 더(→ 덜) 매력적이거나 호감을 주는 것으로 인지된다. 완벽성, 혹은 그 자질을 개인들에게 귀속하는 것은 일반 대중들이 (자신과) 관련지을 수 없는 인지된 거리감을 만들며 실수를 전혀 저지르지 않는 사람들을 덜 매력적이고 덜 호감이 가도록 만든다. 하지만 이것은 또한 정반대의 효과도 가지는데, 인지된 평균 혹은 그 이하의 능력을 가진 사람이 실수를 저지른다면, 그 또는 그녀는 다른 사람들에게 덜 매력적이고 호감을 덜 주게 될 것이다.

문제풀이 완벽해 보이는 사람이 실수를 저지르면 더 매력적이거나 호감을 주지만 정반대의 효과도 있다는 내용이므로 ③ more는 less 등으로 바꿔야 한다.

구문분석

[6행] ... **those** [who never make mistakes] are perceived as being less attractive and "likable" than **those** [who **do** occasionally.]

▶ 두 개의 [ ]는 선행사 those를 수식하는 주격 관계대명사절이다. 「perceive A as B」는 'A를 B로 여기다, 생각하다'의 의미인데 수동태 형식으로 쓰였다. 두 번째 관계대명사절의 do는 make mistakes를 대신해서 쓴 대동사 do이다.

STEP 2 어법 — 대동사와 접속사 (병렬 구조)

PRACTICE p.206

A
1 are → do
2 do → be
3 are → do
4 depress → depressing
5 and → but also

B
1 did 2 shipping

A

1 인간이 그러듯이 동물도 몸짓 언어로 의사소통한다. ▶ 일반동사 communicate를 대신하는 대동사 do
2 나는 최근에 아이들이 예전에 그랬던 것만큼 예의 바르지 못하다는 것을 알았다. ▶ be동사 were를 대신하는 대동사 be
3 카페인이 함유된 탄산음료는 우리 몸에서 수분을 제거하는데 카페인이 함유된 다른 음료도 그렇다. ▶ 일반동사 take를 대신하는 대동사 do
4 긴급 상황에서 여러분은 버튼을 누르거나 레버를 아래로 밀어서 스스로 문을 열어야 한다. ▶ 「by+v-ing+or+v-ing」로 이루어진 병렬구문, by+v-ing: ~함으로써
5 교사들은 가르칠 것뿐만 아니라 가르치는 방법도 배워야 한다. ▶ not only A but also B: A 뿐만 아니라 B도

B

1 사람들은 주로 자신이 실제보다 더 많은 칼로리를 소모했다고 생각하고 다량의 음식을 섭취함으로써 운동을 원상태로 돌리기 때문에 체중을 줄이는 것은 어렵다. ▶ 일반동사 burned를 대신하는 대동사 did
2 귀사의 소매점에서 파는 상품과 귀사의 웹사이트에서 파는 동일 상품 간의 가격 차이를 환불해 주시기 바랍니다. 저는 이 전자 장치를 포장한 후 전액 환불을 위해 귀하에게 다시 배송하는 것이 더 나은 해결책이 될 것으로 생각합니다. ▶ 「전치사+v-ing+and+v-ing (to packing and shipping)」로 이루어진 병렬구문

적용독해 p.207

1 ⑤ 2 ④

1 ⑤

해석 Albert Einstein은 과학자로서의 자신의 삶에 영향을 끼친 것들에 관한 이야기를 했다. 그는 다섯 살 때 작은 나침반을 보고 나침반의 바늘이 항상 북쪽을 가리키는 것에 놀랐던 일을 기억해 냈다. Einstein은 그 당시, "사물의 뒤에 깊이 숨겨진 무언가 대단한 것을 느꼈다"고 회상했다. 여섯 살 무렵, Einstein은 바이올린을 배우기 시작했다. 몇 년 후 음악의 수학적 구조를 인식했을 때, 바이올린은 그의 평생의 친구가 되었다. Einstein이 열 살이 되었을 때, 그의 가족은 그를 Luitpold 김나지움에 등록시켰고, 그곳에서 그는 다른 많은 학생들이 하지 않았던 권위에 대해 의심을 품는 법을 연마하였다. 그러한 특성은 Einstein이 훗날 과학자로서의 삶을 사는 데 큰 도움이 되었다. 그의 회의론적인 습관은 오랫동안 지속되어 온 여러 가지 과학적 가설에 대해 쉽게 의문을 제시할 수 있게 해 주었다.

문제풀이 ⑤ 가목적어-진목적어 구문에서 가목적어와 진목적어 사이에 있는 보어 자리에는 부사가 올 수 없으므로 ⑤ easily는 easy로 고쳐야 한다. ▶ p.28
① 병렬구조(remember+seeing and marveling)
② 부사 deeply가 형용사 hidden을 수식 ▶ p.238
③ his friends를 의미하는 소유대명사
④ developed a suspicion of authority를 대신하는 대동사

2 ④

해석 여러분은 인공 지능으로 구동되는 기계가 할 수 있는 몇 가지 일에 대한 헤드라인을 뉴스에서 본 적이 있을 것이다. 하지만, AI로 구동되는 기계가 실제로 수행할 수 있는 모든 작업을 고려한다면, 그것은 꽤 놀라울 것이다! 인공 지능의 핵심 특징들 중 하나는 그것이 특정하고 새로운 프로그래밍을 필요로 하기보다는 기계들이 새로운 것을 학습할 수 있게 한다는 것이다. 그러므로, 미래의 컴퓨터들과 과거의 그것들 사이의 핵심적인 차이점은 미래의 컴퓨터가 학습하고 스

스로 개선할 수 있을 것이라는 점이다. 가까운 미래에, 스마트 가상 비서는 여러분에 대해 여러분의 가장 가까운 친구나 가족이 아는 것보다 더 많이 알게 될 것이다. 그것이 우리의 삶을 어떻게 변화시킬지 상상할 수 있는가? 왜 이러한 종류의 변화는 정확히 새로운 기술들이 우리 세계에 미칠 영향을 인식하는 것이 아주 중요한가에 대한 이유이다.

문제풀이 ④ 일반동사 know를 대신하는 대동사이므로 ④ are를 do로 고쳐야 한다.
① 「tasks+목적격 관계대명사+불완전한 절」
② 병렬구조 (enables rather than requires)
③ those(computers) ▶ p.198
⑤ it ~ to 가주어−진주어 구문

STEP 3 유형 빈칸 추론 2

pp.208~209

1 ④   2 ②   3 ⑤

1 ④

해석 만약 당신이 10층 건물 꼭대기에서 구슬이 떨어지는 데 시간이 얼마나 걸리는지 물리학자에게 묻는다면, 그는 진공 상태에서 구슬이 떨어지는 것을 가정하고 그 질문에 답할 것 같다. 실제로 건물은 공기로 둘러싸여 있는데, 그것이 떨어지는 구슬에 마찰을 가하며 속도를 떨어뜨린다. 그러나 그 물리학자는 구슬에 가해지는 마찰이 너무 작아서 그것의 효과는 무시할 수 있다는 점을 지적할 것이다. 구슬이 진공 상태에서 떨어진다고 가정하는 것은 그 답에 큰 영향을 주지 않고 그 문제를 단순화한다. 경제학자들도 같은 이유로 가정을 한다: 가정은 복잡한 세상을 단순화하고 이해하는 것을 더 쉽게 만들 수 있다. 예를 들어, 국제 무역의 효과를 연구하기 위해 우리는 세상이 단 두 국가로만 구성되었고, 각각의 국가들이 두 가지 상품만 생산한다고 가정할 수 있다. 그렇게 함으로써, 우리는 문제의 본질에 우리의 사고를 집중할 수 있다. 따라서 우리는 복잡한 세상에서 국제 무역을 이해하는 더 나은 위치에 있게 된다.

문제풀이 가정은 복잡한 세상을 단순화하고 이해하는 것을 더 쉽게 해주며 문제의 핵심에 집중하게 해준다는 내용의 글이므로 빈칸에는 ④ '문제의 본질에 우리의 사고를 집중할'이 들어가는 것이 가장 적절하다.
① 소비자 권리의 침해를 방지할
② 문화적 다양성의 가치를 이해할
③ 실험실 내 실험자들의 안전을 보장할
⑤ 물리학과 경제학 간의 차이를 인식할

구문분석

[1행] If you ask a physicist [how long it would take a marble to fall from the top of a ten-story building,] he will likely answer the question **by assuming** [that the marble falls in a vacuum.]
▶ 첫 번째 [ ]는 「how+S+V」로 이루어진 간접의문문으로 ask의 직접목적어이고 두 번째 [ ]는 assuming의 목적어이다. 「by+v-ing」는 '~함으로써'의 의미이다.

2 ②

해석 다른 과학자의 실험 결과물을 읽을 때, 그 실험에 대해 비판적으로 생각하라. 당신 자신에게 물어라: 관찰들이 실험 도중에 혹은 후에 기록되었나? 결론이 합리적인가? 그 결과들은 반복될 수 있는가? 정보의 출처는 신뢰할 만한가? 당신은 실험을 수행한 그 과학자나 그룹이 한쪽으로 치우치지 않았는지 역시 물어야 한다. 우리가 이렇게 해야 하는 이유는 당신이 실험의 결과로 특별한 이익을 얻느냐 아니냐를 알기 위해서이다. 예를 들면, 만약 한 제약회사가 그 회사의 새로운 제품 중 하나가 얼마나 잘 작용하는지 시험해 보기 위한 실험 비용을 지불한다면, 특별한 이익이 관련된 것이다: 만약 실험이 그 제품이 효과 있음을 보여 준다면, 그 제약회사는 이익을 본다. 따라서, 그 실험자들은 객관적이지 않다. 그들은 결론이 제약 회사에 우호적이고 이익을 주도록 보장할지도 모른다. 결과들을 평가할 때, 있을 수 있는 어떤 치우침에 대해 생각하라!

문제풀이 다른 과학자의 실험 결과물을 읽을 때 있을 수 있는 어떤 치우침에 대해 생각하라고 주장하는 내용의 글이므로 빈칸에는 ② '객관적인'이 들어가는 것이 가장 적절하다.
① 창의적인   ③ 신뢰할 수 없는
④ 믿을 수 없는   ⑤ 결단력 있는

구문분석

[3행] You should also ask [if the scientist or group {conducting the experiment} was unbiased.]
▶ [ ]는 동사 ask의 목적절로 접속사 if를 사용한 '~인지 아닌지'의 의미의 명사절이다. { }는 the scientist or group을 수식하는 분사구문으로 주어와의 관계가 능동이라 현재분사형을 썼다.

3 ⑤

해석 성장하고 있는 유전학 분야는 많은 과학자가 여러 해 동안 의구심을 가져왔던 것, 즉 식품이 유전자 청사진에 직접 영향을 줄 수 있다는 것을 우리에게 보여 주고 있다. 이 정보는 유전자가 우리의 통제하에 있는 것이지 우리가 복종해야 하는 것이 아니라는 것을 더 잘 이해하도록 도와준다. 일란성 쌍둥이를 생각해 보자. 두 사람은 모두 똑같은 유전자를 부여받는다. 중년에, 쌍둥이 중 한 명은 암에 걸리고, 다른 한 명은 암 없이 건강하게 오래 산다. 특정 유전자가 쌍둥이 중 한 명에게 암에 걸리도록 명령했지만, 나머지 한 명에서는 똑같은 유전자가 그러지 않았다. 한 가지 가능성은 쌍둥이 중 건강한 사람이 암 유전자, 즉 나머지 한 명이 병에 걸리도록 명령했던 그 똑같은 유전자를 차단하는 식사를 했다는 것이다. 여러 해 동안 과학자들은 화학적 독소(예를 들어 담배)와 같은 다른 환경적 요인들이 유전자에 작용하여 암의 원인이 될 수 있다는 것을 인정해 왔다. 음식이 유전자 발현에 특정한 영향을 미친다는 생각은 비교적 새로운 것이다.

문제풀이 유전학 분야에서 식품이 유전자 청사진에 직접 영향을 줄 수 있으며 이는 유전자가 우리의 통제 하에 있는 것을 의미한다는 내용의 글이므로 빈칸에는 ⑤ '음식이 유전자 발현에 특정한 영향을 미친다'가 들어가는 것이 가장 적절하다.
① 일란성 쌍둥이는 똑같은 유전적 구성을 지닌다
② 음식에 대한 우리의 선호도는 유전자에 의해 영향을 받는다
③ 균형 잡힌 식단이 우리의 정신 건강에 필수적이다
④ 유전 공학은 몇몇 치명적인 질병을 치료할 수 있다

[2행] This information <u>helps</u> <u>us</u> better <u>understand</u> [that
　　　　　　　　　 V　　O　　　　　O.C.
genes are under our control and not <u>something</u> {we

must obey}].
▶「help+O+O.C.」 구문으로 '~가 …하도록 돕다'의 의미이고
목적격 보어로 동사원형을 썼다. [ ]는 접속사 that이 이끄는 명
사절로 understand의 목적절에 해당하고 { }는 that이 생략된
목적격 관계대명사절로 something을 수식한다.

STEP 1 어휘

26강 환경

PRACTICE
p.212

A	1 ecosystem	2 extinction	3 counterpart
	4 thrive	5 pollution	
B	1 ② 2 ④ 3 ③ 4 ④ 5 ④		
C	1 decrease	2 resilience	

A

1 생물다양성은 해양 생태계에서도 역시 중요하다.

2 불법 조업 때문에 밍크고래는 멸종 위기에 처해 있다.

3 유럽 정상들은 아시아 정상들과 RE 100(재생에너지 100%)에 대해 논의했다.

4 대부분의 식물은 햇볕이 잘 들고 물기가 많은 환경에서 가장 잘 자란다.

5 공장과 농장으로 인한 강의 오염은 갈수록 심각해진다.

B

1 바다의 오염은 물고기에게 위협 요인이다.

2 원전 사고로 후쿠시마는 재난 지역으로 선포되었다.

3 아이들이 노는 공간은 환경친화적이어야 한다.

4 모든 국가는 국제법을 수호할 책임이 있다.

5 올 8월에 해양 활동을 하던 많은 사람들이 해파리에 쏘였다.

C

1 사람들이 어떻게 행동하느냐는 흔히 다른 사람들이 하는 것에 달려 있다. 예를 들어, 만약 나의 동료 시민 대부분이 환경세를 내지 않는다면, 그런 위반자들을 사면해야 한다는 강한 압력이 있을 것인데, 이는 환경세를 내야 하는 나의 동기를 또한 감소시킬 것이다.

2 기후로 인한 교란이 세계 해안의 해양 생태계에 더 자주 그리고 더 큰 강도로 영향을 미치고 있지만, 해양 생태계가 극심한 기후의 사건들에 놀라운 회복력을 보여 주는 경우들이 또한 많다.

적용독해
p.213

1 ③　　2 ④

1 ③

해석 지난 20년 혹은 30년 동안의 상세한 연구는 자연계의 복잡한 형태가 그것의 기능에 필수적이라는 것을 보여 주고 있다. 강을 직선화하고 규칙적인 횡단면으로 만들고자 하는 시도는 아마도 이러한 형태-기능 관계의 가장 막심한 피해 사례가 될 수 있다. 자연 발생적인 강은 매우 불규칙한 형태를 가지고 있다. 그것은 많이 굽이치고, 범람원을 가로질러 넘쳐 흐르고, 습지로 스며 들어가서 끊임없이 변화하여, 엄청나게 복잡한 강가를 만든다. 이것은 강의 수위와 속도 변화를 막을(→ 조절할) 수 있게 한다. 강을 질서정연한 기하학적 형태에 맞춰 넣는 것은 기능적 수용 능력을 파괴하고 1927년과 1993년의 Mississippi강의 홍수와, 더 최근에는, 허리케인 Katrina와 같은 비정상적인 재난을 초래한다. Louisiana에서 "강을 자유롭게 흐르도록 두라.(let the river loose.)"라는 500억 달러 계획은 통제된 Mississippi강이 매년 그 주의 24제곱마일을 유실시키고 있다는 것을 인정한 것이다.

문제풀이 복잡한 형태의 강은 재난을 막는 본연의 기능을 다하고 있기 때문에 인위적으로 강을 질서정연하게 정비하면 큰 재난을 초래할 수 있다는 내용이므로 ③ prevent는 accommodate 등으로 고쳐야 한다.

구문분석

[9행] [A **$50 billion plan** to "let the river loose" in
　　　　　　　S
Louisiana] **recognizes** [that the controlled Mississippi
　　　　　　　　V　　　　　　　　　O
is washing away twenty-four square miles of that state
annually.]
▶ 첫 번째 [ ]는 문장의 주어에 해당하는 부분이고 핵심 주어는
a plan이기에 3인칭 단수 동사를 쓴다. 두 번째 [ ]는 that이 이
끄는 recognizes의 목적어에 해당하는 명사절이다. to let은 '~
할, ~하는'의 의미로 명사 plan을 수식하는 to부정사의 형용사적
용법으로 쓰였다.

2 ④

해석 몇 년 전에 학교 아이들은 산소가 우리에게 꼭 그런 것처럼 이산화탄소가 식물에게 있어서 자연스럽게 발생하는 생명의 원천이라고 배웠다. 오늘날 아이들은 이산화탄소를 독소라고 생각하기가 더 쉽다. 왜냐하면 대기 중의 이산화탄소의 양이 지난 백 년간에 걸쳐서 입자 백만 개당 약 280개에서 380개로 크게 상승했기 때문이다. 그러나 사람들이 모르고 있는 것은 우리 포유류 조상들이 진화하고 있던 약 팔천만 년 전에 이산화탄소 수치가 적어도 입자 백만 개당 천 개였다는 것이다. 사실, 그 수치는 여러분이 에너지 효율이 높은 사무실 건물에서 일하는 경우에 여러분이 정기적으로 내뿜는 이산화탄소의 농도인데, 그것은 난방과 환기 시스템을 위한 기준을 설정하는 기술자 집단에 의해 설정된 수준이다. 그러므로 이산화탄소는 명백히 무독성(→ 독성)을 가지고 있지 않을 뿐만 아니라 이산화탄소 수치의 변

화가 꼭 인간 활동을 반영하는 것은 아니다. 역사적으로 대기의 이산화탄소가 반드시 지구 온난화의 원인이었던 것도 아니다.

문제풀이 오늘날 이산화탄소의 증가가 지구 온난화의 주범이며 독소라고 여겨지지만 이산화탄소에는 독성이 없으며 역사적으로 대기의 이산화탄소가 지구 온난화의 주원인이 아니라는 내용이므로 ④ nontoxic은 poisonous 등으로 바꿔야 한다.

구문분석

[11행] **Nor has atmospheric carbon dioxide** necessarily
　　　　조동사　　　　　　S
been the trigger for global warming historically.
　V
▶ 부정어 nor가 문장의 앞에 위치해 「부정어(구)+조동사+S+V」의 어순으로 도치되었다.

✔STEP 2 어법　　가정법 1

PRACTICE
p.214

A　1 lost　　2 have reached　　3 Had
　　　4 would　　5 have become

B　1 were　　2 have stopped

A

1 만약 그들이 직장을 잃는다면, 그들은 생존할 수 없을 것이다.
　▶ 가정법 과거
2 만약 당신이 그날에 화성 쪽으로 빛을 비췄다면, 그 빛은 3분 만에 화성에 도달했을 것이다. ▶ 가정법 과거완료
3 우리가 피곤하지만 않았다면, 아침에 외출했을 텐데. ▶ if가 생략된 가정법 과거완료
4 네가 없다면, 내 인생은 의미가 없을 텐데. ▶ 가정법 과거
5 세계 야생 생물 기금(WWF)의 도움이 없었더라면, 고래는 멸종되었을 수도 있다. ▶ 가정법 과거완료

B

1 질병 검진 절차와 진단받은 질환에 대한 의학적 치료를 성공적으로 받은 과체중인 사람이 일주일 후에 다시 고열량 식단의 유혹에 빠진다면, 그 사람은 아예 자신의 체중 감량과 조절의 필요성을 받아들이지 않은 경우와 다름없는 실패일 것이다. ▶ 가정법 과거
2 과거에, 열대 지방에 사는 사람들은 병원균의 밀도가 온대 기후나 한랭 기후보다 열대 지방에서 훨씬 더 높다는 것을 알지 못했다. 열대 지방의 사람들이 다른 집단과 교류할 때 병에 잘 걸린다는 것을 알게 되었다면, 그들은 그것(교류한다는 것)을 하는 것을 중단했을 것이다. ▶ 가정법 과거완료

적용독해
p.215

1 ④　　2 ②

1 ④

해석 플라스틱은 매우 느리게 분해되고 물에 떠다니는 경향이 있다. 이는 플라스틱을 해류를 따라 수천 마일을 돌아다니게 한다. 대부분의 플라스틱은 자외선에 노출될 때 점점 더 작은 조각으로 분해되어 미세 플라스틱을 형성한다. 이러한 미세 플라스틱은 일단 그것들을 수거하는 데 일반적으로 사용되는 그물망을 통과할 만큼 충분히 작아지면 측정하기가 매우 어렵다. 미세 플라스틱이 해양 환경과 먹이 그물에 미치는 영향은 아직도 제대로 이해되지 않고 있다. 이 작은 조각들은 다양한 동물에게 먹혀 먹이 사슬 속으로 들어간다고 알려져 있다. 바다 속에 있는 대부분의 플라스틱 조각들은 매우 작기 때문에 바다를 청소할 실질적인 방법은 없다. 비교적 많은 양의 플라스틱을 수거하기 원한다면 우리는 엄청난 양의 물을 여과해야 할 수도 있다.

문제풀이 ④ 주어가 복수명사 particles이므로 is를 복수동사 are로 고쳐야 한다.
① plastic을 대신하는 단수 대명사
② 분사구문의 부대상황 ▶ p.158
③ microplastics를 대신하는 복수 대명사
⑤ 가정법 과거

2 ②

해석 멸종에 이르고 있는 종에게 동물원은 생존을 위한 마지막 기회로 작용할 수 있다. 회복 프로그램이 현장 환경 보호 활동가와 야생 동물 당국의 노력을 통합하기 위해 수립된다. 그 종의 개체 수가 감소하면서 동물원이 포획 사육 프로그램을 시작하는 것은 드물지 않다. 포획 사육은 멸종을 막기 위해 작용한다. 어떤 경우에는 포획 사육된 개체가 다시 야생으로 방생되어 야생 개체 수를 보충할 수도 있다. 이는 개체가 특정 생애 주기 동안에 가장 큰 위협에 놓여 있는 상황에서 가장 성공적이다. 예를 들어 거북이 알은 그것이 부화한 이후까지 고위험 위치로부터 제거될 수도 있다. 이는 성체까지 생존하는 거북이의 수를 증가시킬 수 있다. 악어 프로그램 역시 알과 부화한 유생을 보호하는 데 있어서 성공적이지 않았다면, 일단 그것이 스스로를 보호하도록 더 잘 갖추어진 후 그렇게 많은 부화한 유생이 방생되지 못했을 것이다.

문제풀이 ② If it were not for ～는 가정법 과거구문이므로 주절의 would have been을 would be로 바꿔야 한다.
① it ～ to 가주어-진주어 구문
③ 「관계부사+완전한 절」 ▶ p.182
④ 「선행사(turtles)+주격 관계대명사+복수 동사」
⑤ 가정법 과거완료

✔STEP 3 유형　　빈칸 추론 3
pp.216~217

1 ④　　2 ②　　3 ③

1 ④

해석 일부 심해 생물은 그들이 좋아하는 물고기의 움직임을 모방하는 작은 빛으로 먹이를 유혹하기 위해 가짜 미끼로써, 혹은 반딧불이처럼 짝을 찾기 위해 성적 유인 물질로써 생물 발광을 활용한다고 알려져 있다. 생물 발광의 생존 가치에 대한 많은 가능한 진화 이론이 있지만 가장 흥미로운 것 중 하나는 보이지 않는 망토를 만드는 것이다. 거의 모든 생물 발광 분자의 색깔은 바다 위층과 같은 색인 청록색이다. 청록색으로 자체 발광함으로써 생물은 특히 위쪽의 더 밝은 물을 배경으로 아래에서 보여질 때 더 이상 그림자를 드리우거나 실루엣을 만들어 내지 않는다. 오히려 자신을 빛냄으로써 그들은 햇빛 혹은 달빛의 반짝임, 반사 그리고 분산된 청록색 빛에 섞일 수 있다. 만약 그들이 자신만의 빛을 만들어 내지 못한다면, 보이지 않게 하려는 그들의 목적은 이루어지지 않을 것이다.

문제풀이 동물들이 먹이나 짝을 유혹하려고 생물 발광을 활용한다고 알려져 있지만 일부 생물은 바다 위층과 같은 청록색을 발광하여 자신을 보이지 않게 한다는 내용의 글이므로 빈칸에는 ④ '보이지 않는 망토를 만드는'이 들어가는 것이 가장 적절하다.
① 구조 신호를 보내는 ② 근처에 있는 적들을 위협하는
③ 숨어있는 먹잇감을 찾아내는 ⑤ 항해 시스템으로 기능하는

구문분석

> [1행] Some deep-sea organisms are known to use bioluminescence [**as** a lure, {to attract prey with a little glow ⟨imitating the movements of their favorite fish⟩}], or like fireflies, [**as** a sexual attractant {to find mates}].
>
> ▶ 두 개의 [ ]는 '～로써'라는 의미의 전치사 as가 쓰인 전치사구 2개가 등위접속사 or로 병렬되고 있다. as 전치사구 속에는 to attract와 to find의 to부정사구가 각각 목적을 의미하는 부사적 용법으로 사용되고 있다. ⟨ ⟩는 glow를 수식하는 현재분사구이다.

2 ②

해석 연구원들은 해안가 마을들이 해수면 상승에 어떻게 대비하고 있는지 묻는 프로젝트를 진행하고 있다. 어떤 마을들은 위험 평가를 하고 어떤 마을들은 심지어 계획을 가지고 있다. 하지만 실제로 계획을 실행하고 있는 마을은 드물다. 우리가 기후 변화에 대처하는 데 실패한 한 가지 이유는 그것이 시공간적으로 멀리 떨어져 있다는 일반적인 믿음 때문이다. 수십 년 동안, 기후 변화는 미래에 대한 예측이었다. 만약 과학자들은 미래 시제로 기후 변화에 대해 말하지 않았다면 기후 변화에 더 잘 대처했을 것이다. 불행히도, 이것이 습관이 되어 우리가 기후 위기가 진행 중이라는 것을 알고 있음에도, 많은 과학자들이 오늘날에도 여전히 미래 시제를 사용하고 있다. 과학자들은 또한 방글라데시나 서남극 빙상처럼 위기의 영향을 가장 많이 받는 지역에 초점을 맞추고 있으며, 그 지역은 대부분의 미국인들에게는 물리적으로 멀리 떨어져 있다.

문제풀이 해수면 상승에 대한 해안 마을의 대비 계획과 실행여부가 미비한 이유는 과학자들이 기후 변화에 대해 현재 진행이 아닌 미래 시제로 그리고 멀리 떨어져 있다는 식으로 말하기 때문이라는 내용의 글이므로 빈칸에는 ② '그것이 시공간적으로 멀리 떨어져 있다'가 들어가는 것이 가장 적절하다.
① 그것이 과학과 관련이 없다
③ 에너지 효율성이 가장 중요하다
④ 면밀한 계획이 그 문제를 해결 할 수 있다
⑤ 그것이 발생하지 않도록 하기에는 너무 늦다

구문분석

> [1행] Researchers are working on a project [that asks coastal towns how they are preparing for rising sea levels.]
> I.O.´ D.O.´
>
> ▶ [ ]는 선행사 a project를 수식하는 주격 관계대명사절이며 「ask+I.O.+D.O.」 구문은 '～에게 …을 묻는다'는 의미인데 직접목적어 자리에 「how+S+V」의 어순인 how 간접의문문이 쓰였다.

3 ③

해석 우리의 집은 단순한 생태계가 아니라 독특한 곳이며, 실내 환경에 적응된 종들을 수용하고 새로운 방향으로 진화를 밀어붙인다. 실내 미생물, 곤충, 그리고 쥐들은 모두 항균제, 살충제, 독에 대한 내성을 키우면서 우리의 화학적 공격에서 살아남을 수 있는 능력을 진화시켜 왔다. 독일 바퀴벌레는 바퀴벌레 덫에서 미끼로 흔히 사용되는 포도당에 대한 혐오감을 발달시켜 온 것으로 알려져 있다. 이러한 적응력이 없었더라면, 야외(에 사는) 상대방에 비해 먹이를 잡아먹을 더 적은 기회를 가지는 일부 실내 곤충은 먹이가 제한적일 때 생존할 수 있는 능력을 발달시킬 수 없었을 것이다. Dunn과 다른 생태학자들은 지구가 점점 더 발전되고 도시화되면서, 더 많은 종들이 실내에서 번성하기 위해 그들이 필요로 하는 특성들을 진화시킬 것이라고 말해 왔다. 충분히 긴 시간에 걸쳐, 실내 생활은 또한 우리의 진화를 이끌 수 있었다. 아마도 실내 생활을 좋아하는 내 모습은 인류의 미래를 대변할 것이다.

문제풀이 실내 환경이라는 독특한 공간인 인간의 집에는 다양한 종들이 생존을 위해 진화해 왔으며 앞으로도 진화해 갈 것이라는 내용의 글이므로 빈칸에는 ③ '실내에서 번성하기 위해 그들이 필요로 하는 특성들을 진화시킬'이 들어가는 것이 가장 적절하다.
① 자신을 보호하기 위해 화학물질을 분비할
② 서식지 파괴로 멸종될
④ 먹잇감을 찾기 위해 외부 유기체와 경쟁할
⑤ 야생과 인간의 경계를 허물어트릴

구문분석

> [4행] German cockroaches are known to **have developed** a distaste for glucose, [which is commonly used as bait in roach traps.]
>
> ▶ [ ]는 선행사 glucose를 수식하는 주격 관계대명사절이며 '～하는 것으로 알려진'의 의미인 「be known to-v」 구문에서 단순부정사(to develop) 대신에 완료부정사(to have developed)가 쓰인 이유는 문장의 시제(현재동사 are)보다 더 과거에 발생했다는 의미를 나타내기 위해서이다.

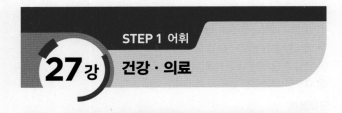

PRACTICE
p.220

A	1 risky 2 elastic 3 optimistic 4 deliberate 5 sanitary
B	1 ④ 2 ③ 3 ② 4 ③ 5 ④
C	1 ceased 2 counter

A

1 의사들은 수술을 시도하기에는 너무 **위험하다**고 말한다.
2 시간이 지남에 따라 고무줄은 점점 덜 **탄력적**이 될 것이다.
3 **낙관적인** 태도가 세로토닌의 분비를 촉진한다고 생각한다.
4 주지사의 연설이 많은 시민을 분노하게 했지만 **의도적인** 것은 아니었다.
5 시 당국은 식당의 **위생** 상태를 개선하기 위해 평점제를 활용했다.

B

1 뇌에 산소가 공급되지 않으면 뇌는 작동을 멈춘다.
2 그 환자는 폐암으로 **오진** 받았다.
3 병적으로 **비만**인 사람들의 수가 젊은 세대에서 더 증가했다.
4 **혈관**이 딱딱해지면 당뇨병이나 고혈압을 유발할 수 있다.
5 공기가 **순환**하도록 문과 창문은 종종 열어 두어야 한다.

C

1 심장 이식을 할 수 있는 능력은 많은 생명을 구할 수 있었던 인공호흡기의 개발과 관련이 있었지만, 심장이 계속해서 뛰는 사람들이 모두 다 어떤 다른 중요한 기능을 회복한 것은 아니었다. 어떤 경우에는 그들의 뇌가 완전히 기능을 **멈추었다**.
2 비서양의 과학적 패러다임을 기껏해야 열등하고 최악의 경우 부정확하다고 일축함으로써, 종래의 서양 의학 연구 단체의 가장 완고한 구성원들은 대체 의학 요법과 연구가 자신들의 연구, 자신들의 행복, 그리고 자신들의 세계관에 가하는 위협에 **반격하려** 한다.

적용독해
p.221

1 ③ 2 ⑤

1 ③

해석 식물로의 영양소 흡수를 막고 우리가 먹는 식품 속 미네랄의 감소를 야기하는 비료가 사용되지 않았더라면 어땠을까? 우선적으로 많은 필수 영양소를 만들어 내는 토양에 있는 이로운 박테리아, 지렁이 그리고 벌레를 죽이는 살충제의 사용이 금지되었더라면 어땠을까? 농작물에 질소와 칼륨으로 비료를 주는 것은 마그네슘, 아연, 철 그리고 요오드의 감소로 이어져 왔다. 예를 들어 밀의 마그네슘 함량에서 평균적으로 약 30%의 감소가 있었다. 이는 부분적으로 칼슘이 식물에 의한 마그네슘 방출(→ 흡수)에 방해물이 되기 때문이다. 토양의 더 낮은 마그네슘 수치는 산성 토양에서도 나타나는데 지구상에 있는 농지의 약 70%가 현재 산성이다. 따라서 토양의 전반적인 특성은 식물 속 미네랄의 축적을 결정한다. 실제로 오늘날 우리의 토양은 덜 건강하고 그 위에서 길러진 식물도 그러하다.

문제풀이 비료와 살충제의 사용이 토양과 식물에 미치는 부정적인 영향에 대한 내용이므로 ③ release는 absorption 등으로 고쳐야 한다.

구문분석

[10행] Indeed, nowadays our soil is less healthy and [so are the plants {grown on it}].
▶ 첫 번째 [ ]는 도치구문으로 「so+V+S」는 '~도 또한 그렇다'라는 의미이며 { }는 앞에 'which/that are'가 생략되어 the plants를 수식하는 수동의 뜻이 담긴 과거분사구이다.

2 ⑤

해석 "잠은 죽어서나 자는 것이다."라는 옛 격언은 유감스럽다. 이런 사고방식을 가지면, 여러분은 더 빨리 죽게 될 것이고 그 삶의 질은 더 나빠질 것이다. 수면 부족이라는 고무 밴드는 그것이 끊어지기 전까지만 늘어날 수 있다. 안타깝게도, 인간은 사실 합당한 이익 없이 의도적으로 잠을 자제하는 유일한 종이다. 건강의 모든 요소와 사회 구조의 수많은 이음매는 인간적 측면과 재정적 측면 둘 다 손실이 큰 우리의 수면 무시 상태로 인해 약화되고 있다. 이제는 세계 보건 기구(WHO)에서 산업화된 나라 전역에 수면 부족 유행병을 선포할 정도였다. 미국, 영국, 일본, 한국, 그리고 몇몇 서유럽 국가들과 같은, 지난 세기에 걸쳐 수면 시간이 가장 급격하게 감소한 국가들이 또한 신체 질환과 정신 질환 비율에서 가장 많은 감소(→ 증가)를 겪고 있는 국가들이라는 것은 우연의 일치가 아니다.

문제풀이 수면 부족이 인간의 건강에 미치는 영향과 손실을 언급하고 있으므로 ⑤ decline은 increase 등으로 고쳐야 한다.

구문분석

[3행] Sadly, human beings are in fact the only species [that will deliberately **deprive** themselves of sleep without legitimate gain.]
▶ [ ]는 선행사 the only species를 수식하는 주격 관계대명사절이고 「deprive A of B」는 'A에게서 B를 빼앗다'라는 의미이다.

A　1 spoil　2 have missed　3 lie
　　　4 had studied　5 be

B　1 impose　2 be

A

1 냉매는 그렇지 않으면 상할 많은 양의 식품을 보존한다. ▶ 「현재 사실＋otherwise 가정법 과거」

2 나는 버스 정류장으로 전속력으로 달려갔는데, 그렇지 않았다면 버스를 놓쳤을 것이다. ▶ 「과거 사실＋otherwise 가정법 과거완료」

3 나는 그녀가 거짓말을 할 때마다 화가 난다. 그녀가 더 이상 거짓말을 안 하면 좋을 텐데. ▶ 「현재 사실＋I wish 가정법 과거」

4 그가 학창 시절에 열심히 공부했더라면 좋았을 텐데. ▶ 「과거 사실＋I wish 가정법 과거완료」

5 판사는 그 범죄자에게 종신형 선고를 명령했다. ▶ 「당위동사＋that＋S＋(should)＋동사원형」

B

1 국가가 개입하지 않으면 공해와 같이 기업이 공공에 부과할 외부 비용에 책임을 지기 위해 민간 부문을 규제할 수 있으며, 기초 과학 연구나 의약품 개발과 같은 시장 잠재력이 거의 없는 공공재에 투자할 수 있다. ▶ 「현재 사실＋otherwise 가정법 과거」

2 1965년에 설립된 하버드 뇌사 위원회는 모든 '식별 가능한 중추 신경계 활동'의 부재는 사망의 새로운 기준이 되어야 한다고 권고했으며, 이 권고가 거의 모든 국가에서 받아들여진 이후로 의학의 새로운 시대를 열었다. ▶ 「당위동사＋that＋S＋(should)＋동사원형」

적용독해   p.223

1 ④　2 ④

1 ④

해석 너무 밝은 빛이나, 눈에 직접적으로 비추는 빛처럼, 나쁜 조명은 여러분의 눈에 스트레스를 증가시킬 수 있다. 어둠 속의 플래시라이트가 그러듯이 형광등 또한 피로감을 줄 수 있다. 여러분이 모를 수도 있는 것은 빛의 질 또한 중요할 수 있다는 것이다. 대부분의 사람들은 밝은 햇빛 속에서 가장 행복감을 느끼는데, 밝은 햇빛이 체내의 화학 물질을 분비하는 것과 관련이 없다면 우리는 정서적인 행복감을 얻지 못할 것이다. 전형적으로 단지 몇 개의 빛 파장만 있는 인공 조명이 분위기에 미치는 효과는 햇빛(이 미치는 효과)과 똑같지 않을 수 있다. 빛이 여러분의 작업 환경의 질을 향상시키는 데 미치는 영향을 알고 싶다면, 창가에서 작업하거나 책상 전등에 있는 모든 파장이 있는 전구를 사용하여 실험해 봐야 한다고 전문가들은 조언한다.

문제풀이 ④ 주어가 셀 수 없는 명사(Artificial light)이면 단수 동사가 와야 하므로 do를 does로 고쳐야 한다.
① 유사 관계대명사 as＋불완전한 절

---

② 「be-v＋명사절 보어」
③ 「현재 사실＋otherwise 가정법 과거」
⑤ 「당위동사＋that＋S＋(should)＋동사원형」

2 ④

해석 어떤 허브는 다소 마법처럼 특정 장기의 기능을 향상시키고, 그 결과 특정한 질병을 "고친다"고 널리 알려져 있다. 그러한 진술은 비과학적이고 근거가 없다. 때때로 허브는 효과가 있는 것처럼 보이는데, 이는 당신의 신체로부터 그것들을 제거하려는 당신 몸의 적극적인 시도 속에서 그것들이 혈액 순환을 증가시키는 경향이 있기 때문이다. 일시적으로 생긴 좋은 기분이 마치 당신의 건강 상태가 향상된 것처럼 보이게 만든다. 또한 허브는, 어떤 다른 방법과 마찬가지로, 위약 효과를 가지고 있는데, 그래서 당신이 더 나아졌다고 느끼도록 도와준다. 어떠한 경우든, 건강을 되찾게 하는 지성을 가진 것은 허브가 아니라 바로 당신의 몸이다. 허브가 어떻게 당신의 몸을 더 건강해지는 방향으로 인도하는 데 요구되는 지성을 가질 수 있겠는가? 그것은 불가능하다. 어떻게 허브가 당신의 몸 안으로 들어가 영리하게 당신의 문제를 해결할 수 있는지를 상상해 본다면, 당신은 그것이 얼마나 불가능하게 보이는지를 알게 될 것이다. 그렇지 않다면, 그것은 허브가 인간의 몸보다 더 지적이라는 것을 의미하는 것이 되는데, 이는 정말로 믿기 어렵다.

문제풀이 ④ 본동사가 따로 없어 동사원형으로 시작하는 명령문이 되어야 하므로 Trying을 Try로 고쳐야 한다.
① 「사역동사 make＋O＋O.C.(동사원형)」
② it ~ that 강조 구문
③ 가정법 과거
⑤ 「현재 사실＋otherwise 가정법 과거」

1 ③　2 ③　3 ④

1 ③

해석 의료에 관한 한, 일반적으로 두 가지 형태의 주요한 진료가 있다. 과거에는 의사와 환자의 관계가 주로 가부장적이었다. 이런 유형의 관계에서 의사는 해야 할 것을 말하고 환자는 많은 질문하고 싶어도 하지 않고 그 지시를 따랐다. 일방적인 의사 전달만을 허용하는 이러한 의료 방식이 일반 대중의 총애를 서서히 잃어가면서, 다른 형태의 진료 방식(정보 제공 방식)이 의사와 환자 관계의 더 일반적인 형태로 점차 정착되고 있다. (많은 연구자들은 환자에 대한 진료를 효과적으로 개선하기 위해 이러한 가부장적 방식이 도입되어야 한다고 주장한다.) 이 경우, 의사의 일은 무엇을 할지를 환자에게 말해 주는 것이 아니라, 다양한 치료 선택 사항에 대해서 환자를 교육하는 것이다. 최종적으로 의사는 환자에게 환자 자신의 건강 상태에 대해 정보에 근거한 결정을 내릴 수 있도록 해준다.

문제풀이 의사와 환자의 전통적인 가부장적 관계의 단점과 이에 대한 대안에 관한 내용의 글이므로, 가부장적 방식을 도입해야 한다는 ③은 글의 흐름과 무관하다.

[7행] Many researchers **insist** [that this paternalistic style **be** introduced to care for patients efficiently.]
▶ [ ]는 당위를 나타내는 동사 insist의 목적절이며 「당위동사 +that+S+(should)+동사원형」 구문으로 should가 생략되어 동사원형 be만 남았다.

2 ③

해석 간호사들은 정신 건강 관리 체계에서 중추적인 역할을 맡고 있으며 의사소통망의 중심에 위치해 있는데, 부분적으로는 그들의 환자들과의 높은 접촉 정도뿐만 아니라 다른 전문직 종사자들과 잘 발달된 관계를 유지하기 때문이다. 이런 이유로 간호사들은 학제 간의(여러 학문 분야가 관련된) 의사소통에서 중요한 역할을 한다. 그들은 다양한 전문직 종사자들 집단과 환자와 보호자 집단 사이에서 중개 역할을 한다. (정신 건강 관리 전문직 종사자들은 법적으로 자신의 환자의 사생활을 보호하기로 되어 있어, 그들은 치료에 필요한 모든 것에 관해 비자발적이라기보다, 말할 수 없을지도 모른다.) 이것은 정신 건강상의 문제를 이해하는 다양한 방식을 가진 사람들에게 납득 가능하고 이해 가능한 언어로 집단 간 의사소통을 번역하는 것을 포함한다. 이것은 고도로 민감하고 숙련된 작업이며 간호사가 대안적 시각에 대한 높은 수준의 관심과 높은 수준의 의사소통 이해도를 가져야 함을 요구한다.

문제풀이 간호사의 중요한 역할 중 하나는 환자 및 보호자와의 원활한 의사소통이라는 내용의 글이므로 환자의 사생활 보호에 관한 ③은 글의 흐름과 무관하다.

구문분석

[10행] This is a highly sensitive and skilled task, [**requiring** that a nurse **have** a high level of attention to alternative views and a high level of understanding of communication].
▶ [ ]는 〈부대상황〉의 분사구문이며 「당위 동사(require)+ that+S+ (should)+동사원형」의 어순으로, '(주어)가 ~해야 한다고 요구하다'의 의미이다.

3 ④

해석 가장 초기의 시대부터, 헬스케어 서비스는 두 가지의 동등한 영역, 즉 병원 치료와 공공 헬스케어를 포함하는 것으로 인식되어 왔다. 고대 그리스 신화에서 의료의 신 아스클레피오스에게는 하이지아와 파나시아라는 두 딸이 있었다. 전자는 예방적 건강과 건강 관리, 즉 위생의 여신이었고, 후자는 치료와 치유의 여신이었다. 현대 시대에, 의료 전문성에 대한 사회적 우세는 아픈 환자들의 치료가 위생 공학자, 생물학자, 정부 공공 건강 관료와 같은 덜 영웅적인 인물들에 의해서 제공되는 그러한 예방적 헬스케어 서비스를 가리도록 만들었다. 그럼에도 불구하고, 인류가 누리는 건강의 질은 공공 위생, 하수 관리 그리고 대기 오염, 식수, 도시 소음을 관리하는 서비스들의 이용 가능성에 비해 수술적 기민함, 혁신적 제약 제품, 그리고 생물 공학적 장비에 덜 기인한다. (공공 헬스케어 서비스는 주로 질병에 걸린 후 치료와 수술에 초점을 맞추는데, 그렇지 않으면 높은 사망률을 낮출 수 없기 때문이다.) 건강에 대한 달성 가능한 최고 수준에 대한 인간의 권리는 의사와 병원의 기술과 장비만큼이나 공공 헬스케어 서비스에 달려 있다.

문제풀이 의료 기술과 장비만큼이나 공공 헬스케어 서비스가 중요하다는 내용의 글이므로 공공 헬스케어 서비스가 사후 치료에 초점을 맞춘다는 ④는 글의 흐름과 무관하다.

구문분석

[13행] The human right [to the highest attainable standard of health] depends *on* public healthcare services **no less than** *on* the skills and equipment of doctors and hospitals.
▶ [ ]는 주어 the human right를 수식하는 전치사구이며 동사는 depends이다. 「A no less than B」 구문은 'B 못지않게 A도'의 의미로 on 전치사구 2개가 A, B로 병렬된다.

STEP 1 어휘

28강 정치 · 법

PRACTICE
p.228

A	1 pursue	2 distribute	3 censor
	4 exploit	5 violate	
B	1 ② 2 ③ 3 ③ 4 ④ 5 ③		
C	1 little	2 challenging	

A

1 경찰은 총기범을 쫓아 버려진 건물로 들어갔다.
2 옷과 담요가 난민들에게 분배되었다.
3 기자들은 정권의 탄압을 받을 때 자기 검열을 한다.
4 노동자들이 근로기준법을 모르면 착취당할 수 있다.
5 사장은 회사에 자금을 공급하려고 부하 직원이 세법을 위반하도록 했다.

B

1 미국의 군사 개입은 그 나라의 붕괴로 이어졌다.
2 한국은 중국과 일본을 연결하는 지정학적 요충지의 역할을 하고 있다.
3 스위스 정부는 공식적인 중립을 지키기 위해 전쟁을 피한다.
4 장관은 신분증 소지를 법적 의무 사항으로 규정하려는 계획을 가지고 있다.

5 일본은 미국과 긴밀한 동맹을 맺어온 나라이다.

C

1 정치학자들이 국제적 활동 무대를 여러 국가들 간의 안보 경쟁으로 보았기 때문에, 국가들은 당장에라도 결렬될 수 있는 일시적인 군사 동맹이나 안보 협정에서 (얻는 이익) 외에, 서로 협력함으로써 얻을 수 있는 이득은 거의 없었다.

2 우주에 대한 당시의 종교적 낙관론을 훼손하고 세력이 있는 귀족들을 모욕하여 수감되었으며 그의 많은 책이 검열받았음에도 불구하고, 그 어떤 것도 그의 주변 사람들의 편견과 가식에 도전하는 것을 멈추게 하지 못했다.

적용독해
p.229

1 ④ 2 ④

---

1 ④

해석 역사적인 증거들을 보면 적절한 법이나 정부 개입의 부재 시 고용주들에 의해 착취당하는 노동자들을 볼 수 있다. 이것은, 노동자들이 경제 이론이 제시하는 것처럼, 그들의 증가된 생산성에 대해, 즉, 그들의 기여분에 대해 항상 보상받는 것은 아니라는 것을 의미한다. 만약 고용주들이 법적으로 제약을 받지 않는다면 노동자들을 착취할 수 있을 것이다. 따라서 최저임금법은 어쩌면 많은 노동자들이 빈곤선 위(→ 아래)의 월급으로 노동하는 것을 못 하게 막는 유일한 방법일 수 있다. 이러한 관점은 최저임금법이 효율적인 결과를 창출해 내는 시장의 힘을 강화시키면서 현존하는 시장의 실패를 수정하는 원천이라는 것을 의미한다.

문제풀이 적절한 법이나 정부의 개입이 없다면 노동자들은 고용주에게 착취당할 수밖에 없으며, 최저임금법이 저임금 노동을 막아 주며 건강한 자본주의로 가는 중요한 원천이라는 내용이므로 ④ above는 below 등으로 고쳐야 한다.

구문분석

[5행] Thus, the minimum wage laws may be the only way to **prevent** many employees **from working** at wages [that are below the poverty line.]
▶ to prevent는 '~할/~하는'의 to부정사의 형용사적 용법으로 the only way 수식한다. 「prevent+O+from+v-ing」는 '~가 …하는 것을 막다'의 의미이고 [ ]는 wages를 수식하는 주격 관계대명사절이다.

---

2 ④

해석 사람들이 서로에게 영향을 미치도록 하는 것은 집단 평가의 정확도를 낮춘다. 증거에 대한 다수의 출처로부터 가장 유용한 정보를 도출하기 위해서, 당신은 항상 이 출처들을 서로 독립적 상태로 만들도록 노력해야 한다. 이러한 원칙은 좋은 수사 절차의 한 부분이다. 한 사건에 대한 다수의 목격자들이 있을 때, 그들은 증언하기 전에 사건에 대해 의견을 나누는 것이 허락되지 않는다. 그 목적은 적대적인 목격자들에 의한 공모를 예방하는 것일 뿐만 아니라, 목격자들이 서로에게 영향을 미치는 것을 막기 위해서이기도 하다. 그들의 경험을 교환한 목격자들은 증언할 때 비슷한 오류를 범하는 경향이 있을 것이고, (이것은) 그들이 제공하는 정보의 전체 가치를 향상시킨다(→ 떨어뜨린다). 개방적인 의견 교환의 일반적인 관행은 먼저 그리고 자신감 있게 말하는 사람들의 의견에 너무 많은 무게를 실어 주고 (이것은) 다른 사람들이 그들 뒤에 줄을 서도록 한다.

문제풀이 집단 평가의 정확도를 높이기 위해서는 사람들이 서로에게 영향을 미치지 못하게 해야 하는데, 그렇지 않으면 서로에게 영향을 미쳐 제공된 정보의 가치가 떨어질 수밖에 없다는 내용이므로 ④ improving은 reducing, lowering, damaging 등으로 고쳐야 한다.

구문분석

[5행] The goal is **not only** [to prevent collusion by hostile witnesses,] it is **also** [to prevent witnesses from influencing each other.]
▶ 「not only A (but) also B」구문으로 'A뿐만 아니라 B도'의 의미로 A와 B에 각각 to prevent ~로 시작하는 명사적 용법의 to부정사가 쓰여 '~하는 것'으로 해석한다. 「prevent+O+from+v-ing」는 '~가 …하는 것을 막다'의 의미이다.

STEP 2 어법 강조·도치·생략

PRACTICE
p.230

A
1 does → did
2 himself → herself
3 this great triumph has
  → has this great triumph
4 are → do
5 did → was

B
1 that 2 does it have

A

1 전쟁이 발발한 1592년보다 180년 전에 거북선은 이미 존재하고 있었다. ▶ 동사를 강조하면서 과거시제

2 그녀는 K-pop 춤과 노래 콘테스트에 직접 참가했다. ▶ 주어 she를 의미하는 재귀대명사의 강조 용법

3 역사상 그러한 대승을 거둔 적은 한 번도 없었다. ▶ 도치문: 「부정어+V+S」

4 물고기는 새들만큼 중력의 영향을 많이 받지 않는다. ▶ 일반동사 fight를 대신하는 대동사

5 중국의 만리장성은 이집트의 피라미드만큼이나 거대하게 만들어졌다. ▶ was made를 대신하는 대동사

B

1 혁신을 촉진하기 위해 국가가 무엇을 해야 하는지에 대한 통념적인 견해는 정부가 민간 부문의 경제적 역동성을 단지 촉진하는 것에서 벗어나는 것에 불과하다. ▶ it ~ that 강조 구문
2 국가 통제주의 사회 체제하에서는 세금, 보조금, 관세, 그리고 규제가 종종 시장에서 기존의 대기업들을 보호하는 역할을 하는 반면, 자본주의 사회는 권리를 침해하는 세금, 관세, 보조금 또는 누군가에게 유리한 규제를 가지고 있지 않고 그것은 독점 금지법도 가지고 있지 않다. ▶ 도치: 「부정어+V+S」

적용독해 p.231

1 ④   2 ③

---

1 ④

해석 토론은 언어 그 자체만큼이나 오래되었고 인간의 역사 내내 많은 형태들을 취해 왔다. 고대 로마에서 원로원에서의 토론은 아주 중요해서 시민 사회의 경영과 사법제도에 큰 영향을 미쳤다. 그리스에서는 정책변화에 대한 옹호자들이 수백 명의 아테네인들로 구성된 시민 배심원단 앞에서 일상적으로 자신들의 주장을 설명하곤 했다. 인도에서 토론은 종교적인 찬반논란을 해결하는 데 사용되었고 매우 인기 있는 오락의 한 형태였다. 인도의 왕들은 승리자들에게 상을 주면서 대규모 토론 대회를 후원했다. 중국은 자국만의 오래되고 훌륭한 토론 전통을 가지고 있다. 2세기가 시작되면서, 도교와 유교의 학자들은 하루 동안 주로 지속되기도 하는 대회의 관객들 앞에서 정신적이고 철학적인 문제를 토론했던 청담(清談)이라고 알려진 관행에 참여했다.

문제풀이 ④ 동시동작을 의미하는 분사구문이 되어야 하는데 의미상의 주어가 Indian Kings이고 둘의 관계가 능동이므로 v-ing형이 와야 한다. offer를 offering으로 고쳐야 한다. ▶ p.158
① 도치: 「보어+be+S」   ② it ~ that 강조 구문
③ 도치: 「부정어+V+S」   ⑤ 관계부사+3형식 완전한 절

2 ③

해석 모든 농부들은 밭이 준비되도록 하는 것이 어려운 부분임을 안다. 씨앗을 심고 그것들이 자라는 것을 보는 것은 쉽다. 과학과 산업의 경우, 공동체가 밭을 준비하지만, 사회는 우연히 성공적인 씨앗을 심은 개인에게 모든 공로를 돌리는 경향이 있다. 씨를 심는 것은 반드시 엄청난 지능을 필요로 하는 것은 아니다; 씨앗이 번성하게 해 주는 환경을 만드는 것은 그러하다. 우리는 과학, 정치, 사업 그리고 일상에서 공동체에 좀 더 많은 공로를 인정해 줄 필요가 있다. 이러한 가장 큰 강점 즉 모든 역경에 맞서, 사회의 인종에 대한 인식과 법의 공정성에 있어 혁명적인 변화들을 성취하기 위해서 사람들이 함께 일하도록 고무시키는 능력을 가진 사람은 바로 Martin Luther King Jr.이었다. 그러나 그가 성취한 것을 진정으로 이해하는 것은 그 사람을 넘어서 보는 것을 요구한다. 그를 모든 위대한 것들의 구현으로 여기는 대신에 우리는 미국이 위대해질 수 있음을 보여 주게 하는 데 있어서 그의 역할을 인정해야 한다.

문제풀이 ③ 일반동사 require를 대신하는 대동사가 쓰여야 하므로 is를 does로 고쳐야 한다.
① 「get+O+v-ed」 ~를 …되게 만들다 ▶ p.52
② 「동명사구 주어+단수 동사」 ▶ p.190
④ it ~ that 강조 구문
⑤ 동사의 강조

pp.232~233

STEP 3 유형   글의 순서

1 ⑤   2 ③   3 ②

1 ⑤

해석 '권력 거리'는 권력의 불평등한 분배가 한 문화의 구성원들에 의해 얼마나 널리 수용되는지를 나타내는 데 사용되는 용어이다. 그것은 권력이 더 적은 사회 구성원들이 그들의 권력에서의 불평등을 수용하고 그것을 규범으로 여기는 정도와 관계가 있다. (C) 권력 거리에 대한 높은 수용의 문화들(예를 들어, 인도, 브라질, 그리스, 멕시코 그리고 필리핀)에서, 사람들은 평등한 것으로 여겨지지 않으며, 모든 사람이 사회 계층 내에서 명확하게 정해지거나 할당된 위치를 가진다. (B) 권력 거리에 대한 낮은 수용의 문화들(예를 들어, 핀란드, 노르웨이, 뉴질랜드 그리고 이스라엘)에서는, 사람들은 불평등이 최소화여야만 한다고 믿으며, 계층적 구분은 오직 편의상 구분으로서만 여겨진다. (A) 이러한 문화에서는 사회 계층 내에서의 더 많은 유동성이 있으며, 개인이 그들의 개인적 노력과 성취를 토대로 사회 계층을 상승시키는 것이 상대적으로 쉽다.

문제풀이 권력 거리라는 용어의 의미와 용도에 관한 내용의 주어진 글 다음에, (C) 권력 거리에 대한 높은 수용의 문화권의 예와 특징을 제시한 후, (B) 이와 대조적인 권력 거리에 대한 낮은 수용의 문화권의 예와 사고방식을 설명하였으며, (A) 그러한 문화의 구체적인 특징에 관한 내용으로 이어지는 것이 자연스럽다.

구문분석

> [5행] ... **it** is relatively easy (*for individuals*) [**to move**
> up the social hierarchy {based on their individual
> efforts and achievements.}]
> ▶ it은 가주어이고 [ ]가 진주어이다. ( )는 의미상의 주어를 나타낸다. { }은 the social hierarchy를 수식하는 과거분사구이다.

2 ③

해석 어떤 사람들은 사회 과학이 자연 과학에 뒤처지고 있다고 믿는다. (B) 그들은 사회 과학이 정확한 법칙을 가지고 있지 않을 뿐만 아니라 인종 차별, 범죄, 가난, 그리고 전쟁과 같은 거대한 사회악을 제거하는 데에도 실패했다고 주장한다. 그들은 사회 과학자들이 그들에게 마땅히 기대되어졌을지도 모르는 것을 달성하는 데 실패했다고 주장한다. (C) 그러한 비판자들은 사회 과학의 진정한 본질과 그것의 특

수한 문제 그리고 기본적인 한계를 절대로 알지 못하고 있다. 예를 들어, 그들은 사회 문제에 대한 해결책은 지식 위의 사람들에게 영향력을 행사할 수 있는 능력도 필요로 한다는 사실을 잊는다. (A) 비록 사회 과학자들이 사회적 발전을 이루기 위해 마땅히 따라야 할 절차를 발견한다 할지라도 그들은 좀처럼 사회적 행동을 통제할 위치에 있지 않다. 그 점에서는 심지어 독재자들도 사회를 변화시키는 자신들의 권력에 한계가 있다는 것을 알게 된다.

문제풀이 어떤 사람들은 사회 과학이 자연 과학에 뒤처지고 있다고 믿는다는 글 다음에, (B) 왜 뒤처졌는지 구체적으로 그들의 주장을 제시하였고, (C) 그들의 주장이 갖는 한계를 반박한 후, (A) 반박의 근거를 제시하는 내용으로 이어지는 것이 자연스럽다.

구문분석

> [6행] They maintain [that **not only** <u>does</u> <u>social science</u>
>   V   S
> have no exact laws, **but** it **also** has failed to eliminate
> great social evils such as racial discrimination, crime,
> poverty, and war.]
> ▶[ ]는 접속사 that이 이끄는 maintain의 목적어이다. 「not only A, but also B」의 구문인데 부정어 not only가 문두로 나와 「not only+do/does/did+S+동사원형」의 어순으로 도치된다. 주어(social science)가 3인칭 단수이므로 does가 쓰였다.

3 ②

해석 독립적인 민족(사회) 정신을 유지하려고 할 때, 문화는 결정적 질량(임계 질량)의 문제에 직면한다. 자신 혼자서 행동하는 어떤 한 개인도 민족(사회) 정신을 만들어 낼 수 없다. (B) 오히려 민족(사회) 정신은 많은 개인의 상호의존적인 행위에서 비롯된다. 생성된 의미의 이러한 군집은 더 크고 더 부유한 외부 힘으로부터 어느 정도의 단절을 필요로 할 수 있다. 캐나다 이누이트족은 비록 2만 4천 명에도 불과하지만 그들만의 민족(사회) 정신을 유지하고 있다. (A) 그들은 삶을 유지하기 위해 무역과 지리적 고립의 조합을 통해 이러한 업적을 해낸다. 이누이트족은 캐나다의 주요 인구 중심지에서 따로 멀리 떨어진 영토를 차지하고 있다. 만약 문화 간 접촉이 충분히 긴밀해진다면, 이누이트인들의 민족(사회) 정신이 사라지게 될 것이다. (C) 비슷한 규모의 다른 문화 집단은 캐나다 토론토 도심에서는 결국 지속되지 않는데, 거기에서 그들은 많은 외부 영향과 접촉하고 그들의 삶을 위해 본질적으로 서구적 방식을 추구한다.

문제풀이 혼자서 행동하는 개인은 민족 정신을 만들어 낼 수 없다는 주어진 글 다음에, (B) 민족 정신은 많은 개인의 상호의존적인 행위로 만들어지며 이누이트족을 그 예로 든 후, (A) 이누이트족이 민족 정신을 유지하는 이유로 지리적 고립을 들었으며, (C) 이누이트족과 비슷한 규모의 집단이라도 대도시에서는 문화 간 접촉으로 민족 정신을 유지하지 못한다는 결론으로 이어지는 것이 자연스럽다.

구문분석

> [5행] If <u>cross-cultural contact</u> **were** to become
>   S   V
> sufficiently close, <u>the Inuit ethos</u> **would disappear**.
>   S   V
> ▶「If+S+동사의 과거형, S+조동사의 과거형+동사원형」의 가정법 과거 구문이 쓰였다. 가정법 과거 표현에서 be동사는 주어의 인칭과 수에 상관없이 보통 were를 쓴다.

STEP 1 어휘

29강 사고·판단

PRACTICE
p.236

A   1 evidence   2 insight   3 stereotypes
           4 categories   5 enlightenment

B   1 ④   2 ①   3 ③   4 ②   5 ①

C   1 weakens   2 overestimating

A

1 현재로서는 다른 행성에 생명체가 존재한다는 증거는 없다.
2 벨기에의 한 신부가 최초로 우주의 탄생에 대한 통찰력을 보여 줬다.
3 페미니스트들은 기존의 성별 고정 관념을 따르지 않는 사람들이다.
4 증거는 두 개의 범주, 즉 객관적인 증거와 정황적인 증거로 나뉜다.
5 '브나로드 운동'은 1930년대 문맹을 퇴치하고자 했던 농촌 계몽 운동이다.

B

1 변호사가 의뢰인의 정보를 누설하는 것은 법적으로든 윤리적으로든 잘못된 것이다.
2 심리학자들은 여자의 직감이 남자의 직감보다 더 정확하다고 생각한다.
3 전문가들은 내수 진작을 위해 기존 세금 공제 혜택을 확대해야 한다고 주장했다.
4 국회의원들은 그 제안을 뒷받침하는 논리로 저조한 투표율을 제시했다.
5 여론 조사는 유권자들이 의견을 결정하는 가장 객관적인 방법은 아니다.

C

1 거짓말이 어느 특정한 경우에 어떤 해로운 영향도 미치지 않는다 할지라도, 그것은 여전히 도덕적으로나 윤리적으로 옳지 않은데 왜냐하면 밝혀질 경우 거짓말은 인간의 의사소통이 신뢰하는 진실 말하기의 일반적 관행을 약화시키기 때문이다.
2 우리는 왜 실제로 그들이 그러한 것보다 다른 사람들이 우리에게 더 많이 주목하고 있다고 종종 느끼는가는 조명 효과로 설명될 수 있는데, 조명 효과는 우리 자신을 무대의 중앙에 있다고 보는 것이고, 그러므로 다른 사람들의 주목이 우리에게 향해 있는 정도를 직관적으로 과대평가하는 것을 의미한다.

적용독해
p.237

1 ④   2 ⑤

1 ④

해석 때때로 자신에 대한 우리의 판단은 터무니없이 부정적이다. 이것은 자존감이 낮은 사람에게 있어 특히 그러하다. 몇몇 연구는 그런 사람이 자신의 실패의 중요성을 확대하는 경향이 있다는 것을 보여주었다. 그들은 자주 자신의 능력을 과소평가한다. 그리고 직장에서의 나쁜 평가나 아는 누군가로부터의 무례한 말과 같은 부정적인 피드백을 받을 때, 그들은 그것이 자신의 자존감을 부정확하게(→ 정확하게) 반영한다고 믿을 가능성이 있다. 자존감이 낮은 사람은 또한 우울해질 위험이 평균보다 높다. 이것은 한 개인의 정신적 그리고 정서적 안녕뿐만 아니라 그 사람의 신체적 건강과 사회적 관계의 질도 또한 해친다.

문제풀이 자존감이 낮은 사람은 자신의 능력을 과소평가하며 상대방의 부정적 피드백을 정확하다고 믿어버리는 경향이 있다는 내용이므로 ④ inaccurately는 accurately 등으로 바꿔야 한다.

구문분석

[7행] This hurts **not only** [an individual's mental and emotional well-being] **but also** [his or her physical health and the quality of his or her social relationships.]

▶ 'A뿐만 아니라 B도'의 의미인 상관접속사 구문 「not only A but also B」가 쓰였으며 A와 B의 자리에는 문법상 대등한 요소가 와야 한다. 여기서는 각각 명사구가 왔다.

2 ⑤

해석 여러분은 아마도 '첫인상이 매우 중요하다'라는 표현을 들어본 적이 있을 것이다. 삶은 실제로 많은 사람들에게 좋은 첫인상을 만들 두 번째 기회를 주지 않는다. 누군가가 또 다른 개인을 평가하는 데 단지 몇 초만 걸린다는 것이 밝혀져 왔다. 이것은 채용 과정에서 매우 두드러지는데, 채용 과정에서 최고의 모집자는 (지원자가) 자신을 소개하는 몇 초 안에 지원자에 대한 자신의 최종 결정의 방향을 예측할 수 있다. 따라서 후보자의 이력서가 지식과 능력을 '진술'할지도 모르지만, 그들의 외모와 소개는 신체 조정 능력의 부족, 불안, 그리고 형편없는 대인 관계 기술을 알려 줄지도 모른다. 이런 식으로 빠른 판단들이 단지 채용 문제에만 관련된 것은 아니며 이것들은 또한 사랑과 관계 문제에도 똑같이 적용된다. 여러분이 몇 달간 공들여 찾아낸 멋진 누군가와의 데이트에서, 입 냄새 또는 구겨진 옷과 같은 미묘한 것들이 여러분의 숭고한 노력을 배가시킬지도(→ 망칠지도) 모른다.

문제풀이 누군가에 대한 첫인상은 아주 짧은 시간 안에 형성되므로 부정적인 첫인상을 다시금 만회하기는 어렵다는 내용과 첫 데이트에서 부정적인 첫인상이 가져올 불행한 상황을 예시로 들어주었으므로 ⑤ double은 spoil 등으로 고쳐야 한다.

구문분석

[2행] **It** has been determined [**that** it takes only a few seconds *for anyone* to assess another individual].

▶ It은 가주어고 접속사 that이하 [　]가 진주어이다. 진주어절에는 '(~가) …하는데 시간이 ~걸린다'의 의미인 「it+takes+시간+의미상 S+to-v」 구문이 쓰였다.

PRACTICE
p.238

A
1 specifically → specific
2 unscientifically → unscientific
3 keen → keenly
4 hardly → hard
5 free → freely

B
1 true　2 entirely

A

1 여러분이 세운 목표를 모두 목록으로 작성할 때, 가능한 한 구체적으로 작성해라. ▶ 「be 동사+형용사 보어」
2 과학자들은 그 영화의 일부 장면들이 비과학적이라고 생각했다.
▶ 5형식 동사 「consider+O+O.C.(형용사)」
3 우리는 건강을 잃고 나서야 건강의 중요함을 절감한다. ▶ 형용사 aware를 수식하는 부사
4 학생들은 전문 용어로 가득한 그 책은 읽기 어렵다는 것을 알았다.
▶ 5형식 동사 「find+가목적어+O.C.(형용사)+진목적어(to-v)」
5 천재 작곡가인 슈베르트는 우리가 친한 사람에게 편지 쓰듯이 자유롭게 작곡했다. ▶ 3형식 완전한 문장+부사

B

1 연구 설계가 타당한 연구 결과에 대한 합리적 기대를 허용하지 않는다면 인간을 위험에 빠뜨리는 것은 결코 윤리적이지 않으며, 이는 많은 사람들이 '좋은 과학은 좋은 윤리이다'라는 말이 사실이 아니라고 생각한다는 의미이다. ▶ 5형식 동사 「consider+O+O.C.(형용사)」
2 근대적 사상가들이 연역의 논리에 따라 나아갔든 혹은 경험적 자료 분석을 통해 나아갔든, 그들이 발전시켰던 근대의 과학적 방법은 전적으로 이성에 따라 그리고 이용 가능한 증거를 고려하여 이론을 검증하는 것에 있다. ▶ 1형식 완전한 문장이므로 부사 적절

적용독해
p.239

1 ④　2 ②

1 ④

해석 인간들은 도덕성을 가지고 있고 동물들은 그렇지 않다는 믿음은 너무나 오래된 가정이라서 충분히 그것은 습관적 사고로 불릴 수 있고, 우리가 모두 알다시피 나쁜 습관은 고치기가 극도로 어렵다. 많은 사람이 이러한 가정에 굴복해 왔는데, 왜냐하면 동물들이 도덕적 태도를 가진다는 가능성의 복잡한 영향들을 다루는 것보다 동물에게서 도덕성을 부정하는 것이 더 쉽기 때문이다. 우리 대 그들이라는 시대

에 뒤처진 이원론의 틀에 갇힌 역사적 경향은 많은 사람들이 현재 상태를 고수하도록 만들기에 충분히 강력하다. 동물들이 누구인가에 대한 부정은 동물들의 인지적, 감정적 능력에 대한 잘못된 고정 관념을 유지하는 것을 편의대로 허용한다. 분명히 중대한 패러다임의 전환이 요구되는데, 왜냐하면 습관적 사고에 대한 안일한 수용이 동물들이 어떻게 이해되고 다루어지는지에 강한 영향을 미치기 때문이다.

문제풀이 ④ 1형식 완전한 문장이므로 convenient를 부사 conveniently로 고쳐야 한다.
① 2형식 완전한 문장+부사
② 「be동사+형용사 보어」
③ 셀 수 없는 명사(tendency) 주어+단수 동사 ▶ p.190
⑤ 「be동사+형용사(과거분사)」

2 ②

해석 우리들 대부분에게 있어서, 운전은 심리학자들이 과잉 학습된 행동이라고 말하는 것이다. 이것은 우리가 어떤 것에 너무나 잘 훈련이 된 나머지 많은 의식적인 사고 없이도 그 일을 해낼 수 있게 해주는 것이다. 그것은 우리의 삶을 보다 용이하게 해주고, 우리가 사물들을 잘 다룰 수 있게 해주는 방법이다. 전문 테니스 선수를 생각해 보자. 서브는 많은 다른 구성 요소들이 결합된 복잡한 기술이지만, 우리가 그것을 더 잘할수록, 우리는 개별적인 각 단계에 대해서는 보다 덜 생각하게 된다. 학습과 주의에 대한 흥미로운 사실 중에 하나는 일단 어떤 일이 자동적으로 이루어지게 되면, 그것은 빠른 일련의 연속된 행위로 처리된다는 것이다. 만약 당신이 주의를 기울이려고 애쓰면, 당신은 그 일을 망쳐버리게 된다. 이것이 야구에서 최고의 타자들이 반드시 최고의 타격 코치가 되지는 않는 이유이다.

문제풀이 ② 2형식 동사 become 뒤에 보어(형용사)가 오므로 skillfully를 skillful로 고쳐야 한다.
① 5형식 동사 「make+O+O.C.(형용사)」
③ 「the 비교급, the 비교급」 구문 ▶ p.246
④ 「2형식 동사+형용사(과거분사)」
⑤ 완전한 문장(3형식)+부사

STEP 3 유형 **문장 위치**   pp.240~241

1 ③   2 ⑤   3 ③

1 ③

해석 모든 사람들은 항상 자동적으로 분류하고 일반화한다. 무의식적으로 그렇게 한다. 그것은 편견을 갖고 있다거나 계몽되어 있다는 것의 문제가 아니다. 범주는 우리가 (정상적으로) 활동하는 데 반드시 필요하다. 그것들은 우리의 사고에 체계를 준다. 만일 우리가 모든 품목과 모든 있을 법한 상황을 정말로 유일무이한 것으로 본다고 상상해 보라. 그러면 우리는 우리 주변의 세계를 설명할 언어조차 갖지 못할 것이다. 그러나 필요하고 유용한 일반화하려는 본능은 우리의 세계관을 왜곡할 수 있다. 그것은 우리가 실제로는 아주 다른 사물들이나, 사람들, 혹은 나라들을 하나로 잘못 묶게 만들 수 있다. 그것은 우리가 하나의 범주 안에 있는 모든 것이나 모든 사람이 비슷하다고 가정하게 만들 수 있다. 그리고 어쩌면 모든 것 중에서 가장 유감스러운

것은, 그것이 우리로 하여금 몇 가지, 또는 심지어 고작 하나의 특이한 사례를 바탕으로 전체 범주에 대해 성급하게 결론을 내리게 만들 수 있다는 것이다.

문제풀이 범주가 우리의 정상적인 활동에 필수적이라고 설명한 후 ③ 뒤에 분류와 일반화가 오류를 야기할 수 있다는 범주의 부정적인 내용이 오므로 일반화(범주)는 필요하지만 주의해야 한다는 내용의 주어진 문장은 ③에 들어가는 것이 가장 적절하다.

구문분석

> [6행] It can make us mistakenly group together things,
>   V   O   O.C.
> or people, or countries [that are actually very different.
>   ↑
> ▶ 5형식 동사로 사역동사인 make가 사용된 문장으로 「make+O+O.C.(동사원형)」의 구조로 되어 있으며, [ ]는 앞에 있는 things, or people, or countries를 수식하는 주격 관계대명사절이다.

2 ⑤

해석 우리는 우리의 편견들을 완전히 없앨 수 없다는 사실을 알고 있기 때문에, 우리는 편견이 우리의 결정과 판단의 객관성과 합리성에 가질 수 있는 해로운 영향들을 제한하도록 노력할 필요가 있다. 우리가 언제 우리의 인지적 편견들 중 하나가 활성화되는지를 인지하고, 그 편견을 극복할 의식적 결정을 내리는 것이 중요하다. 우리는 편견이 우리의 의사 결정 과정과 삶에 끼치는 영향력을 인지할 필요가 있다. 그때 우리는, 편견과 싸우기 위해 적절한 반편견 전략을 선택할 수 있다. 우리가 전략을 실행해 본 이후에, 우리는 그것이 우리가 희망했던 방식대로 작동했는지를 보기 위해 한 번 더 확인해야 한다. 만약 그것이 그랬다면, 우리는 넘어가서 객관적이고 정보에 근거한 결정을 내릴 수 있다. 만약 그러지 않았다면, 우리는 우리가 이성적 판단을 내릴 준비가 될 때까지 똑같은 전략을 다시 시도하거나 새로운 것을 실행할 수 있다.

문제풀이 편견이 우리의 결정과 판단에 해로운 영향을 미칠 수 있기 때문에 적절한 반편견 전략을 세워 실행하고 한 번 더 확인해야 한다는 내용과 ⑤ 뒤에 '만약 그것이 그러지 않았다면(반편견 전략이 제대로 작동하지 않았다면)'이 이어지므로 '만약 그것이 그랬다면(반편견 전략이 제대로 작동했다면)'으로 시작하는 주어진 문장은 ⑤에 들어가는 것이 가장 적절하다.

구문분석

> [2행] **Since** we know [we can't completely eliminate our biases,] we need to try to limit the harmful impacts
>   S   V   ↑
> [they can have on the objectivity and rationality of our decisions and judgments].
> ▶ since는 '~ 때문에'라는 의미의 접속사이고 첫 번째 [ ]는 know의 목적어로 접속사 that이 생략되었다. 두 번째 [ ]는 선행사 the harmful impacts를 수식하는 that이 생략된 목적격 관계대명사절이다.

3 ③

해석 근거와 주장의 한 가지 이점은 겸손을 기를 수 있다는 점이다.

만약에 두 사람이 논쟁 없이 의견만 다르다면, 그들이 하는 것은 서로에게 고함을 지르는 것뿐이다. 대조적으로, 양측이 자신의 입장에 대한 이유를 분명하게 말하는 주장을 제시한다면, 새로운 가능성이 열린다. 이러한 주장 중 한쪽이 반박된다. 즉, 틀렸다는 것이 보여진다. 이런 경우에 반박된 주장에 의지했던 사람은 자신의 관점을 바꿀 필요가 있다는 것을 배운다. 이것은 적어도 한쪽에서는 겸손을 얻는 한 방식이다. 또 다른 가능성은 어떤 주장도 반박되지 않는 것인데, 둘 다 자신의 입장에서 어느 정도 근거가 있기 때문이다. 대화자의 어느 누구도 상대의 주장에 설득되지 않더라도, 양측은 그럼에도 불구하고 반대 견해를 이해하게 된다. 그들이 약간의 진실을 가지고 있다 하더라도 완전한 진실은 가지고 있지 않다는 점을 그들은 또한 인식하게 된다. 그들은 자신의 견해에 반대되는 근거를 인식하고 이해할 때 겸손을 얻을 수 있다.

문제풀이 양측이 논쟁을 하게 되면 두 종류의 결과가 나올 가능성이 있는데 첫 번째 가능성(한쪽이 다른 한쪽에 의해 반박되면 자신의 틀렸음을 인정하면서 겸손을 배운다)을 언급한 후 ③ 뒤에 양측 모두 상대의 주장에 설득되지 않는다는 내용이 나오므로 겸손을 배울 또 다른 가능성을 언급한 주어진 문장은 ③에 들어가는 것이 가장 적절하다.

구문분석

[3행] If two people disagree without arguing, all [they do] is (to) yell at each other.
        V   S.C

▶ 「all+(that)+S+do/does/did」이 주어이면 보어 자리에 to가 생략되고 동사원형이 온다. [ ]는 목적격 관계대명사 that이 주로 생략되고 핵심 주어인 all를 수식하여 '~하는 것'으로 해석하고 단수 취급한다.

STEP 1 어휘

30강 연구 · 실험

PRACTICE
p.244

A	1 reveal	2 randomly	3 imitate
	4 pretend	5 correlation	
B	1 ④	2 ②	3 ③	4 ④	5 ②
C	1 higher	2 testing	

A

1 그 범죄자는 자신의 의도를 <u>밝히려</u> 하지 않았다.
2 공정성을 담보하기 위해 배심원 후보들은 <u>무작위로</u> 선정되어야 한다.
3 고기처럼 생긴 채식주의자용 식품이 갈수록 인기를 얻고 있다.
4 연구자들은 한 집단에게 그 장면은 못 본 <u>척하라고</u> 요청했다.
5 Dr. Lee는 교육과 부의 대물림 간의 <u>상관관계</u>를 밝혀냈다.

B

1 <u>추가</u> 정보를 원하시면 전화나 문자로 문의해 주세요.
2 학습 의욕을 <u>고취시키는</u> 교사는 학생들의 창의력을 <u>자극한다.</u>
3 오염으로 입은 피해를 <u>원상 복구하려면</u> 수년이 걸릴 것이다.
4 그들의 이론을 실험으로 <u>증명해야</u> 한다.
5 어느 실험자도 분자생물학에서의 그의 업적에 <u>필적하지</u> 못했다.

C

1 사람들에게 하지 말아야 할 것을 말하기보다 해야 할 것을 말하는 것이 훨씬 더 적은 저항을 일으킨다. 그러므로 행동을 지지하는 것은 행동을 금지하는 것보다 더 <u>높은</u> 승낙의 결과를 가져올 것이다.
2 일부 처음 시작하는 연구자들은 좋은 가설은 옳다는 것이 보장된 것이라고 잘못 믿는다. 하지만 여러분의 가설을 여러분이 <u>검사해</u> 보기 전에 그것이 사실이라고 이미 우리가 알고 있다면 여러분의 가설을 <u>검사하는</u> 것은 우리에게 아무런 새로운 것도 말해 주지 않을 것이다.

적용독해
p.245

1 ③   2 ⑤

1 ③

해석 우리가 어떤 주장을 믿고 싶지 않을 때, 우리는 "내가 그것을 믿어야만 하나?"라고 자신에게 묻는다. 그런 후에 우리는 정반대의 증거를 탐색하고 만일 우리가 그 주장을 의심할 단 한 개의 이유라도 발견하면 그 주장을 버릴 수 있다. 심리학자들은 현재 '동기화된 추론'에 관한 수많은 연구 결과를 가지고 있는데 이것은 사람들이 원하는 결론에 도달하기 위해 사용하는 많은 요령을 보여 준다. 실험 대상자들은 지능 검사에서 자신이 낮은 점수를 받았다고 들었을 때, 그들은 지능 검사의 타당도를 <u>뒷받침하는(→ 비판하는)</u> 기사를 읽기로 선택한다. 과도한 카페인 섭취가 유방암에 걸릴 위험을 증대시키는 것과 관련이 있다고 보고한 (가상의) 과학 연구를 읽을 때, 커피를 많이 마시는 여성들은 카페인을 덜 섭취한 여성들보다 그 연구에서 더 많은 오류를 찾아낸다.

문제풀이 어떤 주장을 믿고 싶지 않을 때 그 주장을 반박할 증거를 찾으려 하는 동기화된 추론에 관한 내용이므로 ③ supporting은 criticizing 등으로 고쳐야 한다.

구문분석

[4행] ... showing the many tricks [people use **to reach** the conclusions {they want to reach}].

▶ [ ]와 { }는 모두 「선행사+(목적격 관계대명사)+S+V」로 이루어져 있으며 목적격 관계대명사는 주로 생략한다. to reach는 목적을 나타내는 부사적 용법의 to부정사구이다.

[8행] ... women [who are heavy coffee drinkers] find more errors in the study than do less caffeinated women.
                                          V   S

▶[　]는 women을 수식하는 주격 관계대명사절이며 than 뒷부분은 앞 절과 다르다는 것을 강조하기 위해 주어와 동사가 도치되었다. do는 find의 대동사이다.

2 ⑤

해석 전부는 아니지만 대부분의 믿음은 검증 시험을 받을 수 있다. 이것은 믿음이 옳거나 그른지를 확인하기 위해 시험될 수 있다는 것을 의미한다. 믿음은 그 사람의 외부에 있는 객관적인 기준을 통해 진실임이 입증되거나 거짓임이 입증될 수 있다. 지구가 평평하고 구가 아니라고 믿는 사람들이 있다. 우리는 지구가 사실은 구라는 객관적인 증거를 가지고 있기 때문에, 지구가 평평하다는 믿음은 거짓임이 증명될 수 있다. 또한, 내일 비가 올 것이라는 믿음은 내일까지 기다려 비가 오는지 안 오는지 봄으로써 진실인지 확인될 수 있다. 하지만, (9999년이 되면 지구가 자전하는 것을 멈출 것이라는 믿음이나 1억 광년 떨어진 행성에 생명체가 있다는 것 같은) 어떤 종류의 믿음은 우리가 일생 동안 외부 증거를 얻을 수 없기 때문에 진실인지 확인될 수 없다. 또한, (신의 존재와 본질과 같은) 형이상학적 믿음은 모든 사람이 진리 기준으로 기꺼이 사용할 증거를 만드는 데 있어서 상당한 유용함이(→ 난제가) 된다.

문제풀이 대부분의 믿음은 검증 과정을 거쳐 진실 혹은 거짓으로 입증될 수 있지만 시공간적 한계나 형이상학적 믿음은 입증이 불가능하다는 내용이므로 ⑤ usefulness는 challenges 등으로 고쳐야 한다.

구문분석

[5행] Also, the belief [that it will rain tomorrow] can be tested for truth [**by waiting** until tomorrow and **seeing** {whether it rains or not}].

▶첫 번째 [　]는 the belief와 동격을 나타내는 that절이고, 동사는 can be tested이다. 「by+v-ing」는 '~을 함으로써'의 의미로 waiting과 seeing이 and로 병렬되고 있다. seeing의 목적어인 {　}는 「whether S+V+or not」 구문으로 '~을 할지 안 할지'의 의미이다.

STEP 2 어법　비교 구문

PRACTICE
p.246

A　1 than
　　2 more
　　3 better
　　4 much/even/far/a lot
　　5 least

B　1 much　2 more

A

1 우리 중 더 많은 이들이 어느 때보다도 탐욕스럽다고 주장하고 있다. ▶ 비교급 구문
2 케이블 TV의 광고 수입은 상반기 라디오 광고 수입의 두 배 이상을 넘어섰다. ▶ much의 비교급
3 직원들끼리 더 자주 함께 일할수록, 조직은 업무를 더 잘 수행하게 된다. ▶ the 비교급, the 비교급 구문
4 면밀한 읽기는 표면적인 글 읽기보다는 아이들이 더 깊이 탐구할 수 있게 해준다. ▶ 비교급 강조
5 욕구에 이끌리는 동물로서, 우리는 우리가 필요로 하는 것을 얻기 위해서 저항이 가장 적은 경로를 탐색한다. ▶ little의 최상급

B

1 수렵 채집이 농업보다 덜 생산적이고 훨씬 낮은 에너지 생산량을 발생시킬 수도 있지만, 더 오랜 기간 동안 농경 사회는 수렵 채집인보다 심각하고, 존재적으로 위협적인 기근에 시달릴 가능성이 훨씬 더 높았다. ▶ 비교급 강조 much
2 우리의 얼굴을 만지는 것이 특별한 도움이 되지 않는 것처럼 보여도, 그 연구는 불쾌한 소음에 노출되는 것에 대한 피험자의 스스로 만지는 비율이 높을수록, 그 사람은 더 집중하는 것으로 나타났습니다. ▶ 「the+비교급, the+비교급」 구문

적용독해
p.247

1 ③　2 ⑤

1 ③

해석 전통적으로 대부분의 생태학자는 한 군집이 환경 교란에 견디는 능력인 군집 안정성이 군집 복잡성의 결과라고 추정했다. 즉, 종 풍부도가 높은 군집이 종 풍부도가 덜한 군집보다 더 잘 기능하고 더 안정적일 수 있다. 이 관점에 의하면, 종의 풍부도가 높을수록 어떤 하나의 종은 덜 결정적으로 중요하게 될 것이다. 군집 내 있을 수 있는 많은 상호작용 덕분에, 어떤 단 하나의 교란이 체계의 많은 구성 요소에 영향을 미쳐 그 체계의 기능에서 중대한 차이를 가져올 수 있을 것 같지는 않다. 이 가설의 증거는 파괴적인 해충의 발생이 종 풍부도가 높은 자연 군집에서보다 다양성이 낮은 군집인 경작지에서 더 흔하다는 사실을 포함한다.

[문제풀이] ③ 「the+비교급, the+비교급」 구문이므로 least를 less로 고쳐야 한다.
① 주어 community stability (단수)+단수 동사 ▶ p.190
② 1형식+부사 well의 비교급
④ system을 대신하는 단수 대명사 ▶ p.198
⑤ 동격절 접속사 that ▶ p.166

2 ⑤

해석 나이 든 성인은 종종 젊은 성인들보다 결정을 내리는 데 더 많은 시간이 걸린다. 그러나 그것은 그들이 덜 똑똑하다는 것을 의미하지는 않는다. 오하이오 주립대학의 연구에 따르면, 나이 든 성인의 더

느린 반응 시간이 속도보다 정확성을 더 중요하게 여기는 것과 관련이 있다. *Journal of Experimental Psychology: General*에 최근 게재된 그 연구에서, 대학생 나이 정도의 학생들과 60~90세 나이의 성인들이 단어 인지와 기억에 대한 시간제한을 둔 시험을 치렀다. 모든 참가자들이 동등하게 정확했지만 더 나이 든 그룹은 더 느리게 반응했다. 하지만 그 연구자들이 그들에게 더 빨리하도록 장려했을 때 그들은 정확성을 상당히 희생시키지 않으면서도 젊은 사람들의 속도를 따라갈 수 있었다. "많은 단순한 과업들에서, 나이 든 사람들은 주로 그들의 결정을 내리기 위해 더 많은 증거들을 요구하려고 마음먹기 때문에 더 많은 시간이 걸린다."라고 공동저자인 Roger Ratcliff는 말한다. 그가 말하기를, 어떤 나이든 사람이 속도를 요구하는 과업에 직면했을 때, 더 빨리하려는 의식적인 노력이 종종 효과를 낸다.

문제풀이 ⑤ 주격 관계대명사 앞의 선행사가 단수 명사(a task)이므로 require를 requires로 고쳐야 한다. ▶ p.174
① 일반동사 take를 대신하는 대동사 ▶ p.206
② have more to do with: ~와 더 관련이 있다
③ 비교급 강조 far
④ 형용사를 수식하는 부사 significantly ▶ p.238

---

pp.248~249

STEP 3 유형 글의 요약

1 ①   2 ①

---

1 ①

해석 한 연구에서, 심리학자 Laurence Steinberg는 306명의 사람들을 세 연령 집단(평균 나이 14세인 어린 청소년, 평균 나이 19세인 나이가 더 많은 청소년, 그리고 24세 이상인 성인)으로 나누었다. 피실험자들은 게임 참가자가 도로에 경고 없이 나타나는 벽에 충돌하는 것을 피해야 하는 컴퓨터 운전 게임을 했다. Steinberg는 무작위로 몇몇 참가자들을 혼자 게임하거나 혹은 두 명의 같은 나이 또래들이 지켜보는 가운데 게임을 하게 했다. 나이가 더 많은 청소년들은 그들의 또래들이 같은 방에 있을 때 위험 운전 지수에서 약 50퍼센트 더 높은 점수를 기록했다. 다른 어린 십 대들이 주변에 있을 때, 어린 청소년들은 혼자 운전할 때보다 무려 두 배 더 무모하게 운전했다. 대조적으로, 성인들은 그들이 혼자 있든지 혹은 다른 사람에 의해 관찰되든지 상관없이 유사한 방식으로 행동했다.
→ 또래들의 (A) 존재는, 성인들은 그렇지 않지만, 청소년들이 더 (B) 위험을 감수하게 만든다.

문제풀이 컴퓨터 운전 게임 실험에서 성인들은 혼자 있든지 다른 사람들이 지켜보든지 영향을 받지 않지만 나이가 어릴수록 또래가 주변에 있을 때 무모하게 운전하는 경향이 강하다는 내용의 글이다.

구문분석

[3행] Subjects played a computerized driving game [**in which** the player must **avoid** crashing into a wall {**that** appears, without warning, on the roadway}].
▶「in which+완전한 절」로 이루어진 [　]는 선행사 a computerized driving game을 설명하는 관계대명사절이

며, {　}는 a wall을 수식하는 주격 관계대명사절이다.「avoid+v-ing」는 '~하는 것을 피하다'라는 뜻으로 avoid는 동명사를 목적어로 취하는 동사이다.

---

2 ①

해석 교수 환경에 관한 한 실험에서 5학년과 6학년 학생들이 한 주제에 대해 상호작용을 하게 되었다. 한 그룹에서는 토론이 합의를 도출하는 방식으로 유도되었다. 두 번째 그룹에서는 토론이 옳은 정답에 대해 불일치를 낳도록 설계되었다. 쉽게 합의에 도달한 학생들은 주제에 흥미를 덜 보이고 더 적게 공부했으며 부가적인 정보를 얻기 위해 도서관에 가는 경향이 더 적었다. 그러나 가장 눈에 띄는 차이는 교사가 학생들에게 점심시간 동안 주제와 관련된 영화를 보여 주었을 때 나타났다. 동의한 그룹의 18퍼센트만이 영화를 보기 위해 점심시간을 놓쳤으나 동의하지 않은 그룹의 45퍼센트는 그 영화를 보기 위해 남았다. 그룹 내에서 누가 옳았는지 알기 위해 지식 차이를 채우려는 열망은 미끄럼틀과 정글짐을 향한 열망보다 훨씬 더 강했던 것이다.
→ 위의 연구에 따르면, 주제에 대한 학생들의 흥미는 학생들이 (B) 의견을 달리 하도록 장려될 때 (A) 증가한다.

문제풀이 토론이 합의를 도출하는 방식으로 유도된 실험군과 불일치를 낳도록 설계된 대조군을 비교하는 실험에서 누가 옳았는지 알기 위해 지식 차이를 채우려는 열망이 실험군보다 대조군에서 훨씬 강했다는 내용의 글이다.

구문분석

[4행] Students [who easily reached an agreement] were less interested in the topic, studied less, and were less likely to visit the library [**to get** additional information].
▶ 첫 번째 [　]는 주어인 students를 수식하는 주격 관계대명사절이며 were less interested, studied less, were less likely to의 3개의 동사가 병렬 구조이다.「be less interested in A」는 'A에 덜 흥미가 있다'이고「be less likely to-v」는 '덜 …할 것 같다'라는 의미이다. 두 번째 [　]는 목적을 나타내는 to부정사구이다.

The 상승
어법·어휘＋유형편

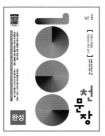